CULTURAL INSANITY

THE KEY TO UNDERSTANDING
OUR WORLD
AND OURSELVES:

WITH CURRENT POLITICAL AND
ENVIRONMENTAL EXAMPLES, AND HISTORICAL
CASE STUDIES IN WITCH-HUNTING,
THE MEDIEVAL CHURCH IMPEDING SCIENCE,
AND THE REJECTION OF GEOLOGIC TIME
& EVOLUTION
(THE ORIGINAL AND DEFINITIVE ACCOUNT)

BY JEFFREY WYNTER KOON
10/28/2020

For copies, inquire at https://store.bookbaby.com/
(electronic copies may be farmed out from there).

Print ISBN: 978-1-09834-159-6
eBook ISBN: 978-1-09834-160-2

Cover photo by the author, 1971, a Berkeley-Emeryville mudflats sculpture; artist(s) unknown.

Printed in the United States of America
First edition

TABLE OF CONTENTS

PART TWO
THE CULTURAL INSANITY OF WITCH-HUNTING

207

PART THREE
CULTURAL INSANITIES DERIVED FROM THE CHURCH'S EFFORTS TO ELIMINATE POSSIBLE THREATS TO DOCTRINE ARISING FROM THE DEVELOPMENT OF (PROTO-)SCIENCE

303

PART FOUR
CULTURAL INSANITY IN THE DENIAL OF GEOLOGIC TIME AND EVOLUTION

513

ACKNOWLEDGMENTS

I want to thank Holland, Nancy J., my wife and professor of philosophy at Hamline University (now deceased) and my son, Justis V. Koon, a Ph.D. student in philosophy at University of Massachusetts, Amherst, for reading and commenting on portions of my earlier drafts. In addition, between 2009 and 2017, Nancy and I managed to get in another 5 months or so of travel, spending time in London, York, Edinboro, Trier, Cologne, Aachen, Paris, and Florence and some countryside areas.

And, later in the writing process, I want to extend my special appreciation to my good friends from Oxford Hall (of the Berkeley Student Cooperative), Lee Shilman, for reading and commenting on semi-final drafts of three parts, and George Gregg, for his review and comments on Part One. Both helped prove to me that the book was well fitted to all "members" of the intelligentsia, and not just those enmeshed in academic pursuits or with political activism in their blood.

And I want to thank the people at BookBaby (especially Isabel) who helped guide me through the process of preparing this complicated treatise for publication. BookBaby's approach—which involves selecting individual items from a menu, rather than an arcane if not indecipherable legal contract that includes some items you can't make good use of—is much appreciated.

Otherwise, any failings are mine (or due to Microsoft's Word). Probably more than in most cases, the author has responsibility for any failings in this book—even the editing.

INTRODUCTION

This book provides a better way of understanding much of what is wrong in our society and in the world today. The cultural insanity perspective offers the mind a pathway to see reality more accurately, especially within one's own country and culture. The concept demonstrated here may well grip your imagination with its possibilities. The explanations I offer, together with the current examples and historical cases studies, will help you to apply the concept correctly and in an enlightening way (rather than merely derogatorily and erroneously for political insults).

Although the focus here is on the kinds and extents of insanity not of individuals, but of *a culture itself*, be forewarned: Where our own culture is involved, *we and all other individuals in our society are party to it, and to varying extents partake of at least some of its madnesses.* Accordingly, correctly grasping the idea of cultural insanity will reveal pathways to improve not only one's worldview but one's self-understanding.

The theory and methods for cultural insanity analyses, along with many examples of current and recent cultural insanities in U.S. political history and the environmental realm, are provided in Part One. Parts Two through Four are historical case studies, the last leading up to the present time. These histories deal with major aspects of our society's heritage, two of them at the bedrock level, with considerable relevance to our culture today. These case studies demonstrate in greater depth the methods of analyzing cultural insanity as well as more of the nuances involved in the proper use of the concept.

Cultural insanity is characterized foremost but not exclusively by features of a culture that unnecessarily thwart the development of human potential in the associated society/societies, where "unnecessarily" means that there must be viable alternatives available. Accordingly, allowances must be made for a culture's level of technology and its people's levels of consciousness. Historically, not to make such allowances is to judge the past using today's values—an ethically unjustifiable stance that is also taboo among historians. For example, for millennia, due to their widespread acceptance, slavery and the oppression of women can qualify only as "buried" cultural insanities—insanities that got exposed only gradually in more recent times—rather like sedimentary rock beds eroding away until the fossils in them are revealed.

The very notion of cultural insanity as unnecessarily thwarting the development of human potential makes us re-reflect on two related questions. What are the purposes/goals of the Nation-state and how should it be designed for best results? And what are these potentials which the State should be fostering and too often doesn't? In this book the former is dealt with only indirectly, by focusing on long-festering problems that need to be dealt with (i.e., maybe shouldn't have arisen in the first place) and occasionally mentioning alternatives. With respect to the latter, I have included an extensive listing of what seem to me to be the principal "elements of human development."

Although cultural insanities, and tendencies toward them, are plentiful and widespread, if you want to assert that some feature of your society is "culturally insane," you will need to make a case for it, not just assert it. Such a case must take account of the relevant historical context(s). It must indicate how human development is impeded. Like a good scientific theory, it must fit all important facts. It may need to face head-on any competing values or worldviews. It will need to reject stereotyping and fake facts or one-sided interpretations based on cherry-picked data or anecdotes/stories. If done well, it will draw on different information silos while cracking them open. More later.

Only a few almost obvious examples of cultural insanity in Part One refer to cultures other than those of Western Europe, but they make it clear that this analysis applies to more than Western culture. Indeed, I claim that virtually (if not) all cultures are, or have tendencies to be, culturally insane in some respects, and that it is immensely important and valuable to analyze and recognize how this is so. The goal is to develop a more realistic worldview, envision alternatives that might improve the development of human potential, and lead to a greater understanding of what people are usually blind to—the culture in which they are enmeshed. Thus one crucial contribution in this writing is to help liberate the human mind from unseen cultural constraints. And, with more of those blinders off, or at least perforated, perhaps we can get a better grasp on the harms that our society has caused and is causing—and see how we need to act to improve the situation. Moreover, some of the environmental harms associated with our society are problems that are common to many cultures—and they are too often denied, ignored, or otherwise given low priority and, hence, are frequently being left in exacerbated forms for subsequent generations—some even potentially endangering all humanity.

But how can cultures be called insane if they don't necessarily account for individual insanities? Well, for one, full-blown cultural insanities are profoundly irrational, where "rational" is one definition of sane. Cultural insanities interfere with our use of reason and thus our problem-solving capacities, and they typically reduce or even foreclose other more viable possibilities. Individual insanities often share those characteristics. Unlike many individual insanities, however, cultural insanity does not necessarily imply that the individuals involved *knowingly* suffer; they may feel or be adapted to their (sub) culture. But the people involved in cultural insanities are not aware how their entanglements negatively affect human fulfillment in the larger society nor how those entanglements often limit them and their progeny as well, though not necessarily in exactly the same ways.

The reader may wonder too, whether my general criterion for identifying cultural insanities—the thwarting of the development of individual potential—involves a modern imposition on the past. But, as described in Part One, some predecessors, some early versions of this criterion, have been available for choosing at least since the time of Aristotle. And there are other examples that also date back to empires before the Romans. Further, as already noted, these analyses do not depend on expecting more than was feasible at the time.

When I asked Google to define "cultural insanity" (as of September 29, 2019), the top ten choices were all focused on individual insanity(ies). Among the top ten, there were no uses of the concept that focused on the problems within cultures generally. The two closest to my usage here spoke to how cultures differ in their stigmatization or interpretation of individual insanity, and to the tendency of the stresses of modern culture to exacerbate depression (specifically). There is no denying that some problems with depression at the individual level are culturally-induced or, at least, culturally-exacerbated. Indeed, as will be seen here, there are a number of cultural insanities that contribute mightily to the sources of stress in modern society.

There are also, of course, histories about the treatment of the insane, as defined at the time, and how the understanding and treatment of insanity have varied over the centuries. But they have only a marginal relevance here. The work closest to mine that I have encountered was published after I had been working on this (for several years). It is Allen Frances' *Twilight of American Sanity: A Psychiatrist Analyzes the Age of Trump* (2017). This work focuses on ten "delusions" that he identifies as common to large numbers of people in this country, where delusions are erroneous understandings of reality that, most crucially, are not readily susceptible to alteration with facts and reason. Frances' work contributes to Part One, but it does not deal with the origin of these delusions nor speak to how they are propagated by people *as part of their cultures*. Moreover, cultural insanity derives from far more than psychiatric delusions; it also festers in realms typically studied by the anthropologist, psychologist, historian, sociologist, philosopher, political scientist and other scientists.

Parts Two through Four are case studies involving major aspects of historical eras lasting from more than 100 years to more than a thousand years. The three case studies involve religion-related topics in the history of the West. They were chosen in part because the vast majority of people in the West have at least some background understanding of the principal religion in the West, such that no case study's material will be entirely unfamiliar to them. Still, religion can be a delicate subject if something written seems to contravene strongly held beliefs. Accordingly, the reader is hereby urged to think of this account as if it were written by a long-lived Martian anthropologist who watched the history of Western Europe unfold from their spaceship. To assist and remind the reader to use this more objective-observer perspective, "Christian" has almost invariably been rendered in the shorthand, as "Xtian"; and most references to "god/God" have been rendered as "the deity." This approach is also meant to remind the reader that the idea of "God" in older times may not have the same meaning as "God" might today. In this then, I have proceeded much as an anthropologist might do when reporting on the deities of a tribe in some rainforest that had had little contact with the outside world.

I have also used historical case studies because, unlike examination of the present or very recent past in Part One, they should prove less likely to trigger people's defenses and biases—where such biases often tend to be rooted at least partly in the cultural insanities in which we are currently enmeshed. These case studies will demonstrate the methodology involved in historical analyses of cultural insanity and, as noted, will help the reader understand more fully the idea of cultural insanity, so that they can apply the concept soundly and more effectively to the present (as I have tried to do in Part One and in Part Four). All three case studies, in addition to applying this new perspective historically, provide what I believe is a more satisfactory resolution to some of the problems with parts of more traditional histories that cover the same topics.

In writing historical aspects of the case studies, *I judged it most important not to make major mistakes.* Although of course I tried to avoid minor errors too, the most important goal was to ensure that the cases were accurate and fair with respect to historical trends most relevant to the analysis of cultural insanity. Given this purpose and the broad sweep of some of the history involved, it also seldom seemed necessary to try to become more up-to-date with the fine points of the academic literature pertaining to the various eras. In addition to general histories, I have relied extensively on re-focusing and re-synthesizing the information in book-length historical accounts of the topics of principal concern in the case studies. Examples include accounts covering topics such as witch hunts, heresy, the Cathars, science and the (Roman Catholic) Church in the Middle Ages, the implications of the re-discovery of Aristotle's work by Europeans in the 1200s, the Reformation(s), the beginnings of the scientific revolution and of the science of geology, and the history of the idea of evolution via natural selection. Where my sources did not agree or otherwise provide synthesizable explanations for what had transpired, I necessarily resorted to yet more histories applicable to that case study. Finally, sometimes it was of course necessary to focus in considerable detail on some events or important themes to assess whether and how some source histories were too weakly tied to those details, too reliant on historical apologia or sources with political axes to grind, or were simply at variance with too many facts and key developments reported in other works. And, with reference to important aspects of a few (sub-)topics, sometimes one historian's account stood head and shoulders above the others because of its comprehensiveness and/or the author's better understanding and integrated explanation of parts of that history that were missing or inadequately explained in others.

More specifically, then, Part Two focuses on witch hunts—in part because it is almost obvious that something went wrong in Western cultures at the time. The history of "witches" provides an example of one way in which a cultural insanity arose by making matters worse. And just as what happens next in our society's history is not foreordained (though some developments are certainly more likely than others), witch-hunting on anything like the scale that actually occurred was not something that was destined to arise from or within Xtianity, or even from the (Catholic) Church. (Many Protestants also joined in the witch-hunting.) Instead, the nature of witchcraft as understood at the time of large-scale witch hunts was largely an invention. The culturally retrograde revisions in the concept of witch(craft) were developed by a specialized second-tier set of leaders in the Church--Dominican inquisitors—who ultimately successfully augmented their dubious case by coaxing a supportive decree from a pope.

However, only slowly did their ideas spread widely among others in the empowered classes, including many secular leaders. And the largest-scale eruptions of witch-hunting very much seemed to be generated by societal leaders' insecurities *after* a reduction in real threats. (Large-scale witch-hunting didn't begin until around 1560, after a peace between Catholics and Lutherans in German-speaking areas.) Leaders' insecurities also seem responsible because most witch-hunting occurred in statelets near realms professing some other variant on Xianity—where conversion of the people or takeover by armed forces of the other side was the real threat. And during some of the witch-hunting era, with the Devil seemingly running rampant in lands adhering to another variant on Xtianity (with witches as his agents), many rulers also tended to fear that the apocalypse was near at hand. In intervals when threats like religious war were reduced, bishops, secular rulers, and even some towns also sought to impose yet greater conformity on behavioral mores to better guarantee their statelet's good standing in the eyes of their version of the deity. And then, sometimes, the underlying insecurities were mentally displaced, deflected onto "witches"—as scapegoats.

Finally, as described in Part One, today we still see considerable use of scapegoating, whether as deliberate attempts to manipulate people's thinking, or by people culturally blinded to understanding the real sources of their problems.

Part Three deals with a topic that has been much disputed over time by historians: the relationship between science and religion in the Middle Ages. The pendulum has swung back and forth between seeing this relationship as "science versus religion" (i.e., mainly the Catholic Church) and the Church as a facilitator of science. From my reading, it seems that only a very few of the most recent historians of science and Church may have a sound grasp of the balance, and even fewer of the larger themes in their picture of the medieval Church's relationship to proto-science/science. And, of course, none of the authors focus on the cultural insanities involved in the dynamics of those relationships.

When Europe began emerging from "darker" times (before the time of Charlemagne), the Catholic Church did help re-establish basic schooling in the reading and writing of Latin, mainly for religious purposes. Also for religious reasons, from the 1200s on, the Church helped to foster the independently evolving universities. But in that latter process, the Church also managed to exercise considerable thought control over them, and over much of knowledge for centuries. In essence, where proto-science or reason(ing) conflicted with Church doctrine, the Church sought to suppress it. Only in the 1600s did heliocentrism/Galileo become the premier example.

The Church in the 1200s was at the height of its power but still needed to find some way(s) to accept the intrusion of the mind-blowing ancient knowledge and wisdom that university intellectuals were finding in the newly re-emerged works of Aristotle. (See text for what was so special.) After initial attempts at suppression and much subsequent debate, the Church opted for considerable integration—albeit while rejecting anything in Aristotle that was not sufficiently compatible with doctrine—all with much assistance from Thomas Aquinas. But its mechanism for thought control remained: *anything opposed to doctrine was regarded as heresy* (which, unless recanted, was ultimately punishable by death). That remains unchanged throughout the Middle Ages and beyond, and it is the effects of that stance, *in interaction with other Church mandates*, that are usually inadequately understood historically.

Moreover, the Church's integration of various parts of Aristotle's thought made it more rather than less difficult to pursue science because many prospective realms of science got entwined with Church doctrines. In the late 1200s, the Church clamped down on university masters (such as Siger of Brabant) endeavoring to teach Aristotle without immediately correcting anything contrary to Church doctrine. Yet, apart from some obvious areas of doctrinal concern, doing so was quite a challenge for the teaching masters because they were not trained in theology. This clampdown terminated some viable alternatives for the advance of proto-science and any associated human development. Among the effects of this sweeping Church restriction on the teaching masters was the suppression of the rational exploration of ideas in (all) areas that might impinge on Church doctrines—and there were many. Even asserting regularities in nature was suspect because the

Church relied heavily on miracles in its sacraments (e.g., thousands of masses offered every day) and in its interventionist deity. To assert regularity in nature was to pin down or limit the deity; it was to deny his omnipotence and his ability to change anything at any time. Fear in Catholic lands of Church prosecution for heterodox works in natural science lasted well into the 1600s.

Aristotle had demonstrated and recommended systematic observation of nature and hands-on efforts. Such ideas were exemplified as well in the early to mid-1200s by Albert the Great and Bacon, Roger. But a far more prominent feature in Aristotle's writings was that he had greatly overdone deducing how the world works from far too little factual information. And this was also the approach adopted in medieval Church scholasticism such that, absent an influx of new information, it led to ever-greater semantic distinctions and obscurantist refinements—with everything put into a doctrinal context (including a few important advances in proto-science). The pattern of ignoring Aristotle's observation-oriented advice, and the two aforementioned exemplars, was reinforced not only by the Church's suppression of reason-based investigations but by an upper-class prejudice against hands-on activities (apart from warfare, hunting, etc.). So the teaching masters did not even encourage their students to try hands-on observations.

To give credit where much of it is actually due, the advance of proto-science and early science in the Middle Ages and beyond was mainly attributable to advances in technology that were separate from the Church and the universities. These advances were abetted in the 1400s and later by some humanist scholars such as Leon Battista Alberti, who learned technologies from artisans and craftspeople, while teaching intellectual skills to those same artisans, and then spread their broadened knowledge to the learned. See the text for some of the details.

Part Four picks up roughly where Part Three left off, but focuses on two related specific areas of science—the age of the earth and the theory of evolution. It starts in the 1600s, with the first comprehensive attack by Frances Bacon on Aristotelean-Church deductive approach to learning employed throughout medieval scholasticism. Over the next 200 years or so, long-buried cultural insanities were slowly brought to life by developments in understanding the true age of the earth, the proper recognition of what fossil shells actually were and, beginning shortly before 1800, amazing new fossil finds. It slowly became progressively clearer that the six days of creation in the Xtian holy book, and the 6,000 or so years since that creation, simply did not allow enough time for the geological record that was emerging, even under the day-age interpretation (with a day being as a thousand years). The ever-accumulating evidence also showed that Noah's Flood, even if something like it occurred, could not be regarded as sufficient—and later was seen as entirely inadequate (and a limited, local flood at most)—as an explanation for much of anything geologically or geographically.

Part Four tracks these early advances in geology, and then shifts to a focus on the evidence slowly accumulating about evolution. Evolution could only occur on a planet much, much older than the one in the Xtian holy book. Despite a well-argued case, Darwin's theory of evolution took many decades to be fully accepted because there were doubts and questions about whether "natural selection" could actually drive evolution and, especially among ordinary people, because Darwin's view did not incorporate any role for a divine providence. But the re-discovery of Mendel's 1865 work on the genetics of peas, advances in statistical analysis, the discovery of DNA, and other key developments in and after the first quarter of the 20th century, left less and less room for doubt except as to the details of exactly how natural selection works. More recent discoveries in geology, paleontology, biology, genetics, statistics, and molecular biology—which I summarize in a table—have fully excavated this once almost totally-buried cultural insanity, in the process overwhelming any possible viability to the mythological biblical account of the creation of the earth and its various life forms, as well as the story of Noah's Flood. And that makes it all the more remarkable that there are still believers in the inerrancy of the Xtian holy book—lots of them. So I took a look at two of their books, one about the Grand Canyon. The many failures in the book by "young-earth creationists" to explain Grand Canyon geology within the biblical timeline, along with Noah's Flood, may not be initially obvious to the scientifically illiterate. But, I must say, it was sort-of "fun" to apply the processes and principles (??) they used to explain the canyon in other geological contexts—and thus demonstrate, using only reason and a little scientific knowledge, how their explanations are concoctions of pure fantasy.

Finally, I proceed to show some of the particulars of this cultural insanity in today's society. These concluding sections show how crucial areas in many sciences, and even the fundamentals of some sciences, must be disregarded, discounted or denied to maintain a cultural insanity that rejects geologic time. I also consider just some of the serious negative effects that advocates of young-earth creationism (and "intelligent design") have had, not only on the children of the believers themselves, but on vast numbers of other students in our K-12 educational systems, and on our society. A major outcome of the continuation of this cultural insanity has been to substantially reduce scientific literacy as well as the development of human potential in many areas of science across much of our society.

PART ONE

FORMULATING THE THEORY
OF CULTURAL INSANITY

CHAPTER 1

Introductory Overview

Almost undoubtedly there have been times when you saw something on TV about somebody, or read a newspaper article about somebody and your reaction was "she's nuts" or "he's insane." And most likely you've said "that's crazy" when the TV or newspaper reported something about some group of people somewhere, possibly even a large group of people, maybe within the U.S.A., but more likely in some other society and culture. For example, it wasn't all that hard to have doubts about the cultural sanity of some policies and practices of the Taliban when they ruled Afghanistan. Or about the extremes of hatred brought forth against a prominent politician in Pakistan who said that blasphemy of Islam should not carry the death penalty (he was assassinated because of that "blasphemy"). Or the genocides in Rwanda and during the break-up of Yugoslavia; or about the massacres that have occurred in the largely tribal power struggles in places such as Kenya and South Sudan; or about Germany as the home of the master race in Hitler's times. I should be clear though that it is not the use of violence per se that is culturally insane. For example, it may have been culturally sane, even if not ideal, when the peoples of former European colonies, with varying degrees of fanaticism and violence, fought to free their lands/countries from the yoke of foreign overlords after World War II.

Despite a bachelor's degree in U.S. history and fairly wide reading in history, as a Westerner born into Xtian family lines in the United States, I don't know non-European cultures at all well. Accordingly, I will limit examples of cultural insanity drawn from non-Western cultures to a few of the most egregious cases. The primary focus in this work will be on cultural insanity in the United States, and in our heritage in the history of Western Europe. If nothing else, this will make quite clear that it isn't only "other" peoples who have such problems. And although I have included a wide range of current and recent examples in this part, my case studies are historical. While I'm sure I will run into some disagreements by some readers in this part, my hope is that the historical approach in the case studies will enable the reader to better understand what cultural insanity is, because potentially emotionally-upsetting current politics are not involved (with one major possible exception).

Overview of Several Contexts

As we grow up, we are invariably influenced initially and extensively by our parents/caregivers. In many respects, our parents, like their parents, are creatures of their/our culture. Each parent tends to pass along their version of the culture. And as we grow, we also come into more and more contact with other cultural institutions—especially via schooling and teachers—that also play a part in developing our minds and our feelings. Parents and these other social institutions are the primary agents by which our culture is inculcated into us. Probably we are all familiar with at least a very few personality and worldview distortions we got from our parents—sometimes serious, sometimes not so serious. Similarly, whatever our broader culture, it too will tend to shape our personality and worldview, promoting various kinds and degrees of culturally-promulgated distortion in that process.

All this occurs within a broad context affected by dimensions such as urban-suburban-rural, and regional and sectional cultural milieus. These contexts result in enculturation pressures that are not entirely uniform and, when that broader variety is considered, offer a somewhat greater range of ways to transmit possible cultural inheritances. Moreover, somewhat different cultural features also tend to be dominant/proffered in schooling, work, religion, etcetera, with at least some variation as well from school site to school site and school district to district, occupation to occupation, church to church.

When we are young, our peers are also great conveyors of culture—especially but not exclusively the culture they are learning at home, and the variation in peers also offers more opportunity for conscious (and subconscious) choice, but still mainly from within the ranges typical of the larger society and culture. There are also older "peers" and siblings who may influence us. If you have had children (or have them now)—especially children older than about 10—you may remember, for example, how at times you bemoaned negative peer influence. Or how many times you told your child that just because a neighbor has one (or does that), that doesn't mean you can have one too (or do that too). Thus peer cultures, though rooted mainly in the rest of society, are a kind of subculture, or set of subcultures really, that in some ways broaden our choices. (See below for more on subcultures.) Some peer cultures tend toward a "rebelliousness" too— which usually still leaves them tied to the aspects of culture against which they rebel, in a way that may or may not ultimately reinforce the existing culture.

<u>Blindness to Our Own Culture</u>. Because we grew up immersed in it, we are usually almost entirely non-conscious about, or blind to, our culture's influence on us and our "possession" of it and by it—it has a kind of a that's-just-the-way-things-are character to us. We regard what we do in our culture as natural—it is the norm and

normal—at least for our primary group(ings) of people. Indeed, our culture cannot even be seen without some kind of comparative context, even if only an imagined one. One example of this cultural blindness should suffice for now—one that I will not pursue in depth. In 1988, Peggy McIntosh wrote an essay called "White Privilege: Unpacking the Invisible Knapsack." She described spending some time deliberately noticing some of the ways that being White gave her extra privileges in her day-to-day interactions. Some of her "White privilege" items did not have seem all that important, but others—like how we as Whites felt safe around police officers—were. Trouble was, she could not later remember the examples she discovered. So she had to make note of them on the spot, as they were discovered. Partly because it is so expectable, this is a fairly convincing (albeit one-person) example that we can be quite blind to the effects of our culture on us.

Some Useful Conceptions of Social Realities

Before I begin to address the nature of cultural insanity, it also seems useful to say a little more about a very few characteristics of the larger society. These characteristics will help to illuminate the sources of culture, and of cultural insanity, especially in the modern world in which ordinary people can play a major role in what ultimately happens.

National, Regional and Other More Obvious Variations in Culture(s). Even in a very large and relatively free society such as the United States of America there are a number of culture-wide traits that are going to be more characteristic of us than they are of people from almost all, if not all, of the countries in Europe. Were we to make such a comparison carefully, we may find that the people here tend to be more capitalistic, more materialistic, more likely to over-eat, more violence-prone and supportive of personal armaments, more nationalistically self-righteous in our justifications of the use of our military force in international political situations, more religious, more likely to hold the individual fully responsible for his/her conduct (i.e., notwithstanding personal or cultural circumstances), more likely to imprison people, and so on. Back in the 1830s, a French aristocrat, Alexis de Tocqueville, toured the U.S.A. for over a year and wrote a classic book about our national character, and how it differed from those of Europe. But Europeans are, for the most part, our cultural forbearers, not to mention among the ancestors of many of us, so it should come as no surprise if they are in many ways not all that different from us either—and that some of those differences have to be characterized relatively narrowly to accurately characterize a *tendency* that distinguishes "us" from "them."

Our strong cultural influence on much of the rest of the world since the close of World War II also has played a role in promoting similarities among many Western cultures. That cultural influence has come via popular music, Hollywood movies, the mass production of consumer goods, huge corporate-capitalistic enterprises with a world-wide presence and the U.S.A.'s promotion and defense thereof, Silicon Valley inventions, the presence of our armed forces in a very large number of countries, etcetera. In the Western and industrially developed world, especially, with the "globalization" of many aspects of life, facilitated by the nearly instantaneous communication currently available to most people, homogenization has very likely increased in the last two decades. As the German rock group Rammstein's song "Amerika" goes, "We're all living in Amerika…." Although China is on the rise and the Russian government is acting roguish again, the United States in recent times has clearly been the world's leading hegemon. But now global "leadership" is becoming more multifaceted, making the political environment more challenging for any would-be world-wide hegemon.

Despite the many forces for increasing cultural homogenization, both at home and abroad, one thing about a large country especially is that there will be regional differences too—though they probably tend, in most respects, to be less strong than earlier in U.S. history. In the U.S.A., for example, such differences presumably peaked at the time of the Civil War, but they remained very strong through the decades of formal "separate but equal"/Jim Crow in the South. Since the time of industrialization, city versus rural differences have been fairly strong too.[1]

And the ethnic/racial minority population of many cities in the last few decades have also become larger. In the U.S., our immense suburbs are largely a post-World War II development. And some once-great manufacturing centers (e.g., Detroit, Pittsburgh) have decayed, with some having since made a substantial revival while others seem to be struggling with that process. Several southwestern states in the U.S. have populations that are becoming more Hispanic

---

1   City-rural differences also appear in other large countries. And regional differences in Western Europe are often at least partly founded in political and social divisions that stem from multiple centuries in the past. For example, at the outset of the 11th century, France, as we know it today, was composed of multiple separate and semi-separate entities/countries: the original Burgundy (to the north of coastal Provence) was populated earlier by a Germanic tribe other than the Germanic Franks who dominated France; Provence and Languedoc in the southeast spoke a different dialect and their cultural ties southward were stronger than those to the north; Aquitaine and Gascony in the southwest were partly Basque and spent some centuries under English control; Brittany in the west was settled long before by many Britons; and Viking-conquered Normandy in the west was only somewhat integrated as of the early 900s.

Throughout the later Middle Ages, the map of today's Germany looked like a 350-piece jigsaw puzzle of small to medium-sized states and city+/bishoprics—after Reformation, some Catholic and some Protestant. The main commonality was the German language. Unification came only in the late 1800s. Britain included several separate entities over the centuries—Wales, Scotland, and Ireland. There were also some fairly strong regional differences among some of the English provinces (and reasons for them). Spain has a history of small independent states in competition with mostly Muslim control until around 1000 CE. Shortly after that, the Muslim-controlled portion fragmented into city-states that before long drew in north African Muslim armies to support resistance to domination by Xtian Spain; slowly there was greater unification among the Christian states and a rollback of Muslim territories; after the Xtian re-conquest concluded in 1492, the Xtian regimes expelled the Jews, with a Muslim expulsion not all that long afterward. Even today there remains considerable tension about Spain's unification because Catalonia, which is centered around Barcelona, includes many people who want it to be independent (even though their original partnership began with the marriage of Ferdinand and Isabella about 550 years ago).

in ethnic background. Evangelical-fundamentalist Protestantism and social and political conservatism generally remains relatively strong in southern, midwestern prairie, and some mountain states, especially in less urbanized or cosmopolitan areas. Big cities and northeastern and western coastal states are becoming more liberal socially and politically, at least relatively.

The Idea of Subcultures

With a country as relatively free as ours, we also have a lot of choices, including as to some or many aspects of culture—though we probably don't often realize when we are "making" (often drifting into) such choices, partly because many of them will have been made in the process of growing up. The socially acceptable variety of choices was much enhanced during the great cultural leap forward starting in the middle of the 1960s, and to varying extents subsequently, initially driven mainly by a rejection of certain aspects of mainstream culture—with demands for civil rights for African Americans, greater sexual freedom, greater equality of opportunity for women, a refusal to adhere to cultural stereotypes for women (and to a lesser extent, for men), and the beginnings of a tentative release of "gays" from the "closet." To this was added a more critical attitude toward government because of the malfeasance associated with its/our immoral War on Vietnam. The sexual revolution part of this cultural shift was greatly abetted by the discovery of the birth control pill (which was first approved in 1960, but progress toward widespread availability was slow at first) and also by a better understanding of female sexuality, for example, as found in the work of Masters and Johnson in *Human Sexual Response* (1966). These great cultural changes opened many more possibilities for the fulfillment of human potential in this country and, over time, to a considerable extent broadened the range of psychological traits and dispositions seen as socially appropriate.

The greater the variation and range of socially acceptable cultural choices within a country/society, the more permutations and combinations there are for alternatives. There would be more choices in values and basic assumptions, attitudes, behaviors, and emotional reactions to a given set of circumstances, event, or other people—and these choices would be available for inculcation by adults into children. Even so, in empirical reality, many choices typically have companion choices with which they tend to be associated, with varying degrees of closeness. A subculture may form around any level of such choices, whether a single choice (e.g., being a music groupie) or a correlated set of choices (e.g., views about "right-to-work" laws). All it takes to form an identifiable subculture is a sufficient emphasis on a particular choice or set of choices together with some number of people involved. Some sets of such choices are typically inculcated by parents, whether deliberately and consciously or otherwise, into their children. They prepare their children to be members of (at least some of) the same subcultures to which they belong. Other sets of subcultural choices arise at school and among peers (e.g., inclusion in a group of athletes, or nerds, or among the popular-social kids).

Let me mention a few more kinds of associated inculcations and/or choices. Another easy-to-see example is that a strong political party affiliation tends to be associated with an array of subsidiary beliefs and feelings (each of which thus tends to be correlated with the others in the set, some less/more strongly than others). Some political party subgroups may even accept (or wink at) severe racial prejudice and thus tacitly include such associated background beliefs and attitudes—about why some racial out-group is inferior or bad, how they harm the society favored by that group, etcetera. Another often-associated set involves specific religious subgroups with correlated beliefs about abortion rights/right-to-life, homosexuality and gay marriage, and feminism. Young-earth creationists are another group that has close ties with the fundamentalist side of that set. For example, in the

1980s and later, Jerry Falwell's "Moral Majority" group's core issues, in addition to its anti-abortion stance (in which conservative Catholics joined), "were evangelical concerns such as opposition to feminism, gay rights, pornography, and the teaching of evolution" [Andrew Hartman, *A War for the Soul of America: A History of the Culture Wars*, 102].

In a large and varied country "established" subcultures are also likely to be more numerous. Compared to the country-wide culture, these will differ to varying but characterizable degrees—even while their adherents will otherwise almost all remain associated with most parts of the broader culture.

So we need to think of subcultures as existing variants on a culture, typically involving one or more cultural themes or sometimes correlated clusters thereof. People can be adherents to a variety of subcultures at the same time. Some people even participate in a mix of subcultures that are somewhat divided with respect to some stances, for example, fundamentalist Xtians who greatly respect the natural environment, or political conservatives (as of 2019) who want the government to act to reduce the likelihood of global warming/climate change in the coming decades. Similarly, one can find both religious conservatives or fundamentalists as well as religious progressives, among members of African Americans' churches, as well as among Protestants, Catholics and Jews.

<u>Subcultures and Their "Members" Vary in Activity Level</u>. Individuals classifiable as adhering to a subculture need not be actively involved beyond a bare minimum, such as sharing opinions to that effect with others, voting for candidates who might best represent that subculture's interests, etcetera. Others may be very active as leaders in a movement to extend the influence and power of a subculture, or spread its beliefs, or write them into laws that affect everyone at a local, state, or national level.

CHAPTER 2

Some Characteristics and Examples of Cultural Insanity

Subcultural Insanity as It Relates to Cultural Insanity

As suggested above, cultural insanity need not be culture-wide. Even when it tends to be culture-wide, it typically arises out of a subculture (at least in modern times in the West). Hitler was once the leader of a small minority group (subculture), but once his group grew in adherents and he came into power and consolidated his dominance, his views tended to be affirmed by great masses of the German people. Particularly powerful subcultures tend to have some shaping influence on the broader culture, so if they are the bearers of one or more cultural insanities, those will also tend to be important within the society as a whole, though sometimes less so if divisions between the powerful subculture and other people or other subcultures are sharp.

Cultural insanity and tendencies toward it often come to reside in broader socio-cultural institutions, including (some of) a country's laws, its schools, etcetera. Laws and social institutions go on transmitting the culture, day after day, whether for good or not. To quote one famous truthful critic or cynic (Anatole France): "The law, in its majestic equality, forbids the rich as well as the poor to sleep under bridges, to beg in the streets, and to steal bread." Implicit here is that the law very much tends to represent and inculcate the views of the leadership, almost always the dominant groups or classes.

In the United States, for example, "separate but equal" was for decades part of the culture of the South. Although it was pretty darn "separate," it was anything but "equal"—its main (only vaguely covert) goal was to eliminate any voting and most economic power held by Negroes, and subject them to control by Whites. Some of the results of "separate but equal" were obvious: It deprived African Americans of their rights as equal and free citizens, including voting and equal educational opportunity (Black children's schools were notoriously inferior to White children's schools). In addition, there were restrictions on occupations for Blacks, channeling them into farm work (usually share-cropping), and menial and service jobs. That there was cultural insanity involved here is further demonstrated in that efforts to overthrow "Jim Crow" laws resulted in decades of social and political turmoil and an as-yet incomplete resolution.

Another example: There was a strong push toward greater cultural insanity in a recent Supreme Court decision ("Citizens United") that granted corporations the right of free speech when it came to spending money freely on election contests and struck down legislated limits on corporate election spending. *At minimum*, the expenditure of corporate money in elections is a problem for informed democracy unless people know clearly (e.g., from timely and accessible public records) which corporations are investing how much in particular candidates (or issues or ballot propositions) in their election-related expenditures. As of this writing, no requirements for disclosure of election-related corporate spending have been adopted federally, and state laws in this regard are also weak or absent. With elections awash in corporate funds and money from very wealthy donors, the money may suffice, through advertisements and propaganda, to influence enough people, sometimes very deceptively, to buy an election result, whether a race for public office or a ballot initiative.

Although the door is now wide open to the influence of money in politics, this influence to a lesser extent made itself felt plenty before that, for example, when corporate leaders, lobbyists, public relations people, and corporate-sourced political donations delayed for decades the legal recognition of the negative health effects of cigarette smoking, and about the health-related effects of over-consuming sugar. More recently, oil industries have spent considerable sums, fairly successfully, to fund biased "research" that they used to arouse *public* doubt on the science of global climate change/warming, though recent weather extremes may now be catching up with these obfuscations. With Citizens United, at its worst, the country may yet become one that is, de facto, ruled more than ever by a corporate oligarchy (from whence most wealthy individual donors also arise)—an oligarchy in which the main public policy debates will be confined to areas in which the interests of corporations differ, and culturally *sanity* will be even harder to sustain.

As the examples above suggest, the degree of a subculture's influence and dominance is what matters in terms of the broader (national) culture. In (quasi-)democratic societies, subcultural insanities become more important when numerous people are involved and/or when their adherents somehow affect or shape the broader culture in ways that substantially deny the potential, or otherwise negatively and significantly affect the fulfillment, of others' lives. But as the corporate tobacco and oil examples, and the Hitler example show, at other times a (sub)cultural insanity may initially be limited mainly to the leadership of a group that exercises power subtly, or subsequently obtains considerable formal power.

In the United States currently, cultural insanity is in part manifested in political campaigning that is low on evidence-based reasoned treatments of real issues, and high on appeal to underlying (often not fully perceived) emotions such as anger, fear and prejudice. Appeals to emotions may subtly or overtly encourage people to overlook real issues and vote almost entirely based on other political pitches and propaganda. Candidates appealing to fear and anger may say that the institution of marriage will be destroyed if "gay" people are allowed to marry, that including some lower-income housing will greatly diminish suburban quality of life (property values, safety, etc.), that immigrants are overrunning our borders and pose a major criminal threat (though immigrant numbers have declined from their peaks and immigrant crime rates are no higher than the general crime rate). Opponents are also lied about (e.g., Obama's birthplace), smeared, guilted by association, quoted entirely out of context, including by internet trolls and, near elections, by anonymous but well-funded private interest groups. (Candidates supported by these interest groups rarely forthrightly disavow such ads.) Fakey congressional hearings may be drawn out over long periods of time with almost no substance, where the real purpose is to discredit a possible political opponent—and continued even when a high dominant party hack admits to their real purpose, as Kevin McCarthy, then likely heir to the House speakership, did with respect to Hillary Clinton and the Benghazi hearings. Issues that didn't matter when a party was in power (e.g., the national debt during two George W. Bush administrations) may with some sleight of hand become crucial when it is out of power (during the two subsequent Obama administrations) and then unimportant again when the party is back in power and is adopting massive tax cuts mainly for corporations (during the Trump administration). This is obviously blatant self-serving hypocrisy, but far too few people seem to notice or expect otherwise, while others may fall for the partisan baiting. Similarly, mainly on the other side of the aisle, skeletons in the closet, some quite old, others long re-hashed, or some slight slip-up in a candidate's words, are often dragged out and ballyhooed to discredit people (e.g., youthful membership in the KKK or blackface costuming from 30-50 years previously, sexist jokes told by a former comedian, insufficient attentiveness to women or ethnic minorities' issues, attending a church or meeting with a controversial minister or spokesperson, etc.). Worse yet, in the Trump presidency, facts are often denied and "alternative facts" (remarkably, often outright lies) are propagated publicly while some kinds of real information, like scientific findings, are suppressed. None of the above involves reasoned treatment of issues.

Virtually all if not all societies/cultures may safely be said to be *culturally insane* to various degrees and in various ways. That does not at all mean that they are all somehow equal in that regard. Almost obviously (e.g., from the Hitler example), there often are very sharp differences between societies/cultures in the types, number and severity of their cultural insanities, and in the extents to which the people partake of them. However, in perhaps all but the smallest tribal groups, these insanities will reside most intensely in one or more subcultures (often including the leadership subcultures), even if that cultural insanity is now shared by a large majority of the people. Technically speaking, *perhaps*, a cultural insanity can only reside in the brain of an individual, but they are propagated by other individuals and the culture. Although culturally insanities in only one individual almost never have important effects (unless that individual becomes empowered), when individuals become masses of individuals they can together be much more empowered as carriers and promoters of a cultural insanity, or tendencies toward a cultural insanity. Cultural insanity is thus something like a communicable disease, but one to which others in the culture may have varying degrees of resistance or immunity.

<u>Leadership-derived Cultural Insanity</u>. Prior to late modern times, society's leaders were primarily responsible for the promulgation and implementation of cultural insanities. In earlier times, society's leadership was largely imposed on the people, originally often as local warlords or generals, or foreign conquerors, became rulers. These warriors then began a line of hereditary rulers. As a result, almost all major decisions about society were in the hands of rulers of state and church, and their associated warrior-aristocracies. These elite, or "nobles," or aristocrats shared some power as advisors and implementers for rulers. Throughout the medieval period, the non-hereditary papal throne of the Catholic Church was unusual in this regard, though it was almost always headed by people from the aristocratic classes. Its considerable long-term stability came from efforts by its leaders to maintain and enhance their/Church power, much like the more typical dynasty. To sustain power, Church leaders used two principal approaches: the development and deployment of doctrines that made the Church seem indispensable to salvation, and indirect and direct coercion, including a number of aggressive wars. In later medieval times, there began to be some exceptions to these simple leadership formulas, but even "republican" city-states were oligarchies ruled mainly by aristocrats and wealthy merchants, sometimes with participation by the upper levels of other important commercial interests (e.g., leaders of some of the most important craft guilds). And from the time of the Late Middle Ages, parliaments, which typically included representatives of aristocrats, churchmen and leading townsmen (the three "estates"), which initially tended to serve as appeal courts and/ or have some control over the taxes imposed on the citizenry, tended in time to gain other powers as well.

Notwithstanding their historical origins as warlords, the king's rule was regarded by most as God-given and natural. The main exceptions involved challenges to the king's rule by high aristocrats (or pretenders to the throne, sometimes from the same family), as in the case of King John I of England, who was coerced into granting the Magna Carta by an uprising of England's barons. Although the power of rulers and the highest aristocrats began to ebb in some realms by the 1600s if not sooner, and most notably in the republican United States after it was founded in the late 1700s, the grip of kings on the populace in many lands can be seen all the way to the end of the monarchical era after World War I.

Until fairly recently, then, it was the leaders/leading classes of society who were almost always the causes of large-scale cultural insanities—apart from those passed along by the entire culture. Even so, when leadership is largely imposed on the people, the extent to which the people come to emotionally incorporate their leaders' culturally insanities or tendencies, however propagated (e.g., via force, early forms of propaganda, the display of leadership grandeur, or the threat of heavenly or earthly retribution), can serve as an indicator of the strength of the underlying cultural insanities, whether traditional or imposed. Later medieval commoners, for example, sometimes went overboard on religious fervors such as apocalypticism, flagellation, and attacks on Jews—but those were also tied in with what the Church had taught them, even if they weren't responses to particular Church initiatives. But many crusades were directly Church-initiated. That so much of human history was forged through its leaders is another reason why I have written parts on witch-hunting, science vis-à-vis the medieval Church and, in treating evolution and geologic time, the very slow recognition that the Bible's creation and worldwide flood accounts were far from correct. These parts provide clear and strong examples of cultural insanity and some of its inhibiting effects on the development of the human potential.

Cultural Insanity Comes in Degrees

Although sometimes an example of full-blown cultural insanity is quite clear, in general it is a concept that is not necessarily easy to grasp accurately, especially with respect to situations in one's own culture. And any given tendency toward a cultural insanity may not have clear or obvious boundaries. But wherever one draws the line(s) intended to designate or encompass a cultural insanity, cultural insanity comes in degrees. Tendencies toward any particular cultural insanity will vary in strength across individuals. Across the society as a whole, sometimes the sum of these constitutes only a minor tendency, sometimes a major tendency, and sometimes a cultural insanity that dominates the society, even if not everyone in it. And some are more dangerous than others. Just as we are almost all at least a little dysfunctional (i.e., almost all have some tendencies toward individual neuroticism and certainly toward mistaken self-perceptions)—though often not so much as to impair us mentally in very important ways in our work or in our interactivity with others—we almost all share to some degree in some cultural insanities or at least some tendencies toward cultural insanities. In terms of measures, therefore, once a dimension of cultural insanity is identified, its measurement must be "continuous" in character (e.g., on a scale of 1-10), not either/or.

Just as the American psychiatric organization identifies, and revises from time to time, a large number and variety of mental illnesses and problems (which are defined in that profession's *Diagnostic and Statistical Manual of Mental Disorders*), some less severe than others or perhaps precursors to or components of others, there are many ways in which cultural insanity or tendencies toward cultural insanity may arise. And cultural insanity may be embedded in attitudes values, in a belief system or worldview, as well as in behaviors and emotions. Accordingly, it may sometimes be necessary to reflect on several aspects of human functioning to understand or diagnose a cultural insanity with a sufficient degree of certitude, and to clarify the major ways in which some mindset creates, or tends to create, unnecessary dysfunctionality for the culture as a whole, and/or a significant proportion of its people. Another reason for considering multiple criteria/ perspectives is to be cautious in judgment and to better identify and assess the likely effects, and their *magnitude*, of a carefully identified mental configuration that seems to be, or tends to be, culturally insane. Cultural insanities can also become much worse once empowered or legally implemented. Yet, clearly, it would utterly destroy the potential meaningfulness of the term if we simply start to go around branding as culturally "insane" things that are simply a matter of legitimate and reasonable differences in political interpretation. Or represent minor foibles or follies.

Cultural Insanity and Reality

From the above it should be clear that tendencies toward cultural insanity typically involve tendencies toward some kind of misapprehension or distortion of reality, not unlike many individual neuroses or insanities. A major difference is that the mistaken worldview (etc.) in cultural insanity is shared by many others; so people adhering to that erroneous belief, worldview, etcetera, may be or feel, or at least seem, fairly well adapted, at least with respect to others sharing that cultural insanity. The same applies to largish subcultures. Such people do not necessarily feel out of place among like-minded people, and are not necessarily alienated except insofar as that subculture tends to be (e.g., the cultural insanity itself may be maladaptive with the dominant culture). Thus the believer may not feel any emotional problem or need for help. Also, the believer may tend accurately to perceive reality in other respects. But that does not prevent the (sub)cultural insanity from having negative effects on human fulfillment among some/many in society, including those involved in it (e.g., see Part Four). Indeed, some cultural insanities may also produce (or at least conceal) some kind of general psychic disquiet because they cannot provide a truly viable resolution in accord with reality. Later we will how the brain can organize our perceptions all too easily to produce conclusions about reality that are erroneous and, in the worst cultural insanities, have gone seriously awry, at least in that respect.

Brief Examples of Cultural Insanity

Although I briefly mentioned some examples above, in order to facilitate further understanding of the idea of cultural insanity, it seems most useful at this point to consider some relatively extreme examples. These are drawn mainly from non-Western cases because those are the easiest for us to see without erecting our own psychological defenses based on nationalism, political leanings, and our own tendencies toward various cultural insanities.

The Cambodian Genocide. However vaguely understandable their general ideology might (or might not) have been, the slaughter of so many Cambodians—1.5 to 2 million, or around 20% of the population—in the mid to later 1970s by Pol Pot and his Khmer Rouge henchmen was monstrously culturally insane. What's the matter with the more traditional "communist" approach—"re-education camps"—or even formal prison terms for the worst offenders? U.S. bombing didn't manage to send Vietnam or Cambodia back to the stone age, but this genocidal slaughter and attempt to force Cambodia to revert to an agrarian society a la Mao, came a lot closer. Considerable built-up human potential was eliminated and potential was reduced for most of those who survived. Moreover, it is even hard to imagine that the killing and conditions imposed on society were appreciated by anyone but the few leading fanatical ideologues. So here we have a case in which the leadership was crazy, but probably only small proportions of the common people shared the same insanity, even if some of them too resented the largely urban and more educated middle and upper classes that the Khmer Rouge tried to eliminate.

China: The Cultural Revolution. Just think of all the lost potential in Mao's "Cultural Revolution"—and how much more progress China might have made if his worldview had not been so distorted, if more of the citizenry's dedication and energies had been put to productive uses instead. Unlike Cambodia, the Cultural Revolution as it occurred could not have come about without the active involvement of large numbers of Mao's ordinary Chinese supporters, whose worshipful stance toward Mao (and hopes for a better China) made them ready followers of what proved to be several really stupid ideas. Among those ideas were a re-channeling of resources into backyard furnaces to make low-grade (useless) steel, and a crippling of human potential by exiling to the countryside as common laborers many educated people who seemed in the eyes of their accusers to be elitist or in disagreement with Mao. Mao's Cultural Revolution also produced a famine that caused millions to die. Even apart from the dead, the Cultural Revolution sacrificed a lot of human potential and set China and its people back a number of years.

The Genocide in Rwanda. In Rwanda, there were long-term cultural resentments by Hutu generally toward Tutsi generally, based in part on the Tutsis having been dominant in the past and on the Tutsis having been a favored class by the old colonial masters, while the Hutu were more numerous. The shortage of land was also a factor, such that, if you were a Hutu, every displaced Tutsi family in your village or town might provide at least some possibility for aggrandizement, either for oneself or your Hutu neighbors. That many of the Hutu who did sympathize with Tutsi neighbors were killed by rampaging Hutu mobs also highlights the contrast between personal integrity and cultural insanity (there was some intertribal marriage too). At the core of the genocidal explosion of this latent cultural insanity was that Hutu resentment against the Tutsi was vigorously egged on by Hutu leaders. Presumably this slaughter would have continued further except that an organized rebel Tutsi armed force brought an end to it, defeating what must have been a very disorganized Hutu-dominated "government." However intractable Rwanda's underlying resentments and problems, there had to have been some better way(s) to deal with them. (Indeed, some efforts had been underway to do so.)

The Fundamentalist Zeal of the Taliban. Now think of the Taliban when they were in power in Afghanistan. In the years before they came to power (and to some extent in some of the Muslim societies that surround it), many restrictions on women had been easing, but among the priorities of the Taliban was a dedication to reversing this trend, per the worst and most reactionary interpretations of Islam. No more schooling for women! Banning women from many existing work roles. Confining women to traditional roles; and requiring them to wear the burqa when outside and to stay in their homes unless they had a male escort. All this raises questions about the mental health of close Taliban supporters but, in any case, it seriously undermined the potential of the society as a whole and, of course, especially the women in it.

Although the Taliban's treatment of women wasn't necessarily a major factor in their ouster (because many Afghani Islamic conservatives lean in some of the same directions), there are other reasons why it's no wonder that the Taliban were expelled from power so easily after Al-Qaeda fanatics flew passenger jets into the World Trade Center buildings and the United States went after Al-Qaeda in a big way—and the Taliban for harboring them. The Taliban's ban on music and television, and some games, and their strict regimentation of society weren't all that appreciated either. Although Taliban leadership's stances presumably found some acceptance initially and surely at least some support among some of the Afghani people, especially among the Pashtuns, Afghanistan's largest tribal group—their acceptance otherwise seems to have been based more on the people being tired of 20 years of war, first against the Soviet Union's puppet governments and then between the regional warlords who had helped to oust the final puppet Communist government (with the help of the CIA in providing armaments such as stinger missiles for use against Soviet Union helicopters). Thus the Afghan people were probably ready to accept almost any group that might bring order and stability, and reduce corruption. To many of them perhaps, the Taliban's youthful fundamentalist idealism seemed to be just the ticket. But the Taliban came with so many cultural insanities as baggage that they made things worse in many respects and so were much less supported by the people when their control of the country was (again) opposed by the other warlords with the help of military support supplied by the United States. Hopefully, if the future brings the Taliban to share in governance or rule again, they will have learned some lessons and their cultural insanities will have abated substantially.

Hitler's Racism Undermines His Own Goals. Just consider this much for now: how much did it cost in terms of lost potential (for building society or even for fighting a war) when Hitler decided to eliminate the roughly 6,000,000 Jews who were or became subjects of the Third Reich? And to eliminate Roma/gypsies, gays, the disabled, and others too. Hitler's policies cost Germany almost all of the more productive labor that the Jews could have offered (instead using only some of them as slave labor), as well as almost all developed intellectual/professional skills that his victims had. Although he may have recouped a little of the wasted resources used to ghettoize, police, and then transport, house, gas, and cremate the Jews by confiscating their belongings and property, the ethno-racist project as a whole clearly detracted from the potential of Germany society, including Hitler's war effort. And, of course, his willingness to persecute the Jews even before the war lead to the exodus of some of Germany's leading intellectuals and scientists. Here we can see leadership that was culturally insane even in contradiction with some of its other goals.

South African Leaders Deny that HIV leads to AIDS. This is an another example of leadership-based cultural insanity where, insofar as any excuse can be offered, the leadership (and presumably too many of his followers) was too hung up on seeing the country in terms of Black-White relations in what had been an apartheid state under White rule (that began converting to democratic governance in 1994). On the issue of whether HIV causes AIDS, President Thabo Mbeki stood strong against virtually the entire medical community from 2000 to late 2004 and beyond, in rejecting that scientific-medical conclusion [Donald R. Prothero, *Reality Check*, 173]. He "installed a health minister, … who was a committed AIDS denier," who prescribed witch-doctor treatments for the disease that was then ravishing Africa [Prothero, 174]. Even though there was at the time no cure for AIDS, a realistic health campaign could have been conducted with respect to safer sex practices. "From 2000 to 2008, when Mbeki and his minions were in power, there were about 340,000 AIDS deaths—and about 171,000 new AIDS infections," many of which might have been prevented [Prothero, 175].

CHAPTER 3

The General Criterion That Defines Cultural Insanity: Unnecessarily Thwarting the Development of Human Potential

Above I have mentioned "human potential" several times. The idea of developing human potential—let alone everyone's human potential—was pretty far removed from the values of pre-modern "civilized" societies' leaders—and they were the ones who really mattered in terms of decision-making. It was not on the agenda of early modern leaders either, except indirectly, for example, in Protestant calls in the 1500s for a church that spent much more of its resources on the public good, or in Francis Bacon's calls in the 1600s for overthrowing scholasticism (then still dominant in the universities) in favor of research programs in science and technology that sought to improve the lot of humankind. And not until around the middle of the 20th century were there efforts to produce a relatively complete compilation of what the potentials in human development were.

So, if historians are not supposed to impose their own values in writing about history, how can I use societies' relative thwarting of the "development of human potential" as the major key to establishing the extent to which they were culturally insane? Or perhaps even the extent to which societies are culturally insane in today's world?

One part of the answer is that this criterion is unbiased relative to historical time—it is the same across time. HOWEVER, the primary analytical focus is NOT on the gap between an ideal and any given reality in a society at some point in time. "Buried" cultural insanities do not count in assessing a historical society's cultural insanity (though probably few are fully buried today, given the immense range of possibilities for communication and for understanding existing cultures and alternatives). So, what counts historically as cultural insanity, and to a lesser extent currently are mainly: 1) movement in directions that make matters worse in terms of the development of human potential; and 2) the refusal to take realistically viable and culturally better alternative paths that history offers them/their leadership.

For example, there were no more than marginally realistic possibilities for the improvement of the lot of women in medieval times, so the lack of progress toward that goal can only be counted with respect to marginal gains and losses relative to any given status quo. Similarly, education for the masses would have been a pipe dream ("what have you been smoking"?). Instead, progress has to be measured by the slow increments in which education spread beyond the upper classes, first mainly to townspeople's sons, and by the extent to which, if any, newly developing educational opportunities in a culture were artificially denied to men on the basis of their class background (even though they continued to be almost universally denied to women except through convents and in some wealthy families).

MOREOVER, it is not correct to say that fulfilling human potential is strictly a modern idea. Indeed, the idea that an empire should rule in roughly the same way over all its subject peoples dates back to Cyrus the Great around 500 BCE [Yuval Noah Hariri, *Sapiens: A Brief History of Humankind*, 196]. Subsequent ancient empires generally followed his model, and that may help account for Rome's tolerance of many religions. Early Xtianity made an important contribution by declaring that everyone was equal in the eyes of their deity. (But despite some important real participation by women in early Xtianity, when the dust of orthodoxy settled, women and lower classes were supposed to stay in their place in society and behave in accord with their lot in life, and Church leaders eliminated most of the implications for the equality of women here on earth.) In the late 700s, Charlemagne mandated that each cathedral develop a school (even if mainly to train clerics, some of whom helped out at the courts of illiterate kings and upper-crust aristocrats). In the late 1100s, the Church also mandated that women have to consent to their marriage—something expected nowadays, but an important precedent and a step forward then—even though a woman's refusal to consent to her father's (usually) choice often met with family pressure and coercion to the contrary. (Also, it seems likely to me that this advance was largely irrelevant to peasants at the time—peasants in their typically small villages—where people rarely strayed far from their villages and would have had few choices when they reached the marriage age range in any case.) And ever since the European educated classes rediscovered, disseminated and digested Aristotle, say by around 1250CE, the concept of human development was no longer absent, even if it was applied first and foremost to the physical unfolding of all plants and animals. "Everything that exists," Aristotle taught, "strives to fulfill itself—to realize (or, in his language, as translated, to "actualize") its inherent potential" [Richard E. Rubenstein, *Aristotle's Children: How Christians, Muslims, and Jews Rediscovered Ancient Wisdom and Illuminated the Middle Ages*, 43].

So perhaps the simplest statement of the criterion as a measuring device involves answering a question about the *extent to which* a society/culture **unnecessarily** thwarts human development, such that people have to settle for second, third, or nth best among otherwise realistic possibilities for developing themselves. Culturally saner societies would tend more toward maximizing human development.

Although the key criterion can thus be stated relatively simply, it is sometimes difficult to apply, in part because there are some important, and almost obvious, additional considerations or provisos (see below). All cultures establish what amount to "channels" for human development. Those channels include everything from social and behavioral mandates and norms to employment roles. And those channels range from very few and narrow—often especially for the lower classes (e.g., slaves, serfs bound to the land, untouchables, peasants)—to many and fairly broad. Obviously, the development of human potential is much more likely to be thwarted when the channels are (unnecessarily) narrow, and the more so yet if the channels are also distorted relative to humanity's natural emotional drives. Sparta's military-only for Spartans society seems to have been something of an epitome of narrow as well as unnatural or warped in its channeling. It is, of course, entirely possible for a culture to have broad choices in some areas of human development and have highly constricted or warped ones in others. This is probably more likely to occur in societies in which religious or secular authoritarian leadership constricts possibilities in some areas of human development, for example, in music, science learning, social-political activism, male-female relationships, or with race/ethnicity-based policies.

Of course some aspects of human development are foundational to survival. These are basic needs such as love, food, and shelter/security. The need for food may imply the necessity of either work opportunities (at least for those able) or some kind of welfare. Obviously, starvation undermines everything else, but the potentials for human development are generally built on top of these minima.

Metaphorically—and to a large extent evolutionarily—**the purpose of life is to grow and to flower**. Evolution is based on a combination of survival and reproduction (passing genes on to the next generation), but in some species, most especially humans, survival of the young depends on the previous generation's support well beyond birth and that requires, at minimum, parental survival well into adulthood. So, in humans, that flowering includes continued adult learning and the teaching of children—which also helps the tribe survive. And this means contributing to the future of humanity through the further development of culture itself. *Apart from rulers and generals*—whose contributions to humanity may be positive or negative—it doesn't take much perusing of the lives of other historically great men and women to discern that most of them were great precisely for their cultural contribution to humankind—the thinkers, the artists, the musicians, the inventors and scientific discoverers, the social justice seekers, and a goodly number of unsung culture heroes and heroines. So everyone is included, not just those who have had more freedom and capacity to contribute to culture directly, but also history's peasants who were oppressed and almost always limited to learning the ins-and-outs of raising the food that the culturally empowered (leaders) depended on, not only for eating but for surpluses to sustain a higher standard of living.

But what are these "human potentials" that societies should foster? The table that follows provides an organized set of concepts that could be said, as a whole, to portray the general range of possibilities in human development, what I call "the elements of human development." In terms of early efforts along these lines, much credit is due to Erik H. Ericson, Abraham Maslow, and Arthur Chickering (see the references at the end of the table). And please don't skip footnote **.

A Formulation of the Elements of Human Development*

"1. Trust/Love**

- Basic trust/security [E*]: the potential for a secure self and the foundation for loving others

- Development of trust/love relationships with parents, siblings, peers

- Capacity to cooperate in work or play with others

2. Basic Autonomy

- Responsibility for oneself (actions not directly dependent on, nor merely rebellious against, parents, peers, spouse, others)

- General self-assertiveness

- Re-evaluation of simplistic goals, beliefs, values, attitudes that were inculcated directly by parents and other socializing agents

3. Initiative

- Sense of initiative [E]: risk-taking

- Growth of self-expressive capabilities and rehearsal/ imagination

- Evolution of patterns of interaction between self and parents (as self grows)

- Reduced self-restriction due to needs for reassurance, affection, and approval [C*]

- Reduced dependence on peers (as adulthood nears) [C]

- Ability to express anger directly

4. Industry

- Capacity for industrious learning [E]; ability to use basic environmental resources
- Ability to plan successfully for the future, and to delay gratification
- Foresight into consequences of one's behavior; capacity to learn from experience [B*]
- Flexible array of general social functioning skills

5a. Psychomotor

- Physical/athletic skills development
- Manual competence
- Development of coordination, grace, balance

5b. Health

- Constructive habits and practices for physiological health (e.g., knowledge of body, hygiene, diet, sanitation, safety precautions, exercise)

6a. Basic Skills and Breadth

- Acquisition of basic skills (understanding of written and oral communications; writing; speaking; quantitative capabilities)
- Acquisition of basic knowledge and understanding of the natural and cultural realms
- Development of practical skills appropriate to life in one's culture (e.g., for effective learning, for using society's basic technologies, for coping with society's requirements, etc.)

6b. Critical, Analytical Thinking

- Development of capabilities for critical, analytical thinking (e.g., abilities to recognize assumptions, purported facts, strengths and weaknesses in argument, etc.)

- Development of abilities to pose and solve problems, including with deduction, inference and hypothesis-testing

- Re-evaluation of basic assumptions (takes up where Element 2, aspect 3, leaves off; see also 9a., aspect 4)

- Development of premises for reasoning; recognizing the contingent nature of truth [B]

6c. Sociocultural Autonomy

- Knowledge/understanding of societal institutions, assumptions, myths, and current issues (e.g., in capitalism, government, social customs and mores, foreign relations, religion, law, etc.)

- Increased resistance to acculturation [M] (advertising, propaganda, authority- or fad-promulgated ideas of "good," etc.)

- Ecological awareness: appreciation of human interdependence with the environment and other forms of life

6d. Aestheticism

- Appreciation of aesthetics and meanings in the various forms of art and architecture, music, literature and drama, dance, etc.

- Appreciation of Nature, natural beauty

- Development of capabilities for artistic self-expression

6e. Experiential Foundation

- Broadened experience with and understanding of social/ societal roles (including work) and human technology and culture; sense of comfort in a greater variety of settings

- Improved capacity for making sound judgments, appreciating quality, refinement of tastes [B]

- Acquiring an experiential foundation for character and personal meanings in life

7a. Empathy and Friendships

- Tolerance/acceptance of others different from oneself

- Empathy: understanding/acceptance/appreciation/sharing of what other individuals are perceiving, experiencing or feeling, and how they view events

- Broadening the variety of friends and acquaintances; increasing the depth of sharing in friendships

7b. Identification with the Species (altruism)

- Care, compassion, altruism

- Understanding cultural relativity: comprehension of the differing ways of humankind (e.g., as possibilities, potentials and actualities within the self); appreciation of all humanity (locally, nationally, internationally)

- Identification with the species [M] and motivation to contribute

7c. Management of Emotions

- Management of emotions [C]: constructive expression of emotions [B] (fit to situation); development of adequate defenses and capacity to selectively apply them (see also 9a., aspect 2)

- Problem-centering: ability to face problems squarely and to cope with them [M]

- Realistic expectations

- Ability to compromise

7d. Accepting Responsibility

- Capacity to fulfill commitments, promises

- Capacity to accept and to delegate responsibility, and to work as a member of a team

- Ability to serve as a leader (with a disposition to seek and take counsel [B])

8. Synthesizing Understandings and Meanings

- Ability to synthesize information in different formats and from various sources

- Development of a coherent worldview – consistent with self's knowledge of history, society and people

- Development of a consistent ethics/morality

- Development of a coherent value system (see also 10d.); development of a life style

- Developing a synthesis of commitments (including 7d. and 10b.) [P]

- Appreciation/development of an integrated meaning in life

9a. Self-Awareness and Insight

- Self-awareness
- Accurate and insightful self-perception (including of one's own defenses and assumptions); ability to introspect
- Conscious access to and acceptance of inner impulses; congruence of that acceptance with self-view
- Insight into and loosening of parentally and culturally-instilled feelings, responses, behavior patterns (see also 11., aspect 2)
- Appreciation of oneself as part of nature

9b. Openness to Ambiguity, Creativity, and Lifelong Learning

- Openness to/welcoming of new ideas, experiences
- Tolerance/acceptance of ambiguity, conflicting ideas, feelings
- Loosely organized perceptions (not bound by object function or role, nonstereotypic, etc.); freely associating mental fields
- Release of creative and imaginative ideas and impulses
- Broad sense of humor; wit; ability to laugh at oneself
- Lifelong learning/growth orientation) (see also 10e., aspect 2)

9c. Sensory and Emotional Richness

- Capacity for full sensory operation (in this highly visual-verbal socioculture); capacity to relate nonverbally
- Appreciation of one's body; sensuality
- Contact with the inner self via dreams

- Development of intuitive capabilities
- Richness of emotional reaction [M]

9d. Spontaneity and Playfulness

- Playfulness; openness to child-like
- Nonself-conscious spontaneity [M]
- Ability to enjoy leisure time and life in general (not fixation on past, future or present, nor escapism)
- Significant degree of focus on living in the present

10a. Sexual Identity and Satisfaction

- Clarification of sexual identity [C]
- Development of capabilities to sustain long-term intimate relationships: full mutual communication; equality in relationships; capacity to give (yield/surrender) and to take (accept/receive); sexual satisfaction (orgasmic potential realized)

10b. Capacity for Intimacy

- Capacity for intimate commitment to another
- Acceptance of others as they are (while encouraging their growth)
- Development of capabilities to foster the development of others (typically including children)
- Mutuality of regard/respect with parents [C] (to the extent possible, given self's integrity, their situation, other life tasks)

10c. Self-Esteem

- Self-acceptance (despite inability to be/do all things, irremediable limitations, errors made)
- Self-esteem; positive self-regard
- Sense of well-being

10d. Integrity and Commitment to Justice

- Internalization of conscience; greater reliance on inner feelings
- Congruence of behavior and values
- Commitment to justice; democratic character structure [M]
- Fulfillment of social responsibilities
- Capacity to take a moral stand

10e. Discovery, Development and Use of Talents

- Discovery and development of one's intelligence, talents (including academic/professional as well as nonacademic specializations, abilities, skills, capabilities)
- Capacity for self-discipline (not compulsivity) in the service of work, avocational, or other activities and goals
- Use of one's intelligence, talents; pursuit of/movement toward a satisfying life's work
- Accomplishments/fulfillment in life/work: contribution to humanity

11. Ego Integrity, Freedom, Wisdom, Fulfillment, and Beyond

- Ego integrity with ongoing evolution/refinement of identity

- Abandonment of self's remaining secondary gain systems (e.g., power, status or money/materialistic orientations; sexism; racism; approval-seeking; nationalism; etc.)

- Realization of free will, self-determination; idiosyncratic individualization

- "Superior" perception of reality [M]; wisdom in judgment

- Satisfaction/fulfillment in life; acceptance of death

- Beyond dichotomies: appreciation of the underlying unity of energy and matter in the universe; the paradox of existential absurdity and meaning in life; the perfect in the imperfect; allowance for mystical experiences

*A number of entries in this table are citations or close paraphrases from Maslow (1968), ... and are flagged with an '[M].' Other entries (marked '[C]') are derived from Chickering (1969).... A '[B]' refers to Bowen (1977)... a '[P]' to Perry (1981)... and an '[E]' refers to Erikson (1968).

**The labels associated with each element of human development ... are intended to facilitate reference to them rather than to be both comprehensive and precise."

End of table and end citation from Jeffrey Wynter Koon, *Assessing Quality and Effectiveness in University and College Academic Programs: A Democratic Theory of Evaluation*, Part 2, pp. 3:142- 3:146. [Bullets have been added here.] The original includes additional discussion about each of the principal sources that precedes this table.

References associated with this table:

Howard R. Bowen, *Investment in Learning.*

Arthur W. Chickering, *Education and Identity.*

Erik H. Erikson, *Identity: Youth and Crisis*.

Abraham Maslow, *Toward a Psychology of Being, 2nd Ed.*

William G. Perry, Jr., "Cognitive and Ethical Growth: The Making of Meaning," in Arthur W. Chickering and Associates, *The Modern American College*, pp. 76-116.

Proviso #1: Level of
Technological Development

There are at least two major provisos that need to be considered in evaluating how well a particular set of cultural behaviors and/or beliefs facilitate or impede human development. The first, which is especially needed in historical analysis and in thinking about less developed countries, is the level of technological development available to a society/culture. Thus, even in modern times, we can and should expect a lot more of the United States than of countries in sub-Saharan Africa, because the former is highly developed technologically (and wealthy) and can apply that potential to the development of its population. Sub-Saharan Africa is more laggard in technology (and poor), where just making major strides toward universal schooling for young people (especially girls) and making birth control available to all women who want it would be big steps forward. A corollary of this proviso is that the level of scientific development and thinking also imposes limits on the possibilities of any given historical time period. We cannot expect a historical culture to facilitate the development of human potential in ways that require a level of scientific knowledge or a technological capability that does not yet exist.

For example, in medieval times, one cannot expect much in the way of sane handling of diseases until people have learned more about them through reason and perhaps proto-science. In medieval times people often attributed diseases such as the plague to the idea that the deity was punishing them or their region for the people's sinfulness. The same was true even of bad weather (drought, crop-destroying hailstorms, floods, etc.). Nevertheless, despite such ignorance and superstition, some people did finally figure out, generally not until after the Black Death of 1349 but long before science explained why, that quarantines could help reduce the spread of plague. Even before that though, nobles often fled to the countryside thinking that might well be a viable avoidance maneuver (knowing that cities were often stricken severely). Thus even in medieval times, at least some kinds of plague were finally recognized in some places as being communicable (though that did not preclude in the minds of the people that a plague might also have been used by the deity to punish sins).

But there's a down side when it comes to materialism in modern industrially- and technologically-advanced cultures. It's vaguely possible now for almost everyone in some societies to be almost literally drowning in material goods, even though those suffering the worst inequalities in those societies may fall well short of that. Our levels of overconsumption and waste are addressed subsequently as is, indirectly, the question of "want" versus "need."

Proviso #2: Level of Consciousness

The second proviso, again especially important in a historical analysis, involves the level of consciousness. This concept is akin (but not equal) to the range of learning at the time upon which the analysis is focused. It applies primarily to whomever has sufficient power to possibly effect change (or preserve the status quo), so, in all but recent history, it applies mainly to leaders of various kinds and the uppermost social-political classes. Often but not always, this proviso boils down to exclude anything that is not in the *realistic* range of possibilities in the minds of leaders. But considering what is realistic does not mean that determinations are bound to declare as unrealistic anything that then-dominant powers did not do or decided to reject or oppose. Just as we cannot predict our future, in part because there are many possible paths [Hariri, 237-239], the same was true in the past, even if there were fewer possible paths and far less input into decision-making. So, if a society's leader(s) rejected an otherwise viable alternative that would have reduced cultural insanity in some important way—and that alternative had substantial support among those who brought it to the attention of leadership or those who were in the (somewhat) empowered classes—that rejection might well count as an add on to, or the unnecessary maintenance of, an existing cultural insanity. (With only a little viability, the events supposed here might simply further reveal a buried cultural insanity.) For example, women's liberation in general was never a realistic possibility throughout medieval times, but new choices for easing up on or increasing restriction of women's activities (even if not their main role as mother and wife) were sometimes in play for leaders to consider. Thus popes had choices about whether or not to crack down on nuns who were active in social service outside their cloisters—where facilitating their human potential (and societal benefits at the same time) requires leaving them alone—a path often not followed by the papacy, making matters worse.

Also required in considering this proviso is an awareness of the role that current perspectives might play in distorting our thinking about what was and was not a realistic or viable alternative in the past. For legitimate judgments about cultural insanity, we obviously cannot simply or automatically impose current values on the past in our interpretation. Thus the Europe-wide array of constraints on women in medieval Europe was Europe-limiting, but it would be erroneous to classify it as an active cultural insanity. It was a buried cultural insanity—it had negative effects, in this case major effects, but effects that were buried deeply in the low level of consciousness at the time. Only later would it come into consciousness enough to enable change. So, when it comes to assessing cultural insanity, ignorance *is* an excuse. Thus, if one expects to be able to fault witch-hunting (and I did), one must do so with reference almost if not exclusively to the range of perspectives of the time. There was some opposition at the time when witch-hunting ideas reared their ugly head, so the problems were far from buried, but the opposition wasn't fully coherent in argumentation and did not retain or attain much viability among the leadership classes once those classes became stressed by and fearful about history's events, and more open to scapegoating. Prior to that time, choices were made that led down the wrong path (a retrogression) to develop the possibility of the witch-hunting cultural insanity (e.g., by exaggerating and distorting an existing belief in witchcraft, per the agenda of some inquisitors in society's second-tier ranks of leaders).

Another part subsequently deals with the cultural insanities imposed on society as the medieval (Catholic) Church rather successfully pursued its desire for power and control, and then used those powers in part to impede the development of reason and proto-science, and thus the potential for greater human development and fulfillment. (And we're talking well before Galileo here.) Nearer in time, extending into today's world, I also take a look at how the young-earth creationists' rejection of evolution and geologic time is a human potential-limiting cultural insanity that affects not only them and their children but the entirety of our modern society and to some extent, the world. But let's take a look at another somewhat familiar example first as a way of illustrating the complexities involved.

African Americans; Huckleberry Finn. In analyses pertaining to cultural insanity it is often important to make note of situations in which there were influential individuals within the society/culture who did not partake as fully of the mainstream culture's defects (or some subculture's defects), and to do so because they might (have) provide(d) an alternative that could instead have been followed. But much depends upon how dim the alternative's prospects were. Here's one example about the level of consciousness that still confuses many people today: Is Mark Twain's *Huckleberry Finn* racist because of his multiple uses of a word in the dialog that is now regarded as almost unprintable—and unspeakable, except among rappers and groups of Black friends? This word, commonly referred to as the "N-word," was in frequent use, especially among southerners, historically. Yet, historically viewed, it is clear that Mark Twain was well ahead of most of the other Whites of post-Reconstruction times (after 1877) in recognizing the legitimacy of Blacks' claim to full humanity (and real equality), in part by his having helped out some individual Blacks. "America's greatest book … by America's greatest writer" … punctured white hypocrisy by showing that 'black lives matter'" [Frances, 92]. *Huckleberry Finn* was published in 1884, but it was set in a time prior to the Civil War in Missouri, a slave state. To write dialog and convey Huck's thinking for a novel that was to be true to its time and place, Twain didn't have any choice but to use the N-word. But in the novel, Huck ultimately learns that the Negro Jim's humanness is as good as anybody else's—a lesson little accepted in U.S. society then. The novel fits in especially well with teaching about the broader realities/history in this country at that time—when southern states had begun to enact laws to control Blacks and their political power. But if it is read without sufficient background knowledge, it could seem shocking to some in today's more racism-sensitive and "politically correct" world. So it also matters how the teaching is handled in high school and now, alas, even in college classes.

Before the Civil War, the cultural insanity of slavery was evident in the tension between "all men are created equal," as the Declaration of Independence put it, and the very idea of an enslaved group of people. Slavery had been built into the Constitution as a compromise with the status quo (a number of leaders in the southern states were slaveholders)—with each slave counted as 3/5ths of a resident for purposes of apportionment of representatives to Congress. According to Alexander Stephens, Vice-President of the Confederacy, Thomas Jefferson thought slavery just might be the rock on which the Union would founder; and the leading statesmen who put the U.S. Constitution together in the late 1780s thought "slavery was wrong in principle, socially, morally and politically" [Stephens, A., "Cornerstone Speech," March 21, 1861]. That is almost undoubtedly an overstatement. It was an evil they did not know how to deal with and thought, or at least hoped, would pass away. Unfortunately, the long-term profitability of slavery became assured with the invention of the cotton gin in 1793 and the spread of cotton plantations throughout the deep south, so it did not fade away. By the 1820s if not before, North-South tensions over the extension of slavery beyond its existing states was a major issue. But later, as secession proceeded, Stephens spoke to how the South's new government was founded on an opposite principle: "Its cornerstone rests… upon the great truth that the negro is not equal to the white man"; further, the Confederacy was "the first, in the history of the world, based upon this great physical, philosophical, and moral truth" [Stephens, "Cornerstone Speech"].

Disapproval of slavery in the North was initially contingent mainly on the dislike of the idea of free men competing with slaves economically, including in newer territories in western areas. But over time, the problem gradually came to be seen by more people in its broader humanitarian context as well, as put forth mainly by abolitionists and articulate escaped slaves like Frederick Douglass. (For decades, however, abolitionists were despised even in the north.) The all-too frequent cruelties against slaves helped to make this broader case (and were all the more widely recognized after the publication in 1852 of *Uncle Tom's Cabin*, a novel by Harriet Beecher Stowe). But when South Carolina attacked Fort Sumter in 1860, a federally-held fort in Charleston harbor, the North went to war to preserve the Union (and its constitution—which incorporated slavery), *not to end slavery*. Only toward the middle of the war did slavery come to the fore as a main issue for the North (a major rationale Lincoln used in emancipating slaves in *rebel-held territory* was to undermine the

South militarily)—even though the defense of slavery was the principal reason the South went to war two years earlier [Harry S. Stout, *Upon the Altar of the Nation: A Moral History of the Civil War*]. At the end of the war, General Grant,U.S., although acknowledging the long and valiant war effort of the South and recognizing the suffering it brought, incisively said that slavery "was, I believe, one of the worst [causes] for which a people ever fought, and one for which there was the least excuse."

Using the cultural insanity lens, it is obvious that the human potential and the development of the Black population during slavery was substantially limited and undermined. To a considerable extent this was done very overtly, for example, by the formal (legal) and informal prohibitions on slaves learning to read. Although ordinary Whites "benefitted" by having a higher status than Blacks and slaveholders benefitted economically, only by twisted thinking could male Negroes not be thought of as fully men—and in the South there was plenty of that.

But regarding Negroes as inferior was very typical throughout the nation, even among many abolitionists. Among the principal objections to Darwin's theories (after 1859) were that they left out a role for Providence and that he argued for the likelihood that humans all came from a single origin [Randall Fuller, *The Book that Changed America: How Darwin's Theory of Evolution Ignited a Nation*]. And, in the relevant sciences of this era, many practitioners began to try to demonstrate that their biases had a foundation in reality, by measuring the head sizes and brain sizes on skulls of European, Black, Mongoloid and Red races (with Blacks almost invariably being placed at the lowest end on intelligence).

After the war, some of the most idealistic northerners went to the South to try to help educate the almost entirely illiterate Black population and to help them in other ways. But a continued Union Army's presence in the South was also needed to reduce or prevent extensive retaliatory violence by Southern Whites against Blacks for their political activities and other self-assertions. After a long and bloody war, continued Southern violence against the freed men and an unchanged leadership class in the South were among the reasons that Northern Republicans for a time took a tough stance against Southern resistance to their changed circumstances (it seemed as if the South hadn't lost the war). Republican members of Congress led the way in adopting constitutional amendments and a variety of legislation supportive of the *civil* equality of, and better opportunities for, Blacks. This is the period known as Reconstruction (1865-1876). But there was insufficient long-term economic and social support from the people of the northern states. After a decade of Reconstruction, many northerners hoped to, or were ready to, get beyond the period of sectional animosity. Slavery had been ended; the Constitution had been amended to give political rights to all people. And Southern complaints about Northern control and the decade-long deployment of contingents of the Union Army in the South slowly undermined much of what idealism there was in the North, but that was possible in part because of the lack of a true appreciation in the north for the equality of Black people.

Thus, if we look at people in the northern states at the time of Twain's writing and subsequently, we cannot make fair historical judgments if we simply condemn their overt racism and discrimination against Blacks—abhorrent though these may seem to enlightened modern conscience and consciousness. That was a time when racist attitudes were still extremely widespread and deep, north and south. "Even after the Civil War resulted in the abolition of slavery, Black Americans existed as an ostracized caste, never considered fully American" [Hartman, 102]. Whites generally were also racial and cultural supremacists when it came to Native American Indians (whose lands were still being taken at the time). Much the same was true about attitudes toward the Chinese who helped build the transcontinental railroad, and toward the original Hispanic denizens in places like California and Texas [Ronald T. Takaki, *Iron Cages: Race and Culture in 19th-Century America*]. And true Black *social equality* was probably never supported by more than a tiny minority of Whites in the U.S. even at the height of abolitionist and post-Civil War idealism. Indeed, it was the voices for true *civil equality*, not social equality, whose influence was waning and then largely collapsed after the election of 1876 in which the Republican candidate, although narrowly the loser, was declared the winner in exchange for an agreement to restore full rights to the states of the rebel South. This was "reconciliation" without much further concern for what would happen to the Negroes under home-state rule in the South.

For many of the Negroes immediately after the Civil War, adjusting to a vastly different absence of formal bondage was a welcome but difficult task, especially in the face of continued sabotage and opposition from most of the White leadership and population in the South (which included the first appearance of the Ku Klux Klan and lynching and the burning down of Black's school buildings). By the early 1890s, many Southern states had already begun to impose highly unequal treatment, often now written into law ("Jim Crow" laws), as well as to deny Blacks' voting rights with poll taxes, arbitrarily enforceable "literacy" tests, etcetera. Over time, more and more occupations were also closed to Blacks. Targeted laws, some as petty as vagrancy, and their selective enforcement, also ensured that many more Blacks became classified as criminals who, once imprisoned, were often hired out to landowners and private corporations (e.g., mining companies) and subjected to slave labor conditions—but now in situations in which the bosses had no monetary interest in preventing harm to their subjects, unlike the original slaveholders. Because this re-constriction of the civil rights of Blacks in the South happened piecemeal and separately by state, it was all the easier for the realities to go largely unheralded and under-reported in the North. Much of the inequality was hidden under the fig leaf of separate but equal, so, to the distant observer, it seemed far less egregious than it was. In time, the South abounded in signs that said, "Whites only," whether affixed to businesses, public water fountains, or sections of beaches. Moreover, throughout this time there was the threat of never-prosecuted White mobs lynching any Blacks who challenged any White-imposed expectations. These actions against the Black population of the Southern states very clearly represented not only a substantial re-institutionalization of the original cultural insanity, but also a considerable exacerbation of the status of Blacks compared to the period of "Radical Reconstruction," which had offered something of a real alternative (even if it didn't provide 40 acres and a mule or social equality). And, as more Blacks made their way North, especially during and after World War I, they ended up in segregated residential ghettoes in the cities and, despite greater opportunities in many workplaces and the freedom to exercise most of their civil rights, there remained lots of prejudice and many de facto limitations too (e.g., deception was needed to buy a house in a "White" area, but even if that was successful, the presence of new Black neighbors would usually elicit a reaction harsh enough to drive the purchaser out). And there were a number of northern cities (and places in the south as well) that were subjected to White mob-led violence on Black districts in and around 1919-1921, with among the worst episodes being in Tulsa, Oklahoma.

Given the inferior or denied education for Blacks in the South, there was a need for, and a very slow emergence of (the Historically) Black Colleges and Universities—which for decades were mainly vocational schools that trained Blacks as somewhat skilled laborers in agriculture and for other low-skilled jobs in which Southern Whites would accept them, and in the domestic/household arts (e.g., to serve as maids), but also, importantly, as Black school teachers. However, until around the time of World War II, most Blacks remained very substantially under-educated, living mostly in rural areas in the South, working as share-croppers dependent on, and typically exploited and often cheated by, and indebted to, large landowner-landlords. De facto, most were trapped there. And thus, for some time, only a few urban and more highly educated Blacks, acting through vehicles such as the National Association for the Advancement of Colored People (NAACP), and through the arts such as music (and eventually, the military and sports), could try to help convince Whites *in general* to see error in ingrained/inculcated attitudes that regarded Blacks as less than equals in so many ways. Real social and interpersonal contact between Blacks and Whites was limited, and the homes of almost all Blacks were confined to Black sections of towns and cities.

The substantial re-institutionalization of the original cultural insanity in the South, along with the continuing extremes of racism among many in the North—and the systemic aspects of it—would come home to roost again in the middle of the 20th century—as if to demonstrate the persistence of this cultural insanity. In sum, we need to be somewhat more aware of the fact that White racism had very deep roots, north and south, and had ebbed only somewhat by the late 1800s when Twain wrote Huckleberry Finn. And when we more fully appreciate this context, we can better see that *Huckleberry Finn* did indeed provide a powerful lesson showing the human equality of Black people. By the same token (history in its chronological context), monuments to the man who, despite feet of clay (slaveholding), perhaps most helped to assert the ideal that all should be free, Thomas Jefferson, still seem appropriate (along with sufficient explanation about his relationship with Sally Hemings, and their children, which, from what I've seen, isn't so bad, especially for the time). Of late, I've even seen a newspaper account questioning whether it is appropriate to name a school after Benjamin Franklin—a man who owned slaves early in his life but by his later years—before 1800!—was a leading abolitionist—making him among the earliest. In context, he should be honored, not faulted [see www.archives.gov>legislative.features.franklin]. Columbus, on the other hand, would seem to have a pretty weak case that is 100% Eurocentric. And confederate generals—well, no—their statues are monuments to the cause of White supremacy (often erected when the South was re-imposing subordinate status on Blacks), to defending slave states/the Confederacy; they are monuments to honor men whose actions were at least bordering on treasonous.

Racism. It should be clear from the above too that racism is not an "either/or" thing. *Racism comes in degrees and almost all Whites are at least somewhat racist—but some are much more racist than others.* If anyone wants to call others "racist," it should be reserved for the worst of the latter set of people. Otherwise, "racist" should be used with respect to *specified* attitudes, beliefs or behaviors. Further, it will become clearer in our subsequent discussion of stereotyping that, when reacting to people of any other "race," everyone, to the degree that they substitute general ideas about "others," or project their own fear(s) of the unknown onto individuals others—a kind of premature "filling in the blanks" (instead of engaging in the reality of other individuals)—can be said to be exhibiting racism. Indeed, some kind of in-group/out-group beliefs and attitudes in human societies are deeply embedded in our evolutionary past. A corollary: Do not expect a racism-free society/culture to evolve any time soon—although perhaps large reductions in racism might be on the horizon.

In any case, once again there seems to be some increased prospects for a reduction in racism among Whites—prospects little seen since the late 1960s—through a growing recognition of the reality of the interactions between all too many police officers and Blacks in this society (and the social structures that support such a status quo). These prospects seem to be attributable partly to a new generation but also to a growing number of instances of *cell phone and body cam videos documenting* police brutality (e.g., Rodney King), itchy police trigger fingers based on race-based fears (e.g., Philando Castile), violent police surprise attacks (e.g., Breonna Taylor), and other totally unnecessary killings of Black people—such as the slow-motion police murder of George Floyd in Minneapolis.

CHAPTER 4

Other Indicators of Cultural Insanity

Continuing to Believe in "Information"
Long Since Revealed to Be Erroneous

What are we to make of information such as this: Even well after the *lack* of evidence was widely discussed in the press and on TV for more than a decade, many supporters of the War on Iraq remained blind to the fact that Saddam Hussein at the time of the U.S. invasion in 2003 no longer had any weapons of mass destruction (none were found by U.S. forces). According to a poll taken as late as 2015, 42% of the U.S. public (and a higher percentage among Republicans and Fox "news" viewers) still believed that the U.S. invasion found an active WMD program in Iraq [Politico]. Many people went right on believing erroneous material that they should long before have come to know was false. Such results definitively show that cultural insanity has little difficulty arising in the United States.

Repeated Failures to Obtain Expected Outcomes
from Particular Actions or Policies

A definition of individual insanity attributed to Albert Einstein says: "Insanity is doing the same thing over and over again and expecting different results." And the same thing might also be said of continuing to believe erroneous information long after it has been widely discredited as false (as above), or continuing to maintain other kinds of strong beliefs that have generally failed to yield the promised results when implemented.

In a democratic society, this maintenance of erroneous beliefs includes recalcitrant government leaders and supporters of a policy or national action who refuse to see (or learn from) multifaceted failures derived from the implementation of that policy, especially when some important negative side effects are quite clear (the dead and wounded in a war are perhaps the most definitive example). Barbara Tuchman identifies four sources of misgovernment: "tyranny or oppression"; "excessive ambition"; "incompetence or decadence"; and "folly or perversity" [Tuchman, *The March of Folly: From Troy to Vietnam*, 5]. In turn, actions that she classifies as folly have three criteria: the actions "must have been perceived as counter-productive" in their own time; "a feasible alternative course of action must have been available"; and the policy "should be that of a group ... and persist beyond any one political lifetime" [Tuchman, 5]. Her history of this country's leadership over the decades of our involvement in the War on Vietnam provides a long-term instance of what she means by "folly." Vietnam is surely an example, the more so because in developing and maintaining its policies in Vietnam, government leaders were reacting "to intimidation by the rabid right at home and to the public dread of Communism that this played on and reflected" [Tuchman, 269]. "Having invented Indochina as the main target of a coordinated Communist aggression" and having in many pronouncements repeated that preserving it from Communism was "vital to American security," our government became "lodged in the trap of its own propaganda" [Tuchman, 258; emphasis added].

Tuchman added the third criterion of folly to "remove the problem from personality," which she sees as needed because "misgovernment by a single sovereign or tyrant is too frequent and too individual to be worth a generalized inquiry" [Tuchman, 5]. However, all people, including current and would-be tyrants, should be able to learn from the histories of tyrants too. Moreover, almost all dictators have some kind of advisory group(s), even if, in some cases, the people in those groups consist almost entirely of sycophants (yes people, usually men, especially historically). Further, presumably even most tyrants want to be seen positively in history. And they also have reason to behave constructively enough toward their people so as not to set off successful revolts against their rule—which might eliminate their dynasty. In any case, it makes no sense to exclude tyrants or their supporters from inclusion in a possible diagnosis of cultural insanity (provided the other conditions for that conclusion are met, including a feasible alternative and effects that hinder the development of human potential).

Finally, not wanting to get into psychologizing, Tuchman says that the source of the various leaders' failures to learn, their source of self-deception, is "wooden-headedness." Wooden-headedness "consists in assessing a situation in terms of fixed notions while ignoring or rejecting any contrary signs" [Tuchman, 7]. As I have begun to show here, with more to follow, this kind of self-deception, especially insofar as it is empowered or has substantial negative effects on others, is readily classifiable as a cause of cultural insanity.

Here's a more current example that has produced repeated failure in most respects, especially relative to the entire society. Although tax cuts for corporations and wealthy individuals may facilitate economic growth and the country's overall prosperity when taxes on high incomes are extraordinarily high and the population has had a build-up in demand as a result of frugality and abstinence—as was the situation after World War II (when marginal tax rates on high-income individuals were 70% and more)—such "supply-side" economics have been a failure as a recipe for whatever ails the economy. The alternative name for this policy is "trickle-down" economics. (Personally, I imagine a male dog and a fire hydrant, where the vast majority of us are the fire hydrant.) Yet many Republican political leaders continued to speak in favor of tax cuts for "job creators" (i.e., corporations and the wealthy) as an alternative way to combat the recession that began in 2008. During recessions, because of reduced demand, there is no economic incentive for corporations to increase production, create new businesses, or hire additional workers, so such tax cuts would mainly increase income inequality, annual government deficits, and long-term debt. In contrast, meaningful government spending (e.g., on infrastructure) without tax cuts will also increase the deficit and debt, but it will create more jobs, raise marketplace demand, bring in some added tax revenues (from those jobs and sales), build useful infrastructure for the future, and, normally, help pull the country out of a recession or depression. Earlier, when Ronald Reagan tried supply-side economics tax cuts, he subsequently said that he would take his Budget Director, David Stockman, "to the woodshed" for, in essence, telling the truth about how those supply-side economic policies were not working, especially relative to rising annual deficits and national debt. (Reagan subsequently increased taxes substantially to counter these negative effects.) The Trump-Republican tax cuts of 2017 also benefited mainly corporations and the wealthy, while emphasizing propagandistically the (small) tax cuts that ordinary people would receive (albeit for only a few years under the law), and that the tax cuts for corporations would spur job creation. But by then the economy had largely recovered from the recession of 2008, and the jobless rate was relatively low compared to historical standards, at 4.8% or lower, down 3 percentage points during Obama's terms (though the percentage out of the workforce was still somewhat elevated), and there was no pent-up demand for goods and services. So, in this case, the economy was boosted a little more (as I write, the unemployment rate is 3.6%), and stocks, made more valuable by corporate tax cuts and higher pay-outs to shareholders, increased in value substantially in the next two years. But increases in wages, as also promised, did not materialize, even with the somewhat more tightened job market. And the supply-side economics recipe all-but failed otherwise because it wasn't applicable to the situation. In sum, the main effects of the tax cuts (given that so little went to the common people) were to increase the monetary holdings of corporations, enabling corporations to return more to their shareholders (mainly the wealthy), make the richest individuals richer while increasing income inequality (which was already very high historically), and to increase annual government deficits while adding to the overall government debt, year after year. Because loopholes in tax laws went untouched, the nominal corporate tax of 21% for high corporate income often resulted in actual rates in the low single digits or even zero. Because the national debt is a loan with mandatory interest payments to owners of government bonds, beyond some reasonable maximum, rising deficits and a rising debt impair a society's capability to fund its other needs—whether social security, Medicare, domestic spending priorities or the military—especially if interest rates rise. Thus one other major effect of the tax cuts was to further impair the government's flexibility to deal with whatever the future holds. In contrast, in times of prosperity the country should be paying down the national debt, so as to retain enough "room" to borrow to increase government spending for emergencies or to help recover from recessions. Indeed, one of the things that slowed the recovery from the 2008 recession was that Republicans refused, after some initial spending on "shovel-ready" infrastructure projects, to continue on that same path for a while longer to help the recovery. As part of their ploy to deny any success to Obama's presidency and the

Democrats, Republicans began emphasizing the perils of government debt. But when Republican Trump was elected to the presidency, suddenly those deficits and debt accumulations again didn't matter in the least (as they also hadn't under President George W. Bush). In 2020, acting Trump White House chief of staff and former budget director Mick Mulvaney even made public mention of the fact that the Republican party's stances on deficits, given the emphasis on to them while Obama was president, amounted to hypocrisy ["Mulvaney says GOP hypocritical on deficits," in the *StarTribune*, Feb. 20, 2020, A4].

And as I am now adding the last few words to this manuscript, what I wrote earlier can also demonstrate its validity. A 10-graph review of the effects of the Trump era tax cuts through 2019 showed almost no longer-term positive benefit for other than corporations and the rich. Otherwise, typically there were no more than short-term positive blips in the first two quarters after the law was passed, *but with longer-term trends largely unaffected* [Kevin Drum, "Death and Taxes," in *Mother Jones*, July-Aug., 2020, 26-31, 66-67]. In other words, economic improvements continued at the same rates they had under Obama. So Republican selling points for the tax cuts did not pan out, for example, in terms of business investment, gross domestic product growth, growth in wages (and bonuses), and share of population employed. And now, with the new COVID-19 virus upon us, already the costs to the economy are immense with some kind of a longer-term recession or stagnation likely in the cards. So President Trump and the Republicans' artificially inflated economy—where Trump, besides agreeing to the massive and deficit- and debt-increasing tax cut for corporations, has also jawboned the Federal Reserve to keep interest rates extra low to keep his much-touted but pumped-up pseudo economic boom going—has left us with less financial flexibility to respond to the crisis than when he and they were elected in 2016. So, with the vast sums of money now being spent to try to reduce the effects of measures needed to deal with the virus, the government will become even more debt-ridden and constrained in the long term than it was before Trump took office. (And, currently, many Republicans are starting to worry again about the government's deficits and debt, in the process jeopardizing the economy.)

Finally, here's a failed example that ranges across centuries and many cultures: The belief that "God is on our side," perhaps especially during wars. In Xtianity, that belief seems to have been taken up from the Hebrews of Old Testament (which probably drew upon religious folklore before that), but it was carried forward for thousands of years within Xtendom (Christendom), to some extent right down to the present day. The belief has also led to aggressive wars. Yet during most of this history, when belief that the deity will enable the triumph of "our" side in war instead fails (i.e., about half the time), it has not provoked skepticism about the belief and associated religious or secular doctrines and practices, but a switch to believing instead that the deity *in this particular instance* was punishing them for insufficient faith or too-sinful ways, or that only over the long term would the people of the deity prevail. The latter was much believed in the South as it began to lose the Civil War [Stout].

Policies and Practices that Produce Gross Injustices or Terrible Side Effects, Such as the War on Drugs

An ongoing failure of a national policy can be illustrated with a policy that persisted through several presidential administrations (emphasized by some more than others): The "war on drugs." President Richard Nixon can be (dis)credited for starting this "war." But the roots of war on drugs go back to the end of alcohol Prohibition, when prohibition police forces suddenly needed something else to do to make their jobs necessary, and they chose to campaign to prohibit drugs, in the process producing propaganda, including films such as "Reefer Madness," that seriously distorted the effects of marijuana (all the way to murder) to help get anti-drug laws enacted. In any case, throughout the war on drugs, the side effects have been worse than any ills it was intended to remedy. By the late 1960s, many voters in this country had started to be full participants in this fiasco because they supported politicians emphasizing anti-crime rhetoric (including drugs), and were happy to crack down on Black power radicals, hippies, and anti-war protestors, and perhaps believed the propaganda associated even with minor drugs such as marijuana. This occurred despite many opportunities in the late 1960s and beyond to have learned otherwise, including by trying marijuana (which was readily available on most college campuses by the late 1960s). The public could also have learned otherwise through a 1972 report by a Nixon commission that unanimously recommended "decriminalizing the possession and distribution of marijuana for personal use" [Drug Policy Alliance website, "A Brief History of the Drug War"]. A high-level Nixon aide, John Ehrlichman, later admitted that the whole Nixon effort was a political ploy to disrupt anti-war protestors' and Blacks' communities and lives, encouraging the public to associate marijuana use with hippies. It was Nixon who first placed marijuana on the Schedule I list of dangerous drugs, pending a review by a commission he appointed. "We could arrest their leaders, raid their homes, break up their meetings, and vilify them night after night on the evening news" [John Ehrlichman; cited in Drug Policy Alliance website, ibid]. Did the Nixon people know they were lying about the drugs? Ehrlichman's response was: "Of course we did." And Nixon paid no heed to the report he had commissioned.

The use of the idea of a "war on drugs" was continued as part and parcel of anti-crime rhetoric in the political fodder through several subsequent administrations, especially with Republican presidents, and in many states, some of which ultimately adopted things like

"3-strikes-and-you're-out" laws, giving life-in-prison sentences for a third conviction, no matter how minor. Cocaine rose to become the chief political target of the drug laws in the 1980s and beyond, and laws typically gave out higher penalties for use of "crack cocaine," a form of the drug which was used primarily in Black communities. And marijuana arrests continued apace. Very much like the Prohibition era in the United States (1919-1933)—which banned alcoholic drinks and generated a black market run by and fought over by criminal gangs—the laws against drugs also generated a black market—a source of money and high profits for those willing to serve that market—and bred criminal gangs from Colombia, through Mexico, to the U.S.A. [Regarding parallel effects during Prohibition, see Daniel Okrent, *Last Call: The Rise and Fall of Prohibition*.] Thus, violent crime actually originated from or was severely exacerbated by our anti-drug laws. Although drug laws have not stopped many U.S. citizens from experimenting and even ongoing use of substances classified as drugs, they have led to millions of people having served prison time and being branded as criminals, for "offenses" that were either harmless or only affected themselves (and affected themselves very little in the case of marijuana—and much less than do alcoholic drinks, at that). In addition, as a result of prejudice and discriminatory law enforcement those arrested for drugs and prosecuted most heavily were Blacks, even for drugs in which Black and White usage rates were the same [Michelle Alexander, *The New Jim Crow: Mass Incarceration in the Age of Colorblindness (revised edition)*, 98-99]. For example, using FBI crime statistics for 2004 to 2012, the Minnesota branch of the American Civil Liberties Union released a set of tables showing Minneapolis police department arrest rates that included data for marijuana [aclu-mn.org, "ACLU releases data showing racial disparities in low level arrests in Minneapolis," 2014]. From that source, in every one of those years, Marijuana arrests were more than ten times greater for Blacks than for Whites, while marijuana usage rates, based on a National Survey on Drug Use and Health, were only slightly higher for Blacks (e.g., 14.0% vs. 11.6% in 2010 and 12.4% vs. 11.7% in 2009).

As if all this wasn't bad enough, the aforementioned black market greatly helped to build and still helps to fund Mexico's crime syndicates that now smuggle several drugs into the U.S.A., including some especially nasty ones like methamphetamines and opiates and even more dangerous substitutes for the latter. One estimate for 2008 (approximately) put these gangs' annual revenue at $23 billion [Drug Policy Alliance, "Drug War Facts," ca. 2010], which is the equivalent of almost 5% of our Department of Defense's budget for that year. These gangs have used this money for many nefarious purposes, including buying guns from little-controlled sources in the U.S.A., and bribing local officials. The gang syndicates have gained control of several large areas of Mexico—areas sufficient to ensure their capacity to operate without real restraints—and those who they deem to have gotten in the way are typically murdered. In recent years, Mexico has used the army to try to regain control in some areas but, at times, ordinary Mexicans have had to live in fear not only of the gangs but of the army's sometimes indiscriminate efforts to suppress the gangs. For a number of years, Juarez, a city on the Mexico-U.S. border, experienced one of the highest per capita murder rates in the world.

Although the minds of most people within our culture are not closely engaged with this craziness, many people have been at least partly involved through their inordinate fear of crime—which has been interactively played upon by politicians who are either similarly ensnared in this insanity or, more dishonorably, seeking to capitalize on the people's fears. Opponents of harsh drug laws have been labeled "soft on crime," and that has made political opposition more difficult. Between 1980 and about 2006, the number of people incarcerated for drug-law violations rose from roughly 50,000 to about 500,000—"more than… Western Europe locks up for everything" [Ethan Nadelmann, *"Drugs,"* in *Foreign Policy*, 26]. Lobbying of governments by those with vested interests in prisons, such as private prison corporations and organizations of prison guards, and their work against efforts to relieve public prison-overcrowding problems, such as an initiative to that effect in California, have also helped to sustain this cultural insanity (though a subsequent initiative in California did pass). Private prisons also make money off confining captured immigrants. Since 2009, for-profit prison industries have spent almost $9 million on campaign contributions; since 2009, they have spent over $25 million lobbying; and, between 2009 and 2016, they contributed more than $7 million at the state level [Alan Zibel, "Corporations Make Billions from Immigration Contracts," in *Public Citizen News*, Vol. 39, No. 6, 7, 13].

So, as the years and decades went by, the country and the states have had to continually build more prisons and/or spend more money to house the inmates in private prisons, some with very bad humanitarian records. In 2015, an estimated $51 billion *per year* was being spent on the Drug War, with 1.5 million arrested annually for drug-law violations [Drug Policy Alliance, "Drug War Facts," mailing, ca. 2017]. By then, judges had begun to rule that prison overcrowding was untenably inhumane and must be corrected—requiring more prison-building and/or reduced sentences and/or alternatives to prison for minor crimes, especially victimless crimes. Finally, the budgetary demands of the "criminal justice system" became so great in many states—especially compared to the real needs of the people—that the problem became more realistically understood, even by many conservatives. Some states eliminated some of their most draconian laws, including some three-strikes laws. For humane reasons, states also began to adopt medical marijuana laws so as to try to decriminalize use by those who were ill (even while possession, growing, etc., remained a federal crime). Finally, some states began to decriminalize marijuana, and now a number have gone on to legalize, regulate, and tax its usage. Even so, data for 2017 show that arrests for simple possession of marijuana totaled 599,282 [Drug Policy Alliance mailing, April 2019]. This was not much of a decline from two years earlier, despite increasing legalization, when marijuana arrests totaled 643,121, with 574,641 of those arrests for simple possession [Drug Policy Alliance, "Drug War Facts," mailing, ca. 2017].

The enforcement of drug laws over the years has wreaked havoc on millions of individuals' lives. As of 2010 or so, 31 million people had been arrested since the Drug War(s) began [Alexander, 60]. Criminal convictions (and to a lesser extent, even arrests), even for victimless drug crimes, make reintegration into society very difficult. Landlords often won't rent to people who have been convicted of any crime, and access to public housing may be prohibited. The vast majority of jobs may be denied based on having any kind of criminal record—and not just jobs where the particular crime might matter. No wonder recidivism rates are high: people have to go on paying for their crime (or, in victimless Drug War cases, "crime") even after their punishment has been completed. College and would-be college students with drug convictions are ineligible for federal student aid, with over 200,000 having been affected [Drug Policy Alliance, "Drug War Facts," ca. 2010]. In many states, voting is barred until any probationary period has ended. And, as above, police enforcement was (and remains) very biased against Black and Hispanic people.

To end the underlying problems even more completely, drug use must be treated as a matter of public and private health, with certain exceptions, for example, where violence is involved. Marijuana must be treated more like alcoholic drinks. In order to kill the black market and the associated criminal gangs, in this country and abroad, some easy-to-access alternatives and support must become available for people who get addicted to methamphetamines, opiates-heroin, or anything else. Some of these alternative policies have long since been explored in countries such as the Netherlands and Portugal (where drugs were decriminalized in 2001), and Uruguay has recently moved in similar directions. And, remarkably enough, some people who once resorted to opium for pain relief have found that marijuana alone suffices.

Failure to Attempt to Solve Problems

Jared Diamond has written about the collapse of a number of once-thriving societies/cultures [*Collapse: How Societies Choose to Fail or Succeed*]. His explication of a number of societal-cultural collapses includes several that involved environmental disasters. When these are unforeseeable—such as a long-term drought the likes of which have not previously been experienced by the living population—there is little that could have been done to avoid them. But from my perspective, ignoring known major problems, including environmental ones, would be a surefire sign of cultural insanity. Diamond's 4-part classification of his set of collapse cases includes the "failure to attempt to solve"—Easter Island being one example [Diamond, 79-119]. A more specific problem of this type is called the "tragedy of the commons" (where commonly owned goods, such as fishing stocks, are harvested to exhaustion, leaving nothing for anybody). These situations require government intervention (e.g., setting quotas for fishermen and/or barring foreign trawlers from national waters) or adequately respected or enforced mutual self-help agreements (e.g., by local fishermen). The Environmental Defense Fund has done some valuable work on establishing local agreements among fishermen, although some have challenged the tendency for consolidation of fishing rights that often results. [For example, see the article on the West Coast, "*A Fishery on the Rebound*" in EDF's *Solutions*, Fall 2014, 8-11.] In international waters, protecting the commons typically requires agreements among all major fishing nations (as has been done with whales, in large part) or to completely prohibit fishing in areas of the ocean which serve as important breeding grounds or sheltering areas for fish.

Similarly, democratic government politicians' undue adherence to ideology instead of efforts to solve long-term problems also typically involve elements of cultural insanity. This is one way to shirk the responsibility to address real problems at hand. All too often though, the presumed "safest" political alternative is to avoid such topics while finding ways to cater to the fear(s), prejudice(s), erroneous beliefs or worldviews, or other distorted attitudes of many in an attempt to ensure re-election. And, alas, to continue the charade once re-elected, sometimes there is an actual denial of known facts, for example, as most Republican leaders did and often still do with many aspects of human-caused climate change.

Not Learning from Other Cultures

In thinking about options available for a culture or its leadership, it is sometimes relevant to consider what possibilities other societies offer that might provide viable alternatives to current practices, even if their cultures differ in important ways. It is the glory of the discipline of an anthropologist that it highlights the different ways that people may be, behave and think and feel—providing us, both individually and as cultural groups, with many more possibilities. Most viable alternatives originating in other cultures arrive through cross-cultural communications, trade, or post-conquest adaptations. Although few in the High and Late Middle Ages (after 1000 CE) in Europe had an understanding anything like an anthropologist of today, sometimes they did find alternatives in other societies, though usually by a kind of osmosis not a directly conscious choosing. For example, architectural elements appropriated from Muslim societies in Spain and Sicily made possible the construction of Gothic churches (see Part Three). Similarly, the concept and the mathematical use of the number zero made its way across the Arab world and into Europe from India, though it took some centuries before it totally supplanted Roman numerals, especially in northern Europe, which was further removed from the more commercial cultures in Mediterranean cities and Atlantic coastal Flanders. But Christian Europe did not seem to learn anything from the Muslim cultures' treatment of Jews. The Muslim's most typical treatment of the Jews—as religiously constrained in the public realm and as subject to higher taxes, but otherwise not *usually* severely mistreated or limited— never caught on in Europe. In Europe, off and on for centuries from about 1096, Jews were occasionally attacked or sometimes even slaughtered by mobs invading Jewish neighborhoods/ghettos. Although the Jews were often protected by society's rulers at the start of the High Middle Ages (and were sometimes of considerable financial benefit to those rulers), later they were driven out of some countries by their kings (often with confiscation of their wealth). Jews were also usually limited in occupational choices. In the Late Middle Ages, they were sometimes forced to wear special identification insignia and forced to live in special Jewish quarters, including in Rome which was run by the pope. And, after the conquest of the last of the Moors' outposts in Spain in 1492, Jews were required to convert to Xtianity or leave that country, at considerable long-term economic and social cost to Spain. Converted Jews also provided a twisted rationale for sustaining the Spanish Inquisition, which, together with its many spies, for decades sought out and persecuted people who had in any way lapsed back into behaviors associated with the Jewish (sub)culture (e.g., avoidance of pork). Nor did any of the subsequent persecutions and pogroms of Jews, including Hitler's, bring any positive results to the persecuting societies. For the most part, when this Xtian cultural insanity flared up, Jews became scapegoats, pure and simple, and the society suffered at least some while the Jews suffered a lot.

CHAPTER 5

The Brain and the Stories It Constructs

In a 24-lecture DVD and course guidebook, Steven Novella, a neurologist (M.D.), provides a thorough look at the foibles of the human mind and discusses how critical thinking skills and scientific reasoning can help individuals manage those weaknesses to develop a better understanding of the realities in the world around them [*Your Deceptive Mind: A Scientific Guide to Critical Thinking Skills*]. His explanations of how the brain and mind work can be used to show cultural insanities can easily arise and why they often do so unless checked.

For starters, then, the human eye is not a video camera that records everything accurately. Instead, it focuses more intensely on a small proportion of its visual field, attending closely to some particular or other. "Peripheral" parts of our perceptions are not noticed or not included in memory. During a hold-up for example, the victim will usually attend visually very closely to the gun, remember its presence strongly and perhaps in some detail, but not be able to describe many other things about the robber. Accordingly, as we assemble our visual perceptions into a whole, our minds must fill in the large gaps in the information actually received by the brain—and they do so with varying degrees of accuracy [Novella, 20-27].

The brain also quickly recognizes patterns or what might be patterns, and it is constantly ready to assign agency to certain kinds of patterns that it assembles from our perceptions [Novella, 36-43]. Agency involves a will, mainly as possessed by life forms. This pattern recognition of agency might have been useful evolutionarily against potential threats, such as a lion in the tall grass. And it is very deeply rooted emotionally, as is suggested by the fact that we can even identify with two-dimensional, odd-shaped cartoon characters because their artists have made them seem to have agency. One more general result is a tendency that humans have to leap to conclusions based on too little evidence. These pattern-seeking mental processes, and our visual-perceptual limitations, work together with human memory, which also has limitations, to construct the brain's woven-together accounts/stories [Novella, 28-35].

Our long-term memory of events is often stored as fragments in various locations in the brain rather than in some more coherent way. Moreover, each time we recall a memory, we are very likely to reshape it some, often embellishing it to make it yet more integrated and complete and detailed as a story, and/or making it more relevant to something at hand and more worth recalling for similar purposes subsequently. Imagine then what multiple police interrogations can do under such circumstances—everything from eliciting conflicting accounts from the same person to inadvertently (or deliberately) coaxing witnesses' memories to agree with police identification of suspects or crime hypotheses. Also, If we hear other accounts of the same events, those too will tend to influence our memories. If we are on one side of a discussion or argument, that is very likely to bias our memory into selectively remembering more of our version and less of the other version of that story. It is even possible, especially in children, to induce entirely false memories (e.g., of childhood abuse). As a result of the many possible slip-ups in our memories, some if not many accounts of "eyewitnesses" have been found partly erroneous and sometimes even totally unreliable/wrong. That is why the Innocence Project, drawing on DNA evidence but necessarily being quite limited in scope because it relies on pro bono legal representation and tends to tackle serious cases, has yielded over 150 exonerations in 13 years, "including many individuals freed from death row," some who were there based on eyewitness testimony [Sean B. Carroll, *The Making of the Fittest: DNA and the Ultimate Forensic Record of Evolution*, 14]. In its "Explained" series, Netflix has now developed a short television program on "Mind" that also covers many of these same points. If identification-inducing practices are used in police line-ups, "a false memory can be created in the victim's mind of who the attacker was" [Andy Mannix, "Eyewitness photo lineups get closer look," in the *StarTribune*, Feb. 20, 2020, B1]. In specific cases in Minnesota, for example, at least two such cases, involving rape, were identified where the suspect was later "exonerated through DNA evidence," and "the true perpetrator was found," while the victim continued to have the false memory [Mannix, ibid]. Police line-ups (and equivalent) need to be such that the officer(s) conducting them do not know anything about the case, especially which photo is the alleged perpetrator, so that they cannot, even subtly, lead the victim to identify any particular suspect.

As suggested by the fact that the brain's perceptual apparatus and long-term memory weave together accounts of events, whether to tell ourselves or others, story-telling has an evolutionary history in humans that is probably as long as our species has had some complex language capabilities. Long ago, as dark fell, humans hovered around their encampment's fire and listened to the re-telling of the tribe's great sagas and to tales from that day's hunt or gathering, or told other stories. And we shared our stories and cleverness with prospective partners [Geoffrey Miller, *The Mating Mind: How Sexual Choice Shaped the Evolution of Human Nature*]. As a result, we also have much greater receptivity to, and potentially empathy for, information that is anecdotal rather than mainly evidence-based. Stories hit us emotionally and can lead to changes in our views or behavior much easier than can reason. Presumably this is why, to keep our attention, newspaper and television journalists have long included "human interest" angles in almost everything they write or say for their readers or their viewers. In general, our brain and its parts are linked up emotionally; the brain does not operate by logic like a computer program with a central processing unit. Indeed, we may well have conflicting emotions that vie for predominance in developing a story or memory.

Let me summarize the above in a different way. External reality does not come with a narrator to tell us exactly what's happening so as to enable a fully organized brain to record it accurately. Instead, the brain can only record snippets of what we select to attend to in our field of vision or that is otherwise available to our senses. Moreover, much of the brain's processing in done at the subconscious level and emotionally, in separate neurological channels, and not in a systematic and rational way. Before the brain's cortex enlarged in human evolution—back when rational consciousness was minimal—this was the way for all mammals. But even now, "much of our behavior is performed automatically and without much conscious control over unconscious hardwired instincts and soft-wired proclivities" [Allen Frances, *Twilight of American Sanity: A Psychiatrist Analyzes the Age of Trump*, 54]. A good example known to many is driving home on a familiar route, largely paying attention to conscious thoughts about whatever, later only vaguely remembering parts of the drive—because the driving was taken care of subconsciously, in habitual ways.

In all, *the brain has to construct everything* we sense, and it does so in a way that somehow constitutes a meaningful account or story for us when it is brought to consciousness. If that story is important enough, the brain will store it, but in multiple locations, thus constituting our long-term memory. However, current perceptual intake may also be (re-)shaped by the past (i.e., as the brain knows it), so as to better fit our ongoing sense of ourselves and the world around us. Finally, each time we recall a memory it is likely to be re-assembled somewhat differently, perhaps even leaving out some facets, and to be re-constructed to varying extents. Without considerable critical thinking about the evidence on a broad scale (rather than just collecting and reacting to a series of anecdotes/stories), often we will not come up with adequate approximations of the real world that is "out there." This is perhaps most easily seen when we have arguments with our significant other that are subsequently renewed (or re-reviewed together)—often both sides remember key features of the argument, and the perspectives involved, but very differently.

CHAPTER 6

Deficiencies in Thinking Processes that Sustain Cultural Insanity

As suggested above, conflicting views of the various aspects of the world may be stored in the brain as if they were kept in separate "compartments." For example, after the civil rights acts in President Johnson's administration, "that the color line remained firmly intact despite the nation's formal commitment to colorblindness was a source of widespread cognitive dissonance" [Hartman, 103]. Didn't colorblindness fix everything? Well, actually, no. And besides many people were by no means rendered colorblind by changes in the laws. Similarly, we may be prejudiced against Blacks but that prejudice may reveal itself only under some circumstances and otherwise be denied. Because we want to appear consistent to others, we resist admitting error because making errors in public is a threat to our self-esteem and ego [Novella, 15]. But if these conflicts are later recognized by the mind, the adaptive approach is to use critical thinking, including scientific methods, to modify one or both of them to eliminate the previous compartmentalization and the underlying cognitive dissonance [Novella, 16].

Rationalization

Unfortunately, a strategy too often used instead of facing dissonance or the many other problems in our mental constructions of life around us is to rationalize away any conflict. Below we'll see that there are many opportunities for rationalization because, in general, "we usually do the things that our experience and synapses tell us to do, without understanding why we are doing them—and then elaborate a plausible story to make it seem that all along we were making free-will choices and really did know what we were doing" [Frances, 54]. As a result, many people have at least some contradictory views and beliefs of which they are not aware. In the worst cases, it almost seems like a person will offer a welter of miscellaneous opinions during the course of a conversation, many of which are at variance with each other. Both compartmentalization and rationalization are among the most important ways in which humans are all too readily enabled to support one or more cultural insanities.

Anecdotal "Evidence"

Our ready empathic engagement with stories was noted above. But such stories are anecdotal evidence *at best*. Given that even accounts by eyewitnesses may have severe weaknesses, that memory of an event may be partly reconstructed each time it is recalled, just how much trust can we place even in the accuracy of any account or story, or even our own recall? Congress may love and need its "horror stories" to take action, but the real questions involving any given story, even if one anecdote is rendered accurately, are *how representative is it, and how widely do stories with similar causes range.* If the story is unusual or perhaps even an outlier it will be especially unreliable to draw conclusions from it. And sometimes stories are deliberately misrepresented as typical when they are not—for example, President

Trump's emphasis on crime and killings by immigrants (e.g., in San Francisco and Iowa) when the rates of such actions by immigrants are the same or lower than among the non-immigrant population. This then is an example of erroneous (or fraudulent) reasoning from stories/anecdotes. *At* most, anecdotal evidence should be used to generate hypotheses [Novella, 80].

Unfortunately, one very typical mental failing that humans have is to generalize based on anecdotal "evidence," to treat a story or a few stories as being typical. As should be clear from testimonials in advertisements for over-the-counter supplements, even multiple similar stories are not adequate, especially if there is any chance that they are a biased selection from a much larger sample. The best generalizations require large samples from which no subjects were omitted, and the closer one can get to that, the better. Because humans have difficulty reasoning on the basis of probability and statistics, the best solution for this deficit is some basic training in their use [Novella, 77-83]. "Our all-too-human love affair with the narrative, rather than statistical truth, has many people swallowing narrative lies that lead to terrible decisions" [Frances, 77].

Confirmation Bias

In today's world, confirmation bias is perhaps the major contributor to cultural insanity. We tend to accept information that is in accord with what we already believe, and reject information—often on the flimsiest of rationalized pretexts—that conflicts with what we already believe [Novella, 73-74]. One way this is done is to examine especially closely the reasoning with which we disagree, searching for any flaws and then overemphasizing those flaws as a way of discounting the whole, while the same application of critical scrutiny to favored information will be absent. As above, events may also be interpreted and memory (memories) re-shaped to fit existing beliefs rather than evaluating them anew on their own merits. We also have a tendency to defensively steel ourselves in our initial position if we are challenged about it (which is why confrontational arguments almost never bring about change).

Modern technology has enabled us to greatly exacerbate this bias. Jeff Bezos, CEO of Amazon, has correctly pointed out that the internet as it now functions is a "confirmation bias machine." It is so because we tend to confine our information sources and internet searches to those likely to confirm our views. We follow links sent by our "friends" who tend to have similar views. Similarly, and all too often, a limited selection of favored television "news" sources (especially insofar as those sources are not actually fair and balanced) lets people more readily confirm biased understandings about life in this society and/or the world. In general, we tend to develop and not venture far away from our "information silos." Too many people also give too much credibility to favored *opinions* of radio, television and newspaper pundits, many of which have an insufficient factual foundation. We also tend to side with authorities and experts with whom we are likely to agree and disregard those with whom we are likely to disagree. But disregarding legitimate scientific expertise on any side of an issue is a particularly bad strategy for developing and maintaining a sound picture of reality. Further, opting for an opposing scientific view when that of scientific experts are very near to reaching a consensus in a different direction is almost always a sure loser in judging reality (more on this below).

At their worst, people will simply and even openly deny or massively distort mountains of evidence to help sustain their own beliefs. That denial will often be linked preordained conclusions—whether political, religious, or otherwise—and then employ confirmation bias and/or rationalization as support. A political example was given earlier that involved a large minority of the U.S. population still believing that Saddam Hussein had weapons of mass destruction. Part Four presents a case such as this involving the all-controlling religious views of young-earth creationists. Rationalization may extend even to extremely unlikely conspiracy theories (such as claiming that there is a conspiracy involving a disparate array of climate scientists from many countries because of their near-consensus agreement that humans are the major cause of global warming). "Our belief systems are structured such that we will almost always find a way to support what we want to believe" [Michael Shermer, *The Believing Brain: From Ghosts and Gods to Politics and Conspiracies—How We Construct Beliefs and Reinforce Them as Truths*, 162]. And "when we believe our own rationalizations, they are a form of self-deception" [William von Hippel, *The Social Leap: The New Evolutionary Science of Who We Are, Where We Come from, and What Makes Us Happy*, 207]. And, as an addendum here, the least competent people (per testing on simple facts) tend to vastly overestimate their performance relative to other test-takers—a phenomenon known as the Dunning-Kruger effect [Angela Fritz, "Why incompetent people think they are experts," in the *StarTribune*, Feb. 3, 2019, SH3].

Receptivity to Emotional Appeals; Advertisements; Consumerism

One cultural insanity bordering on "universal" in the United States and most other developed societies, and even among many of the middle and upper classes in developing societies, involves consumerism. Historically and currently, the development and continuation of our consumer society has been enabled by mass production and abetted by an ever-more sophisticated advertising "industry" that has learned how to stimulate all of our primitive emotional desires. These include the desire to be sexually attractive—both feminine (e.g., perfumes, make-up, clothes) and masculine (e.g., men's after-shave lotions and deodorants, and associations with rugged individualism, like the Marlboro man on a horse). Other desires include those for status and success and to "keep up with the Joneses" (e.g., in possessions of all kinds), for power (e.g., sports cars, large pick-up trucks, SUVs and any possessions associated with a higher social status), and for security. We also have built and occupied ever-larger houses (despite having fewer children); and we have welcomed even marginally greater convenience and easier living with almost every new appliance and electronic device (while disregarding that all too many have a "planned obso-lescence" or other problematic elements, including some discussed subsequently). Our tastes have been manipulated into buying foods that too often fatten us up or otherwise make us less healthy. We even sport advertisements for commercial products on our t-shirts as part of our identity, perhaps somehow hoping that that choice will show that we are cool. (When this approach to advertising first developed in the late 1960s or so, companies had to give their products away to get most people to wear them!) Like the Roman masses at gladiator games, we crave escape from reality and, as part of that, we identify with favorite entertainers, sports stars and celebrities generally, and spend immense amounts of time at vicarious pastimes involving their activities (e.g., following them on the internet or reading about them in a magazine and/or newspaper). We worry about our health and vigor and, with the "help" of advertisements on TV, enough of us follow the directions to "ask your doctor" about new drugs so as to greatly enrich many pharmaceutical and "supplement" companies that sometimes offer products that are no more than tiny advances, if that, or invent new names for ailments or problems that their product will help (maybe). Human conditions that needed fixing go back at least to "body odor" (B.O.) in the 1920s, and later, to Geritol's famous "iron-poor blood." Advertising literally haunts every portal into our lives, both by subtlety and repetition, pounding its way into our minds (much like those former Anacin anvil-headache ads), to convince us that we need more of their product or to try the "new, improved" version. And now, thanks to electronic media's keeping tabs on our every interest and sharing that broadly among companies, ads are targeted to us even more personally, sometimes for days on end. For example, when I recently checked the internet to find what kind of caulking tar I should buy at my local retailer to treat a few questionable places on a flat rubber roof, I was for the next few days bombarded with ads about such inconsequential products every time I went on line, including to play "hearts."

Want to see a consumerist cultural insanity in action? Despite the effects of global warming on our and our children's futures (see below), and despite the higher initial and future costs, consumer demand in the United States has recently risen substantially for low-mileage gasoline-fueled pick-up trucks and large SUVs, some selling at the price of two ordinary new cars. Most are not truly needed for more than occasional personal tasks. Why are people doing this? To maintain powerful, hyper-manly facades? To enable bullying on the roadways? To flaunt their economic status (even though in some/many cases it involves going into long-term debt)? Or what? Our roadways should Instead be filling with smaller hybrids and electricity-powered cars— and bicycles when destinations are nearby.

In general, mass production and advertising have encouraged us to want their products. And in our minds, those wants have often evolved into needs. Life has become more of a pursuit of temporarily satisfying material possessions, sweet and fatty foods, and escapism into sports, celebrities and TV programs, and less of a pursuit of true fulfillments and happiness.

Fear, Hate, Stereotyping, Scapegoating; and Victimization

Another kind of deficiency in our thinking processes and failure to reason is the willingness to act in support (e.g., as we vote) of political pitches meant to gain the adherence of listeners through their emotional appeal to fear, hate, and stereotypes, often in association with some sense of victimhood among the listeners. The fears, hates, stereotypes, and scapegoats associated with victimhood are not always fully conscious to the listener, and may even elicit denials if direct questions about them are raised. Once overt racism was no longer socially appropriate, for example, the term "dog whistle" has been applied, especially in characterizing the history of politics in the south, to somewhat covert political references to attract voters who fear, hate, or have major prejudices against Blacks, allowing both the politicians and their followers enough cover to publicly, but possibly not quite plausibly, deny prejudice or racism.

Most generally, in its early days, Homo sapiens (humans) were based in tribes that often needed to be cautious or fearful about dangers involving competing tribes, even while engaging in trade or other relations with other tribes some of the time. This inheritance contributed greatly to our condition today, in which, without good reason, we all too readily form "us" and "them" perspectives, where "members" of the outgroup are subjects of fear, hate, or blame—and stereotypes. This evolution-based "tribalism may be the most lethal baggage we carry forward from our past" [Frances, 165]. Making matters worse yet, as humanity transitioned from hunter-gatherer to village-town-city dwellers, the social and resources-related equality *within* nomadic tribal societies was supplanted by many more kinds of inequality and much greater degrees of it. "Worldwide, egalitarianism was kicked to the curb, and newfound beliefs in the innate superiority [of some within each culture] led to all sorts of human suffering" [von Hippel, 75]. So we got a sort of fusion of both forces—early tribal us/them and the agricultural transition's acceptance of inequality. We can get a pretty good idea of how the acceptance by those with power of the inequality, inferiority, and otherness played out by examining the history of the people exploited by Europe's imperial colonialism/ imperialism, and by European records of what they thought they were doing at the time [von Hippel, 75]. The subsequent adoption of more republican and democratic institutions has alleviated this situation to a degree, but the two problems are nowhere near being solved.

And if it seems as though minorities' groups have been unduly favored by authority (e.g., by government programs or universities), some Whites may choose to see themselves as victims, and resent everything that appears to support that seeming favoritism, even if any reality to that favoritism results from recent efforts to provide some degree of balance or help to those other groups, directly or indirectly compensating *a little bit* for centuries of governmental favoritism toward Whites, which has benefitted almost everyone with White ancestors in the U.S.A. Heck, even recent White immigrants benefit from the remnants of past favoritisms, even if they don't realize it. (One way they benefit is through "White privilege," which, for example, provides much greater assurance that Whites will be treated fairly and humanely by police.) Native Americans and African Americans especially have suffered a brutal history at the hands of others in this country. Everybody but the descendants of Native Americans still benefit from the lands that were taken away from the Indians (and also, later, taken from some of the former citizens of Mexico who came under U.S. rule, e.g., in Texas and California). The confiscation of Indian lands (and White violations of many a treaty) continued into the late 1800s. Thereafter, Whites attempted to White-civilize Indians by the forced removal of their children to White-run boarding schools at which even speaking in native languages was forbidden. As for the Blacks, almost all but recent immigrants came over on slave ships in conditions that may have killed a third of them. As slaves who received little more than room and board for their long hours of work and whose labor mainly profited their owners over more than two centuries of slavery, they also helped to create the country's infrastructure—such as roads, cleared farm fields, plantation houses, and more (including the White House). And, as well-informed people know, this history didn't stop after the Civil War in 1861-1865 (see also above).

A sense of victimization has also arisen in response to "global-ization." But the problem isn't globalization *per se*. It is that our largest corporations indirectly controlled the outcomes of the negotiations that produced the treaties (large corporations being the main U.S. interests actually "at the table" and in shaping our government's posi-tioning). The resulting trade agreements *favoring the interests of large corporations* made little or no effort to adjust for the higher living standards (including wage rates/costs of labor) in this country and also largely ignored the higher environmental standards here. So the agreements made it all the more profitable for big companies to ship factories and jobs to other countries where the costs of their pollution was lower and the workers more exploited. The resulting decline in manufacturing jobs in this country was also exacerbated by automa-tion-robotization and computerization, some of it encouraged by the cheaper labor costs abroad. As a result, many skilled working people in this country lost their jobs (and were indeed victimized) and the number of unionized, well-paying job opportunities declined. But the true victimizers—the corporations in league with politicians who benefit from their monetary support in elections—are seldom correctly identified. And that makes it easier to pull the wool over people's eyes by scapegoating immigrants or foreigners as blameworthy.

Stereotypes involve our assignment to other people of general characteristics—usually negative ones that are linked to our own neg-ative emotions, such as fear and hate. Stereotypes are often applied to all members of some group or subset of people, necessarily neglecting or disregarding their individual differences and realities. Stereotypes are in essence prejudices (pre-judgments) that are used as a quick-and-easy shortcut that leads to making ill-informed and non-empathic judgments about individuals or, in a worldview, in reference to some broader group. Stereotypes will often be associated with rationalization to support the prejudice. For example, Blacks may be seen generally as unwilling to work and/or lacking in intelligence; Muslims may be seen generally as being supporters of terrorism and/or as intent on implementing strict versions of Islamic/Sharia Law; immigrants, even when decreasing in number, may be seen generally as a threat to society rather than a lot like the people who built the society; liberal Democrats may be portrayed as agreeing with the now-defunct version of despotic "communism" in the U.S.S.R. rather than as favoring the democratic socialist national policies more like one or another country in northwestern Europe.

The mechanisms of stereotyping are simple: Hear or see something negative about a disliked group, it confirms your negative view; hear or see something positive about a disliked group, disregard it, or treat it as an isolated case. Prejudice can also be sustained by isolating oneself from "members" of the stereotyped group (which helps to prevent empathy from arising and the recognition of individual differences). And, once stereotypes are formed, it is easier than ever to sustain them in today's world (e.g., see confirmation bias, above).

And as I write, President Trump is eliciting prejudicial responses from many of his followers using immigrants as scapegoats. I am reminded here of a political cartoon that appeared before the 2018 midterm elections, by Scott Stantis of the Chicago Tribune. In this political cartoon, a mother and child, bundled together in a blanket and labeled "immigrants," are suspended like a piñata; President Trump and an elephant labeled GOP are standing blow them with baseball bats; Trump says, "Whack it hard enough and votes come out!" Over the course of U.S. history many immigrant groups have been scapegoated and mistreated as one or another kind of societal villains—the Irish, the Chinese and Japanese, and the people from Mexico, whether immigrants or otherwise. Now, in a population largely comprised of descendants of immigrants, we are told that somehow immigrants are responsible for undermining America's greatness! Or is that "greatness" a code, another "dog whistle" for "Whiteness"—implicitly portraying the demographic and political dominance of European-sourced Whites as fitting and proper and any reductions in their dominance as their victimization? Yet, in reality, in many places in this country, immigrants are badly needed to work in industries such as agriculture, basic construction (like roofing), many service positions such as maids, janitors and caretakers for the aged, and some high-tech areas. Instead, somehow a larger than usual number of families seeking asylum from dangerous conditions in their home countries—though the totals are well short of the number of "illegal" immigrants some years back—is portrayed as a "national emergency"—even though it is a national emergency that lacks any emergency character (except for the asylum-seekers) and poses no real national threat. But in Trump's mind and speeches, the asylum-seekers include criminals and bad people aplenty—when, in reality, gang-based crime, and governments unwilling or unable to do anything about it—are usually what they are fleeing. And much U.S. policy has supported the governments in the countries from which the people are fleeing to seek asylum. Finally, that so many people respond emotionally to offer support to someone willing to treat innocent work-seeking or asylum-needing immigrants as scapegoats reveals a cultural insanity in action.

Relatedly, Trump recently tweeted that four ethnic/racial minority women in the House of Representatives should go back to the places from which they came. But only one is an immigrant and at least one—representative Ayanna S. Pressley of Massachusetts, a Black, probably has ancestors born in the United States who long preceded any of Trump's people. Trump's pseudo-rationale is, ultimately, if their ideas differ from his, they must hate America. And while at least one of the four has been called out by many in her own party for poorly chosen words about Israel's leaders, because the Democrats in the House also defended the four against Trump's "ship them home" verbiage, Trump proceeded to claim that the entire Democratic Party hates Jews. But didn't Trump show at least as much hatred of Jews when he defended the Nazi and other right-wing provocateurs as "good people" at Charlottesville, Virginia?

Victimization, Multiculturalism, Political Correctness, and Free Speech

Before proceeding, one key point I may need to reiterate is this: It should be utterly clear from what I have already written that *no culture is a sacred cow*. Moreover, with respect to the facilitation of human development, virtually all if not all cultures have their cultural insanities, many unique but some all too typical. All cultures also have other cultural flaws and weaknesses, some of which reflect tendencies toward cultural insanity. The people of these cultures, being individuals (as above), will partake of these cultural insanities and tendencies to varying degrees.

Now, apropos of the idea of victimization, I need to add a few things about multiculturality, "political correctness," and the U.S. Constitution's guarantee of free speech, along with academic freedom. Although much of the situation as I see it probably falls short of full-blown cultural insanity, some of it certainly borders on it. And some frequent practices do not seem to work well because of internal conflicts of principles. And extreme versions of some of these principles have led to coercive rules, informal or even formal, against overt expression of beliefs.

[An important aside: Even though I grant Frantz Fanon's argument in *The Wretched of the Earth* that oppressed minorities are likely to accept and incorporate elements of that oppression into their own psyches and cultures, even to the point of downgrading their own self-worth—and so should perhaps bear less responsibility in those respects—that does not at all preclude cultural insanities carried forward from their original culture(s) or from poor adaptations to the oppressive culture. Perhaps the classic experimental illustration of Fanon's point involved the choices made by little girl African Americans among dollies offered to them, where their usual choice was for a light- rather than a darker-skinned doll. On the other hand, at times oppressed peoples sometimes develop remarkably creative or constructive responses or partial adaptations to their oppression. For example, Blacks in the United States developed Negro spirituals, gospel music, the blues, and jazz, were central in the launch of rock & roll, and initiated rap (to mention only some). Also, because of their low status/ position in society/culture, subordinated groups (such as Blacks) can much more readily see the elements of oppression coming from the people and institutions in the dominant society—elements of cultural oppressiveness that Whites are often blind to and/or in denial about. Similarly, by the third decade of the 20th century, if not earlier, many Jews had become strong supporters of civil rights and liberties because they had seen so much persecution in Europe (and outsider status in the U.S.A. too). But with their rise in status of Jews in this country and perhaps especially the establishment of Israel and its relationship with the Palestinians, the insights stemming from being oppressed and the support for the needs of the oppressed have been weakened.]

The liberals and left tend too readily to overlook the deep roots and ongoing effects of most of the long-term societal failings that have led to the current status of Blacks (and some other ethnic minorities) in this country. They also tend to overlook any maladaptive adjustments those groups may have made in response to those many failings. (Among those societal failings: economics, civil equality, redlining-ghettoizing, shipment of jobs overseas, police rules of conduct, the effects of welfare policies, etc., plus various forms of systemic racism and the long-term denigration of some ethnic minorities by many others, especially historically, but also to varying extents currently.) To counter this situation, many liberals have emphasized respect for these minorities, knowledge of their histories, and their resilience, and an appreciation for the positives in their cultures. One result, though, is a tendency to acknowledge only the positive and see all criticisms of minorities' cultures as "blaming the victim." Yes, minorities have been the victims and they need more support and change in the dominant culture, perhaps especially its economics, but overlooking some of the current realities may be counterproductive with respect to the search for solutions. Among problems too often overlooked, for example, are high proportions of young and often little-educated parents, often single moms ("babies having babies"), homelessness, poverty, low wage jobs and high unemployment levels, the resort to crime and gangs, partly as a survival tactic, police harassment (or worse), and the effects of all those on minorities' communities. Conservatives do tend to blame the victim by overemphasizing the symptoms, which, to varying extents, may also be ineffective, unfortunate, or poor subcultural adaptations, such as gangs, gun violence, and single parenthood. In outstanding displays of survival, resilience, and the overcoming of obstacles, some minority children do well despite such circumstances. And life's circumstances do not define anyone. So, while maximum encouragement for minorities are warranted, their background conditions pose real problems that need to be solved. Instead, if any effort at all is made, it is too often a simplistic approach, such as the expectation that the schools should be responsible for fixing everything. Thus the authors of No Child Left Behind (NCLB)—who included star liberals in the U.S. Senate—thought it could solve educational inequality and possibly lots more when, actually, it could not possibly even do the former, especially by itself. Others have emphasized a greater acceptance of multiculturalism and diversity, and/or greater integration in the schools—but those too are no more than pieces of a far larger entanglement of society's problems in this regard.

To begin to solve the larger problem(s) of this kind, it will require, for starters, something like Andrew Yang's universal guaranteed minimum government payout to everyone in the society (or at least those with low earnings) and/or federally guaranteed employment for everyone who is able to work (and I mean everyone—not just Blacks—including those who are newly released felons). And perhaps the government could also establish a small investment account for each new child born to parents, one or both of whom had ancestors that included slaves—an account that will grow in value until, after age 17, it may be used for postsecondary education or, after age 25, could be put toward the purchase of a home (or saved for retirement). Such a fund would at least begin to compensate for the inability of Black slaves to accumulate any wealth, and thus provide some properly-targeted reparations. Although racism, at best, will only slowly fade from being a prominent feature of people's conscious and unconscious minds (more elsewhere), addressing some systemic aspects of it is long overdue, especially the rules and expectations regarding police conduct. Currently, almost any police killing is considered justified in courts of law. And the police/society need to stop handing out criminal records to ethnic minority youngsters that don't involve violence (or serious crimes) toward others… and make it so that Whites get prosecuted just as often as ethnic minorities for crimes committed in equal proportions… with the same length of sentences. And we need to take the stand that "all is forgiven" when people have served their time in a jail or prison, with their rights (e.g., to vote, to have equal access to rental housing) fully restored upon their release, even if they have to continue to see a probation officer for a time.

One of the partial solutions implied above was a call for White people to recognize how (ideally in considerable detail) the historical and current patterns of discrimination (including socioeconomic deprivation, systemic violence, etc.) against various ethnic minorities have their origin in, and continue to be perpetrated, by many individual Whites and the institutions in the dominant White society. And to recognize that Black lives ought to matter as much as "blue" lives. (The reverse is also true, but phrasing it that way seems to downplay the problem that it is Blacks and not the police who are subjected to systemic racism, including by police practices.) But that recognition necessarily also involves finding and calling attention to the historical and the continuing fault lines and failures in White society's institutions and culture(s). In conjunction with the efforts to do so, however, an imbalance is too often struck: It becomes politically correct to identify, criticize and condemn many negative aspects of White history and culture, but not any of those of ethnic minorities' cultures. While very few of the socioeconomic and cultural problems in the Black community (e.g.) can be *solely* ascribed to Blacks, conversely, Blacks also have agency (even if often impeded by society), so not every problem in their communities can be ascribed purely to discrimination and/or historical oppression by the dominant White society.

Because facing the full truth about Whites' treatment of minorities in this country tends not to occur much before college (and not enough after college either), there is little imbalance in the K-12 schools between the two efforts (i.e., appreciation of diversity/multiculturalism and understanding the fault lines and cultural insanities in White society/U.S. history). In any case, the K-12 schools provide an intensely supervised realm, with teachers and authorities presiding over as-yet children's behavior in what is often intended to be a multiculturally supportive environment (albeit with varying degrees of success). Unfortunately, K-12 schools in some sections of the country (especially outside the cities) continue to perpetuate the dominant U.S. cultural mythology(ies) more than to reveal even sanitized versions of the full complexity of history in the U.S.A. For example, Black history could certainly be more effectively taught in most schools (e.g., as long-term themes extending into the present rather than as problems separated by historical era, and then often treated as resolved, like slavery). The complexities and continuities—and problem-solving—require a better understanding of history across time—as illustrated in my earlier discussion of Mark Twain's *Huckleberry Finn*.

But in universities, the imbalance in the treatment of White and other ethnic groupings is sometimes stark. Among some of the results of this conflict are that the right to free speech and academic freedom by Whites who have not yet become fully aware/politically correct (i.e., including almost all politically conservative-tending students) but who want to express their version of race-related, history-related, or political ideas related to such matters, though often analytically in error, can readily become compromised or even denied in favor of a hypersensitive approach to the feelings of minorities. Part or much of the goal is to enable those minorities to feel fully at home and comfortable in their university setting (i.e., feel no different than the typical White student might feel in the same environment). At the same time, however, some Whites will invariably be upset by having to learn more of the truths about the history and character of the dominant culture. The question is how to make that happen as an educational challenge rather than a personal or political challenge that truncates free speech or academic freedom, or makes more than a very few students feel cornered. Of course I am not writing here about free speech that is an "incitement to riot," or confrontations involving "fighting words," or "shouting 'Fire!' in a crowded theater"—those remain inappropriate if not illegal.

There is no question in my mind that all cultures *and the variations within them* should be seen as accurately as possible (e.g., so as to minimize stereotyping), and that people should be dealt with respectfully, in an unbiased fashion, as the individuals that they are. *All* people need to get used to the idea of their own culture, traditions and history being criticized (including erroneously). The "old" remedy for erroneous free speech was more free speech. There is much to be said for that approach, especially in an educational setting. But in college/university settings, problems can arise when "should" migrates to "must" or when discussion and debate—potentially important parts of the learning process—are suppressed. Too often social media "trolls," faulting any deviations in opinion from their politically correct view, call out individuals who express opinions at variance with their ideals, and seek to get others to join them in their condemnations. The "trolls" approach is also likely to alienate many should-be allies in progressive causes—factions on the left have a long history of cutting each other up over minor doctrinal differences. And students attacked in this manner readily withdraw from further interaction (and learning)—typically while affirming their primitive worldviews (see above re how the brain works). Shutting down discussion and debate (or controversial right-wing speakers) means that there will be an inadequate identification of the scope of the educational deficits among the students, and an inadequate understanding of why some stances are historically in error. And it means that some students will be all the more likely to seek reinforcement for their original views in their own restricted information silos rather than in open discussion and the sharing of evidence and feelings with their fellow students and teachers. (Such discussion must occur without threat of recrimination, and it will do so in carefully taught classrooms.)

Similarly, it is all well and good if college faculty members make every effort to be as "politically correct" as they can be in the classroom and in their relationships with students, so that no student feels out of place or unwelcome. But yet other problems in academic freedom (and free speech) can arise if there are significant consequences when some faculty members fall short of the ideal while transgressing the views of "politically correct" students or administrative mandates associated with them.

From another perspective, "political correctness" can be regarded as an effort to be understanding toward every person, albeit mainly those who have previously been left out. So far so good. But what doesn't work is attempting to coerce others into the same view—or, if nothing else, to silence and/or ostracize them. That is a major part of how attempts to be "politically correct" got a bad name among a large number of people in this society—so much so that Republicans can even run for office using "politically correct" as a foil that attracts some voters! Politically-correct individuals need to use their greater understanding of society and of others' histories and cultures to model better behaviors toward those "others" and, in order to educate the less aware, to speak to the facts of how and why they came to believe what they regard as true, and why they feel as they do. And perhaps colleges/universities can find ways to do anti-racist training that opens rather than closes the students to the appreciation of different others.

As another result of these two conflicting efforts at the university level, we have seen instances in recent history of the anomalous development of conservative culture warriors' pretended support for, and President Trump signing of a proclamation in favor of, free speech. Neither Trump nor, for the most part, Republican stalwarts (apart from some libertarians) actually believe in free speech generally, though they want it *for themselves and their political interests*. Typically it is Republicans and fundamentalist Xtian culture leaders who are among the earliest to condemn and call for censorship or even suppression of countercultural ideas and/or openness about sexuality, *avant-garde* art, feminist thought, rap music, homosexuality, left-wing thought, seemingly anti-Xtian sentiments of any kind, and ideas and policies they see as unpatriotic, from flag-burning to "taking a knee" when the national anthem is played at NFL football games. For a relatively comprehensive treatment of much of this, see Andrew Hartman's *A War for the Soul of America: A History of the Culture Wars*. Republicans have especially often been in the lead to silence others by calling them "unpatriotic" for open expressions of opposition to wars, from the War on Vietnam to the War on Saddam Hussein/Iraq. And before that they were leaders of the bandwagon of anti-Communist purges and professorial loyalty oaths. The most notorious of these efforts was led by Senator Joseph McCarthy of Wisconsin. As conservatives, Republicans very much tend to favor the traditional and the status quo. To them, free speech is more of a threat than not.

Even in an institution like a college or university, the latter of which especially was deliberately designed to research frontiers and seek out new ideas to improve society and the world, Republicans complain about the lack of traditionalists and about the biases against conservativism (though they also tend happily to opt for jobs that make more money on non-academic pursuits instead). Moreover, although there is often at least some range of viable interpretations of U.S. history, for example, it is not clear to me that there are such things as vaguely coherent and historically sound right-wing discourses about the full scope and character of society or U.S. history that might provide viable substitutes in an academic setting. Mainly, there are the simplistic ones taught at lower levels of education. I am reminded here of the fact that the reactionary and highly racist White majority in the South, with its history of justifying separate but (un)equal Jim Crow laws, abandoned the Democrats politically in the late 1960s because of that party's shift to support of greater civil rights, while the Republicans sought and happily accepted into its arms the formerly Democratic "Solid South," and happily took up or substituted "dog whistling" (subtle appeals to prejudice) instead of more direct but by-then less socially appropriate racist appeals, which were left in some but not all cases to overt segregationists such as George Wallace (who late in his life recanted). And it is still true that the south and parts of the rural and small-town Midwest are the bedrock of Republican support in this country. Thus Trump's proclamation in favor of academic freedom is a fig leaf, allowing Republicans to more readily continue to perpetrate and perpetuate the delusion that Whites and conservative ideologies are the primary victims among the people of this country (see below for more on delusions).

Another example of problems arising from an otherwise rea-sonable politically correct idea (assuming no enforcement or on-line berating) involves the notion that Whites should avoid "microag-gressions" against ethnic/racial minorities. This idea can too easily be overextended. Not only might the intents of the person approaching a person of color vary immensely, so might the perceptions of microag-gressiveness vary according to the sensitivities of the individual on the "receiving end," or perhaps even the time of day (though the number of times per day that some get asked roughly the same question could be burdensome or even seem oppressive). For example, the intent of an inquiry as to the national origin of a non-White can be negative or be entirely sympathetic and simple conversation-seeking (just as one White, hearing a different accent, might ask another White where he/she was from while standing in a grocery line). Similarly, some inqui-ries, including about national origin, could be perceived initially as denying, doubting or questioning the citizenship of a minority citizen, even though the inquiry might have been a simple kind of reaching out without bias against anyone, citizen or not. To some, this is still a microaggression because it is an intrusive interruption. So, what is the verdict as to the "right," or at least acceptable range of, conduct here? Don't compliment the young Muslim on her beautifully colored hijab (head scarf) at the grocery store (she smiled and thanked me)? Don't say, in the presence of a Black woman and her two teenage children at the grocery store, as a warning regarding a man in a motorized cart, "Look out! He's gonna back that thang up"? (The mother burst out laughing.) Or, don't ask at the Grand Canyon where some almost obviously foreign Asian tourists might have hailed from, even though the follow-up was to be, "Welcome to the United States." Don't approach the spiffily dressed young, somewhat East Asian-looking couple, the woman with a hijab (very likely Muslim), in the supermarket by asking them, "Do you mind if I try to guess where you're from?" (The guess and answer were both Malaysia.) Don't ask the grocery store checker if he's from Kenya (yes) and then explain that you guessed right because you know someone else from Kenya with an accent much like his? Don't ask the woman checker with an apparently Chinese name who has complimented you on your ability to do arithmetic in your head involving the fractions of a dollar in a cash exchange, "aren't you from China?" while adding, "where they have a long history of being good at mathematics" (she beamed)? What are the alternatives here? Silence? Must all approaches have what amounts to a definite business reason? And otherwise be refrained from, to insure non-intrusiveness? That Whites should not speak to ethnic minority individuals unless spoken to? It seems to me that at a college or university, especially, these alternatives are a sure-fire recipe for making ethnic/racial minorities and many immigrants feel out-of-place if not unwelcome. A simple alternative is to have something positive to say! It is also very helpful to look at things from the other guy's (person's) view.

So, with respect to all of the above and higher education, perhaps it would be better to proceed with the best possible intents and institutional guidance, but without a sense of censorship, coercion, or mandates. Ethnically nasty graffiti on a sidewalk is a matter to take up educationally, while the same on someone's door borders on assault and/or a hate crime. As above, voluntarily politically correct stances are often but not always appropriate as a guide to being respectful (e.g., see re microaggression, above), but mandates and rules too easily and too often result in overdoing it. And maybe expecting perfection is too much to ask, especially if it means that conservative Whites simply hide their opinions and beliefs, stick to fellow travelers using the same information silos, build-up resentment instead of understanding, and then go on to cultivate support among the even more ignorant public on the basis of sometimes legitimate grievances about viewpoint restrictions at their college or university. In fact, all too many White students still arrive at colleges imbued with sociocultural attitudes in part inculcated by prejudiced parents and less than fully adequate K-12 schools. What are they expected to learn from institutional prohibitions and "rules," both formal and informal (e.g., as policed by politically correct peers)—that they had best keep quiet? Or is it better to let them learn and change more naturally and interactively in the classroom (and U.S. history should be required) and outside it, in occasional cross-cultural interactions and sharing. This is what we had to do in times past, despite a status quo weighted down by more conservative elders—where, over time, the society as a whole has shown considerable progress (admittedly, along with some relapses), much of it driven by the young and the minorities themselves?

Suckering for Political Spin

In politics, all parties now engage in putting their own "spin" on events and policy proposals. Although some of this spinning is far more deceptive than other spinning, in general, each major interest group, including large corporations (wherein it is called "public relations"), tries to get their spin to be the predominant way in which some event, failure, product, idea, policy or candidate is viewed by the general public (or, at least, the undecided among them). Among politically sophisticated spinners, often there are misleading interpretations that are also deliberately linked to values many citizens hold dear but which have no real applicability to the subject at hand [George Lakoff, *Don't Think of an Elephant!: Know Your Values and Frame the Debate*]. For example, the spinners might link their web of interpretations to the nebulous idea of "family values" or try to make other interpretations seem racist or opposed to "diversity."

Also, as mentioned earlier, right wing political propagandists try to spin the concept of "socialism" by stirring up a visceral fear and hatred against it. They encourage the population to regard anything with that label as evil—like the former Soviet Union's totalitarian empire and its social system. And once that mental shortcut is established in the minds of followers, the word "socialist" is then used by the spinners as a way of negatively branding many a liberal candidate and policy. Any automatic rejection by listeners of any policy that the spinners brand as socialism helps to lower the likelihood that the opposition can win, or that that policy, or even variants on it, can be considered as a possibility in the United States. Yet almost all of the time, the policies actually in question are variants on the democratic socialistic (human welfare-oriented) societies in Europe, particularly in Scandinavia, and have very little or nothing to do with the actualities in the former U.S.S.R. With his open advocacy of some of these kinds of policies even while accepting the label of "democratic socialist," Bernie Sanders (one of the two main Democrats contending for that party's presidential nomination in 2016 and 2020 and Senator from Vermont) should be given a lot of credit for helping many more people in this country to reject the automatic negative reaction to "socialism," though it is by no means clear that he has overcome most of the negativity that decades of spinning have established with that word. Promoters of this kind of spinning cater to and promote cultural insanities by seeking a de facto prohibition on discussion of a wider range of ideas and policies.

One is readily reminded here too of some of the usual inter-pretations that emerge as to what, if anything, should be done after yet another mass shooting has occurred, where the National Rifle Association (NRA) pretty much argues every time that people, not guns, kill people, and that even attempts to ban rapid-fire weapons with large magazines involves a dire loss of Second Amendment rights and in the long run will result in every gun owner's guns being registered by the government, and subsequently taken away. The NRA's only "solution" to gun-associated violence seems to be to legitimize con-cealed firearms in every setting so that ordinary citizens can intervene against the bad guys. This all-or-none approach, along with advances in conservative regions in "gun rights," can only lead to a worsening of the cultural insanity of the United States being the number one developed country in homicide and suicidal death by gunshot. I see no good reason not to limit long guns to those that can reasonably be used by sportsmen as hunters of animal game or birds—but who do not mow down game species in a fusillade of bullets. Similarly, there is no good reason not to have a much better accounting system of gun purchases and ownership, at least of hand guns. If we can report car sales, car transfers within the family, and car thefts, we can also do that with hand guns. In the days when the Second Amendment to the Constitution was written, most adult males, especially outside our then-small cities, owned a *musket* for hunting and were expected to show up with those guns to help constitute a "well-regulated militia" for use by their state in times of need. (They were also called upon at times for drill and practice as a militia.) We now have a National Guard and a variety of continuous state police forces, and reserves, that fulfill this function. So hunting, marksmanship and, very rarely, self-defense, mainly at home, would seem to be the truly legitimate reasons for owning guns.

Earlier, I discussed some abuses of the words "patriotic" and "unpatriotic." In times of war, those supporting a war will label their critics as "unpatriotic," accuse them of undermining "our boys in uniform" and so forth. Doing so is an appeal to unthinking emotion, a refusal to debate the issues involved. Moreover, true patriotism in a country like this one necessarily involves raising reasoned criticisms of national policies and actions, or of any politician, with which or with whom one disagrees. One of the best comments about such spinning was made by Samuel Johnson in the late 1700s, namely that "patriotism is the last refuge of a scoundrel."

In other spinning mentioned above, the general public generally welcomes pitches for lower taxes, but too often instead the slogans get transmuted by Republicans into laws that mainly benefit large corporations and their wealthy stockholders. The large corporations and wealthy are portrayed as good-guy job creators and, no matter the reality, the tax cuts are certainly not championed as payback for the large donations from wealthy individuals and corporations to Republican politicians and PACs. In truth, though, it is already the large corporations—the special beneficiaries of tax breaks, tax loop-holes, rules that shift what should be regarded as their externalized costs onto the public (e.g., pollution clean-ups), and now extra-low tax rates as well—that are the primary beneficiaries of "welfare" in this country—and that is socialism for the rich.

A localized example of much of this may be drawn from Thomas Frank's *What's the Matter with Kansas?* Frank makes the case that many Kansans have been enticed by conservative Republican politicians into focusing on hot-button cultural issues, such as family values, abortion and reducing taxes, even though the conservatives' social and economic platforms would not contribute to improving the social and economic conditions in Kansas, and even though the actual policies are at variance with a strong populist focus earlier in Kansas history on social and economic equality. The Republican pitch was supported by many lower- and middle-class Kansans. Meanwhile, in reality, the tax cuts that were adopted undermined state funding for public education and other social and economic programming important to the middle and lower classes. Subsequent Republican leadership in Kansas (Governor Brownback) doubled-down on this approach by cutting government spending (with the claim that prosperity would result) until it created so much difficulty that even many of the Republicans in the legislature finally said no in realms such as public education.

In this regard, it is only fair to note that Karl Marx and others developed an idea called "false consciousness." The essence of his concept is that people get inculcated with the ideology or belief systems of the ruling classes, such that many adhere strongly to that ideology, notwithstanding that there may have long since arisen plenty of evidence and reasons—evident to the external observers (whether "objective" or aliens from another planet)—that to do so works against their own interests and their children's futures. One factor in Marx's false consciousness was religion, which he called the opiate of the masses. Much religion still tends to encourage people to focus on the afterlife rather than this life and, as we will see in some of the case studies to follow, can directly lead both the masses and the elite away from higher levels of consciousness, and contribute to parts of an erroneous worldview that promote cultural insanities (e.g., worldviews in which ancient religious texts are considered scientifically correct). Without attempting to formulate a precise definition, I'll just say that higher levels of consciousness reflect a truer understanding of reality, including the social and cultural dynamics of the world around us, and a seeing-through of the many variants on rationalization, pretenses, smokescreens, obfuscations, spins, and deliberate deceptions (lies) propagated by self-interested parties (especially large corporations) and politicians. Good self-understanding is almost necessarily included as part of having higher levels of consciousness as well.

More needs to be said about deliberate deception. Among the archetypal examples are tobacco companies' efforts to discredit the causal component of the correlation between smoking and lung cancer (when their internal memos showed they knew otherwise), by sugar producers and companies to get the country to avoid being concerned about the amount of sugars in our diet (and get any blame laid on fats instead), and by oil companies to fund "research" that deliberately yielded outcomes to cast doubt on the science of global warming. The tobacco companies' effort included the funding of scientists who were willing to do work that raised doubts about the scientific consensus. And this effort by the tobacco companies has been used as the blueprint for all subsequent corporate and political efforts at "science denial" [Lee McIntyre, *Post-Truth*, 22-24]. Later such efforts also involved the funding of "think tanks" designed to be sympathetic to the interests of their corporate funders, thus producing a regular stream of analyses and scientifically biased propaganda from sources that seemed to be independent but were ultimately beholden to their funders' interests. And even if that source of funding dried up (e.g., due to its public disclosure), the staffing and directions of the think tank would be unlikely to change in any short time. Companies have even tried to shape university programs—not without occasional relative success—but universities usually reject grants with too many restrictions as to content or release of findings (while perhaps accepting grants focused on particular topics). Overall, the goal in all these efforts is to deceive the public by stimulating doubts about the extent of the scientific consensus or otherwise promoting the views of the corporate funder. If the public thinks the science is unsettled and that there is no scientific consensus, they are freed to believe what their deceivers want them to believe, and will be more likely to do so if the deceiver can also find ways to associate its lies with the ideological stance of the recipient—such as a belief in free enterprise with minimal government regulation.

Another very typical tactic common to many large corporation playbooks was used by the Western States Petroleum Association which "secretly created 15 fake groups intended to look like grassroots consumer movements, with innocuous names such as California Drivers Alliance" to sponsor advertisements, in this case in a "highly dishonest campaign that succeeded in defeating" a 2015 clean energy ballot initiative in California [Bryan Wadsworth, "Inside the Disinformation Playbook," in *Catalyst*, Winter 2018, 10, 20]. Clearly, considerable caution needs to be exercised before voters "buy into" these spun spider webs, starting with a thorough check on the source of the "information." Because the proponents of the initiative could point to a direct monetary conflict of interest and bias only if most of the major opposition came from the oil companies, the corporations went through considerable effort to conceal who or what entities were putting up the money that generated small, thinly veneered front groups issuing propagandistic press releases, buying advertisements, and using distorted reasoning.

Another famous example of well-funded spin—with conflicts of interest that were disregarded by most of the public—can be seen in a major policy initiative to reform health care during the Clinton administration. The draft of a proposed revision of the law included as one small feature payments for doctors who spend time on voluntary patient-doctor conversations about an "advance directive" (living will)—just like doctors are paid for time spent on almost any other purpose. This idea was severely distorted by entrenched medical interest groups who paid for extensive showings of a television commercial that described that one feature of the bill as a government effort to save money by using "death panels" with their sights on grandma.

Somewhat similarly, but more directly dangerous if practiced by large numbers of people, is adherence to the beliefs or worldview-related propaganda of "authorities" who are known to put forth lies repeatedly, such as President Trump, who has even repeated many a lie after having been called out for that particular lie—even "four Pinocchio" lies. Blind adherence to such an authority is especially likely to give a freer hand to the liar and reinforce errors in the worldviews of the followers. Claims from such authorities about the need for "alternative facts" (rather than alternative interpretations of the same facts—even though that might just involve a different spin) are both appalling and especially dubious to anyone who thinks for themselves. Relatedly, statements by such authorities claiming that information that casts them in a bad light, or reveals their lies, is false, is just another ploy in the effort to sustain adherents' beliefs in the liar and/or the lies. As Nazi propagandists well knew, repeating lies often enough worked remarkably well to convince people that those lies were true. President Trump uses this same playbook as he tweets all manner of outrageous comments and positions in an effort to commandeer the headlines in newspaper and TV. Like many other Hollywood "celebrities," in Trump's case, so far at least, being in the news seems to matter more than what is said, even when he lies or contradicts previous statements (e.g., re Jews and Nazis, as noted above), or when there are yet more revelations about his nondisclosure agreement-based concealments of incidents in his own scandalous past. Moreover, although the press has its weaknesses (see below) and its investigative reporting staff has been hollowed out by new patterns in the flow of advertising money to internet-coordinating corporations, the press is still as close as our society comes to having a bastion of freedom, so a president calling major newspapers the "enemy of the people"—insofar as people believe it—is a sure guarantee that cultural insanity is running rampant. Especially when there are very few good alternatives to the legitimate press and *legitimate* TV news.

One way or another, it takes some degree of delusions among followers to go along with the kinds of propaganda and lies illustrated above and elsewhere here. Delusion is a mental illness that involves a detachment from reality. And, almost obviously, those who heed leaders' lies, showmanship stunts, and propaganda (and, of course, the leaders themselves), when present in large numbers, are likely to be major contributors to cultural insanity in democratic societies.

Overlooking, Disregarding, and Denying the Major Threats to Our Country and Our Planet

Partly as a result of the aforementioned difficulties in our thinking processes, some major world problems have been overlooked, downplayed, or even denied by immense numbers of people. Often, for example, the benefit of one or another destructive industrial or commercial practice in producing some jobs (and sometimes only short-term jobs, such as laying oil pipelines) will be trumpeted as if it were more important than a high probability for longer-term negative effects of the action. Exemplars of this type include hard-rock mining into Sulphur-bearing rocks, roads for logging in (what will no longer be) wilderness habitat, industrial run-off that pollutes rivers and kills much or even all of the fish and other life forms therein, large hog waste lagoons in low-lying riverine environments, tar sands oil extraction in

The Sixth Extinction is an ongoing threat that will continue unless we do a lot more than just dealing with global warming. The extinction process is occurring by way of innumerable processes and effects, some large, some small, that humans are foisting on nature. And that makes it difficult to summarize. Instead, I can only point to some of the most serious effects.

Human causation of this extinction likely goes back to nomads hunting some or most of the megafauna near the end of the Pleistocene Period (e.g., different kinds of mammoth in Europe and the mastodon in the Americas, most large marsupials in Australia, moas in New Zealand). In recent years though, so much evidence has accumulated and been widely made available in various media that there really is no valid excuse for not facing the issue and making much greater effort to deal with it. This is not to say that the people and their representatives in this country have done nothing—for example, we have established wilderness areas, national parks, and passed badly needed laws such as the Endangered Species Act, and the Clean Water Act—but that matters are still getting worse. To varying extents, many other countries have made some efforts too, but some countries have not been able to implement or enforce what they have tried to do and need more outside help of various kinds. In this country, another problem is that the Republican party and some Republican administrations have moved well to the right since the Nixon administration when several important environmental laws were passed with majorities in both major political parties. In recent decades, Republicans have become much stronger in supporting corporate exploitation of the environment. For example, perhaps you too remember the Republican convention of 2008 with its delegates' frequent chanting of "drill, baby, drill"; and now, we have President Trump's zeal to explore/drill for oil on the north coast of Alaska and off the Atlantic coast, and his roll-back of protective standards for off-shore oil rigs in the Gulf of Mexico (despite the immense and costly environmental impact of the

Deepwater Horizon oil spill of 2010). And the Trump administration is now leading efforts to reduce the scope of the Clean Water Act and the Endangered Species Act. Meanwhile, "more than 1,600 U.S. species are already listed under the Endangered Species Act, another 150 are presumed extinct," and the various states have identified thousands of species of concern in their domains [Collin O'Mara, "Support a Game Changer for Wildlife," in *National Wildlife*, Oct.-Nov. 2019, 6]. Although the Endangered Species Act has been a major success in preventing extinction and fostering a few recoveries, it is better to act to preserve habitat before flora and fauna become endangered. To illustrate something of the scale of the problem, an analyst in 2002 estimated that 90% of the weight of all mammals on the planet can be accounted for by humans, "along with their billions of cattle, pigs, dogs, and other domesticated creatures" [Christian Schwägerl, *The Anthropocene: The Human Era and How It Shapes Our Planet*, 43-44].

The onward march of the Sixth Extinction can also be seen in some historical snapshots. In earlier centuries wildlife habitats such as the many forest areas in Europe were slowly but largely destroyed, as were most of the animals that inhabited them. Since the early 1900s or so, the accelerating human population growth and our increase in wants (and our wants becoming "needs") have begun to play an ever-bigger role in this destruction. But well before that, the early wild west economy based on fur trading greatly reduced the number of beavers which also caused many areas to dry out and become non-productive, even for most wildlife. (Some restorative efforts have discovered how much difference beavers can make by ensuring a slowed year-long water flow rather than a complete desiccation during most dry seasons.) By the mid-1900s a number of populations of whales, used as a source of oil and food, had become threatened with extinction by factory whaling ships (and some species are still in that condition)—a process begun in the early 1800s when still primitive whaling vessels were seeking blubber to boil down into lamp oil for human use.

From the late 1860s until the late 1880s, the American bison (buffalo), which had supported a number of plains Indians cultures for centuries if not millennia, was reduced from herds of 30-60 million to the verge of extinction by hunters, initially mainly as a food source, but later also for pure sport—unprecedented and appalling—and ceasing only when there were just something over 100 buffalo left. "Oh give me a home, where the buffalo roam" (as the song goes)—a fertile and erosion-resistant grassland "carbon sink" that supported a diversity of plants and animals—has become monoculture farmland (plus some ranchland and desert) which, especially with mismanagement, became the source of the 1930s dust bowl phenomenon (see below). Similarly, the last of the wild passenger pigeons—a bird that once numbered in the millions but was easily slaughtered for food because of its instinctual mass roosting in trees at night—was killed near the turn of the last century, and the last individual of that species died in the Cincinnati zoo in 1921 (see Plate 1.1).

Plate 1.1: Passenger Pigeons at the Natural History Museum, London. Photo by the author.

More recent and current excesses, atop many others, include exterminating many species by cutting down more tropical rainforest (which harbor the greatest diversity of life), often illegally, in Brazil, to grow soy beans and raise cattle for U.S. and world markets, in Indonesia, to develop environmentally sterile monoculture palm oil plantations, and in Africa, for logs. In Indonesia, these encroachments are threatening orangutans, Asian rhinos, and Sumatran tigers. Extensive destruction of forests in the United States have also contributed to a variety of extinctions and endangered many other animals. And because rainforests and temperate forests (like ours) are also important as a carbon sink, the deforestation, adds to humankind's releases of carbon dioxide and, hence, to global warming/climate change. Between 2000 and 2012, U.S. researchers, in cooperation with Google, estimated that about 880,000 square miles of 'natural forest' were turned into "agricultural areas, residential areas or into wasteland," while only 308,000 square miles were replanted, too often with very little diversity" [Schwägerl, 37].

Poaching of elephants for ivory, rhinoceros for their horns (which are made of keratin, like hair), pangolins for their scales (also keratin), and tigers and bears for various body parts, has run rampant, with some species of each now being threatened or endangered. Pangolins, being small, are the most trafficked animal in the world—so much so that about 2.7 million African pangolins are killed every year; and the largest criminal wildlife bust (in Malaysia) included 30 tons of pangolins [African Wildlife Foundation, *African Wildlife News*, Summer 2019, 6]. Similarly, giraffes, which are now nearing a threatened status, and endangered gorillas are killed for trophies; and many African animals, including our closest living relatives, chimpanzees and bonobos, fall prey to "bush meat" hunters. All too often it is logging roads—often illegal ones—that enable access to the deep recesses of rainforest habitats that enable these depredations.

In the U.S.A., many people have become aware of major threats to the population of monarch butterflies and to bees, where bees are especially important to humans as pollinators for many of our food crops. "Colony collapse disorder," a problem in domesticated bee colonies, seems to be due to multiple causes, *including* the bees' contacts with neonicotinoid insecticides, which plants absorb and retain, even in their flowers, even if only their seeds have been coated with the insecticide. Although Europe in 2018 banned three major "neonics" from all outdoor uses, the Environmental Protection Agency here, and only now (2020) released "preliminary findings and recommendations for public comment" that "fell far short of the dramatic action experts say is necessary" [Natural Resources Defense Council, "NRDC Ramps up Fight to Restrict Use of Bee-killing Pesticides," in *Nature's Voice*, Summer 2020, 2]. In addition, natural insect populations have been reduced by using herbicides used to kill non-crops essential to insects even on roadsides. Some scientists have now reported that a general and continuing decline in the insect population has begun: "About a third of all insect species are threatened with extinction" [in *Population Connection*, June 2019, 4-5] Continuing in that direction will produce a massive decline in many populations of insect-eating animals, including most birds—where a decline in the latter already seems to be underway from many causes (including habitat destruction and "corn deserts"). Recently, scientific estimates have reported a bird population decline of about 2.9 billion for North America—a figure that pertains to long-term populations not annual mortalities, which are high for a number of reasons, including not-very-domesticated cats roaming outside. A classic case that had a direct effect on birds arose from the use of the insecticide DDT. Here the birds' eggs were attacked directly rather than over the long-term via losses of habitat and declines in insects. The problem was exposed in 1962 by Rachel Carson in *Silent Spring*. DDT worked wonders against insect pests such as mosquitos but accumulated in ever greater amounts in the bodies of animals nearer the top of the food chain, and resulted in the thinning of the egg shells of many birds, and especially the raptors at the top of the food chain, including the American eagle. Fortunately, since DDT was banned in the U.S.A. in the 1970s, eagles, peregrine falcons, and other raptors have made a comeback. That was a case where, after considerable prodding over almost a decade, the people and the politicians did pay attention and do something about the problem. (There remain tensions about this ban, however, where malaria is rampant, as in Africa.)

In the oceans, trawlers and other forms of industrial fishing methods and techniques have driven many fish stocks to near extinction and have thinned others into commercial uselessness. As of 2012, the United Nations Food and Agriculture Association classified "eighty per cent of fish stocks as being fully or excessively depleted" [Schwägerl, 36]. Although at times the responsibility has been in the hands of local fishermen (a "tragedy of the commons"), most of these declines, even when involving local fishermen, have been due to a combination of improved technology and industrial-scale fishing (e.g., echolocation of fish schools; large-scale trawlers; immense machine-operated gill nets; thousands of long lines cast), so that everyone catches more until the catch starts to decline and, a short time thereafter, the fish stock collapses. Clearly, these approaches are *unsustainable*. For example, a once-extremely rich New England cod fishery had collapsed by the early 1990s, terminating jobs for about 38,000 fishermen and fish-processing workers in Newfoundland. The entire cod fishery is still very weak and the "northern" cod around Newfoundland have not come back. Other fish are nearing the point of being endangered and are now rarely caught at sizes that were typical a generation of two ago (e.g., bluefin tuna, swordfish, marlin). Sharks have been greatly reduced in number by being slaughtered mainly for their fins (for use in shark fin soup). All too often, lots of other non-targeted ocean inhabitants, including dolphins and turtles, are killed in mass-catching techniques (some as by-catches in nets; some by habitat destruction, especially with bottom trawling; some as avoidable accidents). With respect to dead dolphins, some of this country's tuna canning corporations are still among the responsible parties. In addition, many coastal mangrove forests (which protect against hurricanes and serve as fish nurseries) have been eliminated, most recently for shrimp farms. Dams on free-flowing rivers, whether put there to generate electricity and/or to divert water for agriculture, have the main responsibility for destroying most of the salmon fisheries along the contiguous West Coast states, including "106 runs of Pacific Northwest salmon in the Columbia River Basin," with human work-arounds (breeding and release) managing to preserve some remnant stocks in other cases [Paul Tolmé, "Running the Gauntlet," in *National Wildlife*, June-July 2019, 40]. On a broader scale yet, global warming is now wreaking havoc on coral reefs, which are also among the major fish nurseries (see below). I should add here too that there is a considerable environmental injustice involved in developed countries' commercial factory fishing fleets—because they have often extracted great proportions of the fish and undermined the size of the catch off the coasts of countries in which vast numbers of poor men and their families have for millennia survived as low-tech fishermen.

Another environmental problem to which humans have contributed greatly is desertification. Although well over 100 countries have at least some problem with desertification, the most extensive desertification is underway in northern Africa, along the southern border of the Sahara, which may be partly a result of very long-term environmental change but is also due to human-induced global warming, and the overuse and abuse of the land by (sometimes desperate) people, such that drought takes larger tolls on the landscape than it otherwise might.

In 2004, a Nobel Peace Prize was awarded to Wangari Maathai for her work in Kenya, organizing and coordinating the efforts mainly of many poor women over almost three decades, that resulted in the planting of 30 million trees—which helps to stem the desertification. China is struggling with desertification north of Beijing. Similarly, historically, it was the overuse and misuse of prairie grasslands in agriculture in the United States that contributed mightily to the development of the "dust bowl" in the mid-1930s: much of that land was marginal for the kind of agriculture we practiced on it, especially in periods of low rainfall or drought, and the plowing and lack of cover crops not only helped to ensure that drought continued but led to massive dust storms that reached as far as Washington, D.C. In this case, desertification was halted, but not until a considerable loss in the soil's natural fertility, carbon content, and capacity to store rainwater.

Extinction is the number one unsustainability (even if a few DNA-based resurrections are possible, millions of species are being lost without ever becoming known to humans, many leaving nary a trace). But sustainability problems for humanity occur in many areas. In terms of the "ecological footprint, for example, the amount of usage of land and shallow seas needed to sustain a person: "For every person in the world to reach present U.S. levels of consumption with existing technology would require four more planet Earths" [Edward O. Wilson, *The Future of Life*, 23]. Assuming the technology of the time when Wilson wrote, and no further changes in the rates of forest losses "and other forms of environmental destruction," it could with considerable assurance be said "that at least a fifth of the species of plants and animals would be gone or committed to early extinction by 2030, and half by the end of the century" [Wilson, 102, 150].

The earth provides a limited resource base to which we humans avail ourselves. Advances in mass production, technological innovation, food production, and resource extraction and utilization have so far enabled us to meet our increasing materialistic demands and enable access to food for ever-increasing numbers of people (while reducing the number of starving), even in the face of rising consumption by growing middle classes in many countries. Although early warnings in the 1970s about overshooting resource availabilities and the likely catastrophic collapse of the human population have not yet come to pass, it is all too likely that there is validity in their projection that we had less than 100 years to change course substantially to avoid a drastic crash in the human population—a crash in which billions are likely to die. Please note that the possible immediate causes of this crash include war brought about by national competition for limited resources. (For the classic in this regard, see Donella H. Meadows, Dennis L. Meadows, Jørgen Randers, and William W. Behrens, *The Limits to Growth: A Report for the Club of Rome's Project on the Predicament of Mankind*, 1972.] In other words, so far, humankind has probably only managed to postpone potentially devastating consequences from mauling and ravishing the planet's ecology—some parts of which have been described above here, with others to follow. "The juggernaut of technology-based capitalism ... will very soon either chew up what remains of the living world, or it will be redirected to save it" [Wilson, 156]. Wilson says that a new environmental ethic is needed. "The central problem of the new century, I have argued, is how to raise the poor to a decent standard of living worldwide while preserving as much of the rest of life as possible" [Wilson, 189].

While most authors writing overarching ecological analyses make "it's-not-too-late" suggestions for the improvement of the prospects for life on our planet—including human life—at least one recent author, Bill McKibben, in *Eaarth: Making a Life on a Tough New Planet*, says it is too late, that all we can do is not make it any worse on our already-changed planet Eaarth. Perhaps akin to that, Nathan H. Lents, reflecting on the high probability that there are many inhabitable planets but no detection as yet of any alien civilizations (for which we now have delicate sensors, and as has expected by leading scientists as far back as the 1950s), suggests that all their civilizations may have imploded first. Imploded because of competitive motivation—such as ours—being too strong relative to cooperative motivations [Lents, *Human Erros: A Panorama of Our Glitches, from Pointless Bones to Broken Genes*, 203-207]. So there's a nasty possibility that this analysis might help to avert.

Even humans are at risk of extinction because of our degradation and disregard of the planet and its webs of life. Indeed, even if we humans survive for a very long time yet, "the Sixth Extinction will continue to determine the course of life long after everything people have written and painted and built has been ground into dust..." [Elizabeth Kolbert, *The Sixth Extinction: An Unnatural History*, 269]. Geologists are now contemplating, based on existing strict criteria, whether to declare that the Earth has entered a new geologic period, the Anthropocene, because humans are now the principal agent of change on the planet and, even as of now, will leave long-term effects on its geology—including its climate. (In this regard, see the aforementioned Schwägerl, *The Anthropocene:....*) We have already, for example, changed the character of vast proportions of the earth's land to feed ourselves and our domestic livestock, and transplanted animal and plant species all over the globe. In contrast to environmental pessimists, Schwägerl argued (copyright 2011) that renaming the current (geologic) era as the Anthropocene will help, or at least could help, people to realize and accept their responsibility, and rise to the occasion, despite the many-faceted changes needed. However, Schwägerl is a German, and people of that country seem to have begun to deal with many environmental problems that, eight years later (i.e., as I write) are still largely ignored, downplayed, disregarded, or denied by large majorities in the United States.

Perhaps a new religion is also needed—one that incorporates a new environmental ethic. In several respects, the existing Western religions do not meet current needs. As one author puts it, "The religious dogmas of the Western world ... give humans dominion over nature, but many people no longer use these ancient stories from Bronze Age goatherds as a guide for modern living in an overcrowded planet" [Prothero, 280]. Still, "even massively fictitious beliefs can be adaptive, as long as they motivate behaviors that are adaptive in the real world'" whereas factual knowledge, as we also saw above, may be too weak as a motivator [David Sloan Wilson, cited in Jared Diamond, *The World Until Yesterday: What Can We Learn from Traditional Societies?*, 366]. Clearly, for example, the idea of humans as stewards with respect to the Earth needs to replace the idea of human dominion over the Earth.

One tenet that should be included, whether part of the idea of stewardship or otherwise, involves our need to recognize the holy in aspects of nature. "The natural environment we treat with such unnecessary ignorance and recklessness was our cradle and nursery, our school, and remains our one and only home" [Wilson, 40].

At the base of it all is e = mc2. All life involves a consolidation of energy into matter, plus a way of capturing and using additional energy to enact/perform the functions of life. On Earth, all life, including us, is based on carbon atoms. Our bodies are composed of cells that are specialized versions of single-celled bacteria, again linking us, including evolutionarily, with all other life, plant or animal. Moreover, *every cell* has tiny little organ(elle)s within it—mitochondria—that process energy for that cell and its life form. Thus are we linked to all other animal or plant life—by possessing DNA as a means of reproduction. We may be glorified great apes—apes with language, consciousness and the ability to see ourselves in the future, only smatterings of which are seen in other animals. But we evolved that capacity as a part of nature, not apart from nature, and not as some deity's creation. Religiously, we should worship Nature and Mother Earth.

In recent times, it seems, we have begun to encounter more limits. Up to now, technology has helped us cope with the increases in materialistic and food demands, although at a considerable cost to nature and the future. Sometimes additional discoveries have enhanced our supply (e.g., new oil fields still sometimes get found, shale oil and fracked natural gas became accessible through technology, and solar and wind power became economically feasible). And sometimes human ingenuity with technology finds substitutes for rare or unduly expensive resources (expensive because they are rare and/or difficult to extract, especially if they are becoming rarer due to human consumption). Intensively grown plants (e.g., in vertical structures or in biospheres in which fish produce food for plants and vice-versa, with surpluses from either available to humans) may not require additional arable land devoted to crops (which is in short supply). Plant-based versions of meat may help to produce more protein for humans without having to eliminate yet more natural environments for crops used to feed cattle, pigs and chickens. The same may prove true for lab meat—meat grown directly from cells. And regenerative, organic agriculture combined with good animal husbandry can produce meat at a much lower cost to nature even if not yet at a lower cost for the consumer (in part because the destruction of nature is not counted as part of the costs of industrialized meat production, and in part because many of the techniques of small farmers have been lost in the move to mass-produced food).

Even so, some rare minerals are likely to be in short supply all too soon, or their availability may be limited mainly to one or a very few countries which may not be reliable suppliers. "Rare earths," the vast majority of which are mined in China, might be one example, but many other rare minerals are in short supply too. Some of these minerals are essential to many of the advanced technologies in use today, such as computerized phones and flat-panel televisions, as well as in a lot of military hardware. In any case, ultimately, there are likely to be relatively narrow limits on how much can be found and extracted for some crucial resources, with expensive and less viable alternatives as the only option if any.

The commercial exploitation of fish described above seems to be a major example of unsustainability for which technology will not readily find a replacement on anything like the same scale, even if a few fish species can be farmed commercially. As it is, at least some farmed fish may have reduced purity (e.g., color is added to farmed salmon, disease is far more frequent, and antibiotics are used) and may pose threats to the natural species if they escape their pens.

Also, fresh water supplies are under threat in many places in the world. That human priorities almost always take precedence over nature's needs in the use of river water will speed up desertification (and exterminate more species). Agriculture needs fresh water and considerable effort in some areas has been made to reduce waste— but it is a major user of water. Thus, even if new sources of energy are applied to the task of desalinization and the pipelines to transport it, very severe shortages are likely to continuously develop in the future. Also in jeopardy as cropland are areas that currently rely on subterranean aquifers for water, some of which have been almost drained and will need thousands of years to refill. (Aquifers are "fossil water" left over from ice age meltwater in this country.) In this country, such croplands include important agricultural regions such as the southern great plains and the Central Valley of California. The Central and Imperial valleys of California that lack sufficient water have been among the reasons for the development of vast pipelines that divert river waters from the Colorado River and the Sacramento River (of northern California)—and this reduces water flows that once helped sustain wildlife (fish, migratory birds, etc.) in formerly swampy areas near the deltas of these rivers (in San Francisco Bay, and at the upper end of the Gulf of California). Even now, because of drought, water demands exceed supplies, so further drawdown from the aquifers occurs, and the shortages threaten to dry up portions of California's Central Valley and produce major political struggles over water rights. In some other parts of the world, similar water shortages will produce wars for control of the available water. And wars can be especially hard on wildlife in places like Africa (e.g., Mozambique) because the animals are killed for food by armies operating in the field, by desperate civilians, and by unchecked poachers.

The above represents only the beginning of what could be included among the human behaviors responsible for producing the Sixth Extinction. Several of the sections to follow consider yet other major factors that, because of their relative importance, need separate treatment. But they also include unsustainable human doings that factor into the Sixth Extinction.

Overpopulation

The global human population passed seven billion a few years ago, and projections are for it to reach nine billion by around 2040. But the increases in population are not uniform. People living in highly developed societies have strong inclinations to have fewer children, and many of those countries now have birth rates that are below replacement rates, such that their populations will slowly decline (unless they have enough would-be immigrants and a willingness to accept them). The developing countries have mixed birth rates, some fairly well controlled or stabilized (e.g., Iran, Tunisia, Mexico). But the still largely underdeveloped countries mired in economic poverty typically have high birth rates and population is increasingly rapidly. The last includes many countries in Africa.

Human overpopulation, along with the rise in the number of non-poor people around the globe, has degraded many a natural environment (many of which are discussed in other sections). Technology and Western medical advances (e.g., vaccines, antibiotics) have reduced death rates (especially among children) and lengthened life spans and thus enabled much of the last century's rapid rise in human population. But later medical advances have also provided at least a partial solution to the rising population, namely, various methods of birth control, some of which cost very little and are easy to use. Many people and a variety of non-governmental (charitable) organizations (NGOs) in the developed countries, and cognizant United Nations agencies, have also come to recognize the importance of enabling better education for women in the developing and underdeveloped countries—to provide those women with more choices in life, and to facilitate economic development. Included among the most basic steps here is to enable women in these countries to learn about and gain ready access to birth control. So there is still much unrealized hope for stopping human overpopulation—just a few billion dollars a year more is all that is needed (together with further development of the delivery systems). While I will shortly take up global warming, it is best mentioned here that among the 100 top-ranked ways to reduce global warming, per the remarkable compendium *Drawdown*, are "family planning" (#7) and educating girls (#6) [Paul Hawken, ed., *Drawdown: The Most Comprehensive Plan Ever Proposed to Reverse Global Warming*, 78-82].

Sadly, the kinds of rationalization used to oppose support by this country for stronger worldwide efforts to enable women's access to birth control of various kinds are typically anchored in a cultural insanity with a moralistic-religious character. ("Moralistic" means that they think/feel they know what's right for everyone in all cases.) The Roman Catholic Church, and presumably most conservative Catholics, officially accept nothing other than "natural" family planning (avoidance of sexual intercourse when fertilization might result), excluding even coitus interruptus. Even though the Roman Catholic Church is much more vigorously an opponent of abortion than birth control, it also tends to see most interference with the fertilization process, including many forms of what others see as birth control, as some kind of abortion. (Yet a majority of child-bearing age Catholics in this country use some form of birth control.)

Moreover, to make matters much worse, in the United States, the anti-birth control and anti-abortion stances of the Catholic Church hierarchy and Catholic conservatives have meshed with the anti-abortion stances of most evangelical Protestants, producing a fairly large voting bloc. Probably most of these evangelical Protestants do not oppose birth control per se (though they often oppose premarital sex and sex education other than abstinence-based forms, so they may see birth control as less imperative). Still, the opposition to abortion among conservative Catholics and Protestant fundamentalists has over-ridden any acceptance of birth control measures, such that they oppose Planned Parenthood in this country (one of the few organizations offering complete reproductive services, including abortions at a few locations), and in favor of policies such as the "global gag rule." This global gag rule prevents women's clinics abroad that receive U.S. aid, including via the United Nations, from so much as mentioning abortion as a possibility or from making referrals to abortion providers, let alone providing abortions, even when desperately needed for reasons of the mother's health or survival, or rape. The global gag rule's prohibitions even extend to the (sometimes few) locations that could provide abortion counseling or abortions with other money.

This making-everything-worse policy (i.e., including overpopulation) is fully endorsed by the Republican platform, which uses the issue in part as a dog whistle to keep anti-abortionists enamored of their political party, no matter that party's lack of concern for the poor in many other respects. This party ploy works well because some very large proportion of anti-abortionists are also "single-issue" voters who will only vote for anti-abortion candidates. As a result, many evangelicals/fundamentalists who could never otherwise support a man as flawed in so many ways as Trump have done so because of their cultural insanities involving issues such as this one. In turn, the Trump administration, to sustain and invigorate anti-abortionists' support, has reinstated the global gag rule and has now changed the rules for internal allocation of birth control money so as to extend this ban to Planned Parenthood too.

What, besides the need to reduce the human population (through individual choices, not coercion), makes the Catholic and evangelical/fundamentalist Protestants' willingness to line up behind the global gag rule culturally insane? Notwithstanding the intent to oppose abortion by imposing the global gag rule policy, refusing to help women abroad gain easy access to birth control, especially in underdeveloped countries leads to *more rather than fewer* abortions. Moreover, these abortions are provided by untrained practitioners and charlatans—making them far more dangerous—and, hence, also the cause of more long-term injury and even death to the mother and the unaborted babies (due to reduction in supportive care). In a 2011 study by Stanford researchers of 20 countries in Africa "at highest risk of losing U.S. family planning support aid," abortion rates "more than doubled in the countries most affected by the funding cuts." This analysis was based on a comparison of the two terms of president Bill Clinton (1993-2001) to those of George W. Bush (2001-2009), where the latter had re-imposed the global gag rule ["In the News," *Population Connection*, Sept. 2019, 6].

How can this be? And why don't these clinics simply adhere to the demands of the global gag rule so they can go on providing birth control? In the circumstances of many countries in Africa, refusing even to mention abortion as a possibility is a totally indefensible position to take medically (e.g., it does not minimize harm), because there are so many dire and desperate cases. So clinics cannot take this path, yet, under the global gag rule, these clinics lose any U.S.A.-sourced funding, leaving many a countryside clinic with little or no funding, few or no birth control supplies, and few or no paid staff members, who ordinarily provide most of the information about and the supplies for the available birth control options (some as simple as an inoculation that lasts three months).

What then does the mother of an already-large and near-starving family in Africa do when she becomes pregnant with yet another unwanted child and wants an abortion, lest her several already-living children be more likely to become even more malnourished and be even more deprived of what few chances for a decent life remains to them—not to mention the new baby if the mother can't feed it enough breast milk because she herself is getting too little food? And what if her life is threatened by the pregnancy, for example, because her vaginal canal has already been half-destroyed by one or more previous pregnancies—which often begin at a very young age—or by problems arising from a previous untended birth, or by medical problems arising from a previous back-street abortion? And what will her family do if she dies? What if her pregnancy is due to rape—as many are in areas of ongoing tribal combat and wars for commercial control of natural resources, such as in South Sudan or the eastern Congo? The attitude of many anti-abortion conservative Protestants toward such problems seems to be that the problems of a mother and children in these circumstances are a matter of personal responsibility—the moralistic and self-righteous equivalent of "it's your fault" and "tough!"—imposed on women who typically have very little control over their own lives, often including their sex life.

Of even less concern to anti-abortion zealots is that the lack of birth control is a major contributor to population explosions in many poverty-stricken countries in Africa, many of which have birth rates at five or more children per woman. When population growth keeps well ahead of economic development, as it does in some of these countries, the countries threaten to become further destabilized due to wars, desertification-related crop failures, famines, etcetera. And sometimes thereafter such countries will continue on to become failed states that are safe harbors for terrorists, perhaps fought over by warlords, where the remnants of these states are likely to yield hordes of migrants that then destabilize other nations near and sometimes far (as has now happened in some European countries). Such possibilities have for some time been recognized by the C.I.A. and the U.S. military as a potential security threat to the U.S.A. In addition, every new mouth to feed puts additional demand on the earth's limited resources (and drives up costs), which will ultimately also affect people in this country. And why in heaven's name would we want to impose more children on a mother of many children who could not care adequately for the ones she already has?

So, the human population is continuing to grow at unnecessarily high rates in significant part because Republican administrations and many of their voters in the United States (in contrast to many developed countries in Europe) will not allow this country to do its part to ensure that women around the world have access to knowledge about birth control, and to the birth control devices themselves. Amazingly, we are also not talking about truly large amounts of money being needed here and the culturally *sane* response is to provide more resources than we do under administrations headed by Democrats too, but they have often been limited by Republican opposition in one or both houses of Congress. We can see here that anti-abortion zealotry leads to a near total disregard of the problem of human overpopulation—and of the fact that humans are overrunning the earth and have become the drivers of the Sixth Extinction. This ever-growing human population has also exacerbated global warming. Thus insisting on an anti-abortion stance that in any way, shape or form limits access to birth control is a full-blown cultural insanity that is doing considerable harm to the world.

Overconsumption and Waste(s)

The business section of the major newspaper where I live reminds me at least once a month that 70% of our Gross National Product (GNP) is driven by consumer spending. Around a century ago if not earlier, those in charge of advertising, abetted by new ideas in psychology, began to figure out more about how to steer our inner emotions and drives in directions that led to our buying more goods and, eventually, services. With advances in mass production, they and we built a consumer society. Labor-saving devices like washing machines and advances in technology, from refrigerators and electric typewriters to computers, made our lives better and easier. But we also were persuaded to buy into the materialistic dynamics of a consumer society generally. We bought consumer goods to gratify impulses or even to relieve depression; We ate out more and sought out more entertainment. Our possessions conveyed our status to others as we sought to keep up with the Joneses; we tried to enhance our sexual attractiveness with beauty products; we showed off our power with stronger car engines and fins reminiscent of rockets. We got on the treadmill of buying "new and improved" products. We traded in moderately used cars for new models, bought oversized SUVs, and craved ever bigger televisions. Worse yet, some manufacturers literally built planned obsolescence into their now often flimsier products. Some of us have been buying an expensive new multi-purpose phone every couple of years. Corporations stop supporting their computer work systems after only a few years. Repair shops died out. And in our minds, wants evolved into needs—things we must have. Moreover, our economic system is based on continued growth (or else a recession or depression will result). The economy can't even just coast at a rate that just keeps up with population growth and productivity increases. Apparently, we cannot get off this treadmill without some kind of fundamental changes—in our economic system and in our minds.

Meanwhile, all this time, corporations made every effort to "externalize" costs, and often succeeded to varying degrees—meaning that they escaped paying for any damage caused by their manufacturing. And they have all the more incentive to do so when shareholder interests (and CEO pay) are the principal if not the only factors guiding decision-making—characteristics typical of our capitalism in the last 3-4 decades. Other shareholders could include customers (and they usually matter at least some), employees, the communities in which the corporation is located, the general public, and the environment. But, currently, it is the public, current and future, that is saddled with the externalized costs of any damage done. Corporate bankruptcy often provides an escape hatch for any later efforts to assess the corporation for the full amount of damages done, and even to avoid fulfilling promises the corporation might have made to the public. Externalized costs are perhaps most obvious when taxpayer funds or tax breaks go into supporting new or expanded factories (especially beyond infrastructure costs). Less obvious but more important are the effects on the environment, short-term and long-term, of almost every extractive industry, and every industry that doesn't clean up its contaminants (i.e., pollutes in whatever form). Extractive industries include not only mining and oil and coal, but agriculture that reduces soil fertility, water taken from decreasing supplies (such as aquifers), anything based on timber that is not cut sustainably (often for tissues and toilet paper, no less), and the continuing destruction of rainforest to produce soy beans (mainly to feed pigs) or palm oil (a cheaper and less healthy oil for commercial cookies, etc.). Beyond these, other polluting industries are many (e.g., see below regarding chemicals). But our economic system includes no accounting of successfully externalized costs—except when a corporation takes a financial hit by being fined or made to pay for (typically only some) of the cleanup of the mess it made. Also, the economic system extracts no charges for any resulting loss of "nature's services" (such as cleansing the air or absorbing carbon; or filtering out impurities in our water supplies; or protecting coasts against storms, as marshes and mangrove swamps do). Relatedly, there is no charge assessed when our arable land is plowed from property line to property line and planted with a monoculture that releases the carbon in the soil and has no value to other life forms that once flourished there.

Another aspect of our overconsumption can readily be seen in waistlines and body profiles. The percentage of people who are too fat—overweight or obese—in the United States is now in the vicinity of 70, with nearly half of those being obese. Obesity is also affecting more and more children here. The eating habits of far too many people involve large servings and/or high calorie offerings from restaurants and fast-food places. Those habits are influenced by advertising to eat more convenience foods and snacks that are often based on processed flour and loaded with taste enhancers and sugar (which is added to many foods), and often involve the health-challenging deeply fried foods. All of the resulting fattening-up is bad for our health as well as being wasteful of food that might better feed the truly hungry (though not in the highly processed forms that we eat it). And, as if all this overconsumption wasn't enough, somewhere around a third of all food produced in the U.S. never makes it to our stomachs, but becomes waste somewhere along the line. Indeed, "reduced food waste," is ranked a very high number 3 in *Drawdown* as a way to reduce carbon emissions that contribute to global warming [Hawken, 42-43].

As a way of completely overhauling our economic calculations/system, Allen Frances suggests a combination of higher pay, shorter workweeks, and a life more focused on leisure than on consumption [see Frances' chapter on the "Pursuit of Happiness," 234-267]. A related recommendation is to "accumulate experiences, not stuff," in part because accumulated stuff tends to add nothing to our happiness once it has been accumulated [von Hippel, 256]. Jared Diamond wonders how much of our current consumption levels we can afford to retain in the face of "the seeming political impossibility of inducing First World citizens to lower their impact on the world," while "the alternative, of continuing our current impact, is more impossible" [Diamond, *Collapse*, 524]. Yet few indeed among our politicians seem to express much interest in or concern about addressing any aspect of waste (or overconsumption, except to some extent from a health angle), even though there are a few federal and state agencies that deal piecemeal with the worst episodes of pollution. Meanwhile, growing middle classes in less wealthy countries will be moving up the consumption scale.

Environmentalist Bill McKibben suggests backing off on the global interconnectedness of our technologies, using the problems with too-big-to fail banks in 2008 as an example of how a set of related errors (e.g., the issuance of problematic mortgages and the creation of derivatives based on those mortgages) in only one area can and almost did bring the whole system down [McKibben, 105]. He calls instead for much greater localization of life, including in both national government and the economy, and a greater emphasis on community-level undertakings, from food to energy [McKibben, 106-150]. He is especially fond of one bumper sticker that says "'Think Globally—Act Neighborly'" [McKibben, 137]. As one illustration of the scope of the problem, McKibben mentions that "in 1940, our food system produced 2.3 calories of food energy for every calorie of fossil fuel it consumed"— current estimates are that it takes 10 calories of energy to produce one calorie of supermarket food [McKibben, 157]. Figuratively, "we are eating oil and spewing greenhouse gases" [McKibben, 157].

On the material side, one of the most visible and obvious of our wasteful practices involves plastic pollution. (And plastics are made from oil, no less.) Plastics litter road sides and wash ashore on literally every beach around the world (and may well be at their worst in Asia). There are now some extensive vortexes (gyres) of plastic items, chips, and fragments floating in several areas in the oceans. Similarly, a 2017 study of the remote Cocos Keeling Islands, a little-populated, multi-island linked pair of atolls out in the middle of nowhere (midway between Sri Lanka and Australia, but somewhat closer to Sumatra), estimated that there were 260 tons of plastic in 414 million pieces there, 60% of them microscopic in size [Kendra Pierre-Louis, "Remote islands awash in plastic garbage," in the *StarTribune*, May 23, 2019, A3]. As one result of all this plastic waste, people are now regularly finding both albatross chicks on similarly remote islands and washed-up whales that died because their guts were filled with indigestible plastics that jammed up their digestive tracts. Some sea turtles mistake plastic bags for edible jellyfish. So far, over 90% of the plastic made has not been recycled. Moreover, China recently stopped taking plastics from abroad for recycling (including from us) in large part because the shipments have been overloaded with impurities of one kind or another. Many people in this country have begun (or continue) to complain publicly about the heavy use of plastics, but we have also seen the new fad of buying expensive water in plastic bottles—often mere tap water. Obviously, people need to become aware enough to minimize purchasing such items, and to minimize the buying of goods presented in extensive plastic packaging. Similarly, we can stop using "body wash" in plastic bottles rather than soap bars (at least in the family), which are also probably far more economical. Despite the projections for massive increases in plastic production in the decades ahead, there is at least some hope—arising partly out of public dismay with plastic waste and some public policy rejections of plastic bags, single-use plastics, etcetera. For example, the European Union plans to eliminate single-use plastics in a decade or so and to make all packaging recyclable or reusable. Another valuable prospective way to help is to adopt laws that make corporations take responsibility for the plastics they generate (e.g., for soda making companies, plastic soda containers might be required to have a deposit that is used to help pay for recycling if the container is not returned). Going further yet, we should encourage further research to replace plastic with biodegradable alternatives as well as further research into methods of converting plastic back into its raw materials, which could greatly improve recycling. (There continues to be at least some progress in the technology of recycling plastics.) Nevertheless, we are not anywhere ahead of the problems here. As a more chilling example, microplastics—arising from breakdown of larger pieces of plastic, polyester, and from sources such as commercial use of minute beads of plastic in various cosmetic preparations and toothpaste (now banned in some countries, including the U.S.A.)—are already everywhere, including in our bodies, and moving up food chains, with who knows what long-term effects. Some of these microplastics are carried by the wind and wind up in places like the Alps and Greenland.

As part of our profit-seeking economic system, corporate externalization, and materialistic consuming society, all manner of chemicals are being released into our environments, with almost no meaningful controls on them, not even the new ones. The American

Chemical Society had registered 10 million "different chemicals, the majority of which were synthetically manufactured" in 1990; by late 2009, there were 50 million [Schwägerl, 137]. Insofar as new chemicals are tested, it is mainly done by the corporations that make them, presumably with reference to their designated task and perhaps also regarding the extent to which they might be directly poisonous or carcinogenic (e.g., to mice). Moreover, there is almost no information on the potential interactions of any of these chemicals with each other. As to some of the likely effects of these chemicals-at-large, the pesticide Atrazine, which disrupts hormonally-driven aspects of the lives of some insects, thereby killing them, is thought by some scientists to be one of the sources of the recent scourge of deformities in a variety of amphibian species, though there may be other causes as well. More generally, a variety of endocrine-disrupting chemicals (hormone-like substances) are present in our rivers and thus affect the expression of genes within, and the lives of, animals in that water. Hormones in rivers have at times been identified with changing the proportions of male and female fish born. And this is water many of us may also use to cook with and drink, potentially affecting us as well. Also in this water are trace amounts of a wide variety of medical prescriptions from people's urine, including hormones from birth control pills and mood-altering drugs. In addition, overuse of fertilizers in agriculture has resulted in nitrate pollution in well waters (making them unsafe to drink, as many are in Iowa, Wisconsin, and Minnesota). And the run-off from farm fields of both nitrogen and phosphorus compounds create dead zones at the mouths of many rivers around the world (see below).

Chemicals in our fresh waters are not the only concern. "Approximately 10,000 chemicals are added to our food," including some of those same endocrine disruptors such as BPA which is used in the lining of many of our canned foods [Environmental Defense Fund, *Solutions*, Summer 2017, 14]. BPA is found in the bodies of 9 out of 10 Americans [EDF Special Report, "Don't Assume the Chemicals in Household Products You Use Every Day Are Safe," Spring 2015, 5].

Among potentially dangerous *nonfood* chemicals are PFAs/PFCs (which have been used in clothing and non-stick cookware, food containers and carpets), formaldehyde (used in carpets, some wood products and adhesives), Phthalates (used in air fresheners, paper), Toluene (used in paints and adhesives), and PBDEs (used in furniture and electrical equipment) [EDF, "Don't Assume …", 5]. Various states and cities are currently suing the manufacturers of some PFAs for pollution, and the Environmental Protection Agency and some researchers have linked them to a number of health problems even at very low levels of exposure. PFAs/PFCs, PBDEs, and phthalates have been found in 99% of pregnant women, and 232 potentially toxic chemicals have been found in umbilical cord blood [EDF, "Don't Assume…", 5]. If the opponents of early childhood vaccination (anti-vaxxers) want to look for the most likely source of the rise in autism, I think they should look here, but they may have to find the proverbial needle in the haystack. After decades of inaction (since the Toxic Substances Control Act of 1976), a law was finally adopted in 2016 that requires the Food and Drug Administration (FDA) to review the toxicity of at least 20 chemicals at a time—a start, but not nearly enough given that there are about 80,000 that might be considered [Danette Knickmeier, "Obama Signs New Toxic Substances Chemicals Act," in *Sierra Club North Star Journal*, Winter 2016-17, 12]. This law contains a number of weaknesses, such as an inhibition on state actions while FDA conducts its reviews and that regulation be cost-effective, and much of its limited potential effectiveness will depend on whether the most dangerous chemicals will receive prioritization for review [Knickmeier, 12]—and whether science will prevail over politics.

Lead is a pollutant from the past that still haunts us today. It is a threat to human mental development and health generally. It was formerly added to gasoline to give it more oomph, but that is now banned. It is also now banned in paint. But there are many cities that have some or many lead water intake pipes (like Flint, Michigan), and many older dwellings that were painted with lead-based paints that now slowly flakes off and threatens the inhabitants, particularly the young (who are more susceptible and more likely to spend time on the floor, at windowsills, etc.).

In this country, there are over 1,300 superfund sites needing special clean-up before the land under them can be used again. And there are innumerable other sites from which industries, gas stations, etcetera have departed and must be cleaned up before the land can be used again. Most of the superfund sites are former industrial sites. For example, Butte, Montana is a superfund site at which copper was mined and smelted. And other hard-rock mining sites pose prospective dangers if their wastes are accessible to flowing water (including leakage into aquifers). Waste ponds for other industries, such as coal and pigs, also pose dangers to the fish and drinking water whenever they leak, or overflow, or their dams break. Overall, this country is almost undoubtedly #1 in terms of the *variety* of chemicals loosed in our environment, though parts of the Russian Federation and some of the countries of its former satellite bloc in Eastern Europe are probably more polluted by a smaller number of less exotic chemicals.

Ukraine, when still a part of Russia, also had a nuclear accident at Chernobyl in 1986 in response to which political authorities designated an exclusion zone around it that encompasses 1,000 square miles, though the leftover radiation is now abating some. Japan recently had nuclear accident problems due to an earthquake and tsunami. Similar problems are not entirely precluded in any country using nuclear power (and the United States does have some defense and atomic-testing-related nuclear waste superfund sites). Nor have we resolved the problem of storing radioactive wastes from nuclear power plants, where storage sites will need monitoring and controls for centuries. In *Drawdown*, the greater use of nuclear power to alleviate global warming is ranked #20, but it is also one of their very few "regrets" solutions because of such drawbacks [Hawken, 19-21].

Air pollution derived from intemperate and unwise use of resources remains an important problem, including for human health—a causative factor in asthma, heart attacks, and lung diseases—but at least it is being dealt with to some extent. The smog in Los Angeles is still bad some or much of the time during the year, but not as bad as it once was. Now Houston and the Central Valley of California are among our kings of smog. But cities in some other countries have become much worse, Beijing and Mexico City being among the most well-known examples. And seasonal wildfires in the western U.S.A. produce smoke as well as making the smog extra bad there at times. Smog was reduced in part by controls on automobile emissions, and the air was also improved by the removal of lead from gasoline. And the U.S. and Europe have greatly reduced the extent of acid rain with requirements for "scrubbers" that remove sulfur (which yields sulfuric acid in the rain) in coal-burning smoke(stacks). But much more needs to be done, including the removal of more mercury—a poison that accumulates in our food chain, especially in fish—from coal-burning power plants worldwide. As for coal itself, see the next section.

Global Warming

Our demand for fossil fuels and their carbon compound-based energy is the chief cause of the increase in carbon dioxide in the atmosphere over the last two centuries and, hence, of global warming. (Oil and gas extraction are also a source of methane, another climate warmer—see below). Coal, and oil and gas, are derived from plant life, which like all life is carbon-based, and so burning them—a process in which the carbon combines with oxygen—releases carbon (CO2) into the atmosphere. "Global warming is perhaps the most egregious case of modern science denial" [McIntyre, 27]. As noted elsewhere, fossil fuel companies, following the blueprint developed by tobacco companies, have spent millions to promote pseudo-scientific views and exaggerate the importance of any remaining scientifically legitimate but peripheral questions to cast public doubt about the degree of scientific consensus on this matter. The success of this deception can be seen in the metanalyses of scientific papers in 2004 and again in 2012, which found a truly miniscule proportion of the scientific literature that did not support the idea that human-caused climate change was real [McIntyre, 28]. And in 2013, a "survey of 4,000 peer-reviewed [scientific, published] papers that took a position on climate change found that 97% agreed with the position that global warming was caused by human activity." Meanwhile, however, only 27% of U.S. adults agreed that "'almost all climate scientists agree that human behavior is mostly responsible for climate change'" [McIntyre, 29].

"Global warming," also called "climate change" because the changes will exaggerate current weather and not be uniform, has already begun to wreak (additional) havoc on many environments, both human-built and natural. Examples are legion, including rising seas and more forceful periods of rain and floods, and more destructive hurricanes and typhoons. Rising seas will of course imperil low-lying island countries and many coastal areas around the globe—areas that include many very large population centers. Global warming is threatening the long-term water supplies for China, India, Bangladesh, and Pakistan that are derived in dry seasons from Himalayan-area glaciers, which have been receding for several decades now. Indeed, almost all glaciers around the globe are now in retreat—and that is just one source of rising sea levels. The extra warmth is also melting more of the sea ice near the north pole, threatening habitat(s) of spectacular species such as polar bears and walruses, while at the south pole melting ice shelves are threatening the under-ice algae and plankton species that are at the base of much of the ocean food chain. And it is melting Greenland's ice sheets. Meanwhile, the oceans are absorbing some of the extra carbon dioxide and, in the process, becoming more acidic—and this acidification eats away at shells or prohibits their formation, thus imperiling creatures that make shells for their homes, including some that number in the billions near the bottom of the food chain, ultimately supporting many other forms of life. The warming-based acidification also affects the continued growth of coral reefs, and existing coral organisms are imperiled as well with "bleaching" associated with the increasing warmth. Corals could also be threatened by drowning if there is a rapid rise in sea levels. Coral reefs are the nurseries, havens and homes for perhaps 25% of all marine fish and many other kinds of sea life, so as they decline in viability entire ecosystems, with varying degrees of uniqueness values as well, are threatened. Please note that in several respects above, we are jeopardizing our own food supply.

The land in the far north (e.g., in Alaska) is warming much faster than elsewhere and the additional heat is changing more and more of the permafrost landscape back into (peat) bogs, which will release more carbon dioxide and methane. Parts of Siberia even reached 100 degrees Fahrenheit in 2020! Although the amounts involved are much smaller, methane is a more persistent (long-lasting) and powerful greenhouse gas than carbon dioxide; it is also released by unburnt gases released in the process of oil and gas extraction (including fracking), as well as by the off-gassing of cattle (cows) chewing their cuds. As noted earlier, our wants for more beef, soy beans, palm oil, and wood/fiber have led to destruction of tropical forests in Brazil, Indonesia, central Africa and elsewhere, reducing their functioning as a "carbon sink" and their ability to continue to be the "lungs of the planet," so our demand for beef has made things worse in that respect too.

Global warming will also imperil species and ecosystems, including in temperate climate regions such as the U.S., that do not have migration corridors in which they can move north or further up their mountainous home regions to escape the additional heat. Similarly, forests will be on the move northward and, over time, will move much farther than Birnam Wood in Macbeth. In this northward move, pines will be replaced by advancing deciduous forests, which, in turn, will be replaced by prairie, while some if not many existing prairies (mostly farmland) may well be threatened by desertification. Invasive species (including diseases), most introduced by humans, have already been turned loose almost everywhere, and some have global warming to thank for their ability to flourish in new environments. These invasive species (like the python in the Florida Everglades) are also often a major threat to some native species. And invasive species include some human diseases that are moving out from equatorial regions (like the mosquito-transmitted zika and dengue fever viruses).

Global warming/climate change is now the most obvious and immediate threat that warrants our combined attention, whatever the number of political parties in a country. Many more people in this country, especially the young but with the noteworthy exception of President Trump and a slowly shrinking minority of conservative Republicans, have recently begun to stop denying, disregarding and overlooking global warming, or at least its effects (such as sea level rises), even if they haven't affirmed it as a reality or proposed doing anything about it. Denials have become much less frequent (except for President Trump), mainly because of the severity of changes in climate/weather, and not for reasons that should have caused them to become aware of the problem and willing to do more sooner. Although the time frame may now be short, it is relatively easy to make important progress on global warming in societies like ours. We can start by dropping all forms of subsidies and tax breaks given out to oil companies and continue by putting a tax on carbon dioxide emissions (or some other form of carbon tax) and then continue periodically to raise it (and use the proceeds in part to counter the economic impact on ordinary folks and to decrease the federal deficit and debt). We can prohibit the release or burning of methane gases that are often associated with oil extraction (as the Obama administration had begun to do with oil extraction on federal lands—which Trump has tried to reverse). We can accelerate the conversion to more benign energy sources—such as wind and solar—and start buying only electricity-driven cars. Efforts by energy interests (mainly coal and oil-gas corporations), along with inertia and other factors, mostly based in denial and delusions (see below), have hitherto combined to slow or block these pathways and can be expected to continue to do so. But vastly greater numbers of people may soon start ignoring them instead of joining in their pretense that there is doubt among climate scientists. And if the costs of action are claimed to be too high (one very typical public relations strategy for many a corporation's interests), the costs of inaction will be much higher. But at this writing, the Trump administration is attempting to "edit and ultimately suppress" yet another recent report (and associated testimony), this one prepared by a branch of the State Department, that warned of many dangers associated with global warming, including nine "tipping points" whose thresholds are not fully known—including "rapid die-offs" of corals and insects, and massive releases of methane currently held in place by freezing temperatures [Juliet Eilperin, Josh Dawsey, and Brady Dennis, "White House blocked document warning about climate change," in the *Star Tribune*, June 9, 2019, A13]. So, although the Trump administration is leading the charge on behalf of cultural insanity here (while many states and cities are doing the opposite), under better leadership, this country, especially if it rejoins the world's other countries in their efforts, could have a much bigger influence on reducing the chemicals that cause global warming precisely because the U.S.A. and China are the world's two largest emitters.

The worlds' nations that were responsible for the problem joined together to stop the erosion/thinning of the ozone layer high in the atmosphere that protects the earth's life forms (us too) from too much exposure to infrared radiation from sunlight, the effects of which posed special dangers to plankton at the bottom of many food chains. The ozone hole at each of the two poles is now slowly returning to normal thanks to great reductions in the releases of a couple of chemicals, especially chlorofluorocarbons, which were then used extensively in refrigerators. The world, with the U.S.A. remaining among its leaders, needs to repeat such performances in a number of other cases, starting with global warming.

But the management of chemicals used in refrigeration remains a very important concern in global warming—and one on which global efforts have begun. The major problem is that the refrigerants that substituted for chlorofluorocarbons "have the capacity to warm the atmosphere [that] is one thousand to nine thousand times greater than that of carbon dioxide" [Hawken, 164]. Most of the threat occurs as old appliances are disposed of. So, providing for the proper disposal of refrigeration-related appliances, although it will cost some money net, is actually the number one way to reduce the threat of global warming in *Drawdown* [Hawken, 165].

The other most-important ways calculated in *Drawdown* to reduce global warming are: Onshore and offshore wind turbines (at #2 plus #22, respectively) [Hawken, 2-4]; reductions in food waste (#3, as noted earlier); a diet that draws more on plants, which reduces the use of cropland to feed livestock and frees it to grow food (#4) [Hawken, 39-40]; restoration of tropical forest areas (#5) [Hawken, 114-116]; improving access for women to education and family planning (#6 and #7, as noted earlier); solar farms and rooftop solar (# 8 and #10, respectively) [Hawken, 8-11]; "silvopasture," which involves mixed trees and pasture that better sequesters carbon, protects against desertification, shields cattle/cows from yield-reducing excess heat, better supports biodiversity, and more (#9) [Hawken, 50-51]; "regenerative agriculture," which occurs as a result of no-till farming, diverse cover crops, multiple crop rotations, no use of insecticides or herbicides or synthetic fertilizers, etcetera (#11) [Hawken, 54-55]; and temperate forest restoration (#12) [Hawken, 128-129]. With reference to eating more plants and fewer industrial animal products: fires this year in the Amazon areas of Brazil are sending carbon dioxide into the air, in order to create more room for beef ranching, and for growing soy beans, most of which go to feed domestic animals; this is occurring at least partly as a result of President Trump's tariffs, together with Xi's (China's) retaliatory tariffs on crops from the U.S.A., and the consequent need for other sources for soy beans (Brazil); and the poor leadership of Brazil (President Jair Bolsonaro), which has openly accepted the flouting Brazil's laws to restrain development in the Amazon region. So here we have some major world leaders doing exactly the opposite of what is needed to forestall and reduce global warming. In any case, all Drawdown's calculations also assume, of course, reductions in the use of fossil fuels as fast as reasonably possible (including greater efforts to facilitate the development of alternative power sources noted). Beyond the highest priorities, large amounts of carbon dioxide-producing energy generation could still be saved by better insulation of our (and other nations') old buildings, both to reduce longer-term costs to the user and global warming. Although many utilities for some time have been persuaded, if only by public regulators, to offer building insulation tests and programs, more needs to be done.

Cultural sanity requires that we *recognize and start to deal more effectively with the Sixth Extinction; the unsustainabilities involved in the size of the human population, overconsumption, and human wastes of all kinds; and global warming.* If humans in this country and elsewhere continue to ignore or discount the many threats to the world's environments, there is the possibility, or perhaps a strong likelihood, of major ecological collapse(s) of entire webs of life that will affect humans severely, much more than just some additional heat, coastal inundations, and more violent storms. For example, the food supply for people might suddenly get a lot smaller (e.g., if major oceanic food webs collapse, eliminating almost all fishing, or if the honey bees that pollinate a lot of our crops almost die out). As noted, as many as a third of major fisheries have already collapsed or become commercially useless, while others have had to settle for going after juvenile fish— thereby making the stock even more endangered. Insects in many areas may also be similarly threatened, but here knowledge is less complete.

Apart from dealing with global warming, among the other steps that could be taken to help slow and ultimately stop the Sixth Extinction are the development of migration corridors to connect areas still suitable for wildlife, establishment of more wilderness areas and ocean preserves (especially encompassing coral reefs, mangrove swamps, and other areas important to the survival of fish), better enforcement of laws prohibiting rainforest destruction, reforestation efforts on more land in more countries, and the return of more lands to their natural state (including some prairie and prairie pothole regions in the U.S.A.). In addition to their intrinsic value for wildlife, nature preserves also protect us from some of "the consequences of our mistakes" [Schwägerl, 126].

And we need to more rapidly move away from coal, oil and gas as energy sources, abandoning any new attempts to seismically test for oil in the oceans and on nearby coastal lands (including, immediately, on the north and west coasts of Alaska where a massive caribou calving area is also threatened). The incredibly loud noises associated with seismic testing for oil (e.g., in the Atlantic) also carry a threat of major injury or death to marine mammals (which rely heavily on hearing to navigate and communicate), including some endangered whales, and other animals. We do need to move forward with some kind of "green new deal"(s).

Popular Delusions that Support Culturally Insane Policies and Lies

The material to follow draws extensively on, and notes some contrasts with, the perspectives in Allen Frances's, *Twilight of American Sanity: A Psychiatrist Analyzes the Age of Trump*. Frances has very conveniently (for me) come to recognize as delusional a broad group of problems within the thinking *among the people* in this country, a characterization which, as a psychiatrist, he is more qualified than I am to make. "In psychiatry, a delusion is defined as a fixed false belief that is firmly maintained and resists correction by overwhelming evidence and rational argument" [Frances, 10]. If such major deficiencies in the thinking process occur in the populace or leadership in ways that impact public affairs or policies, they are almost necessarily culturally insane as well. Thus, Frances' listing of delusions also represents a certain subset of cultural insanities. However, as can be seen in the subheads under deficiencies in thinking (above), and in the various examples already given, and as we will see in subsequent parts, delusional thinking is by no means the only pathway to cultural insanity. Further, for the most part, Frances has restricted his list of delusions to those most associated with the Trump presidency. For example, "delusional denial" could certainly be used as a characterization of at least some, and perhaps the great majority, of the young-earth creationists leaders and followers considered in Part Four (though it is not at all unique to the Trump presidency).

Frances discounts the possibility that Trump himself is insane because he does not suffer any negative symptoms from his narcissistic personality; instead he profits from it. But Trump "has revealed and unleashed a deeper streak of *delusional denial* in a larger segment of U.S. society than even I would have thought possible" [Frances, 98; emphasis added]. In contrast, I would say that President Trump does share some and perhaps most of the cultural insanities associated with these delusions—even though it can be difficult to ascertain the differences between Trump's actual beliefs and when he is mainly playing to and trying to manipulate the masses (e.g., when he led the "birthers" in challenging President Obama's citizenship, or when he shifted to an anti-abortion stance).

In accord with the idea of cultural insanity presented here, I agree that Frances' societal delusions, along with other cultural insanities, are blinding us to the urgency of dealing with the realism-based necessities "that will determine whether we deserve to survive as a civilization, and perhaps as a species" [Frances, 52]. He notes too that: "We have so far been mostly unable to figure out a way of living peacefully and sustainably; of controlling our desires and living within our means; of balancing our current needs with our responsibilities to the future" [Frances, 51-52].

Here are my encapsulations of Frances' summaries of the delusional denials and beliefs to which he refers and which, in each case, he contrasts with the real issues facing the country. 1) Denial of the destruction of the environment (including global warming and environmental pollution), particularly in the expectation that the deity or technology will provide a fix. 2) Denial that world population and its continued growth are leading to the depletion of resources, global warming, provoking wars & mass migrations, pandemics and famines. 3) Belief that trickle-down economics works, that making the rich richer will help us all. 4) Belief that the U.S.A. has the best health system in the world. 5) Belief that it is okay for the U.S.A. to bully other countries into doing whatever we want. 6) Belief that "our country can only be great again if you build walls around it" [Frances, 36]. 7) Belief that mankind's being given dominion over the earth means that "our needs are paramount; the survival of other species need not concern us" [Frances, 38]. 8) Belief that it is worth trading away privacy for convenience, security and research data. 9) Beliefs that more guns are better, that an armed population is a safer population, or that "guns don't kill people, people do" [Frances, 44]. 10) Belief that "the technological revolution can do no wrong," with special emphasis on the potential dangers of artificial intelligence [Frances, 47].

Regarding Frances' delusions number 1, 2 and 7: As described earlier, I would put natural habitat destruction—with humans as the drivers of the sixth mass extinction—as the foundational cultural insanity, with global warming being the latest and probably the single most sweeping manifestation thereof thus far. This arrangement seems to be seconded by a 2019 report of the United Nations' Intergovernmental Science-Policy Platform on Biodiversity and Ecosystem Services on which 150 authors worked. The report is focused in large part on the "services" that nature provides to humans and how those are being lost and degraded—presumably because the value of those services will be of some importance even to those who don't give a damn about a situation in which up to a million species of animals and plants are threatened with extinction. As described earlier, the major underlying factors in this Sixth Extinction have been the size of the human population and especially the population increases in the last 150 years. Together the above constitute a set of related concerns that threaten humanity in a number of ways, where overconsumption and wastes are yet another part of the problem which people other than environ-mentalists (mainly) have largely disregarded, ignored, denied, and/or have ongoing delusions about—where any of these is a culturally insane response. Finally, our earlier discussion very much suggests the need for a stewards' approach instead, and/or a yet more worshipful stance toward nature and mother Earth. This is probably the only culturally sane option.

I treated trickle-down economics earlier as an example of opt-ing for a policy that has repeatedly failed. And the matter of guns was treated as political spin, but true believers in that spin likely do have some delusions to overcome. Immigrants were referred to as scape-goats above (a delusion involving misplaced blame, whether by the scapegoater or his/her followers), with more than a hint of racism involved too.

The medical situation in the U.S.A. is a can of worms. People who think medical care is great probably have very good access to the best care available and focus on the advances in treatment. Still, given the practices of other developed countries, there is little question that this country's complex medical (non)system is built on policies some of which are culturally insane or strongly tending to it. An undue pro-portion of what is paid in goes to administration. And to profiteering, especially by pharmaceutical and insurance companies, and probably pharmacy benefits managers too. Despite the high net cost, our (non)system doesn't cover everybody, doesn't cover many fully enough, and for many it is not nearly as good as it should be. Many of our most important drugs are greatly overpriced and prices for *existing* drugs have increased at well above the rate of inflation, too often clearly linked to corporate greed, so negotiating drug prices at the national level—like every other developed country does—is an obvious step to take. Even if we cannot transition relatively quickly to a system of national health care, finding some way to allow people to buy into

Medicare, and to enable employers to offer that option, seems far more sensible than what we do now. Medicare, even with supplementation (e.g., Medicare Advantage plans), is relatively inexpensive now (I pay around $3500 per year for both Medicare and a Medical Advantage plan, plus some modest co-pays), so even raising the price somewhat in order to pay doctors better for Medicare patients (and so that new Medicare patients aren't turned down), seems feasible (especially as more young and healthy people enroll). And, as a sop to the status quo, even in a national health care system, there may be a role for insurers to continue to offer something like the "Medicare Advantage" plans that they now offer, or "Cadillac" plans, or to provide other supplemental coverages like guaranteed private hospital rooms.

Frances' summary version of delusion #5 is better stated in his full chapter devoted to "making America great again" and American exceptionalism [Frances, 79-112]. I have already raised a number of examples of American exceptionalism (really "United States exceptionalism"). Certainly this "exceptionalism" goes way back to the very start of the American colonies, when slavery for Blacks but not Whites became acceptable, and Indians were killed and/or their lands confiscated. And slavery flourished well beyond the time when other European countries had begun to abolish it—despite being in a republic that proclaimed itself a model for government *by the people*. Provoking a war with Mexico and the seizure of California and more in search of our "manifest destiny" represents another major exceptionalism episode. In the War on Vietnam (see above too), this country acted like it had every right to do what it damn well pleased while it imposed a morally-forsaken nightmare on the Vietnamese, starting with the support of French re-colonization efforts after WW II, the canceling of the internationally-agreed upon unification elections in 1954, the support of South Vietnamese dictatorships, and the Bay of Tonkin falsification by the U.S.A.'s leaders. Similarly, that Saddam Hussein actually had no remaining weapons of mass destruction was discovered only because the U.S. assumed it had a prerogative to invade on the pretext that he definitely had some. Our treatment of Latin America throughout the early 20th century and President Reagan's monetary support for the "Contras" in the 1980s to fight against Nicaragua's legitimately-elected leaders also provide evidence of this country's leaders assuming that their views supporting large corporations' interests are right/important enough to try to impose them. Often this happens with little or no consultation/agreement by Congress or the people. Throughout the cold war, this country's leaders supported many a dictatorship simply because they sided with us in the Cold War. In short, this country, albeit with some occasional idealism thrown in and some good done (e.g., support for Latin American independence from Spain, World War II, and perhaps some attempts to help Haiti more recently) has acted very much like any other great power or hegemonic empire (or nationalistic people)—all while the vast majority of the population proceeded under the exceptionalism delusions that we were the good guys, even though much of the time we weren't—and sometimes we were the "bad guys." For more on this, see almost anything written about the international situation by Noam Chomsky. Although some of his interpretations may be tendentious or stretched, he also includes information that should not be ignored.

Frances' #8 is huge, encompassing several major problem areas subject to delusional thinking. Frances titled it "Big Brother Is Watching You" (a la George Orwell's *1984*). Included are the potentials for population manipulation and control by corporations, by organized political interests, and by government and their agencies such as the National Security Agency (NSA). In this case, our exaggerated fear of foreign terrorists (who have taken a small toll compared to several other causes of non-natural death in this country), and of crime or even of immigrants, tends to make us willing to throw away our civil liberties, accept government control over more of our lives, accept government raids on the homes of immigrants, allow S.W.A.T. teams to invade houses with no real warnings (sometimes killing innocent people), and be quiet while NSA and other government agencies monitor our out-of-country e-mails and otherwise spy on large numbers of the people. Enabling all this is a multi-faceted cultural insanity, even if having cameras in many public spaces perhaps strikes an appropriate balance for dealing with some aspects of the real problems involved. But the potentials and early reality for more advanced technological population control (including facial recognition capabilities applied to video camera usage) are now being tested and applied in China, not only to subdue opposition among the Muslim Uighurs in Xinjiang, China's westernmost province, but to try to monitor the social acceptability (per the regime) of every person in China. In this country, there has been some resistance to photographic car license plate-based identification of scofflaw drivers (where the owner is not always the driver) at street intersections. But police agencies such as the FBI have now begun to use still far-from perfect facial recognition technology on large numbers of photos held in state driver's license agencies, in efforts to identify suspects, often with imprecise photos they want to match, and usually without warrants. They compare photos of many innocent people and mis-identify some of those as suspects. Other data available about those "suspects" is then explored and some are subsequently questioned directly. Even if this kind of generalized search can be interpreted as constitutionally justifiable, what is next—and will we find out about it or will it remain secret?

NOVA now has a four-part series on how corporate advertising people have, over the last 100 years, discovered how best to access our subconscious [see NOVA, "Hacking Your Mind—Weapons of Influence"]. Because we act on impulses/feelings/desires, or perhaps choose between the options presented by our subconscious mind, the goal of advertisers, and of newer technologically-sophisticated political propagandists as well, is to establish preferences and desires in our subconscious minds, and/or to implant habitual responses to their stimuli. That way, we are much more likely to almost automatically ask for or select Pepsi or Tide or Marlboro, and to regard Republicans' spin or propaganda, or Democrats' spin or propaganda, as believable and anything else as not believable. Never mind the fact-checking. Stopping to think about every little decision takes time and energy, so proceeding on autopilot, based on the subconscious mind's "gut feelings," is the easier and typical approach.

Netflix also has a program ("The Social Dilemma") on this subject, focused on the age of big data, that includes discussions with a number of people who were once highly-placed in internet corporations such as Facebook and Google. These corporations have grown immensely in size and wealth by exploiting or abusing our personal data for commercial profit. In essence, we are their products which they sell to advertisers. By catering to our existing preferences, they have also created information silos that can easily disregard facts and reality, and instead offer fake information to appeal to our subconscious desires and our fears and prejudices. Their money-making design and algorithms have also greatly reduced our privacy (largely unbeknownst to us) and they are now among the chief manipulators of the desires, feelings, behaviors and the thought processes of virtually every heavy user of small screens. And now, almost the whole of the younger generation is hooked into their systems, and many in the older generations have been taken in by all manner of garbage. As news media people have long known, people are drawn to the sensational, emotional (from cutesy to sob), scandalous, outrageous, divisive, and conspiratorial. Social media (like Facebook, YouTube and Twitter) have designed their algorithms to present this kind of material to people because it keeps them engaged. Keeping people engaged in their platform is what sells advertisements—especially if, with the help of (their own) analyses of big data (and nobody enabled to opt-out), they can target those ads to the most likely consumers. Here then is another cultural insanity that has already overtaken us, and we have only begun to think about restricting, controlling, or eliminating even its most obvious abuses. Moreover, social media corporations are not at all interested in providing us with an "opt out," let alone an easy opt or, best yet, a presumed opt-out unless an uncoerced permission is clearly and explicitly granted. Their corporate decisions and the associated algorithms have enabled the rapid spread of messages generated by people who are spreading lies, deliberately making up truly fake news to support their political favorites and anonymously sabotage (libel?) their opponents, or deliberately stirring up trouble and trying to influence our elections as the Russian government has done, or seeking fame and glory and imitators by publicizing terroristic deeds, whether beheadings in a "caliphate" run by pseudo-Muslim fanatics or attacks on places of worship, including mosques, temples and churches. And social media's "like" buttons, as well as what we "share" with "friends" (and what our friends share with us) help these media to "help" us create our own information silos, adding all manner of "click bait" and otherwise offering material to keep us engaged in our silos.

And it these information silos, abetted by various special interests, from corporate to political to purely disruptive, that have further enabled the growth in the number of right wingnuts and tin-hat conspiracy theories. In earlier times, right wing would-be militias consisting of a modest number of men who were worried about black U.N. helicopters or repressive government; now, despite long-term recognition by the FBI that it is these right-wing groups that pose some danger to society (and more than any left-wing groups), they have been more accepted by President Trump and he is promoting conspiracies about mail-in ballots, where it is Trump himself, especially in actions like that, who is the real threat to a fair and proper election.

President Trump has also promoted this cultural insanity in other ways—using Twitter to pass along all manner of misinformation (mistaken) and disinformation (deliberate). And telling us to ignore Russian tampering with our election seemingly partly in an effort to deny that his tiny margin of victory in the electoral college *may* be attributable to their help (which nobody could ever prove anyway). Instead, he, along with some of his closest minions, have gone off on a wild-goose chase/deception about the Ukraine as the culpable party, trying to smear Joe Biden and his son (Biden was then the most likely opponent in the next election) and, in the process, promoting yet other delusions among his closest supporters, many of whom seem to have fallen for it, hook, line and sinker. Trump's welcoming of Russian spying on the Democrats in the 2016 election was appalling if not quite illegal collusion or treason—it welcomed in-kind contributions (Russian deeds) to help his campaign, whereas accepting direct foreign monetary contributions is illegal. And Trump has said he is willing to accept (non-colluding) foreign help in the 2020 campaign as well. And now it seems quite likely that much of the Trump-Republican campaign in the forthcoming election will be based in substantial part on fake news, ongoing lies, and new and deliberate deceptions [McKay Coppins, "The Billion-Dollar Disinformation Campaign to Re-elect the President," *The Atlantic* website, March 2020].

As an *aside* relevant to this and an earlier topic, there is one thing that Trump did get right in his apologetics for and denials of Russian misbehavior, even though many imbued with "American exceptionalism" were appalled by it: He said that this country too has interfered in other countries' elections. Not only has the U.S. of America monetarily supported its favorites in elections in many countries, but it has even intervened clandestinely to overthrow democratically-elected leaders whom our leaders opposed (e.g., Mossadegh in Iran and Arbenz in Guatemala in the 1950s, to mention a couple more). Indeed, it was the coup against a secular prime minister Mossadegh (launched because the U.S. and Britain wanted to control Iran's oil), and our subsequent support of the Shah of Iran as monarch and dictator for more than a quarter of a century, that was the original source of the Iranian resentment that led to the takeover of the U.S. embassy in 1979. But the historical disinterestedness or denial of exceptionalism in this country (including Trump) made Iran out to be the one-and-only provocateur and the "bad guy."

So far, almost all restrictions on social media in this country have been implemented by the corporations involved, but almost solely because of social and political pressures (or opportunities to cultivate a better image, as Apple has tried to do with privacy). In contrast, Europe has now enacted laws that give its people rights and, absent their consent, limit the use of their personal data [Rhoda Feng, "Public Citizen Pressures Companies to Comply with Europe's New Data Protection Rules," in *Public Citizen News*, July-August 2018, 11]. Only very recently in this country have the Congress and many of the states begun to take a serious look at just what all is going on here. Many states, for example, are investigating Google for monopolistic practices.

In this country, new laws and better monitoring by the corporations involved are both needed, even though laws and practices may need to strike some careful balance to maintain extensive free speech while excluding hate speech, appeals to violence, and deliberate lies posing as news. But what should such a law provide for instances in which a president re-tweets a video about a political opponent to millions of followers when the video contains a major lie—especially if it has already been taken down by its source? A specific example is the showing of Representative Ilhan Omar dancing that claims the date was on the anniversary of the Sept. 11 attack on the World Trade

Center buildings and that, in essence, she was celebrating that attack. In actuality, there was irrefutable proof that the video was taken at an ordinary dance on Sept. 13. Perhaps the internet corporation should intervene to send out a correction to all those to whom the original tweet was sent, as well as to all those to whom it was re-tweeted. As for the original tweet, it seems to me that "libel," a crime that involves deliberately damaging someone's reputation, is often occurring now, even if that needs clarification in our laws. (E.g., is it still libel if it is later removed, when the damage has already been done and is hard to correct?) Examples of the worst kind of what seems to me to be libel even include right wingnuts/propagandists who deny the reality of specific school shooting episodes and—get this—call out as liars the parents of the dead children.

The larger problem is, as a recent article portraying Facebook's history put it, "Facebook talks a good game about connecting us, but it's really tearing us—and our democracy—apart" [Clara Jeffrey and Monika Bauerlein, "With Friends Like These…," in *Mother Jones*, March-April, 2019, 19]. Further, the proliferation of truly fake news (i.e., only very rarely what President Trump labels as fake news) also greatly increases the likelihood of our falling into a world of "post-truth," in which everything is seen as opinion in the minds of a vast majority of people because all facts are equally challengeable (even though, clearly, they are not). Although in some cases political spin may be difficult to sort out from political lies, the danger is well illus-trated in this finding: "Buzzfeed reports that in the three months leading up to the 2016 presidential election, the top twenty fake news stories on Facebook got more shares than the top twenty real news sto-ries" [McIntyre, 109]. Moreover, a Pew poll released in 2016 found that 62% of U.S. adults got their news primarily from social media, and 71% of that group relied most on Facebook [McIntyre, 94]—so, by multi-plying, we find that 44% got their news mainly from Facebook. And as if all this didn't present enough problems already, we are now being challenged by even greater threats to our ability to distinguish between fraud and truth—by "deepfakes." Deepfakes are faked videos, sometimes including audio, that seem like reality, but are altered or deliberately faked—like the mid-2019 slowed-down video of Nancy Pelosi that slurred her words, made her gestures seem awkward, and made her seem like a drunk. Or like a mid-2019 video of Mark Zuckerberg, Facebook's co-founder and CEO, with voice imitation and manipulated photos, saying "whoever controls the data, controls the future."

There are also myriad unknowns and some seemingly dubious effects worthy of closer attention before they get any worse that are due to our ever-greater reliance on social media-based communication as a substitute for direct interpersonal engagement. Except when they were very young, the generation of children nearing adulthood in this country has never known a world without small screens that are now the vehicles for the majority of their non-school-time social exchanges. They may have too little concern about what happens to the data collected on them by internet-facilitating corporations and applications. Is this an interpersonally-alienating cultural insanity under development, or might it yet, once thoroughly regulated, prove to be relatively benign?

Over-reliance on Technology to Come to the Rescue; and Some Other Overlooked and Prospective Cultural Insanities Closely Associated with Particular Technologies

Although Allen Frances makes a general statement about the delusional character of an overly optimistic faith in technology—both the title of the summary of his #10 and the subsequent explication of it apply only to artificial intelligence (AI) and the danger that the silicon-based forms of intelligence and physical capabilities that we develop could come to dominate and perhaps eliminate carbon-based forms of intelligence, such as ourselves [Frances, 47-50]. Clearly, there are potential and real dangers in some uses of artificial intelligence that need at least enough close monitoring to prevent. For example, computers can now be coded to "learn." For example, programs have now been written that can enable their host computer to write coherent sentences, including fake news—all based on a relatively modest sampling of real sentences. And development of functional humanoid robots is well under way. And who knows what awful AI capabilities militaries might come up with to incorporate into the machines of war, where drones may represent an early example. In any case, there are far too many people in the general society who expect that technology of some kind will invariably to come to our rescue in some way, shape or form (e.g., to stem climate change), while seemingly paying much less attention to the many problems that already need solving, including many enabled by or aspects of the current use of technologies (see below).

A decade earlier, Jared Diamond flagged the same erroneous faith that "technology will solve all our problems" [Diamond, *Collapse*, 504]. Despite acknowledging the success of a number of 20th century technologies, he argues that the rapid advances in new technologies also "regularly create unanticipated new problems" (faster than solving old problems), such that "all of our current problems are unintended negative consequences of our existing technology" [Diamond, 505]. Diamond has identified a number of examples of societal failure in handling technology, but he has also found, by comparison, societies that made wiser use of similar technology, thereby avoiding disastrous side effects/consequences. I would argue that Diamond's generalization about "all" of our problems being unintended consequences of technology is something of an overstatement, except insofar as it is a tautology. The tautological truth in Diamond's generalization is obvious when one considers Marx's view. In Marx, advances in technology drive civilization and societies forward. Even if that is only partly correct, it follows that many aspects of *all* societies are inherently involved in whatever level of technology is available, or, historically, was available. Similarly, in our current human world, suffused as it is with all manner of technologies, it might be quite difficult to identify any problem that has no technological aspect or component, such that almost every societal problem is also quite likely to be associated with unintended consequences of one or more technologies. But the technology itself may well be on the periphery of some problems—young-earth creationism is certainly one example. And whatever the extent of the main effects or side effects of the technologies involved in them, most major societal problems, especially long-term or festering problems, will be associated with one or more cultural insanities.

But even when Frances' delusions #8 and #10 are combined, there are a number of other aspects of technology—and varying degrees of directness—associated with cultural insanities that he has not included, some of which we have already reviewed. Among those are the inattention to the effects of chemicals we have loosed on the environment; the continuing serious declines in many fish stocks associated with the technology of industrialized fishing; and the dangers of nuclear war. We avoid thinking about the ghastly threat of nuclear war and we do not demand that our politicians all become crusaders engaging with other nations to jointly eliminate all major weapons of mass destruction. Likewise, we and our politicians have mostly sat on the sidelines while President Trump has engaged in mutually threatening nuclear exchange stand-offs with North Korea, and cancelled U.S. participation in the otherwise widely accepted de-nuclearization deal with Iran—with which Trump has since engaged in threatening displays and maneuvers—which have become mutual. And regarding other weapons of mass destruction, we need more close monitoring of the continuing development of biological diseases and chemical weapons (e.g., nerve gases), together with enforced international sanctions for any use thereof.

So that we can further disabuse ourselves of the notion that technology will come to the rescue, let me mention at least some other technologies that I have not yet discussed that have become drawn into cultural insanities. One example that at minimum warrants closer monitoring by people and politicians is associated with the widespread use of genetically modified (and, in some countries, patented) crops that are heavily promoted by a very few industries. As noted earlier, even before genetic modification, some of these crops (e.g., soy beans, corn) were well along toward becoming like a monoculture which, for purposes of all other life forms, are like "corn deserts" in this country [Schwägerl, 104]. Or, in cases where the GMO crop is associated directly with the applicability of a specific herbicide—"Roundup"-ready soy beans being a case-in-point—the herbicide can destroy nearby non-crop plants and thereby threaten the survival of miscellaneous insects dependent on those plants, including pollinators such as the monarch butterflies (which require milkweed plants for their caterpillars to eat), especially when farmers use the herbicides beyond the edges of the crop fields, creating even more of a "desert" as far as all other plants and plant-dependent life are concerned. Meanwhile, however, some weeds in some areas of the country have also become resistant to Roundup, such that its chief benefit—the possibility of eliminating plowing to kill weeds at the start of the growing season (which costs money and has negative effects on soil fertility)—will likely slowly be lost. That problem has also led to efforts to develop GMO crops resistant to other herbicides as well, so that the weeds can again be controlled without using two herbicide treatments... but is this an endless cycle, as seems likely?

The spread of pollen from some GMO crops such as corn also threatens the purity of nearby non-GMO crops, including those of organic growers, such that before long all readily available corn seed may have some degree of genetically engineered character to it. Interestingly, the genetic modification of corn—the inclusion of a bacterium gene that kills certain varieties of caterpillars such as the corn borer—helped to reduce the use of insecticides (good) but, at the same time (bad), is spread by wind to nearby plants and kills caterpillars there too (including those of the monarch butterfly, a pollinator) and necessarily reduces the availability of yet other caterpillars sought by birds to feed their young. To protect its corn patents (which are granted in the U.S.A. but still disputed territory in Europe), Monsanto (now bought out by Bayer), the maker of GMO corn and soy bean plants, has successfully sued to prevent farmers from using a practice dating back to the dawn of agriculture—selecting their own seeds from their own crop for subsequent planting—if those seeds came from a previous Monsanto crops, or if they were purchased from a silo/storage facility with Monsanto crops inside.

Other dangers that may arise from monoculture crops include reducing the gene pool of any given crop and increasing the danger of famine if, for example, a rapidly-spreading fungus were to descend upon a widespread GMO adoption. (The possible dangers associated with the loss of plant varieties has led to the development of some seed banks—frozen storage places, e.g., in northern Norway—as a back-up for many varieties of plants, though that effort necessarily represents a kind of bare minimum protection of genetic diversity—one that cannot produce enough replacement seed to plant without a multi-year time interval.)

Similarly, on the animal side, we should ask what will happen to wild salmon stocks when genetically engineered salmon (which contain genes from another species of fish that make them grow faster) escape their confines, as some inevitably will. Will they out-compete less hungry salmon and ultimately eliminate natural salmon? Penned fish are also prone to more discases, which presumably could spread. In general, it is difficult if not impossible to know in advance whether some GMO crop or creature will turn out to have a major negative effect on the natural environment. Yet genetic modifications are being carried out in laboratories all over this country and in some other countries as well [Schwägerl, 154-168]. Meanwhile, even small-scale testing may pose some hazards to the natural world. Schwägerl asks whether biologists are "really engineers," as in … "genetic engineering." Or "are they stewards of life?" [Schwägerl, 164]. Very little ethical debate, even among biologists, is occurring. "Without consensus on the aims and limits of cultivating synthetic life, this field will soon simply reflect the ambitions of individual scientists or the profit-hunting instinct of large companies" [Schwägerl., 164]. But some GMO forms of life—those derived from implanting genes from other varieties *of the same plant*—are much less threatening, because they are more like speeded-up traditional crossbreeding. In contrast to the U.S., European countries have been much more resistant to permitting importation or growing of foodstuffs made from genetically engineered crops and they impose a number of requirements, including traceability and labeling. But the U.S., in defense of its big corporations, has gone so far as to sue European countries in World Trade Organization "courts" because they refuse to permit trade as freely as mandated by WTO treaties/agreements. (All nations' sovereignty and environmental, labor, and other laws are weakened by this kind of provision in these agreements.)

Seemingly somewhat more futuristically but present now, geneticists can go in and tinker with individual genes. Before long, genetically designed humans may pose a possible threat (including via researchers who deliberately violate current ethical-legal restrictions, as some have done). Problems will undoubtedly arise at least initially with reference to the equality of access to the technology, even if parts of the technology otherwise prove to be entirely constructive—such as fixing mutated or bad-variant human genes in fetuses or the young, and assisting generally in disease-fighting. Genetically engineered organisms certainly have potential benefits for humanity but, given the loose requirements placed on them, especially in the U.S.A. (and China??), have we also opened Pandora's kettle of worms? We don't know, and in some cases the hour may be growing late to start finding out a lot more.

There is clearly another cultural insanity involved in the abuse of technology in the crowded and germ-filled confinements used in industrialized meat production—with some animals typically given antibiotics in their food as a method of disease *prevention* (i.e., not just for treating diseased animals). A daily regimen of antibiotics will also help to fatten pigs (a boon to the meat company and the drug maker). But this overuse has had the side effect of reducing the effectiveness of these antibiotics against human diseases. The cultural insanity involves the lack of people pressure and the lack of politicians' actions to establish (some time ago) laws that prohibit the use of antibiotics except on veterinarian-diagnosed bacterial infections in sick animals. Recently, though, there have been at least some restrictions placed on the use of drugs that are medically important to humans in some whole-barn uses, but there is considerable leeway. For example, industry can treat lots of animals to prevent the spread of a disease found in one or more animals among them. And the drug companies involved continue to pitch all the possible benefits of their drugs to the meat producers. In any case, the animals' antibiotic-resistant strains of bacteria are already out of the barn: They are present on the surface of much of the meat sold in supermarkets (requiring thorough cooking at high enough temperatures to be sure to prevent potentially severe illness). And some bacteria—such as MRSA (a staphylococcus), Clostridium difficile, and some strains of E. coli—have developed resistance against which few or no remaining antibiotics are invariably effective. And—whoa!—at least some bacteria have also been found to acquire resistance "packages" directly from *different species* of bacteria without having to go through their own, separate evolutionary process. Meanwhile, "drug-resistant infections kill 700,000 people a year around the world, including 35,000 in the U.S." [Andrew Jacobs, "How Denmark raises antibiotic-free pigs," in the *StarTribune*, Jan. 12, 2020, SH2].

And speaking of things overlooked or neglected in medicine, there is some cultural insanity associated with this country's inadequacy of preparation, both long-term and short-term, for a pandemic, as illustrated by the COVID-19 virus. And this occurred despite numerous warnings from disease specialists that just such an occurrence was inevitable, most likely sooner rather than later (with an ever larger and globe-traveling human population to abet its spread).

Relatedly, there has been an overemphasis on insecticides and herbicides to grow many different food crops and cotton (with many a farmer in support, if only for what seem to be short-term financial results). As with diseases, one (entirely expectable) side effect has been the development of biological resistance among some of the targeted insects and weeds and, as noted earlier, some major effects on non-target species.

Similarly, many of our fruits and vegetables are coated with residual amounts of whatever pesticide was applied, where the effects of long-term low-dose exposure and potential accumulation in the human body are unknown (though a few insecticides were eventually withdrawn from the market because of their effects on humans). For years organized farmworkers have complained about the effects of exposure to one or another pesticide on their health (including cancers, miscarriages, etc.). Sometimes this results in closer studies of the pesticide. But if a pesticide is not *clearly* responsible for symptoms occurring in humans, it also often takes years for evidence of its ill effects to be measurable. We do not have good systems for checking on the safety of insecticides and herbicides before they are put to use on a massive scale. Or strong enough requirements to protect agricultural workers.

As noted earlier, there are also substantial and unexpected side effects of the fertilizers we use on farm fields and our lawns—especially from chemical compounds of phosphorous and nitrogen. The fertilizers that are not consumed by the plants end up flowing downriver to the ocean. Less fertilizer escapes if a farm is buffered with natural plantings that extract more of the chemicals before the farm's water— from rainfall, irrigation, or sprinklers—flows into nearby drainage pipes and ditches, creeks, and rivers. But such buffers deprive the farmer of some cropland and may require government subsidies to be sustained. Yet some subsidies have been withdrawn in recent years when the government mandated the inclusion of corn-based ethanol in gasoline, which increased the demand for corn acreage. And where these chemicals' concentration gets too high in the ocean, they overfeed alga, which are then consumed by bacteria, which use up all the oxygen in the water in the process. Because oxygen is necessary for all animal life, including animals such as fish and shrimp that get their oxygen from water, the areas of the oceans most seriously affected by this over-fertilized run-off become "dead zones" for some or much of the year, eliminating some valuable fisheries. "The number of coastal dead zones has doubled every decade since the 1960s; there are now roughly 500" [Abigail Tucker, "The New King of the Sea," in *Smithsonian*, August 2010, 30]. The most well-known of the dead zones in the United States is at the outlet to the Gulf of Mexico off the coast from Louisiana; another occurs in Chesapeake Bay area; and there are lots of other, smaller ones around the country as well. Fertilizer run-off also contributes to harmful algae-and-bacterial "blooms" that can kill fish and make fresh water undrinkable (as recently occurred in Lake Erie, near Toledo) or, in the sea, help to generate "red tides" (as seen recently in Florida), which kill other life by poisoning the waters. In contrast, more traditional agriculture, without the addition of fertilizers except livestock dung, involves practices such as carefully selected and mixed crops, crop rotation and cover crops, some livestock, some trees, constant ground cover (no or minimal plowing), incorporation of plant leftovers into the soil, etcetera—and that facilitates the continuation of local biodiversity, while enriching the soil rather than depleting it. And it produces no harmful run-off.

Finally, as a matter of balance, I should mention that cultural insanity can also involve almost an opposite pathway as well, a kind of Luddite approach. This kind of difficulty can arise when science and technology are rejected almost automatically or for erroneous reasons, and then supported by the promotion of some kind of fear(s) among the people. One modern example comes from the movement against childhood vaccines (the anti-vaxxers), which was initially based on what proved to be erroneous research showing some linkage between autism and the vaccines. But even after this information was thoroughly discredited, some anti-vaxxers continue their crusade. In some cases this has resulted in adding enough children to the few already typically unvaccinated so as to enable the resurgence of a disease—in one recent example, measles—a nasty illness which usually kills a few of its victims. This kind of rejection of (some elements of) modern science and technology is not per se culturally insane however—much depends on the effects of doing so on the individual, the subculture, and the society. For example, there is no inherent problem with subcultures that reject modern technology in the fashion in which the Amish do so, nor, obviously, is there when some hippies or organic farmers try to avoid modern farm chemicals. Cases of Christian Scientists' rejecting modern medicine, especially for seriously ill children who could be easily saved, on the other hand, are much more tending toward a subcultural insanity—but those cases are few and that subculture is very small and not very influential, and so it is unlikely to affect the larger society in any important way.

In general, and irrespective of their benefits, to the extent that technologies yield greater potential to do damage, to a correspondingly greater extent must we monitor and be extra responsible for how we use them. And, as we have seen above, there are indeed a large number of technology-related cultural insanities—both already under way and developing—that jeopardize our and our children's futures in various ways.

CHAPTER 8

Antidotes for Weaknesses in Human Thinking Processes

The Use of Reason and Evidence

One of the special characteristics of Homo sapiens ("wise man" or "thinking man") is our considerable capacity to learn through the use of reasoning rather than relying almost entirely on emotion and instinct, as in most other animals. Moreover, that reasoned learning process also enables us to have the capacity for "conscious restraint"—to avoid making mistakes we might otherwise be likely to make [Wilson, 76]. The outer reaches of the brain—the neocortex—is the source of our executive functioning, including both reasoning and the monitoring of social interactions. Metaphorically, both Stephen Novella and Allen Frances describe our brains as consisting of a human brain atop an ape brain atop a mammalian brain atop a lizard or reptile brain. The amygdala, at the primitive core of the brain (the part dating back evolutionarily to reptiles if not earlier), is the part that deals with fear. "Understanding our animal psychology gives us the potential power to bend its arc to our current survival needs" [Frances, 60].

As human cultures became more advanced and complicated, more and more opportunities presented themselves for the use of reason. For the most part, simple practical reasoning may have sufficed for farmers and artisans in early settlements when all that was needed was handed-down wisdom, mainly parental instruction and demonstration, plus experience, and occasional trial-and-error efforts. (However, that minimum has probably never quite sufficed for leaders of organized societies.) Today, with rapidly advancing technology, ever deeper science, and many intricate and arcane rules of law—including entire sub-systems to regulate the marketplace, to generate taxes, etcetera—effective reasoning/critical thinking is all the more required. And wherever ordinary citizens have at least some kind of roles in governance, effective reasoning is also needed to develop one or another viable worldview if cultural insanity, whether perpetrated on the masses by leaders or by subcultures from within those masses, is to be constrained. Otherwise, people can much more readily become part of the problems, and thereby reduce prospects for solutions. We need to be truly able to think for ourselves, and not just assume that we already are.

Skepticism. Even as a pre-adolescent and adolescent in the 1950s in the U.S.A., we were informally taught by the mass media that all is not as was presented, or seemed. *Mad Magazine* used sarcasm, irony and just plain ridicule to reveal some of society's foibles. The newspaper comic strip *Pogo*, by Walt Kelly, which was filled with ignorant swamp characters, sometimes labeled things incorrectly, but sometimes those labels had more truth to them than did the "right" word. And perhaps the most famous *Pogo* statement, conveying truth in many contexts including the original environmental one, is "We have met the enemy and he is us." And in the 1950s, as now, it wasn't hard to find TV and print advertising that was easier to mock than to believe. So, for kids and readers/viewers or a consumer with a good mind, it wasn't hard to start developing critical thinking—even if we initially bought into much of what we were told about things like religion, our parents' political views, etcetera. (But we weren't as overwhelmed by a flood of advertising, nor was it as sophisticated then.) To varying extents, we learned to be somewhat skeptical, and to wonder about the believability of some of what we read, saw, or heard.

One key to effective reasoning or critical thinking is precisely such doubt or skepticism. How reliable, how trustworthy are the information and purported facts which are presented to us, or that we unearth? How credible are the sources? We need to look for disconfirming evidence and compare reliabilities, particularly with controversial issues [Novella, 172]. The school district in a modest number of locations has now begun to include or require classes in critical analysis of source materials. More should do so. Limiting ourselves to sources that confirm what we already believe is, or abets, confirmation bias rather than knowledge development, and it is an easy way to be led astray and develop or sustain major errors in thinking about the world.

Include All Verified Facts. Another key to effective reasoning is that all demonstrable/verified facts should be incorporated into everyone's worldview about the issue at hand—whatever the source. No fact should be denied for political, ideological, values-based, or other rationales.

After culling whatever is submitted as evidence and eliminating the junk and identifying the questionable pieces (for possible inclusion, or not), we have to take all the good evidence into account. Ideally, we want to arrive at an interpretation that best fits all the evidence, just as a scientific theory would do. So, what especially fails this test is to leave out good evidence, to argue only one side (like a lawyer must do for professional reasons), or to "cherry pick" facts to support the view that we already believe. For example, the most benign interpretation of Vice-President Dick Cheney's efforts to get President Bush and the Congress to authorize a U.S. attack on Iraq in 2003 is that he cherry-picked the evidence in support of his position, ignoring not only serious questions about many of his chosen facts but also all the facts and interpretations that challenged his established beliefs.

However, some of the evidence may best fit one interpretation while other evidence best fits one or more other interpretations. In the complexity of human affairs, especially, it is often the case that multiple social forces are at work which together account for the totality of the observed evidence. And attempts to check questionable information may come up empty. In some cases, then, it may be necessary to stop short of any all-encompassing interpretation while acknowledging a multi-faceted dynamic that is not easily resolved. In such instances, it may be necessary to suspend judgment until more is learned, or to say "I'm not sure," but to do so with a tolerance for ambiguity, a suspension of judgment, not with a relapse into a more simplistic view.

Magnitude of Effects. Another very frequent error in reasoning, one for a long time perpetuated even in scientific journals, especially in the social sciences, is to ignore the magnitude of any cause-effect relationship discovered. Formerly, many studies were accepted for journal publication because their authors discovered a "statistically significant" relationship—never mind the size of that relationship or its associated practical importance. Abandoning this approach was all the more important because it is easier to reach "statistical significance" with larger sample sizes, such that even a tiny and almost meaningless effect could be "significant" with a large-enough sample size. In the past, for example, too many "innovations" in education were put into more general practice (adopted) based on studies that found significant effects the magnitude of which were too small to yield any important differences in results for students (typically in achievement). Many of these effects were also derived from samples not representative of all prospective students, such that the "significant" relationships disappeared entirely in later large samples. Much of the above has been remedied in recent years by an emphasis on "effect sizes." Moreover, effect sizes are usually rendered as ranges to readily convey their reliability, just as is done with "margin of error" (or confidence interval) information provided by higher quality public opinion polls. Similarly, in medicine the field is now in the process of identifying better ways of measuring and conveying just how much additional risk, or benefit, is involved with a new medical device, a new drug, or a vitamin. A 50% decrease in heart attacks in a certain population as a result of taking Drug A is a lot more important, for example, if the usual heart attack rate in that group is 10% than if it is 1%. In sum, simply affirming that A *to some extent* (especially a small extent) is a cause of B (even if true) is not necessarily meaningful as evidence—and it also leaves much room for doubt as to the main causes of B. So considering the magnitude of effects (together with the associated confidence interval) is part and parcel of verifying and assessing the value of facts.

Correlation and Causation. The above also applies to correlation. It is the magnitude of the correlation that is important, not just that there is some degree of relationship, or a "statistically significant" correlation.

But the correlation between any given "A" and "B" does not necessarily imply A causes B (B may cause A), or there may be another factor causing both. Any interpretation of a correlation should include an effort to surmise what all else might have caused the correlation. There are many examples in medicine and nutrition, for example, did eating more roughage cause the fact that there was a correlation between eating roughage and reduced colon cancer rates? Or was eating more roughage simply associated with another factor, such as a better diet overall, or regularly taking vitamin pills, which did the causing? But, if a direction of causation is clear (e.g., socioeconomic status cannot affect race/ethnicity, but race/ethnicity can affect or constrain socioeconomic status), or if it can be safely posited, the magnitude of the correlation does viably express the direction and magnitude of the affecting, even if one or many underlying causal factors remain unknown. For example, the data might show that a correlation between A and B is somewhere between 0.30 and 0.40, using a 95% confidence level.[2]

Because correlation data rarely yields fairly definitive results, you can see why experimental methods, with separate experimental and control group (randomly selected from an initial pool and both blind to whether or not they were receiving the real treatment, such as a new pill), are required for more conclusive proof. Utterly spurious correlations are not hard to find or imagine. For example, viewed over the period 1965-1980, the size of the south pole's ozone hole is very likely to be correlated with any other increase during that time period, such as the proportion of women using birth control pills—where the only factor in common may be due to accidents involving their times of discovery in an ongoing technological society.

Even so, correlational data can be very powerful and important. For example, correlational data constitutes the foundation of the scientific discipline of epidemiology (which involves the tracing of factors associated with negative developments in public health, such as the 19th century discovery that cholera was linked to a contaminated

---

2   The most-used correlation, the "Pearson r," also needs to be squared (arithmetically) for proper interpretation. A squared Pearson r conveys the extent to which the various measurements (observations) of "A" account for the variations in the measurements of "B," and vice-versa if a causal direction is unknown. (So a correlation of 0.30, squared, = 9%, while a correlation of 0.40, squared, = 16%. Thus a correlation of 0.40 also conveys the "fact" that 84% of the reason for the variation in A, and/or in B, remains unaccounted for (absent other measures). In the social sciences, a correlation of 0.50 begins to be fairly high, and a correlation of 0.70 (49% shared variance) begins to be very high. Indeed, alternate versions of a standardized test are often regarded as acceptable (i.e., as more or less "the same") if the two versions, when administered to the same people, are correlated at or above 0.70. This is so because there are many other possible ways—other than student knowledge—to affect those scores, including (e.g.) the particular set of items chosen for Form A and Form B of the "same" test, how much sleep the test-takers got the night before (e.g., was an exciting day coming soon in one case but not the next?), any differences in the extent of disruptions during test administrations (differences in construction noises outside?), and many more.

water source). Further, as in the case of the correlation between lung cancer and smoking, correlations can be used to generate hypotheses that can then be tested in other ways (e.g., that cancers will occur more often in long-term smokers, smokers who consume more cigarettes, etc.) [Novella, 159-160].

When multiple variables are involved, correlations can also convey broad "pictures" of what is "out there." For example, correlations among different attitudes may show general patterns shared more by liberals than conservatives, and vice versa; and the strength of correlation among an array of political beliefs might clarify the extent to which any given political position tends to group with certain other positions or, for that matter, with demographic characteristics, such as race/ethnicity, income or consumption levels, religiosity, political leanings, and more. Indeed, such correlations provide the foundation for most "big data" analyses, allowing for targeting of commercial advertisements, selective or in-silo distribution of political propaganda and deceptive/fake news to those who will believe it, and more. Google expensive suits, you probably have a high income; buy lots of hair straightener on line (or on a rewards card?), you're probably Black, especially if confirmed by other data. Linking a few such (correlated) informational data points together can provide a pretty accurate as to what any given "user" is all about. Privacy has been greatly reduced and the corporations that collect the data can also analyze it and sell it to whomever, for whatever their purposes. So you are being surreptitiously watched (spied on), as well as being packaged and sold.

Bell-shaped (Normal) Curves. Another thing to keep in mind when thinking about the evidence that applies to human beings and most natural phenomena, is that many traits, qualities, characteristics, etcetera, tend to be arrayed in what is called a "normal distribution," a bell-shaped curve (where taller bells indicate a narrower range than broader bells).

Remembering that most distributions tend to be "normal curves" is important in part to avoid two major and related flaws in thinking: 1) either/or classifications; and 2) stereotyping. Almost no general grouping of people (e.g., Republicans or Democrats) is going to do more than tend to share even the most simple or basic characteristics across the entire grouping—unless the general group has been pre-selected by limiting it to people with those specific characteristics. Even then, though, for example, individual Blacks, or individual Trump voters will not share all of the other characteristics which, in varying strengths, have been established as usually being associated with being classified (or self-identified) as Black, or as Trump voters.

Here's a complex example: Maleness and femaleness, for example, come in normal curves which overlap, probably quite a bit, at the ends of the curves that face toward the middle of that joint distribution. Although cultures have major effects on what is regarded as "male" or "female" most people tend to be *predominantly* male or female in sexual orientation, corresponding to their sexual apparatus. But within the *overlapped* ends of these two normal distributions will be some people who will feel that they were born with a sexual apparatus that does not match their feelings-based preference, including a very few who are physically hermaphroditic (have mixed sexual characteristics). Similarly, there will be a range of gayness/homosexuality toward that same side of the distribution, also likely overlapping some with the bell curve for "females." Bisexuality would be more somewhat more toward the middle of the "male" side than homosexuality, but still in the less-stereotypically-masculine half of that distribution. But simply having "homosexual tendencies" would extend well into the more heterosexual range of the "male" distribution. Indeed, it is likely that almost everyone, male or female, whatever their predominant disposition, will have some "homosexual tendencies" (possibly excepting a small proportion of people distributed into the most mutually distant tails of the two bell curves). The characteristics of the bell curve for females would roughly parallel those for males (though the proportions in each subgroup would probably differ a bit), with the most gay/lesbian side of the distribution being the one adjacent to or overlapping with the male curve.

Applying Scientific Reasoning. "Research has shown that the vast majority of people living in industrialized nations do not have the minimal scientific knowledge to participate in important scientific issues of the day" [Novella, 178]. One might add "effectively" in the previous sentence because some or many people will participate in science-related social issues, some quite vigorously, with little or no knowledge, or no sign of having considered facts at variance with their biases. Given the problems in the world and in our society today, and the evolutionary background that gave us minds which have a strong propensity to over-simplify and otherwise distort or disregard those realities, we desperately need proven methods to understand the world around us and ourselves.

Scientific methods represent the epitome of the use of reason. Since about 1543, when Copernicus published his theory that the earth orbited around the sun, or maybe 1600 or 1660, when the Royal Society in England started an effort to do more modern scientific investigations, scientists and their predecessors have slowly developed fairly systematic approaches to the gathering and testing of observational evidence. Testing includes laboratory manipulation, the use of treatment-control groups, and hypotheses that can be confirmed or disconfirmed in the field. Testing makes extensive use of induction (slowly building up generalizations/theories from many facts), mathematics, and more recently, statistics.

But, like statistics, science is also probabilistic. It does not yield definitive, eternal answers—just a confirmation that, at best, is very,

very, very likely to be "true." That is, the most well-established facts and theories can be considered as if they were true, albeit with some hint of reservation yet. See Part Four regarding evolution for a specific example.

Human-oriented science relies heavily on statistical probabilities. But even if it didn't, if we wanted to reason effectively, we would still need to develop some "number sense" and some basic capabilities in simple statistics. Sometimes very simple statistics can tell us a lot. For example, the arithmetic mean from a set of ratings (e.g., 1-5, 1-7, or 1-10 ratings for product quality or pain levels) describes the central tendency among the whole set of respondents. Or, the percentages of cases falling into each subgroup of ratings or categories (such as all those who agree, or disagree) can inform us more about the range of cases. As noted earlier, we readily give emotional attention to stories. Effective reasoning instead requires that we pay attention to the full range and general characteristics of the stories as part of determining just how representative is the one story, or the few stories, that we have heard. For example, Gallup-type pollsters know how to include enough people in their sample sizes to ensure what they deem to be an adequate degree of statistical reliability—the margin of error for the full sample—a form of probability statement. These margins of error will be larger (which isn't always made clear) when the samples are then subdivided for more detailed analyses (e.g., into men and women respondents). Trickier yet for such pollsters is establishing the representativeness of such samples, especially now that many people have given up "land lines" in favor of cell phones. If the accuracy of such polling has been reduced in recent years (e.g., in comparisons of pre-election polling and actual election results), this may be part of the reason why. But there are also other unknowns that could affect the results: What percentage of those included in the initially-selected sample declined to participate at all—and are there any relevant differences between them and those who did respond? If there are, the representativeness of those who responded may be less adequate. Similarly, of those participating in the survey, were there many who "declined to state" or answered "don't know" or had "no opinion" to some of the questions? In the case of pre-election polling or polling about sensitive issues, there may also be some degree of error (reason for a less accurate result) associated with people who are unwilling to express their true feelings about an issue or candidate(s). In election polling, pollsters often attempt to screen for the likelihood that people will actually vote—to avoid using an unrepresentative sample of those who ultimately vote. But if the propensity to vote changes among some sectors of the population, an earlier most-likely-to-vote sampling becomes a little less representative. And opinions may change. That is why we are usually warned by pollsters regarding the dates of the polling. Here I have mainly discussed just one example of why we need to use numerical reasoning as part of drawing conclusions, yet still use care in assessing the resulting data. Above I also included a rather different example from medicine.

There are, of course, some other differences by discipline, e.g., between a laboratory science such as chemistry, observational sciences such as astronomy, and partly historical sciences such as geology or paleontology. But they all use predictions and associated hypothesis testing.

The sciences can also be divided into "harder" and "softer" fields. However, most of the important questions in today's world cannot be answered using only a "hard" approach. For example, climate science relies on combinations of hard data (almost all of which involves sampling and is necessarily incomplete) and computer modeling. Computer modeling is not necessarily biased one way or the other, but it does rely on various assumptions and informed estimates. Results also should include a range (like a margin of error, given the assumptions). In any case, a stronger confirmation may need to be derived from various models yielding similar results. In human-oriented science endeavors, which can range from history to economics, typically there are just too many factors/forces acting on any given outcome to yield any simple or strong cause-and-effect relationships. That doesn't mean that factual evidence is irrelevant (unless it is very weak). Instead, broader searches for more information across possible alternative contributive causal factors may need to be undertaken. Still, often there will be at least some evidence unearthed that will cast considerable doubt on or even discredit poorly-reasoned alternative interpretations or theories among those originally proffered as explanations.

Authority in Science. Of course the statements of authority do not count as evidence per se. Not the Bible, not the pope, not your church's minister, not the president. HOWEVER, a special subset of appeals to "authority" involves appeals to scientific experts. But in many cases, even such appeals must be limited to those in the most relevant disciplines. As discussed earlier, opponents of the scientific consensus that global warming is occurring (i.e., with humans as the driving mechanism) often do not have the scientific credentials that climate scientists have (and even some of those may have potential or clear conflicts of interest—such as oil company funding sources). Although scientific sources (individual scientists, peer-reviewed published manuscripts) may provide good evidence, any conclusions are necessarily tentative until the results are replicated/confirmed and, if not clear cut and of a size that truly matters, confirmed several times. To assist everyone in this regard, scientists have developed "meta-analyses"—published work that summarizes the best studies on a topic in a field to show the *combined* best estimate of the extent to which "A" causes "B," or of the magnitude of the correlation between A and B.

One caution, though, is that there are sometimes different "schools of thought" within a discipline that involve difference in some major approaches, emphases, or interpretations. In many disciplines there are also subfields that focus on different areas within the discipline and, when the whole of the discipline is surveyed, some of these subfields may have less credibility in some areas of inquiry than others—for example, they might be newer/developing subfields, have a focus not germane to the question at hand, or be fading subfields in which expectations about their original potential may not have materialized over time. Such situations are reasons why consensus views and a focus on the work of the most relevant sets of scientists are all the more important.

In general, then, we need to learn about the extent to which a published article, book, or scientist represents the general consensus in their field about the evidence, if such a consensus exists. Where a consensus is absent, we need to be sure that all the disparate scientific evidence of importance is included in our analyses, so that we can do our best to estimate the relative reliability of individual "facts," even if, ultimately, our question cannot be reliably answered because of conflicting evidence. But where there is a scientific consensus, the "burden of proof" falls upon the dissenter, and the effectiveness of any dissent cannot depend upon nitpicking over little inconsistencies or "minor pieces of contrary data" [Prothero, 22]. Having a large majority of the most relevant scientific authorities on one side would also tend to lead to that same conclusion, unless there are particularly well-done recent studies with strong effect sizes that are countervailing.

In addition, perhaps now more than ever, we need to be cautious about taking at face value (or as unbiased) the scientists or scientific findings in which the work was paid for by a corporate entity with a stake in the results, whether the medical device industry's hiring of doctors to demonstrate and tout the benefits of their devices, tobacco companies funding of research findings "showing" that second-hand smoke is not a danger, or Exxon-Mobil-funded studies or oil company executive-funded "think-tanks" raising doubts about global warming. There are many lesser examples that remain largely hidden. [For example, see Wendell Potter, *Deadly Spin: An Insurance Company Insider Speaks Out on How Corporate PR Is Killing Health Care and Deceiving Americans.*] Corporate-funded think tanks (or think tanks funded by biased billionaires) can be especially pernicious, because even if/when the initial funder withdraws, the biases and personnel are likely to remain the same in subsequent output. Unfortunately, think tanks are too readily treated as fully legitimate or neutral sources by the media or, at most, given a "conservative" or "liberal" label. But it has helped some that scientific journals have recently demanded more information from authors about any possible conflicts-of-interest that may be associated with a study submitted for publication (e.g., who funded the study and whether the author has any personal stake in the outcome of the study).

Objectivity. When it comes to interpretation, for all but the hardest and simplest scientifically-demonstrated facts, there is no such thing as "objective." There are always values involved in the use of evidence, scientific or otherwise. Even scientists tend to be bound up in the beliefs of their times, and individual scientists may have personal beliefs or school-of-thought stances that result in overlooked possibilities or otherwise affect the formulation of their studies and their write-ups. For example, ideas about a world-wide flood as the cause of earth's landscapes, even among scientists, were very slow to dissipate (see Part Four). Outside the realm of numerical quantities (some of which may have biases in their definitions) and the hardest and simplest kinds of facts, such as some chemical reactions at a given temperature and pressure range, only long-established scientific conclusions can usually be said to approach a factual or "objective" status.

Indeed, scientific methods, especially over the long term, serve as the model for approximating "objective." Thus, after more than 150 years of evidence piling up, evolution is considered a fact, even though the relative strength of the various mechanisms by which it occurs continues to be a matter of study and debate.

But the word "objective" is also used in other contexts. Consider the ideal of "objectivity" in newspaper reporting—an effort to report "both" sides. In reality, there may be many sides. (I omit TV news from mention here because, apart from mundane coverage and often limited coverage, some networks regularly and deliberately present some "slanted," that is, unfair and unbalanced, "news," with only a pretense at even journalistic objectivity). "Good journalism … should put the opinions of one expert into the proper context" [Novella, 175]—where that context is the totality of expert or scientific opinion. That same context is needed when we are assembling our own views.

Even when there are mainly two sides, sometimes the great preponderance of evidence and sound reasoning may be almost all on one side, or experts actually knowledgeable about the subject may have a 97% consensus on one side, while the other side has 2% (with 1% uncertain, say)—and that may not be clear from news reports. As described above, the status of climate change as an issue, as of about 2017, is a good example involving roughly those percentages yet with a very large proportion of the public in doubt. So, when it was also revealed that oil companies have funded most of the opposition "research," done by carefully selected researchers so as to deliberately try to cast enough public doubt on the virtual scientific consensus to try to prevent any action that might affect oil companies negatively (such as a carbon tax), then we can be pretty sure that it is past time to set aside any political-party or ideological stances to the contrary, and adjust our worldview to probabilistically but strongly conclude that humans are the primary cause of climate change in recent centuries.

Similarly, caution should be exercised before accepting as legitimate the output of think tanks or political organizations that are or have been funded by sources seeking to advance their self-interest, especially their economic self-interest, such as Charles and David [died, 2019] Koch, who have been at it for decades. George Soros also gets blamed by right-wingers of various kinds for all sorts of funding that he seems to have had no part in (e.g., he is smeared as a conspiratorial villain to promote indignation and donations to the right's causes)—so the extent of his involvement (and the goals of any *actual* recipients) need to be verified in response to any such charge. Soros' history also includes many important humanitarian funding efforts, such as reconstituting some of the universities in Eastern Europe to fit the free-world model after the collapse of communism there, and providing some funds for the Drug Policy Alliance's efforts to eliminate the culturally insane "War on Drugs." On the good side, David Koch has helped to fund the PBS "NOVA" program; but he mainly has for years helped create and fund many right-wing "think tanks" and ALEC, a group that drafts model legislation for economically conservative/right-wing causes, with a focus on seeking adoption at the state level.

Weighting Evidence in Evaluation: Fact-Value Interactions

Having assembled all the relevant evidence available, we then need to establish the relative importance of each piece of evidence within the set AND to weight each piece insofar as it pertains to the question at hand. (Fact A may provide better evidence than Fact B, but neither may be as germane to the question as Facts C and D.) This cannot be done with great precision—in part because values are involved. Moreover, especially when the question involves humans, weights for many pieces of evidence will be small because lots of information/data will be relatively tangential to the question. This is another place in the evaluative process in which the question of the magnitude of cause relationships can be especially important. How much does Fact A actually bear on the question at hand? (The quality and reliability of some factual information may also be in question, but this can be further investigated too.) And when the facts/causes themselves are in question, the questions involving the magnitude of their effects and validity generally may need to fall back on the consensus, if any, of experts or scientific authorities who have previously assembled masses of data pertaining to the subject, for example, in a metanalysis (see above). Assuming the weighting process continues, it should be noted that if the reason for an individual's weighting denies the apparent scientific consensus, the set of assumptions/beliefs behind that denial may well be insufficiently correct/accurate as a way of interpreting reality. But where there no scientific consensus or it is very weak, more alternative sets of assumptions/beliefs will be viable competitors to represent reality, such that indecision may result, along with the development of ideas about needs for further research. If action must nevertheless be taken, it is best if that action not be irreversible or have much potential harm associated with it.

The Purview of Various Facts May Overlap. In addressing a problem or question or outcome in the human realm, one major complication in the need to weight factual evidence is that some facts will be somewhat redundant on others. They will overlap, be correlated, typically because they have some degree of shared causation. (Facts that have entirely independent causes but just happen to be correlated can be weighted without reference to each other.) To the extent that two facts share a same cause, to weight them as if they were independent of each other will result in a net overweighting for that cause/source of effects/evidence.

Values and Evidence Together. Assume for a moment that a number of diverse people are meeting to examine the evidence pertaining to a particular problem. Differences often occur among people in the importance (weight) they assign to any given fact in a set. In today's politics, too often there are two sides who offer interpretations based entirely on their own selection of facts and their own values. As above, the facts/evidence need to be merged into one set. Then, in the weighting by the participants in an evaluation, each piece of evidence is subject to whatever array of values is "brought to the table" (ideally, within a group that is broadly representative of the people). Where reasonable consensus on weights cannot be achieved in the evaluation, it is likely that the differences will trace to people having differences in value systems. However, if the relative importance you give to a piece of evidence differs greatly from those of others, you need to be able to explain why in the context of the larger problem under consideration. How is it that you gave Fact A or Evidence Exhibit A so little weight when others think it much more important, or so much weight when others think of it as much less important? Have the views of the most relevant scientific authorities been adequately taken into account? Have overlaps in the causes of data (factual information) been adequately taken into account? And, for that matter, how is it that Value X is so much more important for you than for others, or Value Y so much less important? (See below for more on this.) What we are trying to minimize here, as described above, are the typically biased alternatives—weightings and evaluations of partial sets of factual information the selection of which was based on emotional and only semi-conscious thoughts, stereotypes, beliefs or attitudes associated with some unsound worldview—which are all too often thoroughly bathed in confirmation bias and defensive rationalization. And whenever stereotypes seem to be involved.

For example, with respect to the purported high degree of criminality of would-be immigrants arriving at our southern border, we need especially to consider whether the typicality of the normal-curve distribution has been adequately taken into account. For example, over the years, most immigrants arriving at the U.S.-Mexico border have been seeking a better economic future (and thus represent mostly the needier end of an economic distribution in their home country). But, lately especially, many of them are seeking asylum because of criminal threats or actions against them or their families in their home country (mainly Honduras, Guatemala, El Salvador). And many are women and children besides. Even if the arrivals from El Salvador should be monitored more closely, it is highly improbable that these would-be immigrants will commit more rape, murder, and other violent crimes than people who are already U.S. citizens.

A caution, however: conflicts of interest and vested interests, and corruption in the service of money (including donations to campaign funds), need to be revealed vis-à-vis each issue because they often bias individual participants in any process such as this, and lead to hidden dishonesties in discussions, negotiations, etcetera. If such influences are made clear, the assertions of a potentially corrupted individual can be challenged accordingly. Similarly, if the Supreme Court decision to allow essentially unlimited "independent" funding in elections is unchanged, then action must be taken to force disclosure of all substantial contributions, for or against, to every candidate for office, to every Political Action Committee (PAC) that supports or opposes individual candidates, and to any group taking a public stance on any issue subjected to a vote of the people. (The same should be true of all forms of lobbying expenses.)

Combining evidence and values for one's own evaluations and decision-making requires much the same process, but the individual has to take responsibility for checking and questioning him or herself, including in the realm of values (see below). Per the above, one key requirement is to be able to explain (to yourself and/or others) how you took each and every relevant point of evidence into account (including in its weighting). A reasoned and systematic approach such as described here is needed to link together values and evidence, and it is for everyday use in our thinking as much as for any other purpose.

Can science help here too? Surely! As already noted, scientific thinking provides much of the methodology and raises other key concerns—such as the representativeness of data samples, the specifications needed for an appropriate control group, the adequacy of the measures, the use of normal curves when appropriate, etcetera. But science can help only in limited ways when values are involved. "The position that has the most merit is that science can inform ethical thinking, but there will always be some subjective value judgments in the mix" [Novella, 177-178].

The Need to Re-evaluate Our Basic Assumptions, Values, Beliefs, and Feelings

Even though values, attitudes and emotions inevitably and to varying extents appropriately play a part in all (evaluative) decision-making, reason is often the key to successful results (and cultural sanity). With respect to values, attitudes and emotions, it is crucial to recognize that all of us have initially had these, as well as our beliefs, basic assumptions and worldview, inculcated by our parents (guardians) and culture, mainly early in life. These inculcations are not inherently "ours" or "us"—nor, actually, are "our" feelings. All of these are often and to varying degrees biased, inconsistent, mistaken, irrational and sometimes even "delusional," as described by Allen Frances above. Our initial tendencies toward any given cultural insanity may be strong (and perhaps multifaceted) or weak. And, especially when not re-evaluated, "most of our motivations and behavioral styles reside outside conscious awareness or control and determine much of what we feel, do, and think" [Frances, 56]. Of course we all also have some values that we have arrived at more through our experiences in the world, including from interactions with co-workers and peers. But much of the foundation for how we understand those new experiences was already laid down. Thus many of our later experiences will still tend to be circumscribed or understood in biased, inconsistent, mistaken, and generally irrational ways—especially if we do not consciously call upon reason and full self-re-evaluation(s) to help identify those biases and then minimize or suspend their effects on us, and ultimately, reject them.

Liberating the Mind from the Clutches of Cultural Insanity. The very fact that we have values, ideas and feelings inculcated into us, to which we have added without questioning the foundation and usually without careful evaluation, is why we all need to undertake more generally to "re-evaluate our basic assumptions." We need to re-think that which we have had drummed into us, that which has bombarded us since infancy, and even what we have "learned" since then. That is, we need to suspend all our values, ideas and feelings, and then reassemble and reprioritize them into a revised and largely coherent whole that respects the totality of the evidence now known to us.

Fortunately, most residential traditional-age college students have enough freedom from societal constraints and impingements to enable them to re-evaluate their basic assumptions, and re-consider their values and beliefs. Some modest number now do so fairly fully, and many do so partly, but many do not (especially students not fully immersed in their college community). During college, they have the opportunity to interact with new and often far more diverse peers, and get acquainted with lots of new ideas, facts, and even whole areas of thought new to them. Basic re-evaluations, even partial ones, are how some of the major benefits of attending college actually occur. A broader and more general re-evaluation is probably undertaken mainly when there is a growing realization or recognition of *the need to do so*, sometimes motivated by other questions or turmoil in our lives.

Such broader re-evaluations should be on everyone's "to do" list. For example, many years ago, as my college years progressed, I realized that I was too abstractly rational in orientation (suppressing feelings), fearful of my own homosexual tendencies (as a late bloomer hetero-socially), unsure about the morality of premarital sex, and had some prejudice against Black-White heterosexual relationships. But with the civil rights era and the War on Vietnam at hand, I became aware that my political views were assembled from far too little information and were thoroughly bathed in American exceptionalism. That my father was an alcoholic in denial and a terrible model when it came to relating to my mother accounted for some of my early lack of growth heterosexually, but skipping a grade also put my social maturity level (and athletic capabilities) a year behind all of my same-grade friends.

And in order to do a better job of re-evaluating our values, it also helps if we learn more about our inner feeling-based selves too. As Socrates reportedly put it, "To know thyself is the beginning of wisdom." Inculcated feelings (and associated attitudes) can range from prejudice against people(s) having a different skin color or outward appearance, or particular religious faiths (especially Muslims, in the U.S. case), to our expectations about how both we and the "opposite sex" are supposed to behave and the social roles each "should" take, to how we react to two males kissing, to the goosebumps we might get when hearing the national anthem. Are such feelings and reactions somehow "natural"? Are they even me? Or are they mainly inculcated and quite possibly biased, and not worth re-affirming? Upon thorough reflection and re-evaluation, some of the answers are often obvious.

Sneakier yet in some respects are the likes and dislikes that advertising, often in combination with our social drives, has induced into our subconscious mind. These become our Pavlov's dogs-like default choices for specific things, like certain fattening and unhealthy fried foods, or sugar-sweetened drinks; and for time-sucking efforts to try to become more socially presentable according to our subculture's norms (e.g., grooming); and for some brand of pick-up truck instead of an electric car; and for using bottled water instead of the tap; and for spending way too much time tracking celebrities. I am no guru, but my recommendation would be to take the time to consciously review every semi-automatic decision you make where you have not already done so—at least once. Make sure to use your will to decide, at least once, what you ought to do, what is actually best for you, and to change subconscious-habitual preferences accordingly—to check your e-mail only once a day most days (work excepting perhaps); to answer the phone only for real calls (and check your other phone messages only twice a day); to learn to like 100% whole wheat bread instead of nutritionally poor white bread or to choose a salad instead of French fries; to pick functional/practical options instead of the more prestigious ones; to stop watching "reality" shows and crime dramas; to ease up on the time spent paying attention to sports (you are being assisted here by the COVID-19 virus); to substitute experiences for material goods; and so on. Think too about breaking any habits you happen to have of clicking "like" in response to any communication; and stop opting for any clickbait on Facebook (etc.)—these are the clicks which are used to profile and sell *you* (and to build the walls of your information silo higher and higher while keeping you engaged). Don't forward anything (or links to anything) without checking on it or at least adding a warning that you haven't, and wait until the next day's news cycle to see what if any confirmation you can find before doing so; don't forward anything not confirmed by a second and independent source; check political content against fact-checking websites such as PolitiFact; check many other kinds of information with largely neutral sources such as Wikipedia (which also lists fact-checking resources). Most good newspapers still carry a wider range of content than anything on T.V. Read between the lines—but not just to confirm your existing biases. Read some opinions opposed to yours to try to understand what their best case is.

Re-evaluating feelings is the hardest of all of the needed re-evaluations, so it is not unusual to start with a re-evaluation of our assumptions, values, attitudes and beliefs in light of all the evidence known to us. If we then come up with answers that are at odds with our emotions (e.g., perhaps dominant feelings of negativity toward rather than acceptance of gayness or gay couples or Black-White couples), we should then realize that we have emotional work to do too. In general, then, we need to explore where our feelings came from, and their "whys and wherefores" (all of the underlying causes). This is a task that almost no one ever completes because feelings run deep but, at least ideally, one that is important to be well underway before leaving young adulthood.

Sometimes the lack of self-knowledge is greatest in those who deny they ever have feelings of X, Y, or Z. In reality, we all have an immensely wide range of feelings, though some are likely to predominate. For starters, we need to acknowledge and accept this range of feelings rather than repress those we fear or dislike, and to work to reduce or eliminate the ones that predominate when they are rationally amiss/wrong (and not act on them insofar as they remain). Therapeutic settings can sometimes help with especially stubborn irrational feelings.

Consider this example as it pertains to the previous paragraph. One sees reported from time to time cases involving the struggles of an anti-homosexuality organization *spokesman* who, it subsequently turns out, is more gay than not. Psychologically speaking, he was (unnaturally) repulsed by his own gay feelings, vehemently rejecting them in himself, and thus all the more seeing their presence in others as a threat (e.g., that might elicit his own inner feelings). In some reported cases, the man's own feelings finally broke free of being repressed and he struggled with them in some way that later became public. Of course such people have rightly been called hypocrites (and worse). What was missing, though, was his thorough re-evaluation of basic assumptions, values, beliefs, and feelings *before actions based in bias* and their negative effects occurred, *and before an unnecessary personal crisis* occurred and was exposed publicly.

Wherever one personally falls in the gay-straight distribution (see earlier), it is not appropriate to condemn others within what amounts to a natural spectrum, where the most typical negative reaction is to condemn those who are gay and to try to bar them from relationships of their choice and the opportunity to legally marry. If effective, the main result of such opposition to gayness is to maintain or impose rules and mores that limit the development of the human potential of gays and their contributions to society. And that makes it a cultural insanity. Virtually forcing gays to stay in the "closet," as in times past, did not make for a better world.

Jared Diamond has examined a number of societal collapses. He identifies two choices that are crucial to tipping outcomes toward success rather than failure: "long-term planning, and willingness to reconsider core values" [Diamond, *Collapse*, 522]. The latter, of course, can refer to both the individual and societal level, in parallel to what I have counseled with regard to re-evaluating one's basic assumptions. Diamond summarizes several examples of successfully reconsidered values that occurred at the societal and local levels, some older, some relatively recent. These occurred despite the fact that the decisions involved were "agonizingly difficult" [Diamond, 523-524]. For example, in order to effectively combat climate change/global warming— after having recognized that there is indeed a major problem that must be dealt with—one sometimes-core value that conservatives (and libertarians) may need to compromise on is their preference for a hands-off government and a laissez-faire marketplace (which, actually, needs and already has lots of other rules and treaties enabling it to function). Conservatives will have to yield at least enough to enable the national government to adopt new taxes (and possibly some rules) in the marketplace, such as a carbon tax, that is designed in the not-very-long term to virtually eliminate fossil fuels and their associated pollutions, and to further facilitate alternative energy production while removing existing subsidies and tax breaks for the oil and gas industries.

Long-term planning, coupled with "bold, courageous, anticipatory decisions" is the principal way to make perceptible problems not reach "crisis proportions" [Diamond, *Collapse*, 522]. This links well with the need to avoid developing cultural insanities in the first place. As described above, I have identified several major (and a number of less major) cultural insanities (problems) that we should already have attended to and avoided, and others that are forthcoming. These are problems where we need to ferret out and reject the human foibles and political propaganda that allow them to fester and ultimately threaten us much more seriously. In that process, we will need to rely on reason and scientifically and evaluatively sound approaches to re-evaluate and re-establish some or many of our own values, beliefs, attitudes, assumptions, and even feelings—all of which can contribute to a non-viable worldview. And remember to watch out for your subconscious mind, which could easily have been corrupted by the ever-intensifying world of corporate advertising and political propaganda, especially insofar as we gather information from few sources or information silos, and that our default mode as humans is to allow our subconscious impulses/feelings to become our decisions, bypassing closer conscious scrutiny. Accordingly, as above, we need to re-evaluate those subconscious impulses, feelings and habits. And encourage others to do so. Otherwise, before long we might find ourselves our culture and our world cannot avoid mega-scale disaster(s).

I had hoped to complete this manuscript and have it published well before the November 2020 national election in the U.S.A.—to perhaps help people think through the country's situation a little better. But too many loose ends in the book preparation process took too long. In any case, that election is very likely to be a watershed moment, offering a chance to go back toward repair, reality and evidence-based national policies (i.e., despite some weaknesses, including American exceptionalism). Otherwise, we will likely continue on down the path of truth-avoidance and truth-distortion, ethnic and racial divisions, fear-mongering, authoritarian dictatorship—in other words, another four years of regressing toward greater cultural insanity (that will surely irreversibly harm our country and the world to a substantial degree).

PART TWO

THE CULTURAL INSANITY
OF WITCH-HUNTING

CHAPTER 9

Overview of the Destruction
Wrought by this Cultural Insanity

T he witch hunts of the later middle ages and early modern period
are among the clearest, most amazing, and most sweeping cases
of cultural insanity. *Even given the level of consciousness of the times,*
there was no historical necessity whatever dictating that witch hunts
had to arise out of the Catholic Church or its doctrines—and most
certainly not out of the Xtian religion itself—nor that Protestants
also needed to be drawn into them as well. As we shall see, though, it
was some of the intellectual leaders of the Catholic Church who were
chiefly responsible for developing and spreading this cultural insanity
to society's other educated leaders, some of whom then perpetrated
it on the masses lower in the social hierarchy. The last line of Brian
P. Levack's book fittingly adds that the witch hunts were "one of the
saddest chapters in the legal history of the West" [Levack, *The Witch-
Hunt in Early Modern Europe*, 236].

Although "witchcraft theory" was formulated mainly in the
1400s, in Western Europe, the main witch-hunting period was from
about 1560 to 1670; in Eastern Europe, it continued for another century beyond that. The area with the most witch hunts was greater
Germany, including Switzerland, with perhaps half of them. Roughly

80% of the victims were women. Approximately half of those accused were executed. The rest of the convicted were either banished or forced to perform penance or meet other requirements to regain good standing in their church.

Estimates of those executed for witchcraft have ranged widely, but most historians place the numbers at around 100,000 accused and 50,000 executed. Anne Llewellyn Barstow includes a table conveying the best-known data about the destruction attributable to witch hunts [*Witchcraze: A New History of the European Witch Hunts*, 179-181]. (Her appendix B provides a site-by-site accounting of what she could find about the number of accusations and executions, and their gender breakdown, across the various territories in Europe.) But Barstow believes that there are good reasons to extend those numbers to 100,000 executed (which is also Voltaire's estimate) out of about 200,000 arraigned on the charge of witchcraft [Barstow, 22-23]. Her reasons include that many cases were never recorded; many records have been lost or destroyed; many trial entries do not specify how many were tried; and new cases are still turning up. And, some of the totally missing records are from places known to have had witch hunts. On the death side of the ledger, many records do not give the outcome of the trial(s); accused witches who died in prison are not counted—and, by today's standards, an unexpectedly large number died in prisons which were dark, drafty and often cold, damp, vermin-infested, etcetera, while jailers fed them bread and water and otherwise often treated their prisoners poorly (unless the prisoner had money and outside help for better food, etc.). There were also some suicides (especially where torture was the alternative); some died from the torture; and there were some cases where mobs took matters into their own hands [Barstow, 22-23].

CHAPTER 10

The Original Witchcraft

Some aspects of witchcraft in the human mind are almost undoubtedly rooted in the animism of some of our earliest ancestors struggling to survive in a mixture of grasslands and trees (i.e., a savanna), because some of those aspects are common across many cultures, both "primitive" and more modern. Aspects of the environment were invested with spirit and spiritual powers, and so also were some other people (most obviously, e.g., in the shaman or their equivalent). These spiritual powers could be dangerous, or helpful, or benign. In most cultures, there most likely were all kinds, even if some were located largely at the periphery of the culture.

In medieval Xtian civilization, there was a fear that some people had control, by some magic, over spirits or demons who could be told to bring harm to others, whether directly on the person or as an attack on livestock or crops. For example, fears of magical powers in a neighbor's curses were commonplace among the masses (mostly rural peasants but some townspeople as well) well into the modern period. But amongst these masses, there was also a distinction was made between "white magic" and "black magic." White magic was used for constructive purposes, such as healing the sick. And it was a person sufficiently skilled in maleficia, or black magic, who could call upon evil spirits to do one damage.

Heresy Blended in

Over time, more and more extreme versions of heresy became assigned to witchcraft. That the medieval Roman Catholic Church did not choose either of the more benign methods of reacting to different religious beliefs—such as syncretism (the original Roman model), or tolerance—was a major factor in the development of some if not many of the religious aspects of this cultural insanity. Instead, the Church encouraged the Roman Empire to suppress other religions as well as variants on Xtianity by force, leaving the orthodox version of the Church as the sole authority in religion. In the process, the appropriateness of such Church power-seeking became incorporated as an assumption by almost all Church leaders. In the High Middle Ages (1050-1300) the Church again spread the fear of "heresy" among the secular rulers of society. The Church was the only avenue to salvation/ heaven, and the secular leaders were the deity's choice too, else they would not be in power. Secular leaders, who occasionally had brandished cries of "heresy" in political cases, were easily persuaded that heresy (opposition in some way to their deity, per the Church's rulings) was equivalent to treason, some as early as the late 1100s. Cooperation with secular authorities and the doctrines and procedures developed in establishing the Inquisition to combat heresy, promulgated in the early to middle 1200s—including the use of torture—were important elements over two hundred years later in witchcraft prosecutions. Indeed, as explained below, these "trials" had even fewer protections for the accused.

Moreover, all of the above is occurring in a context of a religion *supposedly* based on two main precepts: loving the Xtian deity first and foremost, and "doing unto others as you would have them do unto you"—while "turning the other cheek" if need be. A great portion of that message was distorted if not almost obliterated by the Church as an institution, in part by its undue inclusion and emphasis on the ways and mores of the Old Testament, despite not only the immense doctrinal differences between that and the New Testament, including (as the Cathars had it) the great differences between the identity, character, attitudes, and the deity's behavior described in the two testaments.

Some decades before the worst of the witch hunts, Desiderius Erasmus' characterization of the Church's behavior in the early 1500s illustrates both the power-hungriness of the Church and the Old Testament character of its justifications. War is bestial, conducted by bandits, and impious, "yet our popes, neglecting all other concerns, make it their only task." Moreover:

"Learned sycophants will be found who will give this madness the names of zeal, piety, and fortitude, devising a way whereby it is possible for a man to whip out his sword, stick it into the guts of his brother, and nonetheless dwell in that supreme charity which, according to Christ's precept, a Christian owes his neighbor." [Erasmus, *The Praise of Folly*, translated, with an Essay & Commentary, by Hoyt Hopewell Hudson, 100-101.]

CHAPTER 11

Several Church Laws & Doctrines Needed Changes to Fit Witchcraft Theorists' Views

In this section, I will show some of the changes in Church/canon law and doctrines that were needed before witchcraft became what it was to become at its height, for the 100+ years following 1560. Apart from the broadening scope of what was heretical, the changes involved more stumbling around than directionality until the early 1400s. It is worth remembering here too that medieval Xtian theologians could interpret Bible passages allegorically whenever they "needed" to do so to make their argument, except that, had other important Church personages treated the same passage earlier, they would be expected to take that into account or show that their case was an exception [Walter Stephens, *Demon Lovers: Witchcraft, Sex, and the Crisis of Belief*, 141. Chicago: University of Chicago Press, 2002].

Magic

People involved with the Church, like others in Xtendom [Christendom], recognized a distinction made between white magic and black magic, but the most official positions, enunciated by Church fathers and doctors were that the source of the *any* magic power was linked to the Devil, and hence heretical. Among the authorities here were Augustine, Bishop of Hippo, during the Xtian Roman Empire period, and Thomas Aquinas, during the High Middle Ages. Thomas Aquinas added that the Devil and his demons cannot be mastered by people [Joseph Klaits, *Servants of Satan: The Age of Witch Hunts*, 36]. *At first though, this kind of thinking was mainly applied to sorcerers—* people purportedly causing evil or suffering to befall others. Vaguely on the borderline here was necromancy. Back when witchcraft trials were few and far between, the Church had forbidden necromancy, a dilettantish practice involving a few learned people (mainly including churchmen) trying to find the incantations to conjure up demons and have those demons do their bidding, but for good. It was the solidifying of the equation, and later the application of it, that all white magic was as bad as black magic—even though the latter supposedly drew on the power of the Devil for *evil* purposes and was necessarily heretical—that ultimately provided the groundwork for defining anyone involved in any way with magic as being not just conjurors of spirits, but heretics too. In a context in which almost all the informal healers of all the lands of Xtendom included white magic as part of their healing arts (such as amulets, charms, special conjurations, incantations, etc.) as part of their healing arts, these altered definitions and practices would have some dire consequences.

Despite the close parallels, Church magic, such as the miracles performed through the priestly administration of the sacraments or the prayers for healing to saints, was not included in the definition of (white) magic. For example, the Catholic priest, using a few formulaic words in Latin and going through certain specific motions, could purportedly convert a wafer to the flesh of Christ. The Church formalized its doctrine about this particular sacrament at the Fourth Lateran Council in 1215, asserting that this transformation, which needed a special name, "transubstantiation," occurred *in reality.* (Aquinas later clarified that the wafer retained its Aristotelean "accidental" properties such as appearance.) Yet this doctrine remained one of the areas of doubt for some of the most learned churchmen, as well as some laypersons. For priests and laypersons alike, the wafer still tasted like a wafer, and for priests, the wine went on tasting like wine and affecting them like wine. (Congregants' partaking of the wine had been discontinued somewhat earlier and was restored only much later.)

People today could also readily apply the term "magic" to some of the other medieval Church doctrines or beliefs. How do the bones of saints, fragments of the true cross, the holy lance, or the Virgin Mary's milk (all relics) help in healing? In actuality, about as well as tiger bones help in Chinese medicine today. Or how does "holy water" help to ward off evil (or wolf bane or garlic, when it comes to werewolves and vampires)? Many a king was even attributed the power to cure scrofula, a form of tuberculosis of the neck with visible symptoms. Though kings had the deity's certification (by virtue of being empowered), it was never, and could never be, clear when healing the sick or otherwise producing good miracles might be drawing on the power of the deity and not the Devil.

The Flight of Witches, and Their Gatherings

In the 1140s, Gratian developed a systematic and convenient compilation of Church law, which is called "canon law." This compilation drew on Roman law, much of which was shared by the Church from the days of its fusion with the Roman Empire, and on the law codes promulgated by Eastern Roman Emperor Justinian while he controlled some or much of Italy from 535-562. On the religious side, canon law drew on the writings of the fathers and doctors of the Church, on decisions by Church councils, and on the bulls and decretals (official statements and decrees) of the popes over the centuries. Drawing on the techniques of the dialectical method demonstrated so effectively by Abelard in the early 1100s (see the next part), Gratian brought the Church sources all together and tried to resolve conflicts or opt for the best path from among them [Nathan Schachner, *The Medieval Universities*, 154-155]. Many of his syntheses proved to be quite satisfactory to the Church.

These earlier syntheses, even as modified by Thomas Aquinas, did not allow for bodily flight of witches. Instead, from canon law around 900, the beliefs of a pagan religious cult involving women who said they rode certain beasts great distances to gatherings with the Roman goddess Diana were deemed "delusional," or a matter of dreaming. It was all in their minds. Bodies did not travel "great distances" thusly. But they were heretics for their belief in another deity [Stephens, 126-127], though not in a way that was a serious threat to the Church.

Accordingly, witchcraft "theorists" had to modify Church doctrine if witches were to be said to engage in flight-related activities in reality, and not simply be delusional. Ultimately, witches were to fly to a sabbat (like the sabbath, but with the Devil), conspire against society in the company of other witches, engage in Devil-worshipping and counter-sacramental activities, join in orgies with each other and with demons and perhaps even have sexual intercourse with the Devil, kiss the Devil's backside, eat unbaptized babies, etcetera. The new version of the Devil was to become the cloven-hoofed, goat like creature with which we are most familiar, as contrasted with an older-style Devil shown in Plate 2.1. (Some or all of these changes became parts of the stereotypes held in various times and places when witchcraft accusations included sabbat-related witch activity.)

Moreover, the witchcraft theorists had to modify and/or distort Church doctrines in spite of some additional information that they knew about.

Early Tests of Witches' Flight

Accounts of observation of women who said they flew to their witchy gatherings are reported in two different works by witchcraft theorists Alonso Tostado (from 1456) and Johannes Nider (printed in 1475 though perhaps written almost 30 years earlier). Both accounts involve people observing a woman who claimed to fly while she slept (possibly anesthetized by some narcotic-like substance in an ointment). In both cases the woman, when she awoke, reported that she had indeed flown and had gone to a witch-like gathering, but the observers in the room disabused her of the notion. "Initially, [such] experiments were interpreted as proof that witches did not and could not fly/go to a gathering. But this failure was a major problem for witchcraft theorists, so such experiments were "interpreted double negatively as evidence that transvection [bodily flight] and the Sabbat were *not unreal*, despite an appearance of unreality" [Stephens, 145]. And witchcraft theorists could and did use their most conclusive "proof," namely the account in Matthew and Luke of the Devil carrying Jesus to the top of a temple, and then to the top of a mountain to show him the whole world that could be his were he to join the Devil's side. Hence, such things must still be occurring in the present time [Stephens, 151]. They could then proceed to offer as proof the confessions of a large number of witches (Tostado claimed 1,000 confessions, an implausibility for his time if it is understood to mean *flying* witches).

Body-to-Body Contact with Demons & the Devil

Early Church doctrines did not allow for body-to-body contact with demons or the Devil because they were purely spirits. They had no corporeal existence. But Aquinas accepted the idea that special agents of the Devil, called incubi and succubi, could interact with people in sexual ways, with incubi engaging sexually with women, and succubi with men (collecting their sperm if needed because these demons don't have sperm).

Plate 2.1: An older-style Devil (eating people, center of lowest panel in the mosaic dome) from the Baptistry building in front of the Cathedral, Florence, Italy. Photo by the author.

Still, this was all pretty much theoretical—derived from the Bible, Augustine, and from wrestling with Aristotle's views about many topics. no one at the time applied it to anything much in reality. But, once Aquinas got sainted in 1323, and as his massive summation of theology got more or less fully but not yet officially accepted by the Church in a fairly short time thereafter, those special agents of the Devil became more important. Although others may have preceded Heinrich Kramer in working with Aquinas' ideas about demons, it was Kramer, in writing the *Malleus Maleficarum*, or "Hammer of Witches" (along with Jacob Sprenger), who wrote the first grand case in support of the idea that demons could take bodily forms, and engage sexually with humans. And those who engaged with these demons were almost exclusively women, because of their susceptibility to demons, due, he said, to their weaker reason and greater emotionality, and their insatiable sexuality (see more below).

Why Suddenly Witches, Starting around 1400?

Kramer also felt obliged to explain why witchcraft, while always present (witches are mentioned in the Xtian holy book), had grown into a much larger scale after about 1400. Kramer argued that sinfulness had increased since 1400. Before around 1400 the Devil had to recruit unwilling victims. Only since 1400, "had large numbers of people actually volunteered for satanic service" [Kramer and Sprenger, cited in Klaits, 45]. And by impregnating a witch, the Devil could produce additional minions to continue his work, accounting for the increase in witches.

Proving It All

Confession was the highest form of proof in Roman law. Starting around 1100, something close to Roman law was slowly adopted all around western Europe, England excepted [Hastings Rashdall, *The Universities of Europe in the Middle Ages, Vol. 1*, edited by F. M. Powicke and A.B. Emden, 87-175]. In Roman law, absent a confession, two eyewitnesses were technically needed for conviction. Witchcraft theorists thought that witches' confessions would demonstrate the reality of demons, and also that witches' confessions of their abuses of the Church's sacraments would prove that those sacraments had real power (why not simply ignore them otherwise). Moreover, if witches also gathered for devilish rites and rituals, then there were eyewitnesses to report on who else had been there and what they did.

What we see here is that witchcraft theorists slowly laid the groundwork (some of it largely without an intended direction at first), and then concocted elaborate scenarios involving witches, partly based on compilations from previous confessions, in order to help prove the truth of Church teachings, including its demonology as a cause of evil in the world, and the efficacy of Church sacraments. Lots more confessions were all that was needed for an even better proof. According to Walter Stephens, for some of these theorists, these efforts were probably to assuage their own doubts, by producing a personalized pseudo-experiment vaguely within the scholastic intellectual tradition of the time, based on the idea of the confession as the standard of truth. But because it ultimately put many innocent lives at stake—the lives almost entirely of powerless people, mostly women at that, particularly those who were despised as dirty peasants by men with power—it was more like a cat playing with toys. The cultural insanity of all this will become even clearer as we proceed.

Early Witchcraft Cases

Occasional cases of maleficia (harmful magic against people or property) were never totally absent. Michael E. Goodich asserts that trials of witchcraft and magic before 1400 were "almost invariably directed against dangerous political foes" [Michael E. Goodich, *Violence and Miracle in the Fourteenth Century: Private Grief and Public Salvation*, 79. Chicago: University of Chicago Press, 1995]. But the most relevant early cases of witchcraft are ones in which it came to pass that more than the simplest maleficia was involved. These are the cases that, in time, would be compiled to a much more all-encompassing version of the witch.

As one might expect, and in parallel with the evolving changes in Church doctrines, the cases that were to be used by witchcraft theorists in developing their theories appeared over a considerable period of time, more than 100 years in all. Because churchmen were linked all across medieval Xtendom, and because all official writing was in Latin, information could circulate among them. However, at the time, everything written had to be copied by hand, so that circulation was slow—until the advent and spread of printing in the late 15th century.

Among the earliest cases of witchcraft that could have been used to cumulate part of the eventual synthesis was one that occurred in Ireland in 1324. Dame Alice Kytler and associates were accused of many maleficia, but "also of belonging to a sect of heretics that met secretly at night, renounced the Christian faith, and made sacrifices to demons. Alice, moreover, was accused of copulating with her own personal demon" [Levack, 38]. Although the charges were likely to have been politically motivated, they demonstrate how maleficia relied on magic, which drew upon the forces of evil (e.g., demons), and could also now involve copulating with the demons. This case for the first time reflects the belief that perpetrators of maleficia could be "organized in a devil-worshipping heretical sect" [Levack, 39]. In fact, this case is so far advanced for its time toward the eventual set of stereotypes imposed on "witches" that it makes me doubt whether it much circulated from a far-off corner of Xtendom to other churchmen or, if it was circulated, whether it was forgotten out of lack of interest at the time.

Another early case, in Bern in 1397-1406, also began with a maleficia charge (destroying crops, killing cattle). But under torture, the man also confessed to "summoning up demons and to membership in a heretical sect of Devil-worshippers. The members of this group also purportedly renounced their faith in Christ, and killed babies by magical means, using the remains to make magical potions" [Levack, 39].

Levack describes the charges of apostasy (leaving one's faith) and Devil-worshipping as having originally been ascribed by monks to heresies, in the 12th and 13th centuries [Levack, 40]. By the 14th century, he says, such charges were associated with magic and maleficia, and no longer with the heresies because more became known about the reality of heretics like the Waldensians (who were true believers, but in an only slightly heterodox version of the faith). And by the start of the 16th century, the witch stereotypes were no longer limited to things like simple ritual magic (the conjuring up of demons); apostasy and Devil-worshipping charges became associated almost solely with witchcraft. Although the basic elements of the cumulative concept of witchcraft, including flight, had appeared by the middle of the 15th century, says Levack, a careful compilation of all the pieces was not yet in place [Levack, 46]. Each would-be witchcraft theorist had a limited set of cases and witch-prosecuting judicial acquaintances to draw upon.

CHAPTER 12

Women; Women and Witch-hunting

The Extreme Focus on Women in Witch-hunting

Almost any historical focus on the treatment of women from a perspective involving cultural insanity is tricky. Historically, at least since the time of the Greek Athenians in the West, and on through the time of the Roman Empire, the treatment of women has involved a kind of ingrained cultural inequality. By our reckoning, we cannot emphasize the common denominator of inequality here as an active cultural insanity, because it is thoroughly buried. That is, we would be imposing modern beliefs and judgments on a time when few if any had any clue about the greater potentials of other forms of social organization in which women were more liberated. Moreover, the conditions necessary to sustain society differed substantially from those in the present day. For example, in medieval times, many more children were needed for enough to survive to maturity to sustain or increase the population. And if many more children are needed, women necessarily will have to bear them, and everyone would have to live their lives in a social organization that somehow accommodates to that fact.

Women's slightly freer status at the outset of Xtianity can be linked at least in part to the fact that they were "technically" equal in the eyes of the deity. At first, some women played important roles by providing a gathering place in their home, and even helped spread the "word." But it wasn't long before their status returned to more typical levels. Early Xtian leaders such as Jerome and Origin, who allegedly castrated himself, wrote of their struggles with sexual desire, and most "projected the fault on women" [Klaits, 67]. "Tertulian told women, 'you are the devil's gateway,' and John Chrysostom called the deceptively beautiful female body a 'white sepulcher'" [Klaits, 67].

Normally, the further back in time you go, the more inappropriate is the judgment of modern times and moral standards. Still, *among the most important questions to ask here are whether there were other realistic options at the time, and to what extent they were selected, or not selected. Another key question historically is whether decisions taken at the time made matters worse.* If historically the leaders/societies chose options that were more rather than less culturally insane, making matters worse in terms of the development of human potential, and those choices and changes persisted, those leaders and societies would have fallen further into cultural insanity—resulting in an even deeper burial of the underlying problem for subsequent generations. So, as we venture a look at the extreme focus on women in witchcraft, we will need to keep the idea of a cultural regression in mind.

But part of the point here is also to remember that we too, in our times, have largely or completely unrecognized cultural insanities that are besetting us, some of them long term (see Part One). For example, it took more than 60 years after early agitation to allow women to vote for that to come to pass. And when that issue was first raised, it was raised by a small number of radicals—and was not at all something that the empowered in society would choose at that time, so they cannot be said to have rejected a viable alternative.

Women in Society

In short, there was apparently never a time in the history of Western civilization—until the late 20th century in most Western countries—when women had anything like equality with men. Of course there were at least some differences over time, but those before the "High Middle Ages" (roughly 1050-1300) will not be of concern here. There were also differences by country and class in gender roles and expectations. Toward the early part of this period, the Church did take a slow-to-develop major step forward in requiring the consent of the woman for marriage. Most "noble" and aristocratic families, and wealthy families, controlled their daughters' marriages to strengthen the long-term power, status and prosperity of the family, construct alliances to avoid war or gain allies in war, etcetera. In cases where a daughter resisted, there was a lot of pressure exerted on her to accede to the family's wishes. Somewhat similarly, free peasants tried to marry other free peasants rather than serfs, who were more bound to the manor house/lord/estate. In many countries, only widows had any real degree of freedom to make their own decisions and own property (prior to its inheritance by one or more of their male children). Women were otherwise legally subject to their fathers or husbands.

The principal roles for women of somewhat high status were more limited in some respects because of social expectations but they also tended to have relatively more power and respect in public, in part because of how they were dressed and who their husbands were. Clothes varied by social rank, so it was easy to tell who merited deference. In terms of actual power, such women would run their far more complicated households, typically directing some or even many servants. While peasant women took on a wider array of work roles, they very seldom had much choice in them. In general, the Church provided little in the way of models—the Church offered virginity and chastity as highly valued (with nothing else except convents to go with that), along with the role of wife and mother [Klaits, 66]. Although the Virgin Mary, who became a much greater object of religious focus and devotion in the early 1100s, was perhaps useful in providing a major female religious figure to whom to appeal in prayer, she wasn't a realistic model for the vast majority of women, except in terms of motherly love and perhaps piety. Similarly, most female Catholic saints were virgins [Klaits, 66].

Through most of this period, the Church recognized sex only for purposes of procreation (i.e., a desire for or at least an openness to having children); indeed, some monks/churchmen wrote against engaging in sex for pleasure, and almost all looked askance (or worse) at any sign of sexuality in women beyond child-bearing age. Church doctrines along with the yearly Church calendar of Sundays, Saints' Days, Lent, etcetera, technically prohibited sex on perhaps half of all days [see the "Sexual Decision-Making Process" table by James Brundage in Steven A. Epstein, *The Economic and Social History of Later Medieval Europe, 1000-1500*, 147]. No sexual position was acceptable except the missionary position, though at least one writer noted that being too fat to engage in missionary-position sex allowed people to resort to the standard animal position instead. Women were never supposed to be on top—that violated all male-dominant norms. Interestingly, Church doctrine did recognize that husband and wife had a sex-related duty to each other to fulfill, barring special circumstances. Women's contribution to the genetic pool/conception (the ovum) was not recognized at the time; sperm were regarded as the generators of new life, while the womb mainly provided the environment (sometimes likened to an "oven") for its growth. Men were more or less spooked by women's menstrual periods, and found them disgusting, impure, and yet more evidence for women's inferiority (Barstow, 136).

In the earliest part of this time period, roughly 95% of people lived in villages, tiny towns, and rural areas, with Italy and later

Flanders (in the vicinity of Bruges and Ghent) being the most citified. In most rural areas, there wasn't much of a money economy until the 1100s. Although agricultural advances would slowly bring important changes to these rural areas (e.g., the spread of water mills, the harnessing of horses to the plow, and changed agricultural practices, including less land left fallow), the development of industry and higher civilization was to occur mainly in the towns, driven in part by wealthier aristocrats wanting what were then luxury goods [Peter Spufford, *Power and Profit: The Merchant in Medieval Europe*]. So, among the vehicles for progress were the changes in expectations of the wealthier classes, especially after victorious papal crusaders established crusader states in the Middle East and fostered the greater development of trans-Mediterranean trade. In time too, craftsmen's production in commercial enterprises in the cities was fostered and, before long, that was occurring in a guild context.

Guilds were organizations of workers in a particular trade or component thereof, somewhat like a union today (e.g., the cloth production trade was subdivided into several guilds). Initially (back around 1100) guilds began as mutual support burial societies with some other social activities for members. From such starts, they then developed additional functions and strengths. By 1200 in many places, guilds had become powerful enough to control production, quality and price in their trade, albeit subject to city oversight. Trade workers were structured into three classes: master, journeyman, and apprentice. Apprentices were mainly adolescents learning the trade; journeymen had learned most of the trade but had not passed the final test(s) of production that would qualify them to be a master and to own a shop or to take on apprentices. Only the masters were likely to be able to do well economically, though journeymen did well enough to support themselves except in harder times. As we move into the 1300s and later, many of the medium to large guilds also developed "confraternities" that supported a chapel and priest for that guild within the local cathedral or church. On some religious festival days in cities and towns, participants in festival processions were arranged according to their status and power in a town, so that the highest ranked nobility and churchmen and city authorities led the procession and the more important guilds marched ahead of the less important ones, each carrying its insignia at the forefront. In many cities, wealthy merchant traders (not craftsmen, though some had leadership positions of the most important guilds), were part of the oligarchy that ran the city.

Although guilds were mainly dominated by men, there were some trades, like work with silk, that were dominated by women and had guilds consisting primarily of women, though they would not be high in any civic power structure. A few guilds were split between men and women if both played a major role in the trade (e.g., tapestry weavers). In addition, in the High Middle Ages (before about 1300) wives whose husbands had died were usually eligible to run their business subsequently and were included in the relevant guild like other members (though not necessarily with full membership rights). Later, however, women were mostly squeezed out of direct participation in guilds. In some countries, women were also responsible for work such as ale-making and many engaged in selling bread in the market.

Although medieval history is not without an occasional well-educated woman, and an occasional powerful woman, usually either in a convent or in a family of high aristocrats or monarchs—for the most part education was much more limited for women, with aristocratic and wealthier merchants' families to some extent excepted (usually per the father's choice). Some women did of course learn in convents. But convents took in few or no poor women—somebody had to provide an endowment to pay their way. Although women in convents were mostly confined there, communications with their families provided an outlet for some, and writing provided an outlet for a very few.

Exclusion of women was also the case in the universities. Because the main goal of a university education was to study to be in the clergy, at least initially, and women could not be members of the clergy, that kind of education was less relevant for women—except that there were no real alternatives to the "general education" aspects of university curricula (though some of them might also be learned in convents), so women's education was often based on what the mother/family could teach. But access to a university education was also essential to become a doctor (such as they were), as well as a lawyer, whether of civil or canon law—professional occupations also denied to women. And, as the High Middle Ages proceeded, a university education became more important for other positions too, such as being on the administrative staff of rulers (such situations had greatly multiplied since being filled almost exclusively by clerics in earlier times). And not until the early 1400s did Christine de Pisan (1364-ca.1430) formally make the argument in her relatively famous (but not yet press-printed) books that women weren't weaker of mind than men, but were simply and typically deprived of the opportunity for an education.

In the early High Middle Ages, peasant women in agriculture shared with men almost all the tasks involved in working the land at least some of the time, though they also regularly had to deal with the young children and the cooking and the cloth-making (especially carding wool, spinning, and weaving) and the garden and the domestic animals—except when work animals were in the field. So women worked nearer the home, and spent much less total time in the fields. They were obliged to be a sort of Jill-of-all-non-trades. Men typically did more of the heaviest labor and engaged in any non-domestic skilled trades that they knew, including doing repairs, building structures, putting in mandatory time for the lord in his fields or at the manor, etcetera. Well more than a few peasant and poor women, and men, became servants or staff at the landowner's manor house, and in the castles of the higher nobility. But female servants as housekeepers, cooks, child care providers, etcetera, were predominant among the wealthier classes in the cities and towns. At the lowest end of the spectrum, besides being servants, women did things like serving as laundresses that accompanied crusades and armies (that was needed to help control the lice), day laborers (though a vast majority of these were men), and prostitutes. Later in the High Middle Ages, with advances in mechanizing looms, weaving was done mainly by men and most cloth was purchased rather than assembled from scratch for purposes of clothes-making.

Among the reasons for including the above sketches is that women's rights in society in many respects tended to be further reduced in the Late Middle Ages and on into early modern times. As noted, for example, their participation in trades and guilds was reduced. After about 1200, though, a number of groups of more independent but pious women called Beguines formed self-controlled communities (beguinages) that supported themselves economically (often with the help of an initial endowment of land and housing from a wealthy widow or other benefactor) and engaged in social service such as hospital work. But suspicions grew as the years went by and the Church clamped down on them to a considerable extent (including tossing around heresy charges and occasionally pursuing them, effectively disbanding some or requiring that they have greater Church supervision). But some survived as largely independent entities, becoming among the few outposts providing some freedom for women without confinement to go with it. Their behavior had to be highly circumspect (including chastity) and their rules were fairly strict, but not without some flexibility. More laxity probably returned as the Church's strength ebbed from a variety of difficulties starting around 1300. but in some respects the crackdown on women's rights and freedoms was to resume with even more vigor during the Counter-Reformation (and Reformation).

In the longer term, the treatment of women by the Church involved a pattern of practices that tended toward the culturally insane, even after discounting the stances toward women that Xtianity inherited, that tended to hold women back where advances might have been made and sometimes further limited the potential of women to contribute to society. For example, in addition to their treatment of the Beguines, the Church on several occasions cracked down on nuns who tried to serve society outside of convents. Still, it was often nuns, supervised by a priest of course, who staffed the hospitals of the day. After the Reformation began, the Protestants were to offer little or nothing in the way of improvement *except* for liberating women in convents and a greater respect for marriage (in part to confine lustful sinning) in the deity's scheme of things. Still, "*Luther* regarded the wife's subordination to her husband as God's curse on the female of the species for the sin of Eve" [Keith Moxey, *Peasants, Warriors and Wives: Popular Imagery in the Reformation*, 121. Chicago: University of Chicago Press, 1989]. And, in time, both Catholic and Protestant states were to crack down on deviation from approved behaviors and mores.

Celibacy's Role in Limiting the Potential for Women's Development

Today Catholic clergy are officially celibate and abstain from sexual activity. They aren't supposed to masturbate either, that too being a sin. I don't know how much self-fondling was required to be labeled as masturbation by the Church in the Middle Ages, but I remember it greatly struck my funny bone many years ago when I went to use a urinal and on the wall above it was written, "more than three shakes is masturbation." Whenever it was that the celibacy-for-all-clergy stance actually became the *official* doctrine of the Church, it was not always so in practice. Monks, given their isolation in monasteries in rural areas, probably were largely celibate, at least with respect to women, and that had likely prevailed for centuries—though not without occasional major transgressive incidents or arrangements or situations involving women (sometimes involving nearby convents).

But one of the papal "reforms" launched in the 1060s was to insist on a celibate priesthood too—no marriages, no concubines (live-in sexual partners), and no unattached live-in female servants. Probably chief among the reasons for this insistence was to have priests devoted entirely to the Church and not to family. But political considerations also entered in as the papacy supported rebel factions in Milan who were opponents of the practices of a bishop who had been appointed by the Holy Roman Emperor. A celibate priesthood may also have been more the expectation among the people, at least in the few cities in Italy, where the history of monasteries and celibacy was longer. But many of the priests were unsatisfactory as conveyors of religious doctrines to the more sophisticated levels of the urban audience too. Indeed, in general, urban dwellers had a questionable place in the great scheme of things. At the time, the sociocultural scenario consisted mainly of people with positions in the Church (people who prayed), knights-nobles (people who fought), and peasants (people who labored). People of the towns were at least somewhat more worried about their status with respect to their Xtian deity. (For example, what exactly was "usury" anyway? Lending at interest was technically forbidden, but what about joint ventures with a higher percentage going to the primary funder? How much profit from a sale of a craft item was usurious? How rich is too rich, when the odds of a rich man getting to heaven were the same as that of a camel passing through the eye of a needle?)

But to this papal insistence on celibacy from the 1060s on, there was considerable resistance, especially in the German parts of the

Holy Roman Empire where priestly marriages were not unusual. And there was considerable resistance from these churchmen and the Holy Roman Emperor. Although being blessed and crowned by the pope added to the aura and sometimes helped ensure the authority and power of the emperor, the first Holy Roman Emperor—Charlemagne— was empowered by virtue of his conquests, including of the Lombards (Germanic tribe that had for about two centuries ruled Lombardy), in response to pleas from the pope. And although the pope crowned him as the first western Holy Roman Emperor, it is disputed historically whether or not he desired that blessing (which could set a bad precedent for the ruling dynasty). In any case, for hundreds of years before that title had been assumed on all sides to belong to the ruler of the eastern Roman Empire (Byzantium), with its capital at Constantinople, who at that time still ruled over parts of Italy. Apart from its usage by the emperor of the Byzantines—who headed both church and state—it was not clear in the West whether the pope or the Holy Roman Emperor had more authority in the eyes of the deity, but the emperors did not see themselves as being below the pope in such authority, particularly in the struggles between the two. Through about 1250, emperors were often in conflict with the pope, mainly on matters such as who can appoint bishops and who rules what parts of the Italian peninsula. And although more than one emperor had replaced a pope, or had intended to but only succeeded in displacing him from Rome for a time—in the early 1000s, the emperor had sometimes done so quite clearly to the benefit of the Church.

The celibacy of the clergy very likely helped to exacerbate the rationales in support of witch-hunting and the practices of the actual persecutions and prosecutions. The clergy being all-male, there were going to be few indeed who could fully empathize with what it was to be a woman in the society, the more so once long-term spousal relationships were barred. Today, of course, priests can at least draw upon their broad experiences taking confession from all classes of people. But then, there wasn't even a mandate until 1215 that everyone should confess their sins at least once a year (and the semi-anonymous cabinet-style confessional did not come into use until the 1500s), so many people did not do confessions, many did so only rarely, and other confessions were surely minimalistic. Plus, spouses probably did not want the other spouse giving confessions about their sex lives.

Also in the early 1200s, the Dominican order of monks was formed, and both they and the Franciscans, unlike other monks, were also chartered as preachers whereas most monks were confined to their monastery estates. Both orders were also mendicants (beggars) and were supposed to mix in with the people, especially in towns and cities—at least partly to provide a counterpart to some heretical preachers (including among the Cathars) who lived a life of truer self-denial. The Franciscans, who arose from a gentle and later sainted Francis of Assisi were well-appreciated by most people for well over a century. The Dominicans were more distant. Their primary work was to know doctrine well in order to better combat heresy, and they were also charged with being inquisitors. Though some Franciscans were also given such assignments and many Franciscans became involved with university education (as had the Dominicans from the start), many Franciscans also tried much more strenuously to adhere to Francis' initial vows of poverty, both in personal terms and as an order, and some later came to adhere to a spirituality that tried to reach the deity without much aid from the Church. The Dominicans were probably at least as removed from the reality of women as secular priests (those not in monkish orders). And some of the leading Dominicans, as inquisitors, were ultimately to have important negative effects on society's perceptions and treatment of women, and especially on the development of an idea of witchcraft in which women, because of their purportedly emotional nature, weak wills, and insatiable sexual desires, were characterized as being drawn to have sex with demons and thus to become the principal plotters in league with the Devil.

Some if not much of what was written about the nature of women was appalling by today's standards. But one can also readily imagine that this is so **in part** because *the monks writing in the High Middle Ages (1050-1300) were writing mainly for each other* (few others could read Latin, and most priests weren't at all well-educated either). In writing they were in essence addressing other monks, trying to help them (and themselves) resist their own sexual urges and, in most cases, that meant their attraction to women. So women were portrayed as over-sexed, beguilers, and evil enticers so as not to blame beleaguered monks trying to live a sin-free holy life of contemplation and prayer and chanting, reading holy texts, practicing ascetic minimalism (sometimes to extremes), and engaging in certain kinds of work. Women were blamed instead of recognizing that the monk's underlying feelings about women were actually the innate drives of a male pushing into consciousness and the direct source of his hunger for sexual activity with women. Never mind too that every Spring (and sometimes other times as well) the monks who worked in the fields undoubtedly saw sexual intercourse among most of the animals around them, including some species with especially randy males. (Almost every monastery had an agricultural estate to support itself, but often that required only a few monks to supervise.) Meanwhile, the official celibacy of churchmen, together with what Jesus reportedly said about lusting after a woman in the heart (it's an adulterous sin, even if the woman is unmarried), undoubtedly contributed to an exaggeratedly negative set of stereotypes about women and their sexuality, most of which came into play in the (later) witch hunts. Thus some or many of these monks' attitudes toward women arose via psychological projection—characteristics they were "obliged" for religious reasons to reject in themselves (sexual desire, seen as lust), they then assigned to women in a very negative way.

Still, it has always amazed me that the medieval Church authors' perspectives on these matters also seem to utterly distort or ignore the realities of adolescent male sexuality, because these writers had to have known about their own physiological history—a history replete with many sexual responses in adolescence, with a physiological-hormonal readiness to launch into an engorgement of the penis at the drop of a bonnet (or equivalent), sometimes resulting in a full erection. In any case, some degree of off-and-on sexual responsiveness is typical during the course of every day for the adolescent male, often as a result of no more than a passing sexy stimulus or thought briefly reflected upon, perhaps the remembrance of the shape or face of some teenaged young lady in the church, in the marketplace, or along the village lanes. Plus the fact, as almost all monks knew from their experience as youths, especially after about 1200 when education became concentrated in the early universities, that the same was true for other young men. The sirens calling to them were in their own mind, even if many females did do some things to maintain some degree of attractiveness (for which they were also condemned in many a sermon against decoration, deception, etc.). Moreover, by the time we have records in the early 13th century of students attending universities—at ages as young as 12-14—it is by no means unexpected that they will seek sexual out-lets/pleasures in the town *even though many if not most of them were studying to be clergy* (most often targeting careers above the level of priest, if only because of their class status). And, in most countries, they were treated legally as clerics (clergy), subject to ecclesiastical/Church law (canon law), not secular law, the minute they enrolled (so punishments tended to be penances and less harsh). Indeed, prostitu-tion, though of course condemned officially by the Church, was seldom heavily suppressed in medieval times, though it was often controlled somewhat with sumptuary (dress) code requirements, restricted to certain portions of a city or kept just beyond city walls. Somewhat later, in London, for example, the baths and prostitutes were even housed on the bishop's land in the suburbs, just across the Thames from the city.

Women were also seen as much less rational and much more emotional, despite some examples of high-status women that didn't fit the stereotype, including noble women who would administer their estates while their men were away at war or for even longer periods while on crusade. Occasionally, women even coordinated the resistance to their besieged castle! There were also examples like the Basque fishermen's wives who would fill almost all of a small community's roles while the men were at sea (attracting the witch-hunter de Lancre in the early 1600s) [Klaits, 70]. No doubt the experiences of Viking wives in the 900s and 1000s had had similar responsibilities. And fishing was a big occupation in the Netherlands in the later parts of the time period here. Women were also weaker physically, of course, which may have helped to promote the other stereotypes in men's minds, since they were clearly "inferior" to men in that regard. Women were also seen as having weaker wills and as being more easily led into temptation, a la the Bible story of Adam and Eve. That women's capacity for orgasm, and sometimes even multiple orgasms, seems to have been recognized in medieval times [Klaits, 68-69], at least in some quarters (including by Albert the Great, ca.1193-1280), may also have contributed to a deeply hidden sense of inferiority among learned men, which, under the circumstances in that patriarchal system, was turned against the women (i.e., who were seen as susceptible to sexual desire and temptation), whilst the men proclaimed themselves better. Later, there were even questions about whether demons could better satisfy women sexually than could men.

Incorporating Stereotypes of Women
into Witchcraft Theory

In sources such as Barstow, Klaits, Levack, Stephens and Waite, much of the "credit" (blame) for compiling an array of negative stereotypes against women into a witch-oriented context goes to Heinrich Kramer and Jacob Sprenger, officially co-authors of the *Malleus Maleficarum*. The *Malleus* is almost exclusively Kramer's doing and was to some considerable extent disavowed by Sprenger. While misogyny in witch-hunting is given primacy by some historians (e.g., Barstow), Walter Stephens is more convincing that Kramer's project was not mainly about blaming women as witches for the world's ills, but about proving Kramer's demonology, which takes up most of the *Malleus*— but that is often disregarded because demons are a non-issue today. Indeed, according to Stephens, the other "witchcraft theorists," both before and after Kramer, were also engaged in the same project— proving that demons existed and that the Church was correct in its demonology, sacraments, and doctrines. Kramer was out to prove demonology, but these demons had to be interacting with someone, and women, more clearly for this Dominican inquisitor-monk than for his predecessors, were the primary somebodies, so he proceeded to catalog every one of the stereotypes imposed on them that would dovetail with his belief in demons.

So Kramer did indeed aggregate much of, and substantially exaggerate, and add to, the specific misogynistic stereotypy of the time (much of it having been generated by monks), that in time came to be associated with witches (and to some greater extent yet with women generally as well). Yet his work did not yet encompass all of the stereotypes that came to be associated with witchcraft. Some other features in time closely associated with witches were even mentioned by others earlier—but perhaps they seemed too far-fetched even for Kramer. For example, Kramer does not include the witches sabbat (a sabbath-like gathering), nor the ideas about witches flying to conspiratorial and orgiastic gatherings of many other witches and the Devil. Kramer makes only a backhanded provision for flight by agreeing with canon law that flight can be delusional, "But who is so foolish as to conclude from this that they cannot *also* be bodily transported?'" [cited in Levack, 43]. It was Martin Del Rio (see table of witchcraft theorists), whose work went through multiple editions, "who systematized the belief which remained vague and marginal in the *Malleus* that witchcraft involved sabbats, that is ritual devotional meetings with Satan himself" [Diarmaid MacCulloch, *Reformation: Europe's House Divided, 1490-1700*, 567].

If the actual situation was indeed as sketched above, then for our purposes we need to take a further look at what the heck these other "witchcraft theorists" thought they were doing, and why. We must do so because, whether they were mainly trying to assuage their own doubts, or had other reasons (including misogyny or simply proving Church doctrines), what they helped launch and perpetrate ultimately produced an extreme and grossly evil cultural insanity. But this cultural insanity could only arise full force *after* their ideas had spread among the other elite who ruled the societies in Europe. Together, they imposed it on the common people.

CHAPTER 13

Sources of a Few Churchmen's Worry and Doubt Arising from Society and from within the Church

I am not as convinced as is Stephens that all of the witchcraft theorists were themselves full of doubts about the validity of Church doctrines, and their own beliefs. As we shall see, many of them are Dominicans—and inquisitors at that—which means they are all among the most highly educated in theology with a charge from the papacy to preach, defend the faith against all comers, and ferret out heresy. It is highly relevant too that a dialectic writing style was the standard for almost all if not all of these writers of theological treatises (disputations). That means that authors laid forth a series of questions, and then set forth all sides of a case, and proceeded to answer those questions (argue) as effectively as they could in support of their favored position (including if they were truly trying to attempt a new synthesis). So what Stephens regards as their "worries" are necessarily included in their writings because that's what the theorists were arguing against as they attempted to prove their own case. Several even bent over backwards to make the opponent's case as strongly as possible, but then went on at great length to counter it, even if most of their arguments were weak (from a modern perspective) and even if, by modern standards especially, they all too often ultimately had to fall back primarily on the views of authority—Church fathers and doctors, and the Bible. The only thing that was tricky was that sometimes they would need to work around or go beyond the interpretation of an important Church father or doctor.

Semi-finally, it seems likely to me that, as Dominican inquisitors, the witchcraft theorists might have had too much time on their hands, and needed more to do. Much of the time period when "witchcraft theory" was written (Stephens' 1430 to 1530) was a relatively slow time for the heretical inquiries and prosecutions, unlike the glory days of inquisitions among the Cathars (1230 to about 1320) and the Waldensians perhaps. The hunts for deviant Beguines and beghards (their male counterparts), and the Spiritual Franciscans as the 14th century got under way had long since finished. And although the Bohemians were a bit of a challenge from about 1410 on, doctrinal differences were small and by about 1440, the moderate Bohemians had won out over the Church-sponsored military crusades against them, garnering an agreement granting acceptance to their variant on Catholicism. What good then were inquisitors if there was nothing to investigate and prosecute?[3] Thus almost all of the early theorists were writing before the Protestant Reformation when there would arise serious challenges to Catholic Church doctrines.

Finally, even if those witchcraft theorists couldn't be sure of the extent to which demons and the Devil played a role in earthly life, they had plenty of proof in their own backyard (i.e., within existing Church records) of the immanence of the Xtian deity, and of the "reality" and importance of their saints as intercessors with that deity. Those proofs

---

3   The absence of much in the way of inquisitorial work reminds me of the very recent opposition of California prison guard unions to easing strict laws because of the likely reduction of the prison population with the associated job losses, and also of the prohibition police many of whom, upon repeal of Prohibition, shifted their focus to exaggerating the harm of drugs (including marijuana) and sought new laws against their purported evils.

were in the form of the thousands of miracles performed in response to supplicants' appeals not only to officially-designated saints, the Virgin Mary, and to Jesus or even the deity, but to local and seemingly holy men or leaders (some of whom were would-be saints for local people). These miracles mostly involved healing of one kind or another, but also "rescue" phenomena, in which supplicants' appeals saved their already-drowned and seemingly dead children, or seamen from shipwrecks, or captured prisoners from execution, or victims of the plague from death [Goodich]. The original reports were not necessarily accepted at face value; instead, they were carefully scrutinized to ensure they met Church criteria. This undoubtedly yielded rejection for most such reports, which were much too spotty and incomplete, but over time thousands were fully certified as meeting the Church's requirements. And might the seeming doubts conveyed by the very nature of their dialectical system for argument, insofar as the doubts actually applied to the witch theorist, mainly involve the author's wondering about the extent of the role of demons in a belief system in which the witchcraft theorists were otherwise satisfied? So, as you can see here, the argument that all or most witchcraft theorists had important doubts about Church doctrine has important weaknesses.

In addition, it may shed some light on the situation to look retrospectively at what happened when witch hunts were abandoned, when any hope for the witch-driven, confession-based proof of demonology was no longer considered viable. Did this change in the status of witches, from real to not real, affect Catholic doctrine substantially? Although I have not pursued this topic—apart from recognizing that Catholics too abandoned any emphasis on witches and witchcraft prosecutions, it is not clear to me that Catholicism abandoned much in the way of fundamental doctrines—at least as a result of the fading of ideas about witchcraft. (Some of its more peripheral doctrines were abandoned as a result of the Reformation/Counter-Reformation [Mark

Greengrass, *Christendom Destroyed: Europe 1517-1648*, 493], but that was before the main era of witch-hunting.) Even if over a long period of time demons faded into the shadows to again become rare (e.g., in an occasional exorcism), saints are still thought to help parishioners communicate with the deity or possibly even intervene on the supplicant's behalf, the Virgin Mary perhaps even more so. Miracles are still required for sainthood. Therefore, it was almost undoubtedly *not* essential to prove demonology in the fashion intended by the witchcraft theorists in order for them to override their doubts and retain their beliefs—although, who knows, some of them might have opted for some Protestant sect if they had had the chance.

Serious challenges to Catholic doctrine did get under way with the start of the Reformation, in 1517. But by about 1524, the last of Stephens' witchcraft theorists had largely completed his work. If there is anything odd going on here, it is that this Protestant challenge did not in any important way deny Catholic demonology or witchcraft theory (see below), even though the *self-selected* Dominican "witchcraft theorists" (a modern label) were on the extreme edge of a spectrum in their own time and otherwise almost totally rejected by Protestants. This thinly-spread second-tier leadership subculture of Dominican inquisitors took an already-considerable degree of (mostly buried) cultural insanity regarding women (one shared by many subcultures), combined with one regarding the existence of witches, to yet greater extremes in both cases. Beyond that, Kramer himself was a poster-boy for all manner of personally questionable and disreputable behavior (see below).

Doctrinal Concerns Affecting the Development of Witchcraft "Theory"

In the High and Late Middle Ages, there were as yet no scientific or widely accepted rational explanations for the natural disasters that befell humankind, or for any of the many other "evils" that occurred. Accordingly, there became a need for some way to resolve "the problem of evil," especially when humans were not directly and clearly the cause, as in war. Why did a hailstorm, or a drought, or rain that wouldn't let up, destroy our crops? Why did this plague beset us, seemingly striking down some good people along with the bad? Why were so many innocent children lost to disease in their earliest years? Why did a pregnancy end in a stillborn baby, or a newborn baby die, especially before baptism (thereby depriving it of access to heaven)? Why did all too many a mother die in giving birth?

And yet such things occurred under the dominion of an Xtian deity who was thought to be good and benevolent (differences between the New and Old Testament were somehow not particularly salient in this regard). This deity was both omniscient/all-knowing (so it knew ahead of time what would happen), and also omnipotent/all-powerful (so it could control anything that it desired to control). If evil occurred, the Xtian deity at least had to have allowed it to happen. The only vaguely viable answer that could be supplied was that the deity worked in mysterious ways that humankind could not fully comprehend; so human inability to understand its purposes was often among the "solutions" offered to the problem of evil.

In fact, this Xtian deity was involved in *everything*. This was not a passive deity just looking down on earth from heaven and watching what happened. The deity wrought several miracles in the sacraments, some administered many times each day. The deity was thought to answer (at least some) personal prayers. Sometimes the deity was thought to have healed the sick, often in response to prayerful requests seemingly conveyed to it by long-dead saints at some shrine, or by Jesus' mother Mary to whom many addressed their prayers asking for intercession. The deity was often thought to be responsible for which side won battles (although this seldom lessened the need for having well-armed and numerous armed forces that were well-led and well-fed), and for relieving sieges by the bad guys by having their army come down with dysentery or some debilitating plague (although such problems mainly happened in the summer, and army commanders certainly knew that). Indeed, until 1215 (when clerical involvement in "ordeals" was banned by the Fourth Lateran Council), the deity could be depended upon to decide for the right in "ordeals by battle," in which one party to a dispute, or his surrogate, physically fought the other party to a dispute, or his surrogate. But that kind of ordeal normally required two fighting men (knights) from the nobility to be involved.

The common people's ordeals were rather different. At least two types have come down to us. One involved grasping a chunk of red-hot fire-heated iron and transporting it a very short distance. If, after 3 days or so, the wound had disappeared or showed little scarring, the person was innocent. Another involved binding a person hand and foot and throwing him or her into deep water. If they sank they were innocent, but if they floated, they were guilty. In a way, this was a kind of community judgment because people from the community stood by to rescue the half-drowned person who sank and likely as not, sometimes community views about the person being tried undoubtedly shaped the decision as to whether the person floated or sank. Indeed, this form of ordeal was even used occasionally in witch trials in the 16th and 17th century.

The principal explanations to solve the problem of evil were three [Klaits, 13]. Perhaps the Xtian deity was responsible for some particular disaster because it was punishing us for our excessive sinning or waywardness from belief in it. Or perhaps the deity was testing us, testing our faith, as it reportedly did with Job, with whom it seemed to have been rather cruel. Or perhaps the deity has given considerable freedom to the Devil/Satan and his demons to wreak havoc on earth, perhaps as a way of challenging our faith or our will. But, if so, why? And why, still, were so many innocents allowed to be afflicted? One way or another though, the theology had to leave the Xtian deity with ultimate responsibility.

The Albigensian/Cathar heresy brought some of these questions to a head among some churchmen, because the Church came to regard the Cathars as dualists (Manicheans). Dualists believe in two gods, one of which was evil and created the world and everything in it—such that all material existence was also ultimately evil (including Institutions such as the Catholic Church)—and the other of which was good and pertained to the realm of souls and spirit. Perhaps the label seemed appropriate to the accusing Churchmen because the Cathars did reject the Old Testament. They did so in part because the deity of the Old Testament seemed very different from the deity of the New Testament. But this purported dualism[4] did fully explain why there was evil in the world (though perhaps not why there was also good in the world), and thereby solved the problem of evil in Xtianity (which the orthodox version of the omnipotent deity, even combined with a Devil, could not quite do). Because the Church had no real solution to the problem of why there was evil in the world, anxiety about it may have been heightened by the purported beliefs of the Cathars. Thus one goal of natural philosophy as pursued by the Church and its

---

4   In reality, according to R.I. Moore, probably only a few of the later Cathar perfecti—those at the highest levels of sanctity—*might* have subscribed to this doctrine [R.I. Moore, *The War on Heresy*. Cambridge, MA: Belknap Press of Harvard University, 2012]. But Church theologians, feeling a multi-faceted threat in any religious dissent, simply compiled a wide-ranging list of heresies to ascribe to anyone they considered heretical (i.e., not only to the Cathars)—a list which included the dualist heresy, borrowed from Augustine's writings (Augustine was once a Manichean dualist), that they then ascribed to the Cathars too. Other add-ons typically included sexual orgies as well.

chief theology school in Paris was showing that God and his creation is good [Stephens, 31].

So the problem of evil was one of the major underlying intellectual problems with which the witchcraft theorists were dealing. And over time, it came to be that witchcraft theory would provide at least a bit more of a solution for the problem of evil: The Devil recruited human apostates to do his dirty work—whether involving natural disasters or individual humans. Heretical human witches who voluntarily cooperated with the Devil were the cause of the evil. The Xtian deity still allowed it to happen, because it had allowed the Devil the freedom to wreak havoc via witches, even if the Devil had to capitalize on "original sin" and its stronger association with Eve, and other purported weaknesses of women, in order to do so.

Another factor potentially involved in the problem of evil was that the Church ascribed to humans an original sin—a sin that humans were born with by virtue of being human. This was one of the reasons why baptism of infants was thought to be important (because they were too young to be sinful except for that original sin, but they would not get to heaven without the baptism that forgave that original sin). As it became interpreted by Augustine and others, this original sin had a lot to do with human sexuality, even though it came about from Eve and Adam eating fruit from the forbidden tree of knowledge. Part of that knowledge, apparently, was recognizing and being shamed that they were naked rather than accepting it as a matter of course, like earth's other creatures. Oddly enough too, little children have no shame about their nakedness [Goodich, 58]. Yet, somehow, the biblical shame about nakedness (whatever its actual source) brought all sexuality under suspicion in the eyes of the Church's interpreters. So, although there seems to be a relatively skimpy link between being embarrassed by nakedness and it being a sin to seek out and enjoy sex for its own sake, that too came to be regarded by the Church as a sin.

In any case, this was another way in which the deity was not exactly directly responsible for the problem of evil—humans had brought it upon themselves with one act of disobedience by the supposedly first two humans. So, even though one might remorsefully confess every last sin one committed, it wouldn't be long before one had sinned again by thinking lustful thoughts, or by being prideful, envious, avaricious (greedy), wrathful (angry), slothful (lazy), or gluttonous (over-eating). But only one of those "seven deadly sins" got much play when it came to witches—their insatiable sexual desires. (And, of course, their apostasy in consorting with demons to fulfill those desires.)

CHAPTER 14

A Review and Somewhat Closer Look at the Development and Progress of Witchcraft "Theory"

As noted near the outset, the origins of what might be regarded as witchcraft are obscured in the mists of time. But as to the Late Middle Ages, as also pointed out earlier, Walter Stephens argued that a small number of clerics, some of whom had already engaged in leading witch hunts, publishing from 1430 through 1530, were the early developers of witchcraft "theory" [Stephens, 7]. According to Stephens, these witchcraft theorists were interested primarily in proving the reality of the existence of demons and the Devil. In turn, this would prove not only the existence of the spirit world in general but its involvement in earthly affairs. And this would help to prove Catholic doctrines as a whole, especially those that pertain to the efficacy of the seven sacraments—Baptism, Eucharist, Confirmation, Penance (confession, reconciliation, punishment), Anointing of the Sick (including extreme unction), Marriage, and Holy Orders (to become a member of a Church order such as the Dominicans). According to Stephens, these witchcraft theorists were dealing with "scientific problems of being and knowledge, concerning devils, angels, the human soul, the truthfulness of the Bible, and the evidence of God's existence and presence in the world" [Stephens, 30].

As to the "science" of it, because one of the norms in Roman law was that confession is the highest form of proof, if confessions that witches had consorted with evil spirits could be obtained, it would provide the strongest evidence to erase any doubts by helping to prove Catholic demonology-angelology. Plus, of course, god-fearing men of faith could not go out and experience these evil spirits on their own, so they could only rely on the testimony of those who had fallen prey to evil. (Why their testimony would be considered trustworthy is another matter—especially in view of the earlier Church perspective, that people who thought they had these experiences were deluded or had dreamt it.)

We can see how this works toward the latter part of the witch-hunting era. "With each trial, the belief in the diabolical Sabbath conspiracy was confirmed, the skeptics denounced, and the reality of the supernatural realm proven" [Gary K. Waite, *Heresy, Magic, and Witchcraft in Early Modern Europe*, 155]. Confession by victim-witches that they had desecrated the Eucharist (that is, the "host," an already-blessed wafer constituting the flesh of Christ in Church dogma) and/ or other sacred objects was frequently a mandatory component of a witch confession in Catholic lands—a confession to be elicited from a grueling protocol of questions to be asked, the threat of torture, and the torture routine itself. This desecration of sacramental objects (the host, the cross, etc.) was usually a part of the witches having attended a sabbat ("witches sabbath") where the Devil or demons were present. It was of course the Devil who mandated this desecration of the sacred, and that he did so was thought to prove the efficacy of the sacrament or object.

In the table below, we can see a very large influence of Dominican inquisitors in shaping this cultural insanity. After about 1530, the people shown in the table became somewhat more secular, but by then most of the theory was done and what followed were works that are less oriented toward proving demonology (etc.) and more often designed as trial-and-question manuals, providing more comprehensive descriptions of witchcraft, compilations of the experiences of those who have sent many witches to the stake, etcetera. These implementers of witch hunts are much more secular for at least two main reasons: city and town, regional/principality, and some yet-higher authorities wanted to run their own court systems without interference from outsiders; and *the elite ruling classes had become largely convinced of witchcraft theory and the jeopardy in which witches placed their domain.* We will return to this subject shortly.

The *Malleus Maleficarum* and the Papal Bull Affirming the Existence of Demons Having Sex with People

Heinrich Kramer (and, Jacob Sprenger, but apparently only nominally) authored the most famous witch-hunting manual, the *Malleus Maleficarum* (the "Hammer of Witches") in Latin in 1487, and it was subsequently reprinted a number of times in the years soon after that. Reprintings then ceased for about 40 years, after which a number of additional printings were done. Little of the contents of the Malleus itself was all that new [Klaits, 45]. However, the compilation of anti-women (misogynistic) material was the most extensive yet, the structure was useful for guiding witchcraft prosecutions, and the timing was right for the availability of the printing press—which substantially abetted its circulation, and may have helped to account for its rise to special fame. As above, Kramer was first and foremost trying to prove the existence of demons, but his work is now most famous for its misogyny. To complete his demonology arguments, Kramer apparently felt he had to show why women were readily susceptible to sexually-oriented demons, and so spared no effort in assembling negative stereotypes about women to make his case. As a kind of summary, as the *Malleus Maleficarum* put it, "all witchcraft comes from carnal lust, which is in women insatiable" [Barstow, 135]. At the same time, however, "like the rest of the activities of the Sabbat, demonic copulation served to *anthropomorphize demons*"—they certainly weren't purely spirits [Stephens, 19].

Table Showing Stephens' Principal Witchcraft "Theorists" and Their Successors

Witchcraft Theorist	Affiliation(s)	Date of Work	Stephens' Page No.	Main Emphasis
Nider, Johannes	Dominican	~1437 (printed, 1475)	154-159	Doubted "it's all a dream" canon
Tostado, Alonso	Teacher w/ theology degree	1456	146-159	Some reputed witch flight is real
Jacquier, Nicholas	Dominican inquisitor	1458	21-22	Handbook for inquisitors; it's all real
Visconti, Giralamo	Dominican	1460 (printed, 1490)	23	Demons→sexual pleasure; sabbat
Vineti, Jean	Dominican, inquisitor	1450-1470	23-25	Demons real
Kramer, Heinrich	Dominican, inquisitor	1487	32-57	Demonology "proof" ←→ women
Sprenger, Jacob	Dominican, inquisitor, prof. of theology	1487*		See Kramer entry & text
Mazzolini, Silvestro	Dominican inquisitor	1521	164	Flight to sabbat is real
Spina, Bartolomeo	Dominican hierarchy, inquisitor, prof. of theology	1523	168-175	Witch confessions are good evidence
Pico della Mirandola, Gianfrancesco	Ruler of small territory in Italy	1523	87-94	Many-sided dialog to change skeptics;
with Alberti, Leandro	Dominican inquisitor who translates Pico into Italian	1524	89	witch= expert (+ transl. widens audience)
Grillandus, Paulus	Papal judge	1524	50(Levack)	Became a main source re sabbat
Bodin, Jean	French philosopher	1580	175 (Barstow)	Updates Kramer for secular courts
			Levack's Page No.	
Remy, Nicolas	Judge from Lorraine	1595	51	Detailed sabbat activities; key source
Del Rio, Martin	Belgian/Spanish Jesuits	1595*	51	Encycl.; instructs judges; into French
King James	King of Scotland (VI), then England (I)	1597	59	Witchcraft, demonology [Ackroyd]
Boguet, Henri	Franche-Comte (Habsburg Burgundy) judge	1602*	51	Writes up his judicial experience
Guazzo, Francesco Maria	Milanese Friar	1608	(Stephens 281 or) 51-52	Encyclopedia of witches; illustr.
De Lancre, Pierre	French judge	1612	51	More detail on sabbat; impt etching
Carpzow, Benedict	Lutheran judge from Saxony	1635*	51	Witches in Leipzig courts; Prot. source

*These works (and some of the others after 1487 as well) were printed in multiple editions over time. The date of Del Rio's publication and the "Spanish" identification is from MacCulloch [566]. Ackroyd is not very specific [Peter Ackroyd, Rebellion: The History of England from James 1 to the Glorious Revolution, 9].

The other thing that was special about the *Malleus* is that it was the first work that could include among its arguments that the pope had already issued a decree (papal bull) that supported Kramer's argument. All editions after the first included a reprinting of that papal bull from 1484. The pope's proclamation affirmed the existence of incubus and succubus demons copulating with humans, and a wide variety of maleficia that occurred as a result, such that "they cause and procure the perishing, suffocation, and extinguishing of the offspring of women, the young of animals, the produce of the earth, the grapes of the vine, the fruits of trees...." [cited in Stephens, 55]. The papal bull's list of damages done goes on a while longer in a similar fashion. Innocent VIII's bull (*Summis Disiderantes*) was a milestone in obliging Europe to recognize the existence of a now revised view of witches and their deeds [Stephens, 55].

Even this near-joint appearance of bull and book and their somewhat closely shared basic content can be attributed in large part to the machinations of Kramer (with Sprenger's support?), who sought justification for his witch-hunting after he had run into opposition in Germany for over-doing it and usurping local authority, including of a bishop—who released all 50 of Kramer's suspects [Waite, 43]. Kramer had earlier complained to Pope Innocent VIII that "other authorities were obstructing his inquisitions" [Stephens, 56] and, with the help of a few others, had urged the pope to issue a detailed bull condemning the crime of witchcraft, in order to better support inquisitors in the field who were ferreting out witches. Pope Innocent VIII seems to have become willing to support Kramer because Kramer (who had been on the Pope's negativity list) wrote a piece against another bishop who had called for a Church council meeting independent of the pope, and so the pope expected Kramer to do more writing in that vein rather than write about witchcraft [Waite, 43]. Instead, Kramer not only wrote the *Malleus* but forged documents indicating support for his views by the

University of Cologne faculty, which infuriated Sprenger, who was the provincial vicar of southern Germany [Waite, 43].

The *Malleus* also argued that those who dissented from its view were supporting the evils of witchcraft.[5] And so did most subsequent witchcraft theorists and their supporters.

Getting the Beliefs in Witchcraft into the Minds of Secular Authorities Too

According to Gary K. Waite, "many Church and secular officials preferred the approach of Ulricus Molitor" (or Ulrich Miller), whose 1489 publication on witchcraft re-asserted the older Church stance against the "realist" interpretation [Waite, 44-45]. Infertility in couples was not due to witches. Witches could not control the weather, or fly, and only demonically caused delusions could make them think they did so, because demons "could not suspend the course of nature." But Molitor like Kramer thought women were "incredibly susceptible to the Devil's charms" and that female sorcerers deserved "harsh treatment" [Waite, 45]. Among the most important reasons for secular officials to accept Molitor and reject Kramer was the latter's "advocacy of inquisitorial supremacy over local lords" [Waite, 45]. But, because almost everyone at the time believed in "the reality of magic and demonic forces," it was difficult for opponents to find convincing arguments against Kramer's views [Klaits, 46].

So, then, what else had to happen before occasional witch prosecutions, and even occasional witch hunts by overzealous few inquisitors, became full-blown witch crazes, waxing and waning in many

---

5   History later records a number of stellar examples of this type, including anti-communist witch hunts by Senator McCarthy of Wisconsin and the House Committee on Un-American Activities in the 1950s and 1960s, and the accusations of lack of patriotism cast at opponents of the War on Vietnam in the 1960s and 1970s. Indeed, much the same occurred during President George W. Bush's (and Vice-President Dick Cheney's) attack on Iraq.

places? Printed works by witchcraft theorists had to attract interest or otherwise be circulated and read widely among the elites of societies. Some of those publications would need to be done by secular magistrates who had prosecuted alleged witches, and be written in the vernacular, maybe even with a how-to manual structure adapted to secular courts. Because Church inquisitors could not do it all by themselves in many lands (especially without secular leaders being willing to allow their presence and then to execute the inquisitor-identified witches), time would be needed for the newer witch-related ideas to spread (especially if there were no consistent papal and/or monarchical pushes of some kind in that direction). Indeed, given the *Malleus'* reception at the University of Cologne, more time was needed just to get the university theology and canon law faculties on board. But by a few decades later, the Germany-wide Carolina law code revision of 1532 called for using professional jurists (necessarily having a university background and a church-oriented education) as resources for the prosecution of serious crimes, including witchcraft [Klaits, 138]. And the Carolina's penalty for witchcraft was death [MacCulloch, 567]. These professional jurists, often with Church (or Protestant church) support, were to become the primary inquisitor-prosecutors in Germany—and Germany accounted for about half of all executions for witchcraft [Klaits, 138]. And by the 1570s, law codes in Protestant Saxony, which was often used as a model by other Protestant areas in Germany, no longer even required harm to have been done by the accused witches—their heretical involvement with the Devil was enough to warrant death [Klaits, 57, 134]. Before the 1560s surge in witch-hunting, the punishments of many convicted witches without evidence of harm done to animals or people might include "life imprisonment, public flogging and banishment" [Rothenburg Medieval Crime Museum, *Criminal Justice Through the Ages*,186].

But what is most surprising is the 40-plus year hiatus in publications relating to witchcraft—especially after additional published work on the subject, including by lay authorities, up through the early 1520s. What intervened was the Reformation, such that witchcraft-related concerns were set aside. For that 40-year plus interval, there were some witch prosecutions; but there were relatively few large witch hunts until the 1560s, and then all hell started to break loose, so to speak. After 1560, there is a revival of demonology [Klaits, 47]. The Peace of Augsburg in 1555, which accepted Lutheranism, settled much of the conflict between Catholics and Protestants in which rulers had been engaged. Until then, leaders had their hands full with other concerns. "However, during the 1540s to 1560s, the countless sermons and pamphlets warning the populace of the Devil's evil plots and the nearness of the Antichrist's arrival had worked their magic, reviving fear of diabolical conspiracies" [Waite, 231]. And that helped to bring the new version of witchcraft to the forefront.

Although Protestant theologians rejected Catholic demonology, that was not necessarily true of all of society's leaders in what were to become Protestant lands. In any case, Protestants retained a great emphasis on the Devil and its/his efforts to separate people from their deity via sin. And that emphasis made it all too easy for some Protestant lands to take up witch-hunting too.

CHAPTER 15

Real Threats to Secular Authorities Put Them on Edge; Concern about Witches Fades

As above, but before proceeding, it is important to note that, of the scholars I've read, no one has proposed anything particularly *definitive* as to *why* witch hunts sprang into large-scale existence starting in the 1560s or so. However, there are a number of factors that those who examined this question tend to cite as being relevant to the resulting history.

Most of the sources that I have read (e.g., Klaits, Waite, Stephens, Levack, Barstow) do assign much of the responsibility for the large-scale prosecution of witches to society's elite—after widespread acceptance of witchcraft theory by more of the clergy, the university faculties, and rulers and their magistrates (judge-prosecutors). These rulers include kings, dukes, counts, and princes of all sorts ("prince" is the generic term for all of these rulers), as well as "prince-bishops" who were both rulers of territory and bishops of the Catholic Church. As above, it is mainly the magistrates (judge-prosecutors) of these rulers, or of the cities/towns, who pursued the actual cases. The concern among the rulers seems to have arisen from the fear of a diabolical conspiracy to undermine or overthrow them and their realm. In areas where major witch hunts occurred (i.e., not just prosecution of an occasional alleged witch), most elites were in support—that is, people such as noble and wealthy advisors, town councilors and their advisory councils, local clergy, and most of the educated elite—although that support might dissipate rapidly if prosecutions began to reach the higher echelons of society. The common people, with rural peasants at the end of the line, were the last to know about the aforementioned new views/theories about witch behaviors and deeds. The common people still saw witches as sorcerers who engaged in maleficia. But it was frequently the case that the identification of such seeming evil-doers provided the launching pad for the prosecution of what proved to be a rather different version of "witch."

First though, between the time the Reformation (beginning around 1521, say, when Luther was condemned as a heretic because he was not willing to recant) and the Peace of Augsburg in 1555, there arose a rather large number of real threats to secular authorities. Among those "threats" were the very existence of people of different Xtian religious persuasion in nearby lands ruled by Catholics or, in time, Protestants, with hundreds executed—especially Anabaptists [Lee Palmer Wandel, *The Reformation: Towards a New History*, 151-154]. Before the Peace of Augsburg, whole units of government (cities, states, etc.) would sometimes shift majority religious adherence or change enough to produce a divided population. But in Germany, after the Augsburg peace treaty, Catholic rulers affiliated with the Holy Roman Empire (Germany-Spain and more) no longer prosecuted Lutherans as heretics and Lutherans no longer prosecuted Catholics as heretics. Until then, most likely, this and other threats (see below) kept secular authorities busy during much of this time. Moreover, in France, the Low Countries, and England, active threats involving conflicts between religious groups, or rulers and some of the populace, continued after 1555.

Belief Systems

The Reformation upended the *security* of Europe's *unitary* religious belief system. Yet, as before, secular authorities themselves continued to be endorsed by the Xtian deity—or else they wouldn't have been in the positions that they were in. For many centuries and continuing in Catholic societies, hierarchy was biblically sanctioned and was generally not to be contravened. But there was some social mobility, mainly at the interfaces between social classes (e.g., rich merchants moved into the aristocracy by marrying families with aristocratic pedigrees that were pressed for money). What about Protestants? Until the peasants' revolt of 1525 (see below), Luther sounded more egalitarian than he was to become. However, he had to adjust his theology to disavow the peasant rebellion in order to retain the support of the ruling aristocracies favorable to his religious movement in Protestant-leaning territories in Germany. (In the end, his stance became that any rebellion against state authority was illegitimate.) Overall though, and entirely apart from threats from armed forces allied with the other religious group, no one was as secure religiously as before. After all, which denomination really had the sure route to the afterlife? And what does one do while on earth to ensure one's salvation?

Thus, even where people stayed Catholic, they knew that there was now an alternative, a somewhat different version of Xtianity that some princes/territories, cities, and even countries had adopted. Moreover, the Catholic Church did not finish developing its definitive response at the Council of Trent—the "Counter-Reformation"—until 1563, and there were still attempts to bridge the gaps between Luther and the Catholics at least through the start of Trent in 1545 [MacCulloch]. Similarly, the Protestants necessarily were aware of the system from which they were breaking away. Many common people were hearing sermons like they'd never heard before, that challenged their previous religious beliefs, and sometimes made them angry that they had been duped by the Catholic Church. But were they all sure they were right, especially those less trained in theology? And, again apart from opposing armed forces, some Catholic rulers near to the centers of Protestant changeovers were in danger of being subverted and ultimately ousted from power by religious conversions within their own lands—unless they too converted.

And there was a harsh war of words between the two sides, much of it done with propaganda broadsides (single sheets, usually with an engraved or wood-block drawing), which were relatively accessible to the masses, especially if they could but find someone to read a short piece to them. To Protestants, the pope was the Antichrist or something close to it and the Catholic Church was both corrupt and had massively distorted what the Bible said in developing its dogmas; and the institution's claims about itself were preposterous. In contrast, for example, Luther initially proposed that each man should be his own priesthood—a stance that necessarily leads to splintering and promptly did so as scholar-preachers in various cities (e.g., Zwingli in Zurich) argued over correct interpretation of the Bible. To Catholics, all the Protestants were heretics, technically deserving of death by Church standards of the High Middle Ages and Late Middle Ages (unless they recanted—and did not thereafter relapse). In fact, the German Diet (a parliament-like assembly technically encompassing the whole of Germany in 1529 had declared that all non-Catholics were heretical. It was a this point that the Lutheran princes in Germany, who were in a minority, drew up a formal protest (thus arose the term "Protestants").

In addition, the Anabaptists—one of those splinter groups that differed from other Protestants especially in favoring adult rather than infant baptism—were beyond the pale, reviled and/or seen as heretical by Catholics and Protestants alike. (For the more orthodox churches, infants "had to be" baptized to keep them out of hell should they die soon, to cleanse them of original sin, and/or to bring them into the church community. Most Protestants retained at least the last feature.) Anabaptists were typically driven out of town—the mildest response—and sometimes killed—even in Protestant lands. Presumably they simply left Catholic lands, having no chance of survival there.

Rebellions and Wars

The Peasants Revolt. The remarkably organized rampage that first put Germany's secular leaders on edge, especially in areas that turned Protestant early, was the peasants revolt of 1525. This revolt involved many thousands of peasants arming themselves as best they could, affixing themselves to leaders, plundering the possessions of the aristocracy—and killing some that they caught unawares—and developing lists of demands. Some looked to leadership from Luther or Luther's preachers. This revolt was larger and more organized, at least in terms of military efforts, than any others yet. But there were peasant predecessors in England in 1381, France (Jacqueries) in 1358, and among lower-class townsmen (Ciompi) in Florence in 1378-82. The ruling classes in Germany, especially in the areas affected, after being stunned initially, organized sizable-enough armed forces to attack and destroy the peasant armies which, as usual, had great difficulty standing up to warriors (knights) leading quasi-military forces. The judicial system was then used to pursue and execute escapees and others involved.

Munster. As Anabaptists were driven out or scared out of many a place, often only after becoming somewhat organized and visible (and, hence, sometimes involving a fair number of people), they tended to congregate where persecution was low or absent (usually in more isolated rural areas, away from authority). Preachers of radical equality, nominally still Lutheran, along with some Anabaptist preachers helped to draw more such egalitarians to Munster, a small city in northern Germany. There in time the newcomers supplanted the ruling mayor and the Lutheran magistrates (judges, city councilors), and in 1534 began attracting yet more Anabaptist leaders/preachers and some followers. Because they allowed divorce when one party chose Anabaptism and the other didn't, they drew disproportionate numbers of women unhappy with their spouses to the city such that, ultimately, the population was about two-thirds women. And because of that disproportion, they assigned each woman to at least one male guardian which in some cases produced a kind of legitimated polygyny, or so it seemed to horrified outsiders. Opponents outside the city drummed up support from nearby local rulers to re-take the city by force while the Anabaptists set up a special governing structure to deal with the forthcoming siege. The city fell in 1535 and the Anabaptist leaders were killed. The entirety of the Anabaptist takeover was terribly shocking to outsiders, producing a kind of "never again" reaction. And Catholics also used it as an example of the evils in Protestant lands.

Charles V versus the Schmalkaldic League; France's Attacks on Spain; the Ottoman Empire. As more of the prince and prince-bishop led territories in central, northern and Western Germany went Protestant, they began to fear an attack by Charles V, Holy Roman Emperor & Spanish King, and the dominant power in Italy. He was known as The Catholic Majesty. Charles was the head of the newly-expanded Habsburg empire (the Habsburgs having recently inherited Spain and all its overseas possessions by marriage, after Ferdinand and Isabella left no fully competent heir. Charles let his brother Ferdinand rule over the German portions of Habsburg possessions, and other agents ruled in his stead over the Low Countries, his personal possession by yet another inheritance. So, in 1531 the Protestant territories, already branded as heretics in 1529, banded together into the Schmalkaldic League in case they needed to defend themselves. While the League did little to challenge Charles directly, it did help to continue to convert north German territories and cities to Protestantism, which was economically profitable for rulers and/or ruling bodies because of the sometimes-extensive abandoned Catholic properties, such as monastery lands, that came with a such a religious conversion. Meanwhile, Charles V was otherwise occupied in conflicts with France and with the Ottoman Empire centered in Turkey. France was surrounded on all sides on land by Habsburg possessions and so French kings felt threatened and sometimes took aggressively defensive, or offensive, action against Spain, including with multiple attacks on Italy and Charles' lands to their north and south. Each time France lost in battle to Spain, it shortly recovered enough to attack again, sometimes reneging on promises to the contrary elicited after an earlier defeat. At the same time, Charles was obliged to deal with the expanding Ottoman Empire, and not only in the Mediterranean. The Ottoman Empire had conquered the Balkans south of the Danube in 1459, and their army conquered a large portion of Hungary in a battle in 1526. The Turks then renewed that advance by besieging a German-Habsburg home base, Vienna, Austria, in 1529. Denmark also became Protestant (and was something of a power then with control of much of the Baltic Sea) and Charles V negotiated a separate treaty of peace between Denmark and the Holy Roman Empire, to try to ensure it would stay out of any conflict between him and the Schmalkaldic League.

Although the Schmalkaldic League had sufficient troop numbers and resources to defend itself—partly because it was not easy for Charles V to get a big army there—Schmalkaldic League armies were much less experienced and coordinated and they lost a major battle at Muhlberg in 1546 [Waite, 82]. Charles terms for peace involved punishing Philipp of Hesse and Elector John Frederick of Saxony by stripping them of their estates, but world distractions elsewhere kept Charles from pressing his advantage at the time, and a more modest defeat for Charles in war with the League in 1552 resulted instead in the Peace of Augsburg in 1555. This treaty stipulated that Lutheranism was to be tolerated, thus canceling the decision of the Diet in 1529. But as a treaty applicable within the German Empire, the treaty left out the "Reformed Church" and Anabaptists/Mennonites entirely, even though the Reformed Church was by then well-established in Geneva (under John Calvin) and some other Swiss cities/cantons, and was rapidly spreading elsewhere, including into France and the Low Countries. But in the Low Countries, Charles V had installed a branch of the Spanish Inquisition in 1545—to reconvert or terminate the heretics (many of whom fled those provinces). The Treaty of Augsburg also said that the prince of a territory determined its choice of religion but, once established, that wasn't supposed to change [Waite, 82-83]. Although this provision may have been intended to prevent further loss of Catholic territories, evangelizing and proselytizing continued on all sides, with the relatively new Jesuits Order being assigned to take the lead on the Catholic side.

Is the Apocalypse Getting Under Way?

With all the turmoil associated with the opening of so many questions about what the true faith actually amounted to (even if a person remained Catholic), and with the disorder involved in the Peasants Revolt and Munster, the military advances by the Ottoman Empire in southeastern Europe, plus the long-term threat of a first Catholic-Protestant war that in time occurred, one ready conclusion that some of society's leaders might draw was that the apocalypse might be expected soon. The apocalypse, per a number of fuzzy and figuratively-interpreted "prophesies" in the book of Revelations in the Bible, was to herald the end of time, leading up to the Last Judgment. That it might be underway would seem to appeal especially to Catholics firm in belief because they would have a surer sense that the Protestant confessions were wrong/heretical and, indeed, that their very existence was part of the evidence. The Protestants, having identified the problem as the Catholic Church and its Antichrist-type leadership, also saw apocalyptic times ahead. Interpretations along these lines by either Catholics or Protestants also involved a major role for the Devil, who was to orchestrate the forces of evil, behemoths, the Antichrist, and the armies of Gog and Magog—all of which were finally to be defeated in the end, just before Christ's "Last Judgment." Among Protestants, "Reform Church" leaders perceived a greater, a more immediate threat from the Devil than did Lutherans, and they were more likely than Lutherans in the Holy Roman Empire to resort to witch hunts [MacCulloch, 568]. Accordingly, the fear that the apocalypse was under way, and that the Devil would likely be making extraordinary efforts just now [Waite, 145-146], necessarily threatened civil order. This threat encouraged the elite to promote righteousness in their lands and to find and thwart the mechanisms whereby the Devil sought to overthrow Xtianity in their realm, whatever their version of Xtianity. "Many lords therefore became more amenable to the clergy's warnings of Satanic activities" [Waite, 146].

Jesus had failed to return (let alone as a king or the deity's equivalent thereof) during the lifetime of at least some of the people at first-century Xtian gatherings (who were told by apostles that Christ would return before their entire congregation had died). And he had also failed to come at the millennium (i.e., in 1000 and/or 1033). But those failures did not seem to deter belief in a second coming. Similarly, various smaller segments of the population throughout the High and Later Middle Ages also had thought the apocalypse was at hand and, of course, were wrong. None of this undermined the ready resort to an apocalyptic second coming as a way of explaining the situation at the time. (Almost obviously, there is a major buried cultural insanity involved in apocalyptic thinking—buried because it is both far from consciousness and from any potential for rejection.)

To rulers, this "widespread belief in the nearness of the apocalypse intensified the drive to purify society and establish or reinforce a uniform and unchallenged belief system." And this "required the demonization and eradication of anything that could be construed as offensive to God, especially since" there were already so many natural disasters taken as indicators of "divine displeasure" [Waite, 232]. And those symptoms could easily be attributed to the activities of the Devil and his agents. Thus, to some considerable degree, witch-hunting "demonstrates the success of reforming efforts to energize the lay elites with the ideology of spiritual purification" [Klaits, 71].

So, the Catholic Church, the Lutheran Church and the Reformed Church sought for a clearer and better definition of how a community of the faithful should behave, both religiously and socially. And they tended to impose much stricter codes of conduct during this time period. John Calvin's leadership in Geneva provides an excellent example of the effort to define expected community behaviors in many aspects of life, a development occurring over many years. And a variety of stricter codes were incorporated into Catholicism as a result of the nearly two decades of off-and-on work by the Council of Trent. And so the religious leadership tried to bring into accord with doctrine what their adherents actually believed and practiced and, hence, to eradicate 'peasant superstitions' [Waite, 191]. Similarly, both the religious and civic leadership sought to reduce disorder; they wanted to foster "law and order" (not their phrasing, but their intent). Among the more specific crackdowns were those on blasphemy [Waite, 45-47], and on vigorous earthy dances and public baths in Germany. "The bathhouses ... were very popular and a visit to them was not only a hygienic necessity, but also one of the biggest amusements of those times." The bathhouses, in which both beer and food were available, went from sexually integrated to sexually segregated, including with respect to attendants [Rothenburg Medieval Crime Museum, 275].

CHAPTER 16

Who Is to Blame for the Threat to the Ruling Classes?

The most logical candidates for being the Devil's agents clearly were the leaders in (heretical) denominations outside the prince or ruler's religious orthodoxy. These people were to remained condemned by each other—without a prayer to get to heaven, for example—but sometimes, in some lands, they got a sort-of free pass in terms of direct persecution as long as they avoided public evangelizing in a territory ruled by leadership with a different orthodoxy. In Germany, the Catholics and Lutherans had reduced the threat from each other by treaty. By the 1560s, the "problems" involving denominational differences no longer had much currency within German-speaking lands [Waite, 146]. In contrast, France was soon to break out in decades of intermittent direct conflict between Catholics and Huguenots (French Protestants in the Reformed Church "tradition," a la Calvin), which would keep authorities in the central areas of France fairly fully occupied for several decades (so there were to be few witch hunts there then). Meanwhile, the Spanish Inquisition went on persecuting former Jews and Moors who had converted to Catholicism but retained aspects of their previous culture or religion—which made them heretics. They also did their best to stamp out anything Protestant (including books) and anyone practicing a more liberal version of Catholicism. But in the Low Countries, as noted earlier, the Spanish Inquisition was used to pursue Protestants who had made extensive inroads in many of the larger cities. In time, such practices and Spanish rule generally (which tended to override local rights that had accumulated over centuries) led to a rebellion, especially in the northern provinces, and a long-term, off-and-on war, so witch-hunting very much took a back seat.

In some German-speaking territories, Lutherans and Catholics were both tolerated, at least for a while—most often because the ruler had little alternative other than civil war, given the relatively large size of the both groups or the war-making strength of the aristocratic faction supporting the minority group. In Poland, which was earlier divided between Eastern and Western Xtianity, one aristocratic right for centuries had been to set the religion in their own lands [O. Halecki, *A History of Poland*]. But, almost 100 years after western Europe stopped witch hunts, Poland was to execute perhaps 15,000 witches [Barstow, 181] after a Roman Catholic King managed to enforce that religion in the country.

Where direct threats from other denominations and the threat of war were on the back burner, elites in some one-confession lands still worried about too little respect for authority, too much disorder, insufficient piety, or too little attention to right beliefs among their citizens. Was the Devil doing his work there? But because there was no Devil in reality, any search for the Devil's agents within a principality could only draw a blank *or come up with some scapegoats.*

However, there would have been a lot more blanks drawn, a lot more single prosecutions that didn't become witch hunts, had not the safeguards in laws in many places been overridden in favor of the use of torture based on little or no evidence other than the confessions of others who had already been tortured into confessions. Among the rationales for short-circuiting or changing legal requirements in the case of witches was the possibility that the accused was under the protection of a demon, making them less likely to confess, such that torture was needed to oust the demon, to get to the truth [Rothenburg Medieval Crime Museum, 112, 186]. In England, which did not adopt Roman law, torture was prohibited, so witch-hunting mainly occurred on a small scale, albeit with at least one exception.

Who Specifically Was Victimized, and Why

The initial accusations in witch hunts typically involved maleficia: Something bad had happened to someone or some family, or to the community, and they accused some disliked person or "enemy," typically of low(er) social status, of being the cause of that event. The event might be a serious illness or accident that befell the accuser, or the death of a child or even a cow. Or it might be a broader community disaster, such as a hailstorm that ruined the crops, a disease that killed livestock, or the arrival of some version of some plague. Because people still believed in the power of a curse, if a personal or family disaster struck soon after someone cursed at them, the curser might be accused of maleficia (even years afterward). "In the case of the witch craze, it appears that anxieties felt at the lower end of the social hierarchy were focused by the upper strata into distinctive patterns of scapegoating" [Klaits, 94]. That is, an accusation of maleficia didn't just mean that the accused drew on God or occult powers to do bad things to someone who had they thought had wronged them, or who was an enemy. Now such a charge also meant (as we saw above)—to the elites at least—that the accused foreswore Xtianity, was in league with the Devil (usually including sexually, in orgies, or with his demons), and that s/he was therefore a sorcerer/sorceress and heretic deserving of being burnt at the stake.

While there is no such thing as complete data in this subfield of history, partial data from varying numbers of sites very strongly suggest that victims of witch trials and executions tended to be "selected" from certain demographic groups. Around 80% were women, but these women were by no means randomly chosen. Probably 90% or all alleged witches or more were poor, often but not always from the lowest tiers of village peasants and townspeople. When witch accusation sequences began to include leaders in large towns and especially, the higher nobility, they were almost always soon thereafter brought to an end. Female victims were disproportionately widowed in comparison to the adult population [Levack, 132]. They were disproportionately old [Levack, 129], ugly, disliked and quarrelsome or outspoken, and handy with curses for those who treated them abusively or dismissively (including sometimes when they begged for food). Some might have been objects of suspicion for years before being accused, with others in the community likely to agree with that accusation.

Being weaker, women were thought to be more likely to resort to sorcery for revenge or protection [Levack, 126-127]. Beyond cranky "old crones," among other women who might be targeted were cooks (with their knowledge of herbs and their work over hot cauldrons—much as witches are sometimes portrayed)—and the servant/maid who took over infant and child care in the homes of those who were better off [Stephens, 4]. After the work of midwives was done, the nursemaid or these longer-term care women might be seen as responsible for any bad fate that befell the children of their higher status employers.

Further, witch allegations also tended to targeted disproportionately at the modest number of community healers (or "wise women" or "cunning women") who necessarily had some failures under their belt, such that others might attribute these failures to the healer's malice. These healers used a wide variety of methods in their practices, including: plants thought to have medicinal properties; ointments;

prayer (probably almost invariably); magic aids such as amulets and special rituals and incantations (likely usual); and close psychological attention of various kinds. (Placebo effects were an important but unrecognized component of their work.) Many surely tended with some success to small wounds and sores of various kinds, and to boils and minor infections. Most surely knew how to ameliorate some childhood diseases. Some of the women in this group were also mid-wives as part of their practice, and some surely could be consulted for recommendations about contraceptives and abortifacients (though whether or how well those worked is probably totally unknown). But most of them were also older and often largely independent of the kinds of male control exercised over all but widows in most societies. Because most probably used what amounted to "white magic" (not that they called it that) they were all the more vulnerable to charges of maleficia (= witchcraft) if something they did seemed to the patient or his/her relatives to have produced an unexpectedly bad outcome. Although some midwives were protected by their special status (e.g., certification by a city, perhaps), and most undoubtedly kept the mother well-informed of ongoing developments during the birth process (and so would be less likely to be seen as being at fault if something bad developed), most midwives might still be potentially vulnerable to witchcraft allegations if a child was stillborn, strangled by his/her umbilical cord, or a newborn or very young infant died, as some invariably did.

Although most healers' skills were probably passed along from generation to generation in the family or to informal apprentices, heal-ers' practices undoubtedly varied considerably, even within a single country. Even if information circulated to some extent between heal-ers, it probably did so slowly because they were widely dispersed across rural and village areas, and seldom literate. It is almost impossible even to develop an estimate of how much real folk wisdom, especially of the botanical world but also of tending to sores and wounds (and possibly infection), and even of guiding a child's birth, was lost in the elimination of many of these healers and midwives, but some certainly was, presumably at some net cost to society (including the lives of some of the people who instead resorted to doctors).

I have seen few/no generalizations about the male victims of witch hunts, but some were husbands of wives who got accused first. Others, no doubt, were practitioners of white magic and/or the healing arts. And the overwhelming majority were surely from the lowest and nearly lowest strata of peasant, village and town society.

Reflecting on the totals estimated earlier for a minute: With 100,000-200,000 executed, but stretched over 100+ years, that's less than 1,000-2,000 per year, where some of the largest witch crazes in a single vicinity might execute 200 or more. None of these numbers are large compared to losses in many wars of the time (especially the Thirty Years War of 1618-1648), or to some visitations by one or another plague. Given that 100+ years encompasses four generations or so, perhaps the terrorization of women that Barstow sees as a *general* offshoot of the witch craze is not really all that generalizable to the whole female population, though it may well have arisen among women in the immediate vicinity of a thinly populated rural area in which a large hunt for witches is occurring [Barstow, 148-150]. (Occasionally, almost every adult woman in a small village would be convicted.) Although each and every woman not yet accused would *not* identify herself with the witch-ness of those so far accused, she might be at least subliminally conscious that people who were disliked and nearer the bottom of the social hierarchy might be among the next to be accused by those currently being tortured for confessions (will frau X give them my name?). Anyway, Barstow's citation from Anderson and Zinsser seems to me to come much closer to hitting the spot: "'The witchcraft persecutions remain the most hideous example of misogyny in European history"' [Barstow, 148]. As we have seen and will see again below, there is no question that misogyny was rampant in witchcraft theory and practice, even though the first-order motives of the persecutors/prosecutors (such as eliminating heresy, or ending the Devil's threats to a realm or town, or helping to prove the righteousness of a particular branch of Xtianity, especially Catholicism) may not have inherently involved gender.

Equally pertinent, it seems to me, is that the 1,000-2,000 people a year tortured and then executed *were all innocent*. But that at least 100,000 innocents were executed by state and religious authorities makes it clear that the larger-scale witch hunts, especially, were an all-but obvious full-blown cultural insanity even for the time. Moreover, this full-blown insanity bloomed on top of a 150-year regression in that direction. No one among the elite believed in torturing and executing innocent people, but the evidence that this is what was occurring was disregarded long after it should have been recognized, until the witch hunts disappeared around 1660 (except in Poland, eastern Europe and a few in the Americas) almost as mysteriously as they had sprung to life in the 1560s.

Along with the "theory" developed initially by Church inquis-itors, the techniques developed by the Inquisition also played an important role in large-scale witch hunts. The Inquisition, having largely failed to crack the Cathar heresy due to resistance by the pop-ulation of Languedoc, was allowed by the pope in 1252 to use torture. Given sufficient suspicion, using torture to gain a confession was also part of Roman law. The inquisitors among the Cathars have been reported to have been generally somewhat respectful of their instruc-tion to have strong suspicions of heretical beliefs, but they also prose-cuted *former heretical beliefs* and even hints thereof, and accumulated evidence (testimony, often secret) for decades in building cases. The Cathar inquisitors also required their victims to name others who had in almost any way supported Catharism (sometimes almost trivially, e.g., by making respectful gestures to the Cathar holy men/perfecti).

When these same torture-until-you-confess-and-name-names techniques were applied by inquisitors and magistrates much later to accused witches, it made it easy to identify other witches. And they in turn were tortured, forced to confess, and forced to name others. This modified torture routine was *the* key piece of the "recipe" enabling a large-scale witch hunt. And it is another reason for the viability of the culturally-insane label: given all that will be pointed out subsequently here, how could the authorities at the time not see this and stop? Actually, they did stop (although, like lightning, they might later strike in the same place), occasionally before the urge to eliminate witches was spent. For example, when a long-lasting witch hunt occurring in a city made it seem to outsiders as though that city was crawling with witches, and commerce began to suffer too much, sometimes witch hunts were wound down. And, as mentioned, the same was usually true when accusations started reaching into the ranks of prominent citizens or nobility.

The Rarest of Tales: Johannes Junius. A former mayor of the city of Bamberg in the prince-bishopric of Bamberg (in Germany), was one of a very few higher status individuals caught in a witch craze. But the most amazing aspect of this case is that there is a written record from the victim! Some combination of his literacy, his high status, and a bribe, enabled Johannes Junius to get his jailer to smuggle a secret letter out to his daughter on July 24, 1628, telling her that he was in fact innocent and detailing what he had gone through in order to extract a confession from him. Although one case like this is necessarily "anecdotal," and certainly not representative of all cases everywhere, Junius' description of what happened very much seems to be fairly typical in many respects, at least in Catholic Germany (which produced a majority of Germany's cases).

Junius protested his innocence to his accusers (as did virtually all others accused in Bamberg and elsewhere), of course, "and challenged the court to bring forward a single witness who had seen him at the witches' meetings" [Waite, 160]. Alas for Junius, a former city council member "denounced him to his face." Anyway, that witness was sufficient to get Junius tortured, initially with thumbscrews and leg-screws, "leaving him unable to use his hands for a month" [Waite, 160]. But it didn't cause him enough pain, according to court records (was he under the protection of a demon?), "thus explaining his reticence to confess" [Waite, 161]. Hence he was stripped and searched for the "Devil's mark," and a birthmark having been found, it was tested for pain with a sharp needle, which, like a vaccination, can be relatively painless. And since it was interpreted to be painless enough, he was advanced to the next level of torture, the dread strappado. This device is usually a simple hoist, using a rope around a drum that can be cranked. People are tied, typically by their wrists—which are tied together behind their back—to one end of this rope and cranked up, suspended in a painful position for a while, and then dropped, but stopped short of the ground. Unwillingness to confess would get the procedure repeated, often with weights attached to their feet as well. This procedure readily caused results such as a dislocated shoulder. Junius was raised and dropped "eight separate times, an experience which caused him 'terrible agony.'" At the end of that day, June 30, the executioner begged him to confess something, "whether it be true or not." He was told to "Invent something, for you cannot endure the torture you will be put to" [Waite, 161]. "One torture will follow another until you say you are a witch. Not before that," he said, "will they let you go, as you may see by all their trials, for one is just like another" [Klaits, 129].

Continuing in his letter to his daughter, Junius summarized his confession, writing that he confessed to signing a pact with Satan, attending sabbats, and attempting to kill his children. But his interrogators insisted that he denounce others as well. When he said he didn't recognize others at the sabbats, they made him go through sections of the city and its streets, naming people. His letter also noted that others in prison for witchcraft had begged his forgiveness before they were executed for having named him under torture [Klaits, 129-130].

"And, when his interrogators were dissatisfied with his confession … and about to raise him again on the strappado, he admitted to desecrating 'a sacred wafer'" [Waite, 161]. When he had said this, they left him in peace. "In the German prince-bishopric panics, the most important service that accused witches could perform was to confirm the reality of the sacraments" [Waite, 161-162].

Bishop Friedrich Forner of Bamberg believed that witches abused all seven sacraments. Moreover, the bishop countered nearby Protestant propaganda with the argument that there are more witches in Catholic areas because the Devil can only recruit apostates from the true religion. Accordingly, the heavy presence of witchcraft in a Catholic area was "'an infallible sign that the true … sacraments, the true religion are found among Catholics'" [Waite, 162].

Questions to Be Asked of Alleged Witches. Lest the Bamberg account seem too incredible to the modern reader, *Criminal Justice Through the Ages* includes a record, translated into English, of the "Interrogatories at Eichstatt Witch Interrogations under the Rule of Prince Bishop Johann Christoph von Westerstetten, 1612-1636" [Rothenburg Medieval Crime Museum, 188-190]. Eichstatt was a small city within a small region that is now within Bavaria. Here's a quick overview of the 84 questions:

These "interrogatories" start with the accused name, birthplace, parentage and their estate/occupations, the occupation of the accused, married or not. All the questions about the accused are phrased as "she"—and it doesn't seem as though the English translation had an effect here, but I can't be sure. There are a variety of questions about the sex and personal life of those of the accused who were married, ranging from items about premarital sex (including a willingness to get together carnally even if it did not occur) to discord in the relationship; and questions about, children and their situation or illnesses and attempted remedies for those who had already died (and the same for the spouse). The interrogators want to know with whom the accused keeps company, and whether any executed witches are known to her. The next 60 questions get right down to business, and all of them are phrased as if the accused is guilty, starting with "How long is it since she succumbed to the vice of witchery?" And where did that occur, and when; and in what manner had she communed with the Devil the first time (and in what form he was). There are inquiries about all sorts of details in the witches' gathering(s), from what was served to the dinnerware, what and who she saw while there, whether she was taught to blaspheme, and so on. Following that are items about her subsequent reactions at mass, communion, etcetera. And then there are a number of questions about what evil the witch has done with her powers, such as causing bodily harm to anyone, killing her own or other children, causing barrenness, causing bad weather, and whether she was capable of shifting to different shapes. Semi-finally, the interrogators want to know if she regrets giving in to vice. The last five questions are reserved for those who have confessed and then revoked their confession: Does she remember the confession? Did the evil one manifest himself with advice regarding the revocation, or did some other persons do so? In answering that, the interrogator is told that "she should give the right reason so that it is not necessary to extract the truth by torture and pain." Finally, the interrogator is to remind her to think about the salvation of her soul, and because she cannot evade the authorities, "it is better to suffer a slight earthly punishment than eternal damnation in the hereafter." Note that these questions, as a whole, cover almost every possible aspect of witchcraft as imagined by the witchcraft theorists. As was seen in Junius' case from Bamberg (above), affirmative (witchy) answers to some of them would likely be required for a confession to be considered complete, including the naming of names. Finally, it must be said that the extent of the divorce from reality here is appalling.

If these prosecutions followed standard procedure, any confession obtained with torture had to be repeated subsequently (e.g., the next day) without torture. When this procedure was used, people did sometimes retract their confessions (hence the provision for it in the Interrogatories above)—among the most famous historically were the retractions by some leading Knights Templar in the early 1300s. Why people convicted of witchcraft did not retract confessions the vast majority of the time was because if they retracted the confession the authorities would typically send them back to the torture chamber to try to get a more honest confession. (Clearly, the first one was in some way dishonest or it wouldn't have been retracted.) At best, one could try to make a futile point about one's innocence in a public setting. Ultimately though, most simply opted for death so that the torture would end. Still, that some people did retract their confessions, saying they were only given because of the torture, should have roused suspicions about the initial confessions among more magistrates in the court and among authorities in the region. Similarly unconsidered were the statements and behavior of people prior being taken to torture, probably almost all of whom would have professed their innocence.

CHAPTER 17

Questioning Catholic Iconography, Demonology, and Ultimately Witchcraft

In his famous satire, *The Praise of Folly*, published in 1511, Desiderius Erasmus all but explicitly criticized much of entire status quo, including religion. According to the modern editor in the book's introductory essay, those criticisms were mainly for the Church following the ways of the world [translator's essay/commentary, xxxvi-xxxvii]. For example, immediately after the (Roman) Goddess Folly considers gamblers, she treats men who "find joy in hearing or telling monstrous lies and strange wonders," such as stories of "banshees, goblins, devils, or the like." These stories "serve very well to lighten tedious hours, but they also provide a way to make money, particularly for priests and pardoners" [Erasmus, 55-56].

Also followers of Folly are the people who gaze on pictures or statues of saints with the "gratifying belief that they will not die that day," or that the "image of [Saint] Barbara" will enable them to "come through a battle unharmed" [Erasmus, 56]. Others "happily fool themselves with forged pardons for sins, measuring out time to be spent in purgatory as if with an hour-glass, and figuring its centuries, years, months, days, and hours as if from a mathematical table" [Erasmus, 56]. After a little more detail, Folly continues:

"I fancy that I see some merchant or soldier or judge laying down one small coin from his extensive booty and expecting that the whole cesspool of his life will be at once purified. He conceives that just so many perjuries, so many lustful acts, so many debauches, so many fights, murders, frauds, lies, and so many breaches of faith, are bought off as [if] by contract; ... And who are more foolish, yet who more happy, than those who promise themselves something more than the highest felicity if they daily recite those seven verses of the *Psalms*? Things like that are so foolish, ... yet they stand approved not only by the common people but even by teachers of religion.... One saint assists in time of toothache, another is propitious to women in travail, another recovers stolen goods, a fourth stands by with help in a shipwreck, and still another keeps the sheep in good repair; .... [56-57].

Yet the book was done subtly enough, with the goddess Folly as narrator, pointing out how almost everybody actually worshipped her and the ways in which they did so, such that Erasmus himself could not be challenged as a heretic. This book was widely read by educated people. It conveyed the questioning and humanistic spirit of the Renaissance, likely one that would not have countenanced large-scale witch-hunting had it not been overwhelmed by other events.

Thus, even before any Protestants existed, Erasmus had criticized the overemphasis on images as opposed to purer forms of devotion to the deity (his preferences were for a form of Devotio Moderna). A few years after *Folly*, Erasmus completed a translation of the Bible from more of its original sources (drawing in part on the work of others) and showed how the Vulgate Bible, the official Church translation for centuries, was sometimes in error. Overall, his record was such that many Protestants were subsequently disappointed that he did not convert. Erasmus remained committed to a purer version of the Bible's teachings, even if not some of the elements of Catholicism as practiced.

The (Protestant) Rejection of Icons

Catholics venerated the paintings and sculptures of saints, and the saints' relics, very much as if those were direct corridors to those saints who could plead for divine mercy for the prayerful petitioner. Protestants did not accept much Catholic doctrine except where it stemmed directly from the Bible or from the Church fathers and doctors from Augustine's time or *earlier*. Protestants rejected saints in favor of directly accessing the deity and Jesus in their praying. Especially despised was the veneration of images/icons/relics of saints and the containers for revered and blessed objects. Such images and artifacts were nothing short of plentiful in all Catholic churches. Protestants also rejected the buying of indulgences as forgiveness for sins, and the idea of Purgatory.

Thus, as areas turned Protestant, the former priests and/or the people themselves tended to remove or sometimes destroy most such images in their churches, sometimes with considerable anger after having been told by preachers that they had been deceived for their entire lives. Advocating the destruction of such objects and any actions pursuant thereto is called "iconoclasm." Among the earliest noteworthy occurrences of iconoclasm were those in Protestant-turning areas of Germany, including in Luther's church in Wittenberg in 1522 [MacCulloch, 142], and in Switzerland. Luther's preaching associates were presiding at the time. Whatever his initial views about the destruction of icons, Luther came out in opposition to iconoclasm because the destruction of items of value in their realms upset his noble supporters.

Probably the idea of iconoclasm would be frowned upon today too, if only because of the destruction of the artistry and its associated history. But in Switzerland, especially in territories reached by Reformed Church founders such as Ulrich Zwingli, preaching against icons and idolizing was often used as an early step in the reform of, or movement away from, Catholicism. And those lessons in the years 1524-1530 and beyond might then be followed by iconoclastic actions—sometimes initiated by only a small number of people [Carlos M. N. Eire, *Reformations: The Early Modern World, 1450-1650*, 227-232, 235-241].

In England, in the 1530s, iconoclastic feelings among the people were also stimulated by Protestant preachers during the Protestant-Catholic struggle for influence over Henry VIII's religious directions. (Henry had opted for a king-run church, mainly to enable his divorce from Catherine of Aragon, who had not borne him a son. The pope, who was dominated by Holy Roman Emperor Charles V of Spain, a relative of Catherine of Aragon, would not grant Henry permission to divorce.) And in the late 1530s, instances of fraud discovered at some Catholic shrines—such as faked blood of Christ and an image of Christ in which the eyes moved (per a mechanical device)—both thoroughly publicized by Protestant leaders, also aroused popular indignation and helped discredit Catholic iconography [Wilson, Derek, *A Brief History of the English Reformation*, 209].

Only rarely were the most spectacular displays of iconoclasm seen as clearly as in Amsterdam in 1566. Although the proof could hardly be called a scientifically valid, Reformed Church advocates there (by then considered followers of Calvin) planned an attack on the sacred images for one night in summer. The point was to prove that the images were inanimate, incapable of response, unable to act as conduits, unworthy of veneration [Waite, 143]. A purposeful "mob" of Calvinists stripped the churches of all of their statuary and images, and piled those images in the town square. Also included in the pile were the special little containers for the already-consummated Eucharistic host, the "sacrament houses" (or pyxes) for transporting the host to the sick, holy oil, holy water vessels, etcetera. Other citizens had been warned to stay indoors during the night and the police said they did not interfere because no one was threatened and the police did not want to escalate matters. In the morning, "like executioners finishing off the wounded, the iconoclasts moved about the sacred objects stabbing, chopping, and smashing them, so that not a single one was left whole." As the Calvinists thus demonstrated, "Not one saint cried out in protest; not a single 'sacrament house' oozed blood or water" [Waite, 143].

Demonic Possession Cases

One of the ways in which Catholics, often led by monks in the Jesuits Order, tried to demonstrate the validity of their religious views was with exorcism efforts in cases in which demonic possession was purportedly involved. Possession differed from witchcraft in that it was involuntary, whereas witchcraft involved a voluntary agreement with a demon or the Devil. In any case, the possessed were usually nuns, and/or higher-status people, and others for whom an accusation of witchcraft apparently made no sense to the elite. Those "possessed" by demons often acted out by blaspheming the deity or invoking the Devil, laughing or shrieking continuously, talking gibberish, acting out sexually in some ways, going into trances, having convulsive fits, etcetera, though they rarely did so constantly [Goodich, 77-78]. In some cases, priests and sexuality were involved in ways that supposedly set off the possession [Michel de Certeau, *The Possession at Loudon*, 53-64]. Psychologically, it might be fair to say that at least some of these cases involved people who had burst the unconscious bounds of their own repressive containment of their sexuality (but had no idea about that link), and did so in a neurotic way. In any case, there came to be a sort of war of propaganda over exorcisms, with Catholics claiming that successful exorcisms showed their religious interpretation's validity (and bemoaning the cases that couldn't be solved and cases that relapsed), and with Protestants claiming the whole thing was fraudulent—as a few possession cases were clearly shown to be. Discoveries involving fraud were especially painful for the Catholic side. Yet a few Protestants too tried their hand at exorcisms, sometimes as medical doctors or psychic counselors, but also, among English Puritans for example, as holiness- and religion-proving preachers [Darren Oldridge, *The Devil in Tudor and Stuart England*, 157-161].

Although Protestants tended to reject demons, English Protestants might still have their "familiars"—demonic animal assistants as a sort of pet [Oldridge, 84], as seen in some witchcraft prosecutions. But the Protestant version of the Devil tended to be much less of a corporeal agent than a subtler influence on the mind, a deceiver and tempter "who sought to exploit the innate depravity of human beings" [Oldridge, 40]. With the pope and/or Catholic Church (an institution) often already depicted as the Anti-Christ, strong beliefs about the Devil still enabled Protestants to see witchcraft as another way in which Devil operated. Witch-hunting in Germany was fairly high in some Protestant territories, and in Scotland, where John Knox fostered Calvinism. In general, adherents to the Reformed Church (Zwingli, Calvin, Puritans, et al.) put the greatest emphasis on the Devil. King James VI of Scotland, who became King James I of England, even wrote a book about witchcraft and its associated evils, but England's laws that restricted torture meant that chain-reaction witch hunts were not as easily launched there (and, as a new ruler in a different kingdom, King James had a lot of other things to attend to).

The Amazing Disproof of Witchcraft in Spanish Basque Lands, 1611-1612

The Spanish Inquisition—a separate branch since it was started under Ferdinand and Isabella in the late 1400s—was under the control of the

Spanish monarchs rather than the pope. It was highly centralized, with a supreme council (the Suprema) as the ultimate authority. It had been used primarily, and extensively, to investigate the Jewish-background "Conversos"—Jews who had converted to Xtianity or whose progenitors had converted to Xtianity (almost always under duress, sometimes even under the threat of death; others converted when they were given the choice to convert or leave Spain). It was in 1492, just after the completion of the Xtian re-conquest of Spain, that all Jews remaining in Spain were forced either to convert or leave the country. Any retention of features of Jewish culture, such as the avoidance of pork or other Jewish customs, let alone the conduct of secretive Jewish rituals in their home, were of concern to this Spanish Inquisition. The ones who were such crypto-Xtians were called Marranos. Because they were now technically Xtians, the people with Jewish backgrounds who in any meaningful way still practiced Judaism or were considered to be heretics! (For Jews, the charge of "heresy" was not applicable.) The Spanish Inquisition maintained a very large network of spies to help ferret out such deviation. Roughly the same fate befell the Muslims in Spain, starting less than a decade after the expulsion of Jews. The most typical process was a rebellion, its defeat, and then more forced conversions or expulsion. The Muslim converts were called Moriscos. In 1609, all remaining Moriscos were forced to leave the country [Klaits, 170]. Thus for decades since its beginning in the 1470s, the Spanish Inquisition kept busy with purifying the country of borderline Xtians, initially with Jewish backgrounds, but then those with Moors in their backgrounds too. This effort also has the characteristics of clear-cut persecuting or scapegoating, because "pureness of blood" (having no non-Xtian heritage) became an important social and political qualification for acceptance into higher society and public office. Undoubtedly forcing the departure of the Jews and the Muslims, and then persecuting many of those who had converted to Xtianity undermined the potential and capabilities of the Spanish state(s), so that too constitutes a major cultural insanity, but one that is not a direct concern here.

Spain also suppressed its mystically-oriented and liberal Catholics, and imprisoned Protestants who came into its clutches (e.g., English sailors). Although Spain was never really under any serious threat from Protestantism, its monarchs, including Holy Roman Emperor Charles V (1519-1556), and his son Philip II, King of Spain (1556-1598) and also ruler of much more, took it upon themselves to be the leading defenders of the Catholic faith. In contrast to countries, dukedoms, bishoprics, and other statelets where nearby regions did offer alternative religious beliefs, Spain lacked some of the threats that elsewhere seemed to "imperil" rulers, or their territory's religious adherence.

It seems likely that the above factors—the Spanish Inquisition being occupied with other "business" during the early periods of witch-hunting in some northern lands, and the lack of threat to the country's rulers and religion—help to explain Spain's lack of involvement in witch-hunting. (Witch-hunting was also minimal in Italy, which was almost uniformly Catholic, albeit with some liberals, and under control of Spain for much of the 1500s.) In any case, "as early as 1526, the Suprema had ordered an inquiry into witchcraft, deciding that witches reconciled to the Church may have suffered delusions and were not therefore to be handed over to the secular arm" to be burnt at the stake. "Doubt was even cast on the authority of the *Malleus*" [Edward Burman, *The Hammer of Heresy*, 181].

However, because there had been very well-known and serious witch hunts-based convictions of witches in the early 1600s in Basque lands on the French side of the border, Spanish inquisitors decided to check for witches on their side of the border. After some initial prosecutions, including a few executions, in 1611 they followed the usual inquisitorial procedure, which was to call everyone in town to the main cathedral square and give a sermon on the evils of heresy (or, in this case, presumably the witchcraft variant on heresy) and *to offer a period of grace (e.g., a week) in which those who came forward to admit their mistaken/heretical beliefs/actions could be forgiven by the Church, usually with no more than minor penances* (assuming the heretic did not subsequently relapse, which could well bring a punishment of death).

What happened on this occasion was that 1,802 people admitted to witchcraft [Burman, 181], 1,300 of whom were minors [Levack, 131], many of them young and unmarried women and even children [Klaits, 169]. Inquisitor Alonzo Salazar de Frias was commissioned to investigate further and report. What he did to check surpassed the best experimental science of the time. "Chemists checked on the so-called magical ointments" [Burman, 181]. When fed to animals, the supposedly hallucinatory ointments had no harmful effects [Klaits, 169]. "And doctors checked the virginity of women who claimed to have had intercourse with the Devil or demons" [Burman, 181]. Salazar de Frias had assistants take those who had confessed to being present at a sabbat to the place where it supposedly occurred and answer questions such as where did the Devil sit and where did they eat, where did they dance, how long it took to get there, etcetera. "The confessed witches contradicted each other in answering nearly all these questions" [Klaits, 169]. It was also discovered that a sabbat was supposed to have taken place at a site on which the secretaries of the Inquisition were positioned at the same time" [Burman, 181-182]. In his report to the Suprema, Salazar de Frias concluded that the agitation about witchcraft contributed to the "diseased" state of the public mind, and "that there were neither witches nor bewitched until they were talked or written about" [Burman, 182].

So Salazar de Frias' report was a potential dagger in the heart of one major cultural insanity of the age—a veritable revelation to disprove witchcraft, rationally demonstrated/proven to all, except perhaps the most weasel-worded scholastic theologians. In the actual event, perhaps the imaginations of the girls and younger women had indeed been stimulated by the frenzy on the French side of the border, and they had had "sinful" thoughts to confess. Or dreams that included them in a witches sabbat. Or daydreams about sex in a witches sabbat. Perhaps they had had fantasies of illicit empowerment, especially given the relative powerlessness of women, young or old. And perhaps they feared the consequences if they didn't confess. Finally, though it seems unlikely that the report of Salazar de Frias circulated much beyond Spain, it may well at least have permanently undermined any lingering pressures for more witch-hunting in Spain.

The Confessor's Anonymously Written Work about Witches' Pre-Execution Confessions

For several years, Friedrich Spee von Langenfelds, one of the Jesuits, served as a confessor for imprisoned witches about to be executed. In Catholic lands, these unfortunates were invariably offered one last chance at confession, that their sins of witchcraft might be forgiven even though they had to die because of the seriousness of their crime— whatever their level of desire to come back into the fold of the Church. Those giving confessions to Spee von Langenfelds had nothing left to lose by telling the truth in their last confession and, as believers in the Catholic system, potentially had much to gain (avoiding eternity in hell). But in the vast majority of witch confessions, what confessor Spee von Langenfelds heard were *NOT* confessions involving what the condemned had done as apostates, heretics, and as demon-consorting witches, but were confessions for the sins of lying under oath in their court confessions to witchcraft [Waite, 222].

As noted earlier, if standard procedure was followed in the trials of these "witches," they were obliged, the next day or so, to admit the same crimes as they had confessed under torture, but on this second occasion, "freely," under oath to the deity in open court. And they very rarely retracted their lies in open court because, had they done so, they would be tortured further (which would produce what the court would then regard as a more accurate confession). Spee von Langenfelds *anonymously* published his critical views of this situation in 1631. Because the Catholic Church under the influence of the Counter-Reformation had doubled-down on its demonology-angelology, this kind of focus on judicial abuses was one of the only ways that offered any prospects of getting the Church to reconsider witch-hunting—if only because it avoided the likelihood of being charged as a heretic for any Protestant-like criticisms of Church demonology. Spee von Langenfelds' work had "considerable influence" [Waite, 222].

CHAPTER 18

Why Were Witch Hunts Abandoned?

There is no need here for further details about how many alleged witches were executed in the various realms, large and small. But from a cultural insanity perspective, it is worth noting briefly some of the major changes that, relatively suddenly (with exceptions for more backward areas), brought a return to much greater degree of cultural sanity in this regard. I have already mentioned the reports of Salazar de Frias and Spee von Langenfelds as contributing factors to ending witch hunts—especially in Catholic lands (which conducted the largest share). Also, although books against the belief in witchcraft were occasionally written, they did not circulate widely until disbelief in witchcraft started to rise among prospective readers among the elite. So, mainly, we need to look at some of the broader social forces at work.

The number one reason for a change in the perspectives/beliefs of the elite was "the calming of confessional conflict and the cooling of religious passion" [Waite, 216-217]. And, most likely, the number one reason for that cooling of religious passions was the experience from the Thirty Years War (1618-1648), a religious-political war in which parts of Germany (such as Protestant Brandenburg and Hesse, and Catholic Bavaria) were devastated over and over with great loss of life [Wilson, Peter H., *The Thirty Years War: Europe's Tragedy*]. The

Thirty Years War was not strictly religious mainly because France was allied with Protestants in its ongoing efforts to reduce the power of the Habsburgs' possessions that still surrounded it. The war featured major involvements by most of Germany and Austria's many statelets, plus Spain's armies, Denmark's armies, Sweden's armies, the Netherlands' armies, and French armies. The armies of the Netherlands (then the United Provinces) were fighting for their independence from Spain. Although witch hunts may have reached their high points in German Catholic lands during the Thirty Years War, by the time it ended it had implicitly suggested that some degree of tolerance might be better than continued warring about religious beliefs—notwithstanding that the others' confessional views were heretical. With the arrival of peace, it was also suggested that maybe greater skepticism was warranted about the apocalypse being at hand, and about the Devil and witches being the cause of the extensive destruction and high numbers of dead in some areas in Germany. And surely the English Civil War, 1642-1648, reinforced the implicit messages from the Thirty Years War. Certainly the latter was highly influential in the development of the English-American colonies' traditions and ultimately their decision as a new nation, over a hundred years later to develop a constitution that promised freedom of religion. Indeed, as early as the 1640s, Roger Williams, with the help of a few leading *Puritan* politicians in England—whose views were affected by the tolerance of differences *among* the variety of radical Protestants within Cromwell's victorious New Model Army—had led the way in establishing a religiously open little outpost in North America—Rhode Island.

In addition, the economic success of the Seven United Provinces in the Low Countries, which was finally recognized as independent by the treaty of Westphalia that finally officially ended the Thirty Years War in 1648 (after well over 100 years of religion-related struggle and war), was remarkable. In the Netherlands, a form of Calvinism was the only officially-recognized religion, but Catholicism was unofficially tolerated, if largely under cover (sometimes facilitated by bribes, etc.). There were also Jews in the Netherlands (including philosopher Baruch Spinoza). This situation suggested that religious co-existence was possible and did not impair prosperity. Way back when the conflict between Spain and its Low Country provinces first got under way, William of Orange, the "prince" leading the United Provinces, had seen the importance of not alienating the Catholics—if only to minimize their support for Spanish overlords. So the armies of the United Provinces weren't strictly Protestant, though Protestants provided most of the leadership and the militancy because they had the most to lose if Spain returned to power there, as that would almost undoubtedly lead to the execution of many Protestant leaders, imprisonment for others, confiscation of Protestant property, and an unleashed Spanish Inquisition again.

Another important reason—some historians assign it number one—for the abandonment of witch hunts was the rise of mechanistic-mathematical interpretations of how nature operated, such that the regular intervention of a deity was less needed as an explanation. As early as the 1300s, there were some predecessor hints that the universe might run without constant intervention by a deity—such as the operations of very large clock-planet models in cities beginning in the 1300s—that in time gave rise to the analogy of a "clockwork" universe [Greengrass, 222-223]. But even into the 1600s, the Catholic Church still enforced the doctrine that the sun revolved around the earth. Also, the heavens (from the moon on up) were perfect, being the realm of the Xtian deity. The heavens consisted of tiers of crystalline spheres (that being the most perfect shape) in which planets and stars were embedded. But as the 1600s progressed, Galileo and his telescope found flaws (craters) on the moon, and moons that circled the planet Jupiter—just like earth's moon did. And Kepler found elliptical not spherical orbits of the planets—going around the sun, not the earth. Philosopher Rene Descartes' thought was also important in the shift to viewing the universe mechanistically. And by the late 1600s Isaac Newton had confirmed it. Maybe the deity could still answer prayers but not have to be involved in every iota of nature's operations. Maybe the deity set up nature according to mathematical and physical principles so that it mostly ran on its own. Similarly, perhaps naturalistic forces and not witches and demons or the Devil were responsible for weather-related disasters, and maybe earthquakes and plague too. Even before Newton, this powerful intellectual change reached many of the educated/elite in Western Europe, and it was these people who controlled society and politics, and who served as prosecutor-judges (magistrates), religious leaders, and rulers and advisers to rulers.

Notwithstanding all the confessions obtained from witches, the long drawn out century and more of witch-hunting also produced results that raised questions about the whole operation. We have seen some of these doubts in the work of Spee von Langenfelds and Salazar de Frias (above). And although the fraudulent cases of demonic possession-plus-exorcism, and fraudulent shrines, and icons that did not resist iconoclasts, did not take a big toll, such discoveries and events tended to undermine rather than confirm Catholic doctrine. Another reason: People, including all well-educated churchmen, almost undoubtedly knew that torture can produce false confessions. For example, a book on "rescue miracles" from the 14th century— that is, before the witchcraft theorists—noted that reports submitted in support of candidates to sainthood (pending Church approval of their veracity) included some in which the prayed-to intercessor intervened to prevent injustice due to false confessions obtained under torture [Goodich, 53, 56-57]. There is also an example from 1659 in Bardeleben, Germany of a "common oath of truce" by an accused witch who had not confessed to witchcraft after two hours of torture, and so was acquitted [Rothenburg Medieval Crime Museum, 191]. In this oath the victim swears, "so help me God," that she will not take revenge, or have others do it for her, on any of the court officers or servants, the councilors, or the prince or any of his functionaries. (At that time, apparently, Bardeleben authorities didn't automatically assume guilt and continue torturing until a confession was obtained.) Similarly, as previously noted, what was one to make of all those initial denials and those occasional recantations of tortured confessions anyway? And surely there were places that underwent extensive witch persecutions where natural or other disasters occurred shortly thereafter, casting doubt on the efficacy of the previous witch hunts. Waite summarizes that "the process of prosecuting witches itself raised more doubts about the supernatural than it resolved" [Waite, 216].

In addition, on the social-political philosophy front, secular theories of monarchical empowerment begin to supplant deity-based justifications for rulers, such that the "imperative" for a state to have only one religion was reduced [Klaits, 167; Greengrass, 391-392].

In England, there had been a large witch hunt in 1644-47, during the period in which a Puritan-leaning Parliament and its followers fought a multi-year war against the king (or the king fought this war against Parliament). Once the restoration of the monarchy came in 1660, witch-hunting became identified with the kinds of Puritanism that dominated under Cromwell (England's official Protector/ruler after King Charles' final defeat), and so was largely rejected by the elite thereafter.

Awakened from the Cultural Insanity

Although the cessation of all witch hunts was not immediately forthcoming—for example, the major witch hunt in the Puritan backwater of Salem Massachusetts occurred in 1692 and others were yet to occur in eastern Europe—witch hunts on a major scale disappeared from most of Western culture in what seems to be a relatively short time, given the magnitude of the practice at the height of the witch craze in the century from 1560 to 1660 and the relative paucity of proto-scientific demonstrations of the invalidity of witch "theory" (unlike geocentrism, e.g.). It was almost as if the elite of Western societies had awakened from a bad dream that they did not remember much of.

Overall, the account above has shown the initially slow culturally retrograde movement within the Catholic Church, especially during the 1400s, led by Dominican inquisitors who, if nothing else, had too little to do. Writing as if they were witchcraft theorists, these self-selected inquisitors may also have been out to strengthen the proofs of Catholic dogma about the reality of the sacraments and Church demonology. Despite the failures of the Church-initiated crusades against the Bohemians' variant on Catholicism in the early-middle 1400s and the earlier Great Schism in the papacy from 1378 to 1417, Catholic dogma was at the time little-challenged, even if some people did have their doubts about doctrines like transubstantiation—about the reality of the changeover to the flesh and blood of Jesus in the wafer and wine purportedly produced by the mass.

The yet earlier adoption of Roman law almost everywhere on the continent—law which stressed the surety of confession—better enabled witchcraft theorists to believe that confessions acknowledging the practice of witchcraft were therefore real too. This belief among the zealous arose despite earlier doctrines that witch flight was delusional and also despite evidence of their delusionality (e.g., that individuals who thought they had flown at night were delusional because they did not in fact do so when watched the whole time). And it arose despite the necessity of calling upon Church authorities such as Aquinas to win their own scholastic arguments, and despite some necessity for convoluted reasoning. So, over time, the few early admissions of witchcraft, and the few prosecutorial records that produced confessions (many no doubt emerging under the duress implicit in an uneducated person's appearance in a clerical court), were compiled into a larger picture by the Dominican zealots. And then embellished.

Moreover, rather than just drawing on the power of demons or the Devil to do harm, as sorcerers were thought to do, witchcraft came to be described as even more fundamentally heretical in that they forsook the deity entirely in favor of serving the Devil. In earlier times in some places, proof of harm done was also needed, but heresy trumped that. And even "white magic"—done for good ends—was ultimately included as heresy because it too drew on the power of the Devil, not the deity. The extra layer of witchy evil-doers, opting to serve the Devil out of their own free will, also helped explain away the problem of why the deity allows so much evil to befall people. Supporting arguments also drew on Augustine's ideas about original sin and the greater sin of Eve especially, and from centuries of churchmen fighting off their sexual desires while blaming women as beguilers. Plus the entire fantasy was slathered with yet more misogyny throughout, in the process labeling women as especially weak-willed sexually, and readily tempted to sexual intercourse with demons. But even before that could happen, the Devil and his demons had to evolve into entities that were more corporeal, whereas, earlier, there were only incubi and succubi capable of having sexual relations with people. And then all that was embellished further with flight to a witches' sabbath with its sexual orgies between the witches and demons, the kissing of a cloven-hoofed Devil's backside, and worship involving deliberate violations of the sacraments (such as sacrilegious treatment of already-blessed eucharist wafers). If that much was real, then these witches had signed on as agents of the Devil and could obviously wield considerable power to do harm to individuals and communities. And, of course, just as in the case of dogma-related heresies (such as the Cathars), heresy could be seen as a threat to the state as well, because rulers were empowered only through the grace of the deity in the first place.

Torture had been used in Roman law and in the papally-sponsored inquisitions (from about the middle of the 13th century), in both cases with some constraints, even if those constraints weren't always adequately observed. Those constraints existed because people knew that torture produced false confessions, so sufficient suspicion was needed before torture could be applied. But witches were deemed to be more resistant to torture because they had enlisted the power of the Devil and his demons, and thereby acquired greater resistance to pain. Between that and the dire prospects of witches doing their will on the status quo in town and country, legal constraints against torture were lowered, in many cases to the point of non-existence, apart from the need for an initial accusation, often obtained under torture.

The earliest trials involving chains of torture and confession led by overzealous inquisitors, including witch-hunter Kramer, dated back to the mid to late 1400s. Some of these trials were on occasion condemned for their infringement on local authority and/or preposterousness. To strengthen their desire to proceed without constraints, Dominican witchcraft theorists induced one pope in the late 1400s to put out a bull condemning an extensive set of witch-related activities. This aided European culture's acceptance of the reality of the witchcraft theorists' perspectives. Even so, because major witch hunts could not easily occur without support from authorities of all kinds, the spread of witchcraft theory was slow and came to little until the changed sociocultural circumstances brought on by the Reformation.

Among the common people, accusations of witchcraft often started with simple ideas rooted in old-fashioned sorcery, the doing of harm with the help of occult powers—perhaps some cranky oldster had cursed someone and the curse (coincidentally) seemed to come true, or one or more midwives had overseen a birth in which the infant died before it could be baptized, or some disliked oldster was blamed for a spell of bad weather. But where witchcraft theory was deployed, torture then produced a confession. And one requirement of such confessions, just as with the Cathars, was that the witch name others involved. And if witches flew to assemblies in counter-deity gatherings to worship the Devil, that meant there were witnesses (a rarity in Roman law cases). So once the complete witches sabbat fantasy was installed or adopted as reality in the minds of most of the elite, the magistrates, and the Church and university guidance-providers, there was all the more reason to demand that the confessed witch name others present at a sabbat. And those chains of identification almost necessarily led to the immediate acquaintances of those earlier accused, which tended to keep the accusations from spreading across status lines, at least early in a witch-hunt and in village settings. The spread across status lines could more readily occur in towns. Not all witch prosecutions followed this model, of course, but the model was the principal way in which a prosecution or two turned into far more substantial witch hunts.

Beyond merely believing in the new ideas about witches, the anxieties of the rulers of society had to be engaged. The complete syndrome was apparently not strong enough among the elite before about 1560 for extensive witch-hunting to occur. Where the Reformation took root (after 1517), there were many threats of religious change and strife, and peasant unrest, and wars of religion. To the leaders of the lands most involved, heretics and the minions of the Anti-Christ probably seemed to be running amok. Even the Muslim Ottoman Empire posed a threat reaching as far as Vienna. But, however vaguely viable a linkage to the Devil for these events might have been, any linkage to witches as a cause of them was quite weak. Later, however, if leaders' anxieties continued even when rational causes for fear were not immediately present, their fears could all too easily be displaced onto witches—available scapegoats.

The Peace of Augsburg (1555) which legitimized Lutheranism, calmed religious strife in much of Germany—except that the Reformed Church of Zwingli, Calvin and others was also extending into new areas. But as a result of the Reformation and Counter-Reformation, many rulers and ruling oligarchies became invested in greater behavioral-social-religious conformity as a way to ward off the threat of an apocalypse and punishments by the deity, such as war, or weather, or disease. By this time, witches, linked up with the Devil, might have seemed like the greatest threat to the elite and the status quo. So the scapegoating began in earnest, though almost always intermittently, popping up in one place, and then, later, another. And if the return of war and punishment by the deity were among the greatest underlying fears of rulers, what better time was there than during a lull in the wars to shape up a princely statelet or town. So that might account for witch hunts peaking in Germany during the Thirty Years War (1618-1648), as indicated in the Rothenburg Medieval Crime Museum publication [186].

Very little or perhaps even none of this was implicit in Catholicism itself, or, of course, in New Testament Xtianity. As we have seen, it was almost entirely invented by Dominican inquisitor zealots. But the Church went along with it and cannot be absolved of the development of this cultural insanity (even though witch hunts were almost non-existent in some Catholic lands).

It may seem surprising that many Protestants leaders, religious and secular, went along with witch-hunting (given the Dominicans' involvement in their history and after Protestant condemnations of Catholic iconography). Although Catholic territories accounted for more witch hunts and executions, Protestant rulers and magistrates were also fearful in way much like their Catholic counterparts. And their great emphasis on the Devil as a source of evil, especially in areas dominated by the Reformed Church, could be used to see witches as the Devil's way of implementing his will. And so some of the Protestant elite almost fully adopted the cultural insanities surrounding the idea of witchcraft, and spread the culpability further.

Reasons for the abandonment of witchcraft prosecutions and witch hunts were covered in the section immediately preceding this one.

This history reveals 250-plus years of multi-faceted retreat into a much greater cultural insanity, guided initially by a very few "leaders" near the top of the Catholic religious elite but later adopted and pursued with vigor by some of the empowered elite, religious and secular, Catholic and Protestant. After the Reformation had proceeded for some time, witch-hunting on a large scale intermittently affected many but not all Western Europe's statelets, prince-bishoprics, cities, and countries, especially those in German-speaking areas, Switzerland, and at or near religious interfaces, and elsewhere if/as religious beliefs changed (though open religious conflict, as in France, tended to defer such fantastical undertakings until later in that era). Clearly, executing 100,000+ innocent scapegoats meant their remaining human potential was lost, their families disrupted and negatively branded (with some other family members sometimes convicted as witches too). Although that's "only" 1,000+ people executed per year over a century, locales with larger witch hunts were sometimes disrupted for months, and the phenomenon arose in many places, sometimes more than once. When a chain witch-hunt erupted, many a site experienced a bizarre variant on Roman circuses (in which gladiators fought each other and wild beasts to provide entertainment), where the popular fascination with events was not without a modicum of risk for some of the bystanders. And, of course, whatever the real problems of the time and place, they were largely ignored or at least were less well-attended through the duration of the witch hunt. And cultural insanity that it was, in many places the mind-set persisted; and sometimes that was to produce subsequent witch hunts.

Finally, it seems worth adding that there are parallels today, that scapegoating and regressions to cultural insanity are not just things of the past. One of the most obvious cases here is some of the thinking about, and treatment of, immigrants to the United States of America, as noted in Part One. Without immigrants, where would we get enough workers for our industrial meat processing enterprises, especially in a pandemic? Or caretakers for the elderly and children outside of schools, again in a pandemic? Or as workers for our agricultural enterprises (planters and pickers), or our roofers, or the country's hotels? Does this country not need this work?

Moreover, much the same can be said about scapegoating when it comes to those who ignore the history of Blacks in this society and accept/favor policies that hold Blacks entirely responsible for their status in the U.S.A. today. Equally questionable are attitudes that let the police off the hook almost every time an innocent or trivially guilty African American (usually a man) is killed by some police officer, where the legal standard is that any threat *perceived by the police officer* is a license not just to use force, but to kill. Similarly, Whites who blame Blacks (e.g., for affirmative action policies or arrest rates), or immigrants, for any sense of victimization they feel, are using them as scapegoats because they have identified the wrong villains.

The real problems in the U.S.A. are centered in the control of governments' policies, which are mainly driven by the power of money in the political realm. And most of the money donated is from the very rich and from large corporations, where the latter work to bring about what they want with armies of hired lobbyists with easy access to government policy-makers and direct links to large-scale political funding for the politicians. Ultimately, that's how we got bad trade agreements that enabled/encouraged corporations to ship jobs overseas (because of lower labor costs and fewer environmental protections)—which also promoted automation at home, thereby undermining both the *White and the Black working class.* In terms of governance, the United States of America is very nearly a corporate oligopoly, with Republicans as their mainstay but many a Democrat beholden to corporate money as well. If you blame/attack the country's money-driven system of governance, you won't be scapegoating.

PART THREE

CULTURAL INSANITIES DERIVED FROM THE CHURCH'S EFFORTS TO ELIMINATE POSSIBLE THREATS TO DOCTRINE ARISING FROM THE DEVELOPMENT OF (PROTO-)SCIENCE

CHAPTER 19

Introduction & Purpose

There have been wide differences among historians' views about the contribution to the development and fostering of science by the Latin/Western/Roman Catholic Church during the High Middle Ages (~1000-1300) and Late Middle Ages (1300-1500 or so). My limited review of this history leads to a crucial clarification. Although not inherently hostile toward proto-science (nor much of a facilitator), the Church strongly resisted reason and the development of science insofar as its leaders perceived a threat to Church doctrines, or Church power. In the process, the Church generated some cultural insanities throughout Xtendom, and helped to sustain others unnecessarily.

Although I was obliged to treat some aspects of the most relevant history extensively, I am not attempting to provide a complete account. Instead, I have tried to write a balanced history of mainline developments, drawing primarily on secondary sources, so that the reader can better judge whether or not I have been fair to the Church in the historical debate. Also, I will not regularly be referring to the various aspects of cultural insanity involved. But cultural insanities will be mentioned or highlighted in sections most central to them, and included in some summaries.

Per Part One, though, a cultural insanity involves an important but unnecessary deterring of the potential for advances in the human development of Europe's peoples, in this case via progress in science and technology. The cultural insanities involved here typically arose, or were unduly prolonged, when the ongoing defense of Church power and doctrine took precedence over the pursuit of knowledge and understanding—when the Church did its best to impose limits on the freedom of thought and exploration. In these cases, it resisted or fought against what were *viable alternatives available within the culture of the time.*

As an aside here, I could add that treating all advances in science and technology as necessarily good might be too simplistic for the modern age, when some technologies pose (or also pose) major threats to human well-being, human life, and even life on earth. But that factor was minimally salient in medieval and early modern times, despite some advances in the means for destructive war-making (cannons and the musket didn't seem to make warfare all that much worse than previously).

Many scholars during the (French) Enlightenment in the 1700s harshly criticized the Church for its suppression of science and knowledge, both then and historically, while at the same time having to look over their shoulders lest they be targeted for inquisitional persecution of some kind by the then-somewhat-weakened (Catholic) Church, or by the French state on behalf of its version of that Church's doctrines. And this negative view was stressed even more strongly in the 19th century by historians such as John William Draper Dickson and Andrew Dixon White, who to varying extents cast the historical scenario up to their times as religion *versus* science [Gary B. Ferngren, in Ferngren, Ed., *Science and Religion: A Historical Introduction*, ix]. A contributing factor to the views of these later historians was the papacy's formal claim in 1870 to infallibility [Colin A. Russell, "The Conflict of Science and Religion" in Ferngren, Ed., 3-4]. To some extent these 19th Century works apparently helped to shape what may once have been among the most common perceptions of religion within academe and among historians. Partly as a counter-balance, much (but not all) recent revisionist history has tried to convey how the Church did help to advance science, and how it was open to reason and to proto-science. Some of these works include a cataloging of the proto-scientific and scientific contributions of churchmen, or even medieval times as a whole, often while downplaying the fact that scientific progress was slow, involving a time span of centuries, as well as some major episodes in which the Church inhibited or thwarted the advance of reason and science by the strictures it imposed. Some chapters here will show why we should not regard such recent histories as sufficiently balanced.

Indeed, in the most dubious cases, parts of these more recent histories read as if they were written as apologetics for the Church (i.e., the Catholic Church and its version of Xtianity in the later Middle Ages). In this category, for example, I would include a fairly recent book by James Hannam: *The Genesis of Science: How the Christian Middle Ages Launched the Scientific Revolution*. This title leans strongly toward the tautological. Yes, a scientific revolution *eventually* was launched, but not so much during the Middle Ages (pre-1500) as subsequently; yes, it occurred primarily in Europe which was in time peopled almost entirely by Christians—but they drew heavily on Greek (and Roman) and Islamic foundations, and even the Vikings and some Asian inventions in the process. And the title misleadingly implies that great praise is due to Christianity and to the Catholic Church for that launch, the Catholic Church being the only Christianity available in most of

and much more—all factors in a broad and important cultural insanity. So, in this Part, I will examine how the Church was and wasn't supportive of the advancement of proto-science and science (mainly in the High and Late Middle Ages and shortly thereafter). I will examine most closely the situations and causes where the two have been at odds, and their effects on culture and the prospects for the fulfillment of human potential.

Background to this Part's Subject

The most fundamental and wide-sweeping cultural insanities perpetrated by the (Latin/Western/Roman Catholic) Church during the Middle Ages had their foundation in the Church's elevation of faith over reason, which involved a relatively direct and explicit rejection of the Greek-Hellenistic heritage bequeathed to the Roman Empire—a heritage that early Xtian leaders all too readily associated with paganism. Only a few decades after Xtianity became an accepted religion— when it became the accepted religion—the centuries-old tolerance of diversity in religion in the Roman Republic and Empire was abandoned in favor of Xtianity as an *enforced* state religion, with the Church in full support of suppressing paganism. And although the Roman state crumbled over the next century plus, the model of a secularly *and* temporally empowered Church was retained within the Church and resurrected a few hundred years later, as the Church struggled to become, and then became, a leading power during the High Middle Ages (1050-1300). As a result, until shortly after 1200, with a few special exceptions, Greek, Hellenistic and Roman learning and written works were permanently set aside (and in the early days of Xtian control, burned) or at least left to molder on monastery shelves. The principal exceptions were the use of Roman-era sources to help teach Latin and rhetoric, Hellenistic-era works promoted by certifiably good Xtians such as Boethius and Cassiodorus and Isidore of Seville in their efforts to save what most seemed of value during the collapse of the Empire, and a later effort to copy all works on hand in monasteries during the age of Charlemagne.

Meanwhile, the books that proto-orthodox Church fathers were to *select* for inclusion in a Bible contained a variety of irrational, conflicting, and erroneous beliefs. As the Early Middle Ages progressed, the Church multiplied, exaggerated, and exacerbated many of these irrationalities. Among the most far-reaching of these distortions was that the Church purported to be an indispensable vehicle for access to heaven and the forgiveness of sin. The Church also overemphasized the afterlife *as the purpose of life*, which was already too strong in the books selected for inclusion in the Bible. This was made worse by the ideas/doctrines of Augustine, Bishop of Hippo in north Africa (d. 428), about original sin. And in the eyes of Church writers sin also came to encompass any pleasurable aspects of sexuality, exaggerating people's guilt and shame. Life on earth became mainly a test for whether the believer was going to be admitted into heaven or not. Among the compounded cultural insanities associated with the emphasis on the afterlife was the waste of time, energy and resources focused on alleviating the punishments purportedly awaiting aging and even dead sinners. One major example was that doing good works—to facilitate a good reception by the deity—came to include giving land to the Church in exchange for arrangements in which monks would pray for a person's departed soul—a practice often followed by the warrior-elite (killers) in the Middle Ages. This practice helped to make the Church the largest single landholder in Europe by far.

The deity was omnipotent, omniscient, and good, yet allowed evil and suffering into the world (including the death of innocent children!), perhaps as part of a testing process—or maybe the problem was that humans simply could not understand the deity's purposes. Natural disasters (weather, plague in people or animals, etc.) as well as individual suffering were often seen as punishment by the deity for sin, or for insufficient faith and disobedience at the community level. The deity was thought to be, or at least could readily be, actively involved in every aspect of earthly life.

The Church increased in capability in the High Middle Ages. It clarified its doctrines to better differentiate what was orthodox and what was not—the heterodox. And as it increased in power, it began to increase the persecution of European people with different/heterodox views (heretics), ultimately doing so with a crusading and murderous intent that had the ultimate responsibility for over a million dead. Most heretics actually espoused variants on Xtianity, often relatively minor ones, often with an emphasis on a biblical basis. With so much focus on the afterlife (and Church power and wealth), increasing the potential of humankind and the quality of life on earth generally were of very low priority in the Church, though there was some effort expended in caring for the poor, the aged, and the sick.

In 1215 it became doctrine that Church masses produced miracles each time they were performed, thousands of times a day across Europe. There was also a promulgation of a kind of cult of saints and the purportedly "Virgin Mary" as intercessors with the deity, and as miracle-workers. All of the irrationalities above, together with the Church's inculcation of its dogma generally, induced a wide variety of crazy beliefs and at times bizarre behaviors in some large numbers of its followers, often including the elite (e.g., in ascribing to witchcraft beliefs and behaviors that were preposterous). Other examples include the belief in all manner of miracles accomplished through the deity's (and saints') involvement in earthly life, going on crusades against Muslim forces while armed with farm implements, flagellant movements, possession by demons, and other religion-induced psychosomatic and psychological crises.

And, seemingly to top it off, the emphasis on life as a proving ground for the afterlife was further exacerbated following the fuller development around 1200 of a what had been a rudimentary doctrine of Purgatory. By the Late Middle Ages, relieving one's forbears' (or one's own) punishments in Purgatory (whilst awaiting the "Last Judgment" there) even came to include the purchase by ordinary people of papers with Church guarantees of various amounts of punishment-free time in Purgatory.

CHAPTER 20

Precursor Considerations

How Much Credit Does the Church Get
for What "Churchmen" Do?

One serious problem with the revisionist historical scholarship that has countered the earlier "science versus religion" histories is that the revisionists have seldom considered just how much credit for advancing science should go to the Church *under various general circumstances*. Everyone of course recognizes the Church as an important conveyance of literacy during early medieval times. But beyond that, there are other major and multi-faceted concerns that needs to be considered. Most especially, how much credit should the Church (or, much later, churches) receive for the proto-scientific and technological advances made by churchmen outside the main hierarchy of the Church, where the principal parts of the hierarchy consists of popes and the papal court (cardinals et al.), abbots and monks in monasteries and monks at large in society, archbishops and bishops, and theologians in universities.

Especially but not exclusively in the 9th through 11th century, most higher Church positions, including those as high as abbots and bishops, were appointed by rulers and went directly to sons of high-ranking noble families who were supporters of the appointing authority. For example, Wikipedia has it that all of the canon positions at Notre Dame in the early middle 1100s were relatives of the king or families allied to the king's family by marriage, or relatives of royal officials [Wikipedia article, "Peter Lombard"]. And, however appointed, until well into the 12th century, almost all of the higher positions in the Church were filled by the sons of noble families, many of whom did not have much of a religious background or calling, but, having been trained as "lords," would know how to fight with sword and lance (as knights on horseback) and have had experience in (or observed as trainees) the exercise of authority over other people, for example, as estate managers, administrators, army commanders, etcetera. (Abbots and other churchmen—including an occasional cardinal and pope—sometimes even led armies or components thereof, at least through the 1400s.) Even in Rome, for centuries there was usually a competition between sets of two or three noble families to control who was chosen as pope, by whatever selection mechanisms were in use at the time.

Rulers often made their Church appointments in exchange for money (for what was a well-paid position). But buying a Church office came to be identified with the sin of simony by Church leaders in the mid-11th century, and getting these appointments under the control of the Church/papacy was one of the strongest of the early "reform" efforts. Later in that same century, Pope Urban II could (and did) legitimately accuse almost every bishop of simony. In any case, in the earlier parts of the High Middle Ages, the likelihood that appointees to high Church positions with this kind of background would make a major intellectual or proto-scientific contribution to the future was extremely low. But the rise of the universities, starting around 1140, helped to strengthen the educational backgrounds of almost everyone who later moved into any position, including secular ones in governments. (And for training to work in Church administration, canon law was often far more important than training in theology.)

One way or another, appointments to important Church positions were almost always filled by people with elite backgrounds. By the time universities became available, being a student was usually limited by costs to the wealthier classes, though more students slowly began to come from the rising commercial classes. And a few worked their way through as servants to wealthy students and, somewhat later, some found support in "colleges"—foundations to help students afford attending a university. But very few of these students would have arisen from the peasant classes. So people with backgrounds in noble families, or wealthy families, continued to provide the vast majority of those who came into Church offices of all kinds—with the exception of local priests, whose class status and educational level was pretty low, or even very low.

As the centralized Church slowly gained more control over appointments, it too began to award many of the higher offices under its control, for example, bishops and abbots, as a kind of patronage to its preferred appointees. In the Late Middle Ages, popes even sold the higher-status positions, all but explicitly reinstituting simony to help fill Church/papal coffers. In general, administrative posts in the Church came with a salary based on the size and wealth of the church realm involved (all such posts/postings are called "benefices"), enabling considerable economic freedom for those who obtained a number of types of positions. At times, the papacy would even provide its supporters or favorites with multiple benefices (thereby increasing their wealth). Further, extensive absenteeism from a benefice location was not at all unusual (almost obviously so in the cases possessing multiple benefices). Absentees usually appointed substitutes to perform the job, but the original appointee almost always continued to draw off some or most of the remuneration from the benefice.

Many kinds of Church positions were not inherently all that demanding. So, in many cases, people might serve faithfully in their appointed capacity but have lots of free time to pursue other interests. In such situations, many appointees pursued outside interests, and in a very few cases, those interests involved proto-science, usually speculation about some aspect of knowledge but in a few cases producing advances or an increase in observation-based knowledge. One such case is illustrated below with Copernicus.

But before proceeding to examples from the past, an analogy from modern times will assist our thinking: How much credit should we give to the Austrian government for Kafka's highly creative literary career, given his long-term job as an Austrian government social insurance office bureaucrat? (The job certainly gave him insights into the character of bureaucracy that infuses his writings.) Or, how much credit should we give to Switzerland for Einstein's work from 1901 to 1909—a time period that included his original papers pertaining to the relative speed of light and e=mc2—given Einstein's job in a Swiss patent office during those years? To these questions, my answer has to be "very little."

Copernicus (1473 1543) provides an excellent example of a man supported financially by the Catholic Church system, but whose real interests seemed to be largely elsewhere despite a degree in religion (canon law) sufficient to obtain a position/benefice as a canon (administrative support person) at a Polish cathedral. Apart from allowing his appointment as a church canon, the Church did nothing directly to support his outside work. "These canonries were extremely popular with scholars because they provided a steady income without onerous duties attached" [Hannam, 275]. In the diocese in which Copernicus obtained a position, most of the canons were political appointees with connections (i.e., as usual, sons of nobles), and could not celebrate mass because they were not priests [Dava Sobel, *A More Perfect*

Heaven: How Copernicus Revolutionized the Cosmos, 17]. In addition to Copernicus' work in astronomy (which, contrary to Church doctrine, ended up supporting heliocentrism—the earth rotating as it revolved around the sun), he also served as a political representative for his uncle, the local prince-bishop and his benefactor in getting him his job as a canon within his diocese. In the course of serving as a canon, Copernicus was assigned a variety of tasks over the years, for example, effectively serving as chancellor, chief financial officer, rebuilding castle defenses, and overseeing agricultural lands some distance away from the cathedral [Sobel]. This was in the as-yet wild and wooly east, so canon duties were more varied than in stable areas (with Catholic-Protestant conflicts added to the mix by this time). In addition, like one or two others with a canon position, Copernicus was for a long time unwilling to dismiss his cook (who assisted him in other ways too and was likely his concubine), despite instructions from the bishop of the diocese that he do so [Sobel, 73-74]. So, Copernicus seems to be a good example of someone brought up and trained well beyond the minimum in the Catholic faith, but for whom it is hard to say that the Catholic Church somehow made an important contribution to science through his work. In fact, his knowledge about Church doctrines was almost undoubtedly a major reason why he was reluctant to publish his theory and findings.

Bacon, Roger (1214-1292) provides a seemingly more mixed example. Bacon, R studied under Franciscans from the start, but only formally became a member of the order in his late 20s. He was to become a famous university teacher and proto-scientist. "He was probably the most learned man in Europe, as well as one of the most imaginative thinkers in history," "certain that scientific knowledge would someday give humanity mastery over nature" [Richard E. Rubenstein, 188]. In his writings, he predicted a future with advanced machines resembling cars, submarines, flying machines, devices for walking on water, and other such magical gadgets [Rubenstein, 189]. Bacon, R supported observation and experimentation and mathematical modeling (likely drawing upon optics—see below) at a time when others (except the Dominican Albert the Great with respect to observation) were limiting themselves almost entirely to authoritative religious and Aristotelian texts. Bacon, R had studied (and perhaps translated) the work on optics done by the Muslim Alhacen (Ibn al-Haytham, 960-1045), did some similar or related experimentation, and helped in spreading the understanding of the properties of light [David C. Lindberg, *The Beginnings of Western Science: The European Scientific Tradition in Philosophical, Religious, and Institutional Context, Prehistory to A.D. 1450 (2nd Edition)*, 313-320].[7] Alhacen had developed a correct model of vision—that light reflected from objects to a passive eye (sight was not a function of emanations from the eye), the laws of reflection and refraction (the bending of light in denser mediums, such as water), and the role of conic sections in the mathematics of vision. Bacon, R "was not the first Western scholar to stress the inductive method of investigation," which he called "*scientia experimentalis* (a term which he also used for the intuitive experience of the deity and the mysteries of faith), but he was certainly the first to point his finger at the basic defects of the medieval educational system, and to suggest radical reforms" [Helene Wieruszowski, *The Medieval University*, 61]. At the time, some of the Franciscans closely identified light with the deity ("let there be light" being the deity's first command in the Xtian holy book). But Church authorities were not receptive to the ideas for reform put forth by Bacon, R, and his name "was linked with scholarly activities bordering on black magic and wizardry"

---

7   Bacon, R was from a multi-generational English tradition. He was a student of Robert Grossteste (1175-1253), a bishop and long-term early patron and supporter of Oxford University. The tradition extends back to Adelard of Bath (1080-1152) who was among the earliest to become acquainted with Arab science by visiting the holy lands in the early 1100s, and was among those most responsible for translating Euclid's geometry, while making its understanding easier [Wikipedia, "Adelard of Bath"].

(though Duns Scotus and William of Ockham later "drew inspiration from" his works) [Wieruszowski, 61]. Note: I have only hinted above that a large number of the views and beliefs of Bacon, R can also be regarded as "flaky" (then or now).

In some accounts, Bacon, Roger was imprisoned for 14 years [Wieruszowski, 61]. If so, this was probably some kind of house arrest within a monastery, because few people lasted anywhere near that long in the dungeons of the day. In a more recent book, it says that "some think that he was punished, perhaps even imprisoned" [Rubenstein, 189]. The Franciscans imprisoned him because "after publishing several essays without receiving the required permission, he was commanded to cease publishing—a ban he violated by sending his *Opus Maius (Major Work)* privately to Pope Clement IV at the pontiff's request" [Rubenstein, 189]. (Because the pope rules over the Franciscans via their minister General/leader, however, this doesn't seem like much of a violation to me.)

How much credit, then, should we give to the Church for the assistance given to proto-science by Bacon, Roger? It's a tough call: he was a man taught by Franciscans at the university level (where all university teachers were at least vaguely associated with the Church, if only via the university itself, but Franciscan and Dominican monks, and theology professors, were more closely associated than other teachers); he was a man who opted into the order somewhat later in life, but who was later restricted by them for his writings; a man dedicated to a radical (and mainly Franciscan not Dominican) view of the Church; he was a would-be educational reformer and teacher of renown among students; he was a serious proto-scientist and a wild-eyed visionary; and, lastly, he was a man whose ideas were all but shunned by the Church.

Which Institutions and/or Who Should Get How Much Credit for What University Faculty Do?

Over the period from around 800 to beyond 1520, the cathedral schools and, after about 1200, the universities that were often their offshoots, were the main source of intellectual learning (as contrasted with practical learning), with monasteries playing an ever-smaller role. However, even in the earliest times, there were also independent schools in the cities in Italy [Wieruszowski, 62-63]. Although usually taught by priests, the curriculum of these independent schools was not the same as in cathedral schools; instead, it was adapted to the needs of nobles (who did not look down on education in Italy, unlike most did in other lands) and of city governance, and to the gradually re-developing merchant class, where merchants were ahead of the leading artisans in terms of status and wealth. The curriculum differed in that it added training in formal writing, as preparation for work in composing city rules, contracts, letters, and other judicial and administrative matters. As a result, grammar and rhetoric (sophisticated, persuasive expression) were also given more emphasis than in most cathedral schools.

Further, in both Italy and elsewhere, independent masters (teachers) competed for higher-level students before the universities arose, though typically they tried to obtain a formal recognition by a cathedral school to help attract students. As was true then and subsequently, the students paid the costs of their education, though in time wealthy benefactors endowed parts of some institutions (i.e., established "colleges") to help some of the poorer students (and occasionally also to establish endowed faculty teaching positions or "chairs"). To be clear for our purposes, then, it seems that the Church did not normally fund the universities in any important way (with the possible exception of some of the theology-related training and staffing, perhaps especially that involving Dominicans and Franciscans as masters). However, some of the wealthy benefactors were also churchmen (e.g., local bishops who were often the official overseers of the university in their diocese).

Most important of all, the universities consisted of a corporation of masters—the teachers—much like other medieval guilds. Such a corporation established its own rules that were binding on the membership, and elected its own leaders, giving the organization considerable autonomy [Edward Grant, *Science and Religion, 400 BC – AD 1450*, 171-172]. Bologna and a few universities modeled after it were exceptions initially [Rashdall, *Vol. 1*, 87-173]. Bologna was first constituted by students seeking an education in secular/Roman law—students who were mature adults mostly from families higher in the social scale—and they set the rules, including for the teachers. (In time, the power of the students was to ebb away.) These master-teacher corporations had to negotiate with the cities in which they located for a satisfactory status—where most cities gave second-class treatment to non-citizens (which would include some if not many masters and students). As early as 1158, Holy Roman Emperor Frederick Barbarossa, being from a line of rulers based in German-speaking provinces north of the Alps but also the titular ruler of much of northern Italy, in order to protect the foreign students in Bologna, many of them from Germany, decreed that students who got in trouble had the right to have their cases judged by their teachers rather than the local courts/rules [A. Daniel Frankforter, *The Medieval Millennium: An Introduction*, 209]. The greatest power that the corporation of masters had was the possibility that they—and all their students—would leave the city, which would strike an economic blow against many in the city. And this was a very real power, especially at first, because universities owned no buildings and teachers were essentially footloose scholars. And just as the students had come to study with these scholars, they could easily follow them. For example, Bologna officials tried so hard to control the university that the university's constituents spawned other universities in north Italian cities because groups of students, sometimes along with some masters, left Bologna. Short of departing a city, the corporation of masters could also do things like suspend instruction. If that suspension lasted very long, students might start to drift away or seek another university. Internally, the faculties elected a rector and were typically obliged by oath to obey his/university rules, which might forbid dissent in situations such as a suspension of instruction. Thus, for example, in 1229 the masters in Paris suspended instruction for more than a year, resulting in Church efforts to find a compromise, lest the Church lose the foundational education provided for the theology program there. Nor were these corporations helpless in the face of the Church, even when it was near the height of its power (as it was through most of the 1200s). For example, the Paris masters for a long time resisted the Church-mandated inclusion of a Dominican and a Franciscan faculty member of the theology faculty, and fought long and hard to bring the people in those positions under the authority of the University's rector—a dispute that took decades to settle. The pope mandated their inclusion in 1257, but that didn't entirely settle the matter [Randall Collins, *The Sociology of Philosophies: A Global Theory of Intellectual Change*, 515; Rashdall, 371-381].

By 1200 or so, the University of Paris began both to be taken under the protective wing of the Church and to be put under more control by the Church. (Of course that control was to weaken some whenever the Church's power ebbed, and also as universities slowly proliferated—but the first university didn't get established in German-speaking regions until after 1360, with Prague preceding that only a little, in 1347.) Above all, the Church wanted Paris to be available to educate the higher clergy. And Bologna and others offered training in Church law (canon law), which had Roman law as its basis. So the Church would sometimes intervene to support the institutions when conflicts arose with the local town (as they invariably did, with some of all those young male students—students often enrolled at age 14—occasionally getting into trouble). Such instances usually included civic punishment of students or townspeople counter-violence against students that was unduly harsh or severe (sometimes involving the death of some students). This tended to produce strong university-level threats/actions. In cases such as Paris, papal legates or other intermediaries on occasion helped in the negotiations or coerced city authorities.

And the Church, ultimately in conjunction with the masters at Church-approved universities, developed a certification process by which individual scholars, once officially recognized as masters by their universities, were certified throughout Xtendom [Frankforter, 209-210]. This certification was important for an institution's status and was entirely satisfactory to the faculty as well because it enabled the potential for them to move between universities. In addition, in many if not most institutions, a high local Church official, such as a bishop, was included, sooner or later, among those who had oversight of the institution and final review of a candidate for a higher degree (master's or doctorate), even though that person very rarely exercised their power independently of the other professor-reviewers (who would include the student's master teacher). When the power of this individual (chancellor) exceeded what the masters were willing to cede, it was usually pared back over time or after some kind of flare-up.

The Church reached the height of its power around the time it launched a crusade against the Cathars (early 1200s). The Church or its agents (such as the local bishop) were most likely to intervene at Paris (and to a lesser extent, elsewhere) against what it regarded as heresy or other threats to the Church. The Church also barred the development of a law school at Paris around 1220, lest its attractiveness dilute the importance of training in theology there [Wieruszowski, 39]. Church interventions about heresy and doctrine involved the teachings of the Amalricians in 1207; the teaching of Aristotle in 1210 and again in 1215; and the purely rational explanation of the ideas of Aristotle (384-322 BCE) and his Muslim interpreter Averroes (Ibn Rushd, 1126-1198) by many of the masters in the arts faculty in 1270 and 1277. See below for more on these last two flare-ups.

The 1200s were also a period of great growth for the mendicant monks—especially the Franciscans but also the Dominicans. They "move to where the intellectual action is," all the while debating their doctrinal differences/disputes, both welcoming recruits from the university students [Collins, 462]. With Paris having its only doctoral program in theology, religious control was probably as strong there as anywhere.

In sum, the university corporations of masters had a very considerable degree of independence from the Church, albeit with some very important exceptions that applied more strongly in some universities than in others. The exceptions applied mainly to ideas that came to be seen as heretical vis-à-vis Church doctrines or otherwise threatened the power of the Church, and those exceptions were especially important in the Church's suppression of potentially proto-scientific areas of curriculum and instruction (again, see below). Otherwise, the Church played little direct role in the formation of the early universities, little role in their governance apart from titular oversight roles and sometimes during crises, and little role in their content, apart from mutually interacting with departments of theology, especially at Paris, around topics pertaining to doctrine. Although some sort of accreditation process made sense, and although the Church's imprimatur certifying that a university was good enough to enable its graduates to teach at any university assisted in facilitating many universities, it also delayed the growth of others or led to their dying on the vine.

So, how much credit should the Church receive for the work of the masters and doctors who teach in the universities—where the first four universities began somewhat independently, albeit two with an affiliation of some kind with a cathedral school. The earliest broad-scope university was Bologna, Italy, which began around 1140 (with earlier roots in a teacher whose enlarged systematization of Roman law was a major advance) and emphasized civil and canon law. Even before that, Salerno, in southern Italy where the culture was influenced by Arab and Greek knowledge, became famous for the teaching of medicine, but stayed more narrowly professional in that focus. It had few direct connections with the Church hierarchy though some of the teachers were churchmen, and it later fell under more direct jurisdiction of the kings of Sicily. Otherwise, Paris was second to form around 1200—but it too had early roots with both independent and cathedral school-affiliated masters/teachers [Rashdall; & Wieruszowski].

In the case of universities, it will help to clarify our thinking if we can reflect on how credit is assigned to professor-scholars now. At the highest level—research-emphasizing universities—a professor's publishing of journal articles and books are what count most in his/her reputation within their field/department (and for promotion within their university)—and that is pretty much all that matters. In comparisons between such universities, the institutions are also credited with the work of professors on their staff in part because they provided the salaries and support system for the research that goes into those articles and books (i.e., largely irrespective of the source of that funding). However, nowadays, at least in the United States, if a renown senior faculty member moves to a different university, his/her reputational value is almost 100% immediately transferred to the new institution. This is confirmed by surveys of faculty, in which professors rate other departments in their own field—where such surveys are then often used as the chief determinants of relative university quality.[8] These professor-raters know where the stars in their field are currently "housed." The same is true for religiously-affiliated research universities, including Catholic ones (although the Church occasionally interferes against doctrinal dissenters, especially in religion and philosophy departments).

Of course, credit for work goes first to the individual who did it, so there is a duplicate credit assigned except that, as above, when a stellar professor changes university, credit for his work done at his former department and institution shifts to the receiving department and institution. It seems most sensible to me to use today's practices in the United States as a model, assigning full credit for a medieval master teacher's writings and teachings both to him, and to his university—at least once the university has formally begun. Before that (e.g., with Abelard), the credit would go to the scholar alone. Initially, the reputation of individual scholars as teachers and disputants was important in drawing students but in time most likely shifted to the university and/or its upper-level program(s) in law, theology, and/or medicine.

Thus, although there were no requirements in medieval times for the masters/doctors (university teachers) to do research, the credit for the few who did proto-scientific work—often people unique in their skills and genius—should be assigned to the individuals and the university or doctoral program, with exceptions *usually* for any such work done by Dominicans and Franciscans, which would be credited to the individual, the theology program, and the Church. But some of the crediting for proto-scientific work by the non-monk faculty in *theology* departments would be something of a borderline area that might need to be treated on a case-by-case basis, though credit would

---

8   For example, see the National Research Council's four volume set that constitute *An Assessment of Research-Doctorate Programs in the United States: Humanities* (also: *Engineering, Social and Behavioral Sciences, & Biological Sciences*), edited by Lyle V. Jones, Gardner Lindzey, and Peter E. Coggeshall. Note that this approach to evaluating the quality of departments essentially assumes that the quality of the researchers equates closely to the value (value-added??) to/for the graduate students.

certainly go to the individual and the program/university, sometimes, or perhaps even often, along with the Church. The principal job of university theologians, and of members of the mendicant orders serving at universities, was to train others entering the Church or their religious orders. But a number of them became famous for their written work on doctrine and a very few did some proto-science writing. And, of course, proto-scientific work done in or for the papacy, or by high Church officials such as cardinals, bishops and abbots, or by monks in the various religious orders, would also normally be credited to the writer and to the Church (e.g., the Jesuits developed the Gregorian calendar in early modern times)—but there are surely some exceptions or at least partial exceptions, as with Bacon, Roger. As a whole, this schema seems to be fair way to estimate the Church's contribution to science—a conclusion that seems confirmed by some special features of the history described below.

Cathedral schools, as well as some other sources of schooling (including tutors), did provide the pre-university education for most students, but students typically went on to the university at ages 12-14, and many of those who served as educators at cathedral schools did not have posts as a canon, even though the cathedrals provided the overseer. So giving much credit to the Church for the development of science because it taught Latin and provided the initial educational setting for most students in most lands—young students who could not begin to make contributions until they had also gone to university—would be inappropriate… at least beyond the initial mandates to cathedrals to develop schools instead of trying to rely solely on monasteries. In addition, university masters/teachers were not usually ordained priests either.

The Church as Patron, Generally

For our purposes here, let's define Church patronage as any expenditure (including of time) on social goods beyond the support of the hierarchy and the maintenance and building of basic meeting places. "Social goods" do not include war-making (with clearly defensive or clearly just wars as possible exceptions). But social goods do include hiring sculptors and painters to decorate churches (even though sometimes the décor, containers for relics, vestments, etc., can also be excessive); the building of many hospitals providing care for the infirm or the aged; the building of bridges, aqueducts and other infrastructure; the restoration of Roman and Greek art and architecture; and other such work. Almost all of these examples did in fact arise during the years 1000-1600, but only some of them owe much to the direct patronage of the Church. Although social goods can count to some extent as aiding human fulfillment, our main interest here is on education, and especially proto-science-related patronage, with a subsidiary interest in other artistic kinds of patronage.

The Church derived its income, some modest proportion of which (net) went into patronage, mainly from taxes (tithes) on the people and from the productivity of the laborers on the many lands it owned. Before the High Middle Ages were well underway, much of this income was in the form of agricultural goods, but I will refer to all income simply as "money." Technically, the amount of the tithe was 10% of income. (I've not yet read anything that indicates how successfully this tax was collected across time and countries, but it was not generally neglected insofar as the Church and subdivisions could collect it. Similarly, it is not clear from what I've read how much of the tithing flowed to the papacy as contrasted with how much was used locally, but at least a little of the income from every Church institution was supposed to move up to the papacy.) The papacy itself, like almost all monasteries and most important cathedrals, had substantial agricultural holdings (in the Papal States) that produced income. In the Late Middle Ages and beyond, both the sale of Church offices and the sale of indulgences were other major source of papal income. Throughout the Middle Ages, other sources of income included all manner of special donations. Extra income from donations was also accrued at pilgrimage sites, including Rome (with much of it there helping to fund the papacy). Another important source, especially in the later Middle Ages, were bequests—normally to a local church. The deceased might leave as little as a candle (if he/she was poor) or as much as a substantial cash donation (or even land), sometimes designated for a specific purpose, possibly including care for the poor. Such bequests might seem best credited to the donor, with the Church as a simple middleman, but Church emphases on sin and the afterlife stimulated the donations. In addition, individuals and communities would often make major contributions of labor or money over time to the building of churches in their town or city, though extra civic taxes also played a role to some extent. (I've seen no proportional breakdowns here, only mentions of individual cases.) These contributions, which in part are attributable to competitions between cities, though again stimulated by Church doctrines, are not patronage expenses coming from the Church but are donations to the Church.

Monasteries (like churches and cathedrals) readily welcomed donations of land and other resources from the faithful—and had been doing so for centuries. The resulting monastery estates needed to be farmed, which required having peasants on that land. Indeed, serfs to work the land accompanied many of the donations of land. While some of these peasants were free vassals of the donor and owned a little parcel of land, especially in earlier times, most were (or became) tenants or serfs. In exchange for the land to farm, and the right to pass that land along to their progeny, serfs were obligated to pay rent as a share of the produce they grew and also to work some of the time on the estates of the "lord," whether a noble/aristocrat or a monastery (later, money equivalents were used). Serfs were bound to the land (could not leave). Renters also had obligations to the monastery as part of their rents, but were not bound to the land. Others, mainly peasants of higher status, would sometimes work directly for the monastery for pay, or serve as "lay brothers" who presumably had a closer affiliation, though that also meant they were more directly subject to monastic rules and discipline.

Large landowners (for a long time the only "wealthy" people in society) gave monasteries (and cathedrals/churches) plots of land, often when near death, to have a better chance to avoid hell/get to heaven through such charity—especially if they had been involved in wars and had killed people (i.e., had mortally sinned). In exchange, they would arrange with the monks (or priests) to have someone say prayers for their souls every day (or on some other regular schedule), sometimes until the end of time (second coming of Christ). Sometimes, and in some places fairly often, wealthy landowners would endow a monastery on their land and pretty much reserve the abbacy position for their progeny henceforth. The build-up of monastery estates was not everywhere continuous, but major confiscations were few indeed until the time of Luther in Germany (after 1517) and England's King Henry VIII in the later 1530s. There was an early exception, however: "As the savior of Christendom (having defeated the Arab-Moor invasion from Spain in 732), [Charles Martel] was able to force the Church to disgorge some of its vast holdings of land," which he gave to his most important warriors/knights [Colin McEvedy, *The New Penguin Atlas of Medieval History*, 34]. A graph from David A. Herlihy's work in 1961 shows the amount of land owned by the Church from 701 to 1200 in 25-year intervals, where the amounts owned at times included as much as a third of all the land in continental Europe [reprinted in Steven A. Epstein, 37]. And although there was indeed a dip in Church/

monastery land ownership in the period 725-750, it was only from about 12.5% to about 8%, and the peak ownership during the same 500 years, at about 28% to 33%, was only shortly thereafter, from about 801 to 875. Many monasteries also made loans to freemen, using their land as security, and when such people failed to repay, for example, due to failed crops or depredation by warlords, the monastery would then own the land and the freeman would become a serf. Depredation by warlords became a major problem especially in large parts of France as the post-Charlemagne (Carolingian) monarchy was weakened by many Viking attacks in the 800s and early 900s. Local warlords ("castellans"—the leaders who controlled one or more castles) competed for power with each other by conquest and pillaging, and there came to be considerable danger to many of the peasants and to their livelihood (homes, possessions, crops). That too obliged many peasants to give up their lands in exchange for protection from their local warlord, count, or bishop or monastery. The monasteries probably also lost some lands during this period.

Monastery estates were almost all rural in character and were involved in agriculture and/or animal husbandry and, as noted, with tenant farmers and/or serfs as the labor force (occasionally along with some lay brothers). They reached their heyday around 1200 and slowly became less important thereafter. Monasteries were involved in patronage by paying for work to decorate the chapels and church(es) for monks and their associated community. A goodly number of individual monasteries became relatively rich and spent considerable wealth on religious paraphernalia such as reliquaries made of silver and gold, statuary, and paintings. In these monasteries, the monks typically came to have a life of relative ease (apart perhaps from their religious discipline). And as some monasteries matured and enlarged, the abbots who led them became wealthy in many respects—in terms of expensive be-jeweled religious clothing, fine food, large retinues of servants and guards when traveling, and later, a few had palatial residences in cities such as Paris as well. Given all the forms of exploitation of the peasantry that produced wealth for the monasteries, it should be mentioned too that monasteries were involved in social welfare patronage that helped feed the most destitute in the population in their vicinity (as did richer landowners with manors to a lesser extent). They often provided overnight refuge and some food for travelers, especially people making pilgrimages (with better accommodations for the high-born). And they maintained facilities for sick and dying monks, often with some access to other local people who were seriously sick. Finally, as we shall see in the next section, monasteries also helped to sustain *some* earlier technology during the "darker," early Middle Ages.

Of course, much of the money received by the Church (or its local branches) was used to pay the priests, church or cathedral administrators and functionaries (canons), and bishops. A goodly amount of resources also went into building and upkeep of the churches, statues and paintings, and religious paraphernalia. Religious clothing for the highest functionaries was typically quite expensive and bishops would sometimes travel with large retinues. Some of these expenses could be regarded as patronage related (e.g., for embroiderers and goldsmiths). Moreover, in most of the High and Late Middle ages (say, 1150 to 1500), most of the highest churchmen lived lives little short of opulent for the times. Church money was also used to help fund crusades and wars against Muslim powers, as well as, very frequently, to hire armies in Italy to defend, expand, or regain the pope's control of the Papal States, or even Rome itself. Wars were expensive and sometimes downright wasteful! In the early modern period (1588), for example, the Church helped fund the King Philip II of Spain's attempt to invade England (with the Spanish Armada to convoy the troops across the English Channel). Overall, Church dogma, inculcated into the people and to a great extent taken up by them as truth, and Church power, produced a huge annual income for the Church and its churches, even though churches in many villages and lower-class sections of towns were relatively poor.

In sum, probably most of what could be considered patronage money was used to pay for Church/churches' decorations, fine art, and some buildings, although modest amounts were also spent on alms and other charitable efforts for the poor. Although Rome itself was the location of considerable expenditures of this kind, far more resources were devoted to the many cathedrals and churches where some of the money or labor was given directly for such purposes. "By definition the seat of a bishop, cathedrals were built with funds often donated largely by nobles and merchants" [Garrett, Wilbur E., Ed., "The Gothic Revolution," in *National* Geographic, Vol. 176, No. 1, 113]. The motives for these donations came not only from individuals' religious devotion but from the "need" to do charitable works for deflecting sin and facilitating salvation. (As above, additional city taxes were also used to an unknown extent.) These buildings also conveyed a civic pride, and having a great cathedral, preferably with important relics, helped to bring revenue to the city.

One key question to ask, then, is this: What would, or could, have been done with the money (resources) that went to the Church (and into Church/church patronage) had it not ended up in Church hands, or if the Church had used its resources differently? If something substantially different had been done, we might not now have amazing and splendid Gothic cathedrals (mainly local enterprises), or Michelangelo's Sistine Chapel, or thousands of paintings and altarpieces of Mary and Jesus attended by various and sundry saints, or thousands of gilded, jewel-encrusted reliquaries as containers for a few shards of bone or hair, or whatever, purportedly from one or another saint. See Plate 3.1. It is worth adding that making war unnecessarily is among the worst possible uses of resources—even though it provides jobs for soldiers and sometimes sailors—because much of the funding goes for equipment and salaries which in turn are used to kill people and destroy cultural structures, from city walls and castles to crops, increasing the waste. But nobody can readily or truly answer whether the results would have been much better for societies in the Middle Ages if the Church/churches had not had all those resources, because history would have had to be much different than it was. Economically, presumably some other entity or entities might have been able to accumulate wealth enough to commission artwork, stimulate the economy, provide jobs, promote research, etcetera. (Or perhaps the peasants could have lived better and more secure lives if they had retained more of the wealth they produced—though that might have slowed the growth of crafts and towns.) Indeed, there existed such other entities in the form of the higher nobility and princes/kings and, in time, in the growing cities. Still, a more realistic question probably would address the extent to which Church priorities might have been different. In any case, to raise such a question as part of this simplified overview does tend to produce one conclusion, namely, that it is very difficult to praise the Church for its patronage, because so much money (resources) was wasted on luxury for the hierarchy, unnecessary wars, and gorgeous but excessive display to enthrall the people with the authority and majesty of the Church. The system was more of a "rip-off" than not, and certainly wasn't the most efficient, effective or productive way to redistribute resources to the communities and the artisanal parts of the economy, but there clearly were at least some compassionate undertakings and some trickle-down effects economically. I should add too that princes and wealthy nobles had similar priorities for their patronage, emphasizing excellent quality personally-owned goods, good food, ostentatiousness in the use of wealth as a way to demonstrate how great they were to the masses, and armed support retinues.

Plate 3.1: Example of a Container (within a display case) for Sacred Objects or Relics from the Cathedral at Seville, Spain.

Having now considered the major general factors involving how much credit might be due to the Church for proto-scientific work done in universities, and for Church expenditures on special projects (patronage), we can proceed to review the most relevant historical data.

CHAPTER 21

The Church Sustains Literacy: ~500 through about 1000+

One very important contribution of the Church is that it remained the source of almost all literacy in the Latin/Roman Catholic area through the "darker ages" of early medieval times—when only a tiny percentage of the population, mostly clerics, was literate. But just how much credit for the development of proto-science does the Church warrant simply because it was almost necessarily (as Roman Catholicism spread/expanded throughout Western Europe), almost the only remaining source for training in literacy? Even when most of the rest of society's institutions collapsed or constricted, one cannot maintain a religion based on a book and not have at least some of that religion's shamans, holy men, rabbis, or priests be able to read that book. So, the Church had to preserve some capacity to train its leaders in reading if that was not otherwise being done.

After the fall of the last of the Western Roman emperors, some of whom had no Roman heritage, the (Eastern) Roman Empire, which later history relabeled the Byzantine Empire, ruled some provinces on the east coast of Italy, such as those in the vicinity of Ravenna until 750 and Bari, until the 1070s, and the same was true for parts of southern Italy and Sicily, the last until 902 (with holdouts after that). And it too was a potential source of education and literacy (at least for the elite), not only among its clergy but also within its administrative hierarchies—but literacy in Greek. And many of the people in the mainly Latin areas ruled by the Byzantine Empire also spoke Greek.

After the fall of the Western Roman Empire, the Western Roman Church was the primary organized institution in Europe as a whole, where most realms (principalities, kingdoms, etcetera) were dominated by Germanic tribes in the process of (re-)settling down. These tribes were organized to varying degrees, and were typically headed by a warrior king. When these tribes invaded, they did not simply destroy everything in their path. Indeed, some if not most of them had been sufficiently imbued with the mystique of the Roman Empire that they wanted to be a part of it—often wanting lands within the empire on which to settle. Failing that (most of the time), the winners instead eliminated all direct military opposition, and the leading warriors often got most of the best land. But that usually meant that the churches and their functionaries simply continued on much as before (e.g., in what was to become Spain, France, and Lombardy—northern Italy), but under different rulers who initially typically were non-believers or heterodox believers. For example, the Visigoths in Spain were originally Arian Xtians (having learned that from Byzantium); the Xtianity of the Arians kept more of a father-to-son relationship, and did not adopt the more equal relationship between deity and son as was done in Roman Xtianity. But these tribes were not nearly so numerous that they needed (or could work) all the agricultural land that was available. So a large majority of the people in most places conquered by Germanic tribes were still holdovers from the Roman Empire, though now of lower status, even though the empire itself no longer played any direct role in their lives.

The Church had another advantage in this situation, that is, in addition to its practitioners' ability to read and write. They could usefully serve kings as administrators, communicators, and tutors for their children. Moreover, the social structure of these tribes was such that if the Church could convert the king to Xtianity, the rest of the tribe would, at least in time (e.g., sometimes 2-3 succeeding kings), follow suit, although sometimes coercion by the converted king was also involved. Thus, when King Clovis of the Franks (the Germanic tribe that took over an area approximately like the France of today) converted to Xtianity in 512, the rest of the Franks slowly converted after that. Of course, as in most other cases as well, they mainly converted in name only at first—they were not very familiar with anything but the most basic promises and doctrines of their new religion, and they retained many pagan beliefs and practices.

Charlemagne's Legacy

Major change and a choppy emergence from "darker" ages began with Charlemagne, albeit with roots in the deeds of his immediate ancestors. See Plate 3.2. Briefly, Charlemagne's grandfather Charles Martel defeated the major invasion of the Arabs-Moors from Spain at Tours in France in 732. His son Pepin took over the French kingship (ousting the Merovingian dynasty, the descendants of Clovis), because he and his family, as "Mayors of the Palace" (chief executive officers/military leaders) had provided the real leadership and were the power behind the throne in any case. Before doing so Pepin also garnered the pope's blessing for the takeover (on the grounds that Pepin was already acting as king), with the pope hoping in return that Pepin would be responsive to an appeal by the pope to attack the Germanic Lombard kingdom in northern Italy because it was making more and more inroads into the papal lands to its south. Charlemagne was one of two of Pepin's sons; he inherited half the kingdom in 768 and the rest three years later when the other son died.

Charlemagne (who ruled until 814) reunified what there was of Latin Christendom via conquest, extending its boundaries somewhat, and restored at least the idea of the Roman Empire. ("Latin Xtendom" here excludes Byzantine possessions in Italy.) Charlemagne was even crowned as Holy Roman Emperor (HRE) by the pope. It is unclear whether this coronation was something they together planned, or was a surprise schemed up by the pope. If it was the latter, it was a long-term play for power by the pope/papacy, trying to set the precedent that the pope's blessing was necessary to confer such a title (in a society in which other rulers tended to appreciate the blessing of the local Church leaders because it added to their aura of having a right to rule).

Plate 3.2: The Author Standing by a Statue of Charlemagne (from about 1600), Aachen City Hall, Germany. Photo by the author's wife, Nancy J. Holland.

In any case, it was Charlemagne, even if only by acting on the advice of the educated clergy he had brought into administrative leadership positions, who mandated the development of cathedral schools to educate more clergy to doctrines of Xtianity so as to yield a more uniform and correct belief system throughout his empire and provide more trained people to assist in administering the empire.[9] This seemed imperative because many of the nominally Xtian peoples at this time, as well as newly-converted pagans, were still attached to a wide variety of differing pagan beliefs. Often the "conversion" required little more than baptism, at least initially, to satisfy Charlemagne's conquering army. But relapse into military opposition could bring harsh retribution, as in the case of the Saxons.

Because of the aforementioned clerical advisors (whom Charlemagne was clever enough to employ), it is hard to know exactly how to divide the credit between the Charlemagne as ruler and the Church for the gains made during his reign. In any case, the most important gains, ultimately contributing to the future of knowledge and literacy (and ultimately proto-science) were the development of cathedral schools and a much greater emphasis in the monasteries on the copying of old manuscripts, thereby better preserving the heritage of Xtianity's founding fathers and doctors, and some important writings from the Roman Empire.

But the rule of Charlemagne's heirs, as well as Charlemagne's legacies, were seriously disrupted in the late 800s and 900s, first by infighting, and then by new rounds of "barbarian" raids and incursions that Europe's kings could not successfully resist or repel—incursions by Vikings from the sea, Magyars on horseback from Hungary, and by princes (emirs) and pirates by sea from north Africa and Sicily. Magyar and Viking attacks sometimes reached well into the heartlands

---

9   Charlemagne's empire ultimately included what is now the Low Countries, France to somewhat south of its current border with Spain (and including Barcelona), Germany up to about the Elbe River and also Bavaria, Austria and Bohemia farther east; south of the Danube it reached into Croatia and Italy, stopping just south of Rome. [For a map, see Epstein, 14.]

of Europe. In Western Europe, Vikings raided up the rivers in the Low Countries and as far as *eastern* France (e.g., to the east of Paris along the River Seine), and set up long-term encampments in northern coastal France (what was to become Normandy, home of men from the North). Vikings took control of some or much of Anglo-Saxon England twice and continued attacks there until 1066 [Christopher Dyer, *Making a Living in the Middle Ages: The People of Britain, 850-1520*]; and they raided and colonized parts of Ireland. The Magyars made major raids on Germany, northern Italy and northern France. North African emirs conquered Sicily (from 827 to 902), and later some of the adjacent Italian mainland, and continually raided much of the southern coast of Italy and Provence (in southeastern France). Besides looting what could be carried off they also captured people, especially in Italy, and sold them into slavery in Muslim lands.

As a way of stabilizing and pacifying the situation involving the Viking settlers in western France, King Charles III of France (a Carolingian) granted them official status (technically as a vassal of the king of France) by giving their leader, Rollo, the title of Duke of Normandy in 911. Presumably Rollo was pleased at having a formal, and typically inheritable title, and a place where his followers did not need to fear counterattacks nearly as much as if he remained an enemy of the king of a then-much-diminished France.

In 955, King Otto I of the now-Xtianized Saxons led his forces to a major victory over the Magyars at the battle of Lechfeld (or Lech) in Bavaria, ending 90 years of their raids on western Europe. Xtianization in Hungary would start with the king a few decades later. The Muslims weren't finally ousted from Sicily until 1061-1091 by Xtian warrior-adventurers originally from Normandy, who had first slowly wrested control of most of the mainland of southern Italy. Despite the many disruptions over this period, some of the institutions established by Charlemagne remained (including some cathedral schools), as did many of the ideals from Charlemagne's time. And in 1079 Pope Gregory VII renewed the mandate to have schools in every cathedral [Grant, 149].

Monasteries and Their Contributions into the High Middle Ages

Monasteries were the primary institutions within the Church in early medieval times that helped to preserve literacy and culture to some considerable extent, mainly by educating monks to read and write, and by copying books. Following Charlemagne's lead, many monasteries took the copying of books to be their major form of work beyond religious observances and exercises and, of course, at least the management of the essentials to operate a monastery and its estates (food production, repairs, etc.). However, until the 12th century, the Roman-sourced books were mainly used to learn/teach Latin, and rhetoric, without much attention to the thoughts therein.

Although the copying done in monasteries included works from Roman times such as Cicero (as an explainer of Stoicism), Boethius (the source for the dialectical parts of Aristotle's logic), Plato's *Timaeus*, the work of the Neoplatonist Plotinus, and Martianus Capella's review of the value of each of the seven liberal arts, the emphasis was on copying works that were of interest to the Church/religion, so some ancient works were undoubtedly lost by omission while others would have been lost without Charlemagne's mandate for more copying. Indeed, "between the sixth century and the middle of the eighth century, Greek and Latin classics virtually ceased to be copied at all" [Stephen Greenblatt, *The Swerve: How the World Became Modern*, 42]. Among the reasons for this lack was that there had been pious attacks on pagan authors and an "active campaign to forget" [Greenblatt, 42]. Thus, some of the most important works from Roman and Greek times lay slowly decaying on monastery library shelves, unread and unconsulted, and some were found only after lucky and laborious searching of monastery libraries/archives by "humanist" scholars from about 1330 to 1450 as the Renaissance got underway in Italy (see below).

But beyond helping to preserve literacy and selected books, if we look for Church-related contributions to proto-science in the early Middle Ages, roughly 500-1050+, we find very little. Isidore of Seville (560-636), archbishop of Seville in Visigothic-Xtian Spain, which was still somewhat post-Roman in character (before it fell to the Berbers and Arabs in 711), prepared an extensive but also highly abridged encyclopedia covering much of Roman culture and knowledge, that is, more in summary fashion than in much detail, and that was passed along into medieval times and frequently consulted. In fact, this became the authoritative and entire source book for most non-religious knowledge of the Roman Empire and its capabilities, including in proto-science and technology. But, given the social conditions (invasions/wars, breakdown of the Empire, poverty/subsistence farming, and emphasis on faith/religion not on other learning) throughout the early Middle Ages, monastery copies of other works did provide at least some potential as a prospective starting place for anyone who was literate and wanted to explore beyond Isidore's rudimentary renditions of what the ancients knew.

"There is no question that knowledge of Greek natural philosophy and mathematical science had fallen off precipitously, and few original contributions to it appeared in Western Europe during the early centuries of the medieval period (roughly 400-1000)" [Lindberg, *Beginnings*, 155]. As one specific example, the only original formulation about nature for eight centuries in the Latin West was about tidal phenomena, by Venerable Bede in England in the 700s, but also that that contribution "must have been common knowledge among fishermen and mariners" [Grant, 145].

In fairness to the history here, however, it is important to note that the Romans had already resorted to an emphasis on encyclopedist-like summaries of knowledge derived from Greece and the culture spread by Greece during the Hellenistic/post-Alexander world, in which a particularly strong tradition of learning had developed in Alexandria, Egypt. But during the "darker" early Xtian era, that already-summarized knowledge was boiled down more and much was simply set aside, in part due to its pagan origins.

Although the main "work" of the monks was to pray—6 times in a 24-hour period, they did make some contributions in the early development of music, which was one of the subjects in the seven liberal arts that were used as a basis for education throughout the later Middle Ages. Although music may have a tenuous relationship with proto-science, in the teaching there was considerable emphasis on its mathematical properties. By the 13th century, and quite possibly throughout medieval times, there was also a "great deal" of ordinary people's involvement in secular music, wandering troubadours and minstrels, etcetera. "People have never ceased to sing and to dance, and medieval people had a tendency to accompany all sorts of events with music" [Frankforter, 323]. There is lots of picture and textual evidence as proof of this, and the same is true for the presence of many new instruments [Frankforter, 323]. So the technology of instrument-making advanced as the centuries passed (and undoubtedly affected at least some other developments in craftsmanship).

With reference to the contribution of monasteries specifically, Cluny was especially famous for its monks' singing/holy chanting. Monasteries developed musical notation, with early modern forms first being used with music such as Gregorian chants [mfiles.co.uk, "A Short History of Musical Notation"]. In time, rules of harmony began to be explored, and by the 13th century polyphony was developing. "Paired lines, each of which was an independent melody, worked together to create a complex, harmonious whole" [Frankforter, 323]. However, the Church ultimately became distressed with the misfit between its goals and some of the more advanced forms of music, including some polyphony. According to a papal bull of John XXII in 1322, this music could be seen as "'intoxicating the ear, not soothing it'" while "'devotion, the true end of worship, is little thought of, and wantonness, which ought to be eschewed, increases'" [Alfred W. Crosby, *The Measure of Reality: Quantification and Western Society, 1250-1600*, 158].

One major area of monasterial cultural contribution involved the "illumination" of manuscripts—the addition to book texts of colored and highly decorative lettering, drawings and story depictions. This tradition, which was not entirely monastery-bound especially in the later Middle Ages, lasted until the printing press and its methods supplanted it. Before the printing press, as wealth spread to some degree, many of those with money would buy psalters—books with prayers, Bible stories briefly rendered and some artistic illuminations of those stories, with perhaps the grandest of all perhaps being the one done for the royal family's Duke of Berry in France, but finished only around 1487, well after the book had passed to heirs of the Duke [Musée Condé, Chantilly, *The Très Riches Heures of Jean, Duke of Berry*, 23-24].

In sum, "the contribution of the religious culture of the early middle ages to the scientific movement was ... primarily one of preservation and transmission" [Lindberg, *Beginnings*, 156]: the preservation of literacy and of a smattering of the knowledge of the ancients, via the copying of manuscripts in monastery scriptoria. Otherwise, apart perhaps from a start on music and illuminated manuscripts, the Church's contribution seems to have been only modestly above a kind of relatively bare minimum—almost the least that one could hope for under the circumstances, especially after Charlemagne had launched so many initiatives to strengthen religion, education, and society. But the monasteries (and therefore the Church) can also be said to be at least partly responsible for a number of important areas of technological knowledge that did get transmitted (see below).

Although at least some monasteries took in foundlings (to become monks or become lay brothers), even in their heyday after 1000 or so, they did not endeavor to educate the peasantry generally (despite their mainly rural locations). But they did educate some children, typically of higher status, who seemed especially able and suited to serve as a monk or enter the priesthood. With few exceptions, monastery leaders (abbots, priors, et al.) were drawn from the nobility, or promoted from within (usually drawing upon their higher-class denizens). Other monks were normally drawn from the upper middle range in the social classes, which in time came to include bourgeois city-dwellers, and occasionally some freemen. As primogeniture became widespread, monasteries more frequently took in second and later sons of nobles and knights. Primogeniture spread rapidly after about 1100—leaving second and subsequent sons without estates—because dividing estates led to the weakening of the all the branches of a family, impairing its interest in preserving its fame, power, and posterity. (Insofar as possible, all daughters were married out of the immediate family, ideally into useful family alliances.)

CHAPTER 22

Technology as a Conveyance of Proto-science through the Darker Ages and Beyond

I have begun to mention technology, but why consider technology at all? Today, many technological advances result from an application of scientific knowledge, although the reverse—technological advances leading to new scientific discoveries—occurs too. Indeed, the further back one goes into the darker ages of medieval and late Roman times, the more likely it is that technology was ahead of science. Even as late as the late 19th and early 20th centuries, with inventors such as Thomas Edison and the Wright brothers, it is not clear that science knowledge played a major role in their discoveries. And as one goes back in time, inventors building on the work of previous inventors is even more prevalent. In medieval times, developments occurred in technology in almost if not nearly the complete absence of any associated proto-science. But many of these technological advances became important toward the end of the Middle Ages and into the early modern period because they helped to provide the foundational empirical observations and knowledge that proto-science used to help extract the principles from the technology to begin to formulate scientific principles, theories, and laws. See Clifford D. Conner's *A*

People's History of Science: Miners, Midwives, and "Low Mechanicks", for an especially strong statement of this case.

Monasteries Were Among the Early Conveyors of Subsistence Technology

Among the upper class men in medieval times, there was a long-standing prejudice, dating back to Roman and Greek times, against nobility getting their hands dirtily immersed in any kind of physical work (other than warfare)—and most high clergy and (later) university students came from such non-peasant backgrounds. This prejudice against physical labor was reinforced by a general, clerically-proffered (but not as an official doctrine) tripartite division of society into those who prayed, those who fought, and those who worked. The overwhelming majority were those who worked, of course, and almost all of them were peasants on the land. And the negative attitudes of the higher classes toward the peasants were appalling.

City-dwellers didn't really quite fit into this schema because most of them were artisans/craftsmen and laborers, and the former made a living in a trade and charged money for their goods, where anything even vaguely akin to usury or profiteering, especially but not exclusively via interest on loans, was regarded with suspicion in Church doctrines. And for the craftsmen, exactly how much was a fair price, after all? So, in some respects, their lives did not fit into the existing religious schema, and some very much yearned to know how better to ensure their salvation.

This avoidance of hands-on labor was even true for the most part of monks despite the fact that the Benedictine Rule, formulated in the late 500s as a guide to how to run a Benedictine monastery—the main line of monks for centuries—included physical labor as part of the role of monks. Thus monasteries helped to conserve Roman technology in plant grafting, horticultural arts, and viticulture [Frances & Joseph Gies, *Cathedral, Forge, and Waterwheel: Technology and Invention in the Middle Ages*, 48]. But as time went on—apart from occasional renewals and re-emphases of the Benedictine rule when the monks were accused of having fallen into too much luxury, less and less of their work became physical labor (which was delegated to serfs and peasants on an abbey's estates, or to lay brothers). Among the newer orders emerging, with an emphasis on "the ideals of apostolic life, poverty and penitence, ... were the Carthusians (1084), Cistercians (1098) and Premonstratensians (1120)" [Erlande-Brandenburg, *The Cathedral Builders of the Middle Ages*, 20]. These new orders facilitated the spread of a better understanding of the faith among the masses and a greater degree of participation in it [Collins, 462]. (Implicit here is more indoctrination into the faith and a reduction in folk beliefs.) The Cistercians grew rapidly to have many "daughter" monasteries. They especially wanted to re-emphasize land reclamation, manual labor, animal husbandry, and abstain from rich décor, but in a few decades, they too were much richer and less dedicated to their original ideals (e.g., lay brethren did much of the work and sometimes rebelled). Whether or not the Cistercians made a major contribution to advances in land clearance seems to be disputed by historians, although they did make some advances in sheep/wool production [Pamela O. Long: *Technology and Society in the Medieval Centuries: Byzantium, Islam, and the West, 500-1300*, 44-45; this is Long1].

In general, though, the monkish labors most often came to involve work in the scriptoria, copying books—a much-needed endeavor as well. However, some had little talent for that work (or could no longer see well enough) and at least some monks necessarily had to act as supervisors of the abbey's grounds and buildings and agricultural plots, and of the serfs and tenants on the monastery's estates. In extreme exemplars such as Cluny from about 950 on, the situation evolved so that monks spent vast proportions of their time in oral prayers and prayerful chanting, where all in earshot could hear. This built Cluny's reputation as a holy site close to the deity. And that helped in its peace-making efforts, promoting the "Peace of God," around the countryside where competing warlords (castellans) had sometimes even attacked monasteries' estates or Church holdings. But working mainly in the scriptoria also likely reinforced the separation of the monks and the Church from physical labor, as very few monks would learn the skills and crafts associated with technology (e.g., carpentry, masonry, metal-working, pottery, glazier work, stained glasswork, etc.). For these kinds of work, practical-applied knowledge was essential.

But, in any case, the period from 500CE to about 1050 saw the technological rudiments in some areas of proto-science conveyed along within the culture by the preservation of *some* aspects of (Greco-) Roman technology, including especially the technologies most needed for the facilitation of a largely agricultural subsistence economy. Indeed, the monasteries—often in semi-isolated locations around the countryside—had to strive for self-sufficiency in this economy, and so they had to retain knowledge of the most basic technological skills in their workshops. When jobs were assigned to peasants in this system, the skills would typically be passed along from father to son(s). One way or another, the monastery community as a whole would include the know-how to make "wooden objects such as furniture and barrels, cloth and clothing, pottery, leather goods, and metal objects made by a blacksmith. Some monasteries also supported skilled artisans who produced finely worked liturgical objects, from candlesticks to embroidered garments" [Long1, 52].

In these ways, the Church was also at least somewhat helpful in transmitting some of the most basic (Roman-era) technology to the future as the Latin West slowly emerged from the debilitating attacks by Vikings, Magyars and Muslim princes (emirs) and pirates from the north of Africa throughout much of the 800s and 900s. But it is important to note too that most of this contribution by the Church (monasteries) was shared with secular sources (see below). Also, Long's mention of a blacksmith is NOT equivalent to someone who extracts/refines iron from ores, but only someone who re-works iron that already exists, for example, to sharpen or repair broken tools or fashion new ones from iron rods or bars or, later, ingots.

Other Sources Conveyed Technology Forward in Time Too

The contribution of monasteries to maintaining technology was by no means unique except perhaps with regard to book copying and the making of some religious paraphernalia and perhaps some narrow agricultural specialties. Manors held by nobles also had to maintain enough technology to be largely self-sufficient. For example, most manors of any size had at least a blacksmith shop [Epstein, 50].

And secular settlements (big towns, little cities) and work sites sometimes served especially important roles in the development and conveyance of technology. One way to illustrate this, and the general point here, is to consider the finds from an archaeological dig at Jorvik (York, England). All of the information to follow is derived from the York Archaeological Trust, *Jorvik Viking Centre: Companion Guide*, 2017 or an earlier guide, *Jorvik Viking Centre*, no date, or from my talking with the staff (some of whom act out roles) on a visit there.

The Jorvik finds date from about 975 from an area in England that was for about 100 years ruled by non-Xtian Vikings but had been retaken by English kings in the 950s. The people of York were of mixed heritages. The Vikings, as traders and raiders, would have spread any technology they invented, or learned from trading, to any long-term settlement they made. York may thus have been more advanced in this regard than other areas in England (but not necessarily more than some of the cities in Italy). But keep in mind too that many archaeological sites have limited accessibility (e.g., much of the old city of York is still underneath the current city) and some of the potential finds are permanently lost to the earth, whether through decay, fires, floods, accident, or whatever. However, the sometimes-boggy conditions for preserving lost items were exceptional at Jorvik, so the finds are remarkable in range.

Among the tools and artefacts made of iron (mainly, but also copper and lead) found at Jorvik were one or more of the following: horseshoes, stirrups, spurs and fetters; a small anvil; nails and wires; needles, and awls for leatherwork (also made of bone); pins as clasps for clothes, brooches, and a kind of buckle; tweezers; gouges, shaves, wedges, files, tongs for working with hot iron, shears, hammers, and ax heads (for felling trees); a helmet; knives, some with hardened steel edges; pans and hook-like devices for suspending cooking pots over fires; fascinating small barrel-shaped locks and their keys; and small crucibles. There were also soapstone molds for shaping molten metal. There is evidence that smelting of iron ore was done somewhere in the immediate region.

In addition, there were metal dyes (molds) found for hammer-minting of coins, typically made of silver.

Also unearthed was a hand-held metal balance with some associated weights, used in assessing the extent of value remaining in coins that had been clipped (a standard practice to facilitate payment). In similar fashion, many of the other tools and artefacts above also involve/imply much more than just the items themselves, for example, the leatherwork-connected skills associated with awls, or the wood-working uses of the shaves, gouges and wedges.

Beyond metals, Jorvik tool finds also included a wooden mallet; intricate antler combs (multi-pieced, riveted together) useful in combatting lice and nits; and pottery, including better vessels imported from the Rhineland and locally-made small cooking pots, and pitchers.

More surprisingly, there was a pedal-driven pole lathe (with an iron gouge) for making wooden bowls and spoons, which were plentiful in the dig.

And there was evidence of two kinds of looms, one a "warp-weighted loom" (with pottery-based circles used as weights) and the other a "two-beam vertical loom." Several dyes for coloring clothes were also used locally.

Also made locally were leather shoes, purses, and sheaths.

Finally, finds included small glass beads of different colors (made and colored locally), evidence of beekeeping, and musical instruments. These instruments included boxwood pan pipes, a stringed instrument (for which a bridge was found), a bone whistle, and a tuning key.

In sum, the finds at Jorvik provide a treasure trove of evidence that technology was present and being passed along outside the realms of Church monasteries. And that there was considerable diffusion across cultural and religious divides cannot be doubted.

But Some Technologies Were Lost

Overall, in Xtendom, there was much more technology that was lost than was invented between 400 and 1050. For example, the Romans learned how to make truly excellent concrete (even by today's standards), but how to do it was forgotten. So most bridges could only be made entirely of wood. Ptolemy and others in Roman-Hellenistic Egypt knew how to make maps and had the idea of longitudes, but Xtian maps degenerated to symbolic round circles with Jerusalem at the center of the world that were of little or no use otherwise. Many architectural skills were lost (some are mentioned later). Even though Vitruvius' book on architecture was available in a few monasteries, it was largely beyond comprehension to any likely readers. As noted earlier, much of the knowledge of the ancient world was available only in a boiled-down form through three encyclopedists who further condensed previous condensations—that is, ultimately, often with no remaining practitioners in the Western Roman Empire.

Thus, when Cluny, a Benedictine monastery located in what is now southeast central France and which was to become the parent monastery for many "daughter" houses, first needed to greatly enlarge its church buildings (about 1030?), its leaders called upon master masons from the Lombardy region of Italy to do so [Edwin Mullins, *Cluny: In Search of God's Lost Empire*, 29]. Because some cities had remained more viable in Lombardy and northern Italy, and in areas associated with Byzantium or Sicily, workmen in those areas had retained more of the skills needed in civilized society generally. However, Roman machines for lifting heavy objects in construction projects were another lost technology, so more primitive methods and manpower or animal power had to be substituted [Alain Erlande-Brandenburg].

More pessimistic as to the retention of skills in the cities and more optimistic as to involvement of early patrons in architecture, Erlande-Brandenburg writes: "Whereas in Carolingian times there were trained architects, they no longer existed because ambitious building projects had disappeared; everything had to be learned again." As a result, he says, a patrons such as bishops or abbots familiar with the buildings of antiquity (and some other recently-built cathedrals) "were forced to become architects themselves to realize their vast plans.... They looked to those ancient structures as models for themselves and the architects they wanted to convince" [Erlande-Brandenburg, 42].

But there is an inconsistency in this citation: the patron specifies his desires for a building, but he does very little beyond that. In reading Erlande-Brandenburg, I saw few if any examples in which the patron did more than specifying features such as the rough length and width of the proposed building and some of the main characteristics that he wanted included in it (e.g., by reference to other edifices). In the documents section of this little book, the closest example to churchmen participating in other ways was this: "Laymen and clergy tried to outdo each other in helping him [the abbot, in rebuilding a church in 1039]; several members of the clergy of their own accord used their carts and their oxen for the transport of materials" [Erlande-Brandenburg, 130-131]. But this is basic, unskilled labor—even assuming that the monks did more than just lend the monastery's carts and oxen to others doing the physical work. Also, by "the middle of the 13th century, far fewer men entered the monasteries, leading to the employment of outsiders who had to be paid." And, very near the start of the Cistercian's expansion into many daughter houses: "As early as 1133 St [sic] Bernard had begun to hire workers to help the monks erect new buildings at Clairvaux" [Erlande-Brandenburg, 101]. My conclusion here is that very, very few monks had any of the skills needed to build churches.

Moreover, there were no "architects" at the time. It was the master masons who knew best how to build with stone—and select the stone, extract the stone from the quarry, and then cut it into the necessary shape(s). (My copy of Erlande-Brandenburg is translated from the French, so that may account for the chronologically premature use of the word "architect.") But until the High Middle Ages era of church building got underway, few master masons would have had any experience building Church structures. So the patron had to express what was wanted, and the master mason had to figure out how to do it. But it was the master masons who made the progress toward greater technological capability, not the patrons, even though Abbot Suger

of Saint-Denis in Paris is famed for selecting the particulars that produced the first "Gothic" portion of his church (St. Denis).

Thus, as the Roman empire dimmed, the preservation of technology in virtually all of the Latin West became much more dependent
on capabilities at the village level, at the manor, and at the monastery,
and in the occasional town or city, although there was always some
trade, both locally and in necessities like salt and iron for tools and
weapons. There was also some exchange between the Eastern Roman
Empire (Byzantium) and that empire's several areas of control or
affiliation on the Italian peninsula (see above). Non-Xtianized areas
under control of Germanic (or Slavic) tribes retained their original
trade networks as well. The Vikings not only had their own ironworks
in Sweden, but made major advances in ship-building—including
ocean-going ships—and also began trading along the interior rivers
within the Russian Slav lands by around 700 or so. Their trade networks
occasionally transported items made in the Middle East and parts of
what was much later the southern U.S.S.R., a few of which made it as
far as Jorvik. And there was at least some direct Latin West trade with
the Muslim world in north Africa and Spain.

Also lost was some of the ability to paint in what appears to be
three dimensions and to render the human form proportionately
(e.g., browse web-available paintings of Mary and baby Jesus from the
1200s). This seems irrelevant to technology, but the (re-)discovery of
how to do 3D perspective had surprising technological and scientific
consequences (more later).

Early Advances in Technology Are Mainly Adaptations of Roman, Chinese, or Arab Technology

In addition, a few advances in technology, the ideas for which were
mainly imported from outside Europe or were continued from areas

retaining more Roman heritage, slowly spread over more of the Latin West. From Roman times, swords of Toledo steel (Spain) were known for their high quality, and presumably provided a model of what could be done. (Plus, Xtians took Toledo from Muslims relatively early, in 1085.) Among other transmissions to the Latin West were stirrups from the steppes of Asia. Waterwheels as sources of power for milling grain were a carryover from Rome, but the waterwheels later were built mainly in an upright and much more powerful form, a form that had necessarily been rare in water-poor southern Europe. Monasteries helped to spread this technology, but were not the only ones to do so. One of the best documented examples of the widespread adoption of waterwheels comes from an extensive accounting in England, ordered by William the Conqueror in 1086, and recorded in *The Domesday Book*. That accounting showed 6,000 waterwheels in England, including some horizontal ones [Dyer, 25], where probably very few existed in 900 when individual households ground their own grain using hand mill stones. Also adopted in many more places was the three-field system, which involved a one-third decrease in the time land spent fallow (unfarmed), and enabled the production of more food and thereby the support of a larger population. (In either system, uncultivated fallow land was grazed and defecated upon by livestock to help restore the soil.) In addition, the growing of peas came to be a regular part of agriculture in some areas, and, as a legume that fixes a crucial plant nutrient (nitrogen) into the soil, peas can help to restore soil and better sustain soil fertility with less time spent fallow. The Asian-sourced invention of a shoulder-resting collar that enabled a horse to pull significant loads (rather than choking the horse with a neck-style collar like the ones used on oxen) made possible a conversion from ox to horse in most plowing. The changeover to horses was slow because it also required that oats be grown wherever grasses were insufficient, and in some if not many environments, iron horse shoes were needed as well.

An overview of developments in technology from around the time of Charlemagne until the beginning of the early modern period is presented subsequently.

The Church's Patronage as a Contributor to the Advance of Technology in the High and Late Middle Ages

There simply is no way to judge whether better quality paintings and sculptures would have emerged had the resources of the Church instead been spent by other entities in the realm of Latin Xtendom, let alone the comparative social value had the resources been expended on other endeavors instead. Besides, before the (re-)invention of three-dimensional perspective in the early 1400s, it seems artificial to me to make comparisons *among* Latin/Western Church artists. But within that limited range, I personally have not been impressed by the creativity involved in the innumerable paintings of the Virgin Mary, baby Jesus, and some number of saints, though there was some slow progress toward greater realism. However, the shift of painters from being mainly monks to artist's workshops seemed to improve the results (see below). And as for sculptures in various mediums, the Greek (and Roman) civilizations were well ahead of Latin/Western Church sculptures until at least the later 1400s.

Still, mainly in the High and Late Middle Ages, the Church and its subsidiary centers (bishoprics, cathedrals, etc.), as the single largest patron in society, must be given at least some indirect credit for main-taining and advancing certain areas of technological knowledge. Its monasteries and cathedral centers had to have artisans and craftsmen such as masons and carpenters to build churches and cathedrals, and painters and sculptors to decorate them, and glaziers to install the windows. Church patronage was almost all-important to the modest refinements of glaziers' skills to create and install stained glass windows in churches. Stained glass windows were made by inserting colored pieces of glass, some simply painted glass, others infused with color from select minerals, into a lead frame/skeleton. See Plate 3.3. But with the exception of finding several new colors for the glass itself in the 14th century, there was little added to the original Roman technology [Martyn Barr, *Paintings in Light: The Stained Glass Windows of Canterbury* Cathedral, 5-14]. So, because most Church funds came from taxes on the people in the first place, or from religious pilgrims, it is fair to remind the reader again that, absent the Church, these resources could have been used in similar or different ways that may have advanced these or other technologies, and either more so, or less so.

Moreover, also as noted earlier, direct city and citizen support also contributed substantially to the funding for cathedral and church construction in almost all places. But in some cases, these citizen contributions were obligated by the imposition of additional taxes, whether by a city or a subdivision of the Church. For example, on monastery lands, additional taxes might be imposed on the peasants working the land. At one extreme, for example, in Vézelay, France, "to accommodate the influx of pilgrims a new abbey church was begun, dedicated on April 21, 1104, but the expense of building so increased the tax burden in the abbey's lands that the peasants rose up and killed the abbot" [Wikipedia article on the Abbey Church at Vézelay, accessed 3/28/2017]. So just as the abbots in monasteries funded their many religious structures from revenues from their lands (and donations), Church patronage in terms of funding (in contrast to just sponsorship), especially from the papacy's income, was by no means the major support for church building and decoration, except in Rome, and in Avignon when the papacy was there for about 70 years.

It should be pointed out too that while refinement in artistic techniques was welcome, originality was not a value promoted by the Church/churches. Through much of the time before about the mid-15th century, the goal of painters, fresco artists, and sculptors and even stained glass craftsmen was to replicate the standard model of the religious subject chosen for portrayal by (local) church authorities, partly because the Church was using all the artwork as a means of communicating Xtian religious stories and morals to the illiterate masses, and it wouldn't do to have the same biblical or saintly person look markedly different from place to place, or be simply one among a large number of unrecognizable persons depicted. To assist in this recognition, many of the saints were assigned standard features to accompany their images, even though popular saints or Mary, Mother of Jesus, were used to tell several different stories. For example, the Apostle Peter, who purportedly was given the keys to heaven by Jesus and who, as an early bishop of Rome supposedly passed those keys along to his successors (the bishops of Rome, aka the popes), was typically depicted with a set of large keys. And some Xtian martyrs were almost invariably depicted along with the instruments that killed them—whether by beheading, roasting in a fire, piercing by arrows, or by other means.

There was at least one significant exception to the rejection of many aspects of creativity by the Church: the gargoyles on cathedrals. Gargoyles were known in antiquity and so were still present in some places in Italy (e.g., Pompeii), and one was even included in very early in the High Middle Ages on the Rouen cathedral. Gargoyles were used extensively in Gothic cathedral construction from about 1220 onward. Creating gargoyles was one of the few areas of church "decoration" over which the artisans had considerable freedom if not almost complete control, resulting in a great range of subjects, much less stereotypy, and some remarkable pieces [Janetta Rebold Benton, *Holy Terrors on*

Medieval Buildings, 10-14]. Moreover, in order to give them enough long-term strength, given their constant assault by rainwater (gargoyles serve as gutter spouts), they came to be cut and sculpted from single pieces of stone in which a section of that stone was part of the church structurally.

Plate 3.3: Rosette Stained Glass Window, Notre Dame Cathedral, Paris (before the 2019 fire). Photo by the author.

Moreover, presumably due to the growing expertise and range of artistic capabilities available in artist workshops, paintings done for churches, which had engaged at least some churchmen in the High Middle Ages, became more and more to be produced in secularized workshops. So, despite some early well-known church-affiliated painters (e.g., Fra Angelico, Fra Lippo Lippi), they became a real rarity. Instead, local church authorities would commission an artist's workshop to produce a piece or pieces of one kind or another (e.g., an altarpiece, a set of sculptures) and the master artist would engage the entire shop in the production of the piece(s). Initially, paintings were credited to the workshop by name of its leader but, in most such cases, no one now knows for sure who did what portions of any given work.

This changeover to artists' workshops is associated chronologically with technological-artistic advances, and the artists' interactions likely were contributive in that regard, but the tenor of the times and other discoveries were surely also a major factor. In the 1400s, in Florence, Italy, for example, among the major advances were improvements on doing relief work in bronze. Most crucially, also rediscovered was how to create perspective in drawing so as to convey a three-dimensional impression to the eyes of the viewer (more later). Although churches were usually still involved as recipients of the art, the initial patron was frequently the city of Florence and/or its then de facto rulers, the Medici. And from these Florentine artist workshops there emerged several giants of the revolution in Renaissance art. And cities, city-states, countries, and princely rulers also became more important among the patrons of art—which was also broadened as to subject matter (e.g., in portraiture).

Cathedrals and Churches. In terms of the resources invested, the largest projects were almost undoubtedly the building of cathedrals and churches. There were a great number of churches built between about 1050 and 1350, at first Romanesque in character, later mainly Gothic (except in Italy). For example, in France between "1050 and 1350... [there were built] eighty cathedrals, five hundred large churches and some tens of thousands of parish churches" [Erlande-Brandenburg, 34]. Almost surprisingly, the master masons who worked on these cathedrals did so without knowledge of geometry per se. Instead, they worked extensively with proportions, using a compass to create equal line segments in their plans, and made frequent use of stencils for the replication of repetitive parts of a building. Their designs, incorporating the desire of the patron or sponsor, would then be shared with him/them for final approval.

The technological developments most important for the capability of building "Gothic" cathedrals were the invention of light-weight ceiling supports—vaulted ceilings with thin ribs of support and the stronger pointed arch (Arab-sourced, possibly from India)—as contrasted with the semi-circular Roman arch. See Plate 3.4 and 3.5. The pointed arches thus allowed thinner pillars and enabled greater height but also transferred more of the pressure from the weight of the roof toward the ground, and less horizontally, toward the walls [Frankforter, 222]. The ribs supporting the ceiling vaults rise from pillars on each side, meeting in several places along the central axis of the ceiling. The ceiling vaults and pointier arches that allowed for higher ceilings also enabled large windows within the arches in the upper walls, because massive pillars and mostly solid walls were no longer necessary to support the reduced weight of the roof/ceiling. See Plate 3.5. This enabled much more light to beam into the cathedral's interior, and stained glass windows, some of them huge (but with internal lead skeletons, e.g., as in the rosette shown in Plate 3.3), to cast an array of colors into the church when light shone through them from outside.

Another important invention was the flying buttress, though buttresses were not new. A buttress is basically an exterior support for the side walls, to which decoration could be added. Buttresses weren't exactly fundamental but helped assure a structure's soundness, especially when thinner pillars were used in the interior. However, flying buttresses became more important because some cities tried to outdo each other in building large/tall cathedral interiors, such that some of the most over-reaching and worst-constructed roofs collapsed because there was still too much horizontal pressure pushing the walls outward from the weight of the ceiling/roof. A flying buttress helped. It is much like a person, arm extended, leaning up against a wall to help hold it up. The weight of the pinnacles on top of the flying buttress (if any) add to their strength. See Plate 3.6.

In 1071, pointed arches "were worked into the design of a rebuilding project at the Benedictine motherhouse at Monte Cassino, Italy" [Frankforter, 222]. Probably the idea was borrowed from Sicily most of which was under Muslim domination for 200 years starting in the early 800s. Not long after, pointed arches were used to some extent in rebuilding the large Romanesque monastery church at Cluny. Abbot Suger of the St. Denis monastery in Paris, the burial place of French kings at the time, was the first to plan (with a master mason) a rebuilding that combined the vaulted ceiling and the pointed arch— while including many windows—producing the first Gothic-style edifice [Frankforter, 222]. (The "Gothic" descriptor was not used until much later.)

Finally, clearly, there was little interest *per se* on the part of the Church, or its members, in efforts by artisans or craftsmen that advanced architecture or civil engineering and the associated technologies (e.g., hoists and other mechanical construction devices). Later we will briefly review some of the key advances in technology during this period to better see how independent they were of the Church. In sum, for the most part, Church/church leadership served as very general planners and sponsors, and to some extent as funders for building churches, but mainly acted as conduits for the people's money, and as deciders of what decorative representations/artwork would be included. The resources invested contributed to some technological advances in architecture, engineering, and the decorative arts, but few churchmen were involved in any details beyond making proposals for basic design elements.

Plate 3.4: Forest of Columns and High (double) Arches, 8th-10th Century, Mosque at Cordoba. Photo by the author.

Plate 3.6: Array of Flying Buttresses (the "bone-studded" upward-arcing arms) and Pinnacles, Cathedral at Cologne, Germany (rear view). Photo by the author.

Plate 3.5: Interior of Canterbury Cathedral, England. Note Thin(ner), Tall(er) Pillars, Ribbed Ceiling Vault Supports, and Stained Glass Windows above the Pillars. Photo by the author.

CHAPTER 23

Education Begins to Spread

As we proceed further here, one of the things we want to watch for is the degree of openness to, and acceptance of, the use of reasoning by the Church, especially about the natural world—irrespective of Church doctrines. Will the Church encourage exploration, including in the real world (e.g., to learn about the deity's creation)? Will it fall back on the authority of Church fathers, doctors, popes and previous Church councils—that is, faith, as the primary determinant of what is true and real? Will it opt for some blend of those two? *If the last, to what extent, if any, will the Church do so in a way that forecloses some or many possibilities on the side of exploration and reason?* To what extent will it allow even if not actually welcome persons who are challenging in this regard? Will it tend to shut them down, one way or another, through dismissal or silencing (e.g., banishment to silence in a monastery), forced recantation and the associated burning of the author's works, a destroyed reputation, excommunication (a bar to a heavenly afterlife), prosecutions for heresy, or even death sentences? And to what extent will its rules and actions warn scholars or others "not to go there" (some potential area of study) in the first place? Correspondingly, to what extent will proto-scientists with challenging ideas be forced to self-censor, to portray what they believe in some peculiar format that conceals what they believe, or to publish some materials only after their death, forfeiting any hope of exchanging ideas to improve their work?

Between Charlemagne's mandate to develop cathedral schools and its papal reaffirmation in 1079, there was one outstanding intellectual figure who helped get more irons into the fire. He was Gerbert of Aurillac, who had gone to study the quadrivium—the mathematically-influenced 4-part side of the seven liberal arts—at a monastery in Catalonia. Catalonia in northeastern Spain (surrounding Barcelona) was then on the border between Muslim and Xtian worlds. Most importantly, the monastery could access manuscripts available only in the Muslim world, in this case linked to the Caliphate of Cordoba (Spain)—then one of the leading intellectual centers of the world, with thousands upon thousands of books in its main library. Gerbert came away from that experience with knowledge not possessed by anyone else in the main areas of Latin/Western Xtendom. Before becoming Pope Sylvester II (999-1003), Gerbert helped to establish a strong teaching tradition at Reims, especially in arithmetic, logic and astronomy-astrology. Gerbert also re-introduced the abacus (or counting board) to Latin Xtendom, enabling far faster calculations than with Roman numerals (though it would be centuries before the regular use of Roman numerals ceased), and he wrote a textbook on how to use it—which was widely used in the cathedral schools [Lynn Harry Nelson, *Medieval History Lecture Index*]. Gerbert's efforts may well also have been the start of a changeover in emphasis from rhetoric to logic (the dialectic) in Xtian education [David L. Wagner, Ed., *The Seven Liberal Arts in the Middle Ages*, 24]. Gerbert also built an organ, with mathematically better pipes that improved the harmonics—with a bellows operated by water power, no less, instead of a bellows foot-pumped by an assistant to the organist. In his teaching of astronomy, he used an armillary sphere—a hollow globe-like representation of the earth showing an equator, a tropic of cancer and of Capricorn, and the courses (*around the earth*) of important planets and "northern" and "southern" stars. See Plate 3.7. He is also said to have introduced the astrolabe to scholars of the Xtian world, though few if any could yet use it because it required considerable knowledge of the heavens and earth to construct or appreciate. "The astrolabe functioned as an observational instrument which enabled astronomers to determine the time of sunrise and sunset and the positions of celestial bodies" [Long1, 37]; its primary importance is probably in navigation beyond the sight of land. Given the wonderment of all this, some churchmen suspected this pope of involvement in magic, in engagement with the forces of evil, and many such suspicions lingered even after his death. After Gerbert, there was a long hiatus, but in which some students of his helped keep things percolating below the surface. But even well beyond Gerbert's time, most literate monks or churchmen remained very dubious about any reliance on reason, including the reason-based "proofs" of the deity's existence first offered by Anselm of Bec/Canterbury in the late 11th century.

But toward the end of the 11th century, more contact with the Muslim world had commenced in three different areas. One contact was via the now-fragmented city-states of the Muslims (Moors) in Spain, especially after the fall of Toledo to an Xtian king in 1085, from which came some translations, worked on by combinations of scholarly Jews who knew Arabic and at least some Latin, and Latin scholars. Toledo had been a major center of intellectual life in Muslim Spain, such that its takeover made Xtian rulers the new owners of vast libraries of the works of the Greek ancients, with additions by Arab and Persian scholars in medicine, astronomy, mathematics, etcetera—all in Arabic. Although the heyday of this translation "movement" did not occur until well into the 1100s, some early Xtian scholars did come and go and take home some learning in the process. Second, after the crusaders conquered Jerusalem and a number of other nearby states/

provinces in the Middle East in 1097-99, contacts with Muslim culture and scholarship became much broader and deeper from that source. Third, when the Normans finally conquered Sicily after a long series of intermittent and limited campaigns, they captured a realm with a 250-year history of Muslim control and, in time, Sicily too became a center of translations. As footnoted above, the thin but long-term English tradition of scholars leading to Bacon, Roger was also greatly facilitated by contacts with the Muslim world.

Plate 3.7: Armillary Sphere exhibit at History of Science Museum, Oxford, England. Photo by the author.

Reaching Xtendom at a trickle's pace, the translations eventually introduced to educated Western medieval minds the thoughts of a number of ancient and Muslim-world authorities who were far more advanced in their subject matters than anyone in the Latin Xtendom. Among the ancient works translated were Galen and Avicenna (Greek & Persian, in medicine), Ptolemy (Hellenic-Egyptian, in astronomy and only later, in geography), Aristotle (Greek) and his main interpreter/commentator, Averroes (one of the Andalusian Moors), Euclid (Greek, in geometry), Ibn-Musa-al-Khwarizmi (Baghdad-Arab?, in algebra), and Ibn-al-Haytham (or Alhazen, Iraqi-Egyptian, in optics). Most of these names will reappear later here.

Abelard

Elements of Aristotle's logic, especially the dialectic (but not his syllogistic logic), were passed along from early post-Roman times to medieval Xtianity by Boethius (~480-525), together with some of Boethius' important commentaries. Boethius was an Xtian whose works were copied in monasteries for many reasons (especially *The Consolation of Philosophy*). Aristotle's other writings were not yet available and even his dialectic seems not to have come into extensive use until after 1100. Although the purpose of the dialectic evolved over time, from an emphasis on discovery to an emphasis on the evaluative and confirmatory [Elenore Stump, "Dialectic," 141, in Wagner, Ed.], the first principal way the Church-based educational system and writers used this method was to line up somewhat or starkly conflicting views in or about Bible passages, or propounded by especially renown popes, or by Church fathers and doctors (early church fashioners of doctrine), and to try to find a way in which all of the assembled statements could be understood as true with respect to a revised synthesis, or to generate a synthesis that leaned more one way than the other, with explanations as to why. Peter Abelard (1079-1142) was among the first to use the dialectic with vigor. However, almost everyone he challenged and defeated in disputations, including his own and other respected teachers, were alienated by his harsh or proudly undiplomatic and self-promoting methods, and they often came to be counted among his enemies.

Nevertheless, there was considerable potential in the dialectical method if it is used fairly and properly, especially where some authorities' views are not readily compatible with those of others. Abelard is one of the great culture heroes in the long-term liberation of humanity. He is especially noteworthy for having deployed some of the potential available in Aristotle's dialectic in his book, called *Yes and No (Sic et Non)*, which he wrote as exercises for his students. This was in the days before universities, but at a time when would-be students could go to a very few select towns and affiliate themselves with the most interesting/challenging master (teacher) in those towns, almost invariably a teacher with some kind of clerical background (almost the only ones who then were educated), sometimes operating out of the local cathedral school but occasionally also purely as an entrepreneur, like Abelard some of the time. Abelard's book posed 158 questions directly or indirectly involving Church doctrines. Each was a proposition about which Church authorities had seemed to contradict each other at one time or another, with quotations from those authorities [Frankforter, 196]. Using the criteria for reasoning he had included in the introduction, Abelard "promised his readers that if they employed dialectical methods correctly, they would be able to reconcile contradictions, think things through for themselves, and arrive at truth" [Frankforter, 196]. As examples, the following propositions offered by Abelard are selected from Wieruszowski [133-134]:

1. That faith should be supported by human reason, and the opposite.

14. That the Son is without beginning, and the opposite. [The former better fits the idea of a "trinity"; the latter is nearer to Arian Xtianity.]

38. That God knows everything, and the opposite. [Knowing everything leads to problems about Predestination, whereas the opposite limits the deity's scope.]

55. That Eve alone, not Adam was seduced, and the opposite. [Just how blameworthy is Eve?]

90. That Joseph did not suspect Mary of adultery, and the opposite. [I've wondered about that.]

156. That it is permitted to kill men, and the opposite. [What did Jesus and the Ten Commandments say, versus the Old Testament and the realities of medieval lives?]

108. That small children are not affected by original sin, and the opposite. [The first would challenge the idea of "original sin" put forth by the greatest of the early churchmen, Augustine.]

But unlike the expected approach in teaching, Abelard did not provide answers, the reconciliations of the questions he posed! "Abelard's critics complained that his propositions were unduly provocative, and that his failure to harmonize the opposing statements himself emphasized the inconsistency of the authorities and brought them into disrepute" [Rubenstein, 92]. Abelard's opponents "were infuriated by what they took to be an arrogant attempt to exalt human reason over faith" [Frankforter, 196-197]. Further, if or where Church authorities' differing views could not be reconciled or synthesized, one or more doctrinal statements must ultimately have heretical implications.

Not only did Abelard's method of presentation almost necessarily make the reader think, maybe even "outside the box," but it could do so without the guidance of a more learned masters close at hand. And the printed word was ultimately also much more of a "final" public statement than was an oral discussion behind church doors or within the walls of rooms rented to hold classes. Moreover, the circulation of written material that might lead to heretical thoughts and views (like preaching heretical ideas to live audiences) was starting to be of more concern to a Church slowly growing more powerful, desirous of maintaining that power and, with every increment in power, thus more and more capable of defining and enforcing what was orthodox and what was heterodox/heresy [Jeffrey Burton Russell, *Dissent and Order in the Middle Ages: The Search for Legitimate Authority*]. Also, as can be seen in some of the examples, some of his questions involved settled doctrines (are those supposed to be the easy questions? Or are they being re-opened?).

Abelard was twice charged with heresy before church councils, the first a council of bishops in Soissons near Paris. In this case, he had written a treatise on the trinity, a dangerous topic. He was entirely prepared to defend himself, debating his position with whomever. Rubenstein's account of that occasion, in 1121, says the charges were brought by two of Abelard's former students, one of whom confronted him beforehand and was intellectually demolished. "Fearing a repetition of this scene at the council, but unwilling to permit the philosopher to return in triumph to Paris, the council members hesitated, debated, decided to defer a decision, and finally condemned the treatise without a hearing on the grounds that Abelard had not received the permission required to publish it" [Rubenstein, 118]. Abelard was forced to commit his book to the flames. This result was a nasty reflection on his reputation and he laid low for a number of years at various monasteries, but students sought him out and in less than a decade he was back to teaching out of a monastery in Paris. Because the content of his previous treatise had not been condemned, he went on to expand it in a book on Christian theology. And he wrote other works as well. But an important churchman took his complaints about Abelard and/or Abelard's work to the leading charismatic churchman of his day, Abbot Bernard of Clairvaux. Bernard of Clairvaux (later Saint Bernard) was the leader of the new and expanding Cistercian system of monasteries and widely respected among churchmen. Bernard wrote "a series of letters denouncing Abelard as a heretic, bound them into a treatise called *Against the Errors of Abelard*, and sent the document to the pope with a request that Abelard be investigated and disciplined by the Church"; he also spoke against Abelard's theology at the Notre Dame cathedral school [Rubenstein, 121-122]. Bernard was a spokesman for faith and religious contemplation over analysis and reason. A debate between Abelard and Bernard was planned to occur at a large meeting of churchmen and some secular officials at Sens. However, Bernard, using his stature and influence and friendship with the Archbishop of Sens, arranged a meeting with the bishops the night before and presented 19 charges against Abelard; the charges were discussed and Bernard "almost certainly gained the bishops' promises to support Abelard's condemnation" [Rubenstein, 123]. So when Abelard arrived expecting a debate, he instead found himself a defendant in a trial, with those 19 charges against him read out. Under those probably hopeless circumstances with the bishops already arrayed against him, Abelard departed and the group condemned the allegedly heretical propositions [Rubenstein, 124-125].

(Abelard is also famous for his love affair and marriage to Heloise—while in a clerical teaching position—which got him castrated by thugs hired by her guardian uncle. Uniquely, he also wrote an autobiographical account of these events, something not done since Augustine.)

Gratian's Dialectical Compilation of Church Law

Clearly there was as yet no respectable compilation of Church dogma/ doctrines/law, let alone an official codification. Although some attempts had been made, including upon request by Charlemagne, they had been far from complete or fully accepted. A far more successful attempt was finally completed by a Benedictine Monk, Gratian, around 1140; it was called Gratian's Decretum. It was "a collection of nearly 3,800 texts on all fields of church discipline and regulation" [Editors at Encyclopedia Britannica (.com), "Gratian's Decretum"]. Drawing on many sources, it was intended to harmoniously synthesize the contradictions and inconsistencies in canon law up through the Lateran Council of 1139. It also became and/or was derived from what Gratian taught his students. Gratian's techniques combined those of law and the dialectic. Abelard's work almost undoubtedly played a major role in stimulating such efforts, but I have seen nothing *specifically* to that effect with respect to Gratian. However, Abelard was the teacher of Peter Lombard, who used Gratian and Abelard's ideas to write his *Sentences* (see below).

The Education of Women

For most of the Middle Ages, women were not educated, except at convents/nunneries, or by tutors in some wealthy families (often contingent on a father's preferences). For one example, Abelard was hired as Heloise's tutor. Women were excluded from universities (with the possible exception of a few doctors from Salerno and Montpellier, mainly in their earlier years). Thus women were mostly trained to fulfill women's household-economic roles. Starting around 1200, however, a movement arose in some cities in northern France and Belgium involving women who wanted to live chaste lives of social service (e.g., serving in hospitals for the sick or aged) outside of a convent setting. These were the Beguines. They lived in separate houses or, more typically, in multi-house courtyards (some of which still exist today), with strict rules (e.g., no men except priests were allowed in), and they educated their members as well as some other girls, though probably not to an advanced level.

With so little access to education, women had almost no direct influence on proto-science in the Middle Ages. However, because some women participated fully in some artisan and craft work, and belonged to guilds, especially in the High Middle Ages, some women may have influenced the history of technology to a modest extent. In addition, no doubt some educated women among the merchant/ wealthy classes influenced the lives of some of their spouses (e.g., as bookkeepers) and adult children in ways that contributed to advances in technology. For more on various aspects of women's lives in the Middle Ages, see Part Two.

CHAPTER 24

The Continuing Development of the Universities; Challenges to Church Doctrines and Church Suppression Thereof

Some of the development of the universities was covered earlier here. Doctorates came to be awarded in medicine, law (Roman law and canon law), and theology. The first level of a degree from a university was a bachelor's (baccalaureate) degree, which mainly involved learning a kind of 7 liberal arts subjects (general education curriculum) initially of Roman design, consisting of the trivium plus quadrivium, as follows: Latin grammar, (Latin) rhetoric, and logic; plus arithmetic, geometry, music, and astronomy. Students often started university at a young age, after having attended a cathedral school or been home tutored, and many needed to learn or at least substantially improve on their Latin/grammar before they could do more advanced work. The quadrivium involved the use of numerical or mathematical relationships, and was vaguely along the lines of an upper division curriculum (albeit with considerable time spent on the symbolic-metaphorical-Xtian-mystical-magical meanings of numbers). Originally logic topped out at dialectical reasoning, but Aristotle's syllogistic logic was added after it was discovered. Heavy doses of Aristotle's philosophical works were later added to this traditional curriculum (e.g., see below regarding the University of Paris). A master's degree was the next level up. In some cases it seems to have required additional study in the quadrivium, but in other cases it may have required very little additional student work beyond some practice teaching. Those holding a master's degree usually started as "masters"—teachers of the general education curriculum leading to the baccalaureate. ("Master" is also used to describe the most skilled level of artisan in almost all of the crafts and arts.)

A doctorate in theology required the most time—several years of study of the Bible and of Peter Lombard's *Sentences*, which became the standard university texts for teaching in theology schools and for use in their disputations (see below).

As noted earlier, the first universities were Salerno, Bologna and Paris, with emphasis on medicine, law, and theology, respectively. Oxford also had some early roots; and Cambridge was founded in 1209 for students who fled Oxford because of serious town-gown troubles. Montpellier, in southern France, was another early university that specialized in medicine. Padua was founded in 1222 (per the University's website) when a group of (likely dissatisfied) students and teachers migrated there from Bologna. Toulouse was founded in 1229. After these dates, there began an initially slow but then substantial rise in the number of universities. Later, rulers also got in the act of chartering universities, though those too had/needed the usual Church approvals for viability.

After the universities got well under way and as the decades passed, their graduates, depending on their training, worked in positions such as: doctors; private lawyers; masters/teachers in the universities; administrative or higher ecclesiastical posts within the Church; administrative posts for kings, dukes, counts; administrative and other leadership posts in cities; deans and posts as a canon of a cathedral (administrative functionaries for the bishop); teachers in a cathedral school or a parish church; private tutors for the children of the wealthy; scribes and notaries; etcctcra.

Everyone associated with the universities, from the students on up, was officially designated as a clerk (clerical person) and therefore was under the *legal* jurisdiction of the Church—except in Italy [Wieruszowski, 67]. In any conflict with the law, clerics of all kinds had the "benefit of clergy," meaning mainly that they would be judged by the Church and any wrongdoing would be punished by the Church through penance or other means, and not by the secular authorities.

Aristotle's Work Begins to Arrive in Christendom

Much of the rest of what survived of Aristotle's work began trickling into Xtendom around 1150-1175, possibly initially from a translation of al-Ghazali done by Jews and Xtians in Toledo, Spain, or, mainly later, from translations done in Sicily. Albert the Great (ca. 1193-1280) encountered Aristotle's work at the University of Padua in the early 1220s and became so involved with it that he wrote commentaries on all available Aristotle texts [Catholic Online, "Albert the Great"]. His goal was to help others in the Latin West to read Aristotle in a more accessible (explained) form [Rubenstein, 184]. Aristotle's writings tended more toward (difficult) lecture notes than polished pieces. Albert apparently had access to Latin versions of at least some Arab commentators on Aristotle as well, but not to those that would prove most important—by Averroes (Ibn Rushd). Because translations of Aristotle directly (and more accurately) from the Greek also became available in Venice (which is near Padua) in the period between 1140 and 1286 [Grant, 166], Albert may have had access to some more accurate versions of Aristotle too. Thomas Aquinas was to have access to almost all of these, including Averroes [Grant, 167].

The breadth of Aristotle's "knowledge" was stunning. He understood how the human mind could pursue truth and knowledge, such that "he literally defined thinking" [Frankforter, 201]. His works covered many subject areas with seemingly definitive, reasoned explanations and assertions/conclusions, based mainly on deduction, usually linked to a few basic observations about the real world. In most of the many subject areas covered by Aristotle, the knowledge of learned men in the earlier High Middle Ages was rudimentary or even absent, especially in natural philosophy (i.e., almost all areas of proto-science). And in addition to the dialectic, Aristotle was also the inventor of syllogistic logic [Grant, 39] which, given the right conditions for the equations, could produce iron-clad proofs. In contrast, the dialectic was much less definitive.

Aristotle was of course wrong about almost all science content areas by current standards. But Richard E. Rubenstein's list of what was valuable in Aristotle *even once the many errors are cut away* is illustrative of the overarching importance of his work: "...the ideas that the world our senses show us is real, not just a shadow of reality [as Plato would have it]; that humans using their reason are capable of discovering general truths about this world; that understanding phenomena means comprehending relationships of cause-and-effect; and that natural processes are developmental, revealing to skillful inquirers orderly patterns of growth and change" [Rubenstein, 10]. But Rubenstein omitted other extremely important contributions. To his list must be added "that 'the idea of carrying out systematic research is one that we in the West owe as much to Aristotle and to [his school] as to any other single man or institution'" [Grant, 37, citing G.E.R. Lloyd]. I will have more to say about this later. Aristotle's research efforts were much more detailed and especially noteworthy (and less erroneous) in biology (especially zoology), a discipline of which he was in essence the founder [Grant, 37].

Armand Marie Leroi, a scientist who looked at much of Aristotle's work in depth (and with a different perspective) calls Aristotle the "first true scientist," who invented science "from scratch" [Armand Marie Leroi, *The Lagoon: How Aristotle Invented Science*, 37, 374]. For Aristotle, science "is the explanation of change" [Leroi, 242]. In Aristotle's most in-depth work in zoology, he "hoovers up" all the information he can find from others, rejecting some because it seemed too unlikely [Leroi, 42]. He examines some animals directly, partly as checks on what he had been told, but extending to the point of vivisection in some cases, to set up a remarkably large matrix of data. Aristotle's methods, though not including experiments with a control group, did include extensive systematic observation as well as initial efforts such as modern-day scientists might use in analyzing "big data" by looking for patterns of association [Leroi, 255, 367, 408]. And Aristotle did find some patterns—for example, that animals with longer gestation periods tended to have longer lives—patterns for which he then sought causes (e.g., fecundity costs animals in terms of life span). Aristotle also found similarities between embryos of different species; and although he missed finding evolution, embryology was to provide Darwin with one of his strongest arguments. Further, Aristotle also argued that "nature did not make jumps" and that there were natural groupings of animals [Leroi, 273, 286]. In the late 1700s, Linnaeus drew heavily on Aristotle in beginning his taxonomy of living things, and Georges Curvier, who organized the animal kingdom into a few great groupings, regarded himself as deeply indebted to Aristotle [Leroi, 276, 279].

Although only some of Aristotle's works were heavily read in the Middle Ages, nevertheless, in modern terms, it seems fair to say that at the time the rational sensibleness and extent of coverage in

Aristotle's work simply blew the minds of those who encountered it. Of course Aristotle drew upon the knowledge base in Greece during his time, but the advances he made beyond Plato, who ran the school that Aristotle attended, were immense. Nevertheless, among Aristotle's chief faults, apart from his zoological work, were deriving conclusions deductively based on far too little evidence. Despite Aristotle's genius and his attractiveness to the learned minds at the time of his works' re-emergence, only after decades of struggle within the Church was Aristotle to become regarded as "The Philosopher" and the center of much of the curriculum in the universities.

This struggle arose not so much simply because Aristotle was a pagan, but also because certain of his beliefs and assertions did not fit the Church's nearly as well as did the philosophical views of Plato. More of what Aristotle wrote was contradictory to the doctrines of Xtianity, whereas the major doctrines of Plato could be squeezed to fit, almost surprisingly well, given that he too was a pagan who also preceded Christ. To the medieval churchman's mind—based on faith in the Bible and in what the Church fathers and doctors and other major figures had to say—Aristotle was necessarily wrong where he disagreed with Church doctrines. Thus, for example, the earth was not eternal as Aristotle thought; instead, the deity created it just before human history began, as described in Genesis, seemingly around 5,000 years before their times. Another important Aristotelian error from the Church's perspective was that the soul probably died with the body.

Indeed, there were many conflicting stances and nuances in Aristotle that needed to be addressed—and not every conflict was obvious at first reading. Over the 125 years or so after Aristotle's re-discovery, a great deal of the efforts of some of the best minds in Xtendom was spent wrestling with this particular set of problems. The Dominican scholar and university professor of theology Thomas Aquinas (1225-1274), building on the goals and to some extent on the work of his mentor Albert the Great, devoted much of his professional life to resolving all the important apparent conflicts, ultimately trying to definitively specify how Aristotle and dogma should fit together across many subjects in his *Summa Theologica* (ca. 1273). In general, he included Aristotle's ideas where he could reasonably do so, in part because the doctrines of the Church might be seen as wrong or inadequate in areas where this had not been done well. Thus, he thought some kind of viable fusion of Aristotle's views with Church doctrines was essential but, in all cases, this "synthesis" had to resolve the many controversies and conflicts in a way that was satisfactory to the Church and its leadership's belief system. However, some or much of Thomas Aquinas' work was not accepted right away by the Church hierarchy or by the other teaching masters and theologians at Paris, and there were various challenges to some or most of Aquinas' views in and after the years in which he wrote. For example, in 1277 the bishop of Paris condemned 219 rational propositions derived from the writings of Aristotle and Averroes, and at least a few of those propositions also attacked interpretations/arguments that Thomas Aquinas had made. (See "The University of Paris in the 1270s," below.) Only at the time of the Counter-Reformation (Catholic Reformation) was Thomas Aquinas' work more officially to become the dominant perspective of how Aristotle should be fitted to the dogma of the Catholic Church and of much of that dogma itself.

For his interpretations of and commentary/analysis on Aristotle's writings, the Muslim Averroes was assigned the title the "Commentator" in the Latin West. Averroes was following a scholarly tradition common to Islam and Christendom when he translated and explained Aristotle and included his own comments on Aristotle's doctrines—comments regarding how Aristotle's ideas did or didn't fit into Islamic thought, and why. Thus Averroes tried to do for Muslim societies almost exactly what St. Thomas was to do later for Xtianity, but

Aquinas had the benefit of having Averroes' model and commentary to think about as well (though some of Averroes' commentary, from most Xtian perspectives, of course went wrong in yet different directions from Aristotle). Translations that included Averroes' explanations and commentaries became the most important vehicle by which Aristotle was learned and spread in the Latin West and, though not available when Aristotle's thought first arrived in Europe, were probably fully accessible in Paris sometime after 1231 [Wieruszowski, 41].

The Church's Struggles Against Aristotle

Since 1208 the Church had been calling, via high-level preachers, for secular warriors to form crusading armies against the Cathars in southern France (Languedoc). Beginning in 1209, each year in late spring an army of knights (and adventurers, would-be looters, and others) assembled at a designated meeting place. These men came mainly from northern France, and then, from early summer to late fall, this crusading army would proceed to besiege walled towns and castles, despoil the countryside around areas of resistance, and slowly expand the area under the control of the crusade's leaders. The leadership of this crusade came to center on Simon de Montfort as warrior, along with papal legates directly representing and empowered by Pope Innocent III (ruled 1198-1216). To those deemed heretics or otherwise in disagreement, the Church could be a holy terror. The point for our purposes here is that the Church was at the height of its power through much of the 1200s as the events below were unfolding.

Meanwhile, much of the content of the works by Aristotle, translated into Latin, had reached the universities and been absorbed by more and more of the masters and doctors. As suggested above, Aristotle lit the intellectual atmosphere on fire. Aristotle's philosophy came more and more to be included in discussions and public disputations between masters in theology and, ultimately, throughout much of the university. The University of Paris, became the center of intellectual(-religious) excitement, even affecting many students.

In 1210, "a council of bishops, presided over by the Archbishop of Sens, Peter of Corbeil, decreed that "neither Aristotle's books of natural philosophy nor commentaries (on them) are to be read publicly or privately in Paris, and this under penalty of excommunication" [Rubenstein, 162]. Moreover, in 1215 the ban was extended by a papal legate, in this case a cardinal and former professor at the University of Paris, who "drew up new university statutes that expressly permitted the reading of Aristotle's books on logic by the faculty of arts, but that proscribed his 'books of metaphysics and natural philosophy and summaries of these.'" The liberal arts students were also "obliged to swear an oath stating that they would not read or discuss the works of three recent writers" who had developed heretical interpretations of Aristotle [Rubenstein, 162-163].

Little is known about these three writers, and the general character of the heresy(ies) involved [Rubenstein, 162-167]. Most importantly, both these heretics and the Cathars had used Aristotle to defend themselves. As usual, the various heresies threatened to obviate the "necessity" for people to use the Church as the only pipeline to the deity and salvation, thereby undermining the power of the Church. This gave the theology faculty, and a little later Dominicans and Franciscans, all the more reason to insist on the right to learn Aristotle so as to be able to better refute heretics who drew on Aristotle.

Although Aristotle and Arabic commentators remained banned, a later pope (Gregory IX, r. 1227-1241), under pressure from the masters, "modified the prohibition of 1215 by adding the clause, 'until the books on nature have been examined and purged of all suspicion and error" [Wieruszowski, 41]. The commission that the pope appointed to purge suspicion and error in Aristotle was unable to accomplish its mission, but the ban began to weaken anyway, in part because the universities at Toulouse and Oxford were now teaching Aristotle, and in part because Averroes commentaries had arrived and they made Aristotle more understandable. Wieruszowski says some masters at Paris began to teach Aristotle after Gregory IX died in 1241.

Rubenstein has it that it cannot be determined the extent to which the bans on Aristotle held sway over the years following 1210. But he also says that Bacon, Roger was probably the first master in more than 30 years to lecture on Aristotle in the faculty of arts" [Rubenstein, 188]. Since Albert the Great and Bacon, R arrived at roughly the same time, that would place the year around 1242, such that the Church's suppression of Aristotle was largely effective, except perhaps among theology students and faculty, at least in public (and probably also in much that was private), from 1210 to 1241. Albert was a Dominican, seemingly in the theology faculty; Bacon, R was among the arts masters.

Bacon, Roger "believed that one could not understand Aristotle and the Bible without knowing Greek, Arabic, Spanish, Hebrew, Aramaic, and several other languages, all of which he had mastered while still in his teens" [Rubenstein, 189]. In Paris, he was lionized for his "brilliant and eccentric" teaching [Rubenstein, 189]. He also engaged in debates with Albert the Great. Bacon R's gripes with the Dominicans emphasized otherworldliness along with his version of experimental "science" as contrasted especially with slavish attention given to texts. For more on Bacon, R, see also the chapters on "Precursor Considerations" (above), and "Observational Aspects of Aristotle Ignored" (below).

In any case, in 1255, Aristotle was formally and extensively written into the curriculum at the University of Paris [Wieruszowski, 145].

So the Church much delayed the teaching and debates about Aristotle but, overall, his work was too powerful intellectually to suppress. The rejection of particulars within Aristotle had to be done piecemeal (which Thomas Aquinas took as his task).

The University of Paris in the 1270s

Disputes arose again in the 1260s about the use and interpretation of Aristotle and his major commenter, Averroes (Ibn Rushd). There was considerable division among the faculty of the University about proper interpretation vis-à-vis the Church, but it was mainly within the large non-theology faculty (the masters) that a major problem arose. The "most famous, perhaps because of the relative moderateness of his claims made him especially appealing," was Siger of Brabant; he was the leader of the dissenters and "the personal target of philosophical attacks" as "the public figurehead of the movement" [Collins, 476]. He had had become a master teacher earlier in the 1260s. (Brabant is now the province surrounding Brussels, Belgium.) "The hallmark of his teaching was to present Aristotle's ideas about nature and human nature without attempting to reconcile them with traditional Christian beliefs" [Rubenstein, 209]. Among other things, Siger and his colleagues "taught their students that, according to the Philosopher and his Arab interpreter Averroes, the world and humanity are eternal [clearly revealing the difference with Genesis], [and] that the behavior of natural objects is governed by the laws of their nature" (which, together with Aristotle's non-interventionist prime mover, imposes limits on the Xtian deity's miracles) [Rubenstein, 209]. In Aristotle, the soul "is the form or organizing principle of the body—the full actualization of the potentialities inherent in the matter of the individual" [Lindberg, *Beginnings,* 230], such that the soul died with the body. Averroes offered a collective intellect-based soul instead, such that "immortality is preserved, but not personal immortality" [Lindberg,

Beginnings, 230]. Siger and others' interpretations were apparently well-reasoned from their sources, so, to avoid trouble, they frequently and apparently sincerely made it clear that Church doctrines must prevail if and when their Aristotelian interpretations differed. But they saw two different modes of thinking involved, one involving mainly faith, the other involving reason, and they proposed to focus on explicating the reason-based side in teaching natural philosophy. But if all nature operates (solely) by natural laws, "this leaves no room for divine providence and the thousands of everyday ordinary miracles like the Eucharist, much less the once-in-an-eternity miracles of Christ" [Rubenstein, 210]. More in a borderline area, perhaps, were all the miracles involving healing after people made appeals to relics of saints. But because they were not trained as theologians, it was fitting and proper, said Siger and his colleagues, that they not try to interpret Aristotle and his commentators with respect to Xtian doctrines. **However, this "was the conservatives' nightmare come true"— teaching a variety of interpretations "that seemed to contradict the fundamental teachings of Christianity," and going no further, leaving Church doctrines in the realm of the irrational** [Rubenstein, 210; emphasis added]. Note that we saw a similar stance/phenomenon with Abelard (above).

As in many other instances, the Church's answer was to do its best to suppress what it regarded as erroneous ideas, declaring them to be heretical. And opting for suppression is a major factor showing that cultural insanity was almost undoubtedly involved. The bishop of Paris, Stephen Tempier, after convening a council of conservative bishops, declared some 13 specific propositions to be heretical, such that anyone teaching them was automatically to be excommunicated. The banned ideas included some of the most religiously-threatening ones propounded by Siger of Brabant and his colleagues *as having been derived from Aristotle and/or Averroes*, including, in a few cases as well, ideas accepted into Thomas Aquinas' interpretations [Rubenstein, 216ff]. However, because the controversy did not subside, Rubenstein concludes that there were ways to get around the ban, for example, by making pro forma statements to students about the superiority of Church doctrines where there were disagreements (which didn't actually make the Church's doctrines seem to be any better). At about this time, Thomas Aquinas returned to Paris (1270-72) in part to defend both his interpretations and the Dominicans, but that got him into three-way debates with the Franciscans and the Sigerites about things like the character of the soul, eternity of the universe, the extent to which nature was governed by natural laws, and even about the extent to which humans could be happy during their short lives with suffering aplenty. Indeed, apart from miracles, a "notion of 'dual causation'—the idea that a creative God causes the things of the world to operate as causes in themselves" was the approach used by Thomas Aquinas in his as-yet not finished or accepted effort to reconcile Aristotle with religion [Rubenstein, 188]. "Thomas, like Siger, had developed a large following among the masters of arts" but, at the same time, in the eyes of the conservatives, his "interventions had not served to clear his own followers from the suspicion that they were radicals in disguise" [Rubenstein, 226, 228]. In addition, intellectual conflicts between the Franciscans (who were much greater in number) and Dominicans were to persist for a long time.

In 1272, an election for rector in the arts faculty—the rector being the supreme authority in the institution, including with respect to making laws for the faculty—pitted the conservative candidate Alberic against Siger. (Masters had to take oaths to obey the rector; to disobey the rector was to become "perjured and rebels" [Rashdall, 328-330], where perjury was a very serious sin because the perjurer violated an oath he had made to the deity.) The conservatives won the election, but Siger's supporters claimed "foul play" and elected their own rector, dividing the institution for the next three years [Rubenstein, 228-229]. Alberic, as rector, adopted a rule forbidding the masters to "'teach against the faith,'" which would have been easy to use to oust any more radical master if they were teachers in his domain [Rubenstein, 229]. "If, for any reason, a master found himself unable to avoid a theological issue, he was further sworn to resolve it in favor of the faith" [Edward Grant, "Aristotle and Aristotelianism" in Ferngren, Ed., 40]. This was to be one of the more specific threats to any and all scholars who might want to do work or teach independently of Church doctrines. Such threats, which were subsequently broadened in scope (see below), for centuries made prospective Catholic authors "watch their step." In any event, after several attempts to mediate between the divided masters, a papal legate held hearings and decided in favor of the conservatives [Rubenstein, 229].

Following up on the ruling against the Siger faction's position, Bishop Tempier, urged on by Pope John XXI, a former theology professor at Paris (and perhaps at Tempier's request), convened another council of conservative theologians/churchmen. This time, however, not 13 but 219 much more specific propositions were banned, and anyone teaching them was excommunicated unless he surrendered himself for punishment within a week [Rubenstein, 232]. The Bishop was particularly upset by the idea that two separate truths would be taught, and that the supreme truth, that of the faith and the Church, would come off second best.

The committed Sigerites were obliged to give up and leave Paris, but some of them remained involved in Church positions in their homelands. They were called before the Inquisition on charges of heresy, but were acquitted [Rubenstein, 230-231]. After all, it is indeed difficult to avoid infringing on dogma if one doesn't know the doctrines. Siger's supporters weren't supporters of any heresy; they wanted to explore the potentials for human reason to discover knowledge about the natural world [Rubenstein, 231]. Although the influence of Averroes in the teaching at Paris was much reduced for a while, his ideas did not die out there and he remained The Commentator throughout Latin Xtendom. Still, with the bans on a wide variety of content and with Church views always being right, the quality of teaching and learning necessarily suffered, along with the quality of informal discussions and freedom of thought. The condemned propositions included a number pertaining to "the tendency to assume that nature's workings could be described and even predicted on the sole basis of what Aquinas called 'secondary causes,'" that is, the laws of nature that the Xtian deity had set up [Rubenstein, 234]. For a time, certain key Bishop Tempier-like propositions were used as bans at Oxford too [Rubenstein, 235]. Tempier also forced out Aquinas' chief disciple at Paris, and then "opened a new investigation of false teaching at the faculty of theology, with the aim of censuring Thomas's views," but this investigation was terminated early, quite probably due to the influence of the Dominicans in Rome [Rubenstein, 235].

In 1341, "new masters of *arts* at Paris were required to swear that they would teach 'the system of Aristotle, his commentator Averroes, and the other ancient commentators and expositors on Aristotle, except in those cases that are contrary to the faith'" [Lindberg, *Beginnings*, 251; emphases added]. Although that formally mandated the inclusion of Averroes, it may also be more extreme yet in seeming to require not simply that the Church's position win wherever there was a conflict, but that subjects in which there is conflict simply not be taught except from the faith side.

Meanwhile, the Dominicans had made Thomism their official stance in 1309, and the Franciscans no longer read Thomas Aquinas. And with a fellow Dominican as pope and support from several orders of monks, Aquinas was sainted in 1323 [Collins, 487]. And in 1325 the (now different) bishop of Paris rescinded the condemnations applicable to Aquinas' work.

So, in the 1270s, there were alternative intellectual directions offered, but rejected by the Church, I presume on the basis of two factors: the concern in the Church for the preservation and extension of its own power (with its capability of enforcement as a background known to all), and the Church's dedication to faith alone as the only surety—faith necessarily as interpreted by Church authorities currently and ultimately monopolistically. Lest this statement of the Church's concern for its own power be thought an overstatement, it is worth mentioning that during the reign of Innocent III, at the height of papal power in the early 1200s, the papacy asserted, rather more insistently than ever before, that its spiritual superiority gave it supremacy over all secular authority when that secular authority deviated from Church stances. While that proclaimed power of the papacy was never accepted by kings, at the time they too had to be careful. That Church power took a while to fade but, by 1302, when Pope Boniface VIII asserted it even more vigorously in his *Unam Sanctum* decree (a papal bull), he was thwarted by the growing strength of the monarchies, in particular, the French king. Still, in the long run, we are reassured by several authors, the undercurrents of the day in favor of exploring Aristotle (along with Averroes) were not to be denied. But if the threatening aspects of Aristotle and reason could not be eliminated at the stroke of pen, or even fully smothered, they surely could be stifled, dampened down, and thwarted as much as Church power allowed.

Aquinas' incorporation of an adapted Aristotle into Church dogma—which might at first seem to have been an affable synthesis—would instead continue to leave doctrine as a millstone around the neck of the potential for advancement in science, likely making matters worse. This was so because it linked much of what one might do intellectively in the study of natural philosophy more tightly to

Church doctrines, generating a situation in which many topics were a veritable minefield of possible heresy! As already noted, Church doctrines involving the deity's interventions on earth (e.g., in healing or in punishing sinners), as well as the many everyday Church-certified occurrences of the miracles of transubstantiation during the mass, necessarily conflicted with any generalization about regularity in nature. The Eucharist and the conversion (transubstantiation) of bread and wine into the actual flesh and blood of Christ, where the bread and blood retained (Aristotelean) "accidental" properties such as appearance (per Aquinas' adaptation), but by Church doctrine changed their real properties, could not mesh with the bread and wine having unvarying natural properties. Thus anyone who asserted that naturally-occurring phenomena are stable and unchanging, unfolding in natural development patterns (also a la Aristotle), risked becoming a heretic.

In contrast, **had some way been found to accommodate Siger's perspectives (e.g., via academic freedom or some other kind of co-existence), it would have opened more fully the prospects for the development of proto-science in ways not barred by the Church**. Indeed, as long as such a separation was maintained, it also would not have mattered nearly as much if the Church proceeded to adopt the synthesis developed by Aquinas. So, imagine if the Church instead had had enough faith in its doctrines and its flock to allow university masters simply to choose the extent to which to teach rational natural philosophy without reference to Church doctrines. Similarly, the Church could even have mandated that those who taught natural philosophy without reference to Church doctrine would not be allowed to assert or affirm the truth of what they taught (the teachers not being theologians, after all), but still allow the teacher to assert the adequacy of their derivation from Aristotle, Averroes, evidence, etcetera. Under these kinds of circumstances, Siger and his colleagues—and in this case, many others as well—could simply have gone on to openly and rationally consider evidence about whether the world might be eternal as Aristotle thought, or to explore and speculate about nature without reference to the supernatural (to mention just two of the many possible starting points).

Other compromises were not beyond imagining. The masters could have remained split into two separate groups. After all, there had already been a number of instances, especially at Bologna, in which sections of the faculty and students broke away to form a new university in a nearby city. Similarly, Oxford had greatly benefited in the early 1200s by an influx of masters and students who would have gone to Paris but for the ban on Aristotle. Thus, although it would have set a somewhat different precedent at the time, it would not have been impossible to do something like divide the university into separate "schools," each with its own rector and general method of operating. That is, to accept the divided status quo.

Moreover, Boethius of Dacia (the area north of Greece), another leader in Siger's group, subsequently wrote out the case for leaving the supernatural out entirely. In essence, remarkably enough, he proposed what can be seen as the idea of "methodological naturalism." **"Boethius of Dacia went on to argue that the natural philosopher cannot even consider the possibility of creation, because to do so would introduce supernatural principles that are out of place in the philosophical realm"** [Lindberg, *Beginnings*, 245; emphasis added]. That makes Boethius of Dacia about 300-400 years ahead of his time— assuming, as a general indicator, that "since the scientific revolution of the 16th and 17th centuries, science has been limited to the search for natural causes to explain natural phenomena" [Wikipedia, "Naturalism (philosophy)," accessed 5/4/2017]. As we shall see later, not until the 1660s or so did *some few* of those systematically pursuing observational-experimental science in areas that impinged upon theology actually practice methodological naturalism (though Albert the Great too had leanings in this direction, believing everything would fit together). And letting each approach go its own way, reason and observation of nature on the one hand, and faith and Church doctrines on the other, was ultimately to be the way forward. That is what Siger and his colleagues offered. Sometimes later philosophers, even if only inadvertently (such as Ockham—see below), provided indirect alternative pathways that might ultimately lead in the same direction (separation of faith and reason in a way that enabled proto-science to develop), but any real breakthrough was not soon in coming.

In stark contrast to this perspective, Hannam acknowledges that the condemnations of 1277 did prevent natural philosophy (i.e., proto-science) from impinging on theology (!), but "placing limits around a subject is not the same thing as being against it" [Hannam, 97]. I agree that the Church was not against science per se, but it was defending doctrine and Church power against any possible threat by Aristotle, Averroes, and reasoning. But instead of seeing those limits as being a major problem even if they did not represent opposition to science per se, Hannam adds that those limits "also protected natural philosophers from those who wanted to see their actions further curtailed" [Hannam, 97]— even though it was the conservative (restrictive, censoring) factions that prevailed in the controversy (except for their attacks on Aquinas). And one result was that only theologians (or those very well informed theologically) could write about natural philosophy and still navigate the intricate doctrinal world of the Church without some danger. Moreover, natural science was not of much interest to most theologians. Thus, much potential for advances in reasoning and proto-science was stifled or smothered.

Finally, lest the Church conservatives' defeat of Siger of Brabant and Boethius of Dacia and their colleagues be taken too lightly, or treated as a minor historical aside by the reader, it is worth noting that

Dante Alighieri, writing from 1308 to 1320, portrayed himself being guided through paradise, where he found Siger among the people in heaven's highest realms. In the Henry Wadsworth Longfellow translation of Dante, Siger, in reading lectures, "did syllogize invidious verities"—which also means that they were logically offensive or threatening truths—a kind of speaking truth to power [Henry Wadsworth Longfellow (transl.), *Dante's Divine Comedy: Hell, Purgatory, Paradise*, 313]. For confirmation here, there is also a translation that has Dante saying that Siger "deduced much-envied truths" [Rubenstein, 207].

CHAPTER 25

Observational and Hands-on Aspects of Aristotle Ignored; Aristotle Too Little Tested

But now we need to back up in time a little here to emphasize two important and related cultural insanities that constitute a major failing of the Church and the learned classes. Recall that when Aristotle became available to the universities, almost all the university scholars and churchmen, being otherwise amazed by Aristotle's profundity and reasoning and scope in comparison to their own limited worlds of thinking and understanding, did not take a questioning or skeptical view toward Aristotle's ideas *except* where his pagan thought conflicted with their faith, that is, with the Church's interpretation of the Xtian religion. But if Aristotle was clearly wrong about many statements that conflicted with the Church's doctrines, might not he also have been wrong in some other respects too? Instead the perspective seems to have been that because pagan Greece and Rome had taken civilization to a higher level than had been seen since, here, at last, was more of the wisdom of the ancients! (Ancients in the Church were also highly respected.) So, only rarely at first, and only slowly over the next four centuries did medieval scholars begin to question Aristotle's assertions and conclusions, or, especially, to treat those as hypotheses or theories which they might then test. Hence, very few scholars indeed *developed any kind of systematic program to examine in any detail whether Aristotle might have been wrong in their area of interest!* Similarly, there was no compilation of such errors in Aristotle as were found. This is not to say that at least a few Aristotelian facts and deductions didn't in time come to be recognized as being in error, but that he might often be in error was not generally recognized nor appreciated as a likelihood. And no systematic checking was done (except in a few isolated or highly specialized areas, eventually). Thus, as will be seen in a little more detail subsequently, even 350 years after Aristotle was formally included in the curriculum at Paris, some learned men would deny their own senses in favor of Aristotle when Galileo had them look through his telescope at the moon—even while those same men recognized the legitimacy of the instrument when it was focused upon things on earth with which they were familiar.

Despite the almost worshipful stance of many toward Aristotle, a major, and perhaps the central part of this failure of the Church, churchmen, university scholars, and the upper classes, was the avoidance of a method used in portions of Aristotle's natural philosophy (i.e., proto-science focused on nature). On occasion, Aristotle even used this method in a very *systematic* fashion: observation of the natural world. So, in addition to not otherwise doubting Aristotle's deductive conclusions, they also **ignored that Aristotle sometimes used deliberate and systematic observational methods in the course of his work on natural philosophy,** especially in what was to become zoology. In those cases, Aristotle reasoned from a knowledge base that was often more extensive than usual, and one that he himself had developed. For example, Aristotle had gone as far as examining a batch of chicken eggs laid on the same day, breaking one open each day for 29 days, to follow the developmental path of the embryo. Further, "more than five hundred species of animals are mentioned in his *History of Animals*;

the structure and behavior of many are described in considerable detail, often on the basis of skillful dissection" [Lindberg, *Beginnings*, 61]. But the university masters and churchmen did not use Aristotle's sometimes-meticulous and systematic observations of nature as a model, or as a way of checking Aristotle in other subject areas, and they did not commend its use to the next generation, their students.

Although Aristotle's work on zoology/biology was not a major focus on the scholars of the Middle Ages, it is not as though he made no mention elsewhere of his methods. In his *Nichomachean Ethics*, in Book VI on "Intellectual Virtue," under "The Chief Intellectual Virtues," the first is Science, *which means the development of knowledge about a subject matter* rather than what we mean by the word today [Stump, 130]. There, Aristotle writes that teaching "proceeds sometimes through induction and sometimes by syllogism [a kind of deduction]. Now induction is the starting-point which knowledge even of the universal presupposes, while syllogism proceeds *from* universals" [Sir David Ross, transl., *The Nichomachean Ethics of Aristotle*, 140]. In his books on animal life, the need for systematic observation is made much more explicitly. From "On Generation and Corruption," Aristotle writes that "… those who have spent more time with the natural world are better at suggesting theories of wide explanatory scope. Those who have spent time arguing instead of studying things as they are show all too clearly that they are incapable of seeing much at all" [quoted in Leroi, 375]. (See also the section on Scholasticism and the Disputation, below.)

Moreover, in ignoring Aristotle's observational work as a model, the university masters and doctors also ignored two of the most famous early leaders amongst them who did indeed make use of systematic observation in their work: Albert the Great and Bacon, Roger. Leroi emphasizes that Albert drew the right conclusion when he wrote: "'The aim of natural science … is not simply to accept the statements

of others, but to investigate the causes that are at work in nature'"
[Leroi, 355].

Not using Bacon, Roger as an exemplar might be vaguely understandable given his reputation and despite his effective teaching (see
above), but ignoring the methods of Albert the Great was not. As
noted, Albert was a Dominican, a professor of theology and he wrote
commentaries on almost everything Aristotle wrote. He launched a
synthesizing project at which his student, Thomas Aquinas, proved
more adept (fusing Aristotle, insofar as he was found fitting with
Church dogma, to Xtianity). Most relevantly for the analysis here,
Albert also "was an extraordinary observer and collector—the most
accomplished botanist and zoologist of his day, and a pioneer in the
methods of empirical research" [Rubenstein, 185]. "Albert wrote thir-
ty-eight volumes covering topics ranging from philosophy to geography, astronomy, law, friendship and love" [Catholic Online, "Albert
the Great," accessed March, 2017]. In his commentaries on Aristotle,
Albert also criticized Aristotle wherever Albert understood that he was
wrong—based on his own observations [Rubenstein, 185]. Albert "felt
one must accurately and sensitively observe [nature] before deriving
general principles from [concrete particulars]" [Rubenstein, 186]. The
deity, Albert believed, created every detail in the material world, "but
creation means that God gives each created thing its own reality or
being" [Rubenstein, 186]. The last part of that statement is very much
in accord with Aristotle's view. Leroi says that "*it is hard to resist the
conclusion that the eclipse of [Albert the Great] by [Thomas Aquinas]
retarded the development of natural science by centuries*" [Leroi, 356;
emphasis added].

Among the "reasons" why higher-ranking churchmen and scholars made so little movement in directions requiring the observation
of nature, let alone interaction with it, was their class background
(usually noble, but progressively more upper bourgeois as well as the

medieval years passed). Like the Romans, higher status individuals had a prejudice against working with their hands: that is what slaves did in Roman times and that is what those grubby and stupid peasants (and craftsmen) did in medieval times. (Their views, not mine.)

In general, then, but with a few exceptions (increasing somewhat over time), neither the masters nor the theologians of the university, the monks in the various orders, nor the Church hierarchy itself used Aristotle in a way that would lead to important advances in what ultimately would come to be called science. For many, Aristotle was the authority apart from the Church, even in 1600 and later. Still, as noted, toward the end of the Middle Ages there did come to be more recognition of some of the weaknesses/errors in Aristotle. But apart from Albert the Great, Aristotle's deductions were rarely tested, especially in the earlier times after his rediscovery. And although progress was made in some technological areas (see below), there seemed to be very little cumulative progress in proto-science in the university-Aristotelian-scholastic-Church world. An example about optics is surely worthy of note here (but see below too). Drawing on the foundational work of Alhazen, Bacon, R had actually taken some measurements of angles in optics, one of which involved rainbows. Theodoric of Freiberg, a Dominican who actually did try to follow the ways of Albert the Great and was a subsequent experimenter who wrote on the optics of rainbows in about 1310, erroneously reduced Bacon, R's measurement by half (or else a copying error was made). But Theodoric did the only important work on optics until around 1600, so "what is more important is that the mistake seems to have troubled no one for hundreds of years" [Crosby, 69]. Finally, in 1604, Johannes Kepler again published an important work on optics. Similarly, Peter the Pilgrim investigated how magnets worked, along with some speculations as to how and why, and wrote up his findings sometime around 1269 [Hannam, 134-135]. Little or nothing was done subsequently, despite various known problems in the use of the compass at sea, until Jean Taisnier plagiarized and reprinted Peter's work in 1558 [Hannam, 289-290]. Finally, William Gilbert (1544-1603), an English doctor, who was interested in the occult (magnetism was seen as weird/magic), found the previous work on that subject and proceeded to study magnetism with systematic observation and even experimental work, and offered associated theorizing (e.g., the earth may be a giant magnet), publishing one of the first truly scientific works [Hannam, 290-291]. But not until 1600, over 300 years later.

The Church itself had no particular interest in the pursuit of knowledge per se. De facto, its main interests were to defend the Church as an organization and its doctrines, and the preservation or extension of Church/papal power. Observation of nature was irrelevant to salvation and therefore to society. With so few university faculty members advancing knowledge, progress was slowed. While there was a little progress in thinking about astronomy and its associated mathematics (trigonometry mainly) and motion theory (over two-plus centuries), the planets were still assumed to have circular orbits (*around the earth*)—because circles were geometrically perfect and the heavens were perfect. But the heavens, being within the purview of the "queen of the sciences" (i.e., theology), were of more interest to the Church, so there was openness to better predictions of movement in the skies and other information from astronomy (in part to fix the Julian calendar which was known to be getting more out of synchronization with the seasons and thus also displacing Church holy days from the times/seasons when they should have been observed). Or, at least there was openness to non-threatening aspects of astronomy (but not otherwise in the cases of Copernicus and Galileo—see below). Yet after the mid-1300s with Buridan and Oresme (see below), even the slow advances in astronomy were much less closely associated with the Church.

CHAPTER 26

Scholasticism

Beginning shortly after 1100, what emerged from the more effective use of the dialectic by Abelard, Gratian, Peter Lombard and others, and the subsequent diffusion of more authoritative views about correct Church doctrines, and then the omni-faceted challenges of Aristotle was a general method of considering questions, along with a somewhat revised worldview, that has been labeled "scholasticism." Its practitioners were "scholastics" (or, probably only later, the "schoolmen").

Some Aspects of Scholasticism and the Disputation, and Their Drawbacks

Like most of Aristotle's work, scholasticism relied on *deductions* from things that were known. As above, things that were known were ideas derived from the Xtian holy book, Church fathers and doctors, outstanding popes, Church councils, and Aquinas' careful selection of which of Aristotle's ideas could be "safely" fused with Church doctrines. The role of the "disputation" can provide us with some insights into the character of scholasticism.

The "disputation" was used for philosophical arguments, for example, between professors competing for students or for intellectual supremacy on a topic of dispute, and in some intra-Church confrontations about whether or not something was heretical. Thus, as already noted, Abelard was prepared to defend himself disputationally at a Church council against heresy charges put forth by Bernard of Clairvaux, but Bernard set himself up to win with the other churchmen by successfully scandalizing Abelard's writings the day before, such that the assembly was set to condemn Abelard rather than hearing him defend his views by confronting Bernard directly. The disputational model was also often used in writing, including by the "witchcraft theorists" (see Part Two). In its most basic use by writers, the author would deploy the dialectic after posing a suitable question, and then proceed to review the pros and cons or different views about that question—ideally in a fair and balanced fashion, but realistically often not. Finally, the author/disputant would then proceed to show why one view provided a better answer than the other(s). Occasionally, this yielded an honest synthesis, but sometimes the result was based on demolishing a straw man. And, all too often, when arguments based on faith were all on one side, that side was an automatic winner, no matter the soundness of the reasoning on the other side. An oral disputation (akin to an oral thesis defense today) was also used as the general method for a would-be graduate to demonstrate sufficient competence to be awarded the master's degree. And theology made extensive use of disputations in its lengthy curriculum.

The disputation and scholastic methodology were based on "authority, reason, and experience." "Reason," as noted above, involved deductions from the known. And "experience" was drawn upon almost solely "as an illustration of things known by authority and logical deduction"; it was seldom experience based on systematic observation or inquiry, more often a matter of "common sense" [Alan Charles Kors, *The Birth of the Modern Mind: The Intellectual History of the 17th and 18th Centuries*, 9]. "Authority was either supernatural or natural. Supernatural authority was based on Scripture, as correctly understood by the appropriate authorities. Natural authorities were based on the presumptive authority of the past" [Kors, 9], especially the Greek ancients. Authorities of the past had stood the test of time and their civilization had reached a greater height. Indeed, the evidence of Rome's empire was still present in many areas, from Roman-era paved roads and bridges, to amphitheaters and coliseums and wondrous monuments, to giant sections of aqueducts looming overhead in a few areas (e.g., in Rome; Segovia, Spain; southern France).

University churchmen (and teachers) were much enamored with Aristotle's four types of causes: material, formal, efficient, and final. Material causes are the stuff from which things are made (e.g., the marble for sculptures); formal causes are the forms into which a material is made (e.g., a sculpture itself); efficient causes are the creator (e.g., a sculptor using hammer and chisel); and the final cause is the reason or purpose of the doer [Kors, 9-10]. By analogy, the goal of knowledge, in the eyes of the Church and theologians, was to understand and appreciate the purposes of the doer (the deity) and the relative perfection of all things. The Xtian deity and the heavens represented perfection; all other beings and things were placed in a hierarchy below that deity, starting with angels, passing through humankind and the hierarchy of beings on earth, and ending in stones. From the moon on up was part of the perfection of heaven. Thus the ultimate goal was to know the relative godliness of everything, to understand the roles of the Church and to live the Church-defined good so as to be as close to the deity as possible (and attain salvation), and to teach those things.

The instructional vehicle ("textbook") in the field of theology became Peter Lombard's *Four Books of Sentences* (meaning "opinions" in Latin), which was done around 1158 [Grant, 159], and further systematized somewhat in 1225. Deriving his approach from Abelard—indeed, Lombard produced a gentler version of *Sic et Non* [Frankforter, 197]—Lombard had assembled texts and glosses (opinions/comments on texts) from authoritative Church sources across a wide range of theological issues, arranged them into topic-related groups, and attempted to reconcile or synthesize differences of opinion/interpretation in his compilations. If only because this was not achievable in all of them, there was all the more room for generations of theology students to develop their disputations around his topics. "Book I of the *Sentences* discusses God, the Trinity, divine guidance, evil, predestination; Book II, angels, demons, the Fall of man, grace, sin; Book III, the Incarnation of Jesus Christ, the redemption of sins, virtues, the Ten Commandments; Book IV, the sacraments and the four last things—death, judgment, hell, and heaven" [Editors at Encyclopedia Britannica, "Peter Lombard"]. "Theological students were required to lecture and comment upon these four books" [Grant, 159]. The "*Sentences* formed the framework upon which four centuries of scholastic interpretation of Christian dogma was based" [Wikipedia, "Peter Lombard"]. The years of study for a doctorate in theology involved classes in the Bible and topics from the *Sentences*, and the professors much preferred the reduced routine in teaching the latter.

The "scholastic" methods used in the universities, and even the goals of education, also tended to hog-tie learners when it came to advancing proto-science. Developing new knowledge was decisively not the goal of the education that was offered. Any "innovation" was usually described as "rash" [Kors, 8]. Lectures generally involved the reading of the designated classic/canonical text (partly, no doubt, due to the shortage of books until around 1500), so that nothing was omitted, and then adding the important commentaries ("glosses"), with professors offering non-compulsory "extraordinary" lectures to clarify and elaborate on difficult parts. Although it matters little for our purposes, teaching in law was a partial contrast, with the emphasis instead being on helping to clarify the meaning of the statutes and prior interpretations, such that teaching quality mattered more [Rashdall, 218].

Still, why the focus on theology here? Why not focus on the far more numerous teachers in the masters of arts programs? Among other reasons, as we have seen with Siger of Brabant and Boethius of Dacia, the first is that the Church constrained the masters of arts, denying them the freedom to pursue ideas wherever they liked—when anything theological was involved—*unless* they ultimately and affirmatively sided with the theological view, whether in teaching or in public advocacy, including writing for publication. This stance made venturing into such areas a doubtful enterprise because the masters were not trained in theology and could easily overstep boundaries by accident. Second, absent theological training, the masters' scholastic disputational and writing skills were seldom as refined either, where both those skills and knowledge of Church dogma were needed to pose or examine many kinds of challenging questions while avoiding heresy. Third—and not entirely by happenstance—much of the proto-scientific and scientific advancement that did occur in the Middle Ages, occurred in fields such as architecture and engineering—fields involving technology that in practice were entirely outside the university curriculum (but not beyond possibility of study for any given master). Among university subjects, only astronomy was both a natural science and one of the seven liberal arts, with introductory material taught to students before the bachelor's degree. But astronomy was also in the province of the theologians (given its relationship to the heavens) and to some extent in medical schools (to learn disease-prognosticating astrology). In astronomy, there were a few noteworthy but still limited deduction- and reason-based advances made by Buridan and Oresme (see below). But most of those who dealt with the heavens, other than as a religious ideal, were astrologers (probably often students or doctors of medicine), one of whom was employed by rulers in many courts, usually including the papacy.

One major result of using scholastic methods was often the all-but-meaningless pursuit of finer and finer distinctions in Church doctrine, frequently involving considerable semantic sophistry. Among the most positive views of scholasticism is this one: "By refining definitions of key terms and tracing their logical implications, Scholastics devised extraordinarily subtle solutions for all kinds of intellectual tangles" [Frankforter, 193]. But this made scholastic texts very dense and, as we shall see, the emphasis on Church-related dogma was seldom worth much to posterity (i.e., beyond the continuing refinement of some Church doctrines).

The traditional question, "How many angels can dance on the head of a pin?" was probably invented to denigrate scholasticism, using the question itself as a metaphor for the inconsequentiality of their concerns. So, a more realistic example of that idea might be instructive. Among the main "reasons" given for the Xtian medieval suppression of women and their lower status was their purported leading responsibility, via Eve, for original sin (see also the Part on witches). But there were occasionally raised some Bible-based scholastic-style counterarguments to women's inferior status. A major counterpoint was the very existence of the Virgin Mary, though many of the attributes ascribed to her were invented by the Church, propagated by St. Bernard (of Clairvaux) and others, and not found in the Xtian holy book. (The Virgin Mary outranks angels from the 12th century onward but was of much less importance earlier.) According to Alcuin Blamires, there were also six or seven "privileges of women"—points that suggested female equality or superiority instead of inferiority [Alcuin Blamires, *The Case for Women in Medieval Culture*, 96-115]. One point was that Eve was made from Adam's rib, a higher substance than the muck from which he was made. Moreover, creation from a rib implies more equality, more unity, than would creation from a head bone or foot bone, either of which would suggest one of them should rule over the other. Other points/privileges include that Adam was introduced into paradise, but Eve was created in it. Eve was created last, so she might be the Xtian deity's crowning glory. (However, the Fall, with blame for Eve, came after all these.) Further, a woman gave birth to Jesus, where the Xtian deity need not have chosen the birth process at all (but perhaps did so in order for Jesus to have a fully human side). Finally, Jesus first appeared upon resurrection to Mary Magdalene, who was told to convey the news to others (though she was not allowed to touch Jesus, whereas later male witnesses were, raising counter arguments by some). Many of the Church's most renown fathers, doctors, and theologians at one time or another dealt with at least one of these points, for or against, or often both, including early ones such as Tertullian, Chrysostom, Ambrose, and Augustine, as well as later ones, such as Abbot Odo of Cluny, Hildegard of Bingen, Abelard, Bernard of Clairvaux, Hugh of St. Victor, Aquinas, and the Franciscan Bonaventure. As positive as such points about the "privileges of women" might seem for helping to reduce the prejudice and discrimination against women, or prevent it from becoming worse, they did not seem to have much effect, so they seem to offer a realistic concrete example of why such sophistry had little value. Indeed, the oppression of women did get worse in some respects as the Middle Ages progressed—for example, they were more and more squeezed out of guilds, confinement to convents became stricter for nuns, and they were the main evil-doers in witch-hunting tracts.

The scholastic approach also seemed to be more detrimental than not in the training of medical doctors. Scholastic training fostered critical comparison of statements across purported medical authorities—usually with the hope of reconciling them—and helped to develop rational habits of mind. "But it also encouraged excessive expenditure of ingenuity in elaborating intricate arguments about textual interpretation; and *it focused attention on issues to which observation was largely irrelevant*" [Siraisi, *Medieval & Early Renaissance Medicine: An Introduction to Knowledge and Practice*, 76; emphasis added]. Moreover, given that the medical authorities of the time were so often wrong in so many major ways (see below), attempting to reconcile them was all the more unproductive.

As a result, by the late Middle Ages and early modern times, many Renaissance humanist scholars saw Aristotle as a kind of enemy, though the real "villains" (who were also recognized by the humanists as such) were the scholastics who all too often still swore by Aristotle in a largely straightforward way, as amended by exceptions made by Thomas Aquinas (or others), for purposes of fitting with Church doctrines. Rubenstein sees what happened over the 300-400 years as a "degeneration" of scholasticism. "Once the source of creative speculation and rollicking, no-holds barred debate, the universities now combined an arid orthodoxy in matters of doctrine with absurd theological hairsplitting" [Rubenstein, 9]. In discussing the severe lack of vitality of scholasticism to contribute to intellectual and philosophical life at the start of the 17th century, Kors attributes much of their ossification to an overemphasis on final causes (the deity) and how to attain salvation by living a life closer to that deity, and admirable in the deity's eyes [Kors, 8-10]. Aiding and abetting the degeneration in scholasticism was that, when it came to Aristotle, medieval philosophers "marginalized some works (the treatises on physics, meteorology, zoology, biology and natural history) in favor of others (the metaphysics)" [Greengrass, 185]. Randall Collins sees the height of the creative period *philosophically* as being from 1230-1360; after that, he sees a disintegration into multiple schools of thought, *separate by university*—and a situation in which each was an "intellectual fortress" that worked mainly on refining its own doctrines (with creative debate largely absent), whilst creative advances in philosophy, in his view, depended on their interactive opposition to one another [Collins, 513-519].[10] (The aforementioned schools of thought were Franciscan perhaps nominalist; Scotist; and Thomist, with some of the these accepting Averroism—more below). Further, as emphasized here, also marginalized were Aristotle's thoughts and examples showing the importance of systematic observation, and induction, as other methods of seeking knowledge (i.e., and not only deduction), including in his relatively "mainstream" work, Nichomachean Ethics.

Overall, my judgment is that, compared to the possibilities, there were only very modest contributions to proto-science within the body of works by medieval university masters and Church doctors of theology and high-level Church functionaries (cardinals, bishops, abbots, monks) over four centuries or so. With almost no attention given to augmenting the observational knowledge base, let alone systematically so, there was little potential for contribution to proto-science by those most involved with the Church. With Church strictures playing a role too, the same seems to have been very largely true among the university masters. Even Hannam mentions that Oxford made almost no contribution to mathematics and philosophy for about 200 years, from 1350 on, whereas previously it had made relatively important

---

10   Collins focuses on (the sociology) of philosophy in a way that seems to the general reader as if philosophy is all that mattered for progress in science—though he also mentions that in the Late Middle Ages the area of interactive oppositions (requisite for advances in his view) did shift to astronomy; and he includes some mention of progress in mathematics. Collins faults the humanists' lack of interaction with schoolmen as yet another reason for so little progress in natural philosophy. But the narrow focus of this work utterly misses some other direct contributions of the humanists to advances in the sciences. Even more importantly, he takes no account of advances in technology or in the humanist/intellectual interactions with artisans which ALSO produced creative advancements important to the development of science (see below). His criticism of Humanists may seem to share a commonality with James Hannam's, but that is not really so, or is only very incompletely so. Hannam's complaints are with reference to all humanists and all science in the Middle Ages (*even though at other times he commends individual humanists*), whereas Collins treatment involves a limited perspective, albeit one that seems too readily to presume that no advances in science arise without philosophy preceding them. Below, I have tried to include both the weaknesses and the contributions of the humanists with respect to the advancement of science.

contributions in mathematics and graphing, the physics of motion, and conceptual astronomy [Hannam, 175]. The Oxford masters' emphasis on reasoning was mainly within their theologically-restricted confines and was for purposes of guiding undergraduates in their disputations in natural science, but with no ties to investigatory research [Collins, 493]. And one way or another, Cambridge also went through "a long period of stagnation," which was then further exacerbated by Henry VIII's reforms in the early 1500s [A. C. Grayling, *The Age of Genius: The Seventeenth Century & the Birth of the Modern Mind*, 164].

The Overemphasis on What Happens After Death

As noted earlier, the Church's overemphasis on life after death is a major cultural insanity, but a largely buried one until the Late Middle Ages. For the Church, life, full of suffering and travail as it was, was really all about preparing for salvation, about getting right with the deity (via the Church of course) to better assure resurrection in the future, with one's body fully restored to the height of its capabilities, and thereafter a life eternal with the deity. There had been no need for a purgatory when Christ's return was imminent. However, the increased emphasis by the Church after 1200 on the living assisting the dead in Purgatory and later, on monetary sales of documents (indulgences) purporting to relieve the punishments of those in Purgatory, were culturally active *additions* to this mostly buried insanity. By the time of the Reformation, the Church's selling of indulgences to enable people to buy their way out of various amounts of Purgatorial punishment was little short of a full-blown financial racket in the minds of some. The most famous case here involves papal indulgences hawked in great quantities in the early 1500s to build St. Peter's Cathedral in Rome. Excesses in this regard helped stimulate Martin Luther to launch a protest that, with some help from German nobles also not happy with the Church (and its extraction of resources from their lands), and from the printing press, morphed into the Protestant Reformation. The Protestants fully endorsed the importance of the afterlife, but they also permitted clerical marriage and wanted to divert resources from the Church (e.g., money spent on icons, reliquaries, monasteries, expensive garments and more) into uses for the welfare of people in this life. The problems were also to some extent recognized and clarified by humanist influences, as seen in Erasmus, and the development of "modern" forms of devotion during the late Renaissance. So there began to be challenges to the non-biblical idea of Purgatory and to the purported efficacy of praying for the dead as a way of gaining favor with the deity. On the Catholic side of religion, the reaffirmation of conservative Church beliefs at the Council of Trent in 1545-1563 can be seen, among other things, as the reaffirmation of the cultural insanities it had added to original Xtian doctrines. Changes in consciousness beginning in the early modern period, especially among the educated (such as Francis Bacon in 1600—see Part Four), even more clearly disinterred the entire cultural insanity involving the overemphasis not only on what happens after death but on scholasticism and the disregard of the world of the living.

Ockham and Nominalism

Among the well-regarded dissenters from Aquinas was Duns Scotus (1265?-1308), "the subtle doctor." His philosophy "overturns not only old Neoplatonism and Augustianism, but new Aristoteleanism as well" [Collins, 482]. The particular theological disputes are of little importance per se here, but perhaps it can be said that his interpretations helped clarify the schools of thought that ultimately would emerge, including nominalism, which would come to dominate more university faculties. The conservatives who made the condemnations of 1277 faded away, even as they helped to open the way for nominalism in their insistence that "no restrictions be placed on the omnipotence of God" [Collins, 490]. Thomism became the conservative position, remaining attractive to many, but without the "innovative prestige of the Scotist and especially the nominalist critics"; and, at the far end of the spectrum, was the "Averroist heresy and anti-papalism" [Collins, 490].

More generally, it is certainly possible to question just how much the Church signed on to an ethic of "rational inquiry" as Rubenstein claims. For example, above we have seen Bernard of Clairvaux's reactions to reason as embodied by the thought of Abelard (and that case was not unique). And we have seen the Church's rejection of student and faculty thinking at the University of Paris in the early 1200s when it came to the ideas of Aristotle. And we have seen the Church's refusal to allow Siger of Brabant and Boethius of Dacia in the 1270s to stick to reasoning about Aristotle's views and simply avoid consideration of faith or the supernatural. Another case in point (and there will be more later) involves William of Ockham (~1287-1347). As Rubenstein himself writes, "in the fourteenth century, the brilliant Franciscan scholar William of Ockham insisted that Aquinas had erred in trying to formulate a 'natural theology,' and that science and religion would both be better off if they separated" [Rubenstein, 9]. I haven't read other sources that put Ockham's views in that stark a contrast, especially with the use of the word "science" contrasted so sharply with "religion." Instead, "the study of the natural world" ("natural philosophy") probably would be a better choice of words than "science." (And, in any case, at that point in time, "scientia" meant "knowledge," often a subject area-specific knowledge, but not "science" as we now know it.) Ockham stood for a re-emphasis on faith (including especially as revealed to the Church, its founding fathers and doctors, and the Bible) as the only sure source of knowledge. The problem for Ockham was that because the deity could do anything (e.g., perform miracles, intervene in response to prayer, use whole different alternatives to get to the same end, change how nature operated, etc.), any generalizations about how the world works, or how the workings of the world might reflect on or reveal the character of an unfathomable deity, were not viable as potential truths. Further, every case in nature was unique and could not safely be generalized; there is no essence that can be reached—generalizations are all pragmatic, for human use. This philosophical doctrine/view is part of "nominalism." Nominalist thinking precedes Ockham, but he is typically treated as its pinnacle or chief spokesman.

Remarkably enough though, Ockham's views about faith being the predominant truth and reason untrustworthy as a source of generalizations, especially generalizations about nature that in any way were linked to the deity, may have backasswardly contributed to providing a way in which scholars could investigate the natural world separately from religion, still provided, however, that their writings made no negative connections to Church doctrines. If such investigations were automatically de-coupled from faith/theology because they could not be generalized as Truth—and specified as such—they would at least not be directly threatening, so then there is no harm in doing them (e.g., in case they have value practically) even though, to nominalists, any generalizations are necessarily crude and untrustworthy summations of individual cases, potentially invalid (and readily invalidated by changes the deity might make), etcetera. Please note here that this "proviso" about not impinging upon Church dogma would not have been needed had the truer separation of faith and reason proposed by Siger of Brabant and Boethius of Dacia been pursued. Trouble would only have arisen directly if someone tried to foist some reasoned conclusion into the realm of Church doctrine, or the Church decided anew to suppress reasoning/reasoned conclusions. In time, difficulties would have arisen anyway if only because the Bible has, and Church doctrines had, major scientific errors in them—but those difficulties might have been resolved more as they are today, that is, with the Church/churches slowly retreating from doctrines that apply to the natural world.

Ockham and his predecessors' nominalism became at least somewhat dominant in the universities by the mid-1300s [Rubenstein, 273], though Aristotle remained "The Philosopher" and was much respected if not revered in virtually all if not all of the universities as well, nominalist-leaning or not, and well into the 17th Century at that. Thus, some/many later philosophical speculations notwithstanding, it is not clear to me that nominalism really had much of a positive effect on the actual, historical loosening of proto-scientific thought, even though it presumably had some positive effects in temporarily de-coupling nature from Church dogma in the minds of some (though not officially, in the eyes of Church leaders). Yet, for some at the time, nominalism also could well have provided even more of an excuse not to bother to conduct observations on all those ungeneralizable aspects of the real world at all.

Moreover, nominalist or not, absent some formal agreement with/by the Church (such as proposed by Boethius of Dacia), the proviso about not impinging on Church doctrine (and/or the Church stance toward heterodox beliefs/"heresy") still mattered if any important new findings revealed something less than orthodox about the Xtian deity's purported creations here on earth or in the heavens (and much more). While in theory a nominalist who was wise about Church doctrines might assiduously avoid making any generalizable truth claims in such situations (which is what Buridan and Oresme were soon to do, being sophisticated in such matters), the situation became much trickier as science drew nearer to a convincing proof of a sun-centered rather than an earth-centered universe (solar system). Thus, it must be doubted that even nominalism could succeed in separating proto-scientific work from Church dogma when the work had major implications for Church doctrines and biblical mythology.

So, the fusion of Christian theology to Aristotelian natural philosophy had some important dissenters beyond Siger of Brabant, including William of Ockham. Indeed, as noted earlier, the Church itself officially began to agree with the interpretations of Thomas Aquinas only in 1323, when a former Dominican was pope and Aquinas was sainted. So there came to be a kind of co-habitation for over two centuries and ultimately a Counter-Reformation-era marriage between the Church and Aristotle's texts as interpreted by the Church/Aquinas, but there were some who objected to that wedding when it was still forthcoming. Moreover, some of the writings of the Church fathers and doctors, as well as mistakes in science within the Xtian holy book, also stood in the way. With those sources as additional baggage, once doctrine widely incorporated Aristotle's views (apart from the rejected ones), coupled with his dialectic and deductive approach as deployed in the thinking of scholars (apart from his mandate to expand information), it became harder yet for churchmen and university masters to entertain other sources of knowledge or develop ideas that might contradict Aristotle or Church doctrines. In discussing this situation at the close of the 14th century, Grant wrote that theologians had great latitude to use natural philosophy and analytic methods virtually as they pleased in their theological treatises on Peter Lombard's *Sentences* but, "by contrast, arts masters usually sought to avoid introducing theology into their commentaries and questions on Aristotle's natural philosophy," at least in part because the Oath of 1272 and its successors that were still in effect at the University of Paris [Grant, 189-190]. Similarly, later adherents of one or another version of nominalism might say they aren't so sure about one thing or another, but then add, "but the Church says otherwise."

CHAPTER 27

Medicine, Surgery, Medicinal Plants, and Animals

Medicine would seem to be among the disciplines in which investigation of cause-and-effect is almost inherent or natural. A doctor might try a prescribed cure and, having had it fail once or twice, try something else, or at least try some variant on the original. That statement is, of course, too simplistic because, for example, there might be successes due to spontaneous remission that might be misattributed to the prescribed cure. Unfortunately, though, the same lacks of Church and university support for additional systematic observation were manifested in the areas of medicine- and drug-related inheritances from the Ancients that also came to Europe in the High Middle Ages. And the aforementioned prejudice throughout the elite social classes against hands-on involvement affected medicine too. As described earlier, the Church deserves little or no credit or discredit for what happens in universities—except insofar as it facilitates or detracts from the advancement of knowledge/human potential in them. Thus the brief account of developments in medicine here are mainly to show the (small) effects of Church involvement and the lack of progress in the field as a science during the Middle Ages.

By the mid-900s, there was a recognized medical group of practitioners at Salerno (near Naples) that had at least some reputation for successful cures [Siraisi, 13]. The healers included Xtian monks and at least some women [Siraisi, 13]. Around 1050, the rudiments of what was to become the first medical school arose. When the work of the Muslim Avicenna (Ibn-Sina, ca. 980-1037) and parts of Galen first became available to the West via Sicily (which was formerly ruled by Muslims who had earlier invaded from north Africa), there was then a stronger rationale to establish a more formal education program for doctors because there was now a substantial body of written work and theory to teach. Galen (130-200CE) was a prominent Greek physician in Roman times who drew some of his views from Aristotle. Avicenna had added some important medical knowledge to what he had derived from Galen and from a book about the medical uses of certain plants. Factored in too were some Greek influences [Wieruszowski, 75-76], because the Eastern Roman Empire had ruled much of southern Italy before the Muslims, as well as some of southern Italy until the successors to the early Normans drove them out in the 1000s. But it was not until 1231 that Frederick II, King of Sicily and Holy Roman Emperor, formally chartered Salerno [Wieruszowski, 77], although his supervision and rules were too stringent, such that Salerno began to fade from the first rank of institutions.

Although Xtian monks were among the first practitioners, teachers, and presumably leaders at Salerno (expectedly enough, because monastery infirmaries were the best sources of medical care late in the early Middle Ages), the Church was not directly the source of the school. Other medical schools that were also fairly early historically were in Montpellier (in Languedoc/southern France), which had an informal presence by 1150, and Bologna. Montpellier was chartered in 1170 by the local count in a very free form—with no requirements to teach—partly because Jews and other outsiders had brought much medical knowledge from Spain. However, this policy suffered a "complete reversal" from 1180 to 1220 as the masters and students formed corporations (like guilds); "this change either resulted in or was brought about by the interference of the Church," and a papal legate chartered the school in 1220 [Wieruszowski, 79]. Padua also developed its medical school fairly early on.

As in the (later) case of Aristotle, the Galen and Avicenna texts presented astonishing amounts of information new to the Latin West. (Many additional texts written by Galen were discovered in the Late Middle Ages.) Unfortunately, much of that new information, including its theoretical foundations, was wrong (see below), as were many of the methods associated with it. Even though medical knowledge was very limited, this *textual* foundation was to remain the basis of medical practice for hundreds of years, so the formally trained doctors, though they might recognize certain ailments, had few or no good treatments for most of them, and the patient was often worse off in the hands of a doctor than in the hands of a healer, or even a clergyman. This is not to say that there weren't at least a few doctors who made some progress in the healing arts, typically as evidenced by having helped some important personage recover from some malady—though their knowledge apparently did not tend to become cumulative. Indeed, some treatments used by almost all doctors were harmful and if they or the profession had actually been able to learn from experience, it seems like it shouldn't have taken a great deal of hindsight to recognize that there were inadequacies or even additional dangers involved in these treatments.

The Humors, Temperaments, and Elements

The biggest failure in medical theory was the assumption/deduction brought forward from the Greek ancients, including Hippocrates, that four humors were involved in much of human health, and that much of the point of treatment was to restore balance in these humors. The humors were: hot/warm, dry, cold, and wet/moist. And these four humors were related to four temperaments, where each temperament overlapped with two humors and had associated body parts: yellow bile, liver, choleric (excitable, easily angered); blood, heart, sanguine (sociable, optimistic); phlegm, brain, phlegmatic (even tempered, passive); and black bile, spleen, melancholic (pessimistic, moody, anxious). And all this bore a relationship as well to the four elements: earth (warm and dry), air (warm and moist), fire (hot and dry), and water (cold and moist). Astrological signs also played a role in prognosis and even some diagnoses; in works of art, doctors were often portrayed with their astrological prediction apparatus dangling from their belt.

Checking a patient's pulse, taking a urine sample, and checking for a fever and a pallor were common practices and probably helped with a few easy diagnoses, even if only because the very complicated "theoretical" schema in use in medicine didn't totally preclude figuring out where to start and some sensible linkages. For example, a fever might be regarded as hot, and there might be some foods that a feverish person should avoid (e.g., hot spices), and some treatments known to ease feverishness (e.g., cold, wet compresses on the forehead). Among the most well-known and harmful practices was blood-letting (phlebotomy), which was also among the most common doctor prescriptions (though the actual bleeding of the patient was farmed out to barber-surgeons). Other common procedures were the use of purgatives and laxatives. Prescriptions for other drugs were common too, but the match between many of the drugs' effects, or lack of effects, and the needs of the patients was undoubtedly often lacking because the uses of drugs were also almost always associated with the humors [Siraisi, 142]. Doctors also were trained never to over-promise and to provide a relatively more, rather than relatively less, dire prognoses, so that if treatment failed they could claim it was hopeless by the time they had been summoned. As can readily be imagined, the theoretical schema made it almost impossible to progress in terms of systematic observation—except outside the theories. And too-slavish adherence to the theories of the Ancients meant there was very little progress at all. Instead, the cultural insanities of scholars being unwilling to systematically observe the world, and to do hands-on work, affected medical practitioners too.

Medicine; Galen; Anatomy

"By his own lights, Galen was an experimental physician, constantly appealing to experience" [Daniel J. Boorstin, *The Discoverers: A History of Man's Search to Know His World and Himself*, 346]. Galen summarized what had been known from before him, added to it substantially, and produced sixteen works that were declared by medical professionals as being authoritative. "As Galen's books became sacred texts, his own spirit was forgotten" [Boorstin, 346]. Indeed, Galen "had insisted that his disciples should first study his writings on method," and follow those. In anatomy, dissection was prohibited in Galen's time, so he learned what he could from gladiator's wounds and animal studies (which threw him off sometimes), but he recommended dissection for learning.

But when dissection of humans did finally come to be acceptable practice at the university of Bologna in the early 1300s, it resulted in a slightly improved curriculum but it didn't begin to revolutionize medicine, or even anatomy or surgery. Witnessing a dissection came to be part of the training of some doctors, but it was done infrequently, in part because obtaining corpses was a problem (and their rate of decay was oppressive and limiting). Even corpses from executions (which were typically mutilated or beheaded) were hard to come by, and so they were sometimes purloined by doctors or their assistants from the public displays of bodies used to humiliate criminals and defame the crime. In the course of instructing, normally the professor stood well above the cutting table and spoke to what was transpiring below in the hands of his barber-surgeon or other assistant(s) [Boorstin, 351]; later, the professor might stand closer and use a pointer. The main idea seems to have been to lecture on Galen or Avicenna and show the medical students the real body parts (and if they differed from Galen, it was because of variations in people).

Boorstin says that as a professor Vesalius (some two centuries later) broke with tradition and did the dissection himself. Then, a few years after that, in 1543, having arranged for some of the best artists to assist him, Vesalius left the professorship and proceeded to design an anatomy text with hundreds of artistically wonderful and anatomically correct wood block etchings showing virtually every aspect of the human body in 663 printed pages [Boorstin, 357]. (This would have been impossible 100 years previously, because artists did not yet then know how to depict human bodies in realistic perspective.) Vesalius' work was an almost-immediate sensation in the profession, although it still took 50 years for it to become the standard anatomy text in almost all universities. Moreover, here, finally, was an extensively demonstrated model of a systematic, observation-based study of a natural phenomenon—the human body no less. The human bodies in Vesalius were depicted in stances that reminded the reader of the perfection of Greek statues, though flayed or cut away to expose organs, muscle groups, or bones. So, Vesalius' work helped to really *begin* the scientific revolution. Vesalius hadn't solved all the knowledge problems but he corrected Galen's anatomy in a number of respects and solved some of the unknowns about how the human body worked. However, this is not to say that Galen was abandoned; rather he was mainly supplanted in this one area—human anatomy. And the microscopic capillary connections between the arteries and veins were still a mystery—and not discovered until well after 1628 when William Harvey proved that the volume of blood was so great that it must re-circulate and could not be created anew, over and over again, in the body [Boorstin, 366-368].

Toward the end of the Middle Ages and earlier in urban areas where there were more doctors, the doctors sought laws to limit the rights of other practitioners of medicine, irrespective of testimonials, successful treatments where doctors had failed, and estimates of success rates. By the late 16th century in Nuremburg Germany (and elsewhere), for example, "physicians convinced secular authorities that the diverse and often 'ignorant' methods of 'practical healers'— even including guild-certified barbers, apothecaries, and midwives— required closer regulation and supervision" [Joel F. Harrington, *The Faithful Executioner: Life and Death, Honor and Shame in the Turbulent Sixteenth Century*, 195]. And executioners and barber-surgeons were restricted to treating external wounds "'about which they have some knowledge'" [Harrington, 196]. Thus, doctors used their greater prestige, and their professional training in the universities, as the reason for denying other healers, but their theory of medicine was so bad that they were seldom even marginally competent in most areas of practice. Some people went directly to apothecaries (druggists) for medicines, and they might have been as good a source as any because they handled far more cases, but in at least some times and places apothecaries were not allowed to sell drugs without a doctor's prescription.

As discussed in the Part on witch-hunting, healers were also one of the targets for witchcraft allegations in the Later Middle Ages and after 1560 especially. Many doctors contributed to this persecution directly by alleging, like the Church, that successful healers necessarily drew upon the Devil for their work because the physicians relied on God, and if they couldn't cure somebody, nobody else could do so without having called upon Satan. While some healers undoubtedly had some useful knowledge (e.g., of medicinal plants), some were little more than charlatans, and yet others relied mainly on charms, magic spells, and prayer (ultimately capitalizing on the placebo effect when successful—an effect which no doubt also led to some if not most doctors' successes). Spontaneous remissions benefitted all practitioners. The skills of most midwives, however, were probably far more valuable, useful and attuned to the reality of their work, even if some magic and charms were used in many cases. In their case, skills were often undoubtedly passed from mother to daughter or to (mainly informal) apprentices, and almost undoubtedly to some extent tended to be somewhat cumulative over time, especially within a practice handed down over generations. Progress in this area was almost undoubtedly interrupted and slowed, or quite possibly made worse, by the witch hunts. So that's another way in which the Church, with some help as well from the Protestants in the heyday of witch-hunting, inhibited the development of science.

Paracelsus: The First Major Critic of Medical Practice

I very much suspect that the faith in a doctor's treatment was anything but robust except perhaps among those unfamiliar with them, and those wealthy enough to hire the most renown physicians. Alas, even when some outspoken challenges to doctors' practices were finally raised by Paracelsus (1493-1541), his substitute treatments often weren't any better (e.g., overuse of poisonous mercury pastes). But Daniel J. Boorstin credits Paracelsus with important changes in emphasis, even though these changes were not generally picked up on by others in the profession at the time: The insistence that the cause of disease was *outside the body*, that there was a uniformity to the causes of specific diseases, and that disease was in no way a matter of humors within the body [Boorstin, 342]. This was indeed a part of the direction in which medicine needed to go, but Paracelsus' hyper-provocative approach and his alternative causes ("minerals and poisons borne from the stars in the atmosphere") and treatments might have undermined his message. Further—as a challenge to what is at least a slight overstatement in Boorstin here—it is impossible that doctors at the time of Paracelsus thought that *all* disease was based within the body— because epidemics like the plague were obviously contagious and, indeed, civil authorities began to impose quarantines to prevent or contain the transmission of plague not long after the Black Death raged through Europe the first time, in 1348-1350.

Surgeons the Exception: Some Learning from Experience

Surgeons were the ones who re-set dislocations and treated broken bones, while making splints as needed; they stopped bleeding from wounds and stitched them up and bandaged them; they lanced boils, cut out cancerous growths, cauterized bad wounds/infections (often without anesthesia in the early days—a very traumatic experience that could kill); they extracted painful teeth; some even learned to repair some anal fistula (with techniques derived from those of Arab writers); they tried to deal with skull fractures (common in a violent society) and sometimes practiced trephining; and they dealt with the wounds of war, including amputations. For example, see Carole Rawcliffe's *Medicine & Society in Later Medieval England* [71, 75, 125-126.] "It is testimony to the skill of the medieval surgeon that so many badly wounded individuals actually lived to fight again" [Rawcliffe, 72]. There were also itinerant specialists who couched for cataracts [Rawcliffe, 72], a procedure rather like fine sewing, pushing the opaqueness from the center of the eye, thus allowing light to enter again, but at the cost of a lens. Surgery was very much a hands-on, second-class profession. The Church in 1215 forbad "regular" clergy (clergy in monkish orders— who comprised almost all the well-educated clergy) to perform cautery or make surgical incisions [Siraisi, 26], even though it had been monks who had some history of work in healing. Although a few surgeons were trained in medical schools, most surgeons were trained by a parent or as an apprentice to a master who was a barber-surgeon, or sometimes even an executioner. In England, for example, the barber surgeons often had strong guilds in which apprentices served for five or six years before they became eligible to practice, and some girls were even admitted to apprenticeships [Rawcliffe, 126]. The city executioner in Nuremberg left a remarkably complete diary-journal of his experiences both as a surgeon and an executioner [Harrington]. When so commanded, executioners were responsible for torture, for breaking bodies of criminals by smashing their limbs while they were tied down on large wagon wheels. beheadings, etcetera. It was a serious failure not to decapitate a victim with one blow of a sword. So, executioners learned from their experiences with human bodies and—at least in the Nuremberg case—to be the best surgeon in the vicinity. Whether following a doctor's orders or using the tactic prophylactically, barbers were the principal blood-letters.

Given all the wars—small and large, short and long—going on over the years, and the associated use of swords and arrows, catapults and trebuchets (which threw large boulders at the stone walls of castles and cities) and later cannons and then smaller arms such as the arquebus (an early musket), there was all the more demand for people skilled in surgery. A king fielding an army might take 10-12 surgeons with him. It is not surprising then that there were more knowledge gains in surgery than in medicine. Clearly, among the reasons for this are the hands-on character of the work and the obvious causes of the most of the problems to be dealt with. Trying to adjust bodily "humors" will not extract an arrow(head). Bleeding patients will not fix a slash wound from a sword, or a broken bone that needs to be re-set. Anesthetic preparations were untrustworthy because overdoses of opium or hemlock or henbane might kill the patient instead [Rawcliffe, 77], but they were sometimes used, for example, in the form of (soporific) sponges held under the nose. A vinegar-soaked sponge would be used to snap the patient out of it. Alcoholic drink was also an important anesthetic. In addition, surgeons had to work as fast as humanly possible in doing work such as amputation or cauterization, often while others held the patient down, lest the patient die from shock.

Plants, Drugs

The experience in medicine with Galen was essentially repeated when it came to the question of medical uses of drugs, that is, herbals/plants. In this case, Dioscorides was the ancient authority. And he too had urged his readers not to pay attention so much to the words, "as to the industry and experience that I have brought to bear on the matter" [Boorstin, 420]. Dioscorides urged readers to continue his work on the plants depicted and described in his work and to find other uses and remedies for other plants as well.

A brief example is essential to understanding the breadth of Dioscorides' mission, and the range of problems for which he sought remedies. As translated into English: "The berry of the juniper … is 'good for ye stomach, being good taken in drinck for the infirmities of the Thorax, Coughs, & inflations, tormina, & ye poisons of venomous beasts. It is also … good both for convulsions & ruptures, & such as [have] strangled wombs'" [Boorstin, 421]. Dioscorides undoubtedly got carried away some here in terms of what all the juniper berry is good for, and that seems to have been typical from the other two examples given by Boorstin. So, there was plenty of room for revision. Dioscorides book covered more than 600 herbal remedies. Recognizing the plants depicted was another matter, however, because they typically had undergone several copyings over the centuries, almost invariably departing further and further from the original except when the copyist knew the plant. (And, of course, not all plants were available everywhere, though there were apothecary shops that had some of them.)

Other examples can be drawn from over 200 included in a compilation assembled from somewhat varying copies of a medieval health handbook. Among other goals, this book depicts plants and foods associated with the humors used in medicine. Most of the plants are common foodstuffs, not specifically medicinal. For example:

"#200. TURNIPS (NAPONES)

Nature: Warm in the first degree, humid in the middle of the second degree. *Optimum:* The fresh, sweet, garden variety. *Usefulness:* They cause urination and sediments. *Dangers:* They cause flatulence and swellings. *Neutralization of the Dangers:* With pepper and aromas. *Effects:* ..." [*The Medieval Health Handbook: Tacuinum Sanitatas*, #200].

A second version of turnips, from a different copy of the original, listed as #201, may be a different variety because it has the optimum described as "The kind that is long, wrinkled, and dark." And they have the opposite effects on swelling because their usefulness is that "They increase sperm and make the flesh less susceptible to swellings." The dangers are that "they cause occlusions in the veins and in the pores." But these dangers can be neutralized "by stewing them twice and then cooking them with very fat meats." There is also a third version of turnips [The Medieval Health Handbook: Tacuinum Sanitatas, #201, & #23].

This is not to say that they were pretty much incorrect about most of the effects of almost all of the plants and foods listed. Any summary here is probably beyond the current level of knowledge. But wine (#56), for example, is "warm and dry in the second degree," optimally "yellow-colored and fragrant," and usefully "quenches thirst." The dangers arise "when drunk without measure" and those dangers can be neutralized by "eating something while drinking." Much more dubious is that the usefulness of yellow-colored wine (#58) is that it "removes the danger of poisons." And the danger is that it "reduces the desire for coitus"—though that danger can be neutralized "with sour quince." Evidently, they typically drank wine to excess and thus missed out on wine's potential to lower inhibitions and the desire for coitus in the early phases of the drinking [The Medieval Health Book: Tacuinum Sanitatas, #56 & #58].

In any case, the medical profession would have done well here to systematically elicit and compile and test these and other plants as candidates for herbal remedies, but I have seen little indication that such efforts were made. Indeed, they probably could have started by eliciting more information from each society's healers.

Animals

"For [1500] years the learned of Europe who wanted to know about nature relied on their 'herbals' and their 'bestiaries,' textual authorities whose tyranny was quite like that of Galen over medicine, and whose poetic delights lured readers away from the outdoor world of plants and animals" [Boorstin, 420]. The bestiaries were replete with imaginatively distorted, composite, mythological, fantastic, and otherwise weird animals. Animals were among Aristotle's strongest areas of work, but I've seen no evidence of any of his efforts being pursued after its rediscovery in the early 1200s. Of course some trial and error efforts undoubtedly occurred in animal husbandry, including some undertaken by monks.

Still, when it came to domesticated animals, probably even most of the churchmen and the nobles knew about them in ways much more intimately than most people in U.S. cities do today. Nevertheless, apart from estate managers and peasants, the upper classes (including those in the Church) were probably most likely to know something about animals with which they themselves actually worked, for example, the riding of horses, and perhaps some of the behaviors of animals sought in their hunts. For other purposes, they would employ grooms and trainers to care for the horses and butchers for the kills. And the nobles' wives presumably directed the servants who worked in the kitchen and in food procurement, and undoubtedly had greater familiarity with some of the domestic animals. Similarly, some monk must have at least supervised the kitchen staff at monasteries. But peasants were by far the main ones who knew the behaviors of most domestic animals, as they fished, built weirs, hunted for birds with nets, took care of the livestock, maintained some dovecotes and bee hives, slaughtered some animals on annual schedules, raised, killed and plucked chickens, gathered eggs, and more.

In the late Middle Ages books began to appear on estate management, but I've seen nothing about the extent to which any of those systematically dealt with the animal world, except that some of them in England included management techniques for herds of sheep, an important agricultural industry there.

There was at least one other related exception. Some of the very rich did know something about managing falcons in a hunt, though they otherwise employed falconers to tend to the birds. Most amazing was Frederick II (Holy Roman Emperor and King of Sicily), who wrote a comparative observational treatise on the effectiveness of different varieties of falcons with different prey species—yet another potential model not followed (it probably circulated mainly among the wealthiest literate aristocrats).

CHAPTER 28

Three Important Church-related Contributors to Proto-science and Science

A few educated in scholasticism, some of them theologians, did advance thought in a few areas of proto-science. Among the uppermost heroes of this kind, from the point of view of historians, are Bacon, Roger, Jean Buridan (1295-1363), and Nicole Oresme (1325-1382). We have already discussed Bacon, R including his problems with the Church. Buridan became a master of arts faculty member and university leader at Paris in the mid-1300s, while Oresme, his student, became a theologian and bishop. Buridan and Oresme "took an existing paradigm (the Aristotelian theory of motion) as their starting point, and ended by revolutionizing it" [Rubenstein, 273].

Jean Buridan wrote on many topics but is remembered primarily for his work on motion, which became well known throughout Europe. His initial question involved what moved the heavens (around the earth). Buridan realized that he could do without an active intelligence or intelligences as the mover(s) of the heavens if he assumed that "things once set in motion remain in motion unless they meet resistance" [Rubenstein, 274]. He called this tendency to remain in motion "impetus."

Per the University of Paris history described above, it is no surprise that Buridan was clearly concerned about the orthodoxy of his theorizing. In contrast, "Aristotle's theory seemed almost Xtian, since it made [heavenly] motion dependent upon a sort of divine intervention…, while Buridan's … approach seemed … godless" [Rubenstein, 274]. Buridan of course pointed out that the Bible says nothing about such matters, and further that "one could rather say that God, as he created the world, imparted to each heavenly circle a movement according to his pleasure" [Rubenstein, 274].

"Another factor that made the theory of impetus explosive was its universality. Buridan did not limit his discussion to the heavenly crystalline spheres, which had always been considered radically different in their structure and operations from the earthly (sublunar) realm" [Rubenstein, 274-275]. Aristotle believed that when something is thrown what keeps it going is a replacement of the air behind it, which then continues to push the object forward but with decreasing force until it falls to the ground. Buridan found examples where this was clearly not the case, such as spinning tops and the attraction of certain objects to magnets. And, he wrote, that a ship towed rapidly upstream by horses with ropes, even after the towing has stopped, continues to move forward for a time. "And yet a sailor on deck does not feel any air from behind pushing him. He feels only the air from the front resisting" [Rubenstein, 275].

However, we must be thoughtful about just how much credit we give to the Church for Buridan's accomplishments. True, the Church did not purge him from the masters of arts, as they had Siger of Brabant. But the Church also deserves little or no credit for his rise to become a faculty member at Paris. He was safe at least in part because, though he had corrected Aristotle's theory of motion, he had not directly threatened Church doctrines ("impetus" within the heavens being unproven in any case). Indeed, Buridan is exactly the kind of scholar that, absent

Church impediments and threats, the masters of arts faculties should have produced many more of over 350 years (1200-1550).

"Oresme's work in mathematics developed methods of geometrical representation which anticipate modern graphing techniques" [Rubenstein, 275]. While Aristotle had represented time by a line, and Euclid had used *lines* to represent numerical magnitudes, Oresme added intensities, such as speed, depicted as the height on a vertical line rising above a baseline representing time. Where the intensity was speed, he realized that the area of a figure in which time and velocity were plotted represented the distance traveled [Lindberg, *Beginnings*, 302-304]. In building on the work in early mathematics by the "Merton College Calculators" at Oxford—who "used a calculating approach to theory, but without organized research or a mathematical technique" [Collins, 494]—Oresme's graphing technique applied to motion helped to prove "the 'mean speed theorem' that is substantially the same as that used by Galileo..." over 200 years later [Rubenstein, 275]. The graphing showed that at some point in time a uniformly accelerated object travels the same distance as an object whose speed remained constant at half the final velocity of the accelerated object. The work of the Oxford calculators was recognized as being of value mainly retrospectively, when work began to proceed in mathematics and astronomy; in the interim it largely faded away, and it was rejected (e.g., by humanists) as more "involuted reasoning" [Collins, 493-494]. (More below.)

Oresme's work on the earth's rotation in his *The Book of the Heavens and the Earth* (ca. 1377) is also of considerable importance, building a little further on Buridan's. According to Rubenstein, Oresme concluded "after much ingenious reasoning that the traditional view was correct: the earth remained immobile at the center of the universe" [Rubenstein, 276]. But Rubenstein's wording here is easily misunderstood or misleading, because "Ingenious" is actually only applicable to: 1) Oresme's reasoning that the earth was *not* at the center of the universe; and/or 2) Oresme's careful wording to avoid Church censorship or repercussions. There would be nothing at all ingenious about relying on Church authorities to conclude in favor of the traditional view.

So, did Bishop Oresme's cleverness and knowledge of the Church and its doctrines (including its willingness to engage in allegorical interpretation at times) enable him to get his arguments in circulation without Church censorship or retribution—or did he, given his faith, actually disbelieve his own reasoned arguments despite their ingeniousness? Lindberg does "not believe that we can lightly dismiss his own version" [Lindberg, *Beginnings*, 285]—which is somewhat ambiguous too. Oresme had reasoned that because there were many heavenly bodies out there, some clearly at a very considerable distance, for them to move around the earth every day would require all of them to be going at extreme speeds, with the more distant ones going ever faster—something he called "unbelievable and unthinkable" [James Bruce Ross and Mary Martin McLaughlin (Eds.), *The Portable Renaissance Reader*, 581]. The need for extreme speeds was clear because Oresme was almost undoubtedly aware of Ptolemy's *Almagest*, translations of which had reached Latin Europe by 1200, in which the distance to the sun was estimated at "1,210 Earth radii, while the radius of the [crystalline] sphere of the fixed stars was 20,000 times the radius of the Earth" [Wikipedia, "Ptolemy," accessed 4/19/2017]. Oresme also noted the fact that a person on a ship not in sight of land cannot tell that he is moving (so the same might be true of a person standing on a rotating earth) [Rubenstein, 277]. That idea was part of a broader consideration about which both Buridan and Oresme had written, and the latter also wrote: "'… to an eye in the heavens which could see the earth clearly, it would appear to move; if the eye were on the earth, the heavens would appear to move'" [Rubenstein, 276].

Looking more closely at Oresme's ingeniousness, then, he began his conclusion by saying "it has been shown how it cannot be concluded by reasons that the heavens may be moved [around the earth]," but "nevertheless all hold and I believe that [the heavens are so moved] and that the earth is not: 'God has established the sphere of the earth, which shall not be moved'" [Ross and McLaughlin, 583; source of the interior quote is Psalm 92:1]. Oresme continues thusly: "But considering all that has been said, it is possible to believe that the earth is so moved and that the heavens are not, and it is not evident to the contrary." Yet "it seems on the face of it, as much or more against natural reason [that the earth moves], as are either all or some of the articles [miracles, etc.] of our faith." So, Oresme's "ingenuity" could be said to be the largely new reasoning itself, or it could be said to start with that last clause, indicating that much of the Xtian faith rests on miracles, and then to finish with this: "And thus what I have said for fun in this manner could be of value in confuting or reproving those who would attack our faith by rational arguments" [Ross and McLaughlin, 583.] So, here, after recognizing that miracles are commonplace in his religion, he makes his (ingenious) reasoning into a matter of purely speculative fun that should not be turned against the beliefs of that religion. So, as in the second option above, the (much-needed?) ingenuity seems to have helped Oresme avoid trouble while still getting his heretical reasoning into a book that could be copied and circulated, and did not have to be recanted.

Moreover, late in his life Oresme may have changed his mind at least part of the way to holding that the "case for a rotating earth was as good or better than the case for immobility" [Rubenstein, 276]. It may be noteworthy in this regard that only shortly after the original book was published in 1377, the papacy began its 40-year "Great Schism"— seriously weakening its potential to enforce doctrine except perhaps in very high priority cases when the most applicable of the two popes also had the full support of the relevant secular authorities, under circumstances in which rulers of major national entities subscribed to one pope or the other, but not both.

Buridan had previously argued that "other evidence [also] proved that the earth stood still. For example, he said, an arrow shot straight up on a windless day falls back to its starting point, which it would not do if the earth were rotating." But Oresme came to argue instead that "if the whole earth rotated, an arrow shot up would combine its own vertical motion with the horizontal motion of the atmosphere, and would therefore return to its starting point" [Rubenstein, 276]. "Moreover, he argued, the concept of a rotating earth was far more elegant and economical than the Aristotelian paradigm involving multiple rotating spheres [in the heavens above]" [Rubenstein, 277]. But given what actually happened subsequently (e.g., to Galileo almost 300 years later), it seems quite an exaggeration when Rubenstein goes on to say that "the stationary earth also became a mere hypothesis" [Rubenstein, 277]. To the Church, it was still the Truth. So, although both Buridan and Oresme backed off, they did open the door a little to a rotating earth hypothesis (but not advocacy!), and provided some pretty good thought-experimental reasoned evidence in support of a rotating earth. Moreover, as Copernicus (who was familiar with Oresme's work) later recognized, the same principles used to support the idea of a rotating earth could also be used to support the revolution of the earth and other planets around an immobile sun" [Rubenstein, 278].

Given the limitations of hand copying, the work of both Buridan and Oresme was spread relatively widely throughout Europe. The Church gets a little credit for Oresme's work because he was a bishop. Together, the two were among the very few major Church- and university-affiliated contributors to proto-science in the Middle Ages. Yet when one realizes that there were more than 150 years between Oresme and Copernicus' heliocentrism (which was not yet really proven), and that the Church put Galileo under house arrest almost 80 years after that, for too-obviously advocating the validity of a heliocentric system and a "moving" earth (and disparaging the pope's view to the contrary), one cannot be impressed by the contribution of the Church in this area of the proto-sciences. Among the reasons for this lack that we have already explored is the history of overt Church censorship of a fairly broad range of uses of reason with respect to the works of Aristotle and his commentators, leading to self-censorship, avoidance, and intricate dodging by scholars, including Buridan and Oresme. So one cannot let the Church off the hook for its cultural insanities because Buridan and Oresme knew how to very carefully present their reasoning that was contrary to Church doctrines; nor can it legitimately be claimed on the basis of their work that the Church was a facilitator of proto-science. Indeed, although Buridan's work was printed (not copied) in the late 1400s [Hannam, 206], the use of their thought, except *possibly* as a source of instructional material in astronomy at some universities, was followed by a lapse in progress for much of two centuries until Copernicus (who studied at Bologna and Padua).

And Copernicus

For our purposes, there is no reason to go into any detail about the knowledge of the motions of the stars and planets at the time of Copernicus, most of which had survived from the time of the Roman empire. Much of this knowledge was error-laden, with the assumptions that the earth was at the center of the universe and was unmoving, and that planets and stars had perfectly circular orbits (circles being more perfect). Such assumptions and beliefs led to rather fanciful attempts to explain what was actually seen in the skies, especially the apparently retrograde ("backward") movement at times of the five known planets (Mercury, Venus, Mars, Jupiter, Saturn). Explanations used mathematical-astronomical machinations such as equants, deferents, epicycles, ecliptic, etcetera, that were developed by Ptolemy (100-170 CE) and his predecessors.

But among the important resources for Middle Ages astronomers and astrologers were extensive astronomical tables, which also dated from ancient times and Ptolemy, and had been updated in the Muslim world. These "tables were designed to facilitate the calculation of planetary positions, lunar phases, eclipses and calendrical information" [Starry Messenger: "Astronomical Tables"]. Some tables included descriptions of instruments, or arithmetic or trigonometric aids, or even explained how to calculate lunar or solar eclipses [Starry Messenger].

The Church had been relatively open to astronomy—though the purported predictive capabilities of astrology, including for medical reasons (see above), were surely among the main reasons a few people were drawn to study the skies. And although cosmology and astronomy (the latter requiring more esoteric mathematics) were largely separate [Lindberg, *Beginnings*, 262], theology, as "queen" of the sciences, dealt with the Xtian deity and the heavens (and agreed with circular orbits and a geocentric universe). So, to study the heavens one almost needed to be willing to go a long way into the discipline of theology while having strong capabilities in trigonometry and geometry and an interest in particular in astronomy. Perhaps that is one of the reasons why, in Europe, "until two decades before Copernicus' birth in 1473 there was little concrete evidence of technically proficient planetary astronomy" [Thomas S. Kuhn, *The Copernican Revolution: Planetary Astronomy in the Development of Western Thought*, 124].

As noted, the Church was also somewhat open to astronomy because it needed a better calendar. Church holy days/saints' festivals were every year getting a little further from their intended spots in the seasonal cycles. In addition, the clock, which for practical purposes was a mechanized armillary sphere (see Plate 3.7) that was used to portray the movements of the principal bodies in the heavens around the (stationary) earth—to which hourly indicators were later attached—was also welcomed by the Church so that it could better keep the right intervals in its 6-times-a-day call-to-prayer routines.

Suffice it to say that Copernicus built upon a long but very thin and intermittent tradition of astronomers—including efforts almost up until his time by individuals in the Islamic world. In the Xtian world, Regiomontanus revised astronomical tables, and drew extensively on the spherical trigonometry work of Jabir ibn Aflah (also known as Geber, 1100-1150) in developing instructional manuals in such trigonometry. Buridan and Oresme's work was also known to those astronomers who tried to improve upon the "mathematical structures and nearly all of their data" taken initially from the work of the Greek-Egyptian/Hellenistic astronomical tradition, especially the work of Ptolemy [Lindberg, *Beginnings*, 366]. "Copernicus' contribution was to deploy these resources to build what was ultimately a successful heliocentric model" [Lindberg, *Beginnings*, 366.]. He did make some astronomical observations, but not a lot. Copernicus' book was published in 1543—a date which some historians regard as the start of the scientific revolution—in part perhaps because it was also the same year that Vesalius published his book on anatomy.

What Copernicus came to believe while he was a young man studying some astronomy at Padua was that the earth rotated (and that the heavens didn't), and that the earth revolved around the sun. With his mathematical capabilities, Copernicus, like his astronomy teacher at Bologna, Domenico Maria de Novara (who had been educated in part by Platonists in Florence), had trouble believing the Ptolemaic system because it was so at variance with any mathematically straightforward explanation (Kuhn, 129, 139]. Subsequently, with his capabilities in trigonometry, he recalculated the existing astronomical tables according to this ancient minority "hypothesis," significantly improving the predictability of the tables. It was Copernicus' revisions of these tables that were used in the Jesuits' development of a revised calendar (known as the "Gregorian Calendar") in 1582.

Copernicus wrote a book about his discoveries, which was virtually complete by 1535 [Sobel, 64]. But he knew it was very controversial religiously. Mainly for that reason, but possibly also because his proof was not yet more definitive, he didn't have the book published then, though word of his work on this different theory of the heavens and on improved astronomical tables reached far and wide, including to Rome. Finally, when nearing death, prodded by friends and by a youthful Lutheran acolyte and professor of mathematics, Georg Joachim Rheticus, who had worked with him for several years, he agreed to have it published. Rheticus also published a first account in 1540 of what was in Copernicus' book, profusely praising Copernicus' learnedness on the title page. But it was Andreas Osiander, in writing an unwanted preface to the book, who explained that the work was intended as a hypothesis, thereby reducing the likelihood of repercussions from both Catholic and possibly Protestant leaders. And the position of some of the latter were known. For example, Philipp Melanchthon, who was for many years Luther's right-hand man, in reference to Copernicus' work, was annoyed by his ideas of a moving earth and immobilized sun [Sobel, 178], and thought that the local prince should suppress such folly.

In 1609, Johannes Kepler (1571-1630), using *observational data systematically accumulated* over about two decades by Tycho Brahe (1546-1601, a Danish nobleman), calculated mathematically that the planetary orbit of Mars was elliptical, and concluded that the same was true for the other planets. (Kepler was the son of a soldier, a mathematician who perhaps derived some motivation to study the heavens from an interest in a theology that leaned Lutheran more than Catholic [Hannam, 291-292].)

For much of a century, the Catholic Church did not react negatively to Copernicus' work because his chapter about how the analysis was based on heliocentrism was regarded as dispensable or as offering a hypothesis, not as an integral part of the book. A Dominican who reviewed the book in 1544 thought the heliocentrism hypothesis was too far-fetched and too easily refuted to be of much concern [Sobel, 217]. But Rheticus went on to defend and praise Copernicus and heliocentrism in a variety of related works, including on trigonometry; and others extracted information from Copernicus' book to present the astronomical tables in a convenient form. Everything that Rheticus wrote was on the Index of Forbidden Books of 1559 [Sobel, 217]. In 1616 the Catholic Church "suspended" (Catholic) publication of Copernicus' book until corrections were made, it being hard to condemn for its heretical hypothesis and awkward because it had been of so much value [Sobel, 222-223]. In turn, Kepler's *Epitome of Copernican Astronomy* was put on the Index of Forbidden Books in 1619 [Sobel, 223]. So here again we see the effects of Catholic suppression of ideas inimical to doctrine, both in terms of self-censorship by Copernicus and church follow-through (including early on re Rheticus). We also have Melanchthon's rejection of the non-biblical, with hearsay reports that Luther had a harsher stance [Sobel, 178], though Melanchthon appreciated the advances in astronomical tables [Sobel, 194]. Of course it was still mainly the Catholic Church that threatened proto-scientists and scientists with prosecution for heresy, and possible execution. And each time the Church or churches retarded science, they slowed the potential for science to advance the potential development of humanity and delayed the elimination of the associated cultural insanities.

CHAPTER 29

Most Real Advances in Proto-science
Come Via Artisans and Craftsmen

Steven A. Epstein's economic and social history of later medieval Europe emphasizes in several places that almost all technological advances were made by "nameless tinkerers making small improvements" [Epstein, 191 & 197, 208, 214] and, indeed, that "anonymous tinkerers were taking more of the same technology to the verge of proto-industrialization" [Epstein, 214]. Despite the fact that guilds usually had a local monopoly, improvements occurred in part because "guild members in many trades continued to compete against one another on quality, freshness, or other aspects of reputation that over time established a good position in the markets" [Epstein, 115]. In addition, the marketplaces involved bargaining over prices with customers, and that too created an incentive to improve and innovate to justify higher prices.

As the "High Middle Ages" (ca. 1100-1300) launched into their second century, the primary mechanism for the transmission of the knowledge involved in technology—including design, tools, and the associated skills—was more and more carried out in the workers guilds [Long1, 52]. To summarize, this artisan system worked thusly: master craftsmen (and some craftswomen) trained young apprentices, who graduated to become journeymen. After more experience, these journeymen would then be tested, often with a final project, to become masters. But because the number of masters at times "had" to be limited to protect the ratio of demand to providers (i.e., the income of the master artisans), not all fully qualified journeymen could move up to become masters in all places at all times. So even though some cities, such as Venice, made great efforts not to let their city's special skill sets (e.g., glass-making) get beyond their borders, in many cases, some of these journeymen ended up migrating to other locations, taking the skills that they had learned with them. So even though no books were involved, most artisan technologies were transmitted around Europe.

Optics/Visual Theory

Attempts to understand how the eye works dated back to the ancients. Among the initial questions/problems were whether light from objects impinged on the eyes (intromission) or whether the eyes had rays that reached out to the objects (extramission). If light came from the objects to the eyes, how did the eye manage to perceive them correctly if the eyes were conical as Euclid said [Lindberg, *Beginnings*, 313-315]? Islamic scholars tried to synthesize the differences among Greek theories and then extended their understanding of optics beyond that. In particular, Alhacen (Ibn al-Haytham, ca. 965-1040) solved most of these problems [Lindberg, *Beginnings*, 314-316]. But the peoples of Europe also gained access to other ideas about how the eye worked through translations of works by Plato, Aristotle, Euclid, and other Muslim scholars, including one representing the Galenic tradition [Lindberg, *Beginnings*, 317-318].

Drawing mainly on Alhacen's work (which he could read in the original languages), Bacon R's writings on light and optics were largely responsible for the West's acceptance of Alhacen's conclusions

[Lindberg, *Beginnings*, 318]—and see above. Even so, "when Johannes Kepler began to think about visual theory in the year 1600, ... he took up the problem where Bacon, Roger, together with Pecham and Witelo, and Alhacen had left it" [Lindberg, *Beginnings*, 320]. And although Theodoric of Freiberg carried the study of optics a little further, publishing in 1310, the problem from our perspective is that all the other European proto-scientists mentioned here died about or before 1292. So, for almost 300 years there was little or no major progress in optics— and, overall, very little addition to what was obtained from the Arabs. Finally, in the early 1600s, Kepler published some major advances in optical theory. And later in that century, Newton added some major work on light/optics.

Meanwhile, however, one major advance occurred in optics technology: eyeglasses. Eyeglasses were developed by craftsmen, most probably in Venice around 1286. Because glass could not yet be made clear enough for lenses, rock crystal had to be used [Epstein, 206], making it all the more likely that the invention arose without any reference to any theory or proto-scientific writing. The use of lenses to improve the major problems with vision (farsightedness and the effects of aging) was a great boon to people who had to rely on their eyes, from monks reading books to tailors stitching clothes. Apart from improvements in eyeglasses, though, there was little progress made in optical technology over the next few centuries. But there were many advances in the quality and types of glass used in making a wide array of glass vessels [Dan Klein and Ward Lloyd, *The History of Glass*]. Then there followed some huge advances in optics technology—first, the invention of the telescope by a craftsman in the Netherlands near the start of the 1600s, which was soon thereafter improved upon by Galileo, and used to look at the heavens with devastating effects on Church doctrines and mythology about the perfection of the heavenly realm (and confirming also, via the presence of craters on the moon, that the doctrine of the heavens' unchangeability was also wrong, as had also been shown by two supernovas and a comet after 1572). See Plate 3.8 for a statue of Galileo. And toward the latter middle of the 1600s, a craftsman invented the microscope. Then Leeuwenhoek, a Netherlands optics craftsman, further improved the microscope, and introduced the world to the fact that there were microscopic life forms too, while sharing drawings of them with the world through the publications of England's Royal Society.

Overview: The Development of Technologies, 1000-1600

Frances and Joseph Gies note that Robert Kilwardby, Archbishop of Canterbury, in a book from 1279, said that the mechanical arts were "practical divisions of the speculative sciences" [Gies & Gies, 13]. The "speculative" sciences were what was done by university masters and doctors, some theologians included. Archbishop Kilwardby can be seen as correct in his vision but, as described above, there was very little connection between speculative sciences and intellectuals, until later among some humanists. Until the 1500s, connections between universities and applied science or technology were virtually nonexistent (and stayed that way) *except* for a few subjects, such as medicine (e.g., anatomy for would-be surgeons within and new discoveries about the circulatory system) and some teaching about astronomy. Some of the early history of the natural sciences and earth sciences is covered in the next Part. The first institutes of technology did not appear until the 1700s; sciences weren't generally available in university curricula until the later 1800s; and the research university wasn't even invented until the 1800s in Germany. Today, however, advances in theoretical sciences often lead to many technological spin-offs, but the reverse is still often the case.

As we have seen, the Church emphasized that the surest reality was based on faith—the authority of the Bible, and the interpretations thereof by Church fathers and doctors. This was supplemented by accepting doctrinally-suitable thinking from the ancients, especially Aristotle and his *Metaphysics*, and the error-filled theory of Galen in medicine. And while the Church was willing to incorporate reason into its scholastic theological ruminations (most Church leaders having been convinced that some forms of reasoning would support its doctrines), it also ruled out free-thinking reasoning (a la Siger of Brabant) and removed the freedom of university masters who might in any way give rise to serious doubt on the largely faith-based reasoning of the Church in areas of doctrinal importance. This reaction undoubtedly held back raw theorizing, and at least some observational work in these proto-scientific areas as well (if only because of the large number of university masters), such that even theologians thoroughly versed in doctrinal matters, such as Oresme, were very cautious in how they phrased their conclusions. In addition, the rejection of hands-on observational work (or the application of technology thereto), let alone systematic observational studies of nature, was supported by social class boundaries even though some highly respected exemplars did do such work (e.g., Albert the Great, and Aristotle in biology).

Plate 3.8: Statue of Galileo Galilei by Aristodemo Costoli (1851) outside the Uffizi Gallery, Florence, Italy. Photo by the author.

What was delayed or lost through these cultural insanities was the possibility of making much greater progress sooner, not only through advances in science and technology, but also in releasing minds from the grip of the Church in a number of ways that might improve human welfare, concerns about which had begun to rise in the 1400s among humanists and were also seized upon by early Protestants protesting Church uses of its wealth.

But there were developments on the technological front in the High and Late Middle Ages (and some even before that). These advances were made in the (manual) "arts"—results produced mainly by artisans/craftsmen, and occasionally even by peasants. And with those advances in technology from time to time there also came tacit advances in proto-scientific and scientific understanding and theory, most but not quite all of which went largely unrecognized by society's educated leaders at the time.

The processes by which the advances in technology tended to be achieved are especially important to mention because they offer a sharp contrast to the traditional approach to intellectual life. These processes included the most natural of all human modes—trial and error—that is, experimenting with different possible solutions to see which best solves a problem or improves an existing product. Of course, all of this was hands-on. As already noted, even where craft productions seemed satisfactory and the goal for most artisans was to achieve quality of product according to existing standards (which was supported by the guilds), advances would occasionally be made. Of course, advances in technology might have been hastened in some areas had the craftsmen been literate and informed in applicable university subject matters (e.g., geometry in some cases), but for the most part, they weren't. Even master masons used proportion and a compass in their architectural work, not a knowledge of Euclidian geometry.

Although the major effort to learn what the academy could gain from society's craftsmen was to await the 1600s, there were several areas in which major precedents were set that stretch back to at least the early-middle 1400s. These are discussed subsequently.

First, however, it seems more important to provide some kind of overview of many or the major advances in technology occurring in the period from roughly 1000CE to 1600CE. In most cases it will be fairly obvious that the Church had no role in facilitating development of technology. My hope is that by including a look at technological advances in this period—using a broader, society-wide lens—it will become harder yet to argue, as some revisionist historians have done, that the medieval Church was supportive of science. The extreme weaknesses in systematic observation-based science and any kind of trial-and-error "experimentation" in the universities made it all the more difficult to make connections between proto-science and technology as it went on evolving in society. Still, as we'll see below, that did not entirely prevent outreach from the learned to the artisan—but it was to be an outreach for the most part without involvement of the Church or the universities.

To provide this overview, the table below presents many of the major developments in different areas of technological endeavor for the period pre-1000CE to about 1600CE. Each is described briefly and a likely source of the technology or a technological improvement is given. Most have a reference associated with them.

When a source of a technological development such as "Arab world" or "China" is given, it is to be tacitly understood that someone in the European/Latin-reading world translated an original work (or a translation of that work) into Latin, or brought the idea of the technology, or the technology itself to Western Xtendom. At minimum, minor adaptations to a European context should be assumed to have occurred. But I have tried to include major adaptations and improvements as separate entries credited to European artisans and inventors. In a number of cases, none of my references reported a source, or who was responsible for some advance in technology, so in several of those cases I have inserted guesses (flagged with a question mark). (Note: Authors Gies & Gies are rendered as G&G in the table.)

Developments in Technology and the Arts, pre-1000 to ~1520+

Area of Endeavor	Major Development(s)	Likely Source or Inventor	Reference
Agriculture	Heavy plow pulled by oxen (+/- wheels), esp. needed for land clearance	Roman; in use by 700	[G&G, 44.]
	Greater use of tools, new & old (harrow, pitchfork, scythe, tandem ox harness)	Roman and later	[G&G, 45.]
	Shift to 3-field (one fallow) planting; legumes, oats, animal fertilizer helps	Peasants/lords/monasteries?	
	Dikes	Netherlanders	[G&G, 48.]
	Irrigation	Baghdad→Moors/Spain	[G&G, 103.]
Animal Power	Rigid, padded horse collar (unchoked horse makes for a better draft animal); slow changeover from oxen in agriculture except where more power needed	Asia; arrived ca. 800	[G&G, 45.]
	Nailed iron shoes (protected horse hooves from rot & injury on non-grasslands)	Asia; arrived ca. 900	[G&G, 46.]
Transportation	Roads (incl. wagon-capable; cobble & sand surfacing in north, 12th C & later)	Roman and new	[G&G, 148-149.]
	Collected fees and Church charity credits (indulgences) support building of bridges; buildings atop bridge added (new)	Mainly Roman technol.	[G&G, 149-153.]
	First suspension systems on carriages & wagons, from 1370s	Wheelwrights?	[G&G, 218-219.]
Power, Mechanical	Waterwheels (upright version rare in Mediterranean b/c low river flows)Roman Post-900 emphasis on upright overshot waterwheel (much more powerful); millwrights were first modern mechanics	Roman+ carpenters, millwrights?	[G&G, 33-35.] [Conner, 280.]
	Waterwheel power adaptations: pumping of bellows for iron forges; pounding for wool processing or hammering iron, etc.	Millwrights, carpenters, ironworkers, miners?	[G&G, 111-117; 168; 200-201.]
	Post windmill (entire structure can be turned to face wind), before 1185	Modified from Arab	[Long1, 48; G&G, 117.]
	Turret windmills—turn-able tower rather than turn whole mill; 15th C.	Millwright, carpenter?	[G&G, 264.]
Carpentry (+ see others)	Brace & bit (adapting crank to a drill), 15th C.	Carpenter-blacksmith?	[G&G, 263.]
Metallurgy (see also military)	Steel (e.g., steel-edged swords from the Rhineland were finished by Vikings)	Germanic barbarians	[G&G, 12; Long1, 69.]
	Advances in iron ore-processing techniques, furnaces	Iron smelter men	
	Improved tools and utensils, and quantities thereof	Blacksmiths, tinsmiths, et al.	[G&G, 268.]
	Blast furnace, w/ much improved structure (earliest record in Eur., 1350)	Chinese or independent	[G&G, 200-202.]
	Iron casting (possible via blast furnace, but not immediately discovered)	Iron smelter men?	[G&G, 201.]
	Mechanization for deeper mining; improved ore extraction, new alloys, etc.; greatly enlarged scale of mining	Smelter men, alchemists; capitalists-&-ruler-funded teams	[Long2, 33, 107-110.]

Category	Description	Source	Citation
Cloth-making	All parts of clothing creation are women's work; spinning remains so	From Roman times	[G&G, 49-50.]
	Several variants on looms	Antiquity + Chinese	[G&G, 52-54; 118-120.]
	Spinning wheel, introduced late 13th century	Via Arabs	[G&G, 175.]
	Spinning wheel improved to get better thread quality, faster speed	Carpenters & spinners?	[G&G, 176-178.]
Wool	Specialization & improvements in weaving, fulling, dyeing, & finishing	Flanders, Italy, other Europe	[Long1, 53.]
Alchemy (ancestor of chemistry) (see also metallurgy)	Re-introduction of ideas, texts about alchemy to Europe, 12th century on	Arab written sources	[G&G, 162-163.]
	Laboratory equipment for heating substances, distillation, etc.	Antiquity	[G&G, 163.]
	Many chemicals, reactions (esp. to yield useful salts)	Arab written sources	[Conner, 164.]
	Improvements in processes, furnaces, stills, equipment	Alchemists	[G&G, 163.]
	Distillation of acids that dissolve metals and alcohol	Alchemists	[G&G, 163.]
Shipbuilding, sailing	Small broad & shallow ships, galleys, lateen sail; ocean-going Viking ships	Roman, Byzantium; Vikings	[G&G, 30,71.]
	Improvements in round-hulled cog (larger, keel, ocean-going), by ca. 1300	Shipwrights+merchants?	[G&G, 154-155.]
	Added ship's castle (fore & aft) for bowmen, defense vs. pirates, war	Shipwrights+merchants?	[G&G, 155-156.]
	Multi-mast ships; multi-deck ships	China?Islam? + shipwrights?	[Long1, 158.]
	Framed construction & improved rudder (replaces steering oar)	China?Islam? + shipwrights?	[Long1, 73.]
	Assembly line (for supplying a series of ships about to sail); before 1436	Venice Arsenal	[G&G, 271.]
	Galleon, early 1500s		[Long2, 100.]
Navigation	Chinese astronomy & survey device→compass after modifications for sailing	Captains, pilots?	[G&G, 157, 222-223.]
	Astrolabe (device for figuring time of sunrise/sunset, position of stars)	Arab lands	[Long1, 37.]
	Better coastal navigation charts (re-evolving from portolans' coastal markers)	Captains, pilots	[Conner, 217-220.]
	Better maps including the idea of latitude, longitude	Roman/Alexandria's Ptolemy; rediscovery 1406	
	Discovery of routes to the Far East by sailing around Africa, later 1400s	Portuguese-employed navigators, captains	
	Peoples of Europe find the "New World"	Spanish crown financed Columbus' quest	
	Sailing by stars and figuring latitude w/ them	Navigators, map-makers	[Conner, 226-227.]
Glasswork	Cathedral glasswork: improvements in glass coloration, cuts for depictions	Glassworkers	[G&G, 68, 132-134.]
	Spectacles (ca. 1285), using rock crystal for lenses (clear glass in 15th C.)	Glassworker in Venice	[Epstein, 206.]
	Many advances in mfg. of glass vessels (esp. in Venice)	Glass workshops	[Klein & Lloyd; Epstein, 206.]
	Telescope (early 1600s), then improved by Galileo	Dutch lens maker	[Conner, 233.]
Arts (fine)	Improvements in oil paint	Artists, mainly in Venice	[G&G, 274.]
	(Re-)invention of vanishing point 3D perspective (Roman, Greek were close)	Goldsmith-mason Brunelleschi	[King, 33-35.]
	Treatise on Painting explains for all how to do perspective, 1435	Leon Battista Alberti	[Long2, 70.]
	Re-learning of 3D work in metals, 1400s	Ghiberti, Donatello, et al.	[King 18-19, 40.]
	Humanist painters breakout from religious strictures, portraits	Botticelli	[Strathern, 60-61.]

Music	Development of musical notation (in monasteries); development of musical staff and polyphony, development of composing by ca. 1200	Monasteries originally, music moves to secular world (but hymns later)	[Crosby, 141-147.]
	Bowed Instruments (lute and rebec, ancestors of violin)	Muslim world	[G&G, 102.]
Linguistics	Humanist emphasis on perfect/original Latin shows Donation of Constantine to be a forgery (Latin in it dated from 800, not 300), 1440 (published 1517)	Lorenzo Valla	[Estep, 31.]
	Humanist emphasis on learning Greek, Hebrew, etc., to read ancient texts;	Petrarch and successors; Erasmus,	[McGrath, 23-24.]
	improvements in unreliable Vulgate Bible wordings/meanings, 1516	Complutense Univ.	
Reading, Writing, Communication	Carolingian Miniscule (small, easy to read standardization of writing)	Alcuin/Charlemagne	[Long1, 91.]
	Greater emphasis on (monastery & palace) scriptoria to copy books	Charlemagne	[Long1, 92.]
	Translations from Arabic in Toledo/Spain, Sicily & from Greek via Byzantines	Xtians, Muslims, Orthodox, Jews	[Long1, 96.]
	Technology spreads when journeymen can't become masters locally		[Long1, 52.]
	Paper (start of production in Europe by 1276) + water-powered mills	Chinese + Spain, Sicily (Muslims)	[Long1, 89.]
	Improvements in paper (incl. mfg., sizing/properties, inks), 15th C.	European	[Long1, 89.]
	Wood block printing for art, depictions	Chinese	
	Movable-reusable type, printing press, usage system, mid 1400s	Johannes Gutenberg	
Architecture	Loss of Roman knowledge of how to make concrete; many other losses	"Darker" ages	[G&G, 67.]
	Improvements in architecture, generally	Master masons et al. (by ca. 1450= architects)	
	Bridges	Roman	
	Bridges: better footings, a few taller arches, buildings atop, more	Ex-shepherd; others	[G&G, 149-154.]
	Recovery of some Roman capabilities; master masons & applied	Villard de Honnecourt, Leon Battista Alberti, +	[G&G, 197-199; Long2, 62-66.]
	mathematicians reflect on/update Vitruvius & others		
	New mechanical devices to assist in construction, e.g., Brunelleschi's hoist	Master masons, carpenters?	[King, 56-63.]
	Book re ideal city, planning (influences: Plato, humanists, artisans), c. 1464	Filarete	[Long2, 77-80.]
Gothic Church Structure	Pointed arch (enabled taller & stronger arches; used in Spanish mosques)	India?/Muslim World	[G&G, 131.]
	Thin, multi-rib, spreading roof supports (w/ arches enabled lighter roof)	Roman baths +master masons?	[G&G, 130.]
	A flying buttress (helps keep walls from falling outward due to roof pressure)	Roman+ master masons	[G&G, 134-135.]
Fortifications	City walls of stone (revived due to raids in 10th century)	Roman	[G&G, 59.]
	Motte & bailey fort (high mound and tall wooden fence with dwellings inside)	High ranking warriors?	[G&G, 59-60.]
	Stone castles (more siege-resistant; more dominative of countryside)	Nobility and master masons?	
	Stone castles w/ rounded towers (better vs. siege engines, sappers); post-1100, with central tower, crenelated battlements, gatehouse, arrow loops, machicolations, portcullis, drawbridge using counterweight	Templars, Hospitalers via Arab lands + others	[G&G, 142-144.]
	Star-shaped earthen bastions (to counteract success of cannons on walls), around 1500	Architects, military engineers	[Crowley, 17-22; Long2, 83-84.]

Category	Description	Source
Military, Offensive	Stirrups, contoured saddles, chain-link armor (mainly), weaponry—mostly before 1000	Asia+ knights/smiths/leather workers [G&G, 55-56.]
	Bits enabling one hand control of horse; spurs; charger/destrier (ca. 1000+)	Knights/nobles? [G&G, 57.]
	Crossbow loaded by pinning to ground with foot stirrup	Improved from Roman [G&G, 147.]
	Mangonel/catapult (rock-thrower for sieges); early versions of trebuchet	Romans; antiquity [G&G, 145-147.]
	Trebuchet with counterweight device, ca. 1100 (greater range, rock size)	Byzantium? [Long1, 71.]
	Improvements in chain mail, plate armor & helmets for knights	Blacksmiths/armorers
	Gunpowder (described by Bacon, Roger in mid-13th century)	Chinese [Long1, 65.]
	Long bow (string pulled to ear, not chest; longer range, 2X power, rapid fire)	Welsh
	Gunpowder improved, ca. 1450 ("corning" → greater chemical stability, safer)	Stray experimenter(s) [Long2, 97.]
	Cannon and hand cannon	Chinese
	Improved cannons (e.g., better casting of metals for shot, barrels; calibers; carriages with trunnions (cradle enabling muzzle lifting); work on ballistics	Foundry workers; master gunners; et al. [Long2, 97-99, 106-107; G&G, 248.]
	Small arms (series of modest improvements to the matchlock musket and arquebus, before 1500); handguns (16th century)	Various military engineers? [G&G, 247-250.]
Cities: Services, Laws, etc.	Growth from renewed trade, market town formations, safety of location, etc.	From about 1000 [Spufford; G&G, 186-192.]
	Emph. by city/state/law on records → promotes reading, writing—from ~1000	For contracts, property (Eur.) [Long1, 92.]
	Some trades forced outside town or downwind or downriver; public baths; sewage provisions; paved streets; barring of loose animals; flood control; fresh water supply; regulation of prostitution; re-design of public spaces	Implementation varies by city [Long2, 113.] (Romans had baths, aqueducts, paved streets, sewers, and more)
	Humanist thrust toward gov't for general welfare, from late 1300s	Roman; adoption varies over time & by gov't.
Weights, Measures, Instruments	Water clock timekeeper	Syria-Byzantines [Long1, 101.]
	Abacus/counting board (re-introduced in early 11th C, common by early 13th)	Antiquity, Moors [Crosby, 42-45.]
	Hindu "Arabic" numbers (w/ zero) begin replacing Roman numerals, ca. 1200	Via Arab world [G&G, 225-226.]
	Surveyors' instruments, techniques	?
	Algebra (still without x-y-a-b-c notation/generalization)	Al-Khwarizmi (via Arab world)
	Clock (balance wheel driven armillary sphere, w/ hours added) → city clocks; → change to time-regimented days; → 1st mechanistic universe metaphor	Armillary sphere via Arab world [G&G, 214.]
	Household clocks, mainly metal	Gold/silversmiths [G&G, 215.]
	Watch (mainspring as power source allows miniaturization), mid 15th C	Gold & fine metal workers? [G&G, 273.]
	Financial instruments, bookkeeping (1000-1500), banking	Merchants: Jews, Arabs, Byzantium, Venice, Champagne Fairs, Florence, Flanders
	Insurance, ca. 1370s, possibly starting in Genoa	Merchants, notaries [Epstein, 184.]
	Patents, copyrights, mid-15th C; precursors in Venice and Florence	Cities= granters of monopolies [Epstein, 213.]

Medicine & Surgery	Misc. advances in the treatment of war wounds, bodily conditions	Barber-surgeons, surgeons, executioners, et al. [Conner, 311-312; Harrington.]
	Apothecaries may have done a lot of prescribing	[Long2, 56.]
	Starting recognition of regular nature of external causes of disease, 1520s on	Paracelsus
	Vesalius wonderfully illustrated book on anatomy, 1543	Vesalius + 3D artists [Long2, 50-60.]

Because of their convenient format and foci, the work of Frances & Joseph Gies, *Cathedral, Forge, and Waterwheel: Technology and Invention in the Middle Ages* was especially valuable in assembling this table. They are referred to as "G&G" in the table. Also especially important, both as a check and for additional and more recent information, were works by Pamela O. Long: *Technology and Society in the Medieval Centuries: Byzantium, Islam, and the West, 500-1300* [Long1]; and her *Artisan/Practitioners and the Rise of the New Sciences, 1400-1600* [Long2]. In addition, a number of important developments were also reported in Clifford D. Conner, *A People's History of Science: Miners, Midwives, and "Low Mechanicks"*. Other sources include:

Alfred W. Crosby, *The Measure of Reality: Quantification and Western Society, 1250-1600.*

Roger Crowley, *Empires of the Sea: The Final Battle for the Mediterranean, 1521-1580.*

Epstein, Steven A., *An Economic and Social History of Later Medieval Europe, 1000-1500.* New York: Cambridge University Press, 2009.

William R. Estep, *Renaissance and Reformation.*

Joel F. Harrington, *The Faithful Executioner: Life and Death, Honor and Shame in the Turbulent Sixteenth Century.*

Ross King, *Brunelleschi's Dome: How a Renaissance Genius Reinvented Architecture.*

Dan Klein and Ward Lloyd, *The History of Glass.*

Alister E. McGrath, *Reformation Thought: An Introduction, 2nd Edition.*

Peter Spufford, *Power and Profit: The Merchant in Medieval Europe.*

Paul Strathern, *Death in Florence: The Medici, Savonarola, and the Battle for the Soul of a Renaissance City.*

CHAPTER 30

Renaissance Humanists, Cities, and Rulers Interfacing with Artisans

What we will see in this section is some of the precursor steps and predecessors that were important to the development of proto-science and science, and to bridging the chasm between technology and proto-science. Although extensive efforts were to be made in the 1600s, a major start was underway by around 1430, especially but not exclusively in Renaissance Italy, led by humanists.

Humanists Help Bridge the Gaps

Petrarch (1304-1374) is typically considered the founding father of the humanist "movement." Compared to the glories of Rome and Greece (some still quite visible), humanists saw the present as a "darker" middle age that was backward in many respects. Accordingly, humanists emphasized the rhetorical, linguistic, moral, and the practical value of the study of ancient literature and history. Cicero (106-43BCE) had long been used as an educational medium to help students learn good Latin, but Petrarch rediscovered some letters Cicero had written as well. And he re-assembled Livy's (59BCE- 17CE) monumental History of Rome [Greenblatt, 23]. Among the moral values of attending to Roman history were eloquent arguments by Cicero (106-43BCE) as to the character of virtue, moral political action and good government. This use of Cicero's ideas, as well as the practices of the better/more just Roman emperors, slowly helped re-shape theories and practice of what constituted good government over the next several centuries (including in the United States at its outset), though some monarchies were but little affected.

Petrarch was strong in the Xtian faith but also thought that humans had deity-given intellectual and creative potentials that warranted full development, and he lived a life that exemplified a kind of public search for his identity, his talents, his emotional realities, etc. More generally, "humanists sought to create a citizenry able to speak and write with eloquence and clarity and thus capable of engaging in the civic life of their communities and persuading others to virtuous and prudent actions" [Wikipedia, "Renaissance Humanism"]. In addition, "Petrarch revised the traditional relationship between the present and the ancient past by seeing it as a model eligible to apply to his own times" [Kenneth R. Bartlett, *The Italian Renaissance*, 29]. Petrarch was a kind of celebrity in his own time (epitomized by the idea of a much sought-after dinner companion among the elite), who deliberately modeled a search for oneself.

And for those interested in eloquent expression in Latin, it was obvious that obscurantist scholastic writing was anything but. Humanists regarded the current Latin as corrupted compared to the Latin available in beauty and expressiveness of the writings of the ancients. (Of course it was only the best writing that had been preserved and not all that many Romans had as much eloquence in speaking or writing at the time.) An alternative view is that the current Latin was "untidy" because it was a living, spoken language; and by emphasizing Latin in its "fossilized classical form" (a la Cicero), "the humanists went a long way toward killing it as a living language" [Hannam, 211]. Hannam goes on to say things such as: the humanists were "incorrigible reactionaries" and that their "one positive achieve-ment" was the reintroduction of Greek [Hannam, 211]. As we'll see below, this is very poor history because such a case can be made only weakly, if even then, by simplistically boiling humanism down to one common denominator, the worship of antiquity and its languages, and discounting any associated effects or results from that *and other* emphases, or any contributions made by humanists beyond that. Indeed, that case fails even if the focus is entirely on humanists' con-tribution to science. And it fails despite the fact that, in digging up the past, some of what the humanists found—for example, books on various "short ways to knowledge"—such as works on the occult, astrology, and magic—were for decades a major distraction for some of the intellectual elite, a distraction from the paths that needed to be taken to advance science [Grayling, 141-205]. Nor is it clear that finding more works by Plato was all that helpful as a way of moving forward except as a counter to the narrow and authoritarian focus on Aristotle within universities AND because of Plato's emphasis on the perfection of mathematics and its prospective value as a way to explain the "the imperfect and fluctuating appearances of the terrestrial world," the workings of nature [Kuhn, 128]. Mathematics would come to play an important part in the forthcoming scientific revolution. Indeed, we even see some individuals labeled as "humanists" among Hannam's contributors to mathematics, including the medical doctor Jerome Cardan (1501-1575), and the self-taught and the would-be humanist Niccolo' Tartaglia (1499-1557) [Hannam, 235-242]. And, after a long break, there were also advances in identifying the prob-lems in Ptolemy's *Almagest* (i.e., in astronomy), and in instruction in trigonometry made by *humanist* court astrologer George Peurbach (1423-1461), by his student Regiomontanus (1437-1476), and also by Copernicus [Hannam, 268-269].

While some of what some humanists set out to recapture could be called reactionary, and some of their finds from the ancients were worse than dead ends, they also recovered several lost art-sciences, such as map-making/navigation (from Ptolemy's *Geography*) and the engineering arts involved in building construction, some of which helped to spur substantial advances in science and culture. Among the most important rediscovered writings was a book on architecture by Vitruvius (re-surfaced in 1416)—though it had been available throughout the medieval era, no one until its re-discovery had managed to deal with its complexities or make any significant use of it. See below for more on this.

Moreover, by comparing current and ancient Latin the humanists discovered a whole new field of endeavor—linguistics. One of the earliest and important products of that new field was the proof in 1440 by humanist-priest Lorenzo Valla that the Church had committed forgery in promulgating the "Donation of Constantine," in which Emperor Constantine purportedly gave the Papal States to the pope/papacy [Christopher B. Coleman, *The Treatise of Lorenzo Valla on the Donation of Constantine*]. Valla showed that the Donation of Constantine was written around 800 CE, not 325 CE. Further, linguistics also contributed to the identification of language families (e.g., Romance Languages) which didn't fit the Tower of Babel story in the Bible all that well. And, in the early 1500s, linguistics techniques were used by Erasmus and others to help demonstrate a number of very important errors in the Vulgate Bible used by the Church. See Plate 3.9.

Petrarch's emphasis on ancient Roman and Greek writings spurred a few other humanists with leisure time (due to money or position or patron) to seek out other lost manuscripts. They searched monastery libraries. Some learned Greek. They reviewed materials captured when Constantinople fell to the Fourth Crusade in 1204, made trips to monasteries in Byzantium, and got more ancient writings and language training when scholars began to leave Byzantium as it weakened in the early 1400s. Byzantium's ruler made a special appeal in person for Western Xtendom's military help in 1437, bringing a large and engaging entourage with him, including many who would teach Greek. (Byzantium fell to the Ottoman Turks in 1453.)

Plate 3.9: Painting of Desiderius Erasmus, 1523, by Hans Holbein the Younger, at the National Gallery, London. Photo by the author.

Another important find was the discovery in a monastery library by humanist Gian Francesco Poggio Bracciolini in about 1417 of a book by Lucretius—a long poem done beautifully in Latin—that conveyed the philosophy of Epicurus (341-270 BCE), a Greek. Among other things, Epicurus believed foremost in human happiness, taking pleasure in life and avoiding pain (but not in the excessive hedonism sometimes mistakenly associated with his philosophy—rather a more tranquil contemplative life removed from the pursuit of power or wealth). He rejected any afterlife—the soul died with the body—and he denied that gods, if any, involved themselves with humans—so it is better to appreciate life while you can and not worry about hades (hell) or the afterlife. In science, Epicurus first proposed that something he labeled "atoms," which were invisible, were the smallest units of matter and the constituents of everything else in a "ceaseless process of formation, dissolution, and redistribution" [Greenblatt, 185-186]. Of course Epicurus' ideas about atoms are in some ways different from what we understand about atoms today—for example he asserted that they were made up of like parts yet solid and indivisible [W. H. D. Rouse, *Lucretius De Rerum Natura with an English Translation, 3rd Edition* , 45]. And though Lucretius said that atoms combined with various other kinds of atoms to make everything from the stars on down, they did so based on the compatibility of their differing shapes [Greenblatt, 185-189], rather than mainly on their electrical charges. Although some (minimal?) version of the idea of atoms had appeared in the 1300s [Collins, 491], and although some ideas were derived from Aristotle, the overall content of Lucretius' work was so outrageously heretical (no creator; atheistic-materialistic; infinity of time; the extinction of life forms; atoms; etc.) that it was not printed until the 1500s. But there are 50 hand copies extant today that provide a clear indication that it was at least somewhat widely if sometimes furtively circulated during the 1400s [Greenblatt, 204].

Later, the printed versions typically added "warnings and disavowals" [Greenblatt, 219]. For example, copied versions might be accompanied by a note to disregard the content and instead just appreciate the wonderful Latin eloquence/poetry. And while Descartes in the early middle 1600s used "corpuscles" as the smallest units of matter, Newton, later in the century, used atoms.

Given that it was not okay to cite Lucretius as an ancient authority, it is all the more impossible to know the extent to which Lucretius' slowly diffusing ideas influenced Western culture after his rediscovery. But, one way and another, the modern world did come to place a lot more importance on our senses as a guide to reality, various forms of emotional satisfaction (pleasure), and the development of the mind as part of developing human potential, and, of course, an atomic structure as the building blocks of the material world. In any case, Lucretius-Epicurus provided yet another example of the potential value derived from humanists digging up old manuscripts that had gone unappreciated and/or undiscovered for almost the entirety of the medieval times.

But probably most crucial of all, as we'll see shortly, the Renaissance humanists contributed greatly to ending the separation between the learned and artisans, thereby enabling proto-scientists and scientists to begin to incorporate some foundational knowledge that was already known to the artisans but not to the learned classes.

Reducing the Doctrinal Grip of the Church and Social Class on the Minds and Activities of Humans

Humanism as a movement didn't just involve the leadership of a few intellectuals, though they led the way, including by developing humanism-based schools (most of which were akin to secondary schools) and higher-level discussion groups. These were entirely separate from the universities. Humanism became an ethos, a way of thinking, and the various aspects of it began to diffuse throughout elite Italian society, though not uniformly of course. Later, humanistic respect for ancient/original authorities, the learning of Greek, a greater emphasis on improving life in the present, and a certain disrespect or rejection of scholasticism and the corrupt status quo in the Church would also spread beyond the Alps, becoming an important influence in the thought of many of the religious elite who would subsequently convert to Protestantism [Eire, 4, 86-113].

Even before that, however, humanists had begun to bridge the divide that separated the formally educated and the less-formally educated, between the elite educated and the most advanced artisans. Although people labeled humanists pursued many different paths, this path was especially important in overcoming the culturally insane failure by Church theologians and university masters to explore nature in a search for knowledge about the world.

And, of course, it was the artisans and craftsmen of the medieval Western world (and the peasants) who actually did the hands-on work and, in the process, sometimes had to invent ways to address challenging new tasks, or observe the effects or relative success of different techniques or materials. So, as suggested by the table of developments in technology, it was the experts in many of these artisanal areas who had accumulated reservoirs of proto-scientific knowledge that were almost unknown to the university educated.

Pamela O. Long, in *Artisan/Practitioners and the Rise of the New Science, 1400-1600*, describes three general kinds of "trading zones" that were especially important in bridging the gap between the educated—in this case, people educated in universities *but also* in humanist directions—and the artisans. These trading zones become important in the 15th century and became more so in the 16th. Trading zones were places in which the learned taught the skilled, and the skilled taught the learned. With respect to the crafts and professions involved, this exchange was prior to professionalization in the skill, but also largely post-guilds [Pamela O. Long, *Artisan/Practitioners and the Rise of the New Sciences, 1400-1600*; 113; this is Long2].

Among the leading and earliest practitioners of this bridging was the university-educated humanist Leon Batista Alberti (1404-1472). He arrived in Florence around 1434 and there met Filippo Brunelleschi. Brunelleschi was educated to a point, to be a civil servant, like his father, but then apprenticed, at 15, per his interests and skills in mechanical things, to a goldsmith [Ross King, *Brunelleschi's Dome: How a Renaissance Genius Reinvented Architecture*, 12]. After completing his apprenticeship and placing second best in a competition to do the bronze doors on Florence's Baptistry building, Brunelleschi was to carefully observe the architectural constructions of the ancients in Rome [King, 12]. At the time of Alberti's arrival, Brunelleschi had won the public competition for his plan to put a classical-style dome on Florence's cathedral. See Plate 3.10. Moreover, Brunelleschi had figured out how to portray his architectural plans in a three-dimensional, realistic perspective—a first for medieval times. If you've seen paintings from before this time (especially from before 1300), you've almost undoubtedly noticed how they often tend to seem two-dimensional or flat, with people erroneously proportioned, and with truncated buildings that tend to resemble outhouses, while distant trees may be as large as those nearby. At the previous cutting edge, Giotto (1267-1337) had begun to use shading to give some sense of a third dimension, and a very few others seem to have had some degree of natural inclination to paint with some degree of perspective. See Plate 3.11.

Alberti generalized what Brunelleschi had done by analyzing the mathematics of perspective and included it in his extraordinarily influential treatise on painting. He dedicated the Italian version to Brunelleschi [Long2, 70], but also did one in Latin. In a very few decades there would no longer be a painter worthy of the name who hadn't, one way or another, learned how to do work that seemed three dimensional.

Alberti is equally if not more famous for his 10-part book on architecture (completed in 1452 and first printed as early as 1486), which encompassed everything from building materials, to construction, foundations, walls and arches, to tools and machines for lifting, to roads and canals, to ornamentation [Long2, 71-72]. Alberti was "a learned humanist who had acquired a deep knowledge and interest in the practical and technical arts, who had studied [the work of Roman architect] Vitruvius and other[s] … and transformed the ideas that he had found there for his own original synthesis, and for use in his own technical practice" as an architect [Long2, 73].

Vitruvius too had emphasized both the reasoning and experience in construction processes needed by an architect. Alberti's ways of obtaining knowledge included "that he 'would learn from all, questioning smiths, builders, shipwrights, and even shoemakers lest any might have some uncommon or secret knowledge of his craft'"; and Alberti "'would feign ignorance in order to discover the excellence of others'" [Alberti, in his book on painting, cited in Conner, 268].

Long goes on to say that Alberti had more than just "traversed the boundary between Latin learning and artisan skill"; through his writings and architectural constructions he had "obliterated that boundary" [Long2, 71].

So, now we can add Alberti to Aristotle (who had questioned many others about animals), and to Bacon, Roger and Albert the Great as models for the revitalization of the ways to seek knowledge, using reason, but also systematic observation, hands-on experience, and respectful communication with those who already had hands-on experience and knowledge of the technological implementations of various aspects of proto-science.

Plate 3.10: Brunelleschi-designed and built dome, cathedral at Florence. Photo by the author.

Plate 3.11: Giotto's Painting of St. Francis of Assisi Receiving the Stigmata, at the Louvre, Paris. Note the extensive disproportionality (e.g., the trees at upper left are atop steep hills or mountains). Photo by the author.

Renaissance humanists were also responsible for the professionalization of artists, and the great increase in status of the best of them, where art was formerly regarded as just another craft emerging from a workshop with a master and his helpers in various stages of learning the trade. Sandro Botticelli presumably emerged from such a workshop, but seemingly became good enough at doing religious paintings to become a frequenter of the court of Lorenzo de' Medici in Florence by the late 1470s or early 1480s. There he interacted with highly learned humanists such as the borderline-heretical philosopher Marsilio Ficino and the poet Angelo Poliziano [Strathern, 61]. These humanists must have been his sources for stunning subject matters, in perspective, that hadn't been done for over a thousand years, namely, his paintings of *The Birth of Venus* (ca. 1485) and *Primavera* (ca. 1482). Both subjects are drawn from (Greco-)Roman mythology, and both attempt to portray pagan mythology as the pagans themselves might have done it—"completely devoid of [Xtian] religious overtones, in no evident Christian setting" [Strathern, 67]. Indeed, Greenblatt says that the *Primavera* is right out of Lucretius' description: "'Spring comes and Venus, preceded by Venus' winged harbinger [Cupid], and mother Flora [Roman goddess of flowers], following on the heels of Zephyr [the fecund west wind, who is reaching for the nymph Chloris], prepares the way for them, strewing all their path with a profusion of exquisite hues and scents'" [Greenblatt, 10, 267]. Venus is apparently pregnant. Also depicted are Mercury and the Three Graces, symbolizing Joy, Beauty and Creativity [Strathern, 67]. The reader should definitely look up the Birth of Venus (or both paintings) in a source such as Wikipedia.

Much earlier in the same century, in 1401, Lorenzo Ghiberti had won that competition to put large bronze doors on the Baptistry building in Florence, showing scenes from the Bible *in relief*. Later he (together with help from assistants in his workshop) was to do a second and much more stellar and famous set of doors, this time incorporating a knowledge of (Brunelleschi's) perspective as well. Donatello trained in Ghiberti's workshop. He was to do the first free-standing nude bronze statue since antiquity (a 3-foot statue of David) [Strathern, 12]. Knowledge of the various ways that bronze could be worked became more extensive and spread (making one wonder if such sources as these helped others realize its possible military uses too, e.g., for cannonballs instead of rounded stones). And before Botticelli was gone, Michelangelo and Leonardo, both of whom were also trained in Florence, were embarked on careers that were to make them even more famous. Both were far more than simple, largely under-educated artisans emerging from a workshop, but neither was a university graduate. Leonardo was a "Renaissance man"—a famous painter and sculptor, an engineer-inventor, an architect, and more. Although Leonardo did not know Latin or have a classical education, he took serious issue with those who faulted him for it while having nothing but a classical education without "the light of experience" [Conner, 263]. See Plate 3.12.

From the above you can also see why Pamela Long included cities and rulers' courts among "trading zones." Florence was a city made wealthy on wool and banking, run by a "republican oligarchy" of sorts (one of several in Italy), but one that lacked a traditional university to sustain an older status quo. And even before the events described above, starting before 1400, leaders in charge of Florence's civil service hiring (including Coluccio Salutati, Leonardo Bruni and Poggio Bracciolini) had accepted the ancient/humanists' ideal of public service as a kind of duty of Xtian charity, including the importance of personal integrity, and that the goal of good government was to serve the people. Governance (and political science) may not be much of a "science," but this kind of trading zone helped (re-) introduce a different vision of its purpose.

Long's principal examples of these city-based trading zones are two pertaining to Rome, somewhat later, dating to around 1560. These examples involve how to deal with floods of the Tiber River there, and the competition to design a way to move a fragile, very tall 361-ton Egyptian obelisk, which was among several captured by the Romans in 31 BCE. At the time, it stood in an obscure corner at the side of St. Peter's. Numerous men, possibly as many as 500, put forward different proposals for the project [Long2, 119]. The task, as it was finally performed, involved encasing the obelisk "in reed mats surrounded by protective planking held together by iron chains" [Long2, 119]. A castle like scaffold cradled the obelisk as it was first lowered, and later when it was raised. After first being lowered, it was placed on a platform that could be rolled from log to log. The raising (and lowering) of the obelisk used 40 capstans (vertically-standing rope winding devices, as seen on ships), strong ropes and pulleys, with "each [capstan] turned by three or four horses assisted by a number of men and two supervisors," all carefully coordinated [Long2, 119]. And the point here is that, for so many serious proposals to have been prepared (even though the most serious ones numbered well under 500), the proposers needed to have a blend of architectural and engineering expertise, and the ability to write their expertise into a coherent proposal, most likely illustrated in three-dimensional perspective—something virtually unthinkable until a considerable time after Alberti, or for anyone who maintained a separation between artisan and literacy.

Plate 3.12: Statue of Leonardo DaVinci by Luigi Pampaloni, 1842, in the ground floor courtyard outside the Uffizi Galleries, Florence. Photo by the author.

Another trading zone situation was associated with arsenals, whether for ship-building (a long-standing institution in Venice) or developing materials for land warfare (especially uniform styles and sizes of cannons and cannon shot, gun carriages, etc.). Arsenals required the cooperation of a number of artisan specialists in casting metals for cannons, shipwrights and an extensive supply network in the case of ships, procurement people and connections with mines and ore-processing facilities, military advisers, and more, including some formally educated people. These arsenals, or components thereof, were in all the major lands of Europe—the Empire

(Austria-Bohemia-Germany), France, England, Spain, and Bavaria [Long2, 96-100]. The formally educated need to learn about what was currently possible as the group together explored how they might improve preparations for subsequent warfare by the leaders of their country, dukedom, or city, and the artisans gained a broader perspective on their work so as to be better able to select improvements to try. Where cannons were made, they were also tested; sometimes training in the use of the armaments was included too [Long2, 96]. Note that "trial and error" is a major mode of knowledge-seeking here.

A related kind of trading zone involved the mines themselves. With the increasing emphasis in warfare on cannons and shot, more metals were needed, especially bronze and iron, and silver (for money). Given the increase in demand, "scarcity provided princely and wealthy investors with motivation to take on the cost and technical problems associated with the digging of deeper mines," which radically changed mining [Long2, 107]. Technical problems included ventilation, and water and ore removal from deeper in the earth. These were capitalist enterprises with shareholders that proved to be quite rewarding from about 1450 to 1550 when there was a "European mining boom with greatly increased production of silver, copper, iron, tin, and lead" [Long2, 108]. "In 1442 at Kremnica [in Hungary/Slovakia], eight hundred miners were matched by four hundred smelters" [Spufford, 364]. The largest were typically mines of silver and copper, where there would be many "hearths, furnaces, bellows, hammers, stamping machinery (most driven by waterwheels), crucibles, and many other kinds of tools" [Long2, 108]. (Bronze is made mostly from copper, along with tin, and various additives.) And as to iron, the invention of taller and hotter blast furnaces greatly accelerated refining because they produced molten iron that needed less refinement subsequently and could be shaped by molds.

Experimentation was involved in testing the viability of new alloys. Long gives an example in which people managed to figure out that silver-bearing copper ores could be more successfully refined by the addition of lead; subsequent heating freed the copper and, then more heating was used to separate the silver from the lead. "The elements of this complex system developed from alchemical traditions and from the expanding cumulative knowledge acquired from minting coins" [Long2, 110]. For example, building on Hellenistic and Islamic foundations, particularly Rhazes (al-Razi), and bridging the hands-on artisanal and intellectual realms, alchemists conducted many trial-and-error experiments on metals and were responsible for improving or developing many of the apparatuses later used in their successor discipline, chemistry [Lawrence M. Principe, *The Secrets of Alchemy*, 46, 208, 15]. The pursuit of how to turn base metals into gold, however hopeless and made worse by deliberate obscurantism in many texts associated with that pursuit, was not without some fruits, and some alchemists were heavily involved in the applied facets of this proto-science.

We have already discussed Vesalius' wonderful groundbreaking tome on anatomy from 1543. While he was educated in medicine as a surgeon and taught at Padua, he was heavily influenced by humanism. His *On the Fabric of the Human Body* was profusely illustrated in perspective by artists who collaborated very closely with him—another epitome of the mixing of the learned and the artisan. Although Vesalius did not credit them by name [Conner, 272], the school of Titian seems to have been a/the major source [Hannam, 257-258].

Before leaving this subsection, I should note that a number of the developments in technology that are included in the table above are also based on similar collaborations. For example, Prince Henry the Navigator (1394-1460) of Portugal, working with ship captains and navigators to map the west coast of Africa, is one historically renown case of a ruler-based bridging or trading zone that is not otherwise discussed here.

Printing and the Vernacular as Important Vehicles for Releasing Artisans' Knowledge

Latin, as the universal language of the literate, was especially valuable in medieval times in that it provided a way of communicating across regions with different vernacular languages (including several that had diverged from Latin). But increasingly, by the Late Middle Ages, the emphasis on Latin became a barrier to the development of literacy on a broad scale. This is so because, for all but would-be higher-level churchmen (very few of whom were of peasant or even artisan stock) and some of the nobility or the wealthy, who could choose to have a child trained in Latin, it required the learning a second language well, and better yet to communicate in writing. For all sorts of purposes— from commerce to descriptions of artisanal processes to manuals for management of estates, it became ever more imperative for people to learn to read in their own language, even if they could not write in it. Without the use of the vernaculars, only those trained in Latin had access to most written material, whether the Vulgate Bible, Roman classics, Roman law, hagiographies of saints and Bible stories, or a great number of Church-related writings. But artisans, some of whom were able to read and to varying extents write in the vernacular, especially in Italy which had a long tradition of secular education for merchants and upper-level craftsmen and would-be city administrators, could not access these sources. In France, several Arthurian romance poems, written by Chretien of Troyes in the late 1100s, were among the first works to be done in the vernacular and helped to promote learning to read in French. In Italy, Dante Alighieri helped to fix the importance of the vernacular by writing his *Divine Comedy* in the Tuscan dialect around 1321. And Alberti's work on painting (see above) was done both in Latin and Italian versions, in 1435 and 1436. Few artisan or estate management books in the vernacular in any country appeared when copies could only be made by hand. But when the printing press became more readily available, more began to be written. And, of course, it was an artisan, Johannes Gutenberg, who is often considered responsible for the most important invention of the last thousand years—the printing press—which was first used in about 1452. Before long, printing presses began to proliferate into the hundreds, appearing in Italy in the late 1470s. A few examples of some of these kinds of later vernacular written works will suggest more of the kinds of proto-scientific learning (including engineering) that most university theologians and masters had been missing out on.

The printing press and the vernacular allowed fully literate artisans to describe the various aspects of their arts and share it with their vernacular world. And a number of important works were done, some in conjunction with humanists (especially in Italy), between the 1470s and 1600. For example, Long describes Francesco di Giorgio's books on machines as evolving from a culture of practice as an engineer in *Trattato I* (ca. 1480) to a culture of learning in *Trattato II* (ca. 1490) [Long2, 41]. The former includes sketches of a few types of machines (military, lifting, etc.) plus 58 water mills, each with discussion of relevant engineering specifications. In contrast, *Trattato II* is much more systematized. It consolidates machine types and explanations (e.g., how gears work). Where there were many minor variations included previously, in *Trattato* II there are only 18 drawings in all, and the text is more learned in character, including references to antiquity [Long2, 44-47]. The changes made between these two volumes "indicate Francesco's efforts to write a more learned treatise, efforts that were influenced by humanist practices of authorship" and "to provide a general understanding of machines and mills to the unskilled," contributing to "natural knowledge as it pertained to the power and motion of machines" [Long2, 47].

Indeed, as described above, it was the developments around the rediscovery of Vitruvius that were "particularly influential in bringing together skilled practitioners and university-educated men" [Long2, 61]. Alberti's architectural writings made Vitruvius accessible. Partly under the influence of humanists and Plato, sculptor and architect Antonio Averlino, also known as Filarete, wrote the first vernacular architectural treatise of the 15th century in about 1464—with a focus on planning and building an ideal city, called Sforzinda, named after Francesco Sforza, Duke of Milan [Long2, 76-77]. Several other people worked independently on developing vernacular editions of Vitruvius, with varying emphases on illustrations (which were a big help when done well). Also in the vernacular, in about 1537, Sebastiano Serlio, who was trained as a painter, produced a highly illustrated and carefully labeled depiction plus description of the five architectural orders, drawn from examples in the ancient buildings and ruins (e.g., multiple sketches showing labeled close-ups of the parts of Doric columns, Corinthian columns, etc.) [Long2, 50-56]. It is very likely that the anatomist Vesalius (see above) used this model to convey each body part or component thereof—each of which was labeled in the artwork with a letter of the alphabet or number, which the reader could reference in the descriptive text, necessarily in Latin given its medical school audience [Long2, 50-59]. Andrea di Pietro della Gondola (son of a mason who was dubbed "Palladio" by the humanist teacher who invited him to join a learned academy for young nobles) ultimately designed and built many classical countryside villas, helped a learned humanist to produce a famous commentary on Vitruvius, and published *Four Books on Architecture* in 1570 [Long2, 120-121]. "Palladio, influenced by Roman and Greek architecture, ... is widely considered to be the most influential individual in the history or architecture"

[Wikipedia, "Andrea Palladio"]. All of his buildings are in the Veneto (Venice-controlled territory on the landward side of the city), and they are now UNESCO World Heritage Sites.

In the 1500s, as Venice became a major center of printing (and one relatively free of censorship by higher authority, whether Church or state), it published a large number of books, often on arsenal-related subjects. A book on pyrotechnics by metallurgist Vannoccio Biringuccio (published in 1540) "contained the first description of casting bronze cannon and also described boring methods [for cannons] and explained how to produce standard calibers" [Long2, 106]. This woodcut-illustrated book also "treated ores and ore processing, assaying, gold and silver refining, the art of casting, methods of melting metals," and more [Long2, 111]. Georg Agricola published another famous book on mining in 1556 (*De Re Metallica*), which included pictures of "piston pumps made from hollowed-out tree trunks, endless bucket chains, and reversible hydraulic wheels" [Long2, 108]. Niccolo' Tartaglia was a self-taught math teacher who worked his way up from misfortune (injury as a boy during a war) published books (in 1537 and 1546) having to do with ballistics, using a common device, the dialog, in this case between gunners and nobles, where the latter were among the audiences for such books [Hannam, 241; Long2, 106-107].

Although dates later than about 1500 are not typically considered part of the "Middle Ages," you can nevertheless see here how technology and proto-science and science (including engineering) were moving along in the kinds of books published and in the work and interactions involved in the "trading zones" described before that. But universities, except in some cases when individual masters were heavily influenced by humanism and perhaps nominalism (mainly in Italy but also in Germany), tended to be responsible for little of the progress in this regard. In Italy, the university at Padua was almost surely the most exceptional: both Vesalius and Copernicus studied and/or taught there, as did Galileo subsequently. But "it was the interaction of artisans and humanists in trading zones bound by common interests and goals (and the blurring of the differences between them) that brought about profound changes in outlook, changes that favored empirical approaches to investigating buildings, ... and eventually, the natural world" [Long2, 129]. At last, the culturally insane prejudice against systematic observation and trial-and-error experimentation (even if yet only rarely induction-oriented experimentation), and hands-on activity, were being overcome. For the most part, the Church itself was on the sidelines of these developments in architecture, engineering and art—apart from patronizing painters, sculptors and architects—because there was *as yet* little threat to doctrine from advances in those areas, though Copernicus' work was sleeping in the wings, supernovas appeared in the 1570s, and Galileo would start wielding his telescope in 1610.

CHAPTER 31

The Reformation and Counter-Reformation

In many respects, the Protestant Reformation was a movement to get back to the basics of Xtianity, albeit with some innovations—to get back before the time of the imposition of so many Church doctrines (e.g., only 2-3 of the 7 sacraments were regarded as based on the Bible in Protestantism). Protestantism initially involved a return to greater simplicity of belief, with emphasis on what Scripture said. In Luther's early pronouncements, the Bible was to be interpreted by the reader, without the need for priests, or the trappings and hierarchy of the Roman Catholic Church, and among his early actions was to translate the Bible to better enable German-readers to do so. However, it rapidly became apparent to Protestant leaders that their adherents needed plenty of guidance too, and that only highly trained ministers, preferably fluent in several languages (to read the various versions of the Bible), would suffice to provide it [Alister E. McGrath, *Reformation Thought: An Introduction, 2nd Edition*, 151-152].

Luther's protests in 1517 caught the Catholic Church and its defenders off guard and, in any case, were initially regarded as unimportant. But the time was ripe for reform in that some rulers (princes, dukes, counts, etc.) were willing to support rather than suppress this particular form of dissent, in part because it was in their own interests to do so. The leadership of the Catholic Church had been corrupt for some time. Although several popes before this time had advanced the beautification of Church architecture in Rome, most of the popes since about 1464 had also pursued ill-gotten revenues (e.g., selling Church offices and selling indulgences), publicly gloried in self-indulgent excess and/or utterly disregarded the ideal of priestly chastity, bribed the other cardinals as a way of gaining the papacy in the first place, openly favored their own children and nephews in high Church appointments, and more than one even started wars to advance the interest of his family (e.g., to procure a dukedom for a nephew). By the time the Church sought to try Luther as a heretic, Luther had obtained a lot of popular support and an important secular prince to protect him, Frederick III of Saxony (1486-1525), who was one of the 7 electors who choose the German/Holy Roman Emperor. And one of the strong defenders of the Church, Charles I of Spain, was young and in the process of trying to become elected to be the emperor, making him more diplomatic initially, and making an immediate crackdown more difficult. (Ultimately, Charles I of Spain became Charles V, Holy Roman Emperor, in 1519.) More importantly, Spain was off-and-on engaged in a struggle with France for land, power and hegemony in Europe. Plus, Spain and especially parts of Charles's Germanic-Austrian lands were also threatened both in the Mediterranean and on land by the Ottoman Turks. The Ottoman Empire had conquered Constantinople/Byzantium in 1453; early in Charles' reign, they took Belgrade in Serbia (1521), eastern Hungary (1526), and they first laid siege to Vienna in 1529.

The kings of France, besides having their own long-term designs on additional territory (to the east and north), felt all the more threatened because of a marriage that put the Spanish throne in the grip of the Habsburgs (due to the lack of an effective heir to Ferdinand and

Isabella, the previous rulers of Aragon and Castile ~ Spain), where the Habsburgs already ruled in Austria-Bohemia-Hungary and were establishing a tradition of becoming Holy Roman Emperors as well (i.e., to rule over the many German statelets). In addition, the Low Countries (now Belgium and the Netherlands) were "privately" owned by Charles V of Spain (and Holy Roman Emperor), so France came to be almost surrounded by Habsburg-family territories. The competition between France and Spain began to heat up in 1494 when France invaded Italy (initially with Milan's support), to enforce its claims on Naples, where Aragon was a direct competitor for control of Naples (both monarchies had some history of familial ties to rulers there). Also, the Habsburgs needed safe land corridors from south to north (through Milan and on to the Alpine passes) to be able to move armies (especially from Spain) to help protect its possessions in the Low Countries (against France) and be able to take joint action with Charles' brother, Ferdinand, to whom Charles had passed his rule in the Habsburg's Germanic possessions. In the latter case, the Ottoman Empire was among the threats. (France also had dynasty-based claims on Milan.) French success in that first expedition was short-lived and after some major victories over French armies in the next three decades, Spain gained almost complete control of Italy, including, in many respects, at least at times, the papacy.

By the time Charles V went after Luther (as a sort-of enforcer/ defender of Catholicism), Luther's popular support was much stronger and Charles felt obliged to honor the "safe conduct" pass he had issued for Luther to come to Worms in Germany for a heresy trial. After Luther left and before agents of Charles could pursue him, he was hidden away by the aforementioned Frederick III (the Wise) of Saxony. It was during that time, that Luther translated the Bible into German (thereby standardizing the language in the process). That Bible was a big hit, as were many of Luther's short pamphlets. Printers had a field day with Luther's content. Luther was the first real "celebrity," and his pamphlets gave many a printer a market in which to sell his writings.

Only a little later, in the 1530s, because Catharine of Aragon, who had married Henry VIII of England, did not produce a male heir for Henry, he sought to divorce her. (Among his rationales was that he had gained special papal dispensation to marry her in the first place, needed because the would-be marriage was defined as "incestuous" because she was originally betrothed to his older brother, Arthur, who was slated to be king of England but instead died.) Popes would normally manage to grant a special dispensation to allow Henry VIII to divorce or annul his marriage to Catherine, but Pope Clement VII was under the thumb of Charles V, and Catherine of Aragon was Charles' aunt. Plus, the marriage gave the Habsburgs bloodline ties to the English monarchy. The pope's unwillingness to grant the requested dispensation led to Henry VIII's movement of England out of the Catholic Church's grip and into a status of a king-home-ruled church. Much to his economic benefit, Henry confiscated the lands of the monasteries in England but maintained a religion that was still fairly Catholic in character. Later, his one son, Edward VI, who ruled as a child and teenager for about five years before dying, was a more thorough-going Protestant who (along with his similarly-minded regents/advisers) pushed England strongly in that direction. After his death, Queen Mary, who was married to King Philip II of Spain (the successor to and son of Charles), did the opposite, moving strongly back toward Catholicism, but she too died after about 5 years. Queen Elizabeth then came to the throne, ruling from 1558 to 1603, and she moved the country back toward Protestantism while retaining some/many ceremonial trappings that resembled Catholicism. Throughout her reign, she was under pressure from external Catholic sources, including the popes and Spain (ruled by Philip II from 1556-1598), who regarded Elizabeth as illegitimate (especially as ruler) and demanded the restoration of

Catholicism/Catholic rulers. An invasion plan, using the Spanish Armada, went awry in 1588, in large part due to naval harassment by the more modest English fleet. The pressure and plotting and war-making by Catholic powers against Elizabeth/England, including efforts by the papacy, which supplied considerable funding, and by some Jesuits to serve as secret Catholic agents within England, led to the further movement of England in Protestant directions, a ban against Catholic religious services and priests, a mandate to attend Church of England services (with fines for refusals), and crackdowns on any aspect of Catholicism that could be seen as traitorous. But Elizabeth's kill rate per year was considerably lower than that of Queen Mary ("Bloody Mary"), and simply being Catholic was not made illegal per se.

By the 1530s, much of northern, western and some of southern Germany, plus Denmark, Sweden, and Norway had become Lutheran. Also in the 1520s, various Swiss and German city-states evolved into early variants on what was to become the Reformed Church (e.g., in Geneva, Zurich, Bern, Nuremberg, Strasbourg). Under threat from Charles V, the German Protestant states formed a defensive alliance (Schmalkaldic League) and built up their troop levels to respectable numbers, but were defeated in 1547 in the battle of Muhlberg. However, Charles followed up on this victory in ways that regenerated much opposition while he turned his attention to other fronts, and his forces lost an important battle to the Protestants in 1552, leading to a settlement (Peace of Augsburg) that recognized the Lutheran states in Germany, and set forth the general expectation that whichever religion a prince preferred (i.e., Lutheranism or Catholicism but not Reformed), that would be the religion of his lands.

A number of historical theories have been put forth regarding the long-term effects of Protestantism on subsequent economic development, the progress of science, and more. It is not clear to me, however, that there were much in the way of short-term effects on science one way or the other, though a few tendencies did seem to emerge fairly early. We have seen above that Copernicus' heliocentrism was not viewed particularly positively by at least some Lutheran leaders, per their belief in the inerrancy of the Bible. Still, unlike areas under control by Catholicism, the works of Rheticus conveying Copernicus' heliocentrism were not censored. And the United Provinces (Netherlands), which seemed to be slowly winning a fight for freedom from Spanish domination by the early 1600s (though more wars for independence were to come), slowly came to harbor a wide variety of refugees and viewpoints, even though Calvinism was the official religion and Catholics had to avoid noticeable public presence. Similarly, by the early 1600s, Galileo's startling findings about the moon were received relatively positively in Protestant lands and Descartes was to find a place of greater security by residing in the Netherlands rather than in France. But Protestants in many lands engaged in varying degrees of witch-hunting (an anti-scientific pursuit if ever there was one), and neither Protestant nor Catholic lands were acceptant of any hint of atheism.

Anti-Science Institutions of the Catholic (Counter-) Reformation

Whatever their openness and attitudes toward, and range of views about science in later history, at the outset Protestants were too focused on other matters for science to be much of a concern. As literal believers in the Bible, they would be expected to agree with the erroneous scientific statements in that book, but these were by no means central concerns in 1517. Science-related concerns were mostly tangential to early Protestantism, albeit with some negative exceptions such as Copernicus' heliocentrism.

But on the Catholic side, there came in time to be a renewed papal emphasis (which had grown lax during the Renaissance) on stances and actions against any natural philosophy or science in which there was a challenge to Church doctrines. Conservative forces within Catholicism began to coalesce to reinforce the prior status quo as discussion and debate about Luther's views seemed to evoke too many sympathetic responses in too many places. Evidence of this sympathy was quite strong in Germany, especially, where a goodly number of monks and nuns went over to some Protestant version of Xtianity. And there were also some supporters of a more "liberal" version of Catholicism within the more thoroughly Catholic countries, including Italy and Spain.

The rejection of Luther's heretical ideas provided an important rationale to re-establish a papacy-centered inquisition—which was done in 1542—to root out the most heretical deviants in realms under Catholic control. (There was already a Spanish Inquisition—established in 1478 under Ferdinand and Isabella—and Portugal also was granted one from the pope in 1560.) Although some dialogues between leading theologians in Protestant and Catholic areas did occur, Catholic conservatives used the new Inquisition to help fight against the most liberal leanings in the Catholic Church, thereby helping to besmirch the reputations of some Catholics who were not so "extreme" but who had associated with others who were, which helped to consolidate conservative control of the Church [MacCulloch]. In time, Pope Paul III was persuaded to call a council meeting to re-address just what Catholicism stood for and how the Church should react to the changed conditions. This was the Council of Trent, which met intermittently over the period from 1545 to 1563 (under three popes); its work set forth the doctrines that were to represent the Counter-Reformation or Catholic Reformation. Although some hoped initially for a Protestant-Catholic dialogue and compromise solutions, the conference was stronger on the conservative side and ended up, relatively early in its history, affirming Catholic beliefs and doctrines largely as they had existed, and also adopted a number of reforms to clean up the corruption in the Church. An important new religious order of monks was also established, the Jesuits. Their charge rapidly evolved into an "educational" one, which included spreading the faith, both in Europe and abroad. Just as the Dominicans were the principal shock troops in the Inquisition in the Middle Ages, the Jesuits were now the leaders in trying to reverse Protestant gains, in part by educating the children of rulers of Catholic countries to be true to the faith (and thus support counter-actions against Protestants), in part by serving as confessors for Catholic rulers (e.g., the Habsburgs—and thus directly or indirectly lobbying them to support actions favored by the Jesuits and Catholic Church), and in part by risking their lives where they weren't always welcome (e.g., in non-Xtian lands being colonized by Catholic Europe, and in England while the Catholic powers, including the papacy, were trying to overthrow Queen Elizabeth I there). One way that the Jesuits succeeded in reclaiming some of Germanic and Slavic Europe for Catholicism was by offering higher forms of education to the children of leaders there, whereas Protestants offered little competition in that regard. The Jesuits emphasis on education also led to some serious scientific work at the university level (while avoiding topics that might be a threat to the Church), including the establishment of a new and better calendar (based on Copernicus' data)—the Gregorian calendar—which is the one currently in use and which was adopted by Catholic countries in 1582.

But in doubling-down on its conservative doctrines and re-establishing a now more-centralized Inquisition, the Catholic Church was also seeking to suppress not only Protestant-favoring thought and publications but also any proto-scientific and scientific information that posed a challenge to its doctrines. Nor were people in Catholic lands who made advances in science free from the danger of prosecution for heresy by the Church. For example, in 1600 Giordano Bruno was condemned to death, in essence for his forthright advocacy of many heresies—which included being the first person "of renown to proclaim unrestrainedly the implications of Copernican theory for the nature of space," presumably including heliocentrism [Crosby, 105].

The Index of Forbidden Books. With the formal institutionalization of the Inquisition under an executive committee at the Vatican in Rome came more censorship, along with an official bureaucracy for censoring. "The first Index of Forbidden Books was issued in 1559, under the Inquisition's auspices; it would be followed by revised and expanded versions" [Cullen Murphy, *God's Jury: The Inquisition and the Making of the Modern World*, 118]. The Council of Trent formally approved having such an index. The Index was circulated to most Catholic authorities; enforcement was not confined to the Papal States. At times, publishers in Italy were visited by Vatican teams; often they needed prior approval to print books; booksellers were expected to know when a particular title was on the Index and not to sell it. Similarly, at times authors were expected to submit their books for prior approval, and censors might demand certain changes before allowing publication. With varying degrees of thoroughness over time, and as in the case of Copernicus' work, expurgators would read existing books and flag deletions and alterations necessary were the book ever to be published again. Also with variations over time, forbidden books were sought out (e.g., in private libraries), confiscated and burned. "Agents traveled to the Frankfurt Book Fair, held twice a year, to keep track of new and shocking titles" [Murphy, 120]. Over many decades in Spain and Portugal, incoming ships and individuals were searched for forbidden books. In 1572, a separate Congregation of the Index was created, though it continued to work closely with the Inquisition itself. "The Master of the Sacred Palace, the Vatican's original censor, served as a member of both congregations" [Murphy, 118]. The Congregation of the Index or its successors remained active for centuries. The 20th edition of the Index, published in 1948, contained more than 4,000 titles. The Index not was finally abolished until 1966.

Even so, it wasn't all that hard for a dedicated author to circumvent the Inquisition to get a book published in one or another Protestant country, but that book might not freely circulate or be purchasable in Italy or Spain or Portugal or some other Catholic countries. (After his sentence to house arrest for "vehement suspicion of heresy," Galileo had some less controversial work published outside Italy.) Nevertheless, among the possibly extensive consequences that cannot be known were books that were not written. "The importance of self-censorship, writes one scholar, remain 'major imponderables'" [Murphy, 125].

Because of the Index, the writings of Protestants, along with works of science (including Rheticus' explanations of Copernican heliocentrism), Erasmus, vernacular versions of the Xtian holy book, and much more, were listed and then targeted in many places, sometimes relatively effectively. Again, at times, "Inventories of books confiscated in Spain suggest Inquisition censors could be surprisingly diligent, removing scientific books regardless of whether they were officially proscribed" [Murphy, 125]. In addition, even as late as 1624 the French Parlement (court/parliament), upon the urging of the theology faculty in Paris, "banned the teaching of any doctrine opposed to [Aristotle's] on pain of death" [Leroi, 354].

So, the Inquisition's suppression of Galileo and Copernicus and the idea that the earth revolved around the sun, which was contrary to Catholic Doctrine about the earth being the center of the universe, was not the only information officially barred to adherents of Catholicism in post-Reformation years. As the decades and centuries went by, the list was expanded more and more. For two hundred and fifty years or so, Spain had its own *Index* with a somewhat different focus, that maintained what amounted to a "cordon sanitaire" around the country, rather effectively barring the entry of all manner of publications/ideas from outside the country and requiring prior clearance of publications within the country [Edward Burman, *The Hammer of Heresy*, 197]. For some time, even Protestant seamen manning trading vessels were policed, with heretical books confiscated and burned, and their possessors sometimes imprisoned at the hands of the Spanish Inquisition [Burman, 197].

The Inquisition; Galileo. Galileo remains the most famous case of the continuing use of the papal Inquisition to suppress science. Various facets of the case of Galileo (1564-1642) have been mentioned a number of times earlier, given their relevance to the issues being discussed. So a summary here of the case and some of the Church doctrine-related aspects of it should suffice. Long before the heresy charge, Galileo's improvement of the telescope had enabled him to discover things about the heavens that were entirely new (e.g., Jupiter had moons), and that Earth's moon was pock-marked with craters and was not the perfect heavenly sphere that it had to be per Church doctrines.

Galileo also believed fairly early on that the earth rotated and revolved around the sun (heliocentrism as contrasted with geocentrism, the latter being in accord with Church doctrine, in which the earth stands still while all the heavens revolve around it). There is some dispute about the clarity with which the Church officially told him to discontinue any advocacy in that regard when its inquisitors reviewed the idea of heliocentrism in 1616. In 1616, the Inquisition's investigative commission concluded not only that heliocentrism was philosophically erroneous but that it was heretical because it explicitly contradicts the Bible. But papal sympathies with Galileo as a scholar and person also waxed and waned as popes came and went, and when Galileo wrote his most doctrinal-challenging book (published in 1632), the pope had seemed open to treating heliocentrism as a hypothesis. However, adding to the stresses of the Catholic Church was the Thirty Years War (1618 to 1648), which was the most devastating European war to date, especially in German lands. To a large extent, it was a religious war between Catholics and Protestants—albeit in time with critical balance-of-power dimensions between France and the Habsburgs—a war in which the popes and Jesuits, as confessor-coaches to Habsburg and other Catholic rulers, were often heavily invested.

Galileo's book employed the subterfuge of being a three-person dialog (*Dialog Concerning the Two Chief World Systems*), with one person for each stance (heliocentrism and geocentrism), and an interlocutor (facilitator/questioner). The book received pre-publication approval from the Inquisition. Perhaps unwisely, the winner of the dialog in Galileo's book was all too clearly the advocate for heliocentrism. Moreover, the advocate for geocentrism, some of whose wordings were much like those used by the then-current pope about the issue, was given the name that, although historically the same an Aristotelean-era philosopher, was also the equivalent of "Simpleton." So, Galileo, who was already an old man by the life spans of the day, was tried before the Inquisition in 1633. He was forced to recant to save his life and was sentenced to confinement under house arrest for the rest of his life and denied permission to write anything more. The rationale for Galileo's sentence was that he was "vehemently suspect of heresy."[11]

Finally, Galileo also advanced science in ways that were tangential to Catholic doctrines, so the Church was neither supportive nor condemning in those respects. Some of that work was done while

---

11 Actually, Galileo erred in his book about *how* he concluded the universe was heliocentric. He based heliocentrism on evidence from tidal movements (which are actually associated with the gravitational effects of the moon on earth). Yet by 1621 Kepler, based on the work of Brahe, had already published a mathematically sound demonstration of heliocentrism, but his ideas were not quick to be studied or accepted (including by Galileo).

Galileo was prohibited from doing so, so Galileo had to have it published abroad to minimize the chance of further retribution. And, of course, Catholic dogmatists were simply stuck with facts such as the moon having craters (facts which were slowly gaining acceptance).

Ways Used All Along by (Proto-)Scientists to Minimize Threats of Church Retribution for Disapproved Ideas

There were many times in the stretch of time from 1100-1600 (and beyond) when it was dangerous for independent thinkers to disagree with the Church and most of those who ventured furthest into dogmatically sensitive areas were in some kind of danger. After the Reformation, the danger was mainly a function of whether the writer was a Catholic or, at least, living in a Catholic country where the Church (or State) could get to him (or her). But over the centuries there were also a variety of creative ways discovered for reducing the threats posed by the Church and its interpretations of Xtianity.

Among the ways of minimizing the threat was to state the case the writer was making, and then throw in the towel in favor of Church doctrines and/or biblical texts. Both Buridan and Oresme did this, whether or not they believed it. (But Oresme seemingly reversed himself near the end of his life.) Relatedly—at least by the time of the second Inquisition—an author could more safely write up a conclusion as a hypothesis (i.e., without formally denying it) but not as a would-be statement of fact. (Osiander's preface did that to/for Copernicus' heliocentrism work.)

Another way to reduce the threat from the Church was to write books with characters in dialog form, where one character gives the ideas of the author but the book as a whole is not fully specific as to which set of ideas the author believed to be correct. Galileo made it too obvious when he did this and also offended the pope by identifying the pope's views as coming a participant named, albeit somewhat ambiguously, as a simpleton in the dialog. Erasmus, in *The Praise of Folly* very cleverly put his thoughts about society's many corruptions into the mind of the Greek-Roman Goddess Folly, who explained, for a very broad range of social positions and roles, including some in the Church, how each group/role paid homage to Folly or her ways, as reflected in duly enumerated follies (hypocrisies, etc.), each of which conveyed real-life truths about that group or role. Yet another way to minimize threats from the Church/state was to write books as if they were a compilation of letters sent to you by one or more foreigners, as Montesquieu did in 1721.

One could also have potentially challenging work published posthumously so as to avoid retribution—but then one misses out on all the legitimate feedback. Examples here include Copernicus and Descartes. However, this strategy might well not have been effective during the first Inquisition, which, when it "proved" too much attachment to the Cathar heresy by (many a) deceased person, would disinherit that person's heirs of everything bequeathed to them, including the dead person's abode (and also dig up the dead person's body and burn it).

And, sometimes one could do one's work in a location or country somehow made safer. For example, at various time, Venice managed to be relatively independent of papal control. Jan Hus indirectly helped make Bohemia safer for some variants on Catholicism. He was lured, under what turned out to be a false promise of "safe conduct" from Emperor Sigismund, to a defense of his doctrines at the Council of Constance, which instead led to his condemnation and execution there. That started a war in which Bohemia in time wrested some degree of independence from the Church in Rome. This is the fate that Luther managed to avoid, perhaps narrowly, by being forcibly taken to a refuge provided by his protector, Frederick III of Saxony. In the 1600s,

Descartes did this more successfully by living in the Netherlands, a non-Catholic country (instead of France, his homeland). But, as noted earlier, the action strongly in favor of Aristotle (backed up by a death threat) by the Parlement in Paris in 1624 provided a demonstration that Descartes was probably right about concerns for his safety when he declined to publish some of his works during his lifetime and was slow to publish others, and when he visited France with caution when he wanted to confer with other scholars about his work. In addition, the potential danger is further shown by the fact that "his *Meditations* and his Metaphysics, along with other works, were placed on the Index in 1663," more than a decade after Descartes' death [Murphy, 110]. Alternatively, one might make an extended journey to a freer land outside Catholic control, such as England, and write about its virtues implicitly (or sometimes perhaps explicitly) in contrast to disliked aspects of one's own society or its belief systems, as Voltaire did in 1726-1729.

The above is not meant to comprise a comprehensive account of the ways in which proto-scientists and scientists, and Church critics, have endeavored to avoid persecution and prosecution by the agents of the Catholic Church for their beliefs, analyses, or discoveries. Rather, it is to help further convey that when it came to (proto-) scientific ideas in opposition to the dogma of the Catholic Church, the author or proponent was personally at risk, at least of having to recant and usually destroy his copies of his now-deemed heretical work (and probably do penance and be forbidden to advocate the same points again), and at worst of being burnt alive at the stake—especially if he stood behind his work. Similarly, as detailed earlier, written mandates, as in the 1270s in Paris, against teaching or propounding any conclusions, whether directly reasoned from Aristotle or Averroes, or otherwise, that conflicted with Church doctrines undoubtedly served as an effective deterrent for many masters of arts who taught in the universities, and almost undoubtedly contributed to a careful self-censorship by some who might otherwise have been more exploratory, whether by deductively reasoning purely from a natural philosophical premise or, though likely to be rarer, by direct explorations of the natural world.

CHAPTER 32

Summary of Principal Medieval Church-related Cultural Insanities

Final Thoughts on Revisionist Historians Who Assign the Church a Positive Role in Promoting Science

Given the overall situation described above, I find it quite difficult to side with those revisionist historians who argue that the medieval Church (or its version of Xtianity or its holy book) was mainly supportive of proto-science and/or the emergence of science. As noted earlier, they are "revisionist" because the earlier stance of most historians, especially after the (French) Enlightenment, was that the Church was anti-science. And with respect to the Catholic Church after its Reformation (until around the 20th century), there was considerable truth to this Enlightenment view.

Xtianity was a faith-based religion with some very major non-rational elements and the medieval Church added to that (just for starters, there was purgatory, the virgin birth by Virgin Mary, a very interventionist deity, and miracles in every mass, and in some other sacraments). Although the Church accepted and occasionally welcomed some proto-science—it mainly did not encourage or discourage it, and seldom participated in it. Some theologians, especially a few Franciscans, did participate in proto-scientific advances in the 150 years starting in the early 1200s. But, in general, advances in the use of reason and natural philosophy (proto-science) were actively opposed by the Church if they were likely to impinge upon doctrine. (However, a very few people—usually people who knew doctrine well—successfully evaded or side-stepped Church prohibitions). In areas of proto-science that did impinge upon doctrine the Church could be a holy terror. It could force recantations, burn every copy of a challenged work, confine people to monasteries, dismiss teachers from their positions, destroy reputations, and it threatened possible eternal damnation (and execution) for heresy. But, mostly, it did not have to do so because its university teaching-related pronouncements told the master-level scholars "not to go there."

At the start of the 1200s, Church leaders tried to resist the consideration of Aristotle in universities. But even at the height of Church power in those times, Aristotle too was an ancient authority; and he had too much new/ancient knowledge to offer, so that straightforward censorship proved impossible. But the Church did ultimately establish rules that barred reasoning directly from Aristotle (and from Averroes, his chief Commentator/explainer) in a university setting unless there was an immediate refutation of any conclusions that emerged which conflicted with Church doctrines. Similarly, Epicurus' ideas (as conveyed by Lucretius), which began circulating in the 1400s, including people dying without leaving a soul and atoms as the basic and unchanging building blocks of everything, could not be fitted into Church doctrines so, for that and many other reasons, Lucretius could only be circulated clandestinely (while being praised for its use of the Latin language). Although Church doctrines most likely to conflict with reality didn't seem all that numerous, some had sweeping implications. In many areas of possible scientific endeavor involving nature—including humans—it was all but guaranteed, if one argued in favor of regularities in nature, to run afoul of doctrines that affirmed miracles. And, of course, there were emerging and potential conflicts with any proto-science or science supporting a sun-centered "universe" (solar system), that is, heliocentrism, or, for that matter, an old earth or universe (Aristotle asserted an eternal one as contrasted with the Church's estimate of only about 5500 before the Late Middle Ages). How then can revisionist historians discount such facts?

Nor, as discussed more fully in the text, does the Church deserve much credit for what science-related advance emerged from medieval universities. Crediting the Church for everything that did emerge from universities, or from anyone with a Church title, involves a serious misunderstanding of university education (then and now), the extent and character of Church support, and sometimes individual histories (e.g., contrast Bacon, Roger and Copernicus with Buridan and Oresme). It also involves a misreading of history because only a rather modest amount of credit for the advancement of proto-science can legitimately be ascribed to university personnel. And crediting the deeds of any and all cathedral school or university-*educated* people to the Church would maim the reality even more. For example, the contrast with university-educated humanists like Alberti who engaged with artisans is an especially sharp one here... and those humanists even included some with Church positions (e.g., Bracciolini, a papal functionary who found the book by Lucretius, and Valla, a priest whose linguistic skills enabled him to identify a much-appealed-to papal forgery).

As noted earlier too, it is also impossible even to estimate how much credit to give to the Church for its patronage (though its particular choices did produce some wonderful works of very expensive art and architecture). Why impossible? Because it cannot be known how much better or worse society would have fared had that funding been left in the hands of peasants, townspeople, and secular rulers instead. Certainly there was an awful lot of Church money and resources spent/wasted on paying high salaries to Church leaders (sometimes with multiple benefices), and for expensive garments and reliquaries, and for gourmet food for the upper hierarchy, and for administrative staffing and support, and for armed retinues, and for papally-initiated wars (with mercenary troops), and also for financially-supported crusades. And not all that much was spent directly by the Church on social welfare or human development generally let alone on proto-science. Society was also obligated to pay for a large priesthood (which at times is estimated to have exceeded 10% of the total population).

A Broader Context: Other Church-related Cultural Insanities in the Same Time Period

As Latin/Western Europe entered the second millennium since Jesus, it suffered under a major but substantially buried cultural insanity associated with the relatively complete dominance of faith over reason (apart from sectors handling practical matters such as agriculture). Moreover, Church doctrines, though at the time not yet completely formulated, harbored a number of other severe but substantially buried cultural insanities, such as the treatment of life, with all its suffering, as a mere proving ground for accessibility to the afterlife, and their treatment of women.

Exacerbating the entire cultural insanity situation were the successful efforts of leading churchmen to gain much more power for and via the Church, beginning in the mid-11th century. Empowering a Church which was clarifying doctrinal stances made it much easier to use that power against any heterodox (different) perspectives on Xtianity—to define them as heresy. By 1200 Church dogma had gone from being unclear and little-enforced upon the population (which had previously incorporated many pagan beliefs into their versions of the religion) to becoming a far more set and serious matter. As power permitted, Church leaders began to much more actively pursue and persecute anything and everything the Church leaders deemed to be heretical, including even disobedience to the dictates of Church leadership. In doing this, the Church used its full array of threats on those who disagreed, even on those who tried to demonstrate the righteousness of their views by reference to the Bible, and those who felt themselves to be fully a part of the Church.

Enlisting the deity-ordained authorities who were the rulers of princedoms in the crackdowns on heresy made matters considerably worse for anyone disagreeing with the Church. Crusades, initially deployed only against infidels, from 1200 on were also turned against variants on Xtianity within Europe, initially by a pope ironically-named Innocent III. The preaching of these crusades (call to fight) were accepted by secular rulers; and knightly adventurers did the actual crusading (often along with papal legates). Innocent III began a decade-long crusade against the Cathars ("Albigensian Crusade") in southern France that may have cost a million souls their lives, many of them simple peasants who were pretty much entirely innocent apart from many not having much appreciation for highly organized and dogmatic Xtianity (or the northern French knights who invaded). This was the era when the Church was at the height of its power. Needless to say, this crusade involved a considerable loss of human potential.

On top of that, a (papally-endorsed) Inquisition was developed to pursue heresy, and permission to torture was granted when inquisitions proved insufficient to find current *or former* Cathar sympathizers who kept quiet or wouldn't talk once convicted. With torture added in, convictions came with a nearly irresistible requirement to name others who had showed even the slightest acceptance of Cathar holy men. The Inquisition remained vigorous for much of a century.[12]

---

12   The Inquisition was renewed and made papally-centered in the 1500s. Some inquisitors (mainly Dominican monks) were instrumental in developing witchcraft theory in the 1400s (see Part Two). The

A Summary of Cultural Insanities Involved in the Church's Impeding the Development of (Proto-)Science

The above Church belief- and power-related cultural insanities form part of the broader cultural context and the evolving status quo for this Part. Given that, the European intellectuals rediscovered Aristotle and other works by the ancients, mainly through contacts with Muslim- or recently Muslim-ruled areas in Europe, especially Spain and Sicily (and to some extent from Byzantium). Aristotle's works, particularly when accompanied by commentary/explanation from the Muslim Averroes, took European intellectuals by storm.

Aristotle used sense data, combined with reason, to try to discover truths about the natural world, which he said involved regular developmental patterns, where knowledge (scientia) meant knowing cause-and-effect. In trying to deal with almost all knowledge, Aristotle mainly demonstrated the use of deductive reason, almost necessarily from sparse evidence given his era, and therefore almost invariably produced at least somewhat erroneous conclusions (many if not most of which were not recognized as such for centuries). He also was the first true scientist in that he employed systematic observation, mainly in some of his studies of animals. And, in his general comments about methods, he also commended this investigative approach to his readers. To the few educated people of Europe, Aristotle shortly became "The Philosopher."

The Church, with its very considerable and multifaceted powers, was initially relatively successful in 1210-1215 in suppressing public and classroom discussion of Aristotle's works at the University of Paris,

---

papal Inquisition, as applied to "witches" by local bishops, was yet more extreme with looser legal restrictions on the credibility of accusations, the ready use of torture, and belief in the coerced confessions. These inquisitions have been drawn upon as models ever since by oppressive regimes with their spies and secret police.

which it was cultivating as a center for a doctoral instruction only in theology. This ban on teaching and discussing Aristotle, though undoubtedly at least somewhat skirted in private, remained in force until the early 1240s at Paris (but not at the newer universities of Oxford and Toulouse, the latter run by Dominicans involved in the inquisitions in Languedoc there). The vitality, scope, and relevance of Aristotle's use of reason in a society that relied mainly on faith was too much to be fully contained for long, even at Paris.

Meanwhile, Albert the Great had begun a project to better explain Aristotle to all concerned (which the arrival of Averroes' work commenting on and explaining Aristotle presumably rendered largely irrelevant). His pupil, Thomas Aquinas, proceeded to work out an entire system in which Aristotle's views were incorporated into Church dogma insofar as possible, and were excluded as pre-Xtian/pagan heresy where they could not be made to fit doctrine. This synthesis would make it such that Church doctrines no longer stood almost entirely in opposition to reason and even relied on Aristotle's views in some respects. But the real concern/focus of the Church was not on proto-science and reason *per se*, but on any way in which those might impinge on Church doctrine. In any case, Aquinas' integration of Aristotle into Church dogma (which was also aided by Averroes' model) was by no means instantly seen as acceptable, and multi-sided serious debates at the University continued over how best to interpret Aristotle and what was and what wasn't heretical.

The next major Church suppression of Aristotle (and Averroes) occurred in the 1270s. What seems to have been at least a large minority of the teaching masters broke from the Church's ideal/norm in their desire to teach Aristotle (and Averroes) using those sources and reason alone, without reference to any associated doctrinal concerns. Led by Siger of Brabant and Boethius of Dacia they willingly agreed that Church doctrines must prevail whenever there was a dispute but also said that they were not trained in theology and therefore could not be sure to identify every conflict with doctrine that might arise. In essence, they sought a limited kind of academic freedom: let us just pursue Aristotle wherever it leads (having informed our students that the reasoning may be wrong). Boethius of Dacia even wrote subsequently supporting the equivalent of methodological naturalism—proposing to omit everything supernatural in the reasoning of natural philosophy. This is among the most basic of assumptions of modern science (a proposal 400 years ahead of its time). Either of these approaches would have greatly reduced cultural insanity at the time and almost undoubtedly prevented its subsequent build-up (which instead was what occurred).

The teaching of Aristotle and reason, had it been fully unleashed from censorship by the Church, represented a threat to Church dogma, and to the Church's hold on the minds of men and women and, therefore, its power. Every reason-based conclusion that conflicted with Church dogma might have made one or more Church doctrines seem irrational to some people! Having first identified 13 and, later, 219 heretical teachings, Church authorities (including, depending on the occasion, local bishops, papal legates, the pope, and university authorities acting on their behalf) in essence mandated that there was to be no uncorrected teaching that violated Church doctrines (and that ruling implicitly applied in other universities as well). That choked off the use of reason every time it ran into anything opposed by faith, and left the university masters without clarity as to what was and wasn't safe to teach or explore or write about, except insofar as they were sure enough about any applicable theology. Further, this restriction was renewed in the 1340s (even as Aristotle and Averroes were otherwise affirmed as part of the curriculum).

So, if some of the many possible deductively-reasoned explorations a la Aristotle had the potential to yield discoveries in proto-science (which Buridan and Oresme they did), their suppression clearly reveals the cultural insanity involved. Moreover—who knows—in time it seems likely that rational explorations might have gone beyond Aristotle and Averroes. Thus the Church impeded and inhibited, even if did not successfully forever thwart, much of the potential for advances in proto-science and, ultimately, restricted the potential for greater fulfillment of human potential that would have accompanied them. And there were other scientific seeds in Aristotle that were also left high and dry (see below).

As Aquinas' synthesis gained more favor and acceptance (he was sainted in the 1320s but his theological summation wasn't formally adopted until the Counter-Reformation), elements of Aristotle's thought and reasoning became more and more fused into Church dogma. And that made it even harder to discern what, in the course of thinking or teaching about nature (natural philosophy/proto-science), would violate Church doctrines. Indeed, some Church doctrines were contrary to almost any assertion pertaining to regularity in natural processes. For the vast majority of university masters, it was probably simply unsafe to "go there" even if some had an inclination to do so. It was safe only for those well-versed in theology who best knew how to avoid or get around problems with doctrine. As described in the text, examples include both of the men most famous for making proto-scientific advances in the 1300s—John Buridan and Nicolas Oresme. This can be seen in Oresme's "conclusion" that his own reasoning (that geocentrism was contrary to reason) was wrong, because Xtianity did, after all, rely to an important extent on a variety of miracles, so, implicitly, maybe geocentrism too was a miracle foreign to reason.

In another contemporaneous but also Aristotle-related manifestation of cultural insanity, medieval churchmen and university masters payed almost no attention to Aristotle's detailed systematic observation-based examples in biology, or his general recommendation in favor of the use of such observation as part of his methodology. Nor did the university masters and theologians commend the use of systematic observation to their students. They remained largely heedless of the potential value of such methods despite stellar examples in the early and middle 1200s from Albert the Great with nature (who sometimes even corrected Aristotle) and Bacon, Roger who experimented with optics (building on knowledge he acquired from the Muslim world) and used mathematics in some analyses. Instead, the use of "experience" among scholars came to mean little more than incorporating what was known via common knowledge. Accumulated over time (a few centuries), the absence of almost all systematic observation, and the non-pursuit of new information generally, became a cultural insanity of considerable importance in limiting the development of proto-science and human potential—particularly because this lack of exploration involved the vast majority of the best educated people in Western Europe. This problem was compounded further by the absence of any attempt even to systematically compile knowledge about where Aristotle's deductions were dubious or wrong (e.g., as Buridan clearly showed they were with respect to objects impelled into motion through the air).

A class-related cultural insanity exacerbated this particular failure: the prejudice among all those of noble rank—which included a large majority of university masters and almost all churchmen above the level of village priests—against most forms of hands-on activity (excluding nobility-related engagements such as combat and hunting), which they regarded as the domain of the peasant, serf, and slave. Although this prejudice dates back to the Roman nobility, the examples of Albert the Great and Bacon, Roger show that it was not insurmountable by individuals nor so deeply removed from possible cultural choices to classify it as a buried cultural insanity. Moreover, Benedictine monasticism had also emphasized hands-on labor from early medieval times, though that emphasis had greatly weakened over time (while book-copying remained). Then, in the 12th century, Cistercian monastics re-emphasized simplicity in their churches and hands-on labor, and many Cistercian "daughter houses" came into being. But in a century or so, the Cistercians too became wealthy and the prejudice against hands-on work began to prevail there too. But while most university masters remained within their self-imposed cultural constraints, as time passed, more and more use of such techniques would occur in other areas of society, particularly those involving technology.

As noted in the text, doctors and medical schools also took a hands-off, authority-oriented stance toward the physician Galen, and toward the Muslim physician-scholar Avicenna, both of whose main medical writings re-emerged in the 12th century. This rejection of further exploration was also contrary to the urging of Galen, so it too became a more open cultural insanity. As a result, even without Church suppression (other than withdrawing the clergy from anything to do with causing bleeding or death), medicine stagnated for the next 400-500 years because doctors relied on bodily humors, temperaments, and earth's elements for diagnosis, astrological charts for prognosis, and far too often on blood-letting as a prescription. Note here that the theory and assumptions here were far more mistaken than Aristotle's deductions, so they were much more likely to yield nothing than reflecting on Aristotle's wide-ranging proto-scientific beginnings. Although some advances were presumably made in the use of plants medicinally, that too was inhibited by the imposition of the same ancient theoretical framework and too little systematic observation. Absent exploration and systematic observation, there were few viable prospects for major improvements in medicine until alternative theories of disease and bodily functioning began to be considered. Paracelsus began the former process in the 1500s. But perhaps the real driver of at least some very slow progress in medicine turned out to be the advances made in surgery, leading ultimately to a great leap forward in anatomy, in understanding how the human body works, initiated by an unusually hands-on university surgeon, Vesalius, whose book in 1543 displayed all the parts of human anatomy in three-dimensional perspective, with artworks resembling Greek or Roman statues.

The development of scholasticism as the method of intellectual discourse in the universities, and especially their theology departments, and in writing books, also played a role in adding to the build-up of cultural insanity. I will not review the details here that are in the text above. But it may be worth pointing out that theology was the only doctoral level study other than medicine and law, so after the intense internal debates among the expanded number of interested parties about Aristotle and religion of the 1200s, there were few/no intellectual competitors by the early-middle 1300s to challenge doctrine—especially after one or another of the various schools of thought came to dominate in almost every university. And the focus of the highest theologian scholastics was primarily on the refinement of Church doctrines (and/or refinements thereof within their schools of thought), and, in instruction, on understanding the hierarchy of relative holiness on earth, so as to live a holier life more likely to lead to salvation.

Thus scholasticism tacitly promoted the continual refinement of ever more sophisticated Church doctrines throughout the Middle Ages, and even up to at least 1600—in most cases to the point of virtual irrelevance—a dead end, especially with almost no new information coming in. The obscurantism of the scholastic approach and results led more and more of the later humanist/Renaissance scholars, and then the Protestants, to simply ignore or reject the work of scholastics almost entirely, often including its reliance on Aquinas' Aristotelianism. In the process, at least in England, they ignored a few works that included valuable proto-science and Protestants often sought substitutes for Catholic instructional texts, where some of the latter were better with respect to subject contents [Hannam, 216]. But on the whole, the scholastic method as it came to be used under Church guidance developed into a subsidiary cultural insanity that further dragged down any potential for the emergence of science and the associated potential to enhance human fulfillment. It largely wasted the creative potential of generation after generation of the most educated scholars and writers whose primary interest was usually but not invariably religion, but whose secondary interests were sometimes broader (again the only strong examples are Albert the Great, Bacon, Roger, the Oxford calculators, Buridan and Oresme—all of whom wrote well before the 1400s).

In a university world of tunnel-vision Aristotelian scholasticism (including variants on it), together with the Church mandates to avoid conclusions that violated Church doctrines and the rejection of hands-on studies, new discoveries were few and any proto-science was all but guaranteed to stagnate. Medicine suffered the same fate as university doctors sought to refine via sophisticated scholastic-dialectics the awful theories of Galen and the ancients. Nothing could come of that... and nothing did. Even optics, the study of which need not dirty the hands and does not involve peasant-like pursuits, pretty much died on the university vine for most of two centuries. Astronomy made only fitfully slow progress after Oresme, mainly via medical doctors interested in astrology who refined the use and teaching of trigonometry. Some people from the mid-1400s onward would place some or much of the blame on Aristotle (e.g., humanists, Francis Bacon)—and this is not unheard of even in the twentieth century—but Aristotle is clearly not the source nor cause of the various cultural insanities accounted for here.[13]

Only the slowly declining power of the Church after 1300 enabled Western Europe to more fully liberate the potential for advances in proto-science and, in time, science. This decay came about from the rise of an intellectual alternative to the Church (Aristotle, reason), competition with the strongest monarchies (princes) for power, a largely-forced evacuation from Rome by the papacy (to Avignon, 1309-1376), a Great Schism in the papacy (1378-1418), the successful revolt of the Bohemians in installing a minor variant on Catholicism in spite of Church crusades against them (1419-1434), and the opulent, amoral lives of Church leaders and Church corruption during the Renaissance. There was also the rise of humanists (from the middle 1300s), including their discovery of important lost works by other ancients (including Cicero on good government, Vitruvius on architecture, Plato's emphasis on math, and Lucretius/Epicureanism). Their stress on "purer" Latin and Greek (despite its partially reactionary thrust) ultimately contributed to the development of and major findings in the field of linguistics. Last but by no means least, they expressed concern for self-discovery and development *in this life*. Then, building on many factors, from humanists who were religious politicians [Collins, 500], and probably from some alienation among university and monkish adherents of nominalism (especially in Germany), and on resentment

---

13   Nathan Schachner recognized that Aristotle was one of the greatest men who ever lived, the first to attempt an "orderly synthesis of all knowledge" [Nathan Schachner, *The Medieval Universities*, 97]. But for Schachner, to the "newly awakened" 13th century men, the influence of Aristotle's complete system, "dogmatic on every point" and "hallowed by an immortal name," was "pernicious." Aristotle "did more than any other man in … history … to retard the progress of civilization. His authority stayed the progress of all independent thought, all original research" [Schachner, 97]. But wait… was it Aristotle who acted here, 1500 plus years after he died, and for 3-4 consecutive centuries? Or was it the Church (in the persons of bishops in and around Paris, papal legates, popes) that was the pernicious influence? And what about the medieval scholastics at Paris who were perhaps too overawed by their belief system and ancient authority generally and who remained too easily deterred by Church mandates and too immersed in their own social class-related prejudice against hands-on activities? Clearly, notwithstanding the weaknesses in his work, it was not Aristotle who was manifesting or promoting cultural insanity in medieval times.

among northern Europe's secular leaders and masses at the monetary and moral corruption in Church leadership, and even on a desire for more basic forms of piety, or more direct piety (which was in vogue by the time of Erasmus), came the Reformation (starting in 1517).

But also, throughout the High and Late Middle Ages, there were advances in many areas of technology that were driven by observation and trial-and-error efforts, sometimes even experimentation, that was largely foreign to the universities and Church. I will not reiterate here those advances (see the table above). But in the 1430s there began a rise of cooperation between artisans and humanist-intellectuals, most notably initiated by the Alberti-Brunelleschi teamwork, where Brunelleschi had discovered how to do three-dimensional perspective and made advances in masonry/architecture and construction machinery. Alberti developed a formula that successfully conveyed how to convey three-dimensionality throughout the worlds of art and construction (and he also made Vitruvius accessible in architecture). And, once secular powers and capitalists were added in, there developed large-scale projects and major advances in civil engineering, metallurgy and mining technology, and army and navy arsenals—occurring in what Patricia O. Long calls "trading zones." In these trading zones, the scholarly educated the artisans and the artisans educated the scholarly. Among the other stellar examples of this exchange is Botticelli, who in the 1470s produced artistic masterpieces, such as *The Birth of Venus*, that were based on Roman deities/mythology learned from humanists in the court of the Medici in Florence. And yet other artisan and trading-zone advances were waiting in the wings—for example, Vesalius' work on anatomy in 1543, which was marvelously illustrated in three-dimensional perspective, and the telescope in the early 1600s (and, half a century later, the use of the microscope to reveal life that the naked eye could not see). Thus it was the many advances in technology that ultimately drove most proto-science forward. Indeed, by the early 1600s, Francis Bacon in England was deliberately seeking out some artisans to begin to develop a written/scholarly account of their knowledge (and he sometimes extended that knowledge as well), while advocating a systematic and inductive approach to research as a means of further discovery.

And with the advances as well in astronomy by Copernicus (1543), Brahe-Kepler (late 1500s to early 1600s) and Newton (1687), the launches of science and mathematics began their lift-off. By the mid-1600s William Harvey had demonstrated that too much blood was being pumped out into the arteries for it not to recirculate through the veins, where previously veins were regarded as separate systems (our microscopic capillaries remained unknown). And from Rene Descartes' thought, abetted by inventions such as clocks (dating to 1300), there also arose the possibility in the minds of people of thinking in terms of a mechanistic universe without a deity's constant intervention, eventually helping science to become an entity separate from religion, as advocated in the late 1200s by Boethius of Dacia. Ockham in the early 1300s and other supporters of nominalism are sometimes given considerable credit for this eventual separation, but dubiously so it seems to me, because Ockham pretty much disavowed the generalizability of any real-world observations, even if he did offer an alternative to Thomism (Aquinas' integration of some of Aristotle's realism and religious doctrine).

The Reformation led to a Counter-Reformation in the Catholic Church and a firming-up of conservative doctrinal stances, affirmed by the Council of Trent (1545-1563), albeit with some reform in the Church as well. Among the re-affirmations (of sorts) were an endorsement of the already-restarted papal Inquisition and of a new institution, the Index of Forbidden Books. In 1632, the Church's conviction of Galileo on charges of "vehement suspicion of heresy" may have been "the last great push … to stem the advance of science" [Grayling,

76], but Galileo was not the last to feel the potential threat from the Catholic Church (e.g., Descartes was quite concerned). Galileo's and Copernicus' and Kepler's heliocentrism were all placed on the Index. These actions were especially effective in Italy and Spain (with its infamous Spanish Inquisition), but influenced all other Catholic countries to varying degrees as well. For example, in 1624, the Paris Parlement, upon urging of the theology faculty there, established the death penalty for anyone teaching a doctrine opposed to Aristotle.

Finally though, the Church could no longer hold back the tides of scientific revolution(s) that disproved some of the most primitive Church-and-biblically-and-ancients' derived doctrines about the perfection of the heavens and geocentrism. And the newer mechanistic paradigm brought forth new efforts to imagine how the deity might have done things by establishing natural systems rather than via constantly miraculous interventions. (And, around the mid-1600s, witch-hunting began to quietly fall by the wayside.) And, from around 1400 on, Europe began to move slowly toward the humanist-Reformation goals to improve the quality of life and enhance the potentials for humanity *in this life*—though the Catholics kept Purgatory and the power elite, now more than ever including rich capitalists, sucked up much of the economic potential to do so. Ultimately, almost despite very frequent efforts over the centuries to stem heterodox beliefs and reason-based threats to Church doctrines, Church leaders were unable to fully maintain their culturally insane strictures and impediments on studying and learning about the many doctrine-related aspects of the natural world.

But the Catholic Church and Protestant churches' opposition to science wherever it confronted doctrinaire religious views was not going away without further struggle. The Catholic Church did not directly reject evolution but only formally allowed for it in 1950 (apart from the deity's installment of a human soul), and then affirmed it more fully in 1996. Protestant churches for a long time resisted, and many evangelical/fundamentalist ones still do. In a cultural insanity slowly emerging from its buried state, most of the more fundamentalist Protestants reject(ed) geology's findings of an earth that is millions, and later billions, of years old; they insisted on Noah's Flood as a primary shaper of landscapes even after it was shown in science that the evidence could not be fitted to that "hypothesis"; and they continued to vehemently argue in favor of the Genesis account about the creation of all life, including people, while rejecting the idea of evolution by natural selection. See below.

PART FOUR

CULTURAL INSANITY IN THE DENIAL OF GEOLOGIC TIME AND EVOLUTION

CHAPTER 33

The Old Order and Its Deductive Approach to "Science"; Francis Bacon's Challenge and the Inductive Approach

The Old Order in 1600: A Slowly Weakening Foundation

Although a number of individuals and especially the Reformation in the 1500s roiled the intellectual and cultural world, Francis Bacon (1561-1626) was among those who played a very substantial role in conceiving some of the future methodological needs of science if it was to escape from the textual authority of the Xtian holy book and of Aristotle, as upheld by the Church/churches and universities. (See Part Three.) Although Bacon's writings somewhat preceded "their time," his contribution to the scientific revolution was noted later in the Royal Society in England, and remains apparent in John Locke (1632-1704). Locke's approach came to predominate over Cartesianism as the principal philosophical perspective on science, even though the Galileo-Descartes mechanistic-mathematical depictions of how nature operated also remained current. The latter had been reinforced by Newton's discovery of gravity (attraction between masses is relative to their size but inversely proportional to the square of the distance between them), which also explained what Kepler found about planetary orbits. It was the emphasis on the senses and on induction in Locke, rather than the emphasis on deduction in Descartes (though the Cartesian heritage also included an emphasis on exploring the natural world), that was to become the dominant approach to understanding the natural world and that would provide guidance to most would-be scientists in the 18th century [Kors, 40].

Over the period 1300-1600, criticisms of the Aristotelian-Scholastic synthesis were often subtle or evasive, attempting to side-step potential condemnation for violating Catholic Church doctrines; or they raised questions mainly on the periphery; or they were discussed only within the Church. But a few were at least somewhat more straightforward even while their proponents maintained a Church affiliation. Previously, I mentioned examples of caution exercised by early deductive proto-scientists such as Buridan and Oresme, by some nominalists, by some Renaissance humanists, and by Copernicus. In contrast, one outspoken proto-scientist (who included support for heliocentrism), Giordano Bruno, was executed by the Church in 1600. And by Bacon's time, none of these critics had had much long-term success. Among the clearest manifestations of the continuing even if lessened dominance by the old order at the turn of the 1600s is that many university students upon entrance were told (e.g., in their handbooks) to heed the Aristotelian-Scholastic tradition. For example, the charter of Trinity College at Cambridge University in non-Catholic *England* warned that "all students and undergraduates should lay aside their various authors and follow only Aristotle and those who defend him." It also forbade "all sterile and inane questions departing or disagreeing from ancient and true philosophy" [Kors, lecture 3]. And the continuing need for caution, especially in Catholic lands, was the reason why Galileo, like others before and after, was to write a dialog (without being entirely explicit in his advocacy of one of the character's views, though in his case it was too obvious that the pope's view was the mistaken one). His camouflage being ineffective, Galileo was tried by the Inquisition and placed under house arrest in 1633. That same need for caution also explains why Descartes carefully delayed publication of a finished work, withholding parts of it until his death. Descartes of course knew about the Church-provoked French Parlement's rule adopted in 1624 in favor of Aristotle (with the death penalty for violation), and later about what had happened to Galileo in 1633. (See the science-and-Church part for more on this.)

Francis Bacon's Scathing Critique of the Scholastic-Aristotelian System

Englishman Francis Bacon's overt critiques began with a treatise in 1605 which is best "known to posterity as *The Advancement of Learning*; it can justifiably be said to have changed the terms of human understanding and the nature of knowledge" [Peter Ackroyd, *The History of England from James I to the Glorious Revolution*, 26]. And in 1620 Bacon produced *The New Organon*, a more comprehensive analysis that included many examples of the beginnings of an inductive approach to knowledge. Although Aristotelian interpretations remained more likely to be enforced in Catholic lands and still dominated many of universities, England had been continuously not Catholic since 1558. So Bacon did not have to restrain or hide or even disguise his criticisms of the Aristotelian-Scholastic synthesis and its methods.

And he didn't. Bacon launched a "ferocious assault upon authority and deductive logic from received authority" [Kors, Lecture 3]. For 68 pages of Book One of *The New Organon*, Bacon, who had attended Cambridge University, presented 130 overlapping numbered points as an extensive description of faults in the entire Scholastic-Aristotelian approach to teaching and learning, and the acquisition of knowledge.

I will proceed to summarize some of Bacon's main charges against Aristotelian scholasticism—many of which were associated with the cultural insanities described in Part Three (and show that Bacon's criticisms have stood the test of time).

According to Bacon, among the many major faults of the Aristotelian-Scholastic synthesis are these:

The system is based on deduction from generalizations hastily drawn from far too little evidence, and far too few observations. More generally, "that method of discovery and proof according to which the most general principles are first established, and then intermediate axioms are tried and proved by them, is the parent of error and the curse of all science" [Bacon, *New Organon*, 32].

Bacon saw that the generalizations to general principles that had greatly harmed philosophy were based heavily on authority of Greek ancients, and on the authority of the fathers and doctors of the Church, including those who fused Aristotle's and other ancient's views with Church doctrines (while discarding what didn't fit). Plato and his school are regarded as "dangerous and subtle" (presumably because they integrated so readily into Church doctrines). Thus the corruption "shows itself… in parts of other philosophies, in the introduction of abstract forms and final causes and first causes, with the omission in most cases of causes intermediate, and the like" [Bacon, *New Organon*, 28].

Accordingly, Bacon wrote that there is a need to separate theology from natural philosophy, because the fusion of the two has undermined the potential for learning about nature. Indeed, among examples given are that "some of the moderns have with extreme levity indulged so far as to attempt to found a system of natural philosophy on the first chapter of Genesis, on the book of Job, and other parts of sacred writings; … from this unwholesome mixture of things human and divine there arises not only a fantastic philosophy but also a heretical religion." The need is to "give to faith only that which is faith's" [Bacon, *New Organon*, 28]. Although Aristotle and a few others (e.g., Lucretius) believed in an old Earth, Bacon seemed ahead of his time in his specific criticism of Genesis as a source of scientific truth.

"There is a great difference … between certain empty dogmas, and the true signatures and marks set upon the works of creation as they are found in nature" [Bacon, *New Organon*, 13]. One such major difference is between the "anticipation" of nature (jumping to conclusions from few and disparate experiences) and the "interpretation of nature," which is based on many facts and a "just and methodical process" [Bacon, *New Organon*, 14].

The sciences now available, he said, are mainly classification systems (Aristotle having stressed categories).

Bacon argued that the focus of learning was misdirected. There is no focus on improving human understanding of and power over nature, no focus on making life better at a time when conditions often made for a life of hardship, if not debilitation in one form or another, and an early death. "Wherefore, as in religion we are warned to show our faith by works, so in philosophy by the same rule the system should be judged of by its fruits, and pronounced frivolous if it be barren" [Bacon, *New Organon*, 35]. The system thus lacks charity, a Xtian fundamental. (This reminds me of the criticisms of Zwingli and others during the Reformation—that Church wealth was not used enough to help people in need.)

Bacon recognized that the scholastic system is organized around disputations as proof of competence and superiority, and to win arguments. Bacon says that those disputations and the works of the "schoolmen" (university teachers/scholastics) are generally far too heavily engaged in sophistry—sophistry involving the careful selection of words to bridge gaps in syntheses encompassing only very minor questions or questions that had been dealt with thousands of times. "In sciences [thus] founded on opinion and dogmas, ... the object is to command assent to the proposition, not to master the thing" [Bacon, *New Organon*, 14].

Because both the syllogistic logic and the dialectic approach to analysis were adapted to the disputational system, they produced artificial or useless truths or gave "stability to the errors which have their foundation in commonly received notions" [Bacon, *New Organon*, 11] and have seldom been of any value for humans. These syllogisms are based on propositions, which are constituted by words, which are symbols of notions. "Therefore if the notions themselves (which is the root of the matter) are confused and overhastily abstracted from the facts, there can be no firmness in the superstructure" [Bacon, *New Organon*, 11]. Bacon says that our only hope is to rely on a true induction model instead.

Erroneous belief systems have entered "men's minds from the various dogmas of philosophies, and also from wrong laws of demonstration. These I call Idols of the Theater, because in my judgment all the received [i.e., handed-down] systems are but so many stage plays, representing worlds of their own creation after an unreal and scenic fashion" [Bacon, *New Organon*, 18]. The same goes for the "many principles and axioms in science which by tradition, credulity, and negligence have come to be received" [Bacon, *New Organon*, 18]. (Note: "Science" here refers to "knowledge" development of all kinds *hitherto*.)

"The study of nature... is engaged by the mechanic, the mathematician, the physician, the alchemist, and the magician; but by all (as things now are) with slight endeavor and scanty success" [Bacon, *New Organon*, 9]. "A notable instance" of this failure is the empirical philosophy used by the alchemists, which "has its foundations .... in the narrowness and darkness of a few experiments" [Bacon, *New Organon*, 27]. But while Bacon disapproves of the empirically nonsystematic ways in which (certain?) "mechanical" arts have been pursued, because that search is to produce minor improvements in a product rather than toward greater knowledge, he also recognizes subsequently that the mechanical arts, which are founded on nature and the light of new/real experiences, when contrasted with the sciences, "are continually thriving and growing, … and at all times advancing" [Bacon, *New Organon*, 36]. And to some degree too, Bacon proposed (and sometimes sought) to assemble what was known in some of these areas of technology as a foundation for knowledge, from which linking to other knowledge and further experimentation could proceed. As a result, some have charged Bacon and others with plagiarizing craftsmen's knowledge of their work in order to summarize, publicize, and then sometimes experiment to extend that knowledge [Clifford D. Conner, *A People's History of Science: Miners, Midwives, and "Low Mechanicks,"* 21].

Words too often name things which do not exist, such as "Fortune, the Prime Mover, Planetary Orbits, Element of Fire, and like fictions which owe their origin to false and idle theories," or they "are confused and ill-defined, and hastily and irregularly derived from realities" [Bacon, *New Organon*, 24]. Bacon gives an example for the word "humid," because it denotes a wide variety of actions which will not bear to be reduced to any constant meaning"; and he goes on to give seven disparate usages. Another set of faulty words involve comparative qualities such as "heavy, light, rare, [and] dense" [Bacon, *New Organon*, 25].

The focus of the entire Aristotelian-scholastic system can be said to be on contemplating and appreciating the hierarchical nature of the cosmos, from the sub-lunar realms of the ever-changing (and therefore inferior) Earth to the perfection and glory of the heaven above [Kors, 10]. So humans needed to recognize the relative godliness of everything in the great chain of being and, using their soul or will, turn away from the sinful and try for an eternity in heaven. But no advances in science can derive from such foci.

Francis Bacon's Proposed Methodology for Science

Like many other philosophers (at least since Plato's cave in which people dwelled and perceived only shadows from the outside world), Bacon recognized a variety of weaknesses in human perceptions, which he called "Idols of the [human] Tribe" [Bacon, 17]. Humans are prone to anticipate, to suppose more regularity than exists and do not examine more fully the variety of cases in nature that they need to [14, 18]; once they have adopted an opinion, they tend to shape evidence to fit it [18]; they seize upon supportive evidence and disregard or mistreat counter-evidence [18-19]. Human nature is "prone to abstractions and gives a substance and reality to things which are fleeting. But to resolve nature into abstractions is less to our purpose than to dissect her into parts …." [Bacon, *New Organon*, 21]. In addition, "affections color and infect the understanding" [Bacon, *New Organon*, 20]. People reject "difficult things from impatience of research; sober things, because they narrow hope; the deeper things of nature, from superstition; the light of experience, from arrogance and pride, lest [their minds too] should seem to be occupied with things mean and transitory [hands-on experience being beneath them]; things not commonly believed, out of deference to the opinion of the vulgar" [Bacon, *New Organon*, 20]. In his *New Atlantis* utopia, the inhabitants study such deceits of the senses in order to better control them [Francis Bacon, *The Great Instauration and New Atlantis*, 78]. "Deceits of the senses" is an archaic phrasing to be sure but, as Part One shows, they may actually be of at least of as much concern now as ever.

Coupling those weaknesses with his critique of Aristotelian Scholasticism, Bacon concludes "we must begin anew from the very foundations" [Bacon, *New Organon*, 15]. But for Bacon, proper method was the key. Accordingly, he proposed a different pathway to generate knowledge. As mentioned once above, his system relies on induction, reasoning upward from experiences and facts—with an emphasis on lots of carefully designed experiments to generate those facts, and the careful re-checking of results. Experiments are needed to "vex" nature (i.e., with artificial treatments) to see how nature reacts. The goal is to develop sound lower-level axioms first, derive subsequent experiments from those, and then higher axioms subsequently, and thus slowly to build to ever broader understandings. Like scientific articles recommending further research, Bacon's research method is a long-term project of further research, to be built up over generations. Bacon's first attempts to draw conclusions or axioms were called "First Vintage," and they were intended to be still open to emendation by subsequent experimentation. For example, one First Vintage conclusion is that "motion" is the genus and "heat" is a species thereof.

As a starting place for further inquiry, Bacon emphasized assembling "a natural and experimental history" [*New Organon*, 81], arrayed into "tables" of all related aspects of nature and of all that was known about each aspect. Bacon gives an example of heat, for which he offers a "Table of Essence and Presence" [Bacon, *New Organon*, 83]. In it, he lists 27 ways in which heat is generated (or thought to be generated), though he does not much go into what is known about each one. Among these sources of heat are: the sun's rays, including when magnified with glass; "burning thunderbolts" (lightning); volcanic eruptions; "natural warm baths"; some of the seasons; all sparks, fire, furnaces, and anything nearby; hot liquids; air in caves in winter; "hay, if damp when stacked, often catches fire"; "bodies rubbed violently"; "quicklime sprinkled with water"; "iron when first dissolved by strong waters" (acids) and also linen; animals, especially internally, but not insects, which are too small; fresh horse manure; spicy herbs and oil, even though "not warm to the hand" feel hot in the mouth; strong vinegar and acids applied to the skin; and "even keen and intense cold produces a kind of sensation of burning" [Bacon, *New Organon*, 82-83].

The *New Organon* also includes 27 subsequent examples, some with multiple parts, of things to look for that might legitimately be used to help interpret a finding or help to differentiate classification within a large (beginning) table such as the one he prepared for heat. The 27 include a number of very weak examples, but others illustrate a variety of meaningful evidence as well as some of tightly-focused experiments that he proposed, or that he conducted, or supervised, or at least watched. For example, he discusses an experiment in which air is heated in a sealed glass vessel, which is placed upside down in a larger container of water without allowing any air to escape. As the vessel and air cool, water is drawn up into the vessel, the air having expanded with the heat and contracted with the reduction in the heat. As further proof, to the extent that the air in the vessel is re-heated, water gets pushed back out of the bottom of the vessel.

The details above give the reader a better idea of just how little about some causes was really understood in 1620. Given how little Aristotelian Scholasticism had contributed to such learning, a new form of inquiry was needed in almost every aspect of human endeavor that pertained to the quality of human life. In Bacon's uncompleted utopia, *New Atlantis*—the name he assigned to a fictional isolated island well west of Peru—the members of the government's House of Salomon (i.e., approximately the biblical wise man, Salomon) had almost every manner of research program under way. This "House" consisted of organized seekers of the knowledge of causes, the secrets behind all kinds of motion, and, generally, how to enlarge "the bounds of Human Empire" [Bacon, *Atlantis*, 70].

Without trying to provide a full accounting, here is a sense of the range of interests of teams within the House of Salomon: They had studies or experiments (or potential studies and experiments) going on in bakeries and breweries and kitchens; in foundries and on metals (using all manner of different levels of heat); on minerals; in fresh and salt water; in caves; with wind engines; with medicine and health-supporting environments; in orchards and gardens; with beasts and birds and dissections too; in putrefied media (for spontaneous generation of "serpents, worms, flies, fishes"); in fermentation tanks; and within the full range of the mechanical arts, including paper, linen, silk, and dyes; with glass and crystals; and with light and the properties thereof, in this case including telescopes and microscopes as well; with sound and musical instruments; within engine houses and gears to study force; and on motion of every kind; on gunpowder-based weaponry; and even on the communications between animals in the same species [Bacon, *Atlantis*, 70-78]. There is also a mathematical research center. Further, the House of Salomon includes a dozen people who travel to other lands to return with books and information about experiments being done abroad, which are in turn dealt with by teams of three people each (for experiments and for books); plus three who try new experiments, three who classify the experiments and assemble them into "titles and tables," and three who attend to these experiments to identify applications useful for humanity. Beyond these, there is yet another tier of threesomes who do higher experiments, including newly mandated ones, and "raise the ... discoveries by experiments into greater observations, axioms and aphorisms" [Bacon, *Atlantis*, 79-80]. Of course there are also novices and apprentices because this is an ongoing social institution already centuries old! This, then, was the opposite of deduction.

Perhaps the greatest of the weaknesses in Bacon's views was a somewhat minimal appreciation for the potentials of mathematics in areas such as physics and astronomy, even though, by Bacon's time of writing, Copernicus and Brahe-Kepler had begun to demonstrate those potentials, and Alberti had long before used mathematical schema to convey how to render two-dimensional depictions of reality in a way that made it seem three-dimensional.

CHAPTER 34

Beginnings of Systematic Observation of the Earth without Reference to the Supernatural, and of Doubts about the Scientific Adequacy of the Biblical History of the Earth

The Royal Societies

In England, a would-be Royal Society, evolving from recently-formed university and gentry intellectual discussion groups, was established in 1660 immediately after the Restoration of King Charles II. (This restoration occurred after the rule of Cromwell as "Protector" and, briefly, his son, following the English Civil War, 1642-1649, at the end of which Charles I was executed.) The founders' hope for a royal charter was realized in 1662. A royally-endorsed French Academy of Sciences was also established in 1666. Over the next 150 years, men from both groups were to contribute substantially to the forthcoming advances in natural philosophy.

For our purposes, William Poole's *The World Makers: Scientists of the Restoration and the Search for the Origins of the Earth*, homes in on key portions of the late 17th century very well, and I have relied on his work, occasionally supplemented by others, to tell much of the beginning of this history [Poole, xv]. There were more than 300 intermittent contributors to the discussions and researches of the Friends of the Royal Society over the period from 1660-1700, including Newton (1642-1727), with his mathematical calculation showing that gravity was subject to mathematical equations and, as part of that process, how the orbits and movements of the planets were controlled by it. Robert Boyle (1627-91), whose greatest fame is as a chemist, was one of the key founders of the society and helped to shape the character of its work. The basic idea was to faithfully report the results of experiments and (sometimes systematic) observations of nature with little or no reference to unproven beliefs, political aspects, possible biblical conflicts, etcetera. The longer-term goal was to assemble and compile such information, moving toward broader generalizations and theories. Both goals arose from the urgings of Francis Bacon (above). Henry Oldenburg (1619-1677), who understood several languages, engaged in extensive correspondence for the society, sometimes translating the work of people on the continent, and publishing some of those in the society's journal (*Philosophical Transactions*), which he helped design (from 1665). The articles in that journal were the foundational model for the scientific journal articles of today [Poole, xiv].

Among those having an influence on the members of the Royal Society was Thomas Hobbes (1588-1679), who published *Leviathan* in 1651. In a still thoroughly Xtian era—a time when people were much afraid of the Devil, heresy, atheism and even deism—Hobbes argued that sense perceptions provide us with our only understanding and "that we can only conceive and know of material things, and that all language of immateriality is nonsensical and insignificant" [Kors, 23, 25.] This was materialism in spades, "and almost all other English philosophers nervously distanced themselves from his extreme materialistic extrapolation" [Poole, 21]. Hobbes' safety valve (from charges of heresy even in a Protestant land, e.g.) was that "reverence of the incomprehensible is an appropriate religious response" [Kors, 24]. Thus, despite his materialism and mechanistic determinism, Hobbes did not preclude an unknowable god of some kind. When members of the Royal Society were accused of insufficient religiosity in the 1660s, they vigorous disagreed; indeed, a number of them were Anglican churchmen [Poole, 5]. Their approach to the study of natural philosophy was a method, not a belief system.

Another very challenging contributor to thought at the time was Benedict Spinoza (1632-77), a Jew (who was also accused of atheism). He argued in 1670 (English translation 1689) "that the Bible was merely a set of culturally specific books aimed at local audiences" [Poole, 7-8]. Further, "Moses' account of Creation was not a scientific text: 'those Men therefore, who endeavor out of the Books of the *Prophets* to find true knowledge of Natural and Spiritual things, are extremely mistaken'" [Poole, 8]. Spinoza's work was so radical that "Oldenburg felt obliged to break off correspondence with [him] for a few years" [Poole, 8].

Earlier, Hugo Grotius' arguments (1629) that all texts decay in the process of writing them down from the original stories was insufficient to deter beliefs in the inerrancy of biblical wordings, notwithstanding the (differing) translations and the associated problems arising therefrom [Poole, 6]. Linguistics arguments, based on examining the language families in Europe, also came to raise considerable doubt about the Tower of Babel story in the Bible [Poole, 75-83]. Plus, some of those departing from the big Babel mix-up in languages had somehow to have reached places like the Americas, which no people from Europe had reached, or even known about, until 1492. Grotius also argued that the text about the apocalypse in the book of Revelation in the Bible applied at the time it was written, that is, to Rome, and not to the future. But—perhaps in part because of the Protestant split in the

United Provinces (Netherlands) and the Calvinist/Reformed Church rejection of Grotius' theology—his views didn't seem to deter faith nor occasional lapses among common people into apocalypticism. Still, a few others did begin to carry on with such questions and doubts, slowly weakening the grip of inerrancy. Particularly explosive was Frenchman Richard Simon's view (1678) that all books of the Bible are abridgements for public use of much longer texts so, in this view, Xtianity's "inspired writers" necessarily became "inspired editors" [Poole, 6].

Frenchman Isaac La Peyrère in 1643 put into limited circulation a manuscript that derived the idea from biblical texts that people existed before Adam, albeit in a lawless state [Poole, 27-28]. La Peyrère also restricted the flood to the vicinity of Palestine. All this was so explosive that Louis XIII's Chief Minister, Cardinal Richelieu, had the work banned.[14] See Plate 4.1. But La Peyrère extended his work beyond biblical exegesis, "borrowing freely from the literatures of geography, travel, and technical chronology," and this was published in Amsterdam in 1655 [Poole, 29]. As a result, "Catholic authorities arrested La Peyrère, imprisoned him, and forced him to recant.... But ... later manuscripts show that he never sincerely abandoned his [views about] men before Adam" [Poole, 30].

Thus, by the 1660s, at least a few highly-educated people had come to have questions about what seemed to be inconsistencies in the Bible. Another inconsistency was that, according to Genesis, the first book of the Bible, on the sixth day of creation the Xtian deity reportedly created the first man and then woman (Adam and Eve).

---

14   Despite his rank in the Catholic Church, Cardinal Richelieu (1585-1642) was not necessarily acting as a religious figure here. While in power as Chief Minister (1624-1642), he did his best to strengthen the French monarchy against all comers. Although he coordinated the final blockade and siege of La Rochelle, a key Protestant island stronghold in the West of France, he also urged support for the Protestant side monetarily and ultimately with troops in the Thirty Years War (1618-1648)—a realpolitik stance against the Habsburgs and Spanish power.

Their violation of the deity's commandment not to eat the fruit on the tree of knowledge got them expelled from the Garden of Eden (the source of Augustine and the Church's "original sin"). They had two sons, Abel and Cain; the latter killed the former and was further exiled. But where did the people that Cain feared would attack him in his exile come from? (One possible answer raised at the time was that because the Bible made no mention of other people being created after Adam and Eve, maybe Adam wasn't the first man, but the first Jew.)

The members of the Royal Society pursued their many individual interests, including some truly scientific ones. Among their work were studies of animals, plants, and the Earth and its past. And it is to these aspects of science to which we will narrow the focus henceforth. With respect to the Earth, the most fundamental question for some of the Royal Society's proto- scientists was: How did the deity do it? How can natural history be connected to what else we know, that is, biblical history? And in reflecting and discussing and speculating on their own and others' early efforts at more systematic observation and investigation and occasional experimentation, they sought to identify more natural mechanisms by which the Xtian deity might have accomplished what was described in the Bible—or, failing that, be (grudgingly) obliged to chalk it up to being purely miraculous.

So a few men—"The World Makers" in Poole's title—developed speculative, rational-mechanical ways in which the Xtian deity might have accomplished the steps in the creation of the universe, the ways in which Noah's Flood might have come to pass and played itself out, as well as how their deity might bring about the end of the world.

Plate 4.1: Cardinal de Richelieu, Chief Minister to King Louis XIII of France, by Philippe de Champaigne (1633-40), in the National Gallery, London. Photo by the author.

Early Questions about the Age of the Earth and about the Character of Shells on Land

As usual, the principal common background learnings of the Friends of the Royal Society (FRS) included works by Aristotle and, of course, the Bible. Aristotle's theorizing about the Earth (in *Meteorologica*) was in many respects better than his other works on physical science.

Among his conclusions, for example, was that the Earth was eternal—an idea which the Xtians of course rejected. Aristotle also said that the surface of the Earth underwent gradual change continuously, that seas had replaced some dry land, and vice-versa [Poole, 10]. In addition, most FRS members and their associates would have read Rene' Descartes principal work (*Principia,* 1644) or otherwise have learned about the Cartesian system. Descartes (of "I think therefore I am" fame) provided a very strong impetus for the idea that the operation of the universe was based on regular mechanical laws/principles—which was similar to Galileo's views and Kepler's practice of astronomy. As Descartes' thought filtered through to England, especially via another Frenchman, Pierre Gassendi, it became a motivator for these FRS seekers to try to figure out how things in nature worked. Gassendi also helped spread the Epicurean theory of atoms—derived from a Roman era manuscript by Lucretius. And many English thinkers preferred an atoms-based theory to Descartes infinitely divisible corpuscles/matter [Poole, 20].

But head and shoulders above everything else in credibility was the Bible, which for most but not quite all of these men was still a God-inspired document to be taken literally (and with the first five books written personally by Moses). As calculated at the time from the Bible, mainly from the book of Genesis, along with some information from pagan histories, the Xtian deity created the Earth sometime around 4004 B.C. But such calculations ranged from 3600 to 6500 BCE [Hubert Krivine, *The Earth: From Myths to Knowledge*, 8].

Noah's Flood in the Bible was calculated to have occurred 1656 years after creation (i.e., in about 2348 BCE if 4004 BCE is the creation date) and, apart from subsequent effects due to earthquakes and volcanoes, was thought to have left the Earth as it was then known [Poole, 40]. Human efforts after the flood to build a Tower of Babel—to climb in order to save themselves from any subsequent floods—resulted in the Xtian deity's making them speak many languages and thus be unintelligible to each other and unable to continue the work, and their dispersal around the Earth was used to account for the different languages that humans spoke. Problems with that view have already been noted above.

"Fossils" began to be added to the curiosity cabinet collections of gentlemen and aristocrats in the 17th century. But the original definition of "fossil" was almost anything that had been dug up from the earth, including minerals and crystals, while anything that resembled a life form, mostly in the form of shells, were "'figured stones'" [Simon Winchester, *The Map that Changed the World: William Smith and the Birth of Modern Geology*, 34-41]. Because they actually were stone (shells turned into stone), and were sometimes found on high mountains, the early beliefs were that they could not be remains of living creatures. They could be special little replicas made by some plastic force attributed to the deity, directly or indirectly, in the course of creation, perhaps even to remind humans of his power. For example, they could arise like crystals grown from a liquid, or gallstones, or corals.

If "fossils" were of organic origin, rather than "formed stones" or "figured stones" that the Earth produced naturally, why was it that some matched current sea life but others did not seem to match any living creatures, when God would surely not permit animals within his "good" creation to perish/go extinct? (Only sea-based fossils were widely known at the time; large bones found on land, with skeletons apparently never having been systematically excavated, were attributed to the giant humans suggested in Genesis.) Even when fossils were thought to be organic in origin, Noah's Flood was used to explain how petrified versions were so widely distributed. What wasn't so clear was why so many would be near the tops of mountains, including the highest mountains in Europe, the Alps, rather than far downslope or even piled up in watery basins, or maybe even largely unaffected by a flood of the land. Further challenging was that some shells could be found by splitting open other kinds of rocks, and the same was true for some impressions of plant leaves within coal lumps.

Thomas Burnet (1636-1715), whose book, *Sacred Theory of the Earth* (1681 in Latin, 1684 in English), "prompted decades of extensive debate within academic, scientific, and theological communities concerning the proper relation between physical hypothesis and biblical exegesis"—that is, biblical explanation [Poole, 56]. Although he was primarily a man of the church (and an academic and natural philosopher), his Cartesian-oriented efforts to explain the creation, flood, and later the end of the world, also had heterodox ("heretical") implications that gave rise to those longer-term concerns. In Burnet's account, chaos settles out into a smooth egg-shaped paradise before the great flood. In time, the sun's heat at the equator dried the Earth there out, and it cracked, releasing the flood of waters that reshaped the surface of the Earth; this was "providentially coordinated to occur *at the point of man's maximal sinfulness*" [Poole, 58; emphasis added]. (Burnet had calculated that there was not enough water in the oceans, rivers, and rains to cover the Earth as described in the biblical texts about Noah's Flood—so he had to come up with a source for more water.) As for the theologically concerning aspects of such a theory, his position could be seen as limiting how the Xtian god could act, as constraining miracles. More obviously a problem was that if man was at his most sinful at the time of the flood, then Adam's "Fall" as the source of original sin and, therefore, as the ultimate source of man's sinfulness, was being down-played in relative importance. Whoops! Given the reactions of many of his readers to such problems, at the end of his second book, some years later, he proposed "that the opening chapters of Genesis were to be understood allegorically, or as written to be accommodated to a primitive Israelite audience" [Poole, 61]. Burnett also took the one-day-is-as-a-thousand-years in 2 Peter 3:8

to apply to the seven days the deity was said to have created the Earth [Krivine, 14]. Although such allegorical interpretation was not new, the scope of Burnet's idea here was quite outside the interpretation of most Xtians, not to mention the fact that Protestants at this time leaned more toward biblical literalism than did the Catholic Church, which had long used allegorical interpretation, even if often mainly to develop and support Church tradition and power.

A second "World Maker" was John Woodward (1665/68-1728), who improved upon Burnet and also emphasized organically-sourced fossils in his account. His work drew heavily from Nicolaus Steno and Robert Hooke (see below re both), though he was the leading fossil collector in England at the time. His account relied on the Xtian deity's suspension of gravity, which "had the effect of briefly cancelling the cohesion of most bodies," such that "the planet therefore turned into a kind of pudding" [Poole, 64]. And when gravity was re-commenced, previously unaffected organic matter got encased in mud which hardened into stone. Although there were theological problems in Woodward's account as well (e.g., was a second creation thus required?), Woodward's "work remained intellectually alive for decades" [Poole, 65].

The third author of note here is William Whiston (1667-1752) who used comets as the Xtian deity's deus-ex-machina. He used comets in the creation of the Earth, as the cause of the flood, and as the forthcoming cause of the Earth's final destruction—where the effects much depended upon the size of the comet and the angle at which it struck the Earth [Poole, 68-72].

Robert Hooke

Robert Hooke (1635-1703) joined a scientific discussion group when he was in college, and despite his youth became much appreciated by building instrumentation to test the theories of some of the leading gentlemen scholar-scientists of the day, including Boyle [Daniel J. Boorstin, *The Discoverers: A History of Man's Search to Know His World and Himself*, 51-52]. In 1662, when Hooke was 27, Boyle helped to get him chosen to continue this role—as the "Curator of Experiments"—in the newly forming Royal Society. In many respects, he embodied the spirit of the new age, or perhaps of a century later. In his book *Micrographia* of 1665, he wrote, "the truth is the science of Nature has been already too long a work of the brain and the fancy: It is now high time that it should return to the plainness and soundness of observation on material and obvious things" [Boorstin, 52].

Hooke made many of the *initial* advances and efforts to develop what later became Earth science [Poole, xiii]. All of the other works and/or authors cited above (and more, of course) were direct or indirect influences on Hooke's thinking, often no doubt via personal interactions. But one of the most remarkable features of Hooke's thinking, at least as it came to be over time, was that he did not reason from the biblical text, nor did he feel obliged to orient his conclusions to that text (although he did incorporate references to it at times or on occasions that suited him). An important collaborator in Hooke's work was Edmond Halley (1656-1742), renowned mainly for discovering that the comet subsequently named for him made periodic appearances. In general, then, their research was "all but disconnected" from the biblical narrative [Poole, 96].

The most important focus of Hooke's work is on what happened to the Earth between its creation (including any subsequent flooding) and his time. Today this would be called geomorphology—the processes by which the Earth changes, such as earthquakes, vulcanism, subsidence and uplift, plate tectonics, the many forms of erosion, along with the landforms and fossils that provided the evidence of these processes. At the time, only recently had Earth's geographical features even become a largely separate "general geography," as described by Bernhard Varenius (1622-1650). Varenius' tome (800 pages) on all aspects of geography included the fact that in some places the sea had become land, and vice-versa, and he had "proposed that the Earth by the natural wearing down of mountains and silting of troughs might in time revert to its state at creation, a sphere entirely covered by water" [Poole, 97-98]. Ovid—a Roman whose work was well known in the 17th century—had also written of such things, including shells far from the sea, "lakes sucked dry by thirsty sand," or lakes added where once there was dry land; also, high hills washed to the sea and instances where "torrents had made a valley of a plain" [Poole, 98]. More rapidly occurring phenomena, such as earthquakes and vulcanism were well known in Hooke's time; even England had experienced an occasional earthquake. "But the most influential English affirmation of the principle of vicissitude [changing landscapes] was George Hakewill's *An Apologie or Declaration of the Power and Providence of God* (1627, 1630, 1635)" in which a text from Solomon emphasizing great cycles was foundational: "'What has been will be again, / what has been done will be done again' (Eccles 1:9)" [Poole, 99]. Varenius had built on this work; among intellectuals, more were recognizing that a variety of ordinary processes shaped the Earth.

Another major contribution to scientific understanding in what was to become geomorphology was Nils Stensen, a Dane from a Lutheran family whose name was subsequently Latinized to Nicolaus Stenonius (who is known as Steno). His studies were launched when he was asked to dissect the head of a great white shark surprisingly caught in the Mediterranean; he recognized the teeth as being the same as some he had seen in stone versions on land [Brian Switek, *Written in Stone: Evolution, the Fossil Record, and Our Place in Nature*, 25-27]. He published his work based on studies of the Tuscan landscape in 1669 and Oldenburg translated it for the Royal Society's publication in 1671 [Poole, 101-104]. Steno made a very systematic analysis of how formerly organic entities (fossils) and gems got inside rocks—for example, the outer layer must have formed at the same time or later for the inner object to have imprinted its shape on the inside of the outer layer. And rock strata with shells in them that had turned to stone (petrified) always began as horizontal layers because they were constituted by sedimentation from bodies of water. Because these strata aren't all horizontal now, they must have undergone change to get where they are now. Steno also realized that rock layers on top must be newer than rock layers beneath. These are modern geology's laws of "original horizontality" and "superposition" [Charles C. Plummer, David McGeary, and Diane H. Carlson, *Physical Geology (8th Ed.)*, 175]. But Steno still tried to tie his findings to the biblical account of Noah's Flood, thusly: water covered everything first; God then dried out some land; Noah's Flood occurred, covering the Earth in sediment; the land dried out again; and then there were lots of subsequent changes, some of them rapid, with change agents such as earthquakes, erosion (yielding the craggy surface to the Earth again), and the undermining of strata [Poole, 103]. Despite massively erroneous hypotheses/conclusions in accord with the beliefs of his time, Steno's methods were highly reusable anywhere rock strata were exposed. In the end, though, apparently because he changed interests to pursue a "higher calling"—or perhaps because there was just too much tension between his religious beliefs and what he saw—Steno never did any more research and instead became an important functionary in the Catholic Church and was assigned a few years later to try to reconvert people in northern Europe.

Meanwhile, Hooke had for a few years been lecturing on fossils and developing his ideas on earthquakes. By 1678, "Hooke reaffirmed his Aristotelian hypothesis that 'Mountains have been sunk into Plains and Plains have been raised into Mountains,'" with earthquakes, which he postulated as being more frequent in earlier times, and Earth's internal fires as the causative agents [Poole, 15, 105]. "The component of Hooke's theory that had the power to cause the most damage to the biblical model was his notion of the Earth changing over time in ways that were too various to be encompassed under a model involving a unique catastrophe, and, at the same time, had [also] escaped the record of written history" [Poole, 107]. Hooke saw a role for floods, but multiple floods, not one great flood.

Edmond Halley proposed replacing biblical chronology with scientific measurements of the salinity of the oceans [Poole, 36]. His lectures in 1694, which he refrained from publishing for 30 years, declared the biblical account of Noah's Flood was unsatisfactory as an explanation for the Earth as currently observed [Poole, 108]. Ultimately, he advanced a theory of periodic catastrophism, which was in accord with Hooke's views too [Poole, 108.]. For Halley, Genesis "recorded the creation of a new geography out of an old landscape" [Poole, 109]. "Hooke's lectures, too, had to wait until two years after his own death before their publication" [Poole, 109]. Halley also argued, as the Bible says in another context (see above), that the "days" of creation were as a thousand years. Thus a few men, including Hooke, increasingly turned to scientific methods to attempt to date the past [Poole, 43]. Nature was the book of history for the Earth [Poole, 112].

Assertions that what we now call fossils are of organic origin had been made by others before Hooke and had been much debated within the Royal Society in the first half of the 1660s [Poole, 118-119]. In addition to shells, they had discussed petrified wood samples and grey marble, with its signs of cockles and shells. By the time Hooke published *Micrographia* in 1665, "he had settled on the theory that he would defend intermittently for almost four further decades" [Poole, 119]. Hooke also examined petrified wood and cockle and ammonite fossils under the microscope. Hooke became convinced that fossilization was real by comparing fossilized charcoal against wood charred in a fire [Switek, 28]. His book also mentioned fossils of other kinds—nautilus, periwinkles, scallops, etcetera, and he was familiar with plant impressions in coal where the plant itself had "mouldered away." Hooke argued for a three-stage fossilization process, suspecting "that great pressure, great heat, or complex physiochemical reactions had transformed the once organic remains into minerals, just as [certain kinds of] mud had been transformed into peat, the peat into lignite [a soft coal], and the lignite into the solid black rock-mineral called coal," in which there were also fossils, but with all the properties of coal [Winchester, 38]. Later Hooke would also treat extinction and develop an improved understanding of the dynamics of seismic disturbance, but his *Micrographia* already included that "the moon had been wracked over the ages by internal fires and vapours" [Poole, 120], implying a parallel with Earth. Having written his book in 1665, Hooke accused Steno of plagiarism when Steno's work appeared in English in 1671, but plagiarism is unlikely. And although helped by numerous discussions with others, "Hooke's achievement was to systematize a theory of fossils ... in a string of lectures delivered in 1667-8, accompanied by examples of the fossils themselves ... and his own drawings of other specimens" [Poole, 122]. Poole gives 11 steps in Hooke's account, the last of which, the most daring of all at the time, is that: "Finally, many species have been lost; many more species are new" [Poole, 122-123]. Of course some of Hooke's ideas were regarded as too speculative and no one had any idea that tectonic plates might be the major driving force for uplifted mountains and much of the world's vulcanism until the middle of the 20th century, but Hooke had certainly started out on the correct path in many respects.

But the strength of the culture's entrapment in the still largely-buried cultural insanity of a literal biblical interpretation was too overwhelming, even among almost all of these (religious) proto-scientists for Hooke's analyses to gain acceptance by more than a few of them, although some could see that there were still unsolved problems with traditional views. "It was still in practice impossible to decouple zoology from theology" [Poole, 126]. Some opponents allowed as how some shells near the sea may indeed be organic in origin, but the spotty distribution of land-based aggregations of what seemed to be petrified shells (the primary example known) instead suggested two different sources, the second being some kind of naturally formed or figured stones [Poole, 124-132]. Moreover, different quarries yielded different figured stones, raising doubts about a common source. Opponents especially could not accept the idea that the Xtian deity had proclaimed himself satisfied with his creation, as related in the Bible, and then nevertheless proceeded to allow some species to go extinct. Opponents could not find any matches between existing sea life and the "figured stones," so that made the extinction conclusion all the more dubious to them (though it easily supports an extinction hypothesis too). However, the idea that there could be a fairly large variation within single species was accepted, such that some forms of the same species might have died off. But in sum, at the time, there was more a reversal of opinion here about fossils than progress because most of even the most highly educated people at the time could not see beyond their beliefs in various literal interpretations of the Bible [Poole, 128-133]. So much of Hooke's work faded from view for the time being.

Interestingly enough, Lucretius' version of Epicureanism, then in wide circulation among the educated, also included extinction: Early in the Earth's history, "many species of animals must have perished…, unable by procreation to forge out the chain of prosperity: for whatever you see feeding on the breath of life, either cunning or courage or at least quickness must have guarded and kept that kind from its earliest existence;…" [W. H. D. Rouse, 401].

CHAPTER 35

The Challenges Diversify and Extinctions Confirmed

The Comte de Buffon

With foundations such as those described above, the baton of exploration in geology-paleontology seems to have passed to France, and especially the Comte de Buffon (Georges-Louis Leclerc), 1707-1788. From 1739 on, he served as the superintendent of the royal botanical gardens. But Buffon had immediate as well as other earlier predecessors in attempting to extend the time of creation and even to date the Earth, especially Benoit de Maillet (1656-1738). Maillet, using the rate of retreat of the sea from the land (silting ports?), calculated that it would take a then-phantasmagorical 2 billion years for the sea to have receded from the highest mountains [Krivine, 16]. He also "demonstrated" the reality of fossils, thought everything came from the sea, and raised very original questions about why the deity delayed almost forever before creating the Earth—if he wanted it at one time, didn't he want it always? [Krivine, 17]. Implicitly then, maybe the deity did his creation earlier than recorded in the Bible. Because these ideas and others as well were very heretical, Maillet provides yet another example of exercising extreme caution in the face of likely Church persecution for heretical ideas. He made provision to publish under a pseudonym, in the Netherlands, and not until 10 years after he died [Krivine, 17].

Building on various predecessors, Buffon "recognized the powerful erosive ability of streams to destroy the land and thought that the land would eventually be reduced to sea level" [William D. Thornbury, *Principles of Geomorphology*, 5]. Having tried to estimate the age of the Earth in more than one way, Buffon (again) suggested that the six days of creation were not ordinary days, but much more extensive. His observation of the rates of sedimentation led him to calculate an age of several million to as many as 3 billion years—but he was "prudent enough not to publish these results" [Krivine, 17]. In any case, the rate of sedimentation was always highly debatable, especially with a worldwide flood in the mix of possible causes. So Buffon, the "father of scientific dating" went on to study the rate of cooling of metal balls up to 5 inches in diameter, extrapolating the results to the cooling time needed for a much larger Earth—and came up with 74,000 years [Krivine, 18]. But those years encompassed only the time until it took Earth to cool. Ultimately, Buffon wrote that there were seven epochs of creation—covering a time span to which Buffon did not assign a number in a publication [David R. Montgomery, *The Rocks Don't Lie: A Geologist Investigates Noah's Flood*, 100]. Buffon's ideas about the Earth's creation involved a comet striking the sun (borrowed from Whiston, above?), and a topography (landscape) that was shaped by erosion, not Noah's Flood [Montgomery, 99].

The bulk of Buffon's time was almost undoubtedly spent on authoring a 44-volume Natural History (36 of which came out during his life time), opening "a new world of change and progress" and "bringing the whole Earth and all its plants and animals onto the stage of history," in the process earning credit for helping to extend the length of time for the history of Earth to have occurred [Boorstin, 454,

457]. See Plate 4.2. And Buffon's works were best-sellers that rivaled the famous and era-defining French encyclopedists [Boorstin, 448].

But escaping formal theological accusations was not yet possible in Catholic France, and with that came the possibility that Buffon would lose his prestigious position. In response to his first volume of natural history conveying his Theory of the Earth, the theology faculty at the University of Paris "demanded that, to avoid their censure, he clarify certain passages in writing" [Boorstin, 455]. In response, he took shelter in claiming that his hypotheses on the formation of the planets were "'pure philosophical speculation'" and abandoned "'whatever in my book concerns the formation of the earth, and in general all that might be contrary to the narration of Moses'" [Boorstin, 455]. Three decades later, having included this recantation in a reprint of this volume, "a committee of censorship was again appointed, but under pressure from the King they never produced a report" [Boorstin, 455].

Progress in Classification Systems; Genus and Species; Linnaeus; Cuvier

Aristotle was among those who first attempted to classify animals according to various traits. Although Carl Linnaeus (1707-1778), a botanist and medical doctor, had a few immediate predecessors, he drew many of his basic ideas about classification as well as a number of specific animal names from Aristotle, with Plato a contributor as well [Leroi, 276]. Among those ideas was the most basic division into "genus" and "species," where a genus would typically include a number of closely-related individual species. By the time he became rector at the University of Uppsala in 1750, Linnaeus had made many trips to study plant life. At Uppsala, Linnaeus sponsored many student "apostles" to go on trips all over the world to collect more information on plants mainly, and later animals too. This approach became standard for a long time, with many expeditions deliberately including a naturalist—and one of those in the early 1830s was Charles Darwin. Linnaeus' tenth edition in 1758-59 included animals. Linnaeus' work provided the initial foundations for biological classifications.

Buffon, a contemporary of Linnaeus, rejected Linnaeus' taxonomy as being overly-simplified and, in the case of plants, too hinged on microscopic features of their sexuality. Although not directly hypothesizing some form of evolution, Buffon declined to affirm a simple concept of species, instead emphasizing descriptions and animal behaviors. He raised doubts as to whether all species of animals were the same, past and present, and posed questions such as "'at what distance from man shall we place the great apes, which resemble him perfectly in bodily conformation?'" [Boorstin, 450-451]. To Buffon, "'the mule resembles the horse more than the water spaniel resembles the greyhound,'" yet the mule is sterile [Boorstin, 450]. And the fox can be known as different from the dog only by testing their offspring [Boorstin, 450]. "Based on ... vestigial organs that served no apparent purpose, like the sightless eyes of a mole and the wings of flightless birds," he even "suggested that animals [had] evolved" [Montgomery, 99].

Nevertheless, the adoption of a classification system a la Linnaeus was particularly important because its use of Latin names for genus and species could be more readily adopted around the globe, enabling naturalists in any country to refer to an animal or plant and have others be sure about the referent. Plus Linnaeus classified so many animals and plants it only made sense to use his beginnings. Only somewhat later, Georges Cuvier (1769-1832, see below) was to devise an overarching four-part classification system for all the animals. In his publication The Animal Kingdom in 1817, he greatly expanded "the hierarchy of Classes, Orders, Families and Genera," and subsumed those under four branches: Vertebrata (animal with backbones), Articulata (external skeletons), Mollusca (soft-bodied creatures), and Radiata (more primitive organisms, such as sponges [Leroi, 279]. This work became the standard for classification at the broader level [Leroi, 280]. Cuvier's classifications also avoided a high-to-low ordering—from stones on up in line to humans, then angels, then the deity (the "Great Chain of Being" emphasized by medieval Aristotelian scholasticism). However, for Cuvier the boundaries between his branches of life could not be crossed and he refused to recognize the considerable parallelism of internal functioning of the organs across branches (thereby also foreclosing evolution across branches) [Leroi, 280-284].

Plate 4.2: Statue/Monument to the Comte de Buffon, Garden of Plants, Paris. Note the lion and the bird. Photo by the author.

Progress on the Identity of Fossils and Recognizing Extinction; Role of Noah's Flood Becomes Dubious

Although a few naturalists since the mid-1600s concluded that extinction did indeed occur, there was also considerable resistance to the idea based mainly on the notion that the deity would not allow extinction to come to creatures in a world which he had pronounced as "good." But as time marched on, more people also began to notice that some of these figured stones resembled creatures that were altogether unknown in their world. Still, per the general interpretation of the Bible, extinction was impossible, so the stones could not be former life forms. Nor could formerly living shells have become "deeply infiltrated" inside rocks because land was created before life according to the Bible. But as more scientists and educated lay people began to accept that these fossils were formerly alive, Noah's Flood became the omnipresent explanation for fossils by the 18th century, including for shells on mountaintops. "Perhaps the rocks and all that lay inside them—the oyster shells, the fern leaves, and the crystal corals, fish skulls, and lizard bones—had all somehow been precipitated or had crystallized themselves from the fluid of a universal, flood-created sea" [Winchester, 40].

In the early 1700s a number of fossil skeletons (dating to the Miocene, 10 to 20 million years ago) were unearthed by quarry workers near the Alpine Lake Constance that were taken to represent animals killed by Noah's Flood [Montgomery, 82]. The reality of Noah's Flood was at least a little in doubt in that no extensive human remains had ever been found. But one creature removed from the quarry in 1725 looked somewhat like a human skeleton and was named and displayed as such—"*Homo diluvia testis*"—"man who testifies to the Flood" [Montgomery, 82]. But within decades, naturalists mostly came to believe it was a fish, and in 1812 Cuvier made the more definitive identification—an amphibian [Montgomery, 83].

By the 1790s, Cuvier, a budding comparative anatomist who was later to become head the France's Museum of Natural History (which was being added to the botanical gardens in Paris), had begun what amounted to paleontological studies. With the help of Napoleon's empire, the museum began a fossil collection (which included some seizures) from all over the world. This collection enabled Cuvier to fuse anatomy with geography by carefully portraying elephantine skeletons from Africa, India, and Siberia (a wooly mammoth) [Montgomery, 87]. Before this, the large bones found around Europe were typically identified as those of the giants referred to in the Bible [Montgomery, 84]. But in 1796 Cuvier delivered two papers that compared the bones of these elephants (museum specimens) along with the teeth of another elephantine creature from the United States. This fourth pachyderm had very different teeth (it was a bark and limb eater instead of a grass eater), which he later named "mastodon" [Montgomery, 88]. Both the mastodon and mammoth were different from the modern elephants, and that made it highly likely that they were extinct unless live specimens had not yet been discovered. Only three years later a Russian naturalist discovered mammoth remains that included some flesh and fur [Switek, 180], making it even more clear that this was definitely a different elephant. Although "No staunch biblical literalist would like to admit that Noah had decided to leave some species behind, ... the bones were too different from those of living species" to conclude otherwise [Switek, 180]. Cuvier's argument for extinction here was backed up by his description of an accurate drawing of the skeleton of an immense sloth-related creature from South America, recently brought to Spain, which he deemed Megatherium [Switek, 31; Lister, 38]. See Plate 4.3. With his expertise in comparative anatomy, Cuvier, who would come to be recognized as the "founder of vertebrate paleontology," proceeded to analyze other fossils and "found that [some] whole faunas preserved in stone were distinct from living species" [Montgomery, 89].

A decade or so later, Cuvier and a colleague explored the rock beds in the region around Paris and, based on the fossils there, "were able to determine that the area had been subject to alternating inundation by seawater and freshwater" [Switek, 32]. This convinced him that the Earth had been subject to multiple catastrophes. Still, Cuvier can be regarded as the founder of scientific catastrophism as contrasted with the uniformitarianism of Lyell (see below) [Krivine, 24]. Catastrophic in this sense does not reflect a single overwhelming flood (a la Noah) but, given what Cuvier found in the Paris basin, floods were the catastrophes he chose as the drivers of major changes in the Earth's history. Cuvier "outlined the role of catastrophes during the earth's history" in a book on fossils and classifications published in 1812. This book included a "Preliminary Discourse," a preface in which he "pontificated on the pattern of ruin and reform over time… and identified the most recent catastrophe as occurring about 6,000 years ago" [Switek, 33]. This preface was translated into English, with additions and multiple revised editions, by Scottish naturalist Robert Jameson, who believed in the biblical Noah's Flood and asserted that Cuvier's work supported this view [Switek, 33-34]. This translation, with its revisions, helped to prolong the debate in geology in England for many years about the overarching role of a Noah's Flood.

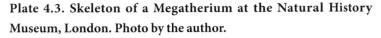

Plate 4.3. Skeleton of a Megatherium at the Natural History Museum, London. Photo by the author.

Cuvier also authored five volumes of comparative anatomy (1800-05), four volumes of The Animal Kingdom, and a 22-volume covering the natural history of fishes (1828-1849). See Plate 4.4 for a monument, presumably representing his work on all of animal life. It was to become "his proud boast that he could classify an animal from only a single bone" [Leroi, 282]. Perhaps what I saw when I visited the National Museum of Natural History in 2010 continued to represent the kind of work being done in Cuvier's time (the museum itself seemed almost historical in character, partly frozen in time), and why he could perhaps legitimately have made such a claim. Upon entering the museum, there is a great hall which is filled almost entirely with columns of skeletons, arranged by type, all facing one way, as if marching toward the viewer. See Plate 4.5.

Examination of the rocks in the Paris basin had a predecessor. Coal beds, which were valuable as a source of energy in England, were seen to contain impressions of what clearly were once plants. And those coal beds sloped down into the earth in some places, going out of sight. One could dig down into those beds to get the coal, but what about situations in which there is no coal on the surface to find? By going down into many a mine, William Smith, a mining engineer and the father of English geology, learned which assemblages of fossilized sea shells were typical of which marine sedimentary rock beds, and he learned the (almost) unvarying order of those and other interspersed rock layers and beds at different sites around Britain. [See Simon Winchester's, *The Map That Changed the World: William Smith and the Birth of Modern Geology*, for a full account of Smith's discoveries.] This regular ordering is called the "fossil column"—an ordering of fossils, from youngest (nearer the surface) to oldest, with particular selections thereof common in similar beds, and always in the same order even in different locations, *provided* that similar ancient environments existed in the same place over the expanse of the lands being examined. And, with that proviso, having learned the order of the rock beds, Smith proved that he could almost always safely conclude that the order was the same below whatever rock was on the surface. This enabled him to determine how far down in the earth the coal beds would be likely to be found, leading to more successful efforts at finding prospective coal mines. Smith went on to complete a huge geologic map showing the surface rock beds across almost all of Britain, with each different rock bed having its own color.

Plate 4.4: Fountain Monument to Cuvier on the Streets of Paris, 1840. The Woman Apparently Represents Natural History (and, in any case, is very Parisian). Photo by the author.

Plate 4.5: Parade of Skeletons (for comparative anatomy) at the National Museum of Natural History, Paris. Photo by the author.

Further, as Smith descended into some deep coal mines around the turn of the 19th century, he observed on some occasions frequent changes in the rock beds, some clearly bearing sea-based fossils and others clearly not—indicating off-and-on kinds of ancient environments—a result not at all resembling what would occur from a single catastrophe, a flood—and similar to what Cuvier was to find in the Paris region. (In Britain's case, when such alternating rocks were found going down in mineshafts, the seashell-bearing rock beds must have been laid down in shallow seas and then, layered atop them, must have been material eroded from highlands and deposited on low-lying but no longer submerged surfaces—the sea having receded or the shallow shoreline having risen; and then, later, these surfaces had to be covered anew by shallow seas for more sea shells to be deposited.)

Moreover, as was potentially clearest to those who studied rock beds with wider spreads in years, the closer one got to the surface, the more the fossils were akin to animals still alive today. And, given the law of superposition, fossils were also necessarily dated (relatively) by their position in the earth, and rock beds elsewhere around the Earth with similar fossils were necessarily of roughly the same age. For example, as Cuvier was to point out, ammonites were found only in older rock beds. See Plate 4.6. The principle involved here is called "faunal succession"—progressively older fossils always occur in progressively older rock beds. The older the sedimentary rock beds, the more the fossils are unlike today's life forms. And the discovery of far more unusual fossils was under way well before Darwin's. *Origin of Species.*

One of England's premier fossil hunters started that career as a young girl. Mary Anning (1799-1847) tagged along with her lower-class cabinet-maker father as he searched during holidays for saleable objects beneath the considerable cliffs that lined the seacoast around Lyme Regis in Dorset County, England [Patricia Pierce, *Jurassic Mary: Mary Anning and the Primeval Monsters*, 5-7]. See Plate 4.7. Among the items more readily found were well-known but attractive ammonites (with coiled shells that people thought were snake-related) and belemnites (with straight shells)—fossils that wealthy tourists sometimes bought as items for their curiosity cabinets, though few of them identified the items as fossilized life forms [Pierce, 9-10]. Mary's father died when she was only 11, and she was all the more obliged to continue with the work of combing the narrow shoreline and scanning the cliffs, in order to help provide for her mother, her 15-year-old brother, and herself.

Good finds were most likely immediately after storms had brought down old and exposed new cliff face. In 1810 or 1811 her brother spotted a newly fallen head of an ichthyosaur in very good condition, and in 1812 Mary spied the other bones of its remains thirty feet up on the face of the cliff [Pierce, 19]. While ichthyosaurs were known and had been previously described in academic circles from partial remains, here was the first very good and virtually complete skeleton of a 17-footer—but another one was soon found elsewhere and made its way earlier to exhibition in London.

Plate 4.6: Fossilized Ammonite at the Natural History Museum in London. Photo by the author.

Mary Anning was also the first to discover a complete skeleton of a plesiosaur, which arrived in London in 1824 [Pierce, 87]. While an ichthyosaur resembles a dolphin, a plesiosaur was like nothing known—though later the fabled Loch Ness monster would often be thought of as one—see Plate 4.8. Mary's find became the "type" specimen for fossilized Plesiosaurus giganteus [Pierce, 197].

Plate 4.7: Painting of Mary Anning in an Exhibit at the Natural History Museum, London. Photo by the author.

Mary learned to do the preparatory work on the fossils she found, and became quite good as a paleo-anatomist. Along the way, she learned to read and write, but all her important work was sold to and transmitted to the outside world by gentlemen and gentlemen-geologist buyers, acquaintances and friends. These men then presented academic papers that described the finds relative to the science and classification systems at the time, receiving credit as the describers (and often as discoverers as well), though Mary was sometimes given some credit. At the time, other "commercial" supplier-finders of fossils were not credited either [Pierce, 200], but many of those arose by accident while Mary became a professional without the formal education normally associated with it—education that was then almost barred to women, especially from the lower classes. And although Mary was sometimes in dire straits financially, she was also sometimes helped out by her friends among this group. Over the years, many of them visited her and her shop in Lyme Regis and her talents and capabilities became more fully appreciated. She was paid what seems to be adequately for most of her best finds, but those were not plentiful. It was Mary about whom it was written, "She sells sea shells down by the seashore."

Among Mary's other nearly-complete and stellar fossils finds were a pterodactyl, a third and fourth ichthyosaur (all different types), a second and different plesiosaur, a recognition of what coprolites were (fossilized excrement), fossilized and reconstitutable ink in pouches from a cuttlefish-like belemnite, and an unusual fossil fish (also a type specimen) [Pierce, 197-200].

Plate 4.8: Fossilized Skeleton of a Plesiosaur at the Natural History Museum, London. Photo by the author.

Despite William Smith's knowledge (as a non-gentleman, his map was plagiarized and he otherwise published little), the idea that Noah's Flood was responsible for the surface of the Earth and the destruction of fossilized life forms lasted longer among the educated in England than on the continent. In England, many a gentleman (i.e., someone with a landed estate and/or a sufficient income/inheritance)

chose to become an ordained Anglican functionary (deacon, vicar, etc.), the principal alternatives being a lawyer or a military man. In looking to nature to help the understanding of the deity's handiwork, a number of these men also became involved in the collection and identification of fossils, sometimes engaging with William Smith and Mary Anning. William Buckland (1784-1856) was one such man. As a geologist he became involved with many a fossil, the geologic society, and Mary Anning (from the time of her first ichthyosaur discovery). But, as might be expected, he, like almost all of the Church-involved men, was reluctant to give up on the Bible as truth, though the accumulating evidence was making it clearer and clearer that the age of the Earth had to be extended, and that not all extinctions could have occurred in one fell swoop (the Flood). Thus Buckland too regarded the rock beds with fossils in them as having originated prior to the flood described in Genesis [Montgomery, 121-122]. Buckland was ordained and was in 1825 to become a canon at Christ Church college; he was appointed as the first reader-professor of geology at Oxford (1818-19). He was the leading defender of the Noah's Flood hypothesis, but he did not believe that the Earth was created in six human-style days [Montgomery, 121]. The Flood, Buckland thought, was responsible for the loose gravelly material and stray boulders found all around the surface of England and on the continent, and for sculpting landscapes [Montgomery, 124]. In 1822, Buckland was directed by workmen to a cave with many bones in it—which he ingeniously proved to be a hyena den, per bones of Africa-style prey—and their death he attributed to the Flood [Switek, 34]. In 1823 Buckland wrote *Relics of the* Flood which brought these and other ideas together in defense of a Noachian Flood as their source. He was not the only academic defender of this view, but some other minister-geologists, such as John Fleming, wrote skeptical articles in response [Montgomery, 126-127]. Although Buckland continued to see the deity's handiwork in the amazing fossil species with which he dealt, by 1836, to his credit, he reversed his view on the Flood as the cause of any extinctions and substituted a tranquil flood that had not created the landscapes which people saw all around them [Montgomery, 128]. And by the 1840s, he was supporting Louis Agassiz's conclusion which attributed the loose gravel and stray boulders around Europe to the action of glaciers. Indeed, by the late 1830s, Buckland came to take up what was by then beginning to be a not unfamiliar stance, that the Bible was a guide to belief and moral conduct, not science; however, to that he added that geology could be used to test the viability of our biblical interpretations [Montgomery, 128-129]. These stances drew attacks from appalled fellow clergy who were, needless to say, much less informed about geology and paleontology. "Outraged traditionalists who insisted on interpreting the Bible literally railed against this compelling dismissal of scriptural geology by a ranking clergyman steeped in Anglican orthodoxy" [Montgomery, 129]. Although the views of the masses undoubtedly lagged far behind the science too, Buckland had published his latest views as one of the volumes in a popular series with otherwise conservative religious leanings.

Among the leading theological critics of Buckland was one William Cockburn of York who "claimed there was no more to earth history than an initial six days of Creation and Noah's Flood about a thousand years later" [Montgomery, 137]. He produced a pamphlet explaining how the flood accounted for various details. Subsequently, in a meeting of the British Association for the Advancement of Science held in York in 1844, Cockburn got to make his case to the audience. In ignoring evidence that had been accumulated over the years, especially in the last few decades, he said that "geologists had to explain everything using Noah's Flood, including layered rocks";… that "there had been no extinctions";… and that "rivers did not cut their valleys" [Montgomery, 138]. Among the results was "raucous laughter"

[Montgomery, 138]. Cockburn continued his campaign for what must surely have been seen as old-time religion by serious scientists in the fields of geology and paleontology.

The British Museum, founded in 1753, offered free entry to the public. So, by the early 1800s if not before, the public did not lack access to some of the best available fossils known at the time. (The museum included a natural history component, which was transferred to a separate building in 1881, and renamed as a separate entity in the late 20th century.) Some fossil finds were the subject of special exhibits and well reported in the newspaper (see below). So even among the common people, fossil finds such as those described here and below made it less and less possible to deny extinction or to affirm that the deity would not extinguish species in a world he deemed as "good."

In addition, it is relevant here to note other important extinctions known by 1859 when Darwin published his *Origin of Species*. These are listed here:

A thirty-foot long mastodon was exhibited in Philadelphia and London in 1841-1842 by Albert Koch, a fossil collector in the U.S.A. who was born in Germany [Switek, 145-146].

But Koch's exaggerated mastodon (with extra ribs and vertebrae) had to compete in the London exhibit with the newly unveiled and more amazing fossil remnants of a carnivorous Megalosaurus (very incomplete) and an herbivorous Iguanodon (somewhat complete) [Switek, 146]. Academically, these had been described in 1824 and by 1834 or so, respectively [Pierce, 88; 60-61]. The term "dinosaur," invented by Richard Owen, was first applied to that group of animals. The Iguanodon and the Megalosaurus were thought to be exclusively four-footed until the discovery in the United States in 1858 of a chronologically much more recent Hadrosaur that must have walked on two legs [Switek, 99]. Hadrosaurs were likely distant descendants of animals that also gave rise to Iguanodons. Moreover, a short-armed predatory dinosaur somewhat akin to Tyrannosaurs (ultimately named Dryptosaurus) was also discovered in 1866 in the U.S.A., and that confirmed that Megalosaurus also walked upright— and thus that neither beast was slow, plodding, or crocodile-like. Its discoverer, Edward Drinker Cope, who was just beginning his career and competition with Othniel Charles Marsh as dinosaur hunters, even envisioned Dryptosaurus as warm-blooded [Switek, 99].

A complete skeleton of a Basilosaurus, exaggerated-in-length to 114 feet (by having vertebrae added from other basilosaurs), was exhibited in Baltimore, Philadelphia, and upstate New York, followed by a European tour that included visits to Dresden and Berlin in 1846-1847 [Switek, 149-152]. It was regarded as a reptilian sea serpent initially but was soon shown to be a mammal (and was later recognized as being in the lineage of whales).

Fossils such as those noted above helped to strengthen the view that the Earth was older than could be calculated using simple 24-hour days from the Bible (or even, many of the educated no doubt saw, by counting each day of biblical creation as a thousand years).

The fact of extinction and its fossil evidence also presented biblical literalists with another challenge. The Xtian deity had purportedly created all the kinds of animals in just a few days, which conflicted with the whole idea of great expanses of geologic time. But if instead some long version of geologic time is accepted with extinctions along the way (including members of the elephants and whales families, and later early horses), with more to be added before the last edition of Darwin's *Origin of Species*, the deity must instead have engaged in multiple creations—which also clearly conflicts with the biblical account.

Progress on the Age of the Earth

Despite a smattering of prior work such as that by Steno and Buffon (see above), and Cuvier dating the age of the Earth to around 80,000 years [Krivine, 24], not until the late in the 18th century was the science of geology really getting underway. For centuries after Xtianity took over in the West, it had been assumed that a single creation event, together with Noah's Flood—both as described in the Bible—had accounted for all but the most recent changing that human history had witnessed in their landscapes, and that the age of the Earth was about 6,000 years old. The most renown of these calculations, which dated creation to 4004 B.C.(E.), was done by Irish Anglican Archbishop James Ussher in the 1650s [Montgomery, 97]. But over the decades in the late 1700s and 1800s, exploring natural scientists began finding evidence that suggested the need to extend the age of the Earth into the millions of years, and then possibly on to hundreds of millions of years. As usual, the most advanced scientists came to realize this before their ideas reached the educated pubic and, even more slowly, the general public. But by around 1800 it began to be acceptable, at least among university students, to think (but not proclaim too strongly) that the world was older than calculated by Bishop Ussher [Winchester, 41].

"As the idea that geologic time involved more than a few thousand years became reasonable, Abraham Werner, a charismatic professor at the Freiberg Mining Academy, began popularizing the idea that the rocks revealed that earth history consisted of four periods" [Montgomery, 101]. Werner (1749-1817) borrowed the idea that a fiery Earth was created by a comet striking the sun. The Earth, once cooled, was covered by a global ocean which precipitated primary/crystalline rocks with fossils in them which, once the mountains had emerged from the sea, explained fossils atop many mountains. Next, horizontal layered rocks were formed by material settling to the bottom of the slowly drying sea; third, Noah's Flood further sculpted the exposed landscape and deposited erosional materials that would form rocks based on gravel, sand, and clay; and finally, the unconsolidated debris on top was derived from erosion from the existing landscape [Montgomery, 101]. Werner, the father of geology in Germany, necessarily expected worldwide consistency in rocks, and demonstrated such a chronological succession in many rock beds, as well as noting fossils atop many high mountains. Although Werner's theories were supported a school of believers called Neptunists and helped to "formalize the basis for evaluating the thickness, lateral extent, and relative age of rock formations," there were a variety of problems with his system so that it faded out as the 1800s progressed [Montgomery, 102]. Werner's views also could be fitted to the biblical view, albeit with more than a few 24-hour days needed for the steps before the creation of humans.

James Hutton. A Scotsman, James Hutton (1726-1797), is in many respects considered the father of geology. Like some before him, especially Steno, he saw that many parts of the current landscape were composed of land that must once have been below the sea, given the signs of sea life similar to what he saw on contemporary seashores embedded in the inland rocks. Therefore, the current landscape was not an original landscape. And, in order for the current landscape to have been produced, land had to coalesce from the loose materials on the bottom of the seas to form rocks, and then had to be elevated above the levels of the oceans in order to become dry land. Under these circumstances, one of Hutton's contributions was to see this as an ongoing and nearly infinite cycle for natural history [Montgomery, 103, 109]. Unlike most, Hutton did not assume a great flood played a major role somehow and, in any case a flood could not account for the consolidation into rock. Hutton's alternative explanation was based on the everyday forces of erosion via wind, water, and waves, along with repeated cycles of uplift. Although Werner's view tended to be predominant among natural philosophers at the time, "Hutton's continual experimentation with mineral chemistry convinced him that rocks contained a lot of material that would not dissolve in water," such that they could not precipitate out of the seas in the first place [Montgomery, 104]. Hutton surmised that heat and pressure—under the great weight of sediments above—were the only viable alternatives for creating rock beds [Montgomery, 104]. Hutton's views were first presented in two lectures in 1784. When published in 1788, his views tended to be received as too dismissive of the idea of creation as well as of more typically acceptable geologic time frames; his views were also seen as too cyclical in character, and too much like a warmed-over Aristotelianism's infinite Earth [Montgomery, 105-106].

Hutton proceeded to try to demonstrate that his theory was better than Werner's. One possible test led to Hutton's search for and discovery of granite lava intrusions into sedimentary rocks, which showed that these intrusions were younger and had to have occurred after the sedimentary rocks were formed [Montgomery, 106]. Such intrusions also supported Hutton's ideas that heat and pressure within the Earth were viable as a force producing uplift.

Among the Earth's phenomena that would totally preclude a short geologic history, or Werner's views, are what geologists call "unconformities." Although unconformities can occur even between nearly horizontal rock layers, such as some of those seen in the Grand Canyon, they are clearest when a horizontal surface layer overlies an underlying sedimentary bed that has been seriously contorted—for example, folded, bent, or even tilted nearly to the vertical, due to extremes of pressure (usually along with heat) having been exerted on them, typically when they were below the surface of the Earth. In 1791, Hutton discovered a very clear unconformity along the eastern Scottish coast at Siccar Point (with a near-horizontal sedimentary rock bed atop a vertical sedimentary rock bed) and realized what it meant.

He also successfully convincingly conveyed the implications/meaning of this discovery to his two traveling companions on a coastal voyage, one of whom was John Playfair, a mathematician and professor.

Given that "the law of superposition" made the horizontal layer on top younger than the bed beneath it, such an unconformity indicated that there had to have been a lot of time elapsed between the time when the lower and upper layers were laid down—otherwise the upper layer would have been similarly contorted, or the lower layer would be horizontal like the upper one.

Hutton's book in 1795, *Theory of the Earth, with Proofs and Illustrations,* has long been recognized as the first real geology book, though he also drew on some French predecessors in realizing the importance of rivers in sculpting valleys [Thornbury, 5-6]. But Hutton died while the work was still incomplete and under-edited, so finalizing that work and explaining Hutton's views became the work of his faithful friend John Playfair who, in 1802, published *Illustrations of the Huttonian Theory of the Earth.* Playfair also strengthened Hutton's arguments about the erosive forces of rivers over time by referring to evidence from mountain valleys. Valleys diverging "in all directions from the center of mountain ranges … could not have been carved … by a single current sweeping across the terrain," nor could mountain valleys at right angles to each other or "perpendicular to the overall trend of the drainage from a mountain range [Montgomery, 112].

Hutton (with Playfair) made an immensely old Earth and the idea of deep time thinkable. However, naturalists in Hutton's time were not yet ready to accept an immensely old Earth, and many were uncomfortable about the absence in Hutton's work of a Noachian Flood as an important geologic force of some kind, and at least one charged Hutton with atheism. Instead, Hutton had faith that "the perfection of God's principles favored slow geological change" [Montgomery, 108].

In any case, "any way one looked at it, the eons necessary to explain … Hutton's two rounds of uplift and erosion [at Siccar Point] did not fit with a literal reading of Genesis" [Montgomery, 109].

Hutton's "greatest contribution came in expounding the concept that 'the present is the key to the past'"—though that wording is from Sir Charles Lyell, Hutton's historically important successor [Thornbury, 6]. This means that the Earth as people see it today resulted from geologic forces in the past that are the same as those in operation today. However, there is a key consideration that is too readily overlooked in this idea. Hutton's stance was that the processes themselves were uniform *but not necessarily the rates.*

Lyell was to become the leading geologist after 1830 when he published volume one of his principles of geology. It was Lyell "who became the great exponent of uniformitarianism" and who established "the doctrine of *uniformitarianism* in opposition to that of catatrophism" [Thornbury, 7]. While Lyell was definitely persuaded by the evidence away from the possibility of a single flood-based geology, the tenor of the times in 1831, when he was just formalizing his career and hoping for a much-need professorial position, resulted in a dilemma. Several clergymen each had a veto over any professorial appointment—and that elicited a letter from Lyell that did an "artful dance" around the issue, saying that "although it was clear that the Flood could not have covered the entire planet, there was no evidence" of an absence of a deluge affecting the Earth in the last 3-4,000 years [Switek, 136].

Evidence, Known Early but Viewed Differently, that Supported an Old Earth. Among the reasons that geologists abandoned flood geology as a major force in creating Earth's landscapes is that many mountains, including the Alps (and Everest), are composed in large parts of limestone with fossils of sea creatures (shells, trilobites, etc.)

embedded in them. While a few geologists as late as the early 19th century still used Noah's Flood to deposit those beds, there were just too many problems with that scenario and it was abandoned (e.g., see the account of William Buckland, above). To ask that a great flood as it receded both deposit sediments in high places, rather than almost exclusively in low places, and carve the mountains at the same time, just didn't make sense. In any case, shells do not float; if anything, they would have been deposited in low places. Moreover, the shells (etc.) in the limestone needed time (and pressure and/or heat—though that mechanism was not then recognized by many geologists) to turn into stone. Similarly, shells and bones needed more than just deposition to get inside solid rock (like shale, as they sometimes do). Impressions of plant leaves in coal posed similar problems. Plus, that some or even many of the creatures embedded in the rocks were extinct didn't fit with anything in the Bible either, or with the human conclusion that the deity would be unwilling to destroy any of the creation he had labeled as good. And if instead the mountains were raised up after the flood, why was there no record of humans perceiving mountain-building on anywhere near such a scale, whether written in the Bible or elsewhere, within a post-flood timeline going back to only about 2600 BCE?

CHAPTER 36

Darwin's Contribution: Identifying and Marshalling Evidence to Show that Descent with Modification (Natural Selection) in an Environment, Acting on Variability within a Species, Is the Mechanism by Which Evolution Proceeds

Darwin's claim to fame is not the idea of evolution, which had predecessors, but that evolution (descent with modification) proceeds mainly by means of natural selection (with "sexual selection" something of a variant). Among the predecessors for the idea of evolution was Jean-Baptiste Lamarck (1744-1829). Lamarck supported evolution via inheritable individual adaptations, meaning, in modern terms, that acquired characteristics could be passed on genetically [Switek, 38-39]. Also important was an anonymously written but easy-to-read, multi-edition book first printed in 1844 by the publisher (and anonymous author) Robert Chambers, which was called *Vestiges of the Natural History of Creation*. The book asserted the reality of evolution, that Providence had established natural laws by which it operated, and that evolution led to higher and higher forms, including humans [Switek, 57]. However, this book provided little or no evidence pertaining to the mechanism by which evolution might occur, and was also scary and scandalizing in that it "bestialized" humans by indicating that they too had evolved from lower forms [Switek, 57]. People were not ready to believe such a bolt-out-of-the-blue, but there were readers aplenty and the arguments in it were included alongside Darwin's in the Chambers Encyclopedia of 1880.

As Darwin accumulated more and more evidence to support his theory and developed his arguments over decades, Alfred Wallace (1823-1913), a naturalist-adventurer and correspondent with Darwin, prepared a short article about his newly developed ideas, including natural selection as the mechanism for evolution, and sent it to Darwin in 1858. In an effort to be fair, Darwin jointly presented some of his preliminary materials and Wallace's paper at the same meeting, and hurried along in finalizing his book, *The Origin of Species* [Switek, 61-62], which was published in 1859.

There is no need here to review piece-by-piece the kinds of evidence for natural selection that Darwin assembled—evidence that was far ranging across the plant and animal kingdoms. There was a lot of evidence but, given the limited knowledge of the time, it necessarily fell short of conclusiveness. A very significant part of Darwin's contribution was pulling together such a wide range of evidence in support of evolution and natural selection, using principles such as faunal succession and superposition, among others, in his reasoning. My purposes here do not involve trying to compare Darwin's version of natural selection with what is believed now. Far more important are the mountains of evidence, some in entirely new areas of research, that have been discovered *since* the publication of the *Origin*. This evidence testifies to the old age of the Earth, the fact of evolution, and the validity of natural selection as the central theme in the theory of evolution. And it is the denial of all the confirmatory evidence, including the old but especially the new, that constitutes one of the major cultural insanities of our time. And, as we shall also see, this denial is no minor matter.

Even in Darwin's time, some kind of inheritability could be safely assumed just by examining characteristics of human families. Those who thought about such matters tended to believe that the characteristics of the two parents were averaged. No one really had any idea yet about genetics or how that process might operate. But many people, educated and uneducated alike, were well aware of the results of the work of selective breeding, especially of animals such as sheep and dogs, where widely divergent breeds of dogs were rapidly proliferating at the time. The history of domesticated species such as these helped Darwin to realize that one key to evolution was that there must be variation within a population for selection to operate, and indeed, insofar as it could be perceived at the time, there almost always was.

Among the most famous evidence for evolution is a number of somewhat similar birds with different beaks, that Darwin had brought back from different islands in the Galapagos. Those birds, upon close anatomical inspection by a specialist in birds, were all labeled as finches (though "tanager" would have been closer). Darwin came to realize that this indicated that they stemmed from one kind of finch and that their beak characteristics had evolved because of the relative degree of success with the differing food sources on each particular island. And thus that environmental change was one of the factors driving evolution.

Another important line of evidence came from the bony structures of vertebrates, with structurally equivalent bones, such as the three major arm bones (with the humerus connecting the shoulder to the elbow, followed by both the radius and the ulna connecting the elbow to the wrist). These bones are all clearly present, with varying degrees of difference according to their usage, in swimmers (fish, whales), flyers (birds, bats), walkers (amphibians, reptiles, mammals), and graspers (monkeys, apes, humans). Embryology provided especially important evidence too because early-life embryos of the vertebrates all look remarkably alike, except for size. Darwin also recognized that there were non-functional vestiges of evolutionary ancestors in many species and that, although animals were well-adapted to their environment, there were also imperfections that made no sense if a creator had been directly involved, but which made good sense if the process was evolution. Darwin also pretty much figured out how sexual selection fit into the overall evolutionary picture—for example, the male peacock is much inhibited in flight by his immense tail feathers, but males with the bigger tails also got the most matings, thus preserving themselves through their genes rather than by longevity.

Darwin was something of a student of geology and found Charles Lyell's 3-volume series on geology (published 1830-1833) very informative, reading each book while sailing around the world as the naturalist on the ship Beagle. As the journey proceeded, Darwin often went ashore, sometimes for weeks on end, to study the geology and search for fossils, especially in South America. In the process, he discovered a number of species new to science, and carefully noted their situation in the rocks in which they were embedded (and the surrounding rocks). Few of the finds involving bones were anything like complete, but many of the shells were wholes. The paleo-anatomists at the time, such as Richard Owen (taking over the mantle of leadership from Cuvier), had become quite good at identifying creatures from limited fossil evidence. Of course some partial fossils were initially misclassified, but many of those were soon adjusted with the benefit of additional specimens. Darwin referred his various finds to a number of specialists, depending on the character of the find.

Darwin's careful study of atolls—on which he was to publish his first book in 1842—helped confirm that some of Earth's rocks resulted from the effects of very slow normal processes (the sinking of a volcanic island core and the corresponding slow build-up of the corals ringing that core). Although Darwin's study led Lyell to modify his next edition (he hadn't been very far off), Lyell "'was so overcome with delight that he danced about'" at hearing from Darwin about his findings regarding atolls (presumably because of the uniformitarian implications) [cited in Adrian Lister, *Darwin's Fossils: The Collection that Shaped the Theory of Evolution*, 177]. While Lyell included Darwin's theory of evolution in his 1863 edition, he was slow to accept the absence of divine providence in nature [Lister, 213]. Clearly though, a long Earth history does give evolution time to occur.

Darwin found marine fossils high in the Andes which were less like fossils of more modern species than the ones he found near the coast. And that meant that the species in the mountains were older and, of course, that the mountains had been uplifted from a once-sunken state. From 1846 to 1854, Darwin undertook a study of barnacles, producing a thousand-page manuscript. He was hoping that a detailed examination of one type of organism would yield evidence to help prove his ideas about evolution [Lister, 204]. (The barnacle fossils spanned 200 million years.) In this study, Darwin found "considerable variation *within* many species" without which natural selection could not occur; and, among living barnacle species, he could see "plausible links in an evolutionary chain" [Lister, 204]. (His evidence on intra-species variation was otherwise restricted to domesticated species—but included the fact that the many varieties of pigeons all came from a single species of rock dove.)

Darwin also drew from Thomas Robert Malthus (1766-1834) the idea that more offspring are born than can possibly survive. (With 100% survival of offspring, many species would in very few generations overrun their food supply, and then the Earth.) Malthus' ideas helped Darwin realize that natural selection was the key to survival/

non-survival. In terms of evolution, the young must survive long enough to successfully reproduce (which in some animals even requires parenting by both sexes up to their progeny's adulthood, in each succeeding generation).

Darwin's fossil evidence constitutes two of the 14 chapters in the *Origin of Species* [Lister, 207]. Darwin was apologetic about the incompleteness and gaps in the fossil record, and the "missing links." But he could explain why there were good reasons for the huge gaps in the fossil record, and he "argues convincingly that the fossil record, as imperfectly known as it was back then, is still strongly supportive of his ideas" [Donald R. Prothero, *Evolution: What the Fossils Say and Why It Matters*, xix]. And as the years passed, more and more fossil evidence came to light, all adding to the credibility of evolution.

Fossils Discovered Shortly After *The Origin of Species* Was Published

Because fossils played such a crucial role in opening human vistas to a longer span of Earth's existence, and in the rejection of simplistic biblical accounts of a worldwide flood as the (assumed) causative agent of the current landscape, I am including additional information about fossils discovered in the first decades after Darwin published *The Origin*. In the year after Darwin first published the *Origin*, the first Archaeopteryx fossil, with impressions of feathers alongside its bones, was discovered. It very much seemed to be a stunning cross between reptiles and birds that the British Museum procured two years later, in 1862 [Switek, 95]. Although this specimen had no head, another complete and confirmatory specimen was discovered in 1877—with clearly toothed jaws and, as before, impressions of feathers [Switek, 105]. The earlier specimen was mentioned cautiously in the 4th edition of Darwin's *Origin of Species* in 1866, and emphasized in the 5th edition as a key new bridge between reptiles and birds [Lister, 208-210]. Moreover, the closeness of Archaeopteryx and Compsognathus skeletons, the latter being a small, fast, meat-eating dinosaur, were also pointed out, though as contemporaries (from the same quarry), the line of descent could not have been direct from that era's Compsognathus to that era's Archaeopteryx [Lister, 209-210]. By 1872, in the last edition (6th) of the *Origin*, Darwin could also cite fossil specimens from the evolutionary lines of whales (Zeuglodon and Squalodon, which had rudimentary hind leg protrusions and non-peg teeth more typical of other mammals than modern meat-eating whales), a sea cow (Halitherium, with rudimentary hind limbs), and an earlier horse (Hipparion, with 3 toes instead of a hoof). Accordingly, he affirmed that the "'great leading facts in palaeontology *agree admirably* with the theory of descent with modification through variation and natural selection'" [Lister, 210; Lister's emphasis].

Although human ancestry is not a subject in the *Origin of Species*, in 1871 Darwin published the *Descent of Man, and Selection in Relation to Sex*. In it he predicted that the remains of human ancestors would be found, and quite possibly in Africa, given that that is the location of animals seemingly most like humans (i.e., more of the great apes that seemed closer to humans than did orangutans). See Plate 4.9 for a statue of Darwin at The Natural History Museum in London.

A Snapshot of Where Evolution Stood in 1880

We can get a sense of where evolution and Darwinism stood in the intellectual community in English-speaking lands if we look to a British encyclopedia, but in this case with additions by American authorities [*Library of Universal Knowledge: A Reprint of the Last (1880) Edinburgh and London Edition of Chambers's Encyclopedia with Copious Additions by American Editors*]. The American contributions are all additions or enlargements, and not changes, within a system which clarifies which source is which. In this encyclopedia, the entry for "evolution" refers the reader to "species," but there are also entries for "Darwin" and "Darwinism." Under "Darwinism" (in an American-only addition), the entry concludes: "It is evident that from his treasury of facts, widely divergent systems of evolution may be drawn, according as the evolution which he has presented as a fact is accounted for by referring its cause or its working force to one or another set of principles" [*Library of Universal Knowledge*, Vol. IV, 617].

Plate 4.9: Statue of Charles Darwin by Sir Joseph Boehm, at the Natural History Museum, London. Photo by the author.

The original British entry under "Darwin" mostly describes his publications, but with respect to the *Origin* describes Darwin's theory, noting too that "this theory has excited controversies which are not yet laid to rest; but it has been embraced by many of the ablest naturalists, and has already induced great changes in the methods of biology and kindred sciences" [*Library of Universal Knowledge*, Vol. IV, 616]. In addition, its publication in 1859 made Darwin's name become "'familiar as a household word' to the mass of educated and semi-educated Englishmen" [*Library of Universal Knowledge*, Vol. IV, 616]. In supporting evolution (and having accepted the fossil evidence for species having arisen at many times in Earth's history), Thomas Huxley (1825-1895), a biologist specializing in comparative anatomy who was also sometimes labeled "Darwin's Bulldog," pointed out too that supposing each species was put in place by a distinct act of a creator was "unsupported by tradition or revelation" [cited under "species," English text, Chambers Encyclopedia, *Library of Universal Knowledge*, Vol. XIII, 692]. In summarizing the reception in Britain of Darwin's "Evolution Theory" as it was then called, the Chambers British version re "species" tells us that "the opponents of Darwinism are perhaps more numerous than its adherents," being concerned about "the foundations of religion and social order" (much like today, it seems). Among scientists, opponents with "legitimate arguments" that were "difficult to answer satisfactorily" emphasized the lack of transitional fossils (the remedy for which was slowly under way), and the need for better proof of how organs evolved from rudimentary to complex; they also expressed doubt about the extent of effects on species of the struggle for existence (i.e., about whether natural selection is the principal agent of species change—which was to remain unsettled for some time yet). The article concludes with "Nevertheless, the doctrine seems to be working its way into general acceptance" [*Library of Universal Knowledge*, Vol. XIII, 694].

CHAPTER 37

After Darwin

With the continuing accumulation of fossil finds, including in the "dinosaur wars" (or "bone wars") before 1900 in the United States (with O. C. Marsh and E. D. Cope competing vigorously for fossils for their museums), the idea of evolution became much more widely accepted. In time, the fossil lineages would be so good that they "would have astonished Darwin and his contemporaries" [Lister, 215]. Lyell, Darwin and their peers knew how hard it was to fossilize land-dwelling specimens. For fossilization to occur, not only is more-or-less immediate burial of a specimen required (e.g., in flood debris, in mud, or by volcanic ash) but, with all but the lowest land subject to erosion, the chances to destroy any such preserved animal are much higher than the chances of its preservation. Further, the fossilized animal would subsequently have to reappear on the surface of the earth within the last 250 years or so (i.e., when at least some people knew enough to extract it carefully and conserve it).

Still, "there was a period from about 1895 to about 1925, when Darwinism came in for a great deal of criticism… from many of the leading biologists" [Julian Huxley, "Introduction to the Mentor Edition," in Charles Darwin, *Origin of Species by Means of Natural Selection…*, xi-xii]. One way or another, for most biologists, natural selection as the driver of evolution was just too speculative. In addition, others gravitated toward a more Lamarckian view of evolution (greater inheritability of individually acquired characteristics).

But the 1866 report of work done by Gregor Mendel on the inheritance of certain characteristics in pea plants was rediscovered in the early 1900s. Mendel had recognized dominant and recessive biological "factors" (later relabeled genes) that served as the conveyances of an organism's characteristics. But his work was initially used to put too much emphasis on mutations as evolution's driving force. Subsequently, advances in "genetics showed that large mutations were rarer and of far less biological importance than those of small extent, and that, apparently, continuous evolutionary change could be, and often was, brought about by the accumulation of numerous small discontinuous mutations under the guidance of natural selection" [Huxley, xii]. In the United States, evolution and a long geologic time span was accepted enough so that fundamentalist-conservative locales, such as Tennessee, passed laws against its teaching (leading to the famous Scopes trial of 1925). Despite the widely publicized failure of the anti-evolutionists to make their case (and the mere slap-on-the-wrist punishment for Scopes), a number of other states went on to pass laws against the teaching of evolution, so evolution tended to become less and less prevalent in high school curricula. Even so, by the 1930s, further advances in statistics applied to biological science helped lead to a new synthesis supportive of evolution together with natural selection as the driving force. Subsequently, great leaps forward in the sciences, especially in genetics and molecular biology, plate tectonics and radiometric dating, the human and animal fossil record, and astronomy, have all been supportive of an ancient Earth, and strengthened the support for an evolutionary process driven primarily by natural selection. The general results from all these advances and more are included in a table summarizing evidence confirmatory of evolution and geologic time (see below).

But there were still distortions prior to very recent times in many scientists' views of evolution—distortions which had come to dominate as far back as Herbert Spencer (in Darwin's time), in which evolution via the guidance of Providence led to progress, to ever higher development, including in the ethical and moral realms [Michael Ruse, *Defining Darwin: Essays on the History and Philosophy of Evolutionary Biology*]. Ruse makes the case that this continued, albeit in an ever-more attenuated state, until recent times. For example, the earliest versions of this treatment had seen humans as the epitome to which evolution was leading, and other current animals as the peak achievements in their realms as well (e.g., horses, elephants). The current scientific view is that evolution is a neutral process as to outcome rather than directional, and not a matter of inevitability nor of the plan of any deity. Evolution is driven mainly by natural selection in changing environments, with random mutations in the gene pool also offering slightly different variations upon which natural selection can act. Although greater complexity has indeed developed over time (given such a low start), already there have been five mass extinctions that each resulted in a substantial do-over that eliminated most species.

Once again, however, the key point here was to sketch important parts of the general history of the idea of evolution and of geologically "deep time" as part of an effort to show how the ever-accumulating evidence has proven that the Xtian holy book is hopelessly misleading as a guide to science in these areas. So now we're ready to look at a summary of the current evidence in support of deep time and evolution, partly to better understand how broadly science as a whole is intertwined with these two ideas. This will shed an even brighter light on why continued opposition to these two ideas partakes of cultural insanity. That is, we're not just talking harmless errors in beliefs or one or another unsound worldview here, but serious distortions of science and reality, and associated political forces that have emerged to cripple the entire society in the United States and undermine the potential for human development in many respects.

CHAPTER 38

Summary of Evidence Confirmatory of Evolution & Geologic Time

Introduction

In *Why Evolution Is True*, Jerry A. Coyne offers six basic components to the modern theory of evolution. These are: "evolution, gradualism, speciation, common ancestry, natural selection, and nonselective mechanisms of evolutionary change" [Coyne, 3]. Evolution is now recognized as both a fact and a theory. "A theory becomes a fact (or a 'truth') when so much evidence has accumulated in its favor—and there is no decisive evidence against it—that virtually all reasonable people will accept it" [Coyne, 16]. And for some time there have been mountains of evidence that make it rationally impossible to deny that evolution is a fact and, for that matter, that natural selection has played a major role in it.

A scientific "theory" also needs to be differentiated from the popular meaning of the term, as "hunch." However, scientific theories do range considerably in the strength of their foundation, at their best having the strength "of general laws, principles, or causes of something known or observed" [*Oxford English Dictionary*, cited in Coyne, 15], even if sometimes being rather small in scope. At the less-supported end, so-called theories probably should be called "hypotheses." In any case, a "theory" should summarize and derive from all that is known to date—although, especially in the early stages of exploration of a subject, that may not preclude competing theories (and hypotheses for study which will shed light on which one is more likely to be correct). Although defenders of the theory of evolution tend to emphasize the strong end of this definition—which indeed the theory of evolution epitomizes—it is nevertheless somewhat misleading to suggest that scientists do not also use the word "theory" to encompass much less and with much less surety as well—perhaps "would-be" theories (e.g., summarizing what little is known so far). For example, in discussing why sexual reproduction is better than parthenogenesis (simple division of one life form into two identical ones), Coyne notes that although we haven't figured out what the advantage is, sexual reproduction "must have some huge evolutionary advantage," about which there are "no shortage of *theories*" [Coyne, 155; emphasis added]. In any case, "for a theory to be considered scientific, it must be *testable and make verifiable predictions* [Coyne, 15; italics in original].

Within the theory of evolution, it is the mechanisms of evolution, and perhaps especially their relative importance, that continue to be debated to varying extents by scientists. For example, considering Coyne's six basic components of the theory of evolution (above), how much evolution occurs gradually as contrasted with (more) rapidly is debated, and can also be seen in terms of geologic time or the number of generations of a species (with microbe evolution obviously not needing all that much time). Similarly debated is how much evolution is "punctuated" (a term used by Stephen J. Gould and Niles Eldredge in a 1972 book), that is, occasionally rapid within a generally slow process. Coyne notes that his "gradualism" does not mean that "each species evolves at an even pace"; rather, "a single species evolves faster or slower as evolutionary pressures wax and wane" [Coyne, 4]. Indeed, "when natural selection is strong, as when an animal or plant colonizes a new environment, evolutionary change can be fast" [Coyne, 4]. When existing variants are subjected to high positive selection pressures, math shows that the DNA (deoxyribonucleic acid) of favored variants produces change remarkably fast [Carroll, 48-50]. Similarly, even Darwin's finches on the Galapagos Islands continued to adapt/evolve when a multi-year drought struck the islands in 1977 and the finches on some islands were forced to adapt to less food or new food sources, or die out [Jonathan B. Losos, *Improbable Destinies: Fate, Chance, and the Future of Evolution*, 117-121]. And some birds have had to adjust their times of migration (or face a serious threat to the survival of their young) due to global warming trends in their environments in order to continue nesting at a time that still corresponds to the peak of food availability (insects) for their young. And though many insects may be becoming imperiled, some have adapted to the new environmental challenge—insecticides targeted to kill them. But apart from viruses, microbial adaptations to antibiotics likely sets the speed record.

Before the middle of the 20th century or so, scientists used to think that all DNA was active, with each gene linked to one trait, with little or nothing of influence on development beyond that, apart from natural selection working on the variation within each species. But in more recent times, scientists have realized that many genes don't act as code for much of anything, or do so for traits that are little involved with selection pressures, while other genes actually (and clearly) do a lot, especially regulatory genes, which are not very numerous at all. Instead, high percentages of DNA, for example up to 90% in humans, is "silent" or "junk" DNA [Prothero, *Evolution*, 95-98] or non-functioning "pseudogenes," some or many having been used in ancestral forms going all the way back, as witnessed in the weird replications of the past occurring in embryos [Coyne, 66-67]. Yet more recently scientists have also discovered master regulatory genes, or homeotic genes

("Hox" genes), that turn other genes off and on in an orchestrated way, initially to build our bodies from egg through embryo through birth [Prothero, *Evolution*, 101]. Moreover, some regulatory genes continue to be active beyond birth, and some have been found to have some responsiveness to our environment, sometimes in ways that are then inherited, affecting how genes play out (are expressed) in subsequent generations [Prothero, *Evolution*, 96].

Apart from the environment and natural selection, probably the most important influences on DNA are random mutation from cosmic and terrestrial radiation, and transcription errors when chromosomes divide as part of fertilization of offspring. Because so much DNA is unused, and because so many traits are coded for by more than one gene, most mutational changes remain both unused (as far as scientists have been able to tell) and unimportant, though a few will be serious or even fatal (e.g., sometimes producing miscarriages). But there has even been a concrete example involving one of the simplest bacterium—one that reproduces asexually—simply divides to replicate itself—in which multiple mutations, the first initially almost if not entirely outside selection pressures, ultimately combined to produce a very significant genetic change [Losos, 258-259]. Further, some amount of genetic drift can occur over time, especially in any small, isolated population. And sometimes this genetic drift potentiates subsequent change.

Competition among males for mates, as in elephant seals and deer, or female choice of males) are both forms of sexual selection, where the latter too is within the bounds of natural selection, even though it may not select for longevity in the males. An earlier example treated by Darwin involved peacocks. In peacocks, more flamboyant tails with more "eyespots" represent better health and strong genes and attract more mates; and since male fowl don't participate in rearing the chicks, they still fulfill the specifications for natural selection by successfully passing on the genes of the hardy, ensuring a strong species (with even gaudier tails). Sexual selection can also be important in driving differences between males and females in traits such as size and physique. Nature selects for breeding and the successful raising of the young.

A major cause of speciation (evolution of new species) arises when portions of a single species get separated from one another such that each begins to evolve separately, developing very small differences at first and then eventually enough to become subspecies and finally to the point where the groups do not, and finally, cannot, interbreed successfully. A species may also respond to environmental changes in ways that lead to changes away from its ancestral species. But the fossil record also shows that some species lasted for millions of years. Absent environmental change, a large interbreeding population is thought to remain more stable over time because conventional DNA configurations overwhelm mutations.

And now that entire genomes can be sequenced (their entire DNA structure known), comparisons of DNA across life forms has become possible, such that the relative proximity of those forms, evolutionarily speaking, can be at least roughly ascertained. As a further confirmation of evolution, however, "these molecular methods have not produced much change in the pre-DNA era trees of life" [Coyne, 10]. For a time, changes in DNA, which seemed initially to occur at a regular rate, were used as geologic "clocks" to estimate how long ago different species diverged from a common ancestor, but doubts about the regularity of such change in some cases have also led to greater caution in interpretation in this regard [Prothero, *Evolution*, 97]. This caution is appropriate, it seems to me, in that it better reflects that evolution may sometimes occur much more rapidly even if random mutation rates are fairly constant. In addition, negative mutations that matter are rapidly weeded out [Carroll]. With so much unused DNA available to draw upon, it seems quite likely to me too that, one way or another, evolution will sometimes be much quicker than "normal"/ gradual—for example, when environmental conditions change, or when unused niches become available for any organism that can make use of them.

The Evolutionary Context for Religion

Science proceeds on the basis of methodological naturalism; its methods assume natural causes; after all, the whole point is to understand how nature works. Accordingly, science leaves the supernatural—deities/gods—out of its examinations and theories entirely. Science also needs to do that because, when a deity is resorted to as the explanation, there is no more cause-effect to study—which is pretty much where things stood back in the Middle Ages (see Part Three).

Because science is also probabilistic, statements about even the strongest and clearest findings are very highly likely to be true, but cannot be proven with a 100% assurance. Prothero calls evolution "proven beyond a reasonable doubt by an amazing convergence of evidence" [Prothero, *Evolution*, 158]—evidence that I will sketch in the table below.

However, scientific theories do arise in part out of their times and the scientists are enmeshed in the culture(s) of those times. Thus, as we saw in the previously, the attachments to the Xtianity of the time led almost all early scientists to attribute fossils to a Noachian Flood—even after fossils were understood as formerly living organisms and after the realization that fossilized shells were found in the highest mountains. But scientific paradigms sometimes shift too, shedding new light on old findings, or even setting some aside, such that the theory and worldview in which they were enmeshed are seen in a new light and sometimes supplanted, much as Copernicus's work launched the paradigm shift from geocentrism to heliocentrism. (See also Thomas Kuhn's *Structure of Scientific Revolutions*.) A more recent example involves plate tectonics (see table below). Who knows, we may yet come to a different understanding of the sun's place in the universe (and ours along with it), but heliocentrism is extremely unlikely to be supplanted. And Newton's mechanics have been qualified by Einstein's relativity and quantum theory at the atomic level, but still seem to work just fine otherwise.

Standing the test of time provides an important confirmation of the viability of a theory, and ideas about an old Earth and evolution with natural selection playing a major role have now more than done that. But there are always questions that remain less than totally resolved in any science, such as the relative importance of the various mechanisms of evolution. And scientific findings often give rise to new questions. The process of science is one that continually updates itself.

Science has also not yet provided a strong possible solution for how life arose on Earth (again see table below). So, some might say that a deity was responsible for creating life, thereby filling in that "gap" in knowledge. Alas, as above, anyone who believes that then has no need to look further because the problem is solved. However, this kind of "god of the gaps" has proven dangerous for religious beliefs because so many gaps that were once thought to need filling by a deity have been eliminated or greatly reduced, including in many fossil lineages, in some cases with stunning mid-lineage fossils like the Archaeopteryx in Darwin's time. The same problem with closing gaps has occurred for other creationist or intelligent design (ID) stances—such as asserting the irreducible complexity of the eye, or of the bacterial flagellum (see below re ID). In any case, it is now very clear that at some early stage in life's history evolution began to operate and carried life to much greater diversity and complexity.

Nevertheless, science cannot offer evidence to prove anything about unexamined or unexaminable phenomena, and so cannot deny that there is a supreme being of one kind or another, a creator perhaps, or a deity that launched the universe with a big bang—even if that universe otherwise seems thereafter to have proceeded according to natural laws. But no clear evidence of an intervention by a deity has been found either (and not all religions have the same time lines or creation stories). Still, science also cannot deny that a deity intervened at selected points in the history of the universe, for example, in an act that launched life on Earth, even though science seems to be making continual progress toward solving that particular one naturalistically (see below). Another typical recourse to a deity involves the transition from apes to humans by the addition of a soul or a kind of self-consciousness. But even the scientific evidence pertaining to the evolution of humans has now discovered steps in that evolution that make any intervention by deities seem less than necessary. Step-by-evolutionary-step, for example, proto-humans made advances in social coordination and interaction, in tool making, in controlling the technology of fire, etcetera—and their progeny proceeded to developed a bigger brain because that helped them survive. Later, Homo neanderthalensis practiced burials and left ceremonial (?) markings on cave walls, while Cro-Magnons (Homo sapiens) made more advanced tools and more sophisticated cave paintings. What is becoming likely for humans is in general what science can do with respect to evolution—to say that so much has been found that there seems to be little or no need for a deity to have intervened. Although a deity's intervention cannot be precluded by science, natural explanations have sufficed and it is far better for advancing knowledge not to short-circuit the searching by resorting to a deity for any missing explanations.

The only religious alternative to evolution and deep time that at first may *seem* to approach viability is the "God the Deceiver" hypothesis—a role not only incompatible with other features usually assigned to deities, but a role usually left to the Devil in Xtianity. And if the Bible is considered inerrant, even the god-the-deceiver hypothesis failed miserably with Noah's Flood—because the Bible's words cannot be made to match the deceiver's made-to-seem-old geology (see below).

Summarizing Evidence Confirmatory of Evolution And Geologic Time

Area of Study & What Learned

Geology and Plate Tectonics

Much of the most relevant aspects of geology has been covered in the text, or in the entries about fossils (but see below too). Nevertheless, plate tectonics should be added because it has come to be able to explain so much of Earth's geology, from earthquakes to the rift valley in Africa, to the volcanic ring of fire around the Pacific Ocean rim and the rise of mountain chains near the edges of continental land masses. Plate tectonics processes are so slow—movement of up to about an inch a year, per modern satellite measurements—as to necessitate an old Earth. Perhaps the most obvious example here is that South America could not have "drifted" as far from Africa as it has in a mere 6-10,000 years. (At their closest, they are now about 1,600 miles apart.) In addition, the Earth undergoes magnetic reversals—where compasses point to the South Pole instead of the North Pole, every 500,000 years or so, on average. Although these have been dated by radiometric methods (see below), which are falsely dismissed by creationists (see below), evidence for them appears in the alignment of magnetizable crystals in lava flows. There have been 23 reversals counted from the last 5 million years [Plummer, McGeary, & Carlson, 429]. Again, there is simply nowhere near enough time for anything like this to have occurred in an Earth that is 6-10,000 years old.

Geographic Distribution of Animals

South America became isolated by movement of tectonic plates in a process beginning well before the demise of the non-bird dinosaurs, disconnecting it from Africa and from Antarctica-Australia. Thus fossil mammals found in South America tend to be unique—and unrelated to the current populations of mammals elsewhere—with the exception of a few of the oldest lineages, including marsupials, which are otherwise common only in Australia. Similarly, in Australia, there are almost no placental mammals either (other than bats, mice and rats), indicating an even earlier isolation. Such results would be very peculiar as an act of a deity distributing his/her animal creations around the world; moreover, it would be utterly impossible as a result of a worldwide flood—that somehow selectively destroyed only certain types of animals on some continents. And only in the last 3 million years, as the North American and South American tectonic plates joined at Panama, has there been a north-south exchange of animals between those continents.

And consider these two preposterous alternatives: 1) After landing on Mount Ararat, the two koalas on board the Ark slowly migrated from eucalyptus tree to eucalyptus tree—what they eat—all the way to Australia—even though there are no eucalyptus trees between Mt. Ararat and Indonesia and even though koalas would have to swim or float across the Torres Strait from New Guinea to Australia. 2) Similarly, after a long shuffle to the west coast of Africa, the Ark's one or two types of extremely slow sloth pairs would have had to swim across the Atlantic Ocean to get to South America.

Even more restricted distributions of animals are found on isolated *mid-ocean* volcanoes and atolls, like the Galapagos and Hawaii, where there were very few or no non-flying mammal natives of any kind. Unlike islands near continents, these islands, with a very few exceptions (animals likely arriving on debris rafts carried by ocean currents), there are no land reptiles, no amphibians, and no freshwater fish [Coyne, 108].

The importance of geography in evolution is also suggested by the fact that molecular biological results (see below) have found that humans, *except those from Africa*, share some human-specific DNA with Neanderthals.

The Fossil Record Generally

Fossils provide a remarkably complete record of hard-shelled and hard-bodied marine life. Sedimentary rock beds follow the geological law of superposition (newer rock beds on top of older), with exceptions associated with severe crustal forces. If evolution rather than (virtually) simultaneous creation is true, older marine sedimentary rock beds will contain fewer fossils like creatures alive today—and indeed, they do. Clearly, no worldwide flood could subside in a way that ordered marine fossils by their relative frequency of being alive today (their age in geologic time). And with so many marine fossil-bearing sedimentary rock beds as a guide, the *relative* date of rocks can be figured with considerable precision. Once this order is known and the much rarer terrestrial fossils have been included in the picture, the order in which evolution brought forth all life forms represented in the fossil record can be estimated fairly accurately. The history of life on earth is of course subject to revision with new fossil finds (e.g., the discovery of an occasional "relic," such as the coelacanth). But with the exception of those few relics that were thought to be extinct but weren't, *every* newly-unearthed fossil that is in its expected sequence in the rocks is another proof of evolution. And for a long time now, it could be said with virtually 100% assurance that there will be no human bones or fossils found in rock beds with dinosaur fossils, notwithstanding fake-science theme parks like the Creation Museum and Ark in Kentucky.

The Fossil Record (Tracing Specific Lineages/Filling Gaps)

As already noted, there have been intermediate fossils found from many animal lineages since the time of Darwin. Darwin found support in the fossil record, but it was a very sparse record when he first published *The Origin of Species*. But by the time of its last edition, several additional important intermediates had been found, including Archaeopteryx with its mixture of dinosaur(-reptilian) and bird characteristics, and an early whale, Basilosaurus. Among other evolutionarily noteworthy intermediate vertebrates now known are those related to today's elephants and horses; between reptiles and "mammal-like reptiles"; between birds and dinosaurs; and between humans and some of our ancestors or their evolutionary cousins. Some lineages of dinosaurs also seem remarkably complete, such as the ceratopsians (horned dinosaurs with neck shields). When Neil Shubin wanted to hunt specifically for new transitional creatures between fish and amphibians, there were only a couple of rock beds of the right age where he could look, one in northern Canada. His expedition found a very near complete specimen of "Tiktaalik." (A few relatives descending from earlier in this transition also survive today, including lungfish and mudskippers [Coyne, 38]). Similarly, newer fossil finds in Pre-Cambrian rocks have changed perspectives on what was once seen as the "Cambrian explosion" (of new life forms); that emergence is now known to have occurred over many millions of years, likely facilitated by so many unoccupied environmental niches.

Radiometric/Isotopic & Other Dating

Because of the imperative creationists feel to reject this evidence of an old Earth, this topic is also elaborated upon in the text below. Isotopes are variants on an element. Radioactive measures of age are based on the decay rates of certain radioactive isotopes into their "daughter" products. For example, over millions of years Uranium-238 decays to Lead. Such "decay" involves the emission of protons and/ or neutrons that reduce the atomic weight of the original substance (electrons are also lost), but "when protons are lost during radioactive decay, the atom becomes a different element" [Plummer, McGeary, & Carlson, 188]. Use of Carbon 14 is probably the dating technique most familiar to the public, but its reach is only about 50,000 years, so assessment of geologic ages requires the use of other, slower-to-decay radioactive elements. Among the most commonly used radioisotope measures (and their daughter products and "half-life") are: Potassium-40➔Argon-40 (1.25 billion years); Uranium-238➔Lead 206 (4.5 billion years); Uranium-235➔Lead-207 (713 million years); Thorium-232➔Lead-208 (14.1 billion years); Rubinium-87➔Strontium-87 (49 billion years); and Carbon-14➔Nitrogen-14 (5,730 years) [Plummer, McGeary, & Carlson, 188]. The "half life" is the amount of time in which half of the initial isotopc will have been converted to its daughter product; the remaining half has the same half-life, so three-quarters of the original isotope will have decayed over two half-lives. Although there will be too little left of the original isotope to enable reliable measurement after multiple half-lives, all but one or two of the half-lives noted above can span the 4.5 billion years age of the Earth. Current measurements of the amount of both the parent isotope and the daughter product, extrapolated backwards mathematically, are used to calculate the age at which the rock became a "closed system," where a closed system is one in which the rock or mineral "was sealed off so that neither parent nor daughter isotopes could enter or leave" [Plummer, McGeary, & Carlson, 190]. The most reliable dates come from lava flows, because systems become "closed" at a certain range of temperatures (and magma intrusions that never reach the surface may stay too hot to consolidate the system for a very long time).

Ensuring a rock sample to be tested comes from a still-intact closed system is important, lest the results be misleading. Comparing radioisotope-ascertained dates with geologically-determined *relative* ages of rock beds is among the ways in which the reliability of the radioactive measures has been determined [Plummer, McGeary, & Carlson, 190]. For example, radioisotope dating when tested on multiple lava flows interrupted by various lengths of time (e.g., with other rock beds between them), must provide results that are youngest for the uppermost lava flow and oldest for the deepest lava flow. In addition, dating often employs the use of more than one radioisotope, and often more than one laboratory too. The relative dates of marine-sourced rock beds all over the globe are readily determined by the fossil column so such comparisons provide a rigorous reliability check. The text below includes an important reference for additional information in this regard.

Finally, radiometric dating of moon rocks and meteorites place the age of the Earth at about 4.5 billion years, where the oldest closed-system rocks accessible and measured on Earth date to date reach almost 4.3 billion years. Earth and the other planets are thought to have consolidated from vast clouds of dust and debris orbiting the sun (clouds something like the asteroid belt remaining between mars and Jupiter), while the moon is thought to have resulted from a collision early on between the Earth and another very large object orbiting the sun.

Ice Core Dating. Ice cores from places such as Greenland and Antarctica extend back at least 800,000 and possibly 2.7 million years, long before the creation dates calculated from the Xtian holy book. (More below.)

Embryology

Some of the clearest evidence for evolution is the fact that the embryonic stages of vertebrate life much more closely resemble each other than do adult life forms. All vertebrates at the earliest stages resemble a fish embryo, with differentiation occurring subsequently into amphibians, reptiles, (dinosaurs)-birds, and mammals. Initially, they all have "a very fish-like body plan… including the predecessors of gills and a long tail" [Prothero, *Evolution*, 110]. There is more on this in the text below.

Vestigial Structures, Imperfections & Evolutionary Atavisms

Vestigial structures are leftovers from ancestors that are no longer needed by a particular animal. There are many. Examples include rudimentary eyes in blind mole rats and some blind cave-dwelling creatures, the retention by some whales and snakes of small hip bones and hind legs, and, at least partly, the human appendix and tonsils (both of which can become deadly when infected), and nipples in men. Similarly, humans often suffer from back pain, foot pain, and knee problems because evolution has not had time to work out all the kinks in our ancestors' evolution from knuckle- and four-legged-to upright walking [Prothero, *Evolution*, 39]. Sometimes animals are also born with evolutionary reversions (atavisms), such as an actual additional toe suspended on the side of the lower leg in horses, hind legs protruding from whales [Prothero, *Evolution*, 108], and even real tails on humans [see the photos in Prothero, *Evolution*, 345].

Morphology (Comparative Anatomy)

Among vertebrates, variations on the *same* bones, whether or not serving different functions in an animal's anatomy, are homologous—and demonstrate a shared common ancestor. Arm bones have not been created anew for each type of vertebrate; instead the same three bones (humerus—upper arm, and radius and ulna—lower arm), modified according to each group or species' nature, constitute the front limbs in fish that emerged from the water, amphibians, reptiles, dinosaurs, birds (wings), and mammals, including bats, whales, and apes/humans [National Academy of Science Institute of Medicine, *Science, Evolution and Creationism*, 26]. Over the history of the efforts in this field of study to depict a "tree of life," some techniques have emphasized comparing as many bones as the evidence allows, while a newer approach is to estimate on the basis of fewer, more recently-evolved characteristics, such as opposable thumbs and stereovision [Prothero, *Evolution*, 124-135]. In addition, there are analogous developments that arose to deal with similar environmental challenges but which did so via *different* ways and at different times in the evolutionary tree of life, such as the wings of birds and of bats, where the former traces back to their dinosaur ancestry and the latter to mammalian ancestry.

Genetics

With the rediscovery around 1900 of Gregor Mendel's work on peas and his recognition of dominant and recessive factors (renamed genes), acknowledgement of the mechanism of heredity started to spread. Similarly, research on chromosomes (the bearers of genes) slowly led to their emergence from obscurity. At first, genes were thought of simply, as one gene yielding one trait or characteristic. But before too long, it was found that many genes are used in the formation of all but some of the simplest traits or characteristics. As the mechanisms of heredity began to be more understood, a neo-Darwinian synthesis arose in the 1930s because it was better understood how natural selection could occur. In the early 1950s, James D. Watson and Francis H. C. Crick (with additional support) solved the puzzle of how genetic instructions were maintained in a double helix structure on chromosomes and how they were transmitted to progeny—which opened the field of genetics to study in ways previously foreclosed. The mystery of how genes were passed across generations was solved by learning how chromosomes divide in half and then re-pair with chromosomes halves from the other sex.

Molecular Biology

Atoms combine to form into molecules, and molecular biology involves the study of life at the level of molecules such as DNA and its chemical constituents. With ever-improving electronic microscopes, molecular biologists have been able to decipher segments that constitute genes on chromosomes, and more recently entire genomes, including the human genome of about 20-25,000 genes (amidst about three billion DNA molecule pairs). Among the fundamental traits shared by all living species "are the biochemical pathways that we use to produce energy," the DNA system of coding, "and how that code is read and translated into Proteins" [Coyne, 4]. This fact leads to the conclusion "that every species goes back to a single common ancestor, an ancestor who had those common traits and passed them on to its descendants" [Coyne, 5].

Molecular biologists use the relative proportion of shared DNA as a gauge of evolutionary similarity. Their studies of the genetic proximity of various animals and plants to each other has revealed evolutionary lineages that, with but few exceptions, matched what had been found by anatomists and paleontologists. For example, such studies have confirmed the greater genetic proximity of humans to the great apes than to other species (and especially to chimpanzees, via a common ancestor about 7 million years ago). Other mammals share less DNA with us (other primates being closest after the great apes), and plants even less—but still as much as half of it.

Molecular biology has also helped identify the very important role of regulatory genes and Hox genes that turn other genes on and off. It has helped in the discovery of the huge cache of "junk DNA" (DNA not used in assembling an organism), which can become a reserve, including of some mutations, that might facilitate occasional relatively quick adaptations (evolutionary change) in response to changes in selection pressure in an organism's environment. Similarly, molecular biologists are seeking to better understand how the expression of genes might be affected by interaction with the environment. A bit more detail on this particular topic was included in the Introduction to this table, above.

Astronomy

The earliest ways astronomers had for measuring the distance to stars relied on trigonometry, with two different observation points around the Earth or along the Earth's orbit, with the point of the triangle being at a star. In that way, even the ancients knew that the planets were closer than the stars. In recent centuries, units of distance measurement came to be light years, where a light year is the distance light travels in a year, at a speed of 186,282 miles per second. For example, light from a star a million light years away took a million years to reach Earth, and such literally "astronomical" distances also help to confirm an old universe (else the light would not yet have reached Earth). Nowadays, many measurements of great distance rely on the relative brightness and wave lengths of light emitted from an object, given what kind of object it is (e.g., the phase in the life of a star or the type of star being observed). For measurement of great distances, astronomers rely on a "cosmic distance ladder"—a multi-faceted set of techniques viable at various ranges. These overlapping ranges and multiple techniques can also be used as a check on one another (a little like radioactive dating of rocks). By the 1920s, telescopes were good enough to reveal that what were thought to be stars in the Milky Way (our galaxy) were instead far more distant whole galaxies. Soon thereafter it was also discovered that galaxies in the universe "are receding from each other in every direction, which implies that the universe is expanding" [National Academy of Sciences Institute of Medicine, 18]. By calculating backwards from known distances and galaxy velocities, astronomers ascertained the approximate time at which the expansion seems to have begun—when there seems to have been a "big bang." The big bang hypothesis has been supported subsequently by other measurements, and so have been the resulting estimates for the age of the universe [National Academy of Sciences Institute of Medicine, 18-20]. The estimate for the age of the universe (i.e., after the big bang) is almost 14 billion years.

Evolutionary Change Demonstrated in Human Time Spans in Medicine & Agriculture

Evolutionary change can proceed fairly rapidly in short-lived creatures with many offspring that breed or divide rapidly. The rise of resistance to antibiotics among many disease-causing bacteria is a human-threatening example. Similarly, even far more complex animals such as insect crop pests can rapidly develop resistance to farm insecticides. All that is required is for some to have survived despite the pesticide application (perhaps on the periphery of a farm field) *because* they had a little more resistance to start with. These will be the ones artificially/naturally selected to breed successfully and, under the same process, each subsequent generation will thereby develop even greater resistance. The same evolutionary process occurs with crop "weeds" and herbicides.

The Origin of Life

The origin of life, or the scientific progress in revealing how it might have occurred, are tangential or even irrelevant to the purpose here. (The crucial concern is the extent and effects of the cultural insanity of denying the immense amount of long-demonstrated evidence for geologic time and evolution after life had arisen.) As always, the lack of sufficient scientific explanation leaves open the possibility of a god-of-the-gaps theological explanation for the origin of life—but that science has not yet discovered everything is par for the course in every branch of science.

Even so, Prothero, [*Evolution*, 145-159] describes, as of 2007 or earlier, many of the advances scientists have made in seeking out how life might have arisen on Earth. Sketching such advances involves technical details that some readers may well want to skim or skip. Among the earliest experiments were those that involved studying what happens in different formulations of a chemical "primordial soup," such as was thought to represent Earth's environment at some point in time, when the soup is heated and/or zapped with electricity (as a substitute for lightning). From far simpler molecules in these soups and their atmosphere, the tests have yielded a variety of amino acids—the basic building blocks of life. The amino acids necessary for life have also been found on meteorites—which indicates they also arose one way or another in conditions prior to the formation of our solar system—so the Earth could also in some way have been "seeded." Other experiments have explored how these essential building blocks might have been assembled into complex chains of molecules. But there are also natural "templates" (special minerals, some clays) that readily assemble amino acids into complex proteins when those amino acids are present. Research reported recently on internet science websites has shown that RNA (the complex molecule that transmits DNA's instructions), which can be self-replicating and can catalyze other reactions (and is currently involved in the regulation and expression of genes), may have come into being in that way. One possible template, for example, is iron sulfide, the electric charge of which might have drawn in organic chemicals that then went on to form more complex building blocks [Prothero, *Evolution*, 153]. Iron sulfide can be found at the bottom of the sea in "black smokers" (chimneys venting hot gases and minerals), which now provide a home for the genetically simplest form of life, an Archaebacteria, that feeds off hydrogen sulfide rather than on the energy of the sun via photosynthesis [Prothero, *Evolution*, 154]. These may even be the founders of life on Earth. The properties of liquid fats in water—which retain a separate identity surrounded by a membrane—suggest a way in which cell wall-like structures might have arisen. Putting RNA inside that fat bubble may draw closer to being a self-replicating entity. Prokaryotes (which include the Archaebacteria) have their RNA and DNA enclosed within a cell, but not in a nucleus. The main step remaining would be the transition to higher forms, the Eukaryotes (all other living organisms), which do have cell nuclei. A nucleus may have arisen via a combination of the simpler cells living communally [Prothero, *Evolution*, 154-155]. In the Eukaryote plant cell, chloroplasts, which do photosynthesis, are very nearly the equivalent of cyanobacteria (a prokaryote); and mitochondria, which do respiration and energy production, are very nearly the equivalent of purple nonsulfur bacteria (a prokaryote) [Prothero, *Evolution*, 154-155]. Even within the Eukaryote cell, these "organelles" (chloroplasts, mitochondria) continue to have their own DNA and reproduce separately by cell division [Prothero, *Evolution*, 155].

Some of the Myths in Genesis

Many stories and myths have a kind of culture-based evolutionary history, some having been selected for inclusion across cultures. Among myths with such a history are the creation myth and flood story that are included in the Xtian Bible. These myths were written into what became the holy book of the Israelites/Hebrews/Jews during or after their captivity in Babylon (approximately 597 to 539 BCE), though some Hebrew writing dates to the 10th century BCE. Not only did Babylon have its own creation myth and flood story, similar to those adopted by the Hebrews but involving Babylonian deities instead, but so did the several predecessor civilizations in the fertile plains of Mesopotamia. Long before the Babylonian captivity, Abraham, the father of the Jewish people, who came from Ur, in southeastern Mesopotamia, where his family worshipped "idols" (and, presumably, would know the stories associated with them), migrated to Canaan. The flood stories are almost undoubtedly based on one or more very severe floods of the Tigris and Euphrates rivers in Mesopotamia—what is now southern Iraq. And elements of a creation myth similar to the Judeo-Xtian one can be dated to the Sumerian civilization around 4000 BCE [Prothero, *Evolution*, 27]; a related creation myth was also an active part of Babylonian culture by the 12th century BCE [Holland, Glenn S., *Religion in the Ancient Mediterranean World*, Part 2, 8], while a similar flood story dates back to 2750 BCE [Prothero, *Evolution*, 27].

CHAPTER 39

The Young-Earth Creationist Contrast

Introduction

As we have seen above, the pre-scientific understanding of the age of the Earth throughout the Middle Ages in Europe was based on the creation story in the Xtian holy book. And as described in the Part on science, after the early 1200s the maintenance of that view required an active rejection of Aristotle's infinite Earth, and that was facilitated through the work of Thomas Aquinas and others. One very important general line of potential dissent did arise in Siger of Brabant, Boethius of Dacia, and others who wanted to do philosophy (especially Aristotle and Averroes) independently of religion, but that was suppressed by Church authorities. As a result, this early opportunity to commence studying natural philosophy independently of the supernatural, and any progress it might have begotten, was delayed for several centuries.

Creationists almost necessarily have to inadequately portray history. As we have seen, for example, in the late 1600s, Hooke and Halley were among the very few would-be scientists who *after 1300 years* did not assume a biblical framework in their scientific studies. But creationist readers are seldom told *why* the challenges to the young-earth view became much more prevalent by the 1800s (hint: more evidence emerged or known evidence became better understood). Instead, as Terry Mortensen explained, "scriptural geologists" "raised biblical, philosophical, and geological objections to... old-earth theories"; these "scriptural geologists were not opposed to geological facts, but to the old-earth interpretations of those facts, which they argued were based on anti-biblical philosophical assumptions" [Mortenson in a subsection "The Rocks," in Tom Vail, writer and compiler, *Grand Canyon: A Different View*, 34-35]. There is no hint given that the evidence itself might point to an old earth—because that very possibility defeats the young-earth creationist position. Indeed, Mortensen then adds that "In this [the scriptural geologists] were correct" and that "Hutton was a deist or secret atheist" [Mortenson, 35]. But by Hutton's time—the late 1700s—serious reasons for an older Earth had also been identified by Buffon and a few others. And by the early 1820s, many more evidence-focused geologists and fossil hunters were stretching out the age of the Earth, typically at first offering "day-age" versions of the biblical creation, in which a day was as a thousand years with the deity (as is indicated in a different passage in the Bible), and perhaps adding that the biblical day may well not have been equal to a human day before the sun had even been put in the sky—which doesn't occur until day four of the biblical creation mythology [Genesis 1:14].

Among the most important evidence that broke through the biblical story line was the recognition that all fossils were derived from life forms, and that their distribution could not be reconciled with an extremely young Earth or a great flood. And as more and more fossil forms came to light—including of animals almost entirely unlike any known at the time, like a giant ground sloth and a plesiosaur—the phenomenon of extinction forced itself into reality (helped along by Cuvier and exhibitions). The idea of extinction was for a long time also resisted because it did not fit with the standard interpretation that since the deity had pronounced his creations as good, he would not have killed some of them off, before or even with Noah's Flood. Nor do creationists tell their readers about reverend-fossil hunter-scientists like Buckland who tried so hard to merge the fossil evidence with Xtian beliefs in a Noah's Flood as the only important event shaping most of the Earth's landscapes, but ended up acknowledging that those beliefs were mistaken.

Some Key Scientific Errors in the Bible

In the United States especially (and to a lesser extent in some other countries of mainly Xtian heritage) there are numerous fundamentalist evangelical sects and denominations whose followers subscribe to one or another of the many variants on the meaning of the Bible, literally interpreted. They believe that the authors of biblical books produced deity-inspired and therefore absolutely truthful accounts, whatever the topic. But among the starkest problems with such literal interpretation are those at the interface with the scientific realizations that have slowly emerged since the Bible was written.

I do not propose to try anything like a full review of creationist (their misnomer is "creation science") writings or deceptions. Nor to deal fully with "intelligent design" (ID), which is primarily a subterfuge offshoot of the former (see below re the Dover, Pennsylvania, case). Both creationism and intelligent design are resurrections of schools of traditional, received thought dating to the early 1800s *and before*. And given the number of their adherents and their effects on modern United States society, these forms of creationism qualify as being near the top in cultural insanities prevalent in the United States (see below for more).

Perhaps the greatest and most overt scientific mistake in the Xtian holy book is in the story about the deity's rapid creation of the Earth and all the beings on it, which, as above, has been calculated from biblical and ancient history sources to have occurred around 4004 BCE, though some young-earth creationists stretch that to 10,000 years. Above, in text and table, I have dealt fairly extensively with many of the principal developments in the scientific history that led to the rejection of the idea of a young Earth. As noted, 20th century techniques estimate the age of the Earth at more like 4.5 billion years.

In addition, some of the biblical order of the purported creation of the creatures that inhabit the Earth is seriously awry. Plants precede animals on land—that is correct—but there is no biblical distinction made between flowering plants which date only to the Jurassic era or so (in the time of the dinosaurs), and other plants on land, some of which date back twice as far. More awkwardly yet, fish and birds are purportedly created on the fourth day, before any creatures of the land. This is the correct timing for fish but very wrong for birds, which, based on evidence from the last few decades, evolved from dinosaurs, themselves the descendants of some reptiles, amphibians, and, before that, fish. And, on the fifth day, the deity is said to have created the creatures of the land, including "everything that creeps upon the ground of every kind" [Genesis 1:25]. That ordering is okay for vertebrate life (but should include birds), but it is very wrong for invertebrate terrestrial life. Arthropods (centipedes, insects, etc.) were actually among the first creatures to colonize the land after plants had taken root there. Creationists seldom if ever deal with such topics, but if they ever did try to fit them into their Noachian flood-oriented pseudo-geologies, they would be confounded by those arthropods appearing in rock layers well below any reptile, mammal, dinosaur, bird, or mammal.

The second but more subtle of the Bible's great scientific mistakes is its geocentrism—the idea that the Earth is the center of the entire universe. In reality, the Earth rotates annually around the sun and revolves daily on its own axis, the latter producing day and night. Beliefs sustained over centuries by the texts from antiquity and from the Bible (though occasionally contrary views were expressed in antiquity) held that the Earth stood still and that the heavens (*sun, planets, and stars*) revolved around the Earth. Beginning in the Late Middle Ages, there was more than a century of controversy that ranged across the lives of Copernicus, Galileo, Kepler, and Newton that finally settled this question: geocentrism was erroneous; heliocentrism—a sun centered-solar system—was true.

Strangely enough perhaps, very few fundamentalists now seem to agree with geocentrism—so somehow they have abandoned biblical literalism in that regard. But it was in defense of geocentrism, that certain biblical texts were cited throughout the Middle Ages, including one in the stories about the Joshua-led conquest of the land of Israel to be the homeland for the Hebrews. Even today the "New Revised Standard Version" of the Bible's Psalm 93:1 does say, "The Lord ... has established the world; it shall never be moved"; Psalm 96:10 says, "The world is firmly established; it shall never be moved." Similarly, 1 Chronicles 16:30 says, "The world is firmly established; it shall never be moved." In addition, Psalm 104:5 says "You set the Earth on its foundations; so that it shall never be shaken"—which is presumably an allusion to the foundations of a dwelling. I do not know whether these texts have been modified from the original Latin Vulgate translation, or translations by Erasmus and Luther and King James but, if so, the current wording (above) may make it more readily possible nowadays to interpret such wordings entirely metaphorically. However, the Church in the Middle Ages, and the Reformation era Lutheran leadership if not other Protestants divisions as well, took those words literally to mean the Earth does not move (i.e., holds still, at the center of the universe). And the text in Joshua is worse yet as regards heliocentrism.

Here is the problem-filled text in Joshua 10:12-14:

[Verse 12] On the day when the Lord gave the Amorites over to the Israelites, Joshua spoke to the Lord; and he said in the sight of Israel, "Sun, stand still at Gibeon, and Moon, in the valley of Aijalon." 13 And the sun stood still, and the moon stopped, until the nation took vengeance on their enemies. Is this not written in the Book of Jashar? The sun stopped in midheaven, and did not hurry to set for about a whole day. 14 There has been no day like it before or since, when the Lord heeded a human voice; for the Lord fought for Israel. [*The Access Bible: A Resource for Beginning Bible Students. New Revised Standard Version with the Apocryphal/Deuterocanonical Books.* The Revised Standard text of the Bible differs very little from this.]

The Access Bible explains further: "a prose framework [Joshua 10:12-13] encloses and reinterprets an older poetic text from the *Book of Jashar*... According to this framework, Joshua's request *to the Lord* ... for extended daylight causes the sun to stop in its noon position (*in midheaven, v.* 13) and delay its setting." Clearly, these words were not written to be interpreted metaphorically.

Granted, it was Joshua who told the sun to stand still in the sky, but it was obviously only the deity who could make it happen—he was, after all, fighting "for Israel." In any case, these verses "played a determining role in the condemnation of Galileo's heliocentrism in 1633" [Krivine, 115].

Also among the scientific problems then is this one: If the sun actually stood still, day would proceed as usual, because the day-night cycle on Earth is contingent on the earth's rotation, not the movement of the sun. And because stopping the sun in the sky would not lengthen the day, one or more things about the account are necessarily wrong scientifically. Thus, even if the deity knew that Joshua's request would not work as worded and instead stopped the rotation of the Earth (along with any associated effects, such as great windstorms if the atmosphere kept moving over the stalled planet), the biblical text is in error about what the deity did (i.e., stopping the sun). Therefore, a literal interpretation of the Bible's science here is simply impossible. But, in this case, the errors reveal hypocrisy because even self-designated literal interpreters of the Bible do not believe in geocentrism anymore. Galileo, who still believed in the inerrancy of the Bible but also recognized that it was written for the people at the time, and thus needed proper interpretation by religious authorities, didn't limit his reasons in this regard to scientific ones. If one limits oneself to the literal wording, he wrote, "there would thus emerge not only various contradictions but also serious heresies and blasphemies, and it would be necessary to attribute to God feet, hands and eyes, as well as bodily and human feelings like anger, regret, hate and sometimes even forgetfulness of things past and ignorance of future ones" [Galileo, cited in Krivine, 120].

Some Specific Literalist Biblical Interpretations That Do Not Work Scientifically, Notwithstanding Rationalizations Concocted by their Purveyors

The purpose in this section is to more conclusively demonstrate the cultural insanity of young-earth creationist-literalist-inerrant belief systems, and reveal some of the rationalization(s) that are used to support them. This is warranted to help ensure that the reader does not just "write off" creationist views as simple differences in religious opinions, but rather will better recognize the dangers to society that are all-but inherent in the spread of these irrational and/or delusional beliefs. As we will explore toward the end here, this cultural insanity has very serious consequences that work to undermine society as a whole, notwithstanding the purported patriotism or nationalism of many of the believers. Further, from its center in the United States, this cultural insanity has to some extent been spread abroad and its presence here is seen to give greater legitimacy to the same and similar cultural insanities elsewhere—with formerly more secular but now Muslim-leaning Turkey being a major example.

I am not expecting more than a few of my readers to believe as young-earth creationists or literal-inerrant interpreters of the Bible do, so any hopes I have of "reaching" them must rely on the concept of cultural insanity itself, and the prospects that it will percolate down to reach more people entrapped by these religious systems that also serve to insulate them from reality. But perhaps the different tack taken in some of what I write will help too.

Let's start first with the utter failure of creationist views to work geologically. Not being a geologist, I will confine what follows to easy-to-understand and relatively unsophisticated examples accessible to the lay person.

The Grand Canyon. The creationist book, *Grand Canyon: A Different View*, written and compiled by Tom Vail, includes many one- and two-page pieces contributed by some of the leading lights of creationism/"creation science," including Steve Austin, Duane Gish, Ken Ham, Henry Morris, John Morris, Gary Parker, Jonathan Sarfati, and Kurt Wise. The effort to include this book among those available in Grand Canyon National Park bookstores involved considerable controversy because our national parks are usually committed to conveying the science of the parks and not creationist-literalist distortions of science. The book can also attract gullible non-literal interpreters—people simply seeking a souvenir because it contains many very nice photographs of the canyon. But a close reading of the fine print on the page devoted to the copyrights and publisher reveals a fuller truth: "All contributions have been peer-reviewed to ensure a consistent and biblical perspective" [Vail, 3]. Although the term "peer-reviewed" is normally used in academic-scientific circles, its insertion here—along with the reputations of the various authors as creationists—lets you know that the parts of the text that I will be examining here are not just me arguing against some "straw men."

Still, given the limited scope of what I propose to do, I will proceed to analyze the principal failings of only two of the most important articles that are part of the book-long effort to dismiss an ancient Earth and evolution and to promote a fundamentalist-literalist interpretation instead. The latter is an interpretation which, among young-earth creationists, is based on the usual mainstays: a recent creation of the Earth by the deity, and Noah's Flood, both as described in the Bible.

There are at least two enormous problems with the assumptions/ perspectives in all of the articles in the creationist *Grand Canyon* book (and many other problems, big and small, as well). The enormous problems are: First, the assumption at the outset that their view is correct, that is, that the Earth is only 6,000 years old, (or maybe up to 10,000 if some "days" of creation are interpreted to represent a thousand years), and that every bit of evidence that challenges that view is by definition misinterpreted or wrong. This approach, as even the Supreme Court has ruled, is not science, but religion (and see below). "Creation science" is fake science. The same is true of "intelligent design," which in some very major respects has been shown to be re-hashed creationism (see below).

The second enormous problem is the implicit assumption in the writing that the reader will not begin to question whether the authors' specially-concocted geological explanations of the Grand Canyon will work worldwide, when in fact, the many failures of creationist geology are precisely the reason why real geologists and paleontologists abandoned Bible-derived hypotheses and perspectives that held universal sway over human minds for well over 1600 years in all of Xtianity.

Some discoveries and people that led to the supplanting of a creationist perspective have been described above; I will add a few others here.

As one thinks about this there is also a simple thought experiment—entirely replicable in reality—to consider. If a mixture of various sizes of pebbles, sand, and clay powder are poured into a glass-walled fishtank, the pebbles will settle out first, then the sand, and last the finest grain clay [Montgomery, 26]. This order is also exactly what one gets with a flooded river; as the floodwaters abate it no longer has the power to move boulders and large rocks, then gravel and pebbles, so these are deposited, in that order, and before the clays/silts. Noah's Flood would be no different. This ordering does not fit the Grand Canyon. So the rock beds in the canyon could not have been laid down by a single flood.

The Tasman Walker piece in the creationist *Grand Canyon* book provides a sterling example of both of the enormous problems noted above. First, after noting that the sedimentary deposits in the Grand Canyon are both thick and extend for thousands of square miles, he goes on to say that "There was not enough time for slow geological processes to deposit such large quantities of sediment" [Tasman Walker, within a subsection "The Rocks," in Vail (compiler), 36-37]. Here we see the automatic assumption that the Earth is only 6,000 years old—hence, not enough time. And that the Bible conveys sound science and that Earth's geological history consists primarily of its creation and a worldwide flood. Yet, as we saw above with the fish tank, and as we'll see yet more, Noah's Flood cannot produce that landscape and an immensity of time is exactly what is required to deposit thick sedimentary rocks made out of fine-grained material, including clay or silt, not to mention much of the Earth's organically-created limestone!

In contrast, Walker's article claims that the Grand Canyon's "horizontal layers were deposited in the first part of the Flood while the waters were advancing" [Walker, 37]. As a real possibility, this one disintegrates merely upon reflecting that the canyon contains not one, but two great limestone layers, widely separated from each other. Even if a rising flood could deposit limestone once, it certainly could not do so twice! But the two separated limestone rock layers could develop with lots of time, including a long interval between them (with changing erosional conditions to generate the rock beds that separated them), and geologically typical processes (e.g., the deposition of shells and the erosion of coral reefs).

Shales are also represented twice in the Grand Canyon, at two different levels. Because shales are composed of fine-grained clays, they too cannot be laid down by a flood, except perhaps as a last layer, and neither of these shale beds are near the top of the canyon.

Moreover, a third, smaller and somewhat different limestone layer occurs in the canyon just below the lower of the two great limestone layers. Geologists have identified an unconformity between the two [Montgomery, 18]—and wouldn't those two layers be pretty much the same otherwise, or at least lack a distinct boundary? Earlier in the text (see re Hutton) I described how unconformities are fatal to a single great flood hypothesis. In claiming there is an unconformity here, scientists are saying that, at minimum, that there are absences in the "fossil column" in the Grand Canyon that are found elsewhere on the Earth—that there is a hole in the "faunal succession"; and at maximum, that geologists know of the *same* rock beds found elsewhere in the general vicinity that have different rock layers sandwiched *between* these two deepest limestone layers in the Grand Canyon.

Similarly, Donald R. Prothero notes that one Grand Canyon layer composed of mudstones and sandstones (the Supai Group) which is between the uppermost limestone below and the Coconino-Toroweap-Kaibab formations above it, differs 80 miles to the East where it is limestone, and 300 miles to the northwest, where it is a boulder conglomerate plus sandstones [Prothero, *Evolution*, 70]. Clearly such changes in a single rock layer could not be an outcome of a single flood, but rather stem from differences along a long-ago shoreline and the associated river deltas. Among Prothero's other examples that help to demonstrate the impossibility of a single flood event are that two Grand Canyon rock beds (Tapeats Sandstone and Bright Angel Shale) "are full of layer after layer of sediments with complex burrows and trackways," showing repeated burrowing and continual or episodic burial of a sea floor, not a single deposition [Prothero, *Evolution*, 68]. Another rock bed (the Permian Coconino Sandstone) is composed of many extensive lightly tilted layers "that could only have formed in desert sand dunes, not under water" [Prothero, *Evolution*, 68]. As we see here, then, creationist concoctions do not really work in the Grand Canyon. And they are utter and miserable failures as generalizations in geology.

I want to deal with one other piece in *Grand Canyon: A Different View*. This piece is by Andrew Snelling and deals with radiometric (or radioisotopic) dating techniques [Snelling, within a subsection "The Rocks," in Vail (compiler), 38-39]. I will first elaborate some on the core of what is described in the table above: Radiometric dating is based on "the spontaneous nuclear disintegration of isotopes with unstable nuclei," which occurs at regular rates from the time that the original characteristics appeared [Plummer, McGeary, and Carlson, 187]. The assumptions needed for accurate measurement based on the decay of some radioactive isotopes into a stable original element, or another element, are usually fairly precise. As described above, the results of an isotope dating show how long ago the rock became a closed system; accordingly, it is important that neither the parent element's isotopes, nor the daughter isotopes, "could enter or leave the mineral or rock" between the time of closure and the measurement [Plummer,

McGeary, and Carlson, 190]. (Because different elements are involved in radioisotopic tests, any given corruption may affect different tests differently.) For an uncorrupted lava flow, the dating gives the date from the time that the lava has cooled below the relevant threshold (which varies by isotope).

The Snelling "different-view" piece includes data from the dating of a sill—a generally horizontal lava intrusion into or between other rock beds. There are several lava intrusions, some clearly related, far down in the Grand Canyon, and Snelling is referring to one at a place he calls Bass Rapids. Claiming the use of four different radio-isotope dating methods, Snelling gives dates of that sill as 840 million years, 1,055 million, 1,249 million, and 1,375 million. However, there are no footnotes given with regard to the source of his data, when the estimates were made (much earlier data may be more suspect; correct utilization techniques took time to develop), or how many radiometric labs were involved. But the bibliography for the Grand Canyon book does include a reference to Vardiman, *Snelling*, and Chaffin, editors, *Radioisotopes and the Age of the Earth: A Young-Earth Creationist Research Initiative*. This book was published by the Institute for Creation Research (ICR), which is very well-known for its invariably creationist output—a bias in this case suggested in the title of this reference. Whether anyone can trust research by biblical literalists who can only conclude that the Bible is correct, or trust their treatment of the materials in the sill (if they actually did the work), is much in doubt. It is also extremely unlikely that the ICR book was reviewed by *independently selected scientific* peers. And, of course, the entire vertical exterior of the sill has been exposed to the weather, and hence is very likely corrupted, so drilling into the sill would be needed for a decent sample (and even that assumes groundwater has not per-colated through any of the sample obtained). In any case, there is no way to confirm the figures given by Snelling, nor to compare them with other efforts at dating the same sill with the same techniques, whereas Plummer, McGeary, and Carlson say that "many thousands of similar [age] determinations have confirmed the reliability of radiometric dating" [Plummer et al., 190].

But based on the variation in the time findings that he reports, Snelling argues that "because all these radioisotopes have been subject to the same conditions within this sill during and since its formation, it is logically difficult to defend the assumption that decay rates have been constant in the past" [Snelling, 39]. In contrast, true geologists say, "It would violate the laws of physics for decay rates (half-lives) to have been different in the past" [Plummer, McGeary, and Carlson, 190]. But Snelling proceeds to write that "the large inconsistencies among these methods show that they are emphatically not providing reliable absolute dates" and thus concludes that "radioactive dating has not proven the rocks of the Grand Canyon to be millions of years old" [Snelling, 39]. Snelling doesn't overtly say that, 'therefore, the earth is about six to ten thousand years old,' but many of the other authors in *Grand Canyon: A Different View* do say that in one way or another. Beyond that, I must point out that the data from Snelling's four radio-isotopic measuring techniques, as cited above, do average 1130 million years (which is pretty far removed from 6,000 years).

The quality of radioisotope dating is explained well on the website of the National Center for Science Education (NCSE), "Radiometric Dating Does Work!" [by G. Brent Dalrymple of Oregon State University]. Besides illustrating the very close convergences of many estimates by a number of different techniques in dating meteorites (with age in the vicinity of 4.5 billion years) and the Cretaceous-Tertiary boundary (when the dinosaurs—except birds—died out, in the vicinity of 65 million years ago), the article notes that a few incorrect radiometrically-calculated ages only indicate "that the methods are not infallible." Some of the possible reasons for errors were noted above (e.g., corruption of the sample, lab errors, etc.). Indeed, people who use such techniques "often test them under controlled conditions to learn when and why they fail so we will not use them incorrectly" [Dalrymple, NCSE website].

A Non-ICR Book Length Creationist Example. The last book I want to consider was sent to me by my youngest sister. She developed a schizo-affective disorder in her middle twenties and the development of paranoia led her to attempt suicide to escape from her guiltiness. Although she survived, she was busted-up here and there for the rest of her life, and developed HIV from a blood transfusion during one of her many surgical operations. Later in her life she became the organist at a very conservative Missouri Synod Lutheran Church (LCMS), and was there enticed, I would say by her need for community belongingness, away from her knowledge of evolution, ultimately to biblical literalism and creationism. A few years before she died, she sent me Erich A. von Fange's *In Search of the Genesis World: Debunking the Evolution Myth*. The author is a professor of education emeritus at Concordia University, Michigan, who has published a number of creationist articles denying evolution. His publisher, Concordia Publishing House, has a long history as an arm of the LCMS. The book includes 341 pages of text, no index, and lots of footnotes, many citing people the author classifies as evolution supporters (mainly non-recent ones) and many citing creationist sources, especially those emanating from the Institute of Creation Research (ICR). And sometimes those latter sources are doing what they may be most infamous for in the eyes of scientists— misquoting scientists or taking what they wrote out of context. The usual scientific context involves debates about the relative strength of the mechanisms of evolution. Creationists who abuse truth then typically go on to treat the authors as if they rejected evolution itself, and twist the scientist's meaning in arguing that here is a well-known scientist who also rejects evolution (and none of their readers know otherwise). Prothero gives several examples of such misuse, including of quotes by Stephen J. Gould [Prothero, *Evolution*, 82]. Of course von Fange treats ICR sources as legitimate. Von Fange too cites or lists controversies among "evolutionists" (see examples below) to show that the science itself is confused, even though such debates are part of the process of advancing scientific knowledge.

Embryology is one area in which scientists in evolution regard as providing evidence so persuasive of the fact of human evolution that "every honest, right-thinking, decent person" should believe it [von Fange, 119]. And von Fange does admit that "embryos of all mammals (including man) pass through a stage of development during which a foundation of gill arches is laid down in the neck region, precisely similar to that which in fishes finally leads to ... gills" [von Fange, 119]. But the idea of "recapitulation" is a "flawed belief" that "keeps reappearing in the writings of evolutionists who demonstrate ignorance of biology" [von Fange, 119]. The idea of recapitulation to which he refers dates to the early middle part of the 1800s and Ernst Haeckel's slogan/"law" 'Ontogeny recapitulates phylogeny'; Haeckel also exaggerated the embryonic similarities across species [Prothero, *Evolution*, 108]. But creationists "such as Jonathan Wells (2000)" continue to "nag" about this [Prothero, *Evolution*, 108-109], even though recapitulation a la Haeckel has not been used by evolutionary scientists for a very long time. That doesn't deter von Fange, however, so, after faulting Carl Sagan for referring to the 'fish stage' of human evolution (the citation being attributed to a William Fix book on *The Bone Peddlers*), he concludes by saying that "biologists have known for almost a century that at no stage of its development does the human embryo have gill slits" [von Fange, 119]. I believe that is all von Fange says about embryology, but there is no index with which to check.

Did you catch the weaseling above? The fact that gill arches continue to evolve to gill slits in fish but not in human embryos does not in any way change the reality of shared gill arches in vertebrate embryos, even though von Fange wants his readers to come to the conclusion that embryology has nothing to offer as a proof of human evolution because of a now long-rejected (over-stated) 19th century idea about individual development as an embryo recapitulating the history of their phylum. (Prothero includes an ultrasound photo of a five-week-old human embryo in which the gill arches are visible [Prothero, *Evolution*, 111].) As you can see here too, even though von Fange maintains an occasional veneer of fairness in his writing (e.g., admitting to gill arches being in common across vertebrates), it is hard to imagine he didn't know he was being deliberately deceptive with his readers here.

Von Fange also spends an entire chapter on the very old news of the Piltdown Man hoax—which was officially declared as such in 1953 [von Fange, 137-160]. He faults the gullibility of scientists who supported the find as real, and the distortions in views of human evolution that it helped to cause in an era when protohuman fossils were still few and far between. Ultimately, to him, his conclusion points to the danger that evolutionary scientists will go overboard on too little evidence—which, to him, in chapter after chapter often ultimately means anything that supports evolution as contrasted with the biblical account. Another chapter on human evolution faults scientists about the squabbles over the exact status of protohuman fossil finds, such as Lucy. "Besides, no two experts are ever in agreement on all points in their interpretation of the meager data available" [von Fange, 123]. Speaking again of weaseling, do note the word "all" in the previous citation—making the statement sure to be true and allowing von Fange to beat up on his straw man. Creationists also sort into ape or human, and never the twain shall meet. Homo erectus, for example, is "fully human" [von Fange, 122]—with no mention of the smaller brain size, roughly 900 cubic centimeters versus 1300 in modern humans.

Because scientists are supposedly extremely strict in their citations, von Fange uses several pages of a short chapter to fault the inaccuracy of scientists' references to Bishop Ussher's creation date of 4004 BCE [von Fange, 101-109]. Some of von Fange's pseudo-problems arise because Britain was still using the Julian calendar rather than the Gregorian calendar (which then differed by about 11 days at the time); and because other religious leaders near Ussher's era amplified the precision within 4004 BCE. But to scientists, the only things of relevance are the startlingly recent date derived in large part from a holy book, and perhaps the precision of Ussher's dating! There is no need to go in any detail, to read any of Ussher's originals, or to seriously distrust other scientists who had previously referred to 4004 BCE. (Still, the occasional sarcasm by scientists that von Fange faults may indeed not be entirely fair, given Ussher's dates of 1581-1656.)

Within the chapter on Ussher, von Fange faults evolutionists' dating of the Earth. In an effort to discredit scientific efforts to date the Earth, he gives 12 examples of age-of-the-earth dates "offered by top scientists of the world in the 1930s" [von Fange, 111]. But these include several that date to early and middle 1800s—including Playfair, Lyell, Charles Darwin, and Kelvin. And, in any case, their estimates necessarily vary a lot because some were based on limited if not rudimentary information available at the time. But now, says von Fange, "scientists no longer dare to deviate on the age question" because of radiometric dating [von Fange, 111]. Needless to say, von Fange does not accept radiometric dating either.

There are two chapters on horses in von Fange. He knows about the chronological overlap of fossil finds of different horse species, so greatly faults early paleontologists for their specification of a simple sequence of evolution in the horse, from small, three-toed to large and one-toed. Long after these initial discoveries, the scientific finds involving overlapping horse ancestors became well known generally too. Among scientists, the finds support the long-term change toward recognizing that the evolutionary tree of life is much bushier than it seemed when the fossil record was still slim. But the general trend in the evolution of the modern horse is still true, even if some of the earlier 3-toed horses did not become extinct until well after others in their lineage came into being over the long stretches of geologic time [Switek, 204-225]. Evolution does not require that ancestral species die out. As mentioned, von Fange is often not very up-to-date in his treatments—hence his attacks on old science. For example, the *median* year for his 54 references in the horse chapter is between 1970 and 1971. Von Fange also includes an entire chapter on Litopterna, an order of mammals found in South America, some fossil specimens of which had remarkably close convergences with "true" horses [von Fange, 199-213]. Von Fange tries to convince his readers that these belong in the same family (in an animal taxonomy) as modern horses (because that would disrupt current views of evolution and the separation, millions of years ago, of South America from all other continents). With respect to one of these Litopterna, there is even a very recent update on the scientific rejection of von Fange's stance. It puts Litopterna in the horse-rhino-tapir line, yes, but from much earlier in geologic time. See the entry for July 9, 2017, in the next table here.

Can you stand a couple more examples? To further mock and denigrate evolution, von Fange quotes a primary source cited by a secondary source written in 1976. The quote involves how feathers might have evolved, which von Fange calls "total nonsense" [249]. Instead, the example might better be said to be "totally irrelevant" as a criticism of evolutionary science today because the original author, likely a Lamarckian (at a time when Lamarck's views were still in contention with Darwin's), wrote the attempted explanation in 1926. The second example comes immediately after the first, both within a chapter entitled "Reflections on Darwin." It is from even further back in time. It is a very brief account of an effort "by evolutionists to evolve a tailless mouse" in which the experimenter cut off the tails of 20 generations of mice, "assuming that eventually mice would be born without a tail. The experiment failed" [von Fange, 250]. The experimenter was August Weismann (1834-1914), a leading Darwinian; but his experiment was actually an attempt to show that acquired characteristics—the Lamarckian stance—*do not* become inheritable [Prothero, *Evolution*, 95]. Whether some actual Lamarckians would actually have expected such extremes of acquired characteristics to be transmitted to subsequent generations I know not, but the experiment was done to discredit Darwin's opponents and, in that respect, it was a success, not a failure. Worse yet for von Fange's twisted view that this last example somehow reflected negatively on Darwin and evolution, people did learn a little something from the experiment, though perhaps cruel or macabre, and would have no matter how the results turned out.

Geological Uniformitarianism and Evolutionary Gradualism. Creationists often assert that supporters of evolution insist on gradual rates of evolutionary change in species, as Darwin, for the most part, did. Such gradualism remained in the new evolutionary synthesis in the 1930s that recognized natural selection as a viable vehicle for evolutionary change (and which incorporated Mendel's genetics and gene-by-gene ideas of species change as a way of modifying the variation within a species). But, as noted earlier, this view was strongly challenged by Gould and Eldredge's "punctuated equilibrium" in *1972* and that challenge seems to have found more and more support in subsequent research, including continuing research on Galapagos finches. So why don't creationists update their views of science?

Many creationists utterly abuse the history of geological thought, especially the distinction between uniform geological *processes* and uniform *rates* of change, as described earlier in the discussion of Hutton and Lyell. Creationists often assert (pretend?) that geologists support uniformitarianism in all respects. But that is simply not true. For example, in a book on geomorphology published almost *60* years ago, the following is the *first* of nine "fundamental concepts" in geomorphology: "The same physical processes and laws that operate today operated throughout geologic time, *although not necessarily always with the same intensity as now* [Thornbury, 1962, 16; emphasis added]. Similarly—a fact well known for millennia—is that the high water flows in rivers in the rainy season, especially when above their "flood stage," tear up their riverbanks and modify their valleys and the landscape much more than lower flows in other seasons. But geologists today still affirm the necessity of very nearly uniform and sometimes almost placid deposition of sediment for millions of years as being required to create some kinds of sedimentary rock beds (e.g., chalk, limestone, thick beds of shale). But it is true that in the last 50-100 years geologists have become more catastrophes-oriented in terms of the rates of change.

Creationists seem to believe that science is weaker if it denies catastrophes altogether (because many Xtians believe in Noah's Flood?), so they try to hold scientists to views that to varying extents may have dominated a century ago or more. But to assert that scientists still take this view, creationists must ignore that it is scientists who over time have identified a number of other catastrophes with a variety of causes, including ice ages (beginning with Agassiz back in the *middle 1800s*). Indeed, it is paleontologists and geologists, not creationists, who discovered the catastrophes involved in the five known mass *extinctions* of life forms on the Earth in the last half billion years—even if they did occur in geologic time unrecognized by creationists. And by shortly after the middle of the 20th century, geologists added on flood catastrophes, albeit on a miniscule scale compared to the mythological Noah's Flood. J Harlen Bretz, a proponent of the idea that glacial-era flooding had a major impact on landscapes in the region south of

Missoula, Montana, was finally and fully vindicated by a group of his peers in *1965* [Montgomery, 203-210]. After personally reviewing the actual landscapes, those peers sent Bretz a telegram that concluded, "We are now all catastrophists" [cited in Montgomery, 210]. So now creationists can only resort to outright denial of scientists' views, or pretense (lies) in the hope that Xtians will reject deep time in favor of an inerrant belief in a flood catastrophe described in their holy book. But the denial of geologically deep time has made the creationist position more and more untenable over time—and the young-earth creationists' denial of science is a large part of the reason that mainstream evangelical Protestant denominations broke away from fundamentalist-literalist groupings in the United States. There is just way too much evidence of many different kinds that supports deep time and a long evolutionary history, and refutes a recent creation.

Much of early geologists' emphasis on uniformitarianism—and the rejection of the idea of catastrophism—was due to science's inability to discover evidence specifically for one giant flood as a shaper of current landscapes. But erosion and deposition processes themselves remain the same; in that way, they are uniform. In any case, uniformitarianism versus catastrophism is a long-dead horse that creationists are still beating.

So, keeping in mind the dates in italics above and the variety of catastrophes identified over time by geologists and paleontologists, let's turn one last time to von Fange, publishing in 2006, for an example of creationist malpractice (though much the same can be seen in the creationist book on the Grand Canyon). Says Von Fange: "The evolutionist cannot stomach the possibility of catastrophes" [von Fange, 168].

<u>A Few More Big Nails in the Coffins of Creationism and Noah's Flood as Science</u>. As described above, young-earth creationist geology fails miserably when confronted with the Grand Canyon's realities. But

beyond the Grand Canyon, any attempt to apply creationist geology results in absurdity, humiliation, and ludicrousness; it is a farce and a fiasco. Among the vast number of examples which added to the evidence that defeats young-earth creationism and Noah's Flood as a major causative agent in the Earth's landscapes are some that almost alone seriously undermine the whole creationist project. Among them are these:

There are major rock beds along some parts of the west African coastline that correspond in composition to rock beds along the eastern coast of South America—one of the proofs of continental drift/ plate tectonics [Plummer, McGeary, and Carlson, 465]. In essence, Africa and South America were for a long period joined but, over many millions of years they drifted apart. The shape of the two coastlines are also remarkably closely matched, after allowing for some rotation of the continents. If a worldwide flood is to account for the similarities in the rocks on two sides of the Atlantic Ocean, then those same rock beds must occur worldwide along the edges of all continental areas similar in slope to these two because a mountaintops-submerging flood must lay down sediments in a fairly consistent order on similar terrain all over the world. Did that in fact occur? Nope.

Relatedly—and far more striking—the land of most of northeastern Canada and western Greenland, apart from some glacial debris and the like on the surface, consists not of sedimentary rock but of primeval rock composed of metamorphic and plutonic rocks (the latter being giant magma intrusions that did not reach the surface as lava). Yet all this land is at a very low elevation [Plummer, McGeary, and Carlson, 501]. A worldwide flood would have made deposits on such low-lying land, not strip it bare (just as creationists assert that a giant flood deposited many of the layers in the Grand Canyon, which is much higher above sea level and therefore less likely to accrue huge flood deposits).

There are marine fossils on many of the highest mountains on Earth, including the Himalayas (and Everest), the Alps, and the Andes. These fossils are not all of the same age geologically—the evidence being differences in the fossils. If the mountains were miraculously pushed up during the Noah's Flood, or if they were simply sculpted by that flood, that is, while the Earth was submerged, there would not be major differences in any of the fossils near the highest points. Plus, the fossils atop these mountains aren't actual remains; instead, minerals have replaced the originals in what is typically a very slow process. Moreover, and equally importantly, shells don't float—in a flood they would be found near the bottom under almost all of the muck, so even mountain-building during a flood, with mountains rising from the sea floor, wouldn't put differing fossils on top.

The Canadian Rockies consist mainly of marine sedimentary rock beds. However, the U.S. Rockies consist mostly of igneous and metamorphic rocks [Michael E. Wysession, *The World's Greatest Geological Wonders: 36 Spectacular Sites*, 38-39.] It is logically absurd to think that a worldwide flood could strip away all its would-be deposits from the U.S. Rockies (and put them around the Grand Canyon) while leaving flood deposits aplenty atop the Canadian Rockies.

Ice cores drilled in places like Antarctica have dated back 800,000 years—not all that long in geologic time, but a lot older than 4004 BCE. Indeed, new techniques may have extended the age of ice cores to 2.7 million years. The accuracy of such readings is very high because each new year in an ice core is marked by factors associated with the change in seasons, for example, evidence of melting-consolidation in the summer, regular intervals at which pollen re-appears in the Spring, etcetera. Similarly, but receiving less press, "cores of deep-sea sediments have provided a fairly precise record of climatic variations over the past few hundred thousand years" [Plummer, McGeary, and Carlson, 306].

There is coal—"metamorphosed, fossilized swamp material" in Antarctica [Wysession, 99]. Coal starts as leaves and other plant material and, under conditions that allows its accumulation, becomes peat; subsequently it proceeds to lignite; then bituminous coal; and, in some cases, to anthracite coal, which is a hard rock metamorphized version [Plummer, McGeary, and Carlson, 530]. Metamorphic rock is sedimentary rock that has been exposed to some combination of heat and pressure that converts it into a different material, but not so much heat and pressure as to convert it all the way back to magma, so anthracite coal is still recognizable as to its peaty source (and includes some fossils of plants mainly). But the development of any kind of coal in Antarctica is precluded in the Bible's literal, young-earth mythology. After all, when in the last 6000+ years has there been enough accumulated plant matter in Antarctica to produce coal? Instead, many millions of years ago Antarctica was joined to other southern hemisphere land masses, all positioned well north of where Antarctica is now, and entirely suited to lots of plant life and animal life (including dinosaurs, the bones of which have also been found there). Subsequently Antarctica began a slow separation from the other continental land masses and drifted southward to become the coldest spot on the globe.

Indeed, roughly the same problem arises for other metamorphic rock that originates from organic sources—for example, marble, which is metamorphosed limestone. The limestone, which is comprised of the remains of marine organisms, must first go down far enough into the earth (e.g., by burial beneath other sedimentary rock or subduction of one of Earth's tectonic plates *under* another), or come into contact with a "hot spot" near the surface, in order to metamorphose. But, again, it must stop short of melting. Once metamorphosed, the marble must somehow make its way to the surface again if humankind is to learn of its existence. For example, in order for marble to be mined by humans and then worked into sculptures by Michelangelo, a subducted plate with limestone in it that slid under a continent would first need to be metamorphized, then to be uplifted substantially, and then the rock atop it would need to be eroded away to bring it back to the surface. Try doing that with a giant flood.

As noted earlier, even in Darwin's time geologists had begun to figure out that some kinds of sedimentary rock beds, such as limestone, take a long time to develop, and that some could not be a product of flood geology. This is so because limestone consists of abraded coral reef fragments, the shells and other remains of mostly small animals that lived within the reef's protection, and the reefs themselves (which the corals built). Corals do not survive massive run-off of erosional debris from the land, so there's no way to hurry the construction of limestone rock beds by adding more dirt. Hence, to build limestone deposits that are many hundreds of feet thick, as in the Grand Canyon, would take millions of years.

A special case of limestone involves reefs attached to mid-ocean volcanoes that are slowly sinking, forming atolls when the volcanoes finally sink entirely beneath the surface of the sea. What very low-lying land remains in an atoll is built from debris/detritus from the reef itself, generated mainly by waves and storms impacting the living corals, which are on the outside edges of the atolls. Further, corals do not survive being out of water more than briefly; and, apart from some deep-water varieties, they do not survive if submerged below about 75 feet deep. So the atolls are built almost entirely by living corals near the surface. In 1952, as part of its atomic bomb testing preparations, the U.S. government drilled deep bore holes into the Bikini and Eniwetok atolls in the Pacific Ocean. The drills reached the original volcanic island "below some 4,000 feet (1,200 m) of shallow-water coral rock" [Lister, 179]. Given the rate that these corals grow, the estimate of the age of this reef was "over 50 million years" [Lister, 179].

Per the above, submerging corals in a long-term Noachian Flood would have killed them all. And then the corals would have been re-killed by the immense amount of muck deposited as that flood subsided over several weeks or months—all purportedly only 4500 years ago. Yet we still have continuously living coral reefs, some of very considerable geologic antiquity. Moreover, if creation was in 4004 BCE and Noah's Flood about 4,400 years ago, that leaves only 1500-1600 years for the world's corals to have built all those immense limestone rock beds found in many places around the world. It cannot have happened that way.

Somewhat similarly, chalk beds are built up mainly from the long-term deposition of microscopic calcium-shelled creatures that float, and upon death, sink to the bottom in seas that are calm, such as well-sheltered bays and inland seas—places where the seas are not subject to other sources of deposition (or the result would not be even vaguely pure chalk). Hence, chalk beds could not have originated from a flood deposition. Moreover, chalk formations several hundred feet thick, such as those in the White Cliffs of Dover in England, which once spanned the English channel to the chalk cliffs on the French side, undoubtedly required millions of years to build.

And as a way to fill in the grave now that young-earth "creation science" in the coffin has been lowered into it, consider this: If there was a worldwide flood a la Noah some 4,400 years ago, why were all of the places on Earth that are now below sea level not filled in with muck and flood debris? Among a number of sites below sea level are those at Death Valley, California (-379 feet) and some rift valley features in Djibouti and Ethiopia in Africa (as low as -502 feet). More amazingly yet are the Sea of Galilee (-696 feet) and the Dead Sea of Bible fame (the latter being the lowest spot on Earth, at -1,411 feet), and the town of Jericho (-846 feet, the lowest town on Earth). Moreover, archaeologists have found at least 20 layers of construction at Jericho, and dated the city to at least 9,000 BCE. Yet Jericho's archaeology shows no signs of having been massively flooded around 2,400 BCE (Noah's Flood). Indeed, if Noah's Flood were real, Jericho would be undiscovered because it would be buried at least 846 feet deep!

Introduction to Table Summarizing Science & Health News Articles

Above we have seen how a number of sciences have provided a multi-faceted confirmation of the truth of geologic time and evolution (per the definitions of "true" given there). Clearly, all of these sciences include subject matter, sometimes as the very foundation of the science, that conflicts with the views of young-earth creationists, believers in the Bible's inerrancy, a variety of other fundamentalist interpretations of Xtianity and, for that matter, deniers of evolution or geologic time of any stripe. But before looking at the general case for the cultural insanity involved in such stances and societally, I want to provide an even more concrete idea of some of what these denials mean in relating to everyday reality in the world.

A major problem for the individuals who deny evolution and geologic time is that *every time* something about an old Earth or evolution appears it must be disregarded, distorted, denied, compartmentalized in a separate part of the mind, or otherwise voided. In the writings of young-earth creationists above we have seen several instances of these kinds of denial and avoidance treatments of the findings of science and of the methods of discovery used by science.

For believers in young-earth creationism, the table which follows suggests the range in which public reports of progress in science would have required denials and avoidance over a recent two-and-a-half-year period. Scientific findings in the fields of paleontology and Earth science (geology and more) must be denied outright, or distorted beyond recognition in writings and theme parks that can only be believed by people who have been heavily indoctrinated or otherwise kept in ignorance. And fields as far apart as human medicine and the search for oil rely on the truths of evolution and/or geology.

When it comes to any of the life sciences, Theodosius Dobzhansky (1900-1975), who helped to shape the post-1930s "modern synthesis" in evolution, famously said, "Nothing in biology makes sense except in light of evolution" [cited in many sources, including Coyne, 55]. For example, all animals and plants are now classified according to their evolutionary heritage. Thus, it should not have been a surprise that the table *above*, summarizing the confirmatory evidence for *evolution*, drew extensively on life-science disciplines: genetics, molecular biology, embryology, comparative anatomy, zoology, medicine and agriculture, and paleontology (which some universities include with geology instead). The table *below*, in contrast, relies most on mentions of geologic time (or even deeper time in the case of astrophysics), because that usually appears wherever it is relevant whereas links to evolution may not.

Examples of Science Parts or All of Which Must Be Denied by Young-earth Creationists or Deniers of Geologic Time

Based on a relatively complete account of relevant articles from the Minneapolis StarTribune Sunday "Science & Health" section, Aug. 28, 2016- Jan. 2019. Each week the section consisted of 3 pages of about 12+ long and short articles, some with large photos or diagrams.

Newspaper Date	Science(s)	How Many Years Ago in Article	Star Tribune Science & Health Article Subject Matter**	S&H Page
2016-17				
Aug 28	Anthro, Paleo	250 Kya	Stone tools have residues of rhino, horse, camel, whether scavenged or killed	3
	Astrophysics	(up to 1 My intervals)	Binary stars observed before & after they go nova; low activity precedes nova	3
Sept 4	Paleo	1 Mya	Austrian museum finds tusks from unusually early mammoth	2
	Astrophysics	300 M light years	Galaxy found, big as Milky Way, but composed almost entirely of dark matter	2
Sept 11	Paleo, Zool	166 Mya	Petite pterosaur (flying reptile) from 77 Mya found; pterosaurs date to 166 Mya	2
Sept 18	Zool, Genetics	1.5-2 Mya	Genetics says 4 species of giraffe, not 3; common ancestor dated	3
Sept 25	Zool, Paleo	13 Kya	Excellent mammoth skull with tusks found on Santa Rosa Island, CA	2
	Astrophysics	no dating*	Black hole burps brilliant and energetic flare after eating a star	2
Oct 2	Anthro, Genetics	200 Kya	Most but maybe not all human ancestry due to Africa outmigration 40-80 Kya	2
Oct 9	Anthro, Zool, Evolution	no dating*	For 1000 mammal types, murder rates vary by similar groups on evolution tree	2
Oct 16	Chem, Genetics, Geol	4 Bya	Thickened not watery primordial soup may have facilitated DNA replication	2
Oct 23	Anthro, Archaeo	14.5 Kya	Cave discovered with 50 "spectacular" etchings by early humans	2
	Paleo, Zool	no dating*	3-D image of Tyrannosaurus arms shows low stress, little actual use	2
	Anthro, Paleo	10-19 Kya	Site with 400+ human footprints in mud found preserved	3
Oct 30	Zool, Anthro, Genetics	no dating*	Auroch cross with larger steppe bison (both cave painted) → European bison	3
Nov 6	Anthro, Paleo	16 Kya	Humans hunted cave lions (up to 500 lbs.), used pelts	3
Nov 13	Geol, Astrophysics	4 Bya	Simulations indicate that collision with Mars-sized object tilted earth, sped up earth's rotation (now slowing slowly), resulted in large moon	2
	Paleo, Biology	66 Mya	4 million years after asteroid killed dinosaurs before high biodiversity recovered	3
Nov 20		none		
Nov 27		none		
Dec 4		none		
Dec 11	Anthro, Paleo	3.18 Mya	CT scans: Lucy had strong bones of a climber, e.g., for food & night safety	2
Dec 18	Paleo, Zool	99 Mya	Baby dinosaur had primitive feather plus bone found inside amber	3
Dec 25	Anthro, Paleo	3.7 Mya	Footprints indicate tall Australopithecus (Lucy's species), weighing 100 lbs.	2
Jan 1	Anthro, Archaeo [accidentally recycled?]	1 Mya	Analysis of teeth plaque shows sticks likely used as toothpicks (like chimps too)	3
Jan 8	Paleo, Zool	66+ Mya	Dinosaur egg hatch times too long to survive unattended after asteroid impact	3

Newspaper Date 2017	Science(s)	How Many Years Ago in Article	Star Tribune Science & Health Article Subject Matter**	Page
Jan 15	Paleo, Botany	52 Mya	Tomatillo fossil pushes lineage back 22 million years	3
Jan 22		none		
Jan 29		none		
Feb 5	Paleo, Zool	6.24 Mya	Extinct Chinese otter grew to 110 pounds, size of wolf	3
Feb 12	Paleo, Zool	540 Mya	Tiny creature found closer to prececessor of all vertebrate (& more) evolution	3
Feb 19	Astrophysics	1.8 Bya	Longest time yet (11 years + of observation) of black hole devouring a star	3
	Paleo, Zool	195 Mya	Older yet soft tissue (collagen) proteins discovered in sauropod to study	2
Feb 26	Astrophysics	no dating*	Supernova images 3-10 hours after explosion—new views on stellar evolution	3
	Geol	no dating*	(New) Zealandia plate seen as part of Gondwana (+ other southern continents)	3
March 5		none		
March 12	Paleo, Genetics, Cepha	160 Mya	Squids (cephalopods) evolved to lack shells for speed in offense, defense	2
	Anthro, Genetics	125 Kya	Human+Neanderthal+(Denisovan?) DNA found in skull DNA fragments in Asia	2
	Paleo, Zool	66 Mya	Better Triceratops skeleton attacked by Tyrannosaurus skeleton, at Smithsonian	3
March 19	Anthro, Archaeo	38 Kya	Pointillist-like cave paintings composed of dots, sometimes connected too	3
	Astrophysics	13.2 Bya	Oldest space dust yet detected already included heavier elements	3
March 26	Paleo, Zool, Genetics	195 Kya	DNA of live and various fossil bison indicates their rapid spread after arrival	3
April 2	Paleo, Zool	247 Mya	Big data analysis suggests revised dinosaur lineage, with theropods (meat-eaters) as offshoots from other bird-hipped dinosaurs, not sauropods	1,3
April 9		none		
April 16	Paleo, Zool	54 Mya	Some mammals shrank in earlier global warming episodes	2
April 23	Paleo, Zool	245 Mya	Teleocrater (pre-dinosaur branch of evolutionary tree) had mix of features	2
April 30		none		
May 7	Anthro, Genetics	550 Kya	Early human DNA extracted from dirt in caves where stone tools found, a first	3
May 14		none		
May 21	Anthro, Paleo	300 Kya	South African human "cousin" (Homo naledi) co-existed with humans	2
	Paleo, Zool	no dating*	Exceptionally well-preserved Ankylosaurus named after movie monster	3
	Paleo, Zool	90 Mya	Fossilized dinosaur embryo from 1990 now identified as an Oviraptor	3
May 28	Paleo, Zool	66 Mya	Location on moving earth that asteroid hit made difference in dinos' fate	2
June 4	Paleo, Zool	30 Mya	Baleen whales grew to jumbo sized only with recent change in food supply	3
June 11	Geol, Ecology	12 Kya	Methane burst explosions during post-glacial warming in Arctic left craters	2
June 18	Paleo, Zool	no dating*	Study of Tyrannosaurus concludes it had scaly skin, not feathered	3
		none		

Newspaper Date 2017	Science(s)	How Many Years Ago in Article	Star Tribune Science & Health Article Subject Matter**	Page
June 25	Zoo, Archaeo, Genetics	10 Kya	Cat genetics tracked from human agricultural hangers-on to domesticated	2
July 2		none		
July 9	Zool, Paleo	78 Mya	Fossil Macrauchenia now est. to diverge from horse-rhino-tapir line 56-78 MYA	3
July 16	Anthro, Paleo, Genetics	765 Kya	Early modern humans and Neanderthals mixed sexually ~270 KYA, per genetics	3
July 23	Archaeo	13 Kya	Experiment showed grooved arrowheads innovation made them less brittle	2
July 30	Anthro, Archaeo	75 Kya	Evidence for human landing date on Australia earlier than heretofore thought	2
Aug 6	Paleo, Zool	no dating*	Study of musculature shows Tyrannosaurus couldn't run, but walked fast	2
Aug 13	Geol	75 Mya	Zealandia a continent, mostly underwater but an unbroken land mass/plate	3
Aug 20	Zool/Arthrods, Paleo	435 Mya	Scorpion ancestors date to 435 million years ago, still finding new species	2
Aug 27	Astrophysics, Geol	4.5 Bya	Article on eclipse dates sun, moon to about 4.5 billion years ago	2
Sept 3	Paleo, Zool	100 Mya	Found: new heavyweight dinosaur champ: Patagotitan at 76 tons	3
Sept 10	[accidentally recycled?]	[accidentally recycled?]		
Sept 17	Astrophysics	100 K intervals	Scientists find evidence of historical nova now gone dim; case yields updated hypotheses on 3 types of novas; explosion intervals to 100,000 years apart?	2
Sept 24		none		
Oct 1		none		
	Zool/Entom, Genetics	50 Mya	Study of butterfly wing color genes refers to 90 Mya start of a genus thereof	2
	Paleo, Paleo	75 Mya	Fossilized feces show plant-eating dinosaurs (hadrosaurs?) ate shellfish	2
Oct 8, 15	Anthro, Paleo	49 Kya	Neanderthal youth skeleton shows slow human-like growth pattern	3
	[missed due to travel abroad]	[missed due to travel abroad]		
Oct 22	Anthro, Paleo, Genetics	300 Kya	Racial categories wrong: Skin color genes found among humanity's ancestors	2
	Anthro, Paleo, Health	1.4-6 Mya	Oral herpes 6 My-old; transmission to hominins around 1.4 Mya	3
Oct 29		none		
Nov 5	Paleo, Zool	120-131 Mya	Feather markings are camouflage in evolution of theropod Sinosauropteryx	3
	Botany, Paleo	374 Mya	Found: fossil trees from the dawn of earth's forests	3
Nov 12	Anthro	40 Kya	Neanderthals doomed because no more immigrants, unlike humans	2
	Zool, Paleo	400 Kya	Third orangutan species, but few and isolated	3
Nov 19	Astrophys	500 M light years	Multiple flare-ups of supernova observed over 1000 days, usually a 100 days	1
	Archaeo, Chem	8 Kya	Chemical evidence of wine extended back another 600-1000 years	2
Nov 26	Paleo, Zool	66+ Mya	Analytic evidence that mammals were nocturnal when dinosaurs ruled	2
		none		

Newspaper Date	Science(s)	How Many Years Ago in Article	Star Tribune Science & Health Article Subject Matter**	Page
2017-18				
Dec 3	Anthro, Archaeo	8-9 Kya	Oldest yet depiction of man-dog relationship found in Saudi Arabia	3
	Zool, Paleo	25 Mya	Skull and rib cage of sea cow found on island 50 miles north of Los Angeles	3
Dec 10	Anthro, Paleo	3.6 Mya	Found: most complete skeleton of human ancestor yet in South African area	3
	Astrophys	13 B light years	Oldest black hole yet found	3
Dec 17	Zool, Paleo	10 Kya	Juvenile mammoth skull found under Los Angeles streets	2
	Zool/Arthropods, Paleo	99 Mya	Found: Tick in amber grasping dinosaur feather, shows early parasitism	3
	Paleo, Zool	75 Mya	Found: flippered duck-velociraptor-like water-living theropod	3
Dec 24	Paleo, Ornith	56-60 Mya	Large (223 lbs.) extinct penguin skeleton found in New Zealand	3
Dec 31		none		
Jan 7		none		
Jan 14		none		
Jan 21	Astro	3 B light years	Some fast radio bursts traced to a host galaxy, but meaning still unknown	2
Jan 28		none		
Feb 4	Astrobiology	4 Bya to now	Earth atmosphere at 3 time intervals may provide clues to life on other planets	3
Feb 11	Paleo, Zool	100+ Mya	Maryland stone slab found with dinosaur and small mammal tracks	2
Feb 18	Astrophys	3.8 B light years	Cluster of planets found beyond our galaxy	3
	Paleo, Ichthy	375, 420 Mya	Skates walk+ like vertebrates; to land ~375 Mya; common ancestor ~420 Mya?	3
Feb 25		none		
March 4	Anthro, Archaeo	64 Kya	Simple cave art done by Neanderthals before humans showed up in Europe	3
March 11	Astrophys	13.6 Bya	Faint radio signal from time of first stars: light; plus likely dark matter effects	3
March 18	Anthro, Med, Genetics	7.3 Kya	Time of origin identified for genetic sickle-cell (defense vs. malaria)	2
	Paleo, Zool	220 Mya	Late Cretaceous Sauropod found in Africa, showing long evolution, connections	3
March 25	Anthro, Genetics, Math	600 Kya	Ancient DNA clarifies our evolutionary mixing w/ Neanderthals, Denisovans	3
April 1		none		
April 8	Entom, Paleo, Genetics	300-360 Mya	Genetic clues found re how insects gained the capability of flying	3
April 15	Anthro	13 Kya	Radiocarbon-dated human footprints found on British Columbia coast (+July22)	3
April 22	Anthro	125-300 Kya	Bony ridges over eyes of skulls tied to expressiveness, having no other function	3
	Paleo, Zool	170 Mya	Sauropod and theropod footprints found on Scottish island	3
April 29	Anthro	85-90 Kya	Evidence humans left Africa earlier than 50 Kya theory	1,3
May 6	Paleo, Anthro	125 Kya	Large mammal extinctions likely due to several early hominins (man-related)	3
May 13	Paleo, Zool	no dating*	Microwear on teeth of 4 predatory dinosaurs shows "puncture and pull" eating	3
May 20		none		

Newspaper Date 2018	Science(s)	How Many Years Ago in Article	Star Tribune Science & Health Article Subject Matter**	Page
May 27	Astron	12.4 B light years	Ongoing cosmic merger of 14 hot star-generating galaxies near edge of universe	1-2
June 3		none		
June 10		none		
June 17	Ornith, Geol, Paleo	66 Mya	Bird survivors of dinosaur-killing asteroid were ground-dwellers	3
June 24	Zool	3.8 Mya	New species Sumatran orangutan designated; Borneo-Sumatran split 3.8 Mya	3
July 1		none		
July 8	Geol, Astron	215 Mya	Earth orbit shifts back & forth every 202.5K years, at least for last 215 m years	3
	Genetics, Paleo, Biol	50 Mya	Search for plesiosaur DNA in Loch Ness as part of larger study of lake biology	3
July 15		none		
July 22	Anthro, Geol	13-17 Kya	Ice-free migration route down west coast of North America likely opened first	2
July 29	Astron	4+ Bya	Asteroids in asteroid belt more like collision shrapnel than aggregated dust	3
Aug 5	Anthro, Paleo	2.1 Mya	Oldest stone tools found outside Africa, probably pre-Homo erectus	3
	Zool, Genetics	350 Kya	Koalas extra genes for enzymes enabled survival for 350K yrs eating toxic plants	3
	Paleo, Zool	200 Mya	Early Argentine sauropod-like dinosaur discovered; it's already fairly large	3
Aug 12	Astrophys	4+ Bya	Detection of neutrino tracked to its source galaxy will help understand universe	3
Aug 19	Zool, Physio, Paleo	up to 50 Mya	Marine mammals lost enzyme ancestors had, now less safe vs. some pesticides	3
Aug 26	Ichthyol, Paleo	25 Mya	Megashark, 30 feet long, 2X great white shark, ate other sharks too	3
Sept 2	Anthro, Archeao	50 Kya	Evidence that Neanderthals could start fires	3
Sept 9	Anthro, Genetics	50-450 Kya	Early humans--Denisovans and Neanderthals--interbred	3
	Entom, Paleo	30-40 Mya	Fossilized parasitic wasps found in fossilized developing flies	3
Sept 16	Anthro, Archaeo	73 Kya	New find of oldest human cave drawing	3
Sept 23	Zool, Paleo, Genetics	25 Kya	Extinct cave bears share some DNA with today's brown bears	1
Sept 30	[accidentally recycled?]			
Oct 7	Anthro, Paleo	7 Mya	Human generosity evolved from 7 Mya ancestors common to chimps, bonobos	1
	Archaeo, Geol	10 Kya	Alpine glacier ice core dates to 10K years, e.g., show evidence of plague in 1349	3
Oct 14	Entom, Paleo	20 Mya	Ants in amber show evidence of fungal cultivation + antibiotic bacteria helpers	3
Oct 21	Anthro, Genetics	40+ Kya	European & Asian people retain Neanderthal DNA, likely helps fight infection	2
Oct 28	none			
Nov 4	Astrophysics	26 K light years	Teams race to confirm black hole at in center of Milky Way	3
Nov 11	none			
Nov 18	Paleo, Ornith, Zool	66+ Mya	Color in bird eggs linked to oviraptor dinosaurs	3
	Ichthy, Paleo	400+ Mya	Fish likely originated in shallow waters along margins of continents	3

Newspaper Date	Science(s)	How Many Years Ago in Article	Star Tribune Science & Health Article Subject Matter**	Page
2018-19				
Nov 25	Paleo, Zool	12.5 Mya	Molar found of smallest ape yet; likely died out competing w/ rise in monkeys	1
	Archaeo, Anthro	40+ Kya	Oldest human cave art yet in Indonesia (animals, hands, people, patterns)	3
Dec 2	Anthro, Paleo	300-500 Kya	Human and pre-human evidence of living in Arabian desert, formerly green	3
Dec 9	Paleo, Cepha	500 Mya	Search for explanation of how octopi, etc., became relatively intelligent	3
Dec 16	Paleo, Anthro, Biol	0-252 Mya	Earth now mirrors conditions that led to largest mass extinction, 252 Mya	3
Dec 23	Anthro, Paleo, Genet	530 Kya	Neanderthal DNA may also have led to rounder skulls in humans	3
Dec 30	Astrophys	3-4 Bya	Computer simulations show large crash long ago into Uranus, uniquely tilting it	1
Jan 6	Microbiol, Paleo	2+ Bya	Some old-earth archaic bacteria & bacteria underground survive differently	3
	Geol	2.6 Mya	Large asteroid likely hit Antarctica during Pleistocene Period, effects unsure yet	3
Jan 13	none			
Jan 20	Geol	580-720 Mya	Missing sedimentary beds in this time slot, including at the bottom of the Grand Canyon likely due to immense "snowball earth" period of glacial erosion	3
Jan 27	none			

Table ends here because I finished the first good draft of it at this point.

*These are usually short articles in which the scientific dating obviously would be 10,000 years or more (i.e., were it included); most of them involve astrophysics (with millions of years required for light to get here), creatures with well-known scientific date ranges (e.g., dinosaurs), etcetera.

**See the end of the references section for greater detail on sources (e.g., new service, author, etc.).

CHAPTER 40

Young-Earth Creationism: The Cultural Insanity of It All

Introductory Summary: Remembering What Got Us to this Point

Above I have illustrated in a variety of subjects and ways how young-earth fundamentalist or literalist creationists must distort, deny, avoid, or otherwise disregard widespread scientific evidence about geologic deep time (and evolution) in order to hold on to their simplistic beliefs that their holy book is inerrant, and/or that creationist concoctions, phrased in pseudo-scientific form, are legitimate. Perhaps the easiest explanation for other Xtians for this easily avoided problem—an explanation several centuries old—is to recognize that the Bible is phrased in ways that would be meaningful for people at the time of its writing. Moreover, the Old Testament stories about creation and Noah's Flood are not original to the Hebrews/Jews, but were borrowed from other cultures. Accordingly, taken literally, they have the same truth value as myths in any other culture: virtually none (possibly there was an extra big local flood once), even though they may promote social solidarity or compliance with the wishes of a king or a priestly class (and attract anthropological-psychological interpretations).

Later, because Jesus was a Jew and his teachings began to be adapted for gentiles some time after his death, those attracted as followers of the new religion worked up some additional basic doctrines and developed religious hierarchies. The leadership of this new religion slowly assembled the writings by his disciples and early followers, selecting some and rejecting others (and reinterpreting some and modifying some), as needed to make them agree with their proto-orthodox views of the religion. They did so at least indirectly to sustain their power as leaders of the priestly class of intercessors, while defining that class as the only vehicle by which to access the purported benefits of the religion. The religion's fusion with the Roman Empire helped the Xtian leadership to consolidate their power, in part by defining what was and wasn't heretical and ultimately by outlawing other religions, reversing Rome's earlier general tradition of tolerance in this regard. While there were several centuries of limited Church capabilities after the fall of the Roman Empire, the (Catholic) Church hierarchy in the High Middle Ages again built up considerable power, formulating doctrines, dogma, and mandates, and defining heresy again in the new context, and again eliminating all "heretical" alternatives. In the Late Middle Ages, Church power ebbed considerably, partly as a result of competition for secular power with rising monarchies, partly as a result of the advance of knowledge and technology, partly as a result of corrupt, amoral, and overbearing Church leaders and the high price of their ambitions, and partly because of the vicissitudes of history (including schisms in the Church and the success of the Bohemians' revolt against the Church's doctrinal rigidity). Finally, with the help of some protective rulers and the new-fangled printing press, one of the religious challenges to Church power was more fully successful, producing the Protestant Reformation. In many respects, this reformation called for a return to the basics, absent the centuries of accreted dogma of the Catholic Church, and absent the papal hierarchy and its priests, in favor of an emphasis on direct interpretation of the Xtian holy book. In response, the Catholic Church underwent a Counter-Reformation in which it cleaned up corruption but doubled-down on much of its existing dogma and associated practices. Although the Catholic Church's willingness to interpret the Bible more allegorically was potentially a plus, its domineering approach to enforcing its doctrines, and its reactionary worldview and attitudes, including a continuing emphasis on heavenly rather than earthly concerns, together with the conservative thrust of the Counter-Reformation, forfeited any hope of long-term leadership in the development of human potential or the advance of science. Until the 20th century, it tried to suppress or otherwise hold proto-science and science at bay whenever it presented challenges to its dogma.

Meanwhile, the Protestants offered more possibilities for the improvement of society and the development of human potential in some areas of life, but their reliance on fundamentalist interpretations of the Bible resulted in new and more closely monitored social strictures in their congregations (with some parallel developments in the Catholic Church). Protestantism also sometimes inhibited advances in sciences, perhaps especially in earth science and paleontology, which were most constrained by the Bible's words and thus by the interpretation by Protestants and Catholics alike (i.e., despite the latter's greater propensity for allegorical interpretation). But, with each person allowed to interpret the Bible for themselves (or, at least, to join a wider range of denominations of their choice), Protestantism was destined to fracture from the start and its fracturing resulted in some cases in greater openness to social, cultural, and scientific advances. In earlier times, there were somewhat freer outposts like Florence and Venice (which, after 1405, included the university at Padua); later, there arose greater freedom in less singularly sectarian realms such as Britain and Amsterdam were becoming. With the help of the discoveries and perspectives of Copernicus-Brahe-Kepler, Galileo, Descartes, and later Newton, science-oriented royal societies in France and England (both after 1660), and then the social-political philosopher John Locke, the educated (intelligentsia) moved toward views of the universe (and human development) which, though still ultimately sourced to the Xtian deity, were more mechanistic and naturalistic in character, and that made it worthwhile to study/learn the ways of nature without reference to possible post-creation interventions by the deity. Still, many of the veils of ignorance, especially in geology, were shed only very slowly. Indeed, as we have seen, a very few, such as Robert Hooke (and Edmond Halley) in the late 1600s were breaking free faster than most, but the intellectual world was not yet ready for them. Over half a century later, the Comte de Buffon, in France, was to re-start the evidence-building process, with Cuvier and Hutton-Playfair making some major contributions in the late 1700s.

From his voyages on the Beagle and shortly afterwards, and from having read Lyell's works in geology and re-reading Thomas Malthus's *An Essay on the Principle of Population*, Darwin came to realize that the idea of evolution by natural selection (together with a long geologic time span) best explained what he had seen and other-wise learned. Over two decades, he continued to research, and learned from others about his collected specimens. He assembled a wealth of evidence—surely most of what was available—to put forth the case for natural selection. And well before the last edition of *The Origin of Species*, exciting new fossil finds continued to revealed unknown creatures confirming earth's long past, some of which even filled gaps in animal lineages (e.g., whales, reptiles/dinosaurs-birds, horses). The idea of evolution became more accepted than natural selection. In time, though, the rediscovery of Mendel's work on genetics and the new science of statistics (showing evolution could arise from variations in a population) helped put natural selection back in the driver's seat. Later still, sexual selection, which was the main topic of Darwin's *Descent of Man*, came to be seen as a viable component of evolution too. Spencerian and goal-oriented evolution that supposedly yielded humans at its pinnacle slowly faded from the picture in favor of directionless multi-branched trees of life. The method by which inheritance was passed along—genes—were discovered to be lodged in double helixes inside chromosomes; subsequently, electron microscopes allowed humans to peer into this previously hidden world and eventually to sequence whole genomes, including that of humans. In geology, plate tectonics and sea-floor spreading were discovered, confirming the movement of continents over the eons. Similarly, in paleontology, eras in which mass extinctions occurred were identified and causes sought. Also in paleontology, many more fossils continued to be found, including, finally, those of a wide variety of early proto-humans, filling gaps in that and many other lineages. Discoveries such as plate tectonics (showing nature's power vis-à-vis environments), ideas such as punctuated equilibrium, and great advances in genetics help to reduce an overemphasis on gradualism in evolution. In physics, the utility of radioactive substances as measures of deep time helped provide good estimates of "absolute" time that matched the relative ages of rocks known from geology-paleontology, and from the moon and meteorites as well, providing a very good age estimate for the earth at 4.5 billion years. In astronomy, many other galaxies were discovered, distances better estimated, and the ever-further distancing of those galaxies showed an expanding universe that might have been set off by a "big bang" around 14 billion years ago.

How the Development of Human Potential Is Thwarted and Cultural Sanity Sabotaged

In *The Rocks Don't Lie: A Geologist Investigates Noah's Flood*, David R. Montgomery provides an account of what happened to creationism and Noah's Flood after it was abandoned by scientists in Britain. He then proceeds to recount what happened in the mid-20th century in the United States that gave rise to the resurrection of those long-outdated beliefs. Although I have covered some of the early history in this regard, so that the reader can better see the scientific fade-out of biblical hypotheses, beyond that I am interested mainly in the effects of belief in biblical inerrancy on cultural sanity today. However, it is noteworthy that around the later middle of the 20th century more liberal Xtian denominations, including Catholicism, did begin to accept both an ancient earth and evolution, in part because not doing so contributed to disbelief in their versions of Xtianity. To these denominations, the holy book is about the teachings of Jesus and his followers, and perhaps about how to get to the Xtian heaven, and not about science. That left only the more fundamentalist denominations and sects to carry on with the long-disproven ideas of an inerrant Bible, a recent creation, and an even more recent and immense worldwide flood. And it resulted in some leaders among those fundamentalists, along with at least some deceptive if not fraudulent power and money-seeking charlatans, to concoct and promulgate creationist pseudo-science, start foundations such as the Institute for Creation Research, and attract donations from the ignorant, and even develop roadside attractions and theme parks based on fake science, that is, presenting their interpretation(s) of biblical inerrancy.

Of course, there are always some Xtian leaders or would-be leaders, and politicians, and a few stray trained scientists, who are so strongly Xtian that they will try to leave room even for fundamentalist doctrines in their scientific or philosophical worldview (as the "intelligent design"/ID contingent does). One avenue by which to do so is to reject the naturalistic methodology used in science, because this methodological approach and most basic of assumptions automatically rules out plugging a deity as the answer to any questions as yet unsolved. Although some of the motivation involved may actually be associated with views that a deity really is needed to fill in gaps in understanding that science cannot (yet) remove, this defeats the whole purpose of science—to find out how nature works. Thus subsequent advances in scientific explanations would be (and formerly were, as we have seen) hindered by a leap of faith to a "solution" based on a deity. Moreover, many once-supposed gaps have a history of being filled later, without having resorted to a deity (and undermining those who did so). But another motive behind some objections to methodological naturalism and unguided evolution is the feeling that Xtian civilization needs defending against materialistic views. Many probably also share the mistaken view that sees the scientific truths in evolution (and/or an old earth) as a primary threat to Xtian civilization. At a deeper level perhaps, in any case among many Xtian adherents, are desires to see humans as special in the eyes of the deity, and to leave room for that deity to intervene, for miracles, and perhaps especially to answer (some) prayers. Although some scientists openly reject a deity and a few have even tried to assemble evidence against a deity's existence, others affirm a belief in a deity, including the Xtian deity. So, the threat is in the eye (and the rigid biblical authority-oriented belief system) of the beholder. In any case, strictly speaking, science can say no more than that it simply proceeds without *assuming* anything supernatural. And that holds even as science has begun to find more evidence, and advance more hypotheses, about how human altruism, human cooperation, and human intelligence arose evolutionarily—the foundations of human civilization and morality in genes that support our capacity for cooperation and our sociability [von Hippel] is not in the Xtian holy book.

Creationists used to claim that many scientists opposed evolution—though they were able to cite only a very, very few, and they often misleadingly included some as opponents who were actually only debating the mechanisms of evolution. "Many" can be a very fuzzy word, quantitatively speaking, yet its use may have made it seem to some true believers that the world of science was in fact divided in its stances on evolution. In response to this falsehood, the National Center for Science (NCSE) in 2005 initiated a "tongue-in-cheek" "Project Steve" (named after Stephen Jay Gould). Figuring that people with the first name of Steve (or variants thereon, including the feminine, such as Stephanie) constituted about 1% of all people, and hence probably 1% of scientists as well, they wrote a basic statement affirming evolution—including that creationism and intelligent design should not be taught as science in public schools—a statement which only people named Steve could sign. Although NCSE has not actively been soliciting signers for well over a decade, people named Steve have been able to sign all along. At last count, in March of 2018, there were 1424 signatories, corresponding to roughly 142,400 scientists if every evolution-supporting scientist were included ["Project Steve," NCSE website]. In other words, scientists overwhelmingly accept evolution, and serious doubters are few (not "many"), especially in the most relevant disciplines.

So, what costs do the denial of the truths of evolution, the fact of evolution, and of deep geologic time impose on our society that make their denial into an especially important cultural insanity?

Undermining the Education of Their Own Children and Grandchildren, and Their Own Interests. As should be obvious from my account above, an Xtian family of anti-evolutionist/young-earth creationist/biblically-inerrant believers that *successfully* transmits its beliefs to the subsequent generations of children in that household come very close to denying them all possibility of becoming scientifically literate, let alone experts in most fields of science. Successful transmission results in avoidances, mental compartmentalization, and denials of facts that are totally unnecessary for other Xtians. (For more on the mental mechanisms involved, see Part One.) Thus, successful transmission of overly fundamentalist religion sustains ignorance in each new generation's perceptions of reality and almost guarantees a warped worldview as well. Of course the reality is that such transmission is only to varying degrees successful and, with the help of education and contact with non-believers, some of each subsequent generation do break free, again to varying degrees, from imprisonment in and by such religious views. But some of the minds even of most of those that break free will be partly hamstrung for life, if only because they got off to such a poor start in understanding science. Of course the direct damage is greatest where inerrant beliefs in the Bible are most successfully transmitted. And this is likely to be where the believers can establish circles of friends and acquaintance with, and live in communities dominated by, similarly limited ranges of beliefs. Then it becomes even easier to maintain the false consciousness involved—the supplanting of reality by an inculcated if not indoctrinated belief system—and to circle the wagons in defense even against other religious perspectives, and find allies to join in attacks on real science.

Undermining the Education of Others' Children. Alas, attempts to transmit Xtian anti-evolutionist/young-earth creationist/biblically-inerrant believers' beliefs are not limited to the younger generations in their own families. Their views are spread and reinforced by the church leaders that arise from among them. And, yet more distressingly, they are also spread via the political realm to the public and private schools that others' children attend—where parents may not know that their child's instruction in biology or earth science is being distorted according to the views of a particular set of Xtian beliefs. Schools face political pressures to exclude evolution from science instruction, and/or to teach "creation science" or "intelligent design" as viable scientific alternatives along with evolution in *science* classes. (Courts have ruled that both "creation science" and "intelligent design" are religion, not science, and so cannot be taught as science in the public schools.) But the efforts to circumvent law still produces pressure on schools that runs the full gamut from individual parental complaints to their children's teacher(s) about evolution being taught and/or the absence of a biblically literalist alternative to that, as well as to well-organized political efforts to elect fundamentalist school board members or members of state boards that have responsibility for curriculum. Elementary school teachers, few of whom have a strong background in science, are most sensitive to such pressures (and not many teach much about evolution or geologic time anyway, especially using the term "evolution"). But in many areas of the country, particularly in the South, Midwest and rural areas, even many middle- and high-school teachers with backgrounds in science (some of whom are also not all that strong on the subject of evolution) would rather avoid controversy than teach evolution, despite it being "a central organizing principle for all of biology"—a key to learning in the life sciences that has long been recognized as such [American Association for the Advancement of Science, *Project 2061: Science for All Americans, Summary*, 7]. So there are many high school biology classrooms in which evolution is treated relatively cursorily (or even not at all). In some cases, teachers may not even be willing to clarify that creationism is not a viable alternative scientifically. And in some cases, the textbook material on evolution is simply skipped as far as the instruction goes, or maybe assigned only as reading. Still, most teachers do try to give students enough information to pass state tests in science (if there are science tests required after biology has been taught in the usual curriculum), but the effectiveness of the inclusion of evolution in state tests also varies widely (and has varied over time *within* some if not many states).

In the United States as a whole, the latest Gallup Poll about evolution, conducted in 2017, asked respondents which of three alternatives came closest to their view, producing the following results: 38% agreed that "God created human beings pretty much in their present form at one time within the last 10,000 years or so"; 38% also agreed that "human beings developed from less advanced forms of life, but God guided this process"; and 19% agreed that "human beings developed from less advanced forms of life, but God had no part in this process"; 5% did not venture a response ["Evolution, Creationism, Intelligent Design/Gallup Historical Trends"; Gallup Poll website]. Since 1982, there has been a 10-point rise in the "God had no part" response; and a 6-point decline in the strict creationist alternative, with some fluctuation within that range; and no net change (with some fluctuation) in the "God guided" alternative. A National Center for Science Education website release on the results of the 2017 poll adds that "acceptance of the creationist option was associated with lower education levels, Protestantism, and weekly church attendance" [Glenn Branch, "The Latest Gallup Poll on Evolution," NCSE website].

Despite the Gallup website headline above, "intelligent design" is not a specific alternative in the poll. The "God guided" response about human evolution could represent some version of ID or it could represent a long-standing stance among many liberal Xtians. Were ID proponents to formally accept that humans evolved from "lower" forms of life, even if guided by a deity, they would seriously jeopardize any possible support from believers in biblical inerrancy. From my perspective, ID itself was designed to accommodate all manner of Xtian views, including if not especially creationism, in part by refusing to provide any specificity, especially as to human evolution in nature and as to the length of time involved in Earth's history. In that way, its modern-day re-founders hoped to be able to unite all Xtians who feel threatened by non-Xtian influences on our culture against the methodological naturalism of science, especially with reference to evolution. In contrast, most liberal Xtian church denominations do not deny science's methodological naturalism. They also recognize geology's "deep time" and probably tend to reserve the deity's subsequent intervention/guidance in evolution to doing something special to convert proto-humans to true humans.

The main arguments that ID proponents advance for their position are untestable and negative—no positive evidence is involved. For example, in support of the necessity of a deity's involvement, some cite seemingly astronomical mathematical improbabilities of aspects of life having occurred/arisen—but calculated in ways that do not take account of evolution as a step-by-step process over millions upon millions of years. And they argue for the idea of "irreducible complexity." Irreducible complexity as seen in some organs, ID proponents claim, cannot have evolved and therefore by default required the intervention of a deity/supernatural entity. The traditional example was the eye, but of late the bacterial flagellum has been offered. However, both examples have now been thoroughly discredited. Regarding eyes, there are lots of intermediate steps that evolution likely followed, as still seen, for example, in the eyes in molluscs today, which range from primitive light-sensing eye spots to sharp-eyed octopi. The bacterial flagellum was addressed in the Dover ID trial (see below). The ID alternative, except perhaps in its worst young-earth variety, also tends to require multiple creations at a very small scale (e.g., the bacterial flagellum!), which to most people nowadays does not seem like a viable alternative either, and certainly does not fit a deity creating all the "kinds" over a few days.

Undermining the Future of the Country and of All Humanity

The concocted inventions of creationist leaders to explain away evolution and geologic time are stretched well beyond sane belief for anyone with an even vaguely adequate foundation in the sciences—unless they have been thoroughly indoctrinated in favor of religious beliefs that mandate rejection or distortion of any Bible-conflicting findings. Given their automatic rejection of so much science, creationists almost had to concoct some fake science(s) because too much real science was becoming common knowledge. Yet, for some creationists, the evolutionary and deep-time-using scientists are regarded as being engaged in a great conspiracy (rather more like the small circle of creationist leadership in actuality). We have seen some of the efforts to undermine real science in the creationist team that wrote the book for sale at Grand Canyon National Park (above). In addition, dinosaurs are so well known even among young-earth creationist youth that many leading creationists have put them onto Noah's Ark, because Noah took two of every kind of land animal, including birds, aboard. But lest the ark get impossibly overcrowded (and food had to be brought along too), "kind" sometimes gets interpreted very broadly so as to exclude many animal species and varieties within kinds, where post-flood "microevolution" (evolution on a small scale) is then used to restore those species—presumably adhering to the old idea that the deity initially regarded his creation as "good," so that "He" wouldn't use "His" flood to eliminate so many animals permanently. (But subsequent extinctions are no longer doubted, notwithstanding the deity's "good" creation.) Although extinctions before Noah's Flood are not supposed to have occurred, some creationists do date some fossils into the 1,500 years or so between the deity's creation of the world and that flood. A one-shot advance of glaciers (rather than several advances and retreats during the recent Pleistocene period) is sometimes crammed into that narrow time slot too. Still, one wonders if the necessarily undersized ark (and creationist theme parks) included, to name a few, pairs of the many different kinds of pterodactyls, "age of mammals" animals such the rhino-sized Uintatherium, wooly mammoth, sabre-tooth cats, Megatheriums and three-toed horse ancestors, or, for that matter, pre-dinosaur animals such as the upwards-of-eight-foot Dimetrodon and the six-foot Eryops (amphibian), and many more. (Extinct species are vastly more numerous than living ones.) And did Noah include any of the 350,000 known species of beetle (or did they all survive via their egg cases remaining unhatched for a long time, until flood waters had fully receded, which in some accounts of the flood was a year or so)? And what did the herbivores eat when they got off the ark, when all the plants were either destroyed or covered in muck sometimes almost a mile thick if the accounts in the creationist Grand Canyon book are to be believed? Did the herbivores wait for plant seeds to germinate and grow (and wouldn't plants with seeds that don't float become extinct)? And the carnivores??—maybe they just twiddled their thumbs while waiting for the pairs of herbivores to breed and produce more food? It is all stupid, and patently absurd.

Yet creationist political attacks on real science that have not been easy to thwart are easy to find. For example, Texas has been a battleground—over and over again—specifically around the treatment of evolution in science texts under consideration for adoption. These textbook reviews are especially important to competing publishers of high school biology texts and, given the size of the Texas market, have sometimes influenced how evolution is treated in publisher modifications to the original text, or in subsequent editions. Indeed, this is roughly how evolution all but disappeared from most high school texts between the mid-1920s until after the U.S.S.R. launched Sputnik, in 1956 (which spurred calls to catch up on science education).

Year after year in many state legislatures bills are introduced that one way or another aim to compromise the teaching of evolution, for example by emphasizing the "critical thinking" value of instructional challenges to the theory of evolution, though there are no such challenges within science (e.g., see most issues of the National Center for Science Education, *Reports*, especially the column, "Update" and its earlier version "Update—News from the Field"). While some are introduced mainly to please religious constituencies in conservative districts, and only a very few of these bills are ultimately passed (and most are then struck down in the courts), others have a real chance of becoming law unless strong organized opposition arises.

The 1987 Supreme Court case on the teaching of evolution (Edwards vs. Aguillard) arose from a law passed in Louisiana that required public schools to teach "creation science" wherever evolution was taught. (The Court ruled that "creation science" was intended to support a particular religion—which is constitutionally prohibited— and so could not be taught in science classes in public schools, though alternative theories that were clearly secular could be taught.) But religious reactionaries in Louisiana did not give up. In 2008, Louisiana adopted a law which apparently allows science teachers to bring in religious materials which are critical of scientific evolution, presumably provided they are willing, at least if it should become necessary, to claim that the added information has a scientific foundation. In large part this was an "academic freedom" (for the teachers) ploy, a subterfuge to undermine the teaching of evolution, as proposed by the Discovery Institute, the key promulgator of ID. But the new law leaves the teachers wide open to creationist parent pressures. And there are, of course, at least some K-12 teachers who are Xtian fundamentalists and will use the leeway given by the law in various ways (where probably the only way to stop erroneous instruction in science is to challenge the teacher to defend his/her materials or expressions according to the law).

In Kansas in 2004, religious conservatives obtained a 6-4 majority on the State Board of Education. In 2005 that majority proceeded to modify science standards by not limiting them to naturalistic explanations and by casting evolution as a theory in distress *scientifically* (which it decidedly is not), and to allow intelligent design to be taught as an alternative, much in accord with a Discovery Institute-earlier recommended subterfuge to "teach the controversy." (The Discovery Institute was very actively involved in these doings, including even in support of some candidates in the election in 2004.) But the state board's actions were so beyond the pale that they made Kansas a bit of a laughingstock and even drew negative reactions from corporations and threats never to consider Kansas locations. A different majority was elected to the board in the next election, and more legitimate science curricula were restored in Kansas.

And in Dover, Pennsylvania, in 2004, the school board promulgated a statement to be read to high school biology classes, despite solid resistance to the interference and the content of the statement by all the high school biology teachers. The statement recommended the book, *Pandas and People,* copies of which, the statement said, were available in the school library, for an alternative perspective on evolution. In the subsequent trial, that book, which comes recommended by ID's Discovery Institute, was shown, through Prof. Barbara Forrest's examination of the many drafts of the book's manuscripts while it was in preparation, to have had two consecutive drafts, straddling the decision in the aforementioned Aguillard case, between which the main alterations were simply changing "creation scientists" to "intelligent design proponents"—which clearly revealed that ID was mainly a cover for "creation science." For a relatively comprehensive account of the development of the case and the evidence in the trial, see the two-hour NOVA production, "Judgment Day: Intelligent Design on Trial." Although a number of states were then attempting to find ways to minimize the teaching of evolution or include religious alternatives, Dover was the first court case involving intelligent design. The school board's policy drew a public endorsement by home-state Pennsylvania Senator Rick Santorum and elicited support for teaching "both sides" by President George W. Bush [NOVA, "Judgment Day: Intelligent

Design on Trial"]. But the school board's defenders of the statement had problems. The problems were not only that there was an Xtian-religious motivation expressed by those who advocated the policy in Dover and in the *government entity* involved (the school board that adopted it), but that intelligent design, which was seen by proponents as accommodating creationist views, wasn't science (as was shown in the trial) and shouldn't be taught as such in science classrooms in public schools.

And even now, as I write, there are at least some colleges—such as Liberty University—wherein young-earth creationist stances and faculty dominate the entire curriculum, including in the biological sciences, in a general attempt to arm and steel the students against evolution's presumed assault on their fundamentalist religious beliefs, including moral beliefs. Extreme creationist backgrounds and training such as this can sometimes harden believers so much that they persist (perhaps under cover) through legitimate graduate training to a Ph.D., and then go on to being credentialed faculty teaching (young-earth) creationist claptrap to new generations of students, adding to the cultural insanity.

Along the same lines, more recently, in a number of states there have been official board-or-advisory group-type challenges to the science-related wordings supportive of evolution (and climate change) found in the New Generation Science Standards (released in 2013). Because these standards are both multi-state/national *in source* and intended use (though not mandatory) and do a best-yet job of clearly including evolution as appropriate (though too delicately and circuitously in elementary school[15]), there is now more hope that some

---

15   I once taught a two-hour "unit" on geologic time and prehistoric life over two days to mostly 3rd graders (4th graders would have been best). Each student was given a portion of an adding machine roll to represent geologic time (back through about 500 million years only). They were also given a chart showing the length of the various important geologic periods. They then sectioned their rolls of paper proportionately (happily taking up floor space throughout the room and in the hall in doing so). They

progress will be made, and less human potential suppressed. In general, it has been harder for states to resist these new standards because doing so brings unwanted disapproval and scrutiny from the outside world. How much difference those new standards will actually make will depend on state science lesson guidelines, state science test design (and scheduling vis-à-vis the high school science curriculum), if any tests are required at that level, the effectiveness of teacher training, teacher beliefs, and local individual and group parental pressures.

Some possible improvements have also been seen in recent international science literacy assessments done by the Program for International Student Assessment (PISA). There were slight gains in science literacy of 15-year-olds in the interval between 2006 and 2018, with the mean score rising from 489 to 502. (All data in this paragraph are from the National Center for Education Statistics [nces.ed.gov]. The Organization for Economic Cooperation and Development countries had a mean score of 489, with a range from 530 to 413. The highest scores came from Estonia, Japan, Finland and Korea, while the bottom two, 413 and 419, from Colombia and Mexico, were 25 points lower than the next lowest, pulling the OECD average down a little. The U.S.A.'s score on scientific literacy was significantly lower than 6, the same as 11, and significantly higher than 19. When countries outside the OECD are included in the picture (many of them with weak educational systems and only partly "developed" economically, expanding the group to 78), 5 more placed measurably ahead of the U.S.A. (i.e., four eastern provinces in China, Singapore, Macau, Chinese Taipei, and Hong Kong). There are, of course, fairly large differences

---

were also given information about the animals that arose and lived in each geologic period, with the task of portraying some of those animals in the right places on their roll. A number of books were available in which they could find depictions of these animals. Some of these children were a little too young to fully understand the concept of a million well (equals 20 full stadiums). But otherwise the unit involved practice in arithmetical scaling (where each inch represented several million years), a beginning familiarity with geologic time periods, and a sense of evolution over those time periods. The kids had a great time and produced a cool product to take home—and refer to subsequently.

in mean scores by poverty level (across all countries). In the U.S.A., there were about 100 points of difference between schools with 75% eligibility for free and reduced lunches and schools with 10-25% eligibility. And, also, "of course," there were similar size differences by race/ethnicity in the U.S.A., with Asians at 49 points above the U.S.A. average, Whites at plus 27, Mixed at minus 1, Hispanic at minus 24, and African Americans at minus 62. ("Of course" is written because there is a large overlap between data about race/ethnicity and data about socioeconomic status.)

One other PISA science literacy score statistic was particularly striking, and perhaps suggests, along with the country's mediocre overall score, some of the effects of the cultural insanity described here. When differences between test scores at the 90th percentile and the 10th percentile on science literacy are examined, the difference for the U.S.A. was 259 points (244 was the mean for the 78 countries). The U.S.A. was in or near the upper fourth of the distribution in overall score. But in comparisons among 78 countries' students of scores at the 90th versus the 10th percentile, the U.S.A.'s score differences were greater than 50 others—so, the U.S.A. placed at about the bottom third. But this involved *difference* scores that were less than only two other countries (with 25 others tied). In effect, the distribution of science literacy difference scores (90th percentile vs. 10th percentile) in the U.S.A. was more strung out, and tied with 25 others with the widest spread!

The cultural insanity described in this Part arises from very large size of the subcultures believing in the inerrancy of their particular "holy" book, and from so much religious-political pressure by "members" of those subcultures either to minimize the inclusion of anything associated with evolution and geologic time in the science curriculum of K-12 students and/or to include that holy book's creation and flood mythology as an alternative "science" alongside real science. As a result, many K-12 students, in generation after generation, have been deprived of a good chance to attain basic science literacy, especially but by no means exclusively in the many disciplines associated with the life sciences. Avoiding instruction in evolution—the idea which unites all knowledge in biology—makes biology seem more like an immense and disparate array of boring facts to memorize. And in the table above, we saw especially how the work in many scientific disciplines includes "deep time"—information that cannot be accepted into the worldview of believers in biblical inerrancy. But all too many of our high school youth then take their science-limited backgrounds to college and often struggle to do well in their very few required science classes, often thereafter abandoning all higher-level courses in those fields. College courses (in all but a few institutions) can help to remedy the deficiencies in K-12 schooling. But it is still more difficult to rise to become an expert in any branch of the biological or earth sciences when a student in the lowest level of college biology classes has to struggle with whether much of his/her religious beliefs are wrong, while students from areas of the country less influenced by fundamentalist religion do not have that obstacle *or the accumulated deficits in science knowledge that accompany it.*

It should come as no surprise then that the emphasis in recent years on getting K-12 students more exposure to STEM (Science-Technology-Engineering-Mathematics) has been slow to produce clear improvements. Similarly, it should come as no surprise that the country has needed many well-educated immigrants to fill its expanding graduate programs in technology/engineering and some sciences in order to develop enough high levels of expertise in those fields. Well over half the graduate students in most fields of engineering are international rather than domestic, including the two largest ones (computer science and electrical engineering, but also in fields like petroleum engineering, which has a foundation in geology).

Potentially making matters worse—in terms of the country's economic needs—are narrow-minded political efforts to reduce the choices that foreign students have to remain in the United States, and to restrict visas for upper level graduate students. (International students do bring more money into universities—helping the U.S. balance of trade—but graduate admissions decisions are departmentalized and their missions involve accepting the best applicants.) But the underlying problem (compounding the effects of poverty) is that we have unnecessarily but substantially diminished the human potentials of many children born in this country with a cultural insanity in which too many people adhere to antiquated religious belief systems that, in effect, seek to discredit if not sabotage foundational evolution-related principles in the life sciences, and the acceptance of deep time integral to many scientific disciplines.

By effectively limiting what so many of our young citizens can learn and achieve in the sciences, this cultural insanity also reduces the contributions that the United States might make to the future of human development, that is, not only for our own direct benefit as a society and country, but for humanity as a whole. The world's nations need to come together to help solve some very important mutual problems, many involving the use of science and technology—not just climate change, but problems that have taken a back seat to climate change, including the fact that habitat destruction and an ever-rising human population are currently interacting to produce a sixth mass extinction, with humans as the driving calamity—where our activities represent the environmental forces to which other creatures must adapt (or die out). And, quite possibly, humans themselves may well ultimately be threatened by collapses in the webs of life. We need more of earth's people to reach closer to their full potential to more effectively address, let alone solve such problems. The U.S.A. has enough wealth to educate its youth so as to ensure some decent level of scientific literacy throughout its population, and to enable many more students to go well beyond that in STEM fields. That we fall far short of that potential is testimony to the effects (and power) of the cultural insanity associated with the denial of geologic time and the rejection of evolution.

REFERENCES CITED

Ackroyd, Peter, *Rebellion: The History of England from James 1 to the Glorious Revolution*. New York: Thomas Dunne Books/St. Martin's Press, 2014.

aclu-mn.org, "ACLU releases data showing racial disparities in low level arrests in Minneapolis," 2014.

African Wildlife Foundation, *African Wildlife News*, Summer 2019, 6.

Alexander, Michelle, *The New Jim Crow: Mass Incarceration in the Age of Colorblindness (revised edition)*. New York: The New Press, 2012.

American Association for the Advancement of Science, *Project 2061: Science for All Americans, Summary*. Washington, D.C.: AAAS, Inc., 1989.

Aristotle, *The Nichomachean Ethics of Aristotle*, transl. by Sir David Ross. London: Oxford University Press, 1959.

Bacon, Francis, *The Great Instauration and New Atlantis*; J. Weinberger, Ed. Arlington Hts., IL: Harlan Davidson, 1980.

Bacon, Francis, *The New Organon*. Seattle, WA: Loki's publishing, undated.

Barr, Martyn, *Paintings in Light: The Stained Glass Windows of Canterbury* Cathedral. Canterbury: Out of the Box Publishing, 2013.

Barstow, Anne Llewellyn, *Witchcraze: A New History of the European Witch Hunts*. New York: HarperOne, 1995.

Bartlett, Kenneth R., *The Italian Renaissance*. Chantilly, VA: The Teaching Company, 2005.

Benton, Janetta Rebold, *Holy Terrors on Medieval Buildings*. New York: Abbeville Press, 1997.

Blamires, Alcuin, *The Case for Women in Medieval Culture*. Oxford, England: Oxford University Press, 1998.

Boorstin, Daniel J., *The Discoverers: A History of Man's Search to Know His World and Himself*. New York: Vintage Books, 1985.

Bowen, Howard R., *Investment in Learning*. San Francisco: Jossey-Bass, 1977.

Branch, Glenn, "The Latest Gallup Poll on Evolution," National Center for Science Education website, accessed 1/18/2019.

Britannica .com, Editors, "Gratian's Decretum," accessed via "Gratian," 8/22/2018.

Britannica.com, Editors, article on Peter Lombard; accessed 8/10/2017.

Brundage, James, "Sexual Decision-Making Process" (table) in Steven A. Epstein (see below

Burman, Edward, *The Hammer of Heresy*. Gloucestershire GL5 2BU, England: Sutton Publishing Limited, 2004.

Carroll, Sean B., *The Making of the Fittest: DNA and the Ultimate Forensic Record of Evolution*. New York: W. W. Norton, 2006.

Catholic Online, "Albert the Great," accessed 4/2/2017.

Certeau, Michel de, *The Possession at Loudon*; trans. Michael B. Smith. Chicago: The University of Chicago Press, 1996.

Chickering, Arthur W., *Education and Identity*. San Francisco, Jossey-Bass, 1969.

Coleman, Christopher B., *The Treatise of Lorenzo Valla on the Donation of Constantine*. Toronto: University of Toronto Press, 1993.

Collins, Randall, *The Sociology of Philosophies: A Global Theory of Intellectual Change*. Cambridge, Mass: Belknap/Harvard University Press, 2002.

Conner, Clifford D., *A People's History of Science: Miners, Midwives, and "Low Mechanicks."* New York: Nation Books, 2005.

Coppins, McKay, "The Billion-Dollar Disinformation Campaign to Re-elect the President," in *The Atlantic*, March 2020—on-line article title.

Coyne, Jerry A., *Why Evolution is True*. New York: Viking, Penguin, 2009.

Crosby, Alfred W., *The Measure of Reality: Quantification and Western Society, 1250-1600*. Cambridge, UK: Cambridge University Press, 1997.

Crowley, Roger, *Empires of the Sea: The Final Battle for the Mediterranean, 1521-1580*. London: Faber and Faber, 2008.

Dalrymple, G. Brent, "Radiometric Dating Does Work!" in website of National Center for Science Education (NCSE), accessed 12/26/2018.

Diamond, Jared, *Collapse: How Societies Choose to Fail or Succeed*. New York: Penguin Books, 2006.

Diamond, Jared, *The World Until Yesterday: What Can We Learn from Traditional Societies*. New York: Viking Penguin, 2012.

Drug Policy Alliance mailing, April 2019.

Drug Policy Alliance website, accessed 4/6/2019, citing John Ehrlichman.

Drug Policy Alliance, "A Brief History of the Drug War, website," accessed 4/6/2019.

Drug Policy Alliance, "Drug War Facts," ca. 2010.

Drug Policy Alliance, "Drug War Facts," mailing, ca. 2017.

Drum, Kevin, "Death and Taxes," in *Mother Jones*, July-Aug. 2020, 26-31, 66-67.

Dyer, Christopher, *Making a Living in the Middle Ages: The People of Britain, 850-1520*. New Haven: Yale University Press, 2002.

Eilperin, Juliet, Josh Dawsey, and Brady Dennis, "White House blocked document warning about climate   change," in the *Star Tribune*, June 9, 2019, A13.

Eire, Carlos M. N., *Reformations: The Early Modern World, 1450-1650*. New Haven: Yale University Press, 2016.

Environmental Defense Fund Special Report, Spring 2015, 5, "Don't Assume the Chemicals in Household Products You Use Every Day Are Safe."

Environmental Defense Fund, *Solutions*, Fall 2014. Articles on the West Coast: "A Fishery on the Rebound."

Environmental Defense Fund, *Solutions*, Summer 2017, 14.

Epstein, Steven A., *An Economic and Social History of Later Medieval Europe, 1000-1500*. New York: Cambridge University Press, 2009.

Erasmus, Desiderius, *The Praise of Folly*, translated, with an Essay & Commentary, by Hoyt Hopewell Hudson. Princeton, N.J.: Princeton University Press, 1970.

Erikson, Erik H., *Identity: Youth and Crisis*. New York: W. W. Norton, 1968.

Erlande-Brandenburg, Alain, *The Cathedral Builders of the Middle Ages*. London: Thames and Hudson/New Horizons, 1995.

Estep, William R., *Renaissance and Reformation*. Grand Rapids, Mich.: Eerdmans, 1986.

Fanon, Frantz, *The Wretched of the Earth*, transl. by Constance Farrington. New York: Grove Press, 1966.

Feng, Rhoda, "Public Citizen Pressures Companies to Comply with Europe's New Data Protection Rules," in *Public Citizen News*, July-August 2018, 11.

Ferngren, Gary B., Ed., *Science and Religion: A Historical Introduction*. Baltimore: The John Hopkins University Press, 2002.

Ferngren, Gary B., "Introduction," ix-xiv, in Ferngren, Ed., *Science and Religion: A Historical Introduction*. Baltimore: The John Hopkins University Press, 2002.

Frances, Allen, *Twilight of American Sanity: A Psychiatrist Analyzes the Age of Trump*. New York: William Morrow/Harper Collins, 2017.

Frank, Thomas, *What's the Matter with Kansas?* New York: Henry Holt & Co., 2004.

Frankforter, A. Daniel, *The Medieval Millennium: An Introduction*. Upper Saddle River, NJ: Prentice Hall, 1999.

Fritz, Angela, "Why incompetent people think they are experts," in the *StarTribune*, Feb. 3, 2019, SH3.

Fuller, Randall, *The Book that Changed America: How Darwin's Theory of Evolution Ignited a Nation*. New York, Viking, 2017.

Gallup Poll website, "Evolution, Creationism, Intelligent Design/ Gallup Historical Trends," accessed 1/18/2019.

Garrett, Wilbur E., Ed., "The Gothic Revolution," in *National Geographic*, Vol. 176, No. 1, 113. Washington, D.C.: The National Geographic Society, July 1989.

Gies, Frances & Joseph, *Cathedral, Forge, and Waterwheel: Technology and Invention in the Middle Ages*. New York: HarperPerennial, 1995.

Goodich, Michael E., *Violence and Miracle in the Fourteenth Century: Private Grief and Public Salvation*. Chicago: University of Chicago Press, 1995.

Grant, Edward, "Aristotle and Aristotelianism,"33-46, in Ferngren, Ed.

Grant, Edward, *Science and Religion, 400 BC – AD 1450*. Baltimore: The John Hopkins University Press, 2006. Unless otherwise noted, all "Grant" references refer to this book.

Grayling, A.C., *The Age of Genius: The Seventeenth Century & the Birth of the Modern Mind*. London: Bloomsbury, 2016.

Greenblatt, Stephen, *The Swerve: How the World Became Modern*, 42. New York: W.W. Norton, 2012.

Greengrass, Mark, *Christendom Destroyed: Europe 1517-1648*. New York: Penguin Books, 2015.

Halecki, O., *A History of Poland*. New York: Barnes & Noble, 1993.

Hannam, James, *The Genesis of Science: How the Christian Middle Ages Launched the Scientific Revolution*. Washington, D.C.: Regnery Publishing, 2011.

Hariri, Yuval Noah, *Sapiens: A Brief History of Humankind*. New York: Harper Perennial, 2015.

Harrington, Joel F., *The Faithful Executioner: Life and Death, Honor and Shame in the Turbulent Sixteenth Century*. New York: Picador, 2014.

Hartman, Andrew, *A War for the Soul of America: A History of the Culture Wars*, 100. Chicago: The University of Chicago Press, 2015.

Hawken, Paul, Ed., *Drawdown: The Most Comprehensive Plan Ever Proposed to Reverse Global Warming*. New York: Penguin, 2017.

Holland, Glenn S., *Religion in the Ancient Mediterranean World*, Part 2. Chantilly, VA: The Teaching Company, 2005.

Hudson, Hoyt Hopewell, "The Folly of Erasmus: An Essay," in *Erasmus*. xi-xli.

Huxley, Julian, "Introduction to the Mentor Edition," in Charles Darwin, *Origin of Species by Means of Natural Selection of the Preservation of Favoured Races in the Struggle for Life*. New York: The New American Library, 1958.

Jacobs, Andrew, "How Denmark raises antibiotic-free pigs," in the *StarTribune*, Jan. 12, 2020, SH2.

Jeffrey, Clara, and Monika Bauerlein, "With Friends Like These…," in *Mother Jones*, March-April, 2019, 19.

King, Ross, *Brunelleschi's Dome: How a Renaissance Genius Reinvented Architecture*. New York: Penguin Books, 2001.

Klaits, Joseph, *Servants of Satan: The Age of Witch Hunts*. Indiana University Press, Bloomington, IN, 1985.

Klein, Dan and Ward Lloyd, *The History of Glass*. New York: Crescent Books, 1989.

Knickmeier, Danette, "Obama Signs New Toxic Substances Chemicals Act," in *Sierra Club North Star Journal*, Winter 2016-17, 12.

Kolbert, Elizabeth, *The Sixth Extinction: An Unnatural History*. New York: Picador (Henry Holt & Co., 2015.

Koon, Jeffrey Wynter, *Assessing Quality and Effectiveness in University and College Academic Programs: A Democratic Theory of Evaluation, Vol. 2*. Ann Arbor, Mich.: University Microfilms International, 1991.

Kors, Alan Charles, *The Birth of the Modern Mind: The Intellectual History of the 17th and 18th Centuries*. Chantilly, VA: The Great Courses, 1998.

Krivine, Hubert, *The Earth: From Myths to Knowledge*, 8. London: Verso Press, 2015. Transl. by David Fernbach.

Kuhn, Thomas S., *The Copernican Revolution: Planetary Astronomy in the Development of Western Thought*. Cambridge, Mass.: Harvard University Press, 1957/1985/2003.

Kuhn, Thomas S., *The Structure of Scientific Revolutions, 2nd Ed.* Chicago: University of Chicago Press, 1970.

Lakoff, George, *Don't Think of an Elephant!: Know Your Values and Frame the Debate*. White River Junction, VT: Chelsea Green Publishing, 2004.

Lents, Nathan H., *Human Errors: A Panorama of Our Glitches, from Pointless Bones to Broken Genes. Boston: Mariner Books, 2019.*

Leroi, Armand Marie, *The Lagoon: How Aristotle Invented Science.* New York: Viking, 2014.

Levack, Brian P, *The Witch-Hunt in Early Modern Europe.* New York: Longman, 1987.

Library of Universal Knowledge: A Reprint of the Last (1880) Edinburgh and London Edition of Chambers's Encyclopedia with Copious Additions by American Editors, Vols. IV, & XIII. New York: American Book Exchange, 1880. [Sic].

Lindberg, David C., "Medieval Science and Religion," 57-72, in Gary B. Ferngren, Ed.

Lindberg, David C., *The Beginnings of Western Science: The European Scientific Tradition in Philosophical, Religious, and Institutional Context, Prehistory to A.D. 1450 (2nd Edition). Chicago:* The University of Chicago Press, 2007.

Lister, Adrian, *Darwin's Fossils: The Collection that Shaped the Theory of Evolution.* Washington, D.C.: Smithsonian Books, 2018.

Long, Pamela O., *Technology and Society in the Medieval Centuries: Byzantium, Islam, and the West, 500-1300.* Washington, D.C.: Society for the History of Technology and the American Historical Association, 2003. This is Long1.

Long, Pamla O., *Artisan/Practitioners and the Rise of the New Sciences, 1400-1600.* Corvallis, Ore.: Oregon State University Press, 2011. This is Long2.

Longfellow, Henry Wadsworth (transl.), *Dante's Divine Comedy: Hell, Purgatory, Paradise.* New York: Chartwell Books, 2012. Edited and introduced by Anna Amari-Parker.

Losos, Jonathan B., *Improbable Destinies: Fate, Chance, and the Future of Evolution.* New York: Riverhead Books, 2017.

MacCulloch, Diarmaid, *Reformation: Europe's House Divided, 1490-1700.* London: Penguin Books, 2004.

Mannix, Andy, "Eyewitness photo lineups get closer look," in the *StarTribune,* Feb. 20, 2020, B1.

Maslow, Abraham, *Toward a Psychology of Being, 2nd Ed.* Princeton, N. J.: D. Van Nostrand, 1968.

Masters, William H., and Virginia E. Johnson, *Human Sexual Response.* Toronto; New York: Bantam Books, 1966.

McEvedy, Colin, in *The New Penguin Atlas of Medieval History*, 34. London: Penguin Books, 1992.

McGrath, Alister, *Reformation Thought: An Introduction, 2nd Ed..* Oxford, UK: Blackwell Publishers Ltd., 1993.

McIntosh, Peggy, "White Privilege: Unpacking the Invisible Knapsack."

McIntyre, Lee, *Post-Truth.* Cambridge, MA: The MIT Press, 2018.

McKibben, Bill, *Eaarth: Making a Life on a Tough New Planet.* New York: St. Martin's Griffin, 2011.

Meadows, Donella H., Dennis L. Meadows, Jørgen Randers, and William W. Behrens, *The Limits to Growth: A Report for the Club of Rome's Project on the Predicament of Mankind.* New York: The New American Library/Signet, 1972.

mfiles.co.uk, "A Short History of Musical Notation," accessed 9/3/2016.

Miller, Geoffrey, *The Mating Mind: How Sexual Choice Shaped the Evolution of Human Nature.* New York: Anchor Books, 2001.

Montgomery, David R., *The Rocks Don't Lie: A Geologist Investigates Noah's Flood*. New York: Norton & Co., 2012.

Moore, R.I., *The War on Heresy*. Cambridge, MA: Belknap Press of Harvard University, 2012.

Mortenson, Terry, 34-35, within a subsection "The Rocks," in Vail (compiler).

Moxey, Keith, *Peasants, Warriors and Wives: Popular Imagery in the Reformation*. Chicago: University of Chicago Press, 1989.

Mullins, Edwin, *Cluny: In Search of God's Lost Empire*. New York: BlueBridge, 2006.

Murphy, Cullen, *God's Jury: The Inquisition and the Making of the Modern World*. New York: Mariner Books/Houghton Mifflin Harcourt, 2013.

Musée Condé, Chantilly, *The Très Riches Heures of Jean, Duke of Berry*. New York: George Braziller, Inc., 1969.

Nadelmann, Ethan, "Drugs," in *Foreign Policy*, Sept.-Oct. 2007, 26.

National Academy of Science Institute of Medicine, *Science, Evolution and Creationism*. Washington, D.C.: The National Academies Press, 2008.

National Center for Science Education website, "Project Steve," accessed 1/16/2019.

National Center for Science Education, *Reports*, especially the column, "Update" and its earlier version, "Update—News from the Field."

National Research Council; Jones, Lyle V., Gardner Lindzey, and Peter E. Coggeshall, Eds., *An assessment of Research Doctorate Programs in the United States: [4 vols.] Humanities; Engineering; Social and Behavioral Sciences; Biological Sciences.* Washington, D.C.: The National Academies Press, 1982.

Natural Resources Defense Council, "NRDC Ramps up Fight to Restrict Use of Bee-killing Pesticides," in *Nature's Voice*, Summer 2020, 2.

National Center for Education Statistics, nces.ed.gov/surveys, accessed 8/3/2020.

Nelson, Lynn Harry, *Medieval History Lecture Index*, hosted at WWW Virtual Library @www/vlib.us.

Netflix, "Explained" series, program on "Mind."

Netflix, "The Social Dilemma."

NOVA, "Hacking Your Mind—Weapons of Influence," credited to the WGBH Educational Foundation.

NOVA, "Judgment Day: Intelligent Design on Trial," credited to the WGBH Educational Foundation and Vulcan Productions, Inc.

Novella, Steven, *Your Deceptive Mind: A Scientific Guide to Critical Thinking Skills.* Chantilly, VA: The Teaching Company, 2012.

O'Mara, Collin, "Support a Game Changer for Wildlife," in *National Wildlife*, 6. Reston, VA: National Wildlife Federation, Oct.-Nov. 2019.

Okrent, Daniel, *Last Call: The Rise and Fall of Prohibition.* New York: Scribner, 2011.

Oldridge, Darren, *The Devil in Tudor and Stuart England.* Stroud, Gloucestershire, England: The History   Press, 2010.

Perry, William G, Jr., "Cognitive and Ethical Growth: The Making of Meaning," in Arthur W. Chickering and Associates, *The Modern American College*, 76-116. San Francisco: Jossey-Bass, 1981.

Peters, Edward, *Inquisition*. Berkeley: University of California Press, 1989.

Pierce, Patricia, *Jurassic Mary: Mary Anning and the Primeval Monsters*. Gloucestershire GL5 2QG: The History Press, 2014.

Pierre-Louis, Kendra, "Remote islands awash in plastic garbage," in the *StarTribune*, May 23, 2019, p. A3.

Plummer, Charles C., David McGeary, and Diane H. Carlson, *Physical Geology (8th Ed.)*. Boston: McGraw-Hill, 1999.

Politico, accessed 2/21/2019.

Poole, William, *The World Makers: Scientists of the Restoration and the Search for the Origins of the Earth*, xv. Oxfordshire X29 8SZ, UK: Peter Lang Ltd, 2010.

Population Connection, June 2019, 4-5, "About a third of all insect species are threatened with extinction."

Population Connection, Sept. 2019, 6, "In the News."

Potter, Wendell, *Deadly Spin: An Insurance Company Insider Speaks Out on How Corporate PR Is Killing Health Care and Deceiving Americans*. New York: Bloomsbury Press, 2010.

Principe, Lawrence M., *The Secrets of Alchemy*. Chicago: University of Chicago Press, 2013.

Prothero, Donald R., *Evolution: What the Fossils Say and Why It Matters*. New York: Columbia University Press, 2007.

Prothero, Donald R., *Reality Check*. Bloomington, Ind.: Indiana University Press, 2013.

Rashdall, Hastings, *The Universities of Europe in the Middle Ages, Vol. 1*, edited by F. M. Powicke and A.B. Emden. London: Oxford University Press, 1936.

Rawcliffe, Carole, *Medicine & Society in Later Medieval England*. London: Sandpiper Books, 1999.

Regnery Publishing website, accessed June 2017.

Ross, James Bruce and Mary Martin McLaughlin (Eds.), *The Portable Renaissance Reader*. New York: Penguin Books, 1977.

Rothenburg Medieval Crime Museum, *Criminal Justice Through the Ages*. Rothenberg ob der Tauber: Medieval Crime Museum, 1993. Translated by John Fosberry.

Rouse, W. H. D., *Lucretius De Rerum Natura with an English Translation, 3rd Edition*. Cambridge, MA: Harvard University Press, 1959.

Rubenstein, Richard E., *Aristotle's Children: How Christians, Muslims, and Jews Rediscovered Ancient Wisdom and Illuminated the Middle Ages*. Orlando, FL: A Harvest Book (Harcourt), 2004].

Ruse, Michael, *Defining Darwin: Essays on the History and Philosophy of Evolutionary Biology*. Amherst, NY: Prometheus Books, 2009.

Russell, Colin A., "The Conflict of Science and Religion," 3-12, in Ferngren, Ed.

Russell, Jeffrey Burton, *Dissent and Order in the Middle Ages: The Search for Legitimate Authority*. New York: Twayne Publishers, 1992.

Schachner, Nathan, *The Medieval Universities*. New York: Stokes, 1938.

Schwägerl, Christian, *The Anthropocene: The Human Era and How It Shapes Our Planet*. Santa Fe, NM: Synergetic Press, 2014; trans. Lucy Renner Jones.

Shermer, Michael, *The Believing Brain: From Ghosts and Gods to Politics and Conspiracies—How We Construct Beliefs and Reinforce Them as Truths*. New York: St. Martin's Griffin, 2011.

Siraisi, Nancy G., *Medieval & Early Renaissance Medicine: An Introduction to Knowledge and Practice*. Chicago: University of Chicago Press, 1990.

Snelling, Andrew, 38-39, within a subsection "The Rocks," in Vail (compiler).

Sobel, Dava, *A More Perfect Heaven: How Copernicus Revolutionized the Cosmos*. London: Bloomsbury Publishing, 2011.

Spufford, Peter, *Power and Profit: The Merchant in Medieval Europe*. London: Thames & Hudson, 2006.

Starry Messenger: "Astronomical Tables," accessed 6/22/2017.

StarTribune article references for the table in Part Four: See the end of these references.

StarTribune, Feb. 20, 2020, A4, "Mulvaney says GOP hypocritical on deficits."

Stephens, Alexander, "Cornerstone Speech," in Wikipedia, accessed 8/12/2020.

Stephens, Walter, *Demon Lovers: Witchcraft, Sex, and the Crisis of Belief*. Chicago: University of Chicago Press, 2002.

Stout, Harry S., *Upon the Altar of the Nation: A Moral History of the Civil War*. New York: Penguin Books, 2006.

Strathern, Paul, *Death in Florence: The Medici, Savonarola, and the Battle for the Soul of a Renaissance City*. New York: Pegasus Books, 2015.

Stump, Elenore, "Dialectic," 125-146, in Wagner, Ed.

Switek, Brian, *Written in Stone: Evolution, the Fossil Record, and Our Place in Nature*. New York: Bellevue Literary Press, 2010.

Takaki, Ronald T., *Iron Cages: Race and Culture in 19th-Century America*. Seattle: University of Washington Press, 1979.

The Access Bible: A Resource for Beginning Bible Students. New Revised Standard Version with the Apocryphal/Deuterocanonical Books. Oxford, England: Oxford University Press, 1999.

T*he Medieval Health Handbook: Tacuinum Sanitatis*, transl. & adapted by Oscar Ratti and Adele Westbrook from the Italian edition by Luisa Cogliati Arano. New York: Georges Braziller, 1976.

Thornbury, William D., *Principles of Geomorphology*. New York: John Wiley & Sons, Inc., 1962.

Tolmé, Paul, "Running the Gauntlet," in *National Wildlife*, June-July 2019, 40.

Tom Vail (writer, compiler), *Grand Canyon: A Different View*. Green Forest, Ark.: Master Books, 2003.

Tuchman, Barbara, *The March of Folly: From Troy to Vietnam*. New York: Knopf, 1984.

Tucker, Abigail, "The New King of the Sea," in *Smithsonian*, August 2010, 30.

Von Fange, Erich A., *In Search of the Genesis World: Debunking the Evolution Myth*. St. Louis: Concordia Publishing House, 2006.

Von Hippel, William, *The Social Leap: The New Evolutionary Science of Who We Are, Where We Come From, and What Makes Us Happy*. New York: Harper Wave, 2018.

Wadsworth, Bryan, "Inside the Disinformation Playbook," in *Catalyst*, the Union of Concerned Scientists, Winter 2018, 10, 20.

Wagner, David L. Ed., *The Seven Liberal Arts in the Middle Ages*. Bloomington, IN: Indiana University Press, 1986.

Waite, Gary K., *Heresy, Magic, and Witchcraft in Early Modern Europe*. Palgrave Macmillan: Hampshire/New York, 2003.

Walker, Tasman, 36-37, within a subsection "The Rocks," in Vail (compiler).

Wandel, Lee Palmer, *The Reformation: Towards a New History*. New York: Cambridge University Press, 2011.

Wieruszowski, Helene, *The Medieval University*. Princeton, N.J.: D. Van Nostrand, 1966.

Wikipedia article on "Adelard of Bath," accessed 12/16/2016.

Wikipedia article on "Andrea Palladio," accessed 7/18/2017.

Wikipedia article on "Naturalism (philosophy)," accessed 5/4/2017.

Wikipedia article on "Peter Lombard," accessed 3/29/2017.

Wikipedia article on "Ptolemy," accessed 4/19/2017.

Wikipedia article on "Renaissance Humanism," accessed 7/8/2017.

Wikipedia article on the Abbey Church at Vézelay, accessed 3/28/2017.

Wilson, Derek, *A Brief History of the English Reformation*. London: Constable & Robinson, 2012.

Wilson, Edward O., *The Future of Life*. New York: Vintage Books, 2002.

Wilson, Peter H., *The Thirty Years War: Europe's Tragedy*. Cambridge, MA: Belknap Press of Harvard University Press, 2009.

Winchester, Simon, *The Map That Changed the World: William Smith and the Birth of Modern Geology*. New York: HarperCollins Perennial, 2002.

Wysession, Michael E., *The World's Greatest Geological Wonders: 36 Spectacular Sites*. Chantilly, VA: The Teaching Company, 2013.

York Archaeological Trust, *Jorvik Viking Centre: Companion Guide*, 2017.

Zibel, Alan, "Corporations Make Billions from Immigration Contracts," in *Public Citizen News*, Vol. 39, No. 6, Nov.-Dec., 2019.

References for the table of StarTribune articles in Part Four [NS= news services]

2016: 8/28, "Human history was written with stone tools" (NS); 8/28, Amina Khan, "A Star Turn: Witness to Nova," Los Angeles Times. 9/4, "Tusks of rare breed of mammoth found" (NS); "Galaxy spotted is mostly dark matter" (NS). 9/11, Rachel Feltman, "Cat-size Creatures Flew in Dino Times," Washington Post. 9/18, "Turns out there are four species of giraffe" (NS). 9/25, Veronica Rocha, "Rare Mammoth Skull Unearthed in California," Los Angeles Times; Sarah Kaplan, "Catch and Release," Washington Post. 10/2, Malcolm

Ritter, "DNA Tied to Single Exodus from Africa," Associated Press. 10/9, Seth Borenstein, "As a Species, Humans Inherit Murderous Tendencies, Study Says," Associated Press. 10/16, Sarah Kaplan, "Thickener Is Key to Primordial Soup," Washington Post. 10/23, "14,500-year-old etchings found in cave in Spain" (NS); "Tiny T.rex arms appear little used, researchers say (NS); Sarah Kaplan, "Footprints a Glimpse at Past," Washington Post. 10/30, "Origins of European bison uncovered" (NS). 11/6, Sarah Kaplan, "Cave Lions May Have Been Made into Rugs," Washington Post. 11/13, Kenneth Chang, "A New Way to Look at Earth and Moon," New York Times; Sarah Kaplan, "After Extinction, a Long Recovery," Washington Post. 12/11, Deborah Netburn, "Lucy Had Strong Bones of a Climber," Los Angeles Times. 12/18, Nicholas St. Fleur, "Amber Preserved Feathered Tail for 99 Million Years," New York Times. 12/25, "Prehuman male was tall for his time" (NS); Cleve R. Wootson, Jr., "Early Humans Used Sticks to Clean Teeth," Washington Post.

2017: 1/8, Sarah Kaplan, "Dinos May Have Been Doomed by Hatch Times," Washington Post. 1/15, "Tomatillo fossil is 52 million years old" (NS). 2/5, Sarah Kaplan, "Over 6 Million Years Ago, Otters the Size of Wolves Roamed China," Washington Post. 2/12, Amina Khan, "Tiny Sea Creature is Human Ancestor," Los Angeles Times; "Black hole takes its time devouring star" (NS). 2/19, Amina Khan, "A Whole New Window Inside Dinosaur Bones," Los Angeles Times; "Supernova aftermath caught in early stage" (NS). 2/26, Avi Selk, "Zealandia, the 'Hidden Continent,'" Washington Post. 3/12, "Figuring out why squids lost their shells" (NS); Ben Guarino, "Skulls Could Be from a New Species," Washington Post; Sarah Kaplan, "Iconic Dino's New Chapter," Washington Post. 3/19, "In ancient caves, stories told dot by dot" (NYT); "Our universe's very dusty beginnings" (NYT). 3/26, "Bison quickly made homes on the range" (NS). 4/2, Seth Borenstein, "Rethinking the Dinosaur Family Tree" (AP). 4/16, "Mammals shrink when Earth heats up." Associated Press. 4/23, Malcolm Ritter, "Reptile Forces a Double-Take" Associated Press. 5/7, Frank Jordans, "DNA Clues Found in Dirt," Associated Press. 5/21, Christopher Torchia, "Humanity's New Cousin Is 'Astonishingly' Young," Associated Press; "Dino's name comes from 'Ghostbusters'" (NS); "After 90 million years, a family for Louie" (NS). 5/28, Peter Holley, "Timing May Have Sealed Dino's Fate," Washington Post. 6/4, Deborah Netburn, "How Whales Got So Big: Climate Shift Contributed," Los Angeles Times. 6/11, Chelsea Harvey, "Long Ago, Methane Popped the Cork," Washington Post; "T. rex had scaly skin and no feathers" (NS). 6/25, Karin Brulliard, "A Look at Cat's Journey toward Domestication," Washington Post.

2017: 7/9, "Mammals that stumped Darwin find a home" (NS). 7/16, Carl Zimmer, "A Clearer Picture of Our Past," New York Times. 7/23, Dake Kang, "Reconstructing a Picture of Ancient Life," Associated Press. 7/30, Nicholas St. Fleur, "Artifacts Push Back Australian Timeline," New York Times; "T. rex couldn't run, but walked fast" (NS). 8/6, Jacqueline Williams, "Exploring Lost Land of Zealandia," New York Times. 8/13, "Scorpions are ancient, but we're still finding new species" (NYT). 8/20, Ben Guarino, "Chasing the Moon," Washington Post; Seth Borenstein, "The New Heavyweight Champion of Dinosaurs: Patagotitan," Associated Press. 9/10, Kenneth Chang, "Astronomers Cast Light on the Mystery of a Vanishing Star," New York Times. 10/1, Nicholas Wade, "Coloring Outside the Lines," New York Times; Amina Khan, "Dinos Changed Up What They Ate," Lost Angeles Times; Ben Guarino, "Similar Beginnings," Washington Post. 10/22, Carl Zimmer, "Study: Genes for Skin Color Rebut Dated Notions of Race," New York Times; Ben Guarino, "Ancient Primate May Be to Blame for Genital Herpes,"

Washington Post. 11/5, Amina Khan, "Dinosaur Markings Hint at Life, Landscape," Los Angeles Times; "374 million-year-old fossils discovered in China" (NS). 11/12, Malcolm Ritter, "No Matter What, the Neanderthals Were Doomed," Associated Press; Ben Guarino and Sarah Kaplan, "New Ape Is Most Endangered on the Planet," Washington Post. 11/19, Marcia Dunn, "Stellar Encore: Dying Star Just Keeps Coming Back," Associated Press; Ben Guarino, "Earliest Evidence of Wine Is Discovered," Washington Post; Amina Khan, "Mammals Mostly Nocturnal When Dinos Roamed," Los Angeles Times. 12/3, "Oldest art of man's best friend" (NS); "25 million-year-old sea cow fossils found" (NS). 12/10, "3.6 million-year-old skeleton revealed" (NS); "Big black hole is farthest ever found" (NS). 12/17, Christopher Weber, "Under Streets of L.A., Fossils Wait," Associated Press; "Ticks likely sucked dinosaurs' blood" (NS); Amina Khan, "Dinosaur Kind of an Odd Duck," Los Angeles Times. 12/24, Malcolm Ritter, "Ancient Penguin Was as Big as a Pittsburgh Penguin," Associated Press.

2018: 1/21, Sarah Kaplan, "Scanning for Radio Bursts," Washington Post. 2/4, Amina Khan, "New Way to Look for Signs of Life," Los Angeles Times. 2/11, Kenneth Chang, "Dinosaurs, Mammals Crossed Paths in Maryland," New York Times. 2/18, "A first beyond our galaxy," Washington Post; "Skates that walk" (NS). 3/4, Deborah Netburn, "Neanderthals Were First Artists," Los Angeles Times. 3/11, Seth Borenstein, "Detecting Dawn of the Universe," Associated Press. 3/18, Carl Zimmer, "How One Mutation Spread," New York Times; Amy B. Wang, "'The Holy Grail of Dinosaurs' Discovered," Washington Post. 3/25, Carl Zimmer, "Ancient DNA Reshapes Story of Our Species," New York Times. 4/8, Asher Elbein, "Clues into How Insects Gained the Ability to Fly," New York Times. 4/15, Nicholas St. Fleur, "Footprints Offer Clues of Earliest Americans," New York Times. 4/22, "The evolution of human eyebrows" (NS);

"Secrets of creatures, big and small: How dinosaurs lived" (NS). 4/29, Sarah Kaplan, "How We Got Here," Los Angeles Times. 5/6, Deborah Netburn, "Last of the Giants," Los Angeles Times. 5/13, "Dinosaur teeth show fierce eating habits" (NS). 5/27, Deborah Netburn, "Cosmic Megamerger," Los Angeles Times. 6/17, Amina Khan, "Surviving Birds Have Common Ground," Los Angeles Times. 6/24, Sean Greene, "The New Wonders of Our World: 5. A New Species of Great Ape," Los Angeles Times.

2018: 7/8, Nicholas Bakalar, "Every 202,500 Years, Earth Shifts Direction," New York Times; Avi Selk, "Scientists on the Hunt for Nessie—this Time its DNA," Washington Post. 7/22, Nicholas St. Fleur, "Rocky Path Reveals Early Migration," New York Times. 7/29, Sarah Kaplan, "New Light on Our Mysterious Origins," Washington Post. 8/5, Carl Zimmer, "Tools Upend Story of Our Evolution," New York Times; "DNA may be key to koala's survival" (NS); "Early rise of gigantic dinosaurs" (NS). 8/12, Sarah Kaplan, "In Cosmic First, Scientists Detect 'Ghost Particle,'" Washington Post. 8/19, Carl Zimmer, "Marine Mammals Lost Gene They May Now Desperately Need," New York Times. 8/26, Nicholas St. Fleur, "A Rare Find of Ancient Shark," New York Times. 9/2, Deborah Netburn, "Neanderthals May Have Started Their Own Fires," Los Angeles Times. 9/9, "Saliva may adapt to bitter flavors" (NS); "Grisly tactics for millions of years" (NS). 9/16, "A 73,000-year-old hashtag drawing?" (NS). 9/23, "Cave bear may be extinct, but its DNA lives on in brown bears," New York Times. 10/7, "Our generosity may be thanks to evolution," New York Times. 10/14, "Ants used antibiotics millions of years ago" (NS). 10/21, Carl Zimmer, "Neanderthal DNA Left Gift for Humans," New York Times. 11/4, Dennis Overbye, "The Monster in the Milky Way," New York Times. 11/18, Ben Guarino, "Origin of Colorful Eggshells: Dinosaurs," Washington Post; "Pinpointing where fish first evolved" (NS).

10/25, "Smallest ape species found hints of rise of the monkeys," New York Times; Sarah Kaplan, "Earliest Evidence of Human Art Is Found," Washington Post. 12/2, Nicholas St. Fleur, "Our Relatives May Have Lived in 'Green Arabia,'" New York Times. 12/9, "The octopus paradox: How smart are they?" (NS). 12/16, Evan Bush, "Reaching Terminal Velocity?" Seattle Times. 12/23, Carl Zimmer, "Neanderthal DNA May Have Shaped Our Brains," New York Times. 12/30, Seth Borenstein, "Giant Rock's Impact Gave Uranus its Tilt," Associated Press.

2019: 1/6, Joanna Klein, "A Hidden World Living Under Us," New York Times; Nicholas St. Fleur, "Scientists for the First Time Discover Impact Crater under Ice Sheet," New York Times. 1/20, Julia Rosen, "Here's How Miles of Vertical Rock Went Missing around the World," Los Angeles Times.

DRAFT INDEX OF PRINCIPAL TOPICS AND REFERENCES

(For entries accidentally omitted or otherwise not shown here—e.g., church, nature—try related topics.)

H